UNDERSTANDING EMPLOYEE BENEFITS LAW

UNDERSTANDING EMPLOYEE BENEFITS LAW

Kathryn L. Moore
Ashland-Spears Distinguished Research Professor of Law
University of Kentucky College of Law

ISBN: 978-1-4224-9495-0

Library of Congress Cataloging-in-Publication Data
Moore, Kathryn L., 1961- author.
Understanding employee benefits law / Kathryn L. Moore, Ashland-Spears Distinguished Research Professor of Law, University of Kentucky College of Law.
pages cm
Includes index.
ISBN 978-1-4224-9495-0 (softbound)
1. Employee fringe benefits--Law and legislation--United States. 2. Pension trusts--Law and legislation--United States. I. Title.
KF3509.M66 2015
344.7301'255--dc23
2015033390

This publication is designed to provide authoritative information in regard to the subject matter covered. It is sold with the understanding that the publisher is not engaged in rendering legal, accounting, or other professional services. If legal advice or other expert assistance is required, the services of a competent professional should be sought.

LexisNexis and the Knowledge Burst logo are registered trademarks of Reed Elsevier Properties Inc., used under license. Matthew Bender and the Matthew Bender Flame Design are registered trademarks of Matthew Bender Properties Inc.

NOTE TO USERS

To ensure that you are using the latest materials available in this area, please be sure to periodically check the LexisNexis Law School web site for downloadable updates and supplements at www.lexisnexis.com/lawschool.

Editorial Offices
630 Central Ave., New Providence, NJ 07974 (908) 464-6800
201 Mission St., San Francisco, CA 94105-1831 (415) 908-3200
www.lexisnexis.com

MATTHEW♦BENDER

Dedication

To

PDH, RMMH, and FGMH

and

In Memory of

RBM and MTM

Acknowledgements

I would like to thank the many people who helped me in writing this book.

First, I would like to thank my research assistants, Eric Biscopink, Chuck Krebs, Gordon Mowen, Young-Eun Park, Darren Smith, and Richard Wooldridge, as well as Franklin Runge, Beau Steenken, and Ryan Valentin who provided valuable assistance with research.

In addition, I would like to thank April Brooks and Richard Wooldridge for their extraordinary assistance in preparing and editing the many charts and diagrams in this book. And I would like to thank Mary Ann Isaacs for her careful typing and editing of the manuscript.

And last, but not least, I would like to thank the many people who offered valuable insights and/or comments on portions of this book. Specifically, I would like to thank Susan Cancelosi, Mary Davis, Josh Douglas, Chris Frost, Izzy Goldowitz, Mike Healy, Nicole Huberfeld, Diane Kraft, Dana Muir, Paul Salamanca, Carol Weiser, and the students in my 2015 Employee Benefits class.

Preface

Employee benefits is a vast and complex area of law. This book is intended to provide readers with a broad overview of the subject as well as a taste of both its breadth and its depth.

In order to assist readers with a broad overview of the subject, the book begins with a detailed table of contents and has many charts and diagrams. In order to help readers understand how the law applies, the book provides many examples. Finally, the book includes an extensive set of footnotes with citations that not only provide readers with support for the statements made in the text but also refer them to additional sources that they can consult for further study of the subject.

The book is designed primarily for use by J.D. students enrolled in an employee benefits course. I hope that LLM students, practitioners, judges, and scholars who need an overview of the law will also find it useful.

Table of Contents

Chapter 1   **INTRODUCTION** 1

§ 1.01   WHAT ARE EMPLOYEE BENEFITS? 1
§ 1.02   WHY DO EMPLOYERS OFFER EMPLOYEE BENEFITS? 2
§ 1.03   HOW ARE EMPLOYEE BENEFITS REGULATED? 3
§ 1.04   HISTORY AND PURPOSES OF ERISA 4
  [A]   Pre-ERISA Regulation of Employee Benefit Plans 4
    [1]   Federal Income Tax Law 4
    [2]   Federal Labor Law 5
    [3]   Welfare and Pension Plans Disclosure Act 5
    [4]   State Law 6
  [B]   Failure of Pre-ERISA Law to Protect Plan Participants and Beneficiaries . 6
  [C]   Purposes of ERISA 8
§ 1.05   OVERVIEW OF ERISA'S REGULATION OF EMPLOYEE BENEFIT
          PLANS 10
  [A]   Statutory Framework 10
    [1]   Title I 11
    [2]   Title II 14
    [3]   Title III 14
    [4]   Title IV 14
  [B]   ERISA's Numbering System 15
  [C]   Coverage 16
  [D]   Risks Against Which ERISA Protects 17
    [1]   Default Risk 17
    [2]   Administration Risk 18
§ 1.06   RELATIONSHIP BETWEEN ERISA AND THE INTERNAL REVENUE
          CODE 20
§ 1.07   OVERVIEW OF TAX RULES GOVERNING EMPLOYEE BENEFITS . 21
  [A]   Tax Exclusion 22
  [B]   Tax Deferral 22
  [C]   Roth Treatment 23

Chapter 2   **PENSION PLANS** 27

§ 2.01   INTRODUCTION 27
§ 2.02   GENERAL INTRODUCTION TO PENSION PLANS AND THE
          DISTINCTION BETWEEN DEFINED BENEFIT PLANS AND DEFINED
          CONTRIBUTION PLANS 27
  [A]   Introduction to Defined Benefit Plans 28
  [B]   Introduction to Defined Contribution Plans 28

Table of Contents

[C]   Distinctions Between Defined Benefit Plans and Defined Contribution
Plans 29

    [1]   Input vs. Output 29

    [2]   Funding 30

    [3]   Investment Risk 31

    [4]   Pension Benefit Guaranty Corporation (PBGC) Guarantee 32

    [5]   Distributions 32

    [6]   Portability 33

    [7]   Older Workers Versus Younger Workers and the Time Value of
Money 35

       [a]   Time Value of Money and its Assumptions 35

         [i]   Positive Interest Rates 35

         [ii]   Compound Interest 35

         [iii]   Discounted Present Value 36

       [b]   Time Value of Money and Defined Benefit Plans 36

       [c]   Time Value of Money and Defined Contribution Plans 37

§ 2.03   A CLOSER LOOK AT DEFINED BENEFIT PLANS — DEFINED
BENEFIT PLAN FORMULAS AND DEFINITION OF
COMPENSATION 38

   [A]   Types of Benefit Formulas 39

    [1]   Fixed Benefit Formula 39

    [2]   Flat Benefit Formula 39

    [3]   Unit Benefit Formula 40

   [B]   Calculating Compensation for Purposes of Benefit Formulas 40

    [1]   Career Average Pay 41

    [2]   Final Average Pay 41

§ 2.04   QUALIFIED PLANS 41

   [A]   Qualification Requirements 42

    [1]   Qualification Rules to Protect Plan Participants 42

    [2]   Qualification Rules to Target Tax Subsidy 42

    [3]   Enforcement of Qualification Requirements 43

   [B]   Tax Benefits of Traditional Qualified Plans 43

    [1]   Employer May Deduct Contributions to Qualified Plans When Made . 43

    [2]   Employees Do Not Need to Include Contributions in Income Until
Contributions are Distributed to Them 44

    [3]   Earnings on Contributions Held by Qualified Plans are Exempt from
Tax 44

    [4]   Participants Can Roll over Distributions from a Qualified Plan to an
Individual Retirement Account or Another Qualified Plan and Further
Delay Taxation of Benefits 44

   [C]   Economic Effect of Favorable Tax Treatment Accorded Traditional
Qualified Plans 45

Table of Contents

[D]   Roth Treatment 45
[E]   Basic Types of Qualified Plans 45
  [1]   Profit-Sharing Plans 46
  [2]   Stock Bonus Plans 46
  [3]   Pension Plans 47
§ 2.05 "ERISA-QUALIFIED PLANS" 49
§ 2.06 SPECIAL TYPES OF QUALIFIED PLANS 49
[A]   401(k) Plans 49
[B]   Employee Stock Ownership Plans (ESOPs) 51
[C]   Cash Balance Plans 52
[D]   Individual Retirement Accounts [IRAs] 54

Chapter 3   WELFARE PLANS 57

§ 3.01 INTRODUCTION 57
§ 3.02 WHAT IS A WELFARE BENEFIT PLAN? 57
[A]   What are Welfare Benefits? 58
[B]   What is a Plan? 58
  [1]   *Donovan v. Dillingham* Test 59
  [2]   Excluded Plans 60
  [3]   Three-Step Inquiry 60
§ 3.03 INTRODUCTION TO EMPLOYMENT-BASED HEALTH CARE
        PLANS 61
[A]   Brief History of Employment-Based Health Care Plans 61
[B]   Reasons for Employment-Based Health Care 62
  [1]   Wage and Price Controls 62
  [2]   Favorable Income Tax Treatment 62
[C]   Types of Employment-Based Health Care Plans 63
  [1]   Conventional Health Insurance 63
  [2]   Health Maintenance Organizations (HMOs) 64
  [3]   Preferred Provider Organization (PPO) and Point of Service (POS)
            Plans 65
  [4]   Consumer-Driven Health Plans 66
[D]   Employers' Methods of Financing Employment-Based Health Plans and the
        Implications of the Financing Methods 67
  [1]   Fully-Insured Plans 67
  [2]   Self-Funded or Self-Insured Plans 68
  [3]   Implications of Financing Methods under ERISA 69
  [4]   Implication of Financing Method under the Affordable Care Act 70
  [5]   Stop-Loss Insurance 71
    [a]   Specific Attachment Point 71
    [b]   Aggregate Attachment Point 71

Table of Contents

[6]   Stop-Loss Insurance and the Distinction between Fully-Insured and Self-Funded Plans 72

§ 3.04   ERISA'S REGULATION OF EMPLOYER-SPONSORED HEALTH PLANS PRIOR TO THE AFFORDABLE CARE ACT 73

§ 3.05   PROBLEMS WITH THE U.S. HEALTH CARE SYSTEM BEFORE THE ENACTMENT OF THE AFFORDABLE CARE ACT 75

[A]   Number of Uninsured Individuals 76

[B]   High Costs 77

[C]   Poorly Functioning Individual and Small Group Markets 78

§ 3.06   THE AFFORDABLE CARE ACT 79

[A]   Broad Overview of the Affordable Care Act 81

[B]   ERISA's Incorporation of the Affordable Care Act's Provisions 81

[C]   Substantive Market Reforms 83

[1]   Provisions Expanding Coverage 84

[a]   Prohibitions on "Cherry Picking" 85

[b]   Coverage of Young Adults 86

[2]   Provisions Improving Coverage 87

[a]   Prohibition on Lifetime and Annual Dollar Limits on Benefits 87

[b]   Prohibition on Preexisting Condition Exclusions 87

[c]   Preventive Care 88

[3]   Summary of Market Reforms 89

[D]   Individual and Employer Mandates and Related Provisions 89

[1]   Overview of Individual and Employer Mandates and Related Provisions 91

[2]   Individual Mandate — IRC § 5000A 91

[a]   "Applicable Individuals" 91

[b]   "Minimum Essential Coverage" 92

[c]   Monetary Penalty 93

[d]   Constitutionality of Individual Mandate 93

[3]   Individual Subsidies 93

[a]   Premium Tax Credit — IRC § 36B 94

[i]   "Applicable Taxpayers" 94

[ii]   Amount of Tax Credit 95

[iii]   Direct Payment to Insurer 95

[b]   Cost-Sharing Subsidy — PHSA § 1402 96

[i]   "Eligible Insureds" 96

[ii]   Amount of Subsidy 96

[iii]   Direct Payment to Insurer 97

[4]   Employer Mandate — IRC § 4980H 97

[a]   "Applicable Large Employers" 97

[b]   "Minimum Essential Coverage" 98

[c]   IRC § 4980H(a) No Offer Penalty 98

Table of Contents

[d]   IRC § 4980H(b) Unaffordable Coverage Penalty 99

   [i]   Unaffordable 99

   [ii]   Minimum Value 100

   [iii]   Amount of Penalty 100

[e]   Effective Date 101

[f]   Summary of Employer Mandate 102

[5]   Tax Credit for Small Employers — IRC § 45R 103

[6]   Excise Tax on "Cadillac" Health Plans — IRC § 4980I 104

[a]   "Applicable Employer-Sponsored Coverage" 104

[b]   "Excess Benefit" 104

[c]   "Coverage Provider" 105

[7]   Summary of Mandates and Related Provisions 106

[E]   Health Insurance Exchanges or Health Insurance Marketplaces 106

[1]   Types of Exchanges or Marketplaces 107

[a]   American Health Benefit (AHB) Exchange 107

[b]   Small Business Health Options Program (SHOP) 108

[2]   Essential Health Benefits Package 108

[a]   Essential Health Benefits 108

[b]   Annual Cost-Sharing Limits 109

[c]   Actuarial Value Requirements 109

[F]   Summary of the Affordable Care Act 111

§ 3.07   RETIREE HEALTH INSURANCE 112

[A]   Types of Retiree Health Insurance 112

[B]   Vesting of Retiree Health Benefits 113

[C]   Retiree Health Benefits and the Accounting Rules 114

[D]   Retiree Health Benefits and the Age Discrimination in Employment
Act 116

§ 3.08   FEDERAL TAXATION OF WELFARE BENEFITS 116

[A]   Contributions to Fund Employer-Provided Health Insurance — IRC
§ 106 117

[B]   Contributions to Consumer-Driven Health Care Plans 119

[1]   Health Savings Accounts (HSAs) 119

[2]   Health Reimbursement Accounts (HRAs) 120

[3]   High Deductible Health Plans (HDHPs) 120

[C]   Group-Term Life Insurance — IRC § 79 120

[1]   Group-Term Life Insurance 120

[2]   Exclusion for Group-Term Life Insurance 121

[D]   IRC § 125 Cafeteria Plans 123

[1]   Premium Only Plans 123

[2]   Flexible Spending Accounts 124

[a]   Use It or Lose It Rule 125

Table of Contents

[b]   Modifications to the Use It or Lose It Rule for Health FSAs 125

    [i]   2 1/2 Month Grace Period 125

    [ii] $500 Carryover 126

[c]   Uniform Coverage Rule for Health FSAs 126

[d]   Limits on Contributions to FSAs 127

[e]   Special FSA Rules for Health Savings Accounts (HSAs) 127

[3]   Full Flex Plans 127

Chapter 4   **PLAN OPERATION** **129**

§ 4.01   INTRODUCTION 129

§ 4.02   WRITING REQUIREMENT — ERISA § 402(a)(1) 129

[A]   Purpose of Writing Requirement 130

[B]   Required Elements of Written Plan Document 130

[C]   Satisfying the Writing Requirement 131

[D]   Effect of Failure to Satisfy Writing Requirement 131

[E]   Oral Representations and Estoppel Claims 132

§ 4.03   REPORTING & DISCLOSURE REQUIREMENTS — ERISA

     §§ 101–111 133

[A]   Purposes of Reporting and Disclosure Requirements 133

[B]   Specific Reporting and Disclosure Requirements 134

[C]   Summary Plan Description 135

§ 4.04   PLAN AMENDMENTS 137

[A]   Plan Amendment Procedure — ERISA § 402(b)(3) 137

[B]   Anti-Cutback Rule for Pension Plans — ERISA § 204(g) 138

    [1]   Purpose of the Anti-Cutback Rule 138

    [2]   Accrued Versus Prospective Benefits 139

    [3]   Protected Benefits 139

§ 4.05   ERISA § 510 141

[A]   Purpose of ERISA § 510 141

[B]   Section 510's Four Prohibitions 141

    [1]   Exercise Clause or Retaliation Provision 141

    [2]   Interference Clause 142

    [3]   Whistleblower Provision 143

    [4]   Multiemployer Plan Provision 144

[C]   Individuals Protected by ERISA § 510 144

[D]   Proving an ERISA § 510 Claim — Shifting Burden of Proof 147

    [1]   Plaintiff's Initial Burden of Proof 147

    [2]   Defendant's Burden of Proof 148

    [3]   Plaintiff's Final Burden of Proof 148

Table of Contents

Chapter 5	**REGULATION OF PENSION PLANS**	**149**

§ 5.01   INTRODUCTION 149
§ 5.02   PENSION BENEFIT SECURITY RULES 149
  [A]   Vesting Requirements — ERISA § 203; IRC § 411 150
    [1]   Vesting Requirements for Employee Contributions 151
    [2]   Vesting Requirements for Employer Contributions to Defined Benefit
            Plans 152
      [a]   Five-Year Cliff Vesting Schedule 152
      [b]   Three- to Seven-Year Graded Vesting Schedule 152
    [3]   Vesting Requirements for Employer Contributions to Defined
            Contribution Plans 153
      [a]   Three-Year Cliff Vesting Schedule 153
      [b]   Two- to Six-Year Graded Vesting Schedule 153
    [4]   Summary of Vesting Schedules 155
    [5]   Forfeitures 156
    [6]   Special Vesting Rules 156
      [a]   Vesting upon Normal Retirement Age 156
      [b]   Vesting upon Plan Termination 157
      [c]   Vesting of Top Heavy Plans — IRC § 416 157
  [B]   Minimum Age and Service Requirements — ERISA § 202; IRC
           § 410 157
  [C]   Benefit Accrual Rules — ERISA § 204; IRC § 410 158
    [1]   Defined Contribution Plans 159
    [2]   Defined Benefit Plans 159
      [a]   3% Method 160
      [b]   133 1/3% Method 162
      [c]   Fractional Method 163
§ 5.03   QUALIFIED JOINT AND SURVIVOR ANNUITY (QJSA) AND
       QUALIFIED PRERETIREMENT SPOUSAL ANNUITY (QPSA) RULES —
       ERISA § 205; IRC § 417 164
  [A]   Brief Introduction to Annuities 164
  [B]   Purpose of Qualified Joint and Survivor Annuity and Qualified Preretirement
           Survivor Annuity Rules 165
  [C]   Qualified Joint and Survivor Annuities 165
  [D]   Qualified Preretirement Survivor Annuities 166
    [1]   Participant's Death After Normal Retirement Age 166
    [2]   Participant's Death on or Before Normal Retirement Age 166
    [3]   Value of Qualified Preretirement Survivor Annuity from Defined
            Contribution Plan 167
  [E]   Plans and Benefits Exempt from the Qualified Joint and Survivor Annuity
           and Qualified Preretirement Survivor Annuity Rules 167

Table of Contents

[F]	Waiver with Spousal Consent	168
[G]	Marriage Requirement	168
§ 5.04	ANTI-ALIENATION PROVISION — ERISA § 206(d); IRC § 401(a)(13)	168
[A]	Purpose of the Anti-Alienation Provision	169
[B]	Definition of "Assign" or "Alienate"	169
[C]	Exceptions to the Anti-Alienation Provision	170
[1]	Loans to Plan Participants	171
[2]	10% Exception for Benefits in Pay Status	171
[3]	Qualified Domestic Relations Orders (QDROs)	172
[4]	Fiduciary Breaches with Respect to the Plan	173
[D]	The Anti-alienation Provision and the Bankruptcy Estate	174
§ 5.05	MINIMUM FUNDING STANDARDS — ERISA §§ 301–305; IRC §§ 412, 430–432	175
[A]	Funding Basics	175
[1]	Funding Defined Contribution Plans	176
[2]	Funding Defined Benefit Plans	176
[B]	Pre-ERISA Funding of Defined Benefit Plans	176
[C]	Purpose of Minimum Funding Standards	177
[D]	Minimum Funding Standards Prior to the Pension Protection Act of 2006	178
[E]	Minimum Funding Standards Under the Pension Protection Act of 2006	178
[1]	Minimum Required Contribution	179
[2]	Benefit Restrictions	180
[3]	At-Risk Plans	181
[4]	Funding Waivers	181
[5]	Effect of Failure to Satisfy Minimum Funding Standards	182

Chapter 6	FIDUCIARY STANDARDS	183
§ 6.01	INTRODUCTION	183
§ 6.02	OVERVIEW OF FIDUCIARY RESPONSIBILITY UNDER ERISA	184
§ 6.03	WHO IS A FIDUCIARY?	188
[A]	Named Fiduciary — ERISA § 402(a)	189
[B]	Functional Fiduciary — ERISA § 3(21)(A)	190
[C]	Summary of Named and Functional Fiduciaries	192
[D]	Determining when a Person is acting as a Functional Fiduciary	193
[1]	Employers	193
[a]	Employer as Settlor	194
[b]	Employer as Fiduciary	194
[c]	Distinguishing Employer as Settlor from Employer as Fiduciary	194

Table of Contents

[2]   Corporate Officers and Directors 196

[3]   Third Party Administrators 196

[4]   Investment Advice 197

   [a]   Investment Advice and Defined Benefit Plans 197

   [b]   Investment Advice and Defined Contribution Plans 198

[E]   Trustees 199

[1]   Directed Trustees . . . . : 199

[2]   Investment Managers 200

§ 6.04   ERISA'S FIDUCIARY STANDARDS — ERISA § 404(a) 200

[A]   Overview of ERISA § 404(a) Fiduciary Standards 202

[B]   Duty of Loyalty — ERISA § 404(a)(1) 202

[C]   Exclusive Purpose Rule — ERISA § 404(a)(1)(A) 204

[D]   The Duty of Prudence — ERISA § 404(a)(1)(B) 205

[1]   General Duty of Prudence 206

[2]   Duty of Prudence and Investment in Employer Stock 207

   [a]   *Moench* Presumption 207

   [b]   *Fifth Third Bancorp. v. Dudenhoeffer* 208

[E]   The Duty to Diversify — ERISA § 404(a)(1)(C) 210

[F]   The Duty to Follow Plan Documents — ERISA § 404(a)(1)(D) 211

[1]   Plan Documents 211

[2]   Conflict with ERISA 212

§ 6.05   ERISA'S EXEMPTION FROM FIDUCIARY STANDARDS FOR CERTAIN
         SELF-DIRECTED PLANS — ERISA § 404(c) 212

[A]   Purpose of ERISA § 404(c) Exception 213

[B]   Significance of ERISA § 404(c) Exception 213

[C]   ERISA § 404(c) Regulations 214

[1]   Opportunity to Exercise Control 214

[2]   Broad Range of Investment Options 215

[D]   Investment Education versus Investment Advice 215

[1]   Investment Education 216

[2]   Investment Advice 216

§ 6.06   PROHIBITED TRANSACTION REGIME — ERISA §§ 406–408 217

[A]   Overview of ERISA's Prohibited Transaction Regime 220

[B]   Section 406(a) Prohibited Transactions Between the Plan and a Party in
         Interest 220

[1]   Party in Interest — ERISA § 3(14) 221

[2]   ERISA § 406(a) Prohibited Transactions between the Plan and a Party in
         Interest 221

[3]   Overview of ERISA § 406(a) Party in Interest Prohibited Transactions
         223

[4]   Supreme Court Cases Interpreting ERISA § 406(a) Party In Interest
         Prohibited Transactions 224

Table of Contents

[a]	*Commissioner v. Keystone Consolidated Industries*	....	224
[b]	*Lockheed Corp. v. Spink*	....	224
[c]	*Hughes Aircraft Co. v. Jacobson*	....	225
[C]	Section 406(b) Prohibited Transactions Between the Plan and Fiduciary	....	225
[D]	ERISA § 406(c) Prohibition on Transfers of Encumbered Property	...	227
[E]	ERISA § 407(a) Limitation on Plan's Acquisition and Holding of Employer Securities and Real Property	....	227
[F]	Exemptions from ERISA's Prohibited Transaction Rules	....	228
[1]	Statutory Exemptions	....	228
[2]	Administrative Exemptions	....	228
[a]	Class Exemptions	....	229
[b]	Individual Exemptions	....	229
[G]	Sanctions and Remedies	....	230
§ 6.07	FIDUCIARY LIABILITY	....	230
[A]	Personal Liability of Fiduciary — ERISA § 409(a)	....	230
[B]	Co-Fiduciary Liability — ERISA § 405(a)	....	231
[C]	Nonfiduciary Liability	....	231
[1]	*Mertens v. Hewitt*	....	232
[2]	*Harris Trust v. Salomon Smith Barney, Inc.*	....	233
[3]	Extension of *Harris Trust* to Breach of Fiduciary Duty Cases	.....	234
§ 6.08	FIDUCIARY LIABILITY AND 401(k) PLAN FEES	....	234
[A]	Plan Fees and their Impact on Retirement Savings	....	235
[B]	Fee Disclosure Regulations	....	235
[C]	Excessive Plan Fee Litigation	....	236
[1]	*Hecker v. Deere*	....	238
[2]	*Tussey v. ABB, Inc.*	....	240

Chapter 7	**CIVIL ENFORCEMENT**	....	**243**
§ 7.01	INTRODUCTION	....	243
§ 7.02	ERISA § 502(a)'S CAUSES OF ACTION	....	244
[A]	ERISA § 502(a)(1)(B)	....	244
[B]	ERISA § 502(a)(2)	....	244
[C]	ERISA § 502(a)(3)	....	244
[D]	Summary of Principal Causes of Action Under ERISA § 502(a)	.....	245
§ 7.03	STANDING — ERISA § 502(a)	....	246
[A]	Participant	....	248
[B]	Beneficiary	....	249
[C]	Fiduciary	....	249
§ 7.04	EXHAUSTION OF ERISA § 503 CLAIMS REVIEW PROCEDURE	..	249
[A]	Exhaustion Requirement for Claims for Benefits Under ERISA		

Table of Contents

		§ 502(a)(1)(B)	250
[1]		Reasons for Exhaustion Requirement	250
[2]		Criticisms of Exhaustion Requirement	251
[3]		Exceptions to Exhaustion Requirement	251
[B]		Exhaustion Requirement for Claims Other than Under ERISA § 502(a)(1)(B)	252
§ 7.05		FEDERAL JURISDICTION UNDER ERISA § 502(e) AND REMOVAL	252
[A]		Removal of Express ERISA Claims	252
[B]		Removal Under Complete Preemption Doctrine	253
[1]		Early Supreme Court Complete Preemption Cases	253
[2]		*Aetna Health Inc. v. Davila*	254
§ 7.06		RIGHT TO A JURY TRIAL	255
§ 7.07		JUDICIAL STANDARD OF REVIEW	256
[A]		Standard of Review Applicable to Claims for Benefits Under ERISA § 502(a)(1)(B)	257
[1]		*De Novo* Default Standard	257
[2]		Deferential Standard if Plan Administrator Granted Discretion	258
[3]		Standard of Review in Cases of Conflict	259
[4]		Standard of Review After Initial Plan Interpretation Rejected	261
[5]		Summary of Standard of Review Applicable to ERISA § 502(a)(1)(B) Claims	263
[B]		Standard of Review Applicable to ERISA Claims Other than Claims Under ERISA § 502(a)(1)(B)	264
§ 7.08		REMEDIES	265
[A]		Claims for Benefits Under ERISA § 502(a)(1)(B)	267
[1]		Available Remedies Under ERISA § 502(a)(1)(B)	268
[2]		Terms of the Plan	270
[3]		Availability of Other ERISA § 502(a) Remedies	270
[4]		Summary of Remedies Under ERISA § 502(a)(1)(B)	272
[B]		Claims for Breach of Fiduciary Duty Under ERISA § 502(a)(2)	273
[1]		*Massachusetts Mutual Life Ins. Co. v. Russell*	273
[2]		*LaRue v. DeWolff Boberg & Associates, Inc.*	276
[3]		Summary of Remedies Under ERISA § 502(a)(2)	277
[C]		Claims Under the ERISA § 502(a)(3) "Safety Net"	277
[1]		Challenges Brought by Plan Participants (or Former Plan Participants)	278
[a]		*Mertens v. Hewitt Associates*	279
[b]		*Varity Corporation v. Howe*	281
[c]		*CIGNA Corporation v. Amara*	282
[2]		Claims Seeking Enforcement of Plan Reimbursement Provisions	284
[a]		*Great West v. Knudson*	284

Table of Contents

[b]   *Sereboff v. Mid Atlantic Medical Services, Inc.* 287

[c]   *U.S. Airways, Inc. v. McCutchen* 287

[3]   Summary of Remedies Under ERISA § 502(a)(3) 290

[D]   Making Sense of the Supreme Court's Remedy Decisions 291

§ 7.09 STATUTE OF LIMITATIONS 292

[A]   Statute of Limitations Applicable to Breach of Fiduciary Claims — ERISA
        § 413 293

[1]   ERISA § 413(2) Three Year Actual Knowledge Limitations Period . 296

[2]   ERISA § 413(1) General Six Year Limitations Period 297

[3]   ERISA § 413 Six Year Fraud or Concealment Limitations Period . . . 297

[B]   Statute of Limitations Applicable to Disputes Under the Multiemployer Plan
        Provisions of Title IV of ERISA — ERISA § 4301(f) 298

[C]   Statute of Limitations Applicable to Other ERISA Claims 299

[1]   Analogous State Statutes of Limitation 300

[2]   "Reasonable" Limitations Periods Set Forth in Plan 302

§ 7.10 ATTORNEY'S FEES — ERISA § 502(g)(1) 303

Chapter 8   **ERISA PREEMPTION** **307**

§ 8.01 INTRODUCTION 307

§ 8.02 GENERAL INTRODUCTION TO PREEMPTION 308

[A]   Basic Types of Preemption 308

[1]   Express Preemption 308

[2]   Implied Preemption 308

[a]   Field Preemption 309

[b]   Conflict Preemption 309

[3]   Effect of Preemption 309

[4]   Complete Preemption for Jurisdictional Purposes 310

[B]   Typical Procedural Posture of ERISA Preemption Claims 311

§ 8.03 OVERVIEW OF EXPRESS PREEMPTION UNDER ERISA § 514 312

§ 8.04 ERISA § 514(a) AND ITS REQUIREMENTS 314

[A]   "State Law" Requirement 314

[B]   "Relates to" Requirement 314

[1]   *Shaw* Two-Prong Test 315

[a]   "Reference to" Prong 316

[b]   "Connection with" Prong 317

[2]   The Future of the Two-Prong *Shaw* Test 321

[3]   Final Thoughts on the "Relate to" Requirement 322

[C]   "Employee Benefit Plan" Requirement 323

§ 8.05 ERISA § 514(b)(2)(A) SAVING CLAUSE 325

[A]   Original Test Defining "Regulates Insurance" 325

[B]   Current Test Defining "Regulates Insurance" 326

Table of Contents

[1]   First Prong of *Miller* Test — Specifically Directed Toward Entities
Engaged in Insurance 327

[2]   Second Prong of *Miller* Test — Substantially Affects the Risk Pooling
Arrangement Between the Insurer and the Insured 328

§ 8.06   ERISA § 514(b)(2)(B) DEEMER CLAUSE 328

[A]   Supreme Court's Interpretation of Deemer Clause 328

[B]   Incentive to Self-Fund Under Deemer Clause and the Affordable Care
Act 329

[C]   Role of Stop-Loss Insurance in Self-Funded Plans 330

[D]   Prevalence of Self-Funded Plans 330

Chapter 9   **NONDISCRIMINATION RULES FOR QUALIFIED
PLANSINTRODUCTION** **331**

§ 9.01   INTRODUCTION 331

§ 9.02   PURPOSE OF THE NONDISCRIMINATION RULES 332

§ 9.03   BROAD OVERVIEW OF THE NONDISCRIMINATION RULES 333

[A]   Three Nondiscrimination Requirements 333

[1]   Overview of IRC § 401(a)(26) Minimum Participation Requirement . 333

[2]   Overview of IRC § 410(b) Minimum Coverage Requirement 333

[3]   Overview of IRC § 401(a)(4) Nondiscrimination Requirement 334

[4]   Summary of the Three Nondiscrimination Requirements 335

[5]   Special IRC § 401(a)(4) Amounts Rule for 401(k) Plans 336

[B]   Preliminary Steps in Applying the Nondiscrimination Requirements .. 336

[1]   Identifying the Employer 336

[2]   Identifying the Highly Compensated Employees 337

[3]   Identifying the Plan 337

§ 9.04   A CLOSER LOOK AT EMPLOYERS 338

[A]   Overview of Employer Rules 339

[B]   IRC §§ 414(b) and (c) Employers under Common Control 339

[1]   Parent-Subsidiary Group 340

[2]   Brother-Sister Group 342

[3]   Combined Group 346

[4]   Advantages and Limits of IRC §§ 414(b) and (c) Controlled Group
Definition 346

[C]   Affiliated Service Groups 347

[1]   *Garland v. Commissioner* 347

[2]   IRC § 414(m) Affiliated Service Groups 348

[a]   IRC § 414(m)(2)(A) Organization 349

[b]   IRC § 414(m)(2)(B) Organization 349

[c]   IRC § 414(m)(5) Management Organization 350

[D]   IRC § 414(n) Leased Employees 351

Table of Contents

[E]   IRC § 414(o) Anti-Avoidance Rule 352

[F]   IRC § 414(r) Separate Lines of Business 352

  [1]   Purpose of IRC § 414(r) Separate Lines of Business Rule 352

  [2]   Treasury Regulations Implementing IRC § 414(r) 353

    [a]   Line of Business 353

    [b]   Separate Lines of Business 353

    [c]   Qualified Separate Lines of Business 354

      [i]   Statutory Safe Harbor 354

      [ii]   Regulatory Safe Harbors 355

      [iii]   Individual Determination 355

    [d]   Summary of IRC § 414(r) Qualified Separate Lines of Business Requirements 356

§ 9.05   A CLOSER LOOK AT HIGHLY COMPENSATED EMPLOYEES — IRC § 414(q) 357

[A]   Ownership Test 357

[B]   Compensation Test 357

[C]   Top-Paid Group Election 358

[D]   Implications of Objective Test 359

§ 9.06   A CLOSER LOOK AT THE IRC § 401(a)(26) MINIMUM PARTICIPATION REQUIREMENT 360

[A]   Purpose of IRC § 401(a)(26) Requirement 360

[B]   Statutory Requirement 361

§ 9.07   A CLOSER LOOK AT THE IRC § 410(b) MINIMUM COVERAGE REQUIREMENT 361

[A]   Plans that Automatically Satisfy IRC § 410(b) 362

[B]   Meaning of "Benefit" Under the Plan 362

[C]   Excludable Employees 363

  [1]   Employees Who Do Not Satisfy Minimum Age and Service Requirements 363

  [2]   Nonresident Aliens 364

  [3]   Employees Covered by Collective Bargained Agreements 364

  [4]   Employees of Qualified Separate Lines of Business 365

  [5]   Certain Terminating Employees 365

[D]   Overview of the Three IRC § 410(b) Coverage Tests 365

[E]   IRC § 410(b)(1)(A) Percentage Test 366

[F]   IRC § 410(b)(1)(B) Ratio Percentage Test 368

[G]   IRC § 410(b)(1)(C) Average Benefit Percentage Test 369

  [1]   Classification Test 370

    [a]   Reasonable Classification Test 370

    [b]   Nondiscriminatory Classification Test 370

      [i]   Nonhighly Compensated Employee Concentration Percentage .. 371

      [ii]   Safe Harbor 371

Table of Contents

[iii]   Facts and Circumstances Test 372
[2]   Average Benefit Percentage Test 374
[H]   Summary of IRC § 410(b) Minimum Coverage Tests 376
§ 9.08   A CLOSER LOOK AT THE IRC § 401(a)(4) NONDISCRIMINATION IN CONRIBUTIONS OR BENEFITS REQUIREMENT 378
[A]   Overview of IRC § 401(a)(4) 379
[B]   Amounts Rule 379
[1]   Safe Harbors for Defined Contribution Plans 380
[a]   Uniform Allocation Formula 381
[b]   Uniform Points Allocation Formula 381
[2]   General Testing of Defined Contribution Plans 383
[a]   Dividing Plan into Rate Groups 383
[b]   Testing Each Rate Group 384
[3]   Flexibility Features 386
[4]   Summary of Amounts Rule as Applied to Defined Contribution Plans 387
[5]   Testing of Defined Benefit Plans 387
[C]   Other Benefits, Rights, and Features 388
[D]   Special Circumstances 389
§ 9.09   A CLOSER LOOK AT THE NONDISCRIMINATION RULES FOR 401(k) PLANS 390
[A]   Overview of IRC § 401(k) Special Nondiscrimination Testing 392
[B]   Special IRC § 401(k)(3)(A)(ii) Nondiscrimination Tests 393
[1]   "Actual Deferral Percentage" (ADP) 393
[a]   Highly Compensated Employees (HCEs) 393
[b]   Actual Deferral Ratio (ADR) 394
[c]   Actual Deferral Percentage 394
[2]   ADP Tests under IRC § 401(k)(3)(A)(ii) 394
[a]   IRC § 401(k)(3)(A)(ii)(I) 125% Test 395
[b]   IRC § 401(k)(3)(A)(ii)(II) Alternative Limitation 396
[c]   Rule of Thumb 398
[C]   Methods for Correcting Excess Contributions 400
[1]   Distribution of Excess Contributions 400
[a]   Step One 401
[b]   Step Two 403
[c]   Step Three 406
[d]   Step Four 406
[2]   Recharacterization of Excess Contributions 406
[3]   Qualified Matching or Nonelective Contributions 407
[D]   Safe Harbors 407
[1]   IRC § 401(k)(12) Safe Harbors 408
[a]   IRC § 401(k)(12)(B) Matching Contribution Safe Harbor 408

Table of Contents

[b]	IRC § 401(k)(12)(C) Nonelective Contribution Safe Harbor	. . . . .	411
[2]	IRC § 401(k)(13) Safe Harbors	. . . .	411
[a]	IRC § 401(k)(13) Automatic Salary Deferral Requirement	. . . . . .	412
[b]	IRC § 401(k)(13)(D)(i)(I) Matching Contribution Safe Harbor	. . .	414
[c]	IRC § 401(k)(13)(D)(i)(II) Nonelective Contribution Safe Harbor	.	418
[E]	Summary of IRC § 401(k) Special Nondiscrimination Requirement	. . .	419

Chapter 10   TAX RULES GOVERNING PENSION PLANS 421

§ 10.01	INTRODUCTION		421
§ 10.02	TAX QUALIFICATION REQUIREMENTS		421
[A]	IRC § 401(a)(17) Annual Compensation Limit		422
[B]	IRC § 415 Limitation on Contributions and Benefits		423
[1]	Purpose of IRC § 415		423
[2]	IRC § 415(c) Limitation on Contributions		423
[3]	IRC § 415(b) Limitation on Benefits		424
[4]	Phased in Limit		425
[5]	De Minimis Benefit		425
[C]	IRC § 402(g) Limitation on Elective Deferrals		426
[1]	Brief History and Purpose of the IRC § 402(g) Limitation		426
[2]	Basic IRC § 402(g) Limitation on Elective Deferrals		427
[3]	IRC § 401(a)(30) Qualification Requirement		427
[4]	Treatment of Excess Deferrals		428
[5]	Correction of Excess Deferrals		428
[D]	IRC § 414(v) Catch Up Contributions		429
[1]	Purpose of IRC § 414(v) Catch-up Contributions		430
[2]	Application of IRC § 414(v) Catch-up Contributions		430
§ 10.03	DEDUCTIBILITY OF EMPLOYER CONTRIBUTIONS		432
[A]	Timing of Deductions		433
[B]	IRC § 404(a)(3) Deduction Limitations on Defined Contribution Plans		434
[1]	Compensation for Purposes of IRC § 404		435
[2]	Compensation and Elective Deferrals		436
[3]	IRC § 404(l) Limit on Compensation		436
[4]	Interaction with IRC § 415 Limits		437
[C]	IRC § 404(o) Deduction Limitations on Defined Benefit Plans		439
[D]	IRC § 404(a)(7) Deduction Limitations on Combined Plans		439
[E]	IRC § 4972 Excise Tax on Excess Contributions		439
[F]	Summary of Deduction Limitations		442
§ 10.04	PLAN DISTRIBUTIONS		443
[A]	Taxation of Distributions under IRC § 72		443
[1]	Amounts Received as an Annuity		444

Table of Contents

[a]	Definition of Amount Received as an Annuity		444
[b]	"Simplified Method of Taxation" under IRC § 72(d)		445
[2]	Amounts Not Received as an Annuity — IRC § 72(e)		446
[B]	Taxation of Qualified Distributions from Designated Roth Accounts — IRC § 402A(d)		447
[C]	Rollover Distributions — IRC § 402(c)		448
[1]	Purpose of the Exception for Rollover Distributions		448
[2]	Eligible Rollover Distributions		448
[a]	Periodic Payments		449
[b]	Minimum Required Distributions		450
[c]	Hardship Distributions		450
[3]	Eligible Retirement Plans		451
[4]	Types of Rollovers		451
[5]	Rollovers of Property		452
[D]	IRC § 72(t) 10% Additional Tax on Early Distributions		453
[E]	Plan Loans — IRC § 72(p)		455
[1]	Advantages and Disadvantages of Plan Loans		456
[2]	Regulation of Plan Loans		457
[a]	Plan Loans and the Plan Qualification Requirements		457
[b]	Plan Loans and the Prohibited Transaction Rules		457
[c]	Plan Loans and the Tax Distribution Rules — IRC § 72(p)		458
[i]	General Maximum Loan Amount — IRC § 72(p)(2)(A)		459
[ii]	Repayment Period — IRC § 72(p)(2)(B)		460
[iii]	Amortization Requirement — IRC § 72(p)(2)(C)		460
[iv]	Special Maximum for Multiple Loans — IRC § 72(p)(2)(A)		460
[F]	Minimum Required Distributions — IRC § 401(a)(9)		462
[1]	Required Beginning Date		462
[2]	Distribution Period		463
[3]	Minimum Required Distributions from Defined Contribution Plans		463
[4]	Minimum Required Distributions from Defined Benefit Plans		464
[5]	Post-Death Distributions		465
[a]	Death after Distributions Have Begun		465
[b]	Death before Distributions Have Begun		465
[i]	Five-Year Rule		466
[ii]	Life Expectancy Rule		466
Chapter 11	**PLAN TERMINATION**		**467**
§ 11.01	INTRODUCTION		467
§ 11.02	REGULATION OF PENSION PLAN TERMINATION UNDER THE INTERNAL REVENUE CODE		467
[A]	Special Vesting Requirement — IRC § 411(d)(3)		468

Table of Contents

[1]   Vertical Partial Termination 468

[2]   Horizontal Partial Termination 469

[B]   Tax on Reversions — IRC § 4980 469

[1]   Qualified Replacement Plan 470

[2]   Benefit Increase Exception 470

§ 11.03   REGULATION OF PENSION PLAN TERMINATION UNDER TITLE IV
OF ERISA 470

[A]   Purposes of Title IV of ERISA — ERISA § 4002(a) 471

[B]   Pension Benefit Guaranty Corporation 472

[C]   PBGC Insurance Programs 472

[1]   Single-Employer Program 472

[2]   Multiemployer Program 473

[D]   PBGC Premiums — ERISA § 4006(a)(3) 473

[1]   Single-Employer Per-Participant Flat-Rate Premium — ERISA
§ 4006(a)(3)(A)(i) 474

[2]   Single-Employer Variable-Rate Premium — ERISA
§ 4006(a)(3)(E) 474

[3]   Single-Employer Termination Premium — ERISA § 4006(a)(7) ... 475

[4]   Multiemployer Per-Participant Flat-Rate Premium — ERISA
§ 4006(a)(3)(A)(v) 475

[5]   Critique of PBGC Premium Structure 475

[E]   Guaranteed Benefits 476

[F]   Single-Employer Plan Terminations 477

[1]   Voluntary Standard Termination — ERISA § 4041(b) 478

[2]   Voluntary Distress Termination — ERISA § 4041(c) 479

[a]   Liquidation Test 480

[b]   Reorganization Test 480

[c]   Business Continuation Test 480

[d]   Pension Costs Test 480

[3]   Involuntary Termination — ERISA § 4042 480

[a]   Mandatory Terminations 480

[b]   Discretionary Terminations 481

[4]   Summary of Single-Employer Plan Terminations 482

[G]   Liability to PGCG upon Plan Termination 483

[1]   Unfunded Benefit Liabilities 483

[2]   Unpaid Minimum Funding Contributions 483

[3]   Unpaid Annual Premiums 484

[4]   Termination Premiums 484

[H]   Distribution of Plan Assets upon Plan Termination 484

Table of Contents

Appendix A   **ERISA** **487**

Appendix B   **ECONOMIC EFFECT OF FAVORABLE TAX TREATMENT ACCORDED QUALIFIED PLANS** **497**

Appendix C   **SAFE AND UNSAFE HARBOR PERCENTAGES** **501**

Table of Cases **TC-1**

Index **I-1**

Chapter 1

INTRODUCTION

§ 1.01   WHAT ARE EMPLOYEE BENEFITS?

Employee benefits are the extras or "perks," over and above wages, that an employer provides to its employees.[1] Employee benefits range from paid vacation to life insurance to Social Security.

Some employee benefits are mandatory, that is, required by law. Mandatory benefits include Social Security, Medicare, and unemployment insurance.

Other employee benefits are voluntary. For example, an employer may elect, but is not required, to provide its employees with health insurance, sick leave, and/or retirement benefits, other than Social Security.

Employers typically offer employee benefits through employee benefit plans. There are two basic types of employee benefit plans: pension plans and welfare benefit plans.

Pension plans generally provide employees with retirement income or deferred income, that is, income after the employee ceases to work for the employer sponsoring the pension plan.

Welfare benefit plans provide employees with a wide variety of other benefits, such as life insurance, medical, surgical, and hospital care, disability benefits, unemployment benefits, vacation pay, and severance pay. Unlike pension benefits, welfare benefits are typically current benefits, that is, benefits that are earned and received in the same year.

---

[1] Employee benefits account for about 30% of the cost of compensation. *See* Bureau of Labor Statistics, *Employment Cost Index News Release Text — Dec. 2014*, USDL-15-0113 (Jan. 30, 2015), *available at* http://www.bls.gov/news.release/eci.nr0.htm.

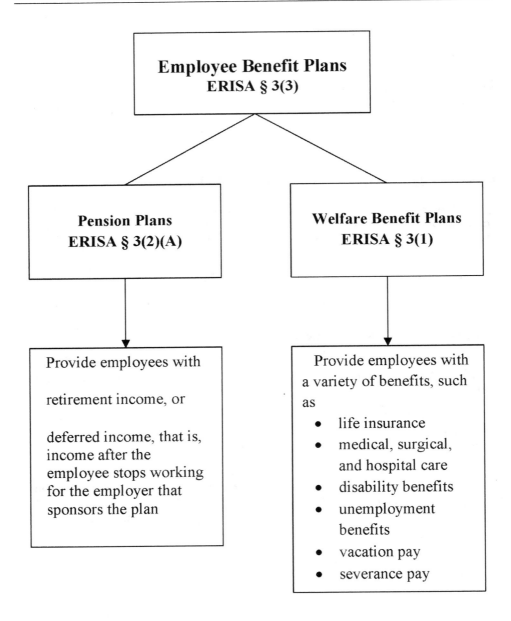

§ 1.02 WHY DO EMPLOYERS OFFER EMPLOYEE BENEFITS?

Employers offer mandatory employee benefits because they are required by law to offer such benefits.

Employers offer voluntary employee benefits for a variety of reasons. For example, an employer may offer a rich employee benefit package to attract and retain good, qualified employees. An employer may offer, or change, its employee benefit package to keep up with workforce competition and/or foster good employee morale. In addition, many employee benefits are eligible for favorable income tax treatment, and an employer may offer these benefits to take advantage of their favorable tax treatment.

Some employers are more likely to offer voluntary employee benefits than others. For example, public sector, that is, governmental, employers[2] are more likely to offer employee benefits than private sector employers, and union employers are more likely to offer employee benefits than non-union employers. In addition, certain employees, such as full-time employees, are more likely to be offered benefits than other employees, such as part-time workers.[3]

In many ways, the law governing public sector benefits differs from the law governing private sector benefits. In addition, in some instances, the rules for benefits provided by union employers differ from those for benefits provided by non-union employers.

For the most part, this book focuses on the regulation of benefits provided by private sector, non-unionized employers.

§ 1.03 HOW ARE EMPLOYEE BENEFITS REGULATED?

Employee benefits are regulated by both federal and state law as well as by a number of administrative agencies.

Federal laws that regulate employee benefits include the Employee Retirement Income Security Act of 1974 (ERISA),[4] the Internal Revenue Code (IRC),[5] the Family Medical Leave Act (FMLA),[6] and the Older Workers Benefit Protection Act (OWBA).[7]

State laws vary by state, but all states have laws that regulate health insurance, and most states require employers to contribute to state workers' compensation programs.

Federal administrative agencies that regulate employee benefits include the Department of Labor (DOL), the Treasury Department, and the Pension Benefit Guaranty Corporation (PBGC).

---

[2] For data on state- and locally-administered public pension systems, see Erika Becker-Medina, *Public-Employee Retirement Systems State- and Locally-Administered Pensions Summary Report: 2010*, U.S. CENSUS BUREAU GOVERNMENTS DIVISION BRIEFS (Apr. 2012), *available through* http://www.census. gov/govs/retire/.

[3] For statistics regarding plan coverage and participation, see, for example, Craig Copeland, *Employment-Based Retirement Plan Participation: Geographic Differences and Trends, 2013*, EBRI Issue Brief No. 405 (Oct. 2014); U.S. Census Bureau, Jessica C. Smith and Carla Medalia, *Health Insurance Coverage in the United States, 2013*, CURRENT POPULATION REPORTS, P60–250 (Sept. 2014).

[4] Pub. L. No. 93-406, 88 Stat. 829 (1974) (codified as amended in scattered sections of U.S.C.).

[5] 26 U.S.C. §§ 1–9834.

[6] Pub. L. No. 103-3, 107 Stat. 6 (1993) (codified as amended at 29 U.S.C.).

[7] Pub. L. No. 101-433, 104 Stat. 978 (1990) (codified as amended at 29. U.S.C.).

This book focuses on the two most significant federal laws regulating employee benefits: ERISA and the IRC. It does not discuss any specific state laws governing employee benefits. Chapter 8, however, addresses ERISA's preemption of state law.

§ 1.04 HISTORY AND PURPOSES OF ERISA[8]

ERISA, the Employee Retirement Income Security Act of 1974,[9] was signed into law by President Gerald Ford on September 2, 1974.[10] It was the culmination of more than a decade of Congressional hearings, reports, studies, and deliberations on the weaknesses and problems with existing state and federal regulation of employee benefit plans.[11]

[A] Pre-ERISA Regulation of Employee Benefit Plans

Prior to the enactment of ERISA, employee benefit plans were impacted by three types of federal laws:

(1) federal income tax laws,

(2) federal labor laws, and

(3) the Welfare and Pension Plans Disclosure Act.[12]

In addition, employee benefit plans were subject to some state law regulation.

Nevertheless, substantive regulation of employee benefit plans was relatively limited.

[1] Federal Income Tax Law

Federal income tax law encouraged the creation of "qualified" pension plans by providing for favorable income tax treatment of such plans.[13] Tax law, however, did not impose much substantive regulation on qualified plans. For example, it did not

---

[8] For an extensive history of ERISA, see JAMES A. WOOTEN, THE EMPLOYEE RETIREMENT INCOME SECURITY ACT OF 1974: A POLITICAL HISTORY (2004).

[9] Pub. L. No. 93-406, 88 Stat. 829 (1974).

[10] *Id.* at 1035.

[11] On March 28, 1962, President Kennedy initiated the first comprehensive study of employee benefit regulation with the creation of the President's Committee on Corporate Pensions. Social Security Administration, *Notes and Brief Reports: Public Policy and Private Pension Programs*, 28 SOCIAL SECURITY BULLETIN 39, 39 (No. 7 July 1965). Eight separate sets of congressional hearing were held between 1968 and 1973. *See* Camilla E. Watson, *Broken Promises Revisited: The Window of Vulnerability for Surviving Spouses under ERISA*, 76 IOWA L. REV. 431, 434 n.18 (1991).

[12] Pub. L. No. 85-836, 72 Stat. 997 (1958), repealed by ERISA, Pub. L. No. 93-406 § 111(a)(1), 88 Stat. 851 (1974).

[13] The Revenue Act of 1921 provided a tax deduction for employers who contributed to employee pension plans. 1921 Revenue Act, Pub. L. No. 67-98, § 219(f), 42 Stat. 227 (1921). The Revenue Acts of 1926 and 1928 extended the favorable income tax treatment by permitting tax-free accumulation of earnings on the contributions while they are held in a tax-exempt trust and delaying taxation of plan participants on contributions to the trust until the money is distributed to the participants. 1926 Revenue Act, § 219(f), Pub. L. No. 69-20, 44 Stat. 9; 1928 Revenue Act § 3165, Pub. L. No. 70-562, 45 Stat. 791. The Revenue Act of 1938 conditioned favorable income tax treatment on the requirement that the trust be

require advance funding of benefits nor did it require that benefits become vested, that is, nonforfeitable, after a certain period of time. Federal tax law was most concerned with targeting the tax subsidy and ensuring that lower-income employees as well as higher-income employees participated in and benefited from qualified pension plans.

[2] Federal Labor Law

The National Labor Relations Act (NLRA),[14] enacted in 1935, established a framework for the bargaining of pension and welfare benefits.[15] In 1947, the Labor Management Relations Act (LMRA)[16] amended the NLRA to require that pension and welfare plans subject to the Act be administered by joint trustee fiduciaries representing both employees and employers.[17] The LMRA also required that plans subject to the Act be written and operated for the "sole and exclusive benefit" of the employees.[18] Case law established principles of fiduciary responsibility governing plan administration and the investment of plan assets.[19] Federal labor law, however, only regulated plans established pursuant to collective bargaining agreements[20] and was not enforced uniformly.[21] For example, the Department of Justice only enforced the labor law provisions when there was evidence of criminality, and participants and beneficiaries were often reluctant to enforce the law because of the fear of retaliation.[22]

[3] Welfare and Pension Plans Disclosure Act

In 1958, Congress enacted the Welfare and Pension Plans Disclosure Act (WPPDA),[23] the first federal statute aimed directly and exclusively at private employee benefit plans. The WPPDA did not impose any substantive regulations on

---

"irrevocable" and for the exclusive benefit of employees. 1938 Revenue Act § 23(p)(3), Pub. L. No. 75-554, 52 Stat. 447, 463–464. The 1942 Act tightened the rules governing favorable income tax treatment by requiring that plans not discriminate in favor of highly compensated employees and imposing limits on tax deductions for contributions to fund pension plans. 1942 Revenue Act § 162, Pub. L. No. 753, 56 Stat. 798, 862. While the tax rules governing pension plans have evolved considerably over the years, these basic elements have not changed.

[14] Pub. L. No. 74-198, 49 Stat. 449 (1935) (codified as amended at 29 U.S.C. §§ 151–169 (2012)).

[15] ABA SECTION OF LABOR AND EMPLOYMENT LAW, EMPLOYEE BENEFITS LAW 1–6 (Jeffrey Lewis et al. eds., 3d ed. 2012). *See also* James A. Wooten, *A Legislative and Political History of ERISA Preemption, Part 1*, 14 J. PENSION BENEFITS 31, 32 (2006); William J. Kilberg and Paul D. Inman, *Preemption of State Laws Relating to Employee Benefit Plans: An Analysis of ERISA Section 514*, 62 TEX. L. REV. 1313, 1313 n.3 (1984).

[16] Pub. L. No. 80-101, 61 Stat. 136 (1947).

[17] David Gregory, *The Scope of ERISA Preemption of State Law: A Study in Effective Federalism*, 48 U. PITT. L. REV. 427, 440 (1987).

[18] ABA SECTION OF LABOR AND EMPLOYMENT LAW, EMPLOYEE BENEFITS LAW, at 1–7.

[19] *Id.* at 1-7–1-8.

[20] David Gregory, 48 U. PITT. L. REV., at 441.

[21] ABA SECTION OF LABOR AND EMPLOYMENT LAW, EMPLOYEE BENEFITS LAW, at c (reprinting introduction to the first ed.).

[22] *Id.*

[23] Pub. L. No. 85-836, 72 Stat. 997 (1958), repealed by ERISA, Pub. L. No. 93-406 § 111(a)(1), 88 Stat.

employee benefit plans. Instead, it sought to regulate employee benefit plans through reporting and disclosure requirements.[24] The theory behind the WPPDA was that "full disclosure to plan participants and beneficiaries of the provisions of their plan and its financial operations would deter abuse ('sunlight being the best disinfectant') and would enable [participants and beneficiaries] to police the plans themselves without requiring greater Government regulations or interference."[25] The WPPDA expressly preserved state authority to regulate employee benefit plans.[26]

[4] State Law

When Congress enacted the WPPDA, six states had already enacted statutes specifically directed at employee benefit plans.[27] For the most part, however, employee benefit plans were regulated by state common law prior to the enactment of ERISA, and little of that common law was directed specifically at employee benefit plans.[28]

[B] Failure of Pre-ERISA Law to Protect Plan Participants and Beneficiaries

By the 1960s, a consensus was beginning to form that state and federal law did not provide sufficient protection of employee benefit plan participants and beneficiaries.[29]

The failure of pre-ERISA law to protect plan participants and beneficiaries was most famously — and starkly — illustrated by the closing of the Studebaker automobile plan in December 1963.[30] Prior to the enactment of ERISA, neither federal nor state law required that pension plans be prefunded, that is, the law did not require that contributions be made during each employee's working life to ensure that the full cost of the benefit promised to the employee was funded when

---

851 (1974). As its name suggests, the WPPDA required that descriptive and financial information about private employee benefit plans be filed with the Department of Labor and made available to plan participants and beneficiaries. ABA Section of Labor and Employment Law, EMPLOYEE BENEFITS LAW, at xcix–c.

[24] In 1962, the WPPDA was amended to provide the Department of Labor with limited investigatory authority and the power to issue regulations. The WPPDA was also amended to require that those handling plan funds have surety bonds and to make theft, embezzlement, and kickbacks involving employee benefit funds federal crimes. Michael S. Gordon, *Overview: Why Was ERISA Enacted*, in United States Senate Special Committee on Aging Information Paper, The Employee Retirement Income Security Act of 1974: The First Decade 1, 7, 98th Cong., 2d Sess. (1984).

[25] *Id.*

[26] Welfare and Pension Plans Disclosure Act, Pub. L. No. 85-836 § 10, 72 Stat. 997, 1008 (1958).

[27] James A. Wooten, *A Legislative and Political History of ERISA Preemption, Part 3*, 15 J. PENSION BENEFITS 16, 16 (2008). All of the state laws included disclosure requirements. *Id.*

[28] Jay Conison, *ERISA and the Language of Preemption*, 72 WASH. U. L.Q. 619, 644–45 (1994).

[29] ABA SECTION OF LABOR AND EMPLOYMENT LAW, EMPLOYEE BENEFITS LAW, at 1–7.

[30] For a detailed discussion of the closing of the Studebaker plant and the galvanizing role it played in the enactment of ERISA, see James A. Wooten, *"The Most Glorious Story of Failure in Business": The Studebaker-Packard Corporation and the Origins of ERISA*, 49 BUFFALO L. REV. 683 (2001).

the employee retired.[31] Thus, when the Studebaker plant closed, and its pension plan terminated, the Studebaker's plan's liabilities (that is, its promised benefits) exceeded its assets by $15 million.[32] As a result, the terminated plan was unable to pay all of the plan participants all of the benefits that they had been promised. Specifically, 4,000 vested employees between the ages of 40 and 60 received 15% of their promised benefits while 2,900 workers under the age of 40 received no benefits whatsoever (regardless of whether their benefits were vested).[33]

The Studebaker plant closing clearly demonstrated the inadequacy of the law to ensure proper plan funding. Inadequate funding, however, was not the only risk plan participants faced. Prior to the enactment of ERISA, some pension plans did not provide for the vesting of benefits.[34] Employers of such plans were free to terminate their plans at any time, and employees had no enforceable rights to their promised pensions. Moreover, plans that did provide for the vesting of benefits could impose age limits and lengthy service requirements. According to one account, prior to ERISA, fewer than 10% of plan participants ever attained benefit eligibility because of lengthy service requirements and numerous disqualification provisions. [35]

In addition to concerns about inadequate funding and vesting of pension plans, "Congress was also concerned that large amounts of money in the hands of plan managers created a temptation for self-dealing and improper handling of these funds."[36] In the 1950s, a special Senate committee was established to investigate improper practices with respect to employee benefit plans. The investigations uncovered "all manner of abuses, ranging from ineptness and lack of know-how to outright looting of benefit funds and corrupt administration."[37] For example, in

---

[31] Indeed, prior to the enactment, the Internal Revenue Code discouraged pre-funding of pension plans by limiting annual deductions for the funding of past-service liability. *See* Kathryn J. Kennedy, *Pension Funding Reform: It's Time to Get the Rules Right (Part I)*, 108 Tax Notes 907, 2005 TNT 162-34 (July 29, 2005).

[32] Wooten, *"The Most Glorious Story of Failure in Business": The Studebaker-Packard Corporation and the Origins of ERISA*, at 726.

[33] Paul Nathanson & Bruce Miller, *Litigation to Compel Pension Payments*, 2 Class Action Reports Art 2 (Issue 4 July–Aug. 1973), *citing*, Staff of Subcomm. On Labor, Senate Comm. on Labor and Public Welfare, 92d Cong., 2d Sess., Private Welfare and Pension Plan Study 1972 — Report of the Hearings on Pension Plan Terminations 1–2 (Comm. Print 1972).

[34] According to the Investment Company Institute, 88% of plans provided for the vesting of benefits by 1974, but the vesting schedules ranged widely, with some plans imposing age and lengthy service requirements. Investment Company Institute, *A Look at Private-Sector Retirement After ERISA*, 16 Res. Persp. 1, 11 (2010).

[35] Mary E. O'Connell, *On the Fringe: Rethinking the Link Between Wages and Benefits*, 67 Tul. L. Rev. 1422, 1454–55 (1993).

[36] Carlton R. Sickles, *Introduction: The Significance and Complexity of ERISA*, 17 Wm. & Mary Law Rev. 205, 206 (1975).

[37] Gordon, *Overview:* U.S. S. Spec. Comm. Aging Info. Paper, at 6.

In addition to embezzlement, kickbacks, unjustifiably high administrative costs, and excessive investment of funds in employer securities, serious examples of improper insurance practices were also found, including exorbitantly high commission and administrative charges, fictitious fees, retention by some insurance carriers of unduly an large share of the premiums, unequal treatment of policyholders, switching carriers to obtain high first-year commissions and

1965, the Senate Permanent Subcommittee on Investigations discovered that George Barasch, the founder of two New Jersey unions, had managed to manipulate and divert the funds of the unions' employee benefit plans so as make himself a prospective multimillionaire.[38] He was both trustee of the plans and owner of a benefit consulting firm which operated the plans and collected huge consulting fees on his behalf.[39] Existing law did not adequately protect against this behavior.[40]

[C] Purposes of ERISA

In section 2 of ERISA,[41] Congress set forth, at length, its findings and declaration of policy in enacting ERISA.

Congress identified four principal problems with employee benefit plans: (1) inadequate disclosure of plan information, (2) inadequate safeguards against inappropriate plan administration,[42] (3) the widespread loss of anticipated retirement benefits due to the lack of vesting provisions, and (4) the inability of plans to provide promised benefits due to inadequate funding.[43]

Congress then identified six ways in which ERISA would address those problems: (1) by imposing reporting and disclosure requirements, (2) by establishing fiduciary standards, (3) by providing for appropriate remedies, sanctions, and ready access to courts, (4) by imposing vesting standards, (5) by imposing minimum funding standards, and (6) by requiring plan termination insurance.[44]

On a number of occasions, the Supreme Court has referred to Congress' purposes in enacting ERISA. For example, in one early case, *Nachman Corp. v.*

---

collusions between insurance representatives, union officials and management.

Id.

See also U.S. Gen Acct. Office, Report to the Permanent Subcommittee on Investigations, Comm. on Governmental Affairs, the Dep't of Labor's Oversight of the Management of the Teamsters' Central States Pension and Health and Welfare Funds App. I, 2–3 (1985), *available at* http://www.gao.gov/assets/150/143210.pdf (describing Teamsters Union's misuse of tens of millions of dollars in Central States pension funds).

[38] Gordon, *Overview:* U.S. S. Spec. Comm. Aging Info. Paper, at 10.

[39] *Id.* at 10–11.

[40] *Id.* at 11. Prior to the enactment of ERISA, federal criminal law classified embezzlement, the filing of false reports, and bribery as felonies. Nevertheless, the Department of Justice found it difficult to convict individuals of these crimes, and the convictions it did obtain were ineffective in correcting such abuses. Thomas C. Woodruff, *The Goals of ERISA and the Impact of ERISA on Plan Participants*, in United States Senate Special Committee on Aging Information Paper, The Employee Retirement Income Security Act of 1974: The First Decade, 26, 27, 98th Cong., 2d Sess. (1984).

[41] 29 U.S.C. § 1001.

[42] Although the statute does not expressly refer to corrupt plan administration, its reference to "the lack of adequate safeguards concerning their operation" in section 2(a) presumably refers to the corrupt practices undercovered in the hearings leading up to the enactment of ERISA. ABA Section of Labor and Employment Law, Employee Benefits Law, at xicx–c.

[43] ERISA § 2(a).

[44] ERISA § 2(b) & (c).

Pension Benefit Guaranty Corp.,[45] the Court declared, "one of Congress' central purposes in enacting [ERISA] was to prevent the 'great personal tragedy' suffered by employees whose vested benefits are not paid when pension plans are terminated."[46] In *Boggs v. Boggs*,[47] the Court announced that "[t]he principal object of the statute is to protect plan participants and beneficiaries."[48]

Not all of ERISA's provisions, however, protect and favor plan participants. For example, ERISA expressly preempts state laws that relate to employee benefit plans. To the extent that state law provides employees with greater protections than does ERISA, ERISA preemption does not protect or favor plan participants. Instead, ERISA preemption favors plan sponsors and administrators by promoting uniformity of law and reducing the administrative burden of complying with multiple laws. ERISA's legislative history makes clear that not only did Congress intend to protect plan participants in enacting ERISA, but it also sought to encourage employers to voluntarily establish employee benefit plans and thus tried not to place undue burdens on plans when enacting ERISA.[49]

Accordingly, ERISA may be said to have conflicting purposes.[50] Indeed, in *Varity Corp. v. Howe*,[51] the Court noted that in interpreting ERISA, "courts may have to take account of competing congressional purposes, such as Congress' desire to offer employees enhanced protection for their benefits, on the one hand, and, on the other, its desire not to create a system that is so complex that administrative costs, or litigation expenses, unduly discourage employers from offering welfare benefit plans in the first place."[52]

---

[45] 446 U.S. 359 (1980).

[46] *Id.* at 374.

[47] 520 U.S. 833 (1997).

[48] *Id.* at 845.

[49] *See, e.g.*, 263 Cong. Rec. 29,928, 29,953 (1974) (statement of Sen. Nelson) ("Congress tried to adopt provisions which strike a balance between providing a meaningful protection for the employees and keeping within reasonable limits for employers"); 120 Cong. Rec. 29,192, 129,198 (1974) (statement of Rep. Ullman) ("these new requirements have been carefully designed to provide adequate protection for employees and, at the same time, provide a favorable setting for the growth and development of private pension plans); *id.* at 29,210 (statement of Rep. Rostenkowski) ("[t]he goal of this legislation was to strengthen the rights of employees under existing pension systems, while at the same time encouraging the expansion of these plans and the creating of new ones").

[50] *Cf.* Pamela D. Perdue, *Overview of ERISA's Legislative and Regulatory Scheme*, ST043 ALI-ABA 1 (May 16–18, 2012) ("In short, the goal of ERISA was to protect participants while also promoting the expansion of the private pension system."); *See* Peter J. Wiedenbeck, *ERISA's Curious Coverage*, 76 WASH. U. L.Q. 311, 312–15 (1998) (identifying four central goals of ERISA: (1) controlling mismanagement and abuse of employee benefit funds, (2) promoting economic efficiency by facilitating improved career and financial planning, (3) assuring the pension promise has some minimum content, and (4) cost containment and the preservation of employer flexibility (which competes with the three preceding objectives which are aimed at protecting plan participants)). *But see* Norman Stein, *An Alphabet Soup Agenda for Reform of the Internal Revenue Code and ERISA Provisions Applicable to Qualified Deferred Compensation Plans*, 56 SMU L. REV. 627, 648 (2003) (asserting that unifying purpose of ERISA as a whole was "providing meaningful protections to the benefit expectations of men and women who participate in employee benefit plans").

[51] 516 U.S. 489 (1996).

[52] 516 U.S. at 497.

§ 1.05 OVERVIEW OF ERISA'S REGULATION OF EMPLOYEE BENEFIT PLANS

Enacted in 1974 and amended a multitude of times since then,[53] ERISA is a very complex and extensive piece of legislation. It contains four separate titles and is administered by four different administrative agencies.[54] Indeed, the breadth and complexity of ERISA can be seen by the fact that six different sections of the American Bar Association have committees on employee benefits and executive compensation.[55]

[A] Statutory Framework

ERISA is not a single statute.[56] Rather, it consists of four separate titles which are codified in three separate titles of the United States Code (U.S.C.):

(1) 29 U.S.C., the labor laws,

(2) 26 U.S.C., the Internal Revenue Code, and

(3) 42 U.S.C., the Public Health Service Act.

---

[53] For a summary of post-ERISA legislation, see ABA SECTION OF LABOR AND EMPLOYMENT LAW, EMPLOYEE BENEFITS LAW, at 1-11–1-23.

[54] Four agencies play a significant role in administering ERISA: (1) Department of Labor, (2) Department of Treasury, (3) Pension Benefit Guaranty Corporation, and (4) Health and Human Services.

[55] The six sections are: (1) the Business Law Section, (2) the Health Law Section, (3) the Labor and Employment Law Section, (4) the Real Property, Trust and Probate Law Section, (5) the Taxation Section, and (6) the Tort Trial and Insurance Practice Section.

[56] Patricia E. Dilley, *Hidden in Plain View: The Pension Shield Against Creditors*, 74 IND. L. J. 355, 377 (1999) ("Strictly speaking, there is no single statute that can be identified as 'ERISA.' ").

ERISA

Title I	Title II	Title III	Title IV
ERISA §§ 1-734, codified in labor laws, 29 U.S.C.	Amends Internal Revenue Code (IRC), 26 U.S.C.	ERISA §§ 3001-3042, codified in 29 U.S.C.	ERISA §§ 4001-4402, codified in 29 U.S.C.
ERISA § 715 incorporates §§ 2701-2728 of the Public Health Service Act, codified in 42 U.S.C.		Allocates jurisdiction between Department of Labor and Department of Treasury for overlapping provisions in Title I and Title II	Creates PBGC and establishes termination insurance for defined benefit pension plans

[1] Title I

Title I of ERISA is entitled Protection of Employee Benefits Rights. It contains definitions,[57] extensive reporting and disclosure requirements,[58] vesting and participation rules,[59] minimum funding standards[60] fiduciary rules,[61] administration

---

[57] ERISA § 3.

[58] ERISA §§ 101–111.

[59] ERISA §§ 201–211.

[60] ERISA §§ 301–308.

and enforcement provisions,[62] and rules governing group health plans.[63]

For the most part, title I of ERISA is codified in 29 U.S.C. as part of the labor laws and is generally administered by the Department of Labor. One section of title I of ERISA, section 715,[64] regarding group health plans, incorporates elements of the Public Health Service Act,[65] which is codified in title 42 of the U.S.C. The Public Health Service Act is administered by Department of Health and Human Services.

---

[61] ERISA §§ 401–414.

[62] ERISA §§ 501–521.

[63] ERISA §§ 601-734.

[64] ERISA § 715 was added by the Affordable Care Act. It is part of Title I, Part 7, Group Health Plan Requirements.

[65] Public Health Service Act, Chapter 373, 58 Stat. 682 (1944) (codified at 42 U.S.C. § 201-300mm-61).

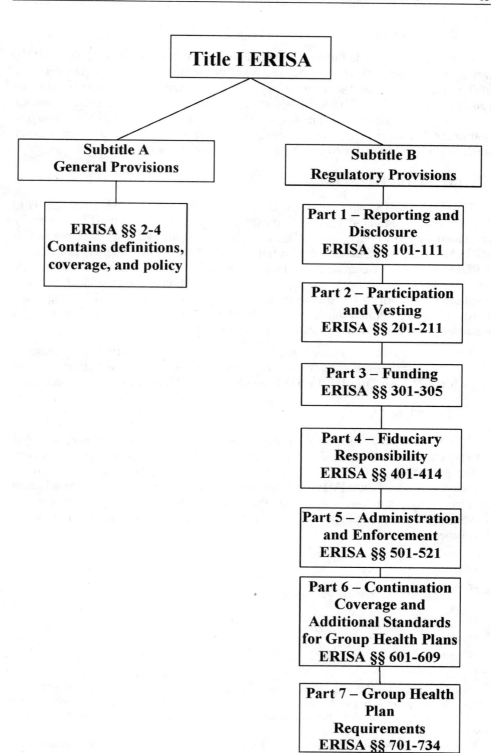

[2] Title II

Title II of ERISA sets forth amendments to the Internal Revenue Code ("IRC"), which are codified in 26 U.S.C., and are generally administered by the Department of Treasury. Many of the provisions in the IRC are substantially parallel to provisions in Title I of ERISA. For example, like Title I of ERISA, the IRC imposes minimum participation,[66] minimum funding,[67] vesting,[68] and anti-alienation requirements[69] on qualified plans. Generally, a plan must satisfy the requirements set forth in the IRC in order to receive favorable income tax treatment.

[3] Title III

Title III of ERISA allocates regulatory jurisdiction over ERISA. Although Title I is generally regulated by the Department of Labor and Title II is generally regulated by the Department of Treasury, this is not always true. With respect to ERISA's provisions that are duplicated in both Title I and Title II, Title III of ERISA directs the Department of Treasury and the Department of Labor to work together to avoid unnecessary expense and duplication[70] and specifically grants regulatory authority over the minimum participation, funding, and vesting standards to the Department of Treasury.[71] In addition, Title III requires that the two agencies provide certain notifications to each other.[72]

Title III is intended to ease plan administration and ensure that plan sponsors are not required to comply with two separate, potentially conflicting, sets of regulations.[73] Like Title I, Title III is codified in the labor laws in 29 U.S.C.

[4] Title IV

Title IV of ERISA governs the termination of defined benefit pension plans.[74] It creates the Pension Benefit Guaranty Corporation ("PBGC") which is then charged with administering a termination insurance program for defined benefit plans in the event of insolvency. Title IV is intended to ensure that participants in covered plans receive a minimum guaranteed benefit in the event their plan is terminated. Covered plans are required to pay annual premiums to fund the PBGC and its insurance program.

---

[66] IRC § 410.

[67] IRC §§ 412, 430, 431.

[68] IRC § 411.

[69] IRC § 401(a)(13).

[70] ERISA § 3004.

[71] ERISA § 3002(c).

[72] ERISA § 3002.

[73] *See* Brian A. Benko, *The Regulatory Systems for Employee Benefits*, 63 Tax Law. 239, 257 (2010) ("The more fundamental reason for splitting jurisdiction was that administration and compliance with two sets of regulations, one from the DOL and another from Treasury, would make providing pensions too costly.").

[74] A defined benefit plan is a type of pension plan in which the benefit is expressed as a certain amount to be paid the plan participant at retirement. For a discussion of defined benefit plans, see Chapter 2 §§ 2.02 & 2.03.

Like Titles I and III, Title IV is codified in the labor laws in 29 U.S.C.

[B] ERISA's Numbering System

ERISA's numbering system is a bit complicated. ERISA has its own numbering system covering titles I, III, and IV of ERISA. It begins with section 1, the short title and table of contents, and continues (with significant gaps)[75] through section 4402, effective date and special rules.

ERISA practitioners always refer to the provisions in titles I, III, and IV of ERISA by their ERISA section number. Thus, an ERISA practitioner refers to ERISA's general preemption provision as ERISA § 514.

Titles I, III, and IV of ERISA are codified in title 29 of the U.S.C., the labor laws. The section number in the codified labor law is quite different from the ERISA section number. For example, ERISA's general preemption provision, ERISA § 514, is codified at 29 U.S.C. § 1144, and ERISA's general minimum funding standards provision, ERISA § 302, is codified at 29 U.S.C. § 1082.

Although ERISA practitioners refer to ERISA's provisions by their ERISA section number, courts often refer to them by their codified labor law number.[76] Thus, for example, courts may refer to ERISA's preemption provision as 29 U.S.C. § 1144.[77] Moreover, courts sometimes erroneously refer to the labor law codification number as an ERISA section number.[78] For example, courts have referred to ERISA § 511, codified at 29 U.S.C. § 1140, as ERISA § 1140,[79] and ERISA § 404, codified at 29 U.S.C. § 1104, as ERISA § 1104.[80]

Throughout the text, this book follows the ERISA practitioner convention of referring to ERISA's provisions using the ERISA numbering system. Appendix A identifies each of the section numbers in ERISA and the corresponding section number in 29 U.S.C.

Title II of ERISA differs from the other titles of ERISA in that it amended the Internal Revenue Code (IRC), which is codified at 26 U.S.C. These sections are not separately included as ERISA section numbers. Instead, they are contained in the IRC and are referred to by the section number in which they are codified in the IRC. Thus, for example, IRC § 401 refers to 26 U.S.C. § 401.

---

[75] For example, the single digit section numbers only go through section 4, coverage. The next section is section 101, the first section of the reporting and disclosure provisions in part I of subtitle B of Title I. The 100s go through section 111, repeal and effective date. Section 111 is followed by section 201, the first section on the participation and vesting provisions in part 2 of subtitle B of Title I.

[76] *See, e.g.,* Cooper Tire & Rubber Co. v. St. Paul Fire & Marine Ins. Co., 48 F.3d 365 (8th Cir. 1995), *cert. denied,* 516 U.S. 913.

[77] *See, e.g.,* Turner v. Fallon Community Health Plan, 127 F.3d 196 (1st Cir. 1997), *cert. denied,* 523 U.S. 1072 (1998).

[78] *See, e.g.,* Concha v. London, 62 F.3d 1493 (9th Cir. 1995), *cert. denied,* 517 U.S. 1183 (1996) (referring to "§§ 1109 and 1132(a) of ERISA" rather than ERISA §§ 409 and 502(a)(3)).

[79] *See, e.g.,* Perdue v. Burger King Corp., 7 F.3d 1251, 1255 (5th Cir. 1993); Molina v. Mallah, 817 F. Supp. 419, 421 (S.D.N.Y. 1993).

[80] *See, e.g.,* Hunter v. Caliber System, Inc., 220 F.3d 702, 717 (6th Cir. 2000); American Flint Glass Workers Union v. Beaumont Glass Co., 62 F.3d 574, 579 (3d Cir. 1995).

[C] Coverage

ERISA's coverage has been described as "curious."[81] In essence, ERISA applies to private sector employee benefit plans but does not apply to governmental plans.[82] Generally speaking, defined benefit pension plans are subject to the most significant regulation under ERISA while welfare plans are least regulated by ERISA.[83]

Congress relied on the Commerce Clause for the basis of its power to regulate employee benefit plans. Thus, ERISA § 4(a) provides that ERISA generally applies to any "employee benefit plan"[84] established or maintained by an employer "engaged in commerce or in any industry or activity affecting commerce" or any plan established or maintained by unions representing employees engaged in commerce.[85] ERISA § 4(b) then expressly excepts from coverage five types of plans, the most significant of which is governmental plans.[86] Thus, ERISA applies to almost all private sector employee benefit plans but does not apply to any public sector plans.

Some of ERISA's provisions apply to all employee benefit plans subject to ERISA. For example, ERISA's reporting and disclosure requirements,[87] fiduciary rules,[88] and administration and enforcement provisions[89] apply to all (or essentially all) employee benefit plans subject to ERISA. Other provisions, in contrast, only apply to a subset of employee benefit plans. For example, the vesting and participation rules only apply to pension plans[90] while the minimum funding rules[91]

---

[81] *See* Wiedenbeck, 76 WASH. U. L. Q., at 311–12.

[82] ERISA § 4(b)(1).

[83] *Cf.* Wiedenbeck, 76 WASH. U. L.Q., at 311–12 (discussing ERISA's four increasingly intense levels of regulation for different types of employee benefit plans).

[84] For a discussion of the meaning of "employee benefit plan," see Chapter 3 § 3.02[B].

[85] ERISA § 4(a).

[86] Specifically, ERISA § 4(b) excepts from coverage: (1) governmental plans, (2) church plans, (3) plans established to comply with workers' compensation, unemployment compensation, or disability insurance laws, (4) plans maintained outside the United States primarily for the benefit of nonresident aliens, and (5) funded excess benefit plans. ERISA § 4(b). For a detailed discussion of the church plan exception, see David Pratt, *Church Pension Plans*, 2013 NYU REV. OF EMPLOYEE BENEFITS & EXECUTIVE COMPENSATION Chapter 16.

[87] ERISA"s "Reporting and Disclosure" provisions, set forth in Part 1 of Subtitle B of Title I of ERISA do not have a section entitled "Coverage." Thus, the provisions apply to all employee benefit plans subject to ERISA.

[88] ERISA § 401, the first section of part 4 of Subtitle B of Title I of ERISA, provides that the part 4 fiduciary rules do not apply to certain unfunded plans and agreements providing for payments to retired partners. Thus, the part 4 fiduciary rules apply to all employee benefit plans subject to ERISA, with these two limited exceptions.

[89] ERISA"s "Administration an Enforcement" provisions, set forth in Part 5 of Subtitle B of Title I of ERISA do not have a section entitled "Coverage." Thus, the provisions apply to all employee benefit plans subject to ERISA.

[90] ERISA § 201, the first section of part 2 of Subtitle B of Title I of ERISA, provides that the part 2 participation and vesting rules do not apply to welfare benefit plans. ERISA § 201(1). Section 201 of ERISA also contains a few other exceptions. *See* ERISA § 201(2)–(6).

[91] ERISA § 301, the first section of part 3, provides that the part 3 funding rules do not apply to

and title IV termination insurance program[92] apply only to defined benefit pension plans. Moreover, some provisions apply solely to group health plans.[93]

[D]　Risks Against Which ERISA Protects

ERISA was designed to address two principal risks plan participants and beneficiaries faced under pre-ERISA law:

(1)　default risk, and

(2)　administration risk.[94]

[1]　Default Risk

Default risk is the risk that the employer (or other plan sponsor) may not honor its promise to provide plan participants and beneficiaries with benefits.[95]

Pension plans[96] give rise to default risk because pension plans promise workers benefits that will be paid in the future. Default risk is much less of a concern in the case of welfare benefit plans because welfare benefits,[97] such as health care benefits, are typically current benefits, that is, benefits that are earned and received in the same year.

ERISA addressed the default risk inherent in pension plans in three different ways. First, ERISA created minimum funding standards[98] that were intended to require that employers (or other plan sponsors) contribute, over time, sufficient amounts to their plans to ensure that the plans have sufficient funds available to pay the plan participants their promised benefits upon retirement.[99] Second, Title IV of ERISA created an insurance system administered by the Pension Benefit Guaranty

---

welfare benefit plans as well as most defined contribution plans. ERISA § 301(1) & (8). Section 301 of ERISA also contains a few other exceptions. *See* ERISA § 301(2)–(7) & (9)–(10).

[92] ERISA § 4021, entitled "Coverage," provides that Title IV only applies to private sector defined benefit pension plans.

[93] The titles of Part 6, "Continuation Coverage and Additional Standards for Group Health Plans," and Part 7, "Group Health Plan Requirements," make clear that the two parts only apply to group health plans.

[94] John H. Langbein, *What ERISA Means by "Equitable": The Supreme Court's Trail of Error in Russell, Mertens, and Great-West*, 103 Colum. L. Rev. 1317, 1322 (2003).

[95] *Id.*

[96] For an overview of pension plans, see Chapter 2.

[97] For an overview of welfare plans, see Chapter 3.

[98] The minimum funding standards are set forth in ERISA §§ 302–305 and IRC §§ 412 and 430–31. The rules apply to all defined benefit pension plans but only one type of defined contribution plan, the money purchase plan. *See* ERISA § 301(a)(8). For a discussion of the minimum funding standards, see Chapter 5 § 5.05.

[99] Although the minimum funding standards, as originally enacted, were intended to ensure that plans were adequately funded, they were, in fact, inadequate, and substantially modified by the Pension Protection Act of 2006, Pub. L. No. 109-280, §§ 101–102, 120 Stat. 780 (2006). For a discussion of the original minimum funding standards and their inadequacies, see Kathryn J. Kennedy, *Pension Funding Reform: It's Time to Get the Rules Right (Part I)*, 108 Tax Notes 907, 2005 TNT 162-34 (July 29, 2005).

Corporation (PBGC)[100] to protect workers' pensions in the event that a pension plan is terminated before it is fully funded.[101] Finally, ERISA introduced vesting rules[102] to ensure that employees' pension benefits become nonforfeitable within a reasonable period of time.[103]

ERISA's rules addressing default risk only apply to pension plans. They do not apply to welfare benefit plans.

[2] Administration Risk

Administration risk concerns the risk that the individuals who are "responsible for managing and investing plan assets and paying claims may abuse their authority."[104]

Unlike default risk, administration risk is as likely to arise in the case of a welfare benefit plan as a pension plan.

ERISA enacted fiduciary provisions to address administration risk.[105] Unlike the rules designed to address default risk, ERISA's fiduciary rules apply to both pension and welfare benefit plans.[106] Thus, despite the fact that ERISA is officially titled the "Employee *Retirement* Income Security Act,"[107] and in its early years was usually referred to as the "*Pension* Reform Act,"[108] portions of ERISA regulate all employee benefit plans, not just pension or retirement plans.

---

[100] ERISA § 4002.

[101] The PBGC only guarantees the benefits of defined benefit pension plans. ERISA § 4021(a). For an argument that its protection should extend to defined contribution plans, see Regina T. Jefferson, *Rethinking the Risk of Defined Contribution Plans*, 4 FLA. TAX REV. 607 (2000). For a more detailed discussion of the PBGC, see § 11.03[B], *infra*.

[102] ERISA § 203.

[103] The minimum participation rules and benefit accrual rules are designed to work with the vesting rules to ensure that participants' benefits will be nonforfeitable. Together, they are sometimes referred to as the "pension benefit security rules." These rules apply to all pension plans, that is, both defined benefit and defined contribution plans. For a discussion of the vesting, minimum participation, and benefit accrual rules, see Chapter 5 § 5.02.

[104] Langbein, 103 COLUM. L. REV., at 1323. *See also* D. Bret Carlson, *ESOP and Universal Capitalism*, 31 TAX L. REV. 289, 301 (1976) ("One of the motivations for enactment of ERISA was to protect employee benefit funds from being exploited for the benefit of employers who maintain them.").

[105] ERISA §§ 401–415. For a discussion of the fiduciary rules, see Chapter 6.

[106] ERISA § 401(a).

[107] (emphasis added).

[108] Carlton R. Sickles, *Introduction: The Significance and Complexity of ERISA*, 17 WM. & MARY L. REV. 205, 206 (1975) (emphasis added).

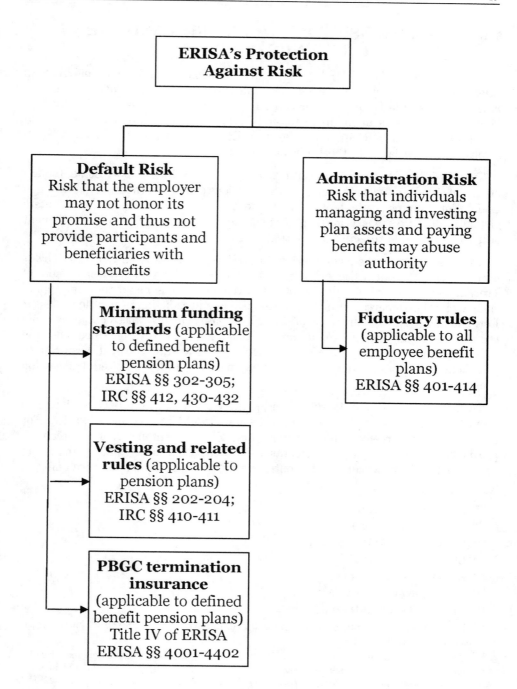

§ 1.06 RELATIONSHIP BETWEEN ERISA AND THE INTERNAL REVENUE CODE

As discussed above, ERISA consists of four separate titles. One of ERISA's titles, title IV, is entirely separate from the Internal Revenue Code. Another of ERISA's titles, title II, only concerns the Internal Revenue Code. Specifically, title II of ERISA contains amendments to the Internal Revenue Code that were enacted in conjunction with ERISA. The other two titles of ERISA, title I and title III, involve some overlap with the Internal Revenue Code.

Title I of ERISA is codified in title 29 of the United States Code. Some, though not all, of title I's provisions overlap with provisions codified in the Internal Revenue Code. For example, title I of ERISA and the Internal Revenue Code contain virtually identical rules regarding participation,[109] vesting,[110] funding,[111] benefit accrual,[112] spousal protections,[113] anti-alienation,[114] and prohibited transactions.[115]

To the extent that the rules overlap, title III of ERISA and an Executive Order issued during President Carter's administration[116] provide that the Department of Treasury has primary jurisdiction over the regulation of some of the overlapping rules while the Department of Labor has primary jurisdiction over other rules.[117] For example, the Department of Treasury has primary jurisdiction to issue regulations regarding the minimum participation and vesting rules and the minimum funding standards.[118] The Department of Labor, in contrast, has primary jurisdiction to issue regulations regarding most of the prohibited transaction provisions.[119]

Even to the extent that the rules overlap, there are distinctions between ERISA's provisions and those of the Internal Revenue Code. First, coverage varies. For example, the enforcement mechanisms vary. ERISA contains civil enforcement provisions that permit plan participants and beneficiaries, among others, to seek to enforce ERISA's provisions.[120] In contrast, the Internal Revenue Service enforces

---

[109] ERISA § 202; IRC § 410.

[110] ERISA § 203; IRC § 411.

[111] ERISA §§ 302–305; IRC §§ 412 & 430–432.

[112] ERISA § 204; IRC § 411.

[113] ERISA § 205; IRC § 401(a)(11).

[114] ERISA § 206(d); IRC § 401(a)(12).

[115] ERISA §§ 406–408; IRC § 4975.

[116] ERISA Reorganization Plan No. 4 of 1978, 43 Fed. Reg. 47,713, Executive Order No. 12,108, 44 Fed. Reg. 1065 (Dec. 28, 1978).

[117] *See* Pamela Perdue, Qualified Pension & Profit Sharing Plans ¶ 2.02 (2014) (discussing allocation of responsibility between Department of Labor and Department of Treasury). *See also* John W. Lee, *The "Elaborate Interweaving of Jurisdiction": Labor and Tax Administration and Enforcement of ERISA and Beyond*, 10 U. Rich. L. Rev. 463, 463–71 (1976) (discussing legislative debate regarding overlapping jurisdiction and enforcement responsibility).

[118] ERISA Reorganization Plan No. 4 of 1978, 43 Fed. Reg. 47,713, Executive Order No. 12,108, 44 Fed. Reg. 1065 (Dec. 28, 1978).

[119] *Id.*

[120] ERISA § 502.

the provisions of the Internal Revenue Code, and plan participants generally cannot compel plans, plan sponsors, or plan administrators to comply with the Internal Revenue Code nor can they compel the Internal Revenue Service to enforce the Internal Revenue Code.[121]

If a plan fails to satisfy a requirement set forth in the Internal Revenue Code, the plan may be subject to an excise tax[122] or disqualified,[123] that is, lose its favorable tax treatment. In contrast, a plan sponsor may, at least under certain circumstances, be compelled to satisfy the requirements of ERISA.[124]

In addition, the focus of ERISA differs from the focus of the Internal Revenue Code. ERISA was enacted principally to protect plan participants.[125] The Internal Revenue Code, in contrast, is a taxing statute designed to collect revenue.[126]

§ 1.07   OVERVIEW OF TAX RULES GOVERNING EMPLOYEE BENEFITS

Section 61(a)(1) of the Internal Revenue Code provides that, absent an express exception, "gross income" includes "compensation for services including fees, commissions, fringe benefits, and similar items." Thus, absent an express provision in the Internal Revenue Code, employee benefits are includible in gross income and subject to regular income tax treatment.

Example

The Internal Revenue Code does not provide for special income tax treatment for vacation pay. Thus, if an employee receives vacation pay, the vacation pay is taxable income, just like regular compensation.

The Internal Revenue Code expressly provides for favorable income tax treatment for some employee benefits. Generally, this favorable income tax treatment takes one of three different forms:

(1)   tax exclusion,

(2)   tax deferral, or

(3)   Roth treatment.

---

[121]   Stein, 56 SMU L. REV., at 648.

[122]   *See, e.g.*, IRC § 4972.

[123]   The Internal Revenue Service developed the Employee Plans Compliance Resolution System to permit plan sponsors to correct plan violations and avoid the draconian remedy of plan disqualification. Rev. Proc. 2013-12, 2013-4 I.R.B. 313.

[124]   *See* Chapter 7 § 7.08 (discussing remedies under ERISA).

[125]   *See* § 1.04[C] (discussing purposes of ERISA).

[126]   Stein, 56 SMU L. REV., at 648. Nevertheless, as Senator Long pointed out in the hearings leading to ERISA, the Internal Revenue Code is not used entirely and exclusively to raise revenues. Rather, it has long been used to achieve other social purposes as well. Lee, 10 U. RICH. L. REV., at 468.

[A] Tax Exclusion

The Internal Revenue Code excludes a number of welfare benefits from taxable income. Benefits that are excluded from taxable income are never includible in taxable income and thus never subject to income tax.

Example

Section 106(a) of the Internal Revenue Code generally excludes employer contributions to fund health care plans from taxable income. Thus, if an employer pays $1,000 toward the cost of health insurance for an employee, the employee is not required to include that $1,000 in gross income and the employee will never be taxed on that benefit.

Although the employee does not need to include that $1,000 in gross income, the employer may deduct the $1,000 it paid as an ordinary and necessary business expense. In addition, the employer's contribution is exempt from Social Security taxes[127] and federal unemployment taxes.[128]

In addition, under IRC § 105(b), benefits paid by employer-sponsored health care plans are excludable from income to the extent that the benefits are paid to reimburse the cost of the employee's medical care or the medical care of the employee's spouse or dependents.

According to the Joint Committee on Taxation, the tax exclusion for employer contributions for health care, health insurance premiums, and long-term care insurance premiums represents the single largest tax expenditure[129] for the years 2014 through 2018, with an estimated $785.1 billion in forgone tax revenues between 2014 and 2018.[130]

[B] Tax Deferral

The Internal Revenue Code defers taxation of pension benefits received from traditional "qualified plans."[131] Qualified plans are retirement plans that meet the 30 or so requirements set forth in section 401(a) of the Internal Revenue Code.

Essentially, the favorable tax treatment accorded traditional qualified plans consists of four elements:

---

[127] IRC § 3121(a)(2).

[128] IRC § 3306(b)(2).

[129] Tax expenditures are defined as "revenue losses attributable to provisions of the Federal tax laws which allow a special exclusion, exemption, or deduction from gross income or which provide a special credit, a preferential rate of tax, or a deferral of tax liability." Joint Committee on Taxation, Estimates of Federal Tax Expenditures for Fiscal Years 2014–2018 2 (Aug. 5, 2014).

[130] *Id.* at 31.

[131] The Internal Revenue Code also provides for tax deferral of pension benefits from other plans, such as state and local plans established under section 457 of the Internal Revenue Code. This book focuses on "qualified plans" and does not discuss other plans that are eligible for favorable income tax treatment.

(1) Employers may deduct contributions to qualified plans when the contributions are made;

(2) Employees do not need to include the contributions in income until the contributions are distributed to them;

(3) Earnings on contributions held by qualified plans are exempt from tax; and

(4) Participants can roll over distributions from a qualified plan to an individual retirement account (IRA) or another qualified plan and further delay taxation of benefits.

As discussed in Appendix B, this tax treatment is economically equivalent to never taxing the earnings on the contribution.

Example

On January 1, 2000, April contributes $1,000 to a 401(k) plan established by her employer. April is not required to include that $1,000 in her taxable income in 2000.

So long as the $1,000 remains in her employer's 401(k) plan, neither the $1,000 contribution nor the earnings on the $1,000 contribution will be subject to income tax.

On April 15, 2015, April, age 65, retires and asks for the money in her 401(k) plan to be distributed to her. She receives a $1,500 distribution from the plan (her $1,000 original contribution plus $500 on earnings on the contribution). April must treat the $1,500 distribution as ordinary taxable income in 2015.

[C]   Roth Treatment

In 2006, a new form of favorable income tax treatment for employee contributions to qualified plans was introduced.[132] Under this method, referred to as "Roth" treatment, plan participants must include their plan contributions in income when the contributions are made, but no tax is imposed on plan earnings or distributions attributable to the Roth contribution (including earnings on those contributions).

As discussed in Appendix B, the essence of the economic effect of the favorable income tax treatment accorded traditional qualified plans is to never tax the qualified plan's earnings. Assuming no change in tax rates, Roth treatment is essentially economically equivalent to this traditional form of favorable tax treatment.[133]

Roth contributions are named after the former Senate Finance Chairman William Roth, who was the principal sponsor of the 1997 legislation that introduced

---

[132] Economic Growth and Tax Relief Reconciliation Act of 2001 § 617, 115 Stat. 38, 103–06 (authorizing 401(k) plans to incorporate a "qualified Roth contribution program" effective for tax years beginning after 2005).

[133] *See* Gregg D. Polsky & Grant J. Hellwig, *Taxing Structured Settlements*, 51 B.C. L. Rev. 39, 47 n.31 (2010); Daniel I. Halperin, *Interest in Disguise: Taxing the Time Value of Money*, 95 Yale L.J. 506, 519 (1986).

this method of taxation for contributions to individual retirement accounts.[134]

Example

On January 1, 2000, Benjamin makes a $2,000 Roth contribution to a 401(k) plan established by his employer. Benjamin must include that $2,000 in his taxable income in 2000.

So long as the $2,000 remains in his employer's 401(k) plan, any earnings on the $2,000 contribution will not be subject to income tax.

On April 15, 2015, Benjamin, age 65, retires and asks that the money in his 401(k) plan be distributed to him. The plan distributes $3,000 to Benjamin (his original $2,000 contribution plus $1,000 in earnings on the contribution).

None of the $3,000 distribution is treated as Benjamin's taxable income. Thus, Benjamin is never taxed on the earnings on his Roth contribution.

According to the Joint Committee on Taxation, the favorable tax treatment accorded employer-sponsored pensions will result in an estimated $647.3 billion in forgone tax revenues between 2014 and 2018.[135]

---

[134] Taxpayer Relief Act of 1997, Pub. L. No. 105-34, § 302, 111 Stat. 788, 825–29.

[135] Joint Committee on Taxation, Estimates of Federal Tax Expenditures for Fiscal Years 2014–2018, at 32 (estimating tax expenditure of $248.3 billion for employer-sponsored defined benefit plans and $399.0 billion for employer-sponsored defined contribution plans).

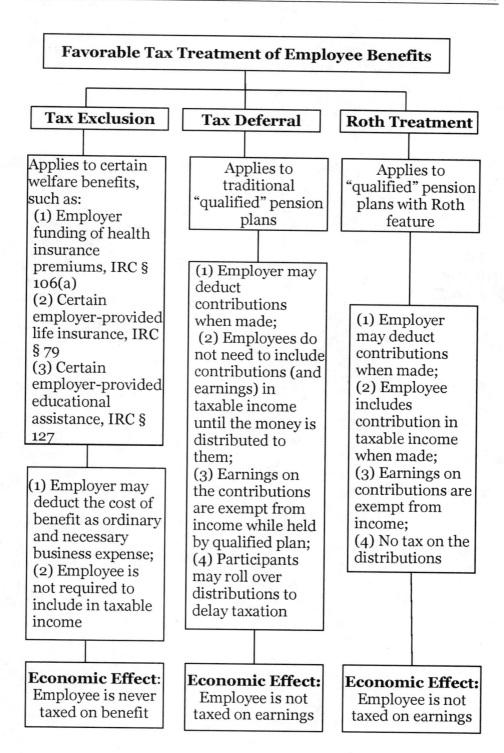

Favorable Tax Treatment of Employee Benefits

Tax Exclusion

Applies to certain welfare benefits, such as:
(1) Employer funding of health insurance premiums, IRC § 106(a)
(2) Certain employer-provided life insurance, IRC § 79
(3) Certain employer-provided educational assistance, IRC § 127

(1) Employer may deduct the cost of benefit as ordinary and necessary business expense;
(2) Employee is not required to include in taxable income

Economic Effect: Employee is never taxed on benefit

Tax Deferral

Applies to traditional "qualified" pension plans

(1) Employer may deduct contributions when made;
(2) Employees do not need to include contributions (and earnings) in taxable income until the money is distributed to them;
(3) Earnings on the contributions are exempt from income while held by qualified plan;
(4) Participants may roll over distributions to delay taxation

Economic Effect: Employee is not taxed on earnings

Roth Treatment

Applies to "qualified" pension plans with Roth feature

(1) Employer may deduct contributions when made;
(2) Employee includes contribution in taxable income when made;
(3) Earnings on contributions are exempt from income;
(4) No tax on the distributions

Economic Effect: Employee is not taxed on earnings

Chapter 2

PENSION PLANS

§ 2.01 INTRODUCTION

ERISA regulates "employee benefit plans."

Under ERISA, there are two basic types of employee benefit plans: pension plans and welfare benefit plans.

This chapter provides a general overview and introduction to pension plans. Chapter 3 introduces welfare benefit plans.

§ 2.02 GENERAL INTRODUCTION TO PENSION PLANS AND THE DISTINCTION BETWEEN DEFINED BENEFIT PLANS AND DEFINED CONTRIBUTION PLANS

Section 3(2) of ERISA defines a pension plan as "any plan, fund, or program which was . . . established or maintained by an employer or an employee organization . . . to the extent that [it provides] retirement income to employees, or . . . . results in a deferral of income for periods extending to the termination of employment or beyond. . . . "

Thus, at its most fundamental level, a pension plan is an employee benefit plan that provides employees with retirement income or deferred income, that is, income after the employee ceases to work for the employer sponsoring the pension plan.

Both ERISA and the Internal Revenue Code distinguish between two basic types of pension plans:

(1) defined benefit plans, and

(2) defined contribution plans.

When ERISA was enacted, defined benefit plans were the most common type of pension plan.[1] Over the last 30 years or so, coverage has shifted so that plan participants are now more likely to be covered by a defined contribution plan than by a defined benefit plan.[2]

---

[1] In 1975, the year after ERISA was enacted, the primary plan for 87% of active plan participants was a defined benefit plan. Investment Company Institute, *A Look at Private-Sector Retirement Income After ERISA*, 16 Res. Persp. 1, 4 (2010).

[2] *See, e.g.*, Dep't of Labor, Private Pension Plan Bulletin, Abstract of 2010 Form 5500 Annual Reports 3 Table A1 (Nov. 2012) (reporting that of the 129,724,000 participants in private sector pensions in 2010,

[A] Introduction to Defined Benefit Plans

Technically, ERISA[3] and the Internal Revenue Code[4] define a defined benefit plan as any pension plan that is not a defined contribution plan. In common parlance, however, a defined benefit plan is defined as a pension plan in which the benefit is expressed as a certain amount to be paid to the participant at retirement.[5] Thus, as the name suggests, a defined benefit plan defines the benefit that the plan participant is entitled to receive at retirement.

Typically, defined benefit plans provide for a fixed amount to be paid annually beginning at age 65 for the life of the retired participant. The fixed amount is often based on a formula that takes into account the participant's years of service and salary.

Example

The Delta Defined Benefit Pension Plan promises plan participants a benefit at age 65 that is equal to 1% of the plan participant's final average pay multiplied by the plan participant's years of service. After having worked for Delta for 30 years, Allison, a 65-year-old single woman, retires from Delta. Her final average pay is $100,000.

Under the Delta Defined Benefit Pension Plan, Allison is entitled to an annual benefit equal to $30,000 (30 x .01 x $100,000). Thus, the Delta Defined Benefit Pension Plan will pay Allison $30,000 per year until she dies.

[B] Introduction to Defined Contribution Plans

ERISA[6] and the Internal Revenue Code[7] define a defined contribution plan as a pension plan "which provides for an individual account for each participant and for benefits based solely upon the amount contributed to the participant's account, and any income, expenses, gains, and losses," and any forfeitures from other participants' accounts that may be allocated to the participant's account.

Conceptually, defined contribution plans are like savings accounts. Money is contributed to each participant's individual account, and each participant's benefit is equal to the total contributions allocated to the account plus any investment earnings (and losses) credited to the account. Under a typical defined contribution plan, the employer contributes a specified percentage of each worker's compensation to an individual account for each worker.

88,301,000 were covered by a defined contribution plan and 41,423,000 were covered by a defined benefit plan); Craig Copeland, *Employment-Based Retirement Plan Participation: Geographic Differences and Trends*, EBRI Issue Brief No. 348, at 6 (2010) (showing that in 2009, the primary plan for 60% of workers was a defined contribution plan while the primary plan for 39% of workers was a defined benefit plan).

[3] ERISA § 3(35).

[4] IRC § 414(j).

[5] Joint Committee on Taxation, Present Law and Background Relating to the Tax Treatment of Retirement Savings, JCX-32-12, at 17 (2012).

[6] ERISA § 3(34).

[7] IRC § 414(i).

Example

Employer establishes a defined contribution plan and promises to contribute 5% of annual compensation on behalf of each plan participant. Benji, an employee of Employer, earns an annual salary of $50,000 in 2015. Under the terms of the plan, Employer must contribute $2,500 ($50,000 x .05) to Benji's individual account in 2015. Benji's ultimate benefit will be based on all contributions made to Benji's individual account plus any earnings or losses on those contributions.

Unlike traditional defined benefit plans, defined contribution plans typically distribute benefits in the form of a lump sum, rather than a life annuity, that is, a fixed amount for life.[8]

[C]   Distinctions Between Defined Benefit Plans and Defined Contribution Plans

Defined benefit plans and defined contribution plans have been described as the "chocolate and vanilla of plan types."[9] Just as there are fundamental differences between chocolate and vanilla, so too are there fundamental distinctions between defined benefit plans and defined contribution plans. This section explores some of the more significant differences between defined benefit plans and defined contribution plans.[10]

[1]   Input vs. Output

As their names suggest, defined benefit plans differ from defined contribution plans in their focus.

A defined benefit plan defines the benefit the plan will provide, that is, the plan's "output."[11] Defined benefit plans may use a wide variety of formulas to define the promised benefit. For example, a defined benefit plan might promise plan participants a specified dollar amount, such as $1,000 per year for life. Or, a defined benefit plan might promise an annual benefit equal to a fixed dollar amount tied to years of

---

[8] *See* Profit Sharing/401k Council of America, 51st Annual Survey of Profit Sharing and 401(k) Plans 49 Table 85 (2008) (reporting that 20.5% of profit-sharing plans offer to distribute retirement benefits in the form of an annuity). *Cf.* David L. Wray, *Testimony Before the ERISA Advisory Council Working Group on Spend down of Defined Contribution Assets at Retirement* (July 16, 2008), http://www.psca.org/psca-president-testified-july-16-2008-before-the-erisa-advisory-council-on-the-spend-down-of-defined-contribution-assets-at-retirement (noting that only about 20% of defined contribution plans offer annuities and these are hardly ever utilized); Investment Company Institute, *Plan Distribution Choices at Retirement: A Survey of Employees Retiring Between 2002 and 2007* (Fall 2008), *available at* http://www.ici.org/pdf/rpt_08_dcdd.pdf (reporting that 52% of DC participants received all of their distributions as a lump sum).

[9] Norman Stein, *An Alphabet Soup Agenda for Reform of the Internal Revenue Code and ERISA Provisions Applicable to Qualified Deferred Compensation Plans*, 56 SMU L. Rev. 627, 634 (2003).

[10] For additional discussion of the differences between defined benefit and defined contribution plans, see, for example, Douglas J. Elliott, *PBGC: Fundamental Questions*, Center on Federal Financial Institutions 2–4 (Apr. 7, 2004), *available through* www.coffi.org.; Jonathan Barry Forman, *Public Pensions: Choosing Between Defined Benefit and Defined Contribution Plans*, 1999 L. Rev. M.S.U.-D.C.L. 187 (1999).

[11] Edward A. Zelinsky, *The Defined Contribution Paradigm*, 114 Yale L.J. 451, 455 (2004).

service, such as $500 times the participant's years of service. No matter the formula, a defined benefit plan always promises a specific benefit determined by the plan's benefit formula.

A defined contribution plan, in contrast, defines the contribution to be made to the plan, that is, the plan's "input."[12] The contribution may be a specific dollar amount, such as $1,000, or a specified percentage of pay, such as 1% of compensation. Or, the plan may reserve the right to determine how much to contribute to the plan each year. No matter how the contribution is calculated, a defined contribution plan always provides for a specific amount to be contributed to the plan rather than a promise regarding the amount the plan will ultimately pay out.

[2] Funding

Funding a defined contribution plan is much simpler than funding a defined benefit plan.

Because a defined contribution plan defines the contribution to be made to the plan, funding a defined contribution plan simply requires that the promised amount be contributed to the plan. A defined contribution plan is never "underfunded" even if the value of the plan's assets fall because the plan's assets are invested in a stock and the price of the stock falls. Similarly, a defined contribution plan is never "overfunded" even if the value of the plan's assets increase dramatically because the plan's assets are invested in stocks that have dramatically increased in value. A defined contribution plan is always "fully funded" so long as the promised contributions are made to the plan regardless of the subsequent value of the assets held by the plan.[13]

Funding a defined benefit plan, in contrast, is much more complex. Because a defined benefit plan promises a specific dollar amount in the future, determining how much to contribute to the plan when the promise is made to ensure that there are sufficient funds available in the future to pay the promised benefit requires complex actuarial calculations.

Example

Suppose that a defined benefit plan promises plan participants a benefit beginning at age 65 equal $1,000 per year for life. Suppose further that the plan has two participants, Aaron, age 50, and Bette, age 40. Determining how much must be contributed to the plan to ensure that there are sufficient funds to pay Aaron and Bette $1,000 per year for life beginning at age 65 depends upon, among other things,[14] (1) how long Aaron and Bette live[15] and (2) current and future interest

---

[12] *Id.*

[13] A defined contribution plan participant, however, may be said to bear "funding risk," that is, "the danger that the funds necessary to finance adequate retirement benefits will not be contributed to the plan." *Id.* at 457.

[14] Additional factors, such as the plan's costs, must also be taken into account in determining how much must be contributed to the plan.

[15] The longer the plan participants live, the more the plan will be required to pay out and thus, the more that must be contributed to the plan to ensure that it is adequately funded.

rates.[16] If the plan's benefit formula were more complex, such as 1% of the plan participant's final average salary times years of service, funding would also depend on additional factors, such as (1) how long Aaron and Bette work for the company,[17] and (2) their final average salaries.[18]

ERISA[19] and the Internal Revenue Code[20] impose minimum funding standards on defined benefit plans to ensure that defined benefit plans are adequately funded.[21] These complex rules, which are mostly the work of actuaries, only apply to defined benefit plans.[22] The minimum funding standards require the use of "actuarial assumptions," that is, educated guesses about future events, such as future interest rates and life expectancy. Although the minimum funding standards are intended to ensure that defined benefit plans are adequately funded, if the actuarial assumptions turn out to be inaccurate, defined benefit plans may be "underfunded," that is, have insufficient assets to pay promised benefits, or "overfunded," that is, have more assets than are necessary to pay promised benefits.

[3] Investment Risk

Defined benefit plans and defined contribution plans differ in who bears the investment risk.

In a defined benefit plan, the employer is responsible for ensuring that there are adequate funds in the plan to pay the promised benefits. If, for example, the plan's assets are invested in a stock and the price of the stock falls so that the plan's assets are insufficient to pay promised benefits, the employer will be required to contribute more to the plan to cover the shortfall. On the other hand, if the plan's assets earn more income than anticipated, the employer will be required to contribute less to the plan to fund the promised benefits. Thus, the employer is said to bear the investment risk in a defined benefit plan.

In a defined contribution plan, the plan participant is not promised any specific benefit from the defined contribution plan. Rather, the plan participant is simply entitled to a benefit equal to the contributions to his account and any earnings or losses on that account. If the assets in a participant's individual account are invested in a stock that increases in value, the participant will receive a larger benefit. If the assets in a participant's individual account are invested in securities that decrease in value, the participant will receive a smaller benefit. Thus, the plan participant is said to bear the investment risk in a defined contribution plan.

---

[16] The higher the interest rate, the less that must be contributed now to pay for a future benefit. Funding also depends on other factors, such as the plan's administrative costs.

[17] The longer Aaron and Bette work for the company, the more that must be contributed to the plan.

[18] The higher their final salaries, the more that must be contributed to the plan.

[19] ERISA §§ 301–305.

[20] IRC §§ 412, 430–432.

[21] The minimum funding standards are discussed in more detail in Chapter 5 § 5.05.

[22] Technically, the minimum funding standards apply to one type of defined contribution plan, a money purchase plan, which is a "pension plans" for qualified plan purposes. The minimum funding standards, however, are satisfied so long as contributions to the plan are made according to the terms of the plan.

Example

Abigail works for Company A while Bennett works for Company B. Both Company A and Company B offer their employees a defined contribution plan, and Company A and Company B each contribute $2,000 per year on behalf of Abigail and Bennett, respectively, for 10 years. The only difference between the two plans is that the Company A plan has had a 5% annual rate of return over the last 10 years while the Company B has had a 10% annual rate of return over the last 10 years. Because Company A's plan has had a 5% annual rate of return, Abigail has $25,833 in her individual account.[23] Bennett, in contrast, has $33,577 in his individual account, about 30% more than Abigail, simply because his account earned a higher rate of return.

[4] Pension Benefit Guaranty Corporation (PBGC) Guarantee

The Pension Benefit Guaranty Corporation (PBGC) guarantees defined benefit plans but not defined contribution plans.

Under Title IV of ERISA, the PBGC guarantees that defined benefit plan participants will be paid the basic pension benefits (up to certain limits) that they have earned prior to plan termination if their defined benefit plan is underfunded and terminates.[24]

The PBGC guarantee does not apply to defined contribution plans.[25] A participant in a defined contribution plan is entitled to a benefit equal to the contributions to the participant's individual account plus any earnings or losses on those contributions. Defined contribution plan participants are not guaranteed any particular benefit.

[5] Distributions

Distributions from a defined benefit plan differ from distributions from a defined contribution plan.

Traditional defined benefit plans provide distributions in the form of a joint and survivor life annuity, that is, a fixed amount per month to be paid for the life of the retired participant and the participant's spouse.[26] Defined contribution plans, in contrast, typically provide benefits in the form of a lump sum distribution, that is,

---

[23] $2,000 x $(1 + .05)^{10}$ + $2,000 x $(1 + .05)^{9}$ + $2,000 x $(1 + .05)^{8}$ + $2,000 x $(1 + .05)^{7}$ + $2,000 x $(1 + .05)^{6}$ + $2,000 x $(1 + .05)^{5}$ + $2,000 x $(1 + .05)^{4}$ + $2,000 x $(1 + .05)^{3}$ + $2,000 x $(1 + .05)^{2}$ + $2,000 x $(1 + .05)^{1}$ = *See* http://www.bankrate.com/calculators/retirement/401-k-retirement-calculator.aspx.

[24] For a discussion of Title IV of ERISA, see Chapter 11 § 11.03.

[25] ERISA § 4021(b)(1). For an argument that the PBGC guarantee should be extended to defined contribution plans, see Regina Jefferson, *Rethinking the Risk of Defined Contribution Plans*, 4 FLA. TAX REV. 607 (2000).

[26] A defined benefit plan may be drafted to permit lump sum distributions. In order for a distribution to be in any form other than a joint and survivor annuity, the plan participant must elect, with the consent of the participant's spouse, to another form of distribution. ERISA § 205; IRC § 401(a)(11). For a study of the frequency of plan provisions offering lump sum distributions and plan participants' elections to take such distributions, see Sudipto Banerjee, *Annuity and Lump-Sum Distribution Decisions in*

a single cash distribution of the plan participant's entire interest in the plan.[27]

Generally, defined benefit plans may not make "in-service" distributions, that is, distributions to plan participants while they are working for the employer that established the plan.[28] Many defined contribution plans, in contrast, permit in-service distributions.[29]

[6] Portability

Defined contribution plans are more "portable" than defined benefit plans; that is, it is easier for employees with defined contribution plans to move their pension benefits from one job to another than it is for employees with defined benefit plans.[30]

A defined contribution plan is portable because a plan participant's benefit is based on contributions made to the plan and any earnings and losses on those contributions. A plan participant is not penalized if she changes jobs. Her benefit from the defined contribution plan remains equal to the contributions made to the plan and earnings and losses from those contributions.

A participant in a defined benefit plan tends to lose benefits if he changes jobs. This is because benefits under a defined benefit plan tend to be tied to the plan participant's years of service and final average pay. Thus, if the plan participant changes jobs, the participant's benefit will be based on her salary with the old employer and will not reflect any salary increases with the new employer.[31]

Example

Allison and Bob have both worked for 30 years and earned identical salaries over those 30 years. Specifically, they each earned $22,000 their first year of employment and earned a $1,000 raise each year of their employment so their lifetime earnings are as follows:

Defined Benefit Plans: The Role of Plan Rules, Employee Benefit Research Institute Issue Brief No. 381 (Jan. 2013).

[27] Just as defined benefit plans may be drafted to permit lump sum distributions, defined contribution plans may be drafted to permit annuity distributions. Annuity distributions from defined contribution plans, however, are uncommon. Jonathan Barry Forman, *Optimal Distribution Rules for Defined Contribution Plans: What Can the United States Learn from Other Countries?* 28 ABA JOURNAL LAB. & EMP. LAW 27, 31 (2012).

[28] A defined benefit plan may, however, permit in-service distributions to plan participants who are 65 or older. IRC § 401(a)(36). The prohibition on in-service distributions also applies to one type of defined contribution plan, the money purchase plan, which is a "pension plan" for purposes of the Treasury regulations. *See* § 2.04[E][3].

[29] *See* Profit Sharing/401k Council of America, 51st Annual Survey of Profit Sharing and 401(k) Plans: Reflecting 2007 Plan Experience 46–47 Tables 80 & 82 (reporting that 41% of stand-alone profit sharing plans and 63% of 401(k) plans permit in-service distributions (excluding hardship withdrawals) and 88% of 401(k) plans permit hardship withdrawals).

[30] *See* Steven L. Willborn, *The Problem with Pension Portability*, 77 NEBRASKA L. REV. 344, 344 (1998) (stating that "[p]ortability refers to the ability of employees to carry their pension benefits with them as they change jobs").

[31] *See id.* at 347–48 (discussing effect of transferring service credit in calculating benefits under a defined benefit plan).

YEAR OF SERVICE	COMPENSATION	YEAR OF SERVICE	COMPENSATION	YEAR OF SERVICE	COMPENSATION
1	$22,000	11	$32,000	21	$42,000
2	$23,000	12	$33,000	22	$43,000
3	$24,000	13	$34,000	23	$44,000
4	$25,000	14	$35,000	24	$45,000
5	$26,000	15	$36,000	25	$46,000
6	$27,000	16	$37,000	26	$47,000
7	$28,000	17	$38,000	27	$48,000
8	$29,000	18	$39,000	28	$49,000
9	$30,000	19	$40,000	29	$50,000
10	$31,000	20	$41,000	30	$51,000

The only difference between Allison and Bob is that Allison has worked for a single company, Company A, for 30 years, while Bob worked for Company A for the first 10 years of his career, Company B for the second 10 years of his career, and Company C for the final 30 years of his career.

Company A, Company B, and Company C all have defined benefit plans that promise a benefit equal to 2% of the worker's final three years' average pay times years of service. Under Company A's plan, Allison will receive an annual benefit of $30,000 (.02 x $50,000 x 30 = $30,000) because she worked for the company for 30 years and her final average salary was $50,000.[32]

Although Bob also has a final average salary of $50,000, and he has worked for 30 years, he will receive a lower total benefit than Allison. First, Bob will receive a benefit from Company A based on his 10 years of service with the company and the average of his final three years' pay with the company, which is $30,000.[33] Specifically, he will earn a benefit of $6,000 (.02 x $30,000 x 10 = $6,000) from Company A. In addition, he will receive a benefit from Company B based on his 10 years of service with Company B and the average of his final three years of pay with Company B, which is $40,000.[34] Specifically, he will receive a benefit of $8,000 (.02 x $40,000 x 10 = $8,000) from Company B. Plus, he will receive a benefit from Company C based on his 10 years of service with Company C and the average of his final three years' compensation from Company C, which is $50,000.[35] Specifically, he will earn a benefit of $10,000 (.02 x $50,000 x 10 = $10,000) from Company C.

Bob's total annual benefit from Companies A, B, and C will be $24,000 ($6,000 + $8,000 + $10,000), which is $6,000 per year less than Allison's annual benefit of $30,000 from Company A. Allison, the employee with longer service with a single employer, will receive a substantially higher total benefit because the benefit is based on final average pay and salaries tend to rise over time.

---

[32] ($49,000 + $50,000 + $51,000)/3 = $50,000.

[33] ($29,000 + $30,000 + $31,000)/3 = $30,000.

[34] ($39,000 + $40,000 + $41,000)/3 = $40,000.

[35] ($49,000 + $50,000 + $51,000)/3 = $50,000.

[7] Older Workers Versus Younger Workers and the Time Value of Money

Defined benefit plans tend to favor older workers while defined contribution plans tend to benefit younger workers. This difference is due to the "time value of money."

[a] Time Value of Money and its Assumptions

The "time value of money" is a basic economic principle that makes two basic assumptions:

(1) positive interest rates, and

(2) interest will compound over time.

In addition, the time value of money principle includes a corollary that a dollar promised in the future must be discounted to its "present value" today.

[i] Positive Interest Rates

The time value of money principle assumes positive interest rates and thus that a dollar today is worth more than a dollar in the future.[36]

Example

Assume that the interest rate is 3% per year. If an individual puts $1 in the bank today, that dollar will be worth $1.03 in one year.[37] If the interest rate is 5% per year, the dollar will be worth $1.05 in one year,[38] and if the interest rate is 10%, that dollar will be worth $1.10 in one year.[39]

[ii] Compound Interest

The time value of money principle also assumes that interest will compound over time, that is, interest will be earned on the interest.

Example

Assume that the interest rate is 5% per year. If an individual puts $1 in the bank today, that dollar will be worth about $1.28 in five years,[40] and that dollar will be worth about $1.62 in 10 years.[41]

---

[36] *See* MICHAEL J. GRAETZ & DEBORAH H. SCHENK, FEDERAL INCOME TAXATION: PRINCIPLES AND POLICIES 826 (5th ed. 2005). Determining the future value of $1 by the end of some number of years is determined by application of the formula $(1 + r)^t$ where r equals the interest rate and t equals the number of years. *Id.* at 828.

[37] The future value of $1 at the end of one year at an interest of 3% = $1 \times (1 + .03)^1 = \$1.03$.

[38] The future value of $1 at the end of one year at an interest of 5% = $1 \times (1 + .05)^1 = \$1.05$.

[39] The future value of $1 at the end of one year at an interest of 10% = $1 \times (1 + .10)^1 = \$1.10$.

[40] The future value of $1 at the end of five years at an interest rate of 5% = $1 \times (1 + .05)^5 = \$1.276$.

[41] The future value of $1 at the end of 10 years at an interest rate of 5% = $1 \times (1 + .05)^{10} = \$1.629$.

[iii]   Discounted Present Value

A corollary of the time value of money is that a dollar promised in the future must be discounted to its "present value" today. The present value is the amount that would have to be invested today at a specified interest rate in order to have a specified amount at some specified future date.[42]

Example

Assume that the interest rate is 5% per year. If a defined benefit plan promises an individual $1 one year from now, that dollar is worth about $.95 today.[43] If a defined benefit plan promises an individual $1 in five years, that dollar is worth about $.78 today,[44] and if the defined benefit plan promises an individual $1 in 10 years, that dollar is worth about $.61 today.[45]

[b]   Time Value of Money and Defined Benefit Plans

Because a defined benefit plan promises a worker a specific benefit[46] beginning at normal retirement age, the older the employee is and thus, the closer the employee is to the normal retirement age, the more valuable the benefit is. Thus, defined benefit plans favor older workers relative to younger workers because of the "time value of money."

Example

Two employees, Anabeth and Byron, have earned a benefit equal to $1,000 per year for life beginning at age 65. Anabeth is 65 and Byron is 55.

Regardless of the interest rate, the present value of the first year of Anabeth's benefit of $1,000 is $1,000 because it does not need to be discounted to present value. She is entitled to receive the benefit this year.[47]

Assuming positive interest rates, the present value of Byron's first year benefit of $1,000 is less than $1,000 because it must be discounted to present value. Assuming an interest rate of 5%, the present value of the promise to pay Byron $1,000 in 10 years is $614.[48]

---

[42] This amount is calculated by discounting the future payment by the interest rate over the relevant period. The formula may be expressed as $PV = C/(1 + r)^t$ where PV equals the present value, r equals the interest rate, and t equals the number of years. *Id.* at 827.

[43] The present value of $1 one year from now at an interest rate of 5% = $1/(1 + .05)^1$ = $.952.

[44] The present value of $1 five years from now at an interest rate of 5% = $1/(1 + .05)^5$ = $.784.

[45] The present value of $1 10 years from now at an interest rate of 5% = $1/(1 + .05)^{10}$ = $.614.

[46] The specific benefit is determined by the benefit formula.

[47] Determining the value of the entire promise to pay $1,000 for life requires that Anabeth's life expectancy be taken into account, and the future years' benefits be discounted to present value.

[48] The present value of $1,000 10 years from now at an interest rate of 5% = $1,000/(1 + .05)^{10}$ = $614. Determining the value of the entire promise to pay $1,000 for life requires that Byron's life expectancy be taken into account and the remaining future years' benefits be discounted to present value.

[c]   Time Value of Money and Defined Contribution Plans

Because a dollar contributed to a defined contribution account today can be invested and earn money so that it will be more valuable in the future, the younger an employee is when a contribution is made, the more valuable the contribution will be to the employee. Thus, defined contribution plans favor younger workers relative to older workers because of the time value of money.

Example

Employer contributes $1,000 to individual accounts for Chloe, age 60, and Devlin, age 40. If both Chloe and Devlin leave the contribution in their individual accounts until they reach age 65, and the contributions earn an annual return of 5%, the $1,000 is worth $1,280 about to Chloe[49] and worth about $3,390 to Devlin.[50]

Moreover, because the essential benefit of a tax qualified plan is the deferral of taxation on earnings,[51] defined contribution plans are even more valuable to younger workers relative to older workers because younger workers can benefit from the tax-free compounding of earnings over a longer period of time.

---

[49] The future value of $1,000 at the end of five years at an interest rate of 5% = $1,000 x (1 + .05)^5 = $1,280.

[50] The future value of $1,000 at the end of 25 years at an interest rate of 5% = $1,000 x (1 + .05)^{25} = $3,390.

[51] *See* § 2.04[B].

DIFFERENCES BETWEEN DEFINED BENEFIT PLANS AND DEFINED CONTRIBUTION PLANS

	Defined Benefit Plan	**Defined Contribution Plan**
Input vs. Output	Defines the output of the plan; that is, defines the benefit that will be received from the plan	Defines the input of the plan; that is, defines the contributions that will be made to the plan
Funding	Requires actuarial calculations to ensure there are sufficient funds available in the future to pay the promised benefit	Requires only that the promised amount be contributed to the plan
Investment Risk	Employer bears the investment risk	Employee bears the investment risk
PBGC Guarantee	PBGC guarantees basic pension benefits	No PBGC guarantee
Distributions	Distributions typically in the form of a joint and survivor life annuity	Distributions typically in the form of a lump sum distribution
Portability	Not portable; changing jobs tends to limit benefits	Easily portable
Time Value of Money	Time value of money favors older workers	Time value of money favors younger workers

§ 2.03 A CLOSER LOOK AT DEFINED BENEFIT PLANS — DEFINED BENEFIT PLAN FORMULAS AND DEFINITION OF COMPENSATION

In order to qualify as a defined benefit plan, the plan must have a benefit formula. The benefit formula specifies the benefit to which the plan participant is entitled upon retirement, that is, it specifies the benefit a plan participant is entitled to receive beginning at the plan's "normal retirement age," which is typically age 65.

[A]   Types of Benefit Formulas

There are three basic types of benefit formulas:

(1)   fixed benefit,

(2)   flat benefit, and

(3)   unit benefit.[52]

[1]   Fixed Benefit Formula

A fixed benefit formula provides that plan participants will be paid a stated dollar amount at the normal retirement age regardless of the employees' years of credited service under the plan (that is, how long the employee has worked for the employer).

Example

Employer's fixed benefit plan promises each employee a benefit of $200 per month beginning at normal retirement age, which is age 65.

Under this plan, both Avery, who has worked for Employer for 25 years, and Brian, who has worked for Employer for five years, will receive a benefit of $200 per month for life beginning at age 65.[53]

[2]   Flat Benefit Formula

A flat benefit formula provides a benefit that is equal to a specified percentage of the employee's compensation beginning at normal retirement age.[54] Like a fixed benefit formula, a flat benefit formula does not take into account a plan participant's years of service in determining a participant's benefit. Unlike a fixed benefit formula, however, it takes a plan participant's compensation into account.

Example

Company's flat benefit plan provides a benefit equal to 25% of compensation beginning at normal retirement age, which is age 65.

Under this plan, Avery, who earns compensation of $100,000, is entitled to a benefit of $25,000 per year beginning at age 65 ($100,000 x .25 = $25,000) while Brian, who earns compensation of $120,000, is entitled to a benefit of $30,000 per year beginning at age 65 ($120,000 x .25 = $30,000).

As this example illustrates, higher-paid employees receive higher benefits under a flat benefit formula than do lower-paid employees. Benefits, however, do not vary based on years of service with the employer.

---

[52] *See* Bender's Federal Income Taxation of Retirement Plans 1-15–1-16 (Alvin Lurie ed., Aug. 2008).

[53] *See id.* at 1–15.

[54] *See id.*

[3] Unit Benefit Formula

A unit benefit formula differs fundamentally from fixed and flat benefit formulas in that a unit benefit formula takes a participant's years of service into account in defining the benefit. Specifically, a unit benefit formula provides a unit of benefit for each year of a participant's service credited under the plan. The unit of benefit may be a fixed dollar amount or a percentage of salary.

Example 1 — Unit Benefit Plan Using a Fixed Dollar Unit

Employer's unit benefit plan using a fixed dollar unit promises workers a benefit beginning at age 65 equal to $50 per month for each year of service with Employer.

Under this plan, Avery, who has worked for Employer for 25 years, is entitled to a benefit beginning at age 65 equal to $1,250 per month ($50 x 25 = $1,250) while Brian, who has only worked for the company for five years is entitled to a benefit beginning at age 65 equal to $250 per month ($50 x 5 = $250).

Example 2 — Unit Benefit Plan Using a Percentage of Salary Unit

Company's unit benefit plan using a percentage of salary unit provides workers with a benefit beginning at age 65 equal to 2% of compensation multiplied by years of service.

Under this plan, Avery, who has worked for Company for 25 years and whose compensation is $100,000, is entitled to an annual benefit equal to $50,000 (25 x $100,000 x .02 = $50,000) beginning at age 65. Brian, who has worked for Company for five years and whose compensation is $120,000, is entitled to an annual benefit equal to $12,000 (5 x $120,000 x .02) beginning at age 65.

As these examples illustrate, unit benefit plans favor employees with longer service with the company relative to employees with shorter service because employees with longer service receive more units of credit than employees with shorter service.

[B] Calculating Compensation for Purposes of Benefit Formulas

Any defined benefit plan that bases benefits on a percentage of compensation, such as a plan using a flat benefit formula or a plan using a unit benefit formula with compensation as the unit of benefit, must define the participant's compensation.

Employers typically use one of two methods to determine compensation:

(1) career average pay, or

(2) final average pay.[55]

---

[55] *See id.* at 1–16.

[1] Career Average Pay

In a plan using career average pay, a plan participant's benefit is based on the participant's average compensation during the entire period in which she is either employed by the plan sponsor or is a participant in the plan.

In order to receive favorable tax treatment, compensation must be capped at the limit set forth in IRC § 415(b)(1)(A), which is $210,000 in 2015 and adjusted for increases in the cost-of-living.[56]

[2] Final Average Pay

In a plan using final average pay, a plan participant's benefit is based on the participant's compensation over a defined period of time rather than the employee's career average salary.

In order to qualify for favorable income tax treatment, compensation must be capped at the lesser of the IRC § 415(b)(1)(A) limit of $210,000 or the average of the employee's three highest years of compensation.[57]

Since employees' salaries tend to increase over time, benefits tend to be higher under final average pay plans than under career average pay plans.

§ 2.04 QUALIFIED PLANS

A "qualified plan" is a retirement plan that meets the requirements of section 401(a) of the Internal Revenue Code and thus "qualifies" for favorable income tax treatment. Although welfare benefit plans, such as employer-provided health plans, receive favorable income tax treatment, welfare benefit plans are not "qualified plans."[58] The term "qualified plan" solely refers to pension plans that meet the requirements of IRC § 401(a).

Employers may establish a variety of other pension plans that receive favorable income tax treatment. For example, governmental employers may establish pension plans that are eligible for favorable income tax treatment under section 457 of the Internal Revenue Code. Although eligible for favorable income tax treatment, so-called "section 457 plans" are not "qualified plans" because they do not receive favorable income tax treatment under section 401(a) of the Internal Revenue Code. The tax rules applicable to section 457 plans are similar, though not identical, to the tax rules applicable to qualified plans.

This book focuses on qualified plans.

---

[56] For a discussion of the IRC § 415(b) limit, see Chapter 10 § 10.02[B][3].

[57] IRC § 415(b)(1)(B).

[58] Wholly separate and apart from the Internal Revenue Code, the Affordable Care Act sets forth requirements that "qualified health plans" must satisfy in order to be eligible to participate in the Health Exchanges. *See* 42 U.S.C. § 18021 (defining "qualified health plan").

[A] Qualification Requirements

Section 401(a) of the Internal Revenue Code sets forth about 30 separate requirements that a plan must satisfy in order to qualify for favorable income tax treatment.[59]

The qualification requirements may generally be divided into two distinct types of rules:

(1) rules designed to protect plan participants and police against employer fraud and misrepresentation, and

(2) rules designed to limit the tax subsidy provided to qualified plans.[60]

[1] Qualification Rules to Protect Plan Participants

Some qualification requirements are designed to protect plan participants. For example IRC § 401(a)(3) requires that qualified plans satisfy the minimum participant rules set forth in IRC § 410(a) and IRC § 401(a)(7) requires that qualified plans satisfy the vesting rules set forth in IRC § 411.

Generally, Title I of ERISA contains rules that are parallel to the tax rules that are designed to protect plan participants.[61]

[2] Qualification Rules to Target Tax Subsidy

According to the Joint Committee on Taxation, the favorable income tax treatment accorded employer-sponsored pensions will result in an estimated $647.3 billion in foregone tax revenues between 2014 and 2018.[62] Some of the tax qualification requirements are designed to limit and target that substantial tax subsidy. The most significant of these rules are the nondiscrimination rules[63] which prohibit qualified plans from discriminating in favor of highly compensated employees.[64] The rules also include limits on the amount of compensation that may

---

[59] Section 401(a) contains 37 subsections. Not all of the subsections set forth separate qualification requirements. For example, IRC §§ 401(a)(5) and 401(a)(6) contain special rules relating to the nondiscrimination requirements set forth in subsections 401(a)(3) and 401(a)(4), and two subsections, 401(a)(18) and 401(a)(21), have been repealed. Moreover, not every plan has to satisfy every requirement. For example, section 401(a)(28) sets forth additional requirements that only apply to employee stock ownership plans (ESOPs).

[60] Joseph Bankman, *Tax Policy and Retirement Income: Are Pension Plan Anti-Discrimination Provisions Desirable?*, 55 U. CHI. L. REV. 790, 795 (1988).

[61] For example, ERISA § 202 contains minimum participation rules that are parallel to the minimum participation rules in IRC § 410(a) and ERISA § 203 contains vesting rules like the vesting rules set forth in IRC § 411.

[62] According to the Joint Committee on Taxation, the favorable tax treatment accorded employer-sponsored pensions will result in an estimated $647.3 billion in forgone tax revenues between 2014 and 2018. Joint Committee on Taxation, Estimates of Federal Tax Expenditures for Fiscal Years 2014–2018, at 32 (Aug. 5, 2014).

[63] IRC § 401(a)(3) (requiring qualified plans to satisfy IRC § 410(b) minimum coverage rules); IRC § 401(a)(4) (prohibiting discrimination in contributions and benefits); IRC § 401(a)(26) (imposing minimum participation standards on defined benefit plans). *See* Chapter 9.

[64] IRC § 414(q) (defining highly compensated employee). *See* Chapter 9 § 9.05.

be taken into account in calculating benefits provided under a qualified plan[65] and limits on contributions that may be made to defined contribution plans.[66]

Unlike the rules designed to protect plan participants, the rules designed to limit the tax subsidy are contained solely in the Internal Revenue Code.[67]

[3] Enforcement of Qualification Requirements

In theory, failure to meet the qualification requirements could mean loss of tax-favored status.[68] As a practical matter, however, the Internal Revenue Service (IRS) rarely disqualifies plans. Instead, the IRS has a well-developed alternative resolution program to address and correct qualification problems.[69]

[B] Tax Benefits of Traditional Qualified Plans

Traditional qualified plans enjoy four principal federal income tax advantages:

(1) Employers may deduct contributions to qualified plans when the contributions are made;

(2) Employees do not need to include the contributions in income until the contributions are distributed to them;

(3) Earnings on contributions held by qualified plans are exempt from tax; and

(4) Participants can roll over distributions from a qualified plan to an individual retirement account (IRA) or another qualified plan and further delay taxation of benefits.

[1] Employer May Deduct Contributions to Qualified Plans When Made

Under section 404(a) of the Internal Revenue Code, an employer may deduct contributions to a qualified plan when made. An immediate deduction of the contributions is permitted regardless of when the employee includes the benefits in

---

[65] IRC § 401(a)(17). *See* Chapter 10 § 10.02[A].

[66] IRC § 401(a)(16) (requiring qualified plan to satisfy limits on contributions and benefit set forth in IRC § 415). *See also* IRC § 401(a)(30)(requiring qualified plan to satisfy limits on elective deferrals set forth in IRC § 402(g)). *See* Chapter 10 § 10.02[B] (discussing IRC § 415 limits); Chapter 10 § 10.02[C] (discussing IRC § 402(g) limits).

[67] Many of those rules are discussed in Chapter 10. In addition, separate and apart from the tax qualification requirements, the Internal Revenue Code contains tax rules that are designed to limit the tax subsidy. For example, IRC § 404 limits the amount employer can deduct for contributions to pension plans. Those limits are also discussed in Chapter 10.

[68] For a discussion of the consequences of loss of tax-favored status, see Pension Plan Guide, *Understanding the Tax Fallout from Plan Disqualification* (CCH Nov. 2012).

[69] Employer Plans Compliance Resolution System (EPCRS), Rev. Proc. 98-22, as amended by multiple Revenue Procedures. For a detailed discussion of EPCRS, see, for example, Richard A. Naegele & Kelly A. VanDenHaute, *Plan Correction Methods — IRS EPCRS and DOL Voluntary Compliance Programs*, presented at The Group 2014 Annual Meeting (Jan. 26, 2014), *available at* www.wickenslaw. com. *See also* Carly E. Grey, *IRS Expands Its Retirement Plan Qualification Correction Program*, 118 J. OF TAX'N 137 (No. 3 March 2013) (describing most recent changes to EPCRS).

income and whether the employee's benefits are vested.[70]

[2]   Employees Do Not Need to Include Contributions in Income Until Contributions are Distributed to Them

Under the traditional tax doctrines of constructive receipt and economic benefit,[71] contributions to fund the benefits of vested employees[72] would ordinarily be taxable to the employees when made. Section 402(a) of the Internal Revenue Code, however, provides an exception to these doctrines for contributions to qualified plans. Specifically, IRC § 402(a) provides that plan participants are not required to include employer contributions to qualified plans in income until the benefits are actually distributed to them.

[3]   Earnings on Contributions Held by Qualified Plans are Exempt from Tax

Section 501(a) of the Internal Revenue Code exempts from taxation income earned by the contributions to a qualified plan while the plan assets are held in a tax-exempt trust. This rule permits a tax-free build-up of investment earnings which is the essence of the favorable tax treatment of qualified plans.[73]

[4]   Participants Can Roll over Distributions from a Qualified Plan to an Individual Retirement Account or Another Qualified Plan and Further Delay Taxation of Benefits

Section 402(c) permits a participant who receives a lump-sum distribution from a qualified plan to further delay taxation by rolling the distribution over into an individual retirement account (IRA) or another qualified plan. The plan participant

---

[70] Under general tax principles, employers should be entitled to deduct contributions to fund vested benefits when made and employees should be required include those contributions in income when made. Deductions for contributions to fund unvested benefits should be delayed until the benefits are vested and thus nonforfeitable. *See* Bruce Wolk, *Discrimination Rules for Qualified Retirement Plans: Good Intentions Confront Economic Reality*, 70 VA. L. REV. 419, 422–24 (1984).

[71] The constructive receipt doctrine focuses on "when" income is taxable while the economic benefit doctrine focuses on "what" income is taxable. Under the constructive receipt doctrine, a cash-basis taxpayer must include in income amounts set aside or otherwise made available when they are set aside or otherwise made available, regardless of when or whether the taxpayer actually receives the income. 26 C.F.R. § 1.451-2(a). Under the economic benefit doctrine, which is derived from the broad definition of income contained in IRC § 61(a), any amount of compensation paid to an individual for services must be included in income regardless of the form it takes, such as cash, bonus, profit-sharing, or compensation in kind. *See* Robert B. Chapman, *A Matter of Trust, or Why "ERISA-Qualified" is "Nonsense upon Stilts": The Tax and Bankruptcy Treatment of Section 457 Compensation Plans as Exemplar*, 40 WILLAMETTE L. REV. 1, 16–18 (2004); Wolk, 70 VA. L. REV., at 422–24.

[72] Contributions to fund benefits that are not yet vested would not be taxable income to the participant when made because the benefits would be forfeitable until vested. Wolk, 70. VA. L. REV., at 422–24.

[73] *See* Regina T. Jefferson, *Redistribution in the Private Retirement System: Who Wins and Who Loses?*, 53 HOWARD L.J. 283, 297 (2010), *citing*, Daniel I. Halperin, *Interest in Disguise: Taxing the Time Value of Money*, 95 YALE L.J. 506, 519–22 (1986). *See also* Appendix B.

will not be taxed on the distribution until the proceeds are distributed from the IRA or new qualified plan.[74]

[C] Economic Effect of Favorable Tax Treatment Accorded Traditional Qualified Plans

As illustrated in Appendix B, the favorable tax treatment accorded traditional qualified plans is, assuming no change in tax rates, the economic equivalent of never taxing the income earned on assets held by the qualified plan; that is, never taxing the plan's earnings.

[D] Roth Treatment

Since 2006, an alternative form of favorable tax treatment has been available for one type of qualified plan, the 401(k) plan.

As discussed below, a 401(k) plan is a special type of qualified plan to which an employee may elect to contribute. If an employee elects to contribute to a traditional 401(k) plan, the employee may exclude the contribution from taxable income when made, but the employee must treat all of the 401(k)'s distributions as taxable income when received. Thus, a plan participant will be taxed on both contributions to a 401(k) plan and earnings on those contributions when the contributions and earnings are distributed.

In contrast, if an employee makes a Roth contribution to a 401(k) plan, the contribution will be includible in taxable income when made.[75] Distributions from the plan, however, will not be included in taxable income.[76] Thus, neither the contributions that were already taxed nor the earnings which were never taxed are treated as taxable income when distributed.

As illustrated in Appendix B,[77] assuming no change in tax rates, the favorable tax treatment accorded traditional qualified plans is economically equivalent to the favorable tax treatment accorded Roth contributions to 401(k) plans.

[E] Basic Types of Qualified Plans

Section 401(a) of the Internal Revenue Code divides qualified plans into three basic types of plans:

(1) profit-sharing plans,

(2) stock bonus plans, and

(3) "pension plans."[78]

---

[74] IRC § 402(a).

[75] IRC § 402A(a)(1).

[76] IRC § 402A(d)(1).

[77] *See also* Gregg D. Polsky & Grant J. Hellwig, *Taxing Structured Settlements*, 51 B.C. L. Rev. 39, 47 n.31 (2010); Daniel I. Halperin, *Interest in Disguise: Taxing the Time Value of Money*, 95 Yale L.J. 506, 519 (1986).

[78] Specifically, section 401(a) of the Internal Revenue Code provides that "a trust created or

Unlike ERISA, which classifies all employee benefit plans that provide retirement income as "pension plans," the term "pension plan" for purposes of the Internal Revenue Code refers to a specific subset of qualified plans that provide retirement income. Except when referring to "pension plans" for purposes of the Internal Revenue Code and qualification requirements, this book uses the term "pension plan" in its broader sense as referring to all employee benefit plans that provide retirement income.

[1] Profit-Sharing Plans

Profit-sharing plans are the most common type of defined contribution plan in operation today.[79]

As their name suggests, profit-sharing plans were originally intended to provide employees with an opportunity to share in their employers' profits.[80] Now, however, contributions may be made to a profit-sharing plan regardless of whether the employer has profits.

Profit-sharing plans may provide for regular annual employer contributions or may be discretionary and permit the employer to decide whether and how much to contribute each year.

Profit-sharing plans must provide a definite formula for allocating the contributions among the participants' accounts, and they must specify which events, such as severance of employment, trigger distributions to plan participants.[81]

[2] Stock Bonus Plans

Stock bonus plans are similar to profit-sharing plans except that benefits are distributable in the form of stock of the employer company.[82]

Although stock bonus plans may provide for distributions in the form of cash, they must also allow participants to receive distributions in the form of employer stock.[83] If the employer stock is not publicly traded, participants generally must be given the right to require the employer to repurchase the stock for fair value.[84]

---

organized in the United States and forming part of a *[1] stock bonus, [2] pension, or [3] profit-sharing plan* of an employer for the exclusive benefit of his employee or their beneficiaries shall constitute a qualified trust under this section" if the plan satisfies the requirements set forth in section 401(a). IRC § 401(a) (emphasis added).

[79] Dep't of Labor, Private Pension Plan Bulletin, Abstract of 2010 Form 5500 Annual Reports 3 (Nov. 2012) (reporting that of the 701,012 private sector pension plans in 2010, 611,366 were profit sharing plans or thrift-savings plans).

[80] Joint Committee on Taxation, Present Law and Background Relating to the Tax Treatment of Retirement Savings, JCX-32-12, at 25 (2012).

[81] Treas. Reg. § 1.410-1(b)(1)(ii).

[82] Treas. Reg. § 1.401-1(b)(1)(iii).

[83] Joint Committee on Taxation, Present Law and Background Relating to the Tax Treatment of Retirement Savings, JCX-32-12, at 26 (2012).

[84] *Id.*

[3]   Pension Plans

All defined benefit plans are "pension plans" for purposes of the Internal Revenue Code and qualification requirements. In addition, a special type of defined contribution plan, the money purchase plan, also constitutes a "pension plan" for purposes of the tax qualification rules.

On their face, money purchase plans closely resemble profit-sharing plans. The fundamental difference between a money purchase plan and a profit-sharing plan is that contributions to a money purchase plan cannot be discretionary. Instead, the plan must provide for a set contribution formula, which is typically a specified percentage of the participant's salary.[85]

Now that profit-sharing plans need not be based on profits and can provide for a set contribution formula, it can be difficult to distinguish between profit-sharing plans and money purchase plans based on the terms of the plan. Thus, in order to ensure that governmental regulators and plan participants can distinguish between profit-sharing and money purchase plans,[86] the Internal Revenue Code requires that the terms of money purchase plans and profit-sharing plans expressly designate whether they are money purchase plans or profit-sharing plans in order for the plans to be qualified and thus eligible for favorable income tax treatment.[87]

Although money purchase plans closely resemble profit-sharing plans, some of the tax rules governing money purchase plans are very different from the tax rules governing profit-sharing plans because money purchase plans are "pension plans" for tax qualification purposes. For example, money purchase plans are subject to the minimum funding requirements,[88] and the employer is generally subject to an excise tax if it fails to make contributions as required by the plan.[89] In addition, money purchase plans are subject to the same rules requiring distributions in the form of qualified joint and survivor annuities as defined benefit plans.[90]

Nevertheless, some of the rules governing money purchase plans are different from the rules governing defined benefit plans because money purchase plans are defined contribution plans. For example, money purchase plans are subject to the same deduction limits as profit-sharing and stock bonus plans,[91] and benefits under a money purchase plans are not guaranteed by the PBGC.[92]

---

[85] *Id.*

[86] Dan M. McGill et al., Fundamentals of Private Pensions 354 (9th ed. 2010).

[87] IRC § 401(a)(27).

[88] Treas. Reg. § 1.412(a)(1)(A).

[89] Joint Committee on Taxation, Present Law and Background Relating to the Tax Treatment of Retirement Savings, JCX-32-12, at 26 (2012). In addition, unlike profit-sharing and stock bonus plans, money purchase plans cannot provide for in-service distributions except at normal retirement age or in the case of plan termination. *Id.*

[90] For a discussion of the qualified joint and survivor annuity (QJSA) rules, *see* Chapter 5 § 5.03.

[91] *See* IRC § 415(c) and Chapter 10 § 10.02[B][2].

[92] *See* ERISA § 4021(b)(1) (excluding defined contribution plans from Title IV coverage).

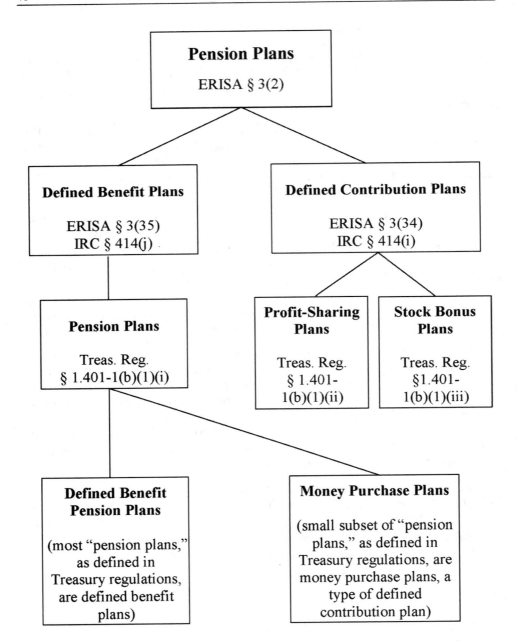

§ 2.05   "ERISA-QUALIFIED PLANS"

Occasionally, courts refer to "ERISA-qualified" plans.[93] Indeed, in *Patterson v. Shumate*,[94] the Supreme Court repeatedly referred to an "ERISA-qualified plan" in applying bankruptcy law.[95]

There is, however, no such thing as an "ERISA-qualified plan." Plans may be subject to ERISA, or they may be "qualified," that is, "qualify" for favorable income tax treatment under the Internal Revenue Code. ERISA, however, does not impose "qualification" requirements.

§ 2.06   SPECIAL TYPES OF QUALIFIED PLANS

Employers may sponsor a multitude of different types of pension plans. This section provides an overview of three particular types of qualified plans:

    (1)   401(k) plans,

    (2)   employee stock ownership plans (ESOPs), and

    (3)   cash balance plans.

In addition, this section provides an overview of individual retirement accounts (IRAs), which are not a type of qualified plan but often hold assets that were rolled over, that is, transferred, from qualified plans.[96]

[A]   401(k) Plans

401(k) plans, which are named for the section of the Internal Revenue Code that regulates them, are the most popular type of qualified plan today.[97]

Technically, 401(k) plans are not a separate type of pension plan. Rather, 401(k) plans are profit-sharing or stock bonus plans[98] that contain a qualified "cash or deferred arrangement" that permits plan participants to choose between receiving

---

[93] Prior to 2005, courts frequently addressed the question whether a plan was "ERISA-qualified" for purposes of the bankruptcy code, and courts applied different tests to define the term. *See* Donna Litman, *Bankruptcy Status of "ERISA Qualified Pension Plans" — An Epilogue* to Patterson v. Shumate, 9 Am. Bankr. Inst. L. Rev. 637, 652 (2001) (discussing various approaches courts applied to interpreting term "ERISA-qualified plan"). In 2005, Congress amended the bankruptcy code to provide a straightforward exemption for a wide range of tax-exempt retirement savings vehicles. As a result, the term has much less significance for bankruptcy purposes. *See* John Hennigan, *Rousey and the New Retirement Funds Exemption*, 13 Am. Bankr. Inst. L. Rev. 777, 797 (2005).

[94] 504 U.S. 753 (1992).

[95] For a discussion of *Patterson v. Shumate*, see Chapter 5 § 5.04[4].

[96] Employers may also use IRAs to provide retirement benefits to their employees. Specifically, employers may use IRAs to provide employees with retirement benefits through simplified employee pension plans, SEPs, under IRC § 408(k), SIMPLE IRA plans under IRC § 408(p), and deemed IRAs under IRC § 408(q). For an overview of these specialized plans, see Employee Benefits Law 6-44–6-47 (Jeffrey Lewis et al., eds., 3d ed. 2012).

[97] *See, e.g.*, Dep't of Labor, Private Pension Plan Bulletin, Abstract of 2010 Form 5500 Annual Reports 2 (Nov. 2012) (reporting that of 701,000 private pensions in 2010, 519,000 were 401(k) plans).

[98] Certain pre-ERISA money purchase plans and rural cooperative plans may include a qualified cash or deferred arrangement and certain small employers may adopt "SIMPLE" 401(k) plans. Joint

a cash payment or having a contribution made on their behalf to a qualified plan.[99] These voluntary contributions are referred to as "elective contributions."

401(k) plans differ fundamentally from other qualified plans in that the decision of whether to participate in a 401(k) plan rests with the individual employee. Employers may encourage participation by offering "matching contributions"[100] or by adopting an automatic enrollment plan under which plan participants must affirmatively opt out of the plan if they do not wish to participate.[101] Nevertheless, the ultimate decision of whether to participate in a 401(k) plan rests with the individual plan participant.[102]

As in all defined contribution plans, the individual plan participant, rather than the employer/plan sponsor, bears the investment risk. In addition, unlike in defined benefit plans and traditional defined contribution plans, in most 401(k) plans, the individual plan participant, rather than a professional investment manager, decides how to invest the plan assets.[103]

Committee on Taxation, Present Law and Background Relating to the Tax Treatment of Retirement Savings, JCX-32-12, at 27 (2012).

[99] According to Professor Norman Stein:

Section 401(k) has an interesting history and the § 401(k) plans, as we know them today, might be thought of as an unintended consequence of legislation designed to address a narrow issue. Prior to ERISA, it had been a practice in the banking industry for firms to offer a year-end bonus, which could be taken in cash or contributed to a profit-sharing plan on a before-tax basis. The IRS had permitted this practice but before ERISA began questioning whether an employee who elected deferral should be considered in constructive receipt of the contribution. In 1978, Congress passed legislation designed to approve such plans if the contributions were not weighted heavily in favor of highly paid employees.

A story, almost certainly true, is that a pension consultant named Ted Benna realized that § 401(k) seemed to authorize plans in which employees could elect to defer a portion of their regular compensation throughout the year. In 1981, the Department of Treasury issued regulations endorsing this reading of the statute, setting the stage for the § 401(k) revolution.

Norman Stein, *An Alphabet Soup Agenda for Reform of the Internal Revenue Code and ERISA Provisions Applicable to Qualified Deferred Compensation Plans*, 56 SMU L. REV. 627, 659 (2003).

[100] Matching contributions are employer contributions made to a 401(k) plan on account of an employee's elective contributions to the plan. For example, a plan may provide that an employer will provide a matching contribution equal to 100% of an employee's contributions up to 5% of compensation. If an employee elects to contribute 2% of pay to the plan, the employer contributes an additional 2% of pay so that the employee's account would be credited with 4% of the employee's pay.

Employers may also make "nonelective contributions" to 401(k) plans. As their name suggests, nonelective contributions are contributions that the employer makes to the employee's individual account, and like contributions employers make to other, more traditional, defined contribution plans, the employee does not have the choice between receiving the money as income or as a contribution to the plan. Instead, the nonelective contribution is simply additional compensation provided to the employee in the form of a contribution to the plan. An employer may decide to make nonelective contributions in order to ensure that the plan satisfies the nondiscrimination requirements. *Cf.* IRC § 401(k)(12)(C) (providing nonelective contribution safe harbor for 401(k) plans).

[101] *See* IRC § 401(k)(13) (authorizing automatic enrollment 401(k) plans).

[102] The sole exception is in the event the employer offers "nonelective" contributions to satisfy the nondiscrimination requirements. If an employer elects to provide nonelective contributions, contributions must be made on behalf of all nonhighly compensated employees eligible to participate in the plan regardless of whether they choose to participate.

[103] *See, e.g.*, Dep't of Labor, Private Pension Plan Bulletin, Abstract of 2010 Form 5500 Annual

[B] Employee Stock Ownership Plans (ESOPs)

An Employee Stock Ownership Plan (ESOP) is a special form of stock bonus plan that is designed to invest primarily in qualifying employer securities,[104] that is, stock of the employer.[105] ESOPs differ from conventional qualified plans in that their principal purpose is not to provide workers with retirement income. Rather, the purpose of an ESOP is to help workers become owners of their employers, that is, merge the roles of capitalist and worker,[106] so that workers have a second source of income derived from capital and need not depend solely on their labor income.[107] ESOPs are intended to strengthen the free market by "transferring the ownership of a company's capital to its workers";[108] they are not intended to serve as a replacement for "traditional pension arrangements."[109]

ERISA's general fiduciary provisions require that the assets of a pension plan be diversified,[110] and its prohibited transaction rules prohibit pension plans from holding qualifying employer securities that exceed 10% of the plan's assets.[111] Those limitations, however, do not apply to ESOPs. Specifically, ERISA § 404(a)(2) provides that "eligible individual account plans," which include ESOPs,[112] do not violate the diversification requirement if they hold qualifying employer securities, and ERISA's prohibited transaction rules provide eligible individual accounts plans, including ESOPs, with a statutory exemption from the prohibition on holding employer securities that exceed 10% of plan assets.[113]

Although ESOPs are not the only type of qualified plan that may acquire and hold employer securities,[114] ESOPs are the only type of plan that may borrow

---

Reports 48 Table D6 (Nov. 2012) (reporting that of the 654,469 private sector defined contribution plans in 2010, 493,460 permitted employees to direct all investments and 18,842 permitted employees to direct some portion of assets).

[104] IRC § 409(a)(2).

[105] IRC § 409(l).

[106] Donovan v. Cunningham, 716 F.2d 1455, 1458 (5th Cir. 1983).

[107] ESOPs are the brainchild of Louis O. Kelso, a San Francisco lawyer who believed that the economic value of a worker's labor would not be sufficient to support the worker and thus, it was essential to encourage more widespread ownership of capital among workers so they would be entitled to second source of income derived from capital rather than labor. Kelso thought that by encouraging pension plans to invest in employer stock ownership of capital could be extended to all workers. Thus, was born the concept of an ESOP. Andrew W. Stumpff, *Fifty Years of Utopia: A Half-Century After Louis Kelso's "The Capitalist Manifesto," A Look Back at the Weird History of the ESOP*, 62 Tax Law. 419, 419 (2009)

[108] Susan J. Stabile, *Pension Plan Investments in Employer Securities: More Is Not Always Better*, 15 Yale J. on Reg. 61, 69 (1998).

[109] *Id.*

[110] *Cf.* ERISA § 404(a)(1)(C), (requiring that fiduciaries diversify "the investments of the plan so as to minimize the risk of large losses, unless under the circumstances it is clearly prudent not to do so").

[111] ERISA § 407(a)(2).

[112] ERISA § 407(d)(3)(A).

[113] ERISA § 407(b)(1). This exemption applies to all "eligible individual account plans," including 401(k) plans.

[114] Many 401(k) plans permit employees to invest in employer stock. *See* David Blanchett, *Employer Stock Ownership in 401(k) Plans and Subsequent Company Stock Performance*, Morningstar Paper 4

funds to purchase employer securities.[115] ESOPs that borrow funds to acquire employer securities are referred to "leveraged ESOPs."[116] Leveraged ESOPs offer employers special tax advantages, such as the ability to deduct contributions to the ESOP to cover loan principal payments, and thus are often used by employers as a corporate finance tool.[117]

[C]　Cash Balance Plans

A cash balance plans is a type of qualified plan that combines elements of both a defined benefit plan and a defined contribution plans. Thus, a cash balance plan is often referred to as a "hybrid plan."[118]

Technically, a cash balance plan is a type of defined benefit plan because it promises plan participants a specific benefit.[119] The benefit, however, is specified in terms of a theoretical account balance;[120] thus, a cash balance plan resembles a defined contribution plan.

Each participant in a cash balance plan has a hypothetical individual account that resembles an individual account in a profit-sharing plan. The participant's promised benefit is then based on two components: (1) a pay or contribution component, and (2) an investment component.[121] The pay or contribution component is determined by the benefit formula specified in the plan document and may require that the employer contribute a percentage of pay or a flat dollar amount. The investment component provides for an investment return based on a defined rate. The rate of return may be a fixed rate or it may be tied to a federal rate of return, such as the yield on 30-year Treasury bonds.

Example

Company sponsors a cash balance plan under which it promises to provide employees with pay credits equal to 5% of their annual wages and interest credits of 3% per year.[122]

---

figure 1 (July 1, 2013) (showing that in 2013 about half of large companies with 401(k) plans permit employees to invest in employer stock).

[115] See IRC § 4975(d)(3) (providing exemption from prohibited transaction rules for qualifying loans to leveraged ESOP).

[116] Steven J. Arsenault, *AESOP and the ESOP: A New Fable About Dividend and Redemptions*, 31 Va. Tax Rev. 545, 552 (2012).

[117] For a more detailed discussion of leveraged ESOPs and their tax advantages, see *id.* at 550 n.17. *But see* Stumpff, 62 Tax Law., at 427 & n.61 (explaining why ESOPs do not "convert" a nondeductible cost such as a loan principal repayment into a deductible expense).

[118] Joint Committee on Taxation, Present Law and Background Relating to the Tax Treatment of Retirement Savings, JCX-32-12, at 17 (2012).

[119] *Id.*

[120] Edward A. Zelinsky, *The Defined Contribution Paradigm*, 114 Yale L.J. 451, 499 (2004).

[121] Dana M. Muir, *Counting the Cash: Disclosure and Cash Balance Plans*, 37 J. Marshall L. Rev. 849, 856 (2004).

[122] This hypothetical is based on the hypothetical presented in Julie A. Roin, *The Limits of Textualism: Cooper v. IBM Personal Pension Plan*, 77 U. Chi. L. Rev. 1195, 1199 (2010).

Arnold, Company's employee who participates in the cash balance plan, earns $50,000 in Year 1 and $60,000 in Year 2. Under the terms of the cash balance plan, Arnold is entitled to receive a pay credit of $2,500[123] at the end of Year 1, and at the end of Year 2, a pay credit of $3,000[124] plus an interest credit of $75.[125] Thus, at the end of Year 2, Arnold has a hypothetical account balance of $5,575 ($2,500 + $3,000 + $75 = $5,575). If Arnold retires at the end of Year 2, Arnold's retirement benefit will be $5,575. If he continues to work for Company and earns another $60,000 in Year 3, his hypothetical account balance will increase to $8,742.25 at the end of Year 3.[126]

Arnold's retirement benefit resembles the benefit he would have earned had Company maintained a traditional defined contribution plan with a 5% contribution rate and the assets in the plan had earned 3% each year, compounded annually.

A cash balance plan differs from a traditional defined contribution plan in two fundamental ways. First, the individual accounts are purely hypothetical. Plan assets are pooled and invested by the plan trustee or investment manager. Second, participants' accounts are credited with interest at the rate guaranteed by the plan regardless of the plan's actual investment return. Thus, as in all defined benefit plans, the employer bears the investment risk, and the cash balance plan is guaranteed by the PBGC.

Like all defined contribution plans, a cash balance plan allows employees to earn their retirement benefits more evenly throughout their careers, as opposed to defined benefit plans pursuant to which employees tend to earn most of their retirement benefits at the end of their careers.

Most cash balance plans are the result of conversions from traditional overfunded defined benefit plans.[127] These conversions raised difficult questions regarding how benefits earned under a preexisting defined benefit plan should be converted to benefits under a cash balance plan and led to considerable controversy[128] and litigation, especially regarding whether employers' conversions impermissibly discriminated against older workers.[129] In 2006, Congress amended

---

[123] $50,000 x 0.5 = $2,500.

[124] $60,000 x 0.5 = $3,000.

[125] $2,500 x 0.3 = $75. In the interest of simplicity, this example assumes that contributions to the hypothetical account are made once a year on the last day of the year. Thus, no interest credits are awarded in Year 1 with respect to Year 1 contributions. In reality, pay and interest credits typically accrue at regular intervals throughout the year. Roin, 77 U. CHI. L. REV., at 1199 n.28.

[126] His $5,575 hypothetical account balance at the end of Year 2 plus the Year 3 contribution of $3,000 ($60,000 x .02) plus $167.25 in interest on his Year 2 account balance (.03 x $5,575 = $167.25).

[127] Roin, 77 U. CHI. L. REV., at 1199 n.28.

[128] For a discussion of the controversy, see for example, Roin, 77 U. CHI. L. REV., at 1199 n.28 (2010); Regina T. Jefferson, *Striking a Balance in the Cash Balance Plan Debate*, 49 BUFFALO L. REV. 513 (2001); Coleman J.F. Cannon, *Cashing in on Older Workers: Age Discrimination Claims in Cash-Balance Pension Plans*, 19 LAW & INEQ. 31 (2001); Edward A. Zelinsky, *The Cash Balance Plan Controversy*, 19 VA. TAX REV. 683 (2000); Jonathan Barry Forman & Amy Nixon, *Cash Balance Pension Plan Conversions*, 25 OKLA. CITY U. L. REV. 379 (2000).

[129] *See, e.g.*, Cooper v. IBM Personal Pension Plan, 457 F.3d 636 (7th Cir. 2006), *cert. denied*, 127 S. Ct. 1143 (2007); Register v. PNC Financial Services, 477 F.3d 56 (3d Cir. 2007); Drutis v. Rand McNally

ERISA to provide that cash balance plan conversions do not (1) violate ERISA, (2) fail to qualify for favorable tax treatment, or (3) discriminate on the basis of age if certain requirements are satisfied.[130]

[D] Individual Retirement Accounts [IRAs]

Individual retirement accounts or IRAs are tax-favored retirement savings vehicles for individuals. There are two basic types of IRAs: traditional IRAs and Roth IRAs. In addition, plan participants may roll over assets from a qualified plan into a third type of IRA, a rollover IRA.

The favorable tax treatment accorded IRAs mirrors that of qualified plans. Specifically, like traditional qualified plans, individuals may deduct contributions to traditional IRAs from their income when the contributions are made,[131] no tax is imposed on IRA earnings so long as the assets are held by the IRA,[132] and distributions from IRAs are subject to tax when made.[133] In addition, like Roth contributions to 401(k) plans, contributions to Roth IRAs are taxable when made[134] but neither the earnings on[135] nor the distributions from Roth IRAs are subject to income tax.[136]

When Congress originally authorized IRAs, they were only available to individuals who did not participate in an employment-based retirement plan.[137] Now IRAs are also available to individuals who participate in employer-sponsored pension plans so long as their income falls below certain indexed income thresholds.[138]

& Co., 499 F.3d 608 (6th Cir. 2007), *cert. denied*, 555 U.S. 816 (2008); *In re* Citigroup Pension Plan ERISA Litigation, 470 F. Supp. 2d 323 (S.D.N.Y. 2006), *cert. denied*, 130 S. Ct. 3506 (2010).

In *CIGNA Corp. v. Amara*, 131 S. Ct. 1866 (2011), the Supreme Court decided a case in which plan participants claimed that their employer violated ERISA's disclosure requirements in conjunction with a cash balance plan conversion. This aspect of *Amara* is discussed in Chapter 4 § 4.03[C].

[130] The requirements are set forth in IRC §§ 411(a)(13) & 411(b)(5), ERISA §§ 203(f) & 204(b)(5), and ADEA § 4(i)(10). Among other things, the rules require that the interest credit be at a rate that is not less than zero and not greater than a market rate of return. IRC § 411(b)(5)(B)(i)(1).

[131] IRC § 219(a). Individuals may also make after-tax contributions to traditional IRAs. IRC § 408(o).

[132] IRC § 408(e).

[133] IRC § 408(d).

[134] IRC § 408A(c)(1).

[135] IRC §§ 408A(a); 408(e).

[136] IRC § 408A(d).

[137] *See* Patricia E. Dilley, *Hidden in Plain View: The Pension Shield Against Creditors*, 74 IND. L.J. 355, 419–24 (1999) (describing history of IRAs).

[138] IRC § 219(g)(3)(B). In 2015, tax deductible contributions are phased out for single taxpayers with modified adjusted gross income between $61,000 and $100,000 and for married taxpayers with modified adjusted gross income between $98,000 and $118,000.

Since their inception,[139] IRAs have been authorized to accept tax-free rollover contributions from qualified plans[140] in order to facilitate the portability of pensions,[141] that is, to make it easier for plan participants to take their pension benefits with them when they move from one job to another. Thus, if a plan participant rolls over an "eligible rollover distribution" from a traditional qualified plan into a rollover IRA, the rollover distribution will not be subject to income tax, and earnings on the distribution will continue to grow tax free[142] until the money is distributed from the rollover IRA.[143] A significant percentage of the assets held by IRAs today are attributable to rollovers from qualified plans.[144]

When IRAs were originally introduced, most employer-sponsored pension plans were defined benefit plans which were not easily portable, that is, the benefit could not easily be transferred from one employer's plan to another.[145] Thus, from a policy standpoint, permitting rollovers into IRAs made a great deal of sense. Today, however, with 401(k) plans the most common type of employer-sponsored pension plan, portability of pension benefits is no longer a significant issue. A plan participant's interest in a 401(k) plan may easily be transferred to another 401(k) plan.[146]

Instead, IRA rollovers now raise serious policy concerns. Because IRAs are not established by employers, they are not subject to title I of ERISA.[147] Nor are they currently subject to much other regulation. Thus, a plan participant who rolls over his or her interest in a 401(k) plan into a rollover IRA loses many of the protections ERISA provides for plan participants.[148] As the "wild west" of the retirement

---

[139] Lemishow v. Commissioner of Internal Revenue, 110 T.C. 110, 113 (1998) (citing Employee Retirement Income Security Act of 1974, Pub. L. No. 93-405, § 200(b), (g)(5), 88 Stat. 829, 959–64, 968–69).

[140] IRC § 408(d)(3).

[141] Lemishow, 110 T.C., at 113 (citing Conf. Rep. 93-1280, 1974-3 C.B. 415, 502; H. Rep. 93-807, 1974-3 C.B. (supp.) 236, 265).

[142] IRC § 408(e).

[143] IRC § 408(d)(3).

[144] Craig Copeland, *Individual Retirement Account Balances, Contributions and Rollovers 2011: The EBRI IRA Database*, EBRI Issue Brief No. 381, at 1 (May 2013) (stating that individuals with rollover contributions had higher account balances than individuals with regular contributions and the dollar amount of rollovers is 13 times higher than the dollar amount of regular contributions to IRAs).

[145] *See* Steven L. Willborn, *The Problem with Pension Portability*, 77 NEBRASKA L. REV. 344, 348 (1998) (explaining that because benefits under a defined benefit plan are typically based on years of service and final average pay, a new employer would be required to give employees credit for years worked for the old employer in order for benefits under a defined benefit plan to be portable).

[146] In order the transfer an employee's interest from one 401(k) plan to another 401(k), the assets in the first 401(k) plan must simply be transferred to the second 401(k) plan. *See id.* at 348–49 (discussing portability of assets).

[147] *See* Kathryn J. Kennedy, *Why Regulators Are Wringing their Hands as to Who Captures the IRA Rollover Market*, N.Y.U. REV. OF EMPLOYEE BENEFITS & EXEC. COMP. § 3.03 (2014) (noting even IRAs funded with assets rolled over from employer-provided plans are not covered by title I of ERISA); Patricia E. Dilley, *Hidden in Plain View: The Pension Shield Against Creditors*, 74 IND. L.J. 355, 430 (1999) (explaining that IRAs are not regulated by ERISA because they are not employee benefit plans established by employers).

[148] IRAs are still subject to the prohibited transaction rules under the Internal Revenue Code, which

world,[149] IRAs have been the subject of considerable scrutiny and debate in recent years.[150]

---

are similar, though not identical, to the prohibited transaction rules under title I of ERISA. *See* Kennedy, 2014 N.Y.U. REV. OF EMPLOYEE BENEFITS & EXEC. COMP., at § 3.03 (noting that "the excise taxes imposed on prohibited transactions by Title II of ERISA (through the federal tax code) are applicable to IRAs"); Chapter 6 § 6.06 (discussing prohibited transaction rules).

[149] John Hechinger, *Retirees Suffer as $300 Billion 401(k) Rollover Boom Enriches Brokers*, Bloomberg News (June 17, 2014) (quoting Karen Friedman of the Pension Rights Center: "You're going into the wild, wild west when you take your money out of a 401(k) and put it into an IRA."), *available at* http://www.bloomberg.com/news/2014-06-17/retirees-suffer-as-401-k-rollover-boom-enriches-brokers.html.

[150] *See* Kennedy, 2014 N.Y.U. REV. OF EMPLOYEE BENEFITS & EXEC. COMP. 3-1 (2014) (discussing governmental agencies' oversight and fiduciary standards and disclosure requirements that should apply to a financial adviser's recommendation to roll money over from a 401(k) plan into a rollover IRA).

Chapter 3

WELFARE PLANS

§ 3.01 INTRODUCTION

Although Congress was most concerned with pension plans when it enacted ERISA, ERISA has always covered both pension plans and welfare benefit plans.[1] Specifically, ERISA's disclosure,[2] fiduciary,[3] and enforcement[4] provisions have always applied to welfare benefit plans.

Initially, ERISA did not impose any additional substantive regulation on welfare benefit plans. Over the years, however, Congress has amended ERISA a number of times to regulate one specific type of welfare benefit plan, the health care benefit plan. Initially, Congress amended ERISA to address discrete problems in our employment-based health care system. Then, in 2010, Congress amended ERISA to incorporate many of the provisions of the Affordable Care Act,[5] the country's most sweeping reform of its health care system since the enactment of Medicare and Medicaid in 1965.[6]

This chapter begins by discussing the meaning of the term "welfare benefit plan" for purposes of ERISA. It then provides a lengthy discussion of health care plans and their regulation under ERISA and the Affordable Care Act. Finally, it concludes with an overview of the favorable income tax treatment afforded certain welfare benefit plans under the Internal Revenue Code.

§ 3.02 WHAT IS A WELFARE BENEFIT PLAN?

Section 3(1) of ERISA defines the term "employee welfare benefit plan" or "welfare plan." Specifically, it defines a welfare plan as

---

[1] The decision to include welfare benefit plans in ERISA has been described as an "ill-considered 'afterthought.'" *See* Brendan S. Maher, *Thoughts on the Latest Battles over ERISA's Remedies*, 30 Hofstra Lab. & Emp. L.J. 339, 342 n.19 (2013), and authorities cited therein.

[2] ERISA §§ 101–111. *See* Chapter 4 § 4.03.

[3] ERISA §§ 401–414. *See* Chapter 6.

[4] ERISA §§ 501–521. *See* Chapter 7.

[5] Pub. L. No. 111-148, 124 Stat. 119 (2010), as amended by Pub. L. No. 111-152, 124 Stat. 1029 (2010).

[6] *See* David Gamage, *Perverse Incentives Arising from the Tax Provisions of Healthcare Reform: Why Further Reforms Are Needed to Prevent Avoidable Costs to Low- and Moderate-Income Workers*, 65 Tax L. Rev. 669, 669 (2012) ("[T]he ACA is the most extensive reform to the U.S. health care system since the creation of Medicare and Medicaid in 1965."). *See also* Janet Cecila Walthall, *New Health Care Law Likely to Pose Challenges for Employers, Attorneys Say*, 37 BNA Pension & Benefits Rep. 1152 (May 18, 2010) (describing the ACA as seminal as the enactment of ERISA).

any plan, fund, or program which was heretofore or is hereafter established or maintained by an employer or by an employee organization, or by both, to the extent that such plan, fund, or program was established or is maintained for the purpose of providing for its participants or their beneficiaries, through the purchase of insurance or otherwise, (A) medical, surgical, or hospital care or benefits, or benefits in the event of sickness, accident, disability, death, or unemployment, or vacation benefits, apprenticeship or other training programs, or day care centers, scholarship funds, or prepaid legal services or (B) any benefit described in section 302(c) of the Labor Management Relations Act, 1947 (other than pensions on retirement or death, and insurance to provide such pensions).

[A]   What are Welfare Benefits?

ERISA § 3(1) does a good job of identifying specific welfare "benefits."

For example, ERISA § 3(1) specifically identifies the following welfare benefits:

> Health care benefits,
>
> Disability benefits,
>
> Vacation benefits,
>
> Prepaid legal services, and
>
> Apprenticeship and other training programs.

[B]   What is a Plan?

Although section 3(1) of ERISA does a very good job of specifically identifying particular welfare benefits, it does not clearly define the term "plan." Rather, the term "plan" is defined in a circular fashion. As quoted above, section 3(1) provides that the term "employee welfare benefit plan" or "welfare plan"

> means any plan, fund, or program which was heretofore or is hereafter established or maintained by an employer or by an employee organization, or by both, to the extent that such plan, fund, or program was established or is maintained for the purpose of providing for its participants or their beneficiaries, through the purchase of insurance or otherwise [specifically enumerated benefits as discussed in § 3.02[A], *supra*]

The question of what exactly constitutes a welfare benefit "plan" for purposes of ERISA is a frequently litigated issue.[7]

---

[7] Occasionally, a question arises as to whether there is a pension plan for purposes of ERISA. *See, e.g.*, Musmeci v. Schwegmann Giant Super Markets, 332 F.3d 339 (5th Cir. 2003) (holding that employer's grocery voucher plan was pension plan for purposes of ERISA); Guilbert v. Gardner, 480 F.3d 140, 146 (2d Cir. 2007) (concluding that "no reasonable fact finder could find that [employer] 'established or maintained' a pension plan under ERISA"). The question, however, arises much more frequently in the context of welfare benefit plans than pension plans because ERISA provides far fewer substantive protections for welfare plans than for pension plans and thus, ERISA preemption, the context in which most of this litigation arises, is much more significant for welfare plans than for pension plans. ERISA preemption is discussed in Chapter 8.

Whether a particular arrangement is a welfare "plan" for purposes of ERISA arises most commonly in the preemption context. In a typical preemption case, a plan participant files suit in state court claiming that his employer violated state law. The employer then raises ERISA preemption as a defense to the state law claim. Specifically, the employer claims that the state law "relates to" an employee benefit "plan" and thus is preempted by ERISA. Whether an arrangement is a "plan" for ERISA preemption purposes is discussed in detail in Chapter 8 § 8.04[C].

Although less common, the question of whether an arrangement constitutes a plan under ERISA may arise if a plan participant or the Department of Labor files suit to enforce ERISA's provisions. In this type of case, the Department of Labor or plan participant contends that a particular arrangement constitutes a plan and thus is subject to express regulation under ERISA. This section addresses this second category of cases in which a plan participant or the Department of Labor claims an arrangement constitutes a plan for purposes of enforcing ERISA.

[1] *Donovan v. Dillingham* Test

In *Donovan v. Dillingham*,[8] the leading case on the question of what constitutes a welfare plan for purposes of ERISA, the Secretary of Labor brought suit against the trustees of a multiple employer trust[9] to enforce ERISA's fiduciary provisions.[10] The district court dismissed the Department of Labor's complaint on the ground that there were no employee benefit plans involved and thus, the court lacked subject matter jurisdiction.[11]

Reconsidering the case *en banc*, the Eleventh Circuit declared that "by definition," a welfare benefit plan under ERISA requires

   (1) a plan, fund, or program,

   (2) established or maintained

   (3) by an employer or by an employee organization, or by both,

   (4) for the purpose of providing [specifically identified welfare benefits]

   (5) to participants or their beneficiaries.[12]

The court noted that the last three elements were either self-explanatory or defined by statute.[13] The first two elements, however, are less clear.[14]

---

[8] 688 F.2d 1367 (11th Cir. 1982).

[9] The purpose of a multiple employer trust is permit "employers of small numbers of employees to secure group health insurance coverage for their employees at rates more favorable than offered directly by an insurer." *Id.* at 1370.

[10] *See also* Musmeci v. Schwegmann Giant Super Markets, 332 F.3d 339 (5th Cir. 2003) (former employees filed suit claiming former employer's grocery voucher program was pension plan and termination of the "plan" violated ERISA's fiduciary provisions).

[11] 688 F.2d at 1370.

[12] *Id.* at 1371.

[13] *Id.*

[14] *Id.* at 1372.

With respect to the first element, the "plan, fund, or program" requirement, the court announced that at a minimum, there must be

(1) intended benefits,

(2) intended beneficiaries,

(3) a source of financing, and

(4) a procedure to apply for and collect benefits.[15]

With respect to the second element, that the plan be "established or maintained," the court declared that a formal written plan is not required but something more than simply a decision to extend benefits is necessary for the creation of a plan.[16]

Combining the two elements together, the court declared that "a 'plan, fund or program' under ERISA is established if from the surrounding circumstances a reasonable person can ascertain the intended benefits, a class of beneficiaries, the source of financing, and procedures for receiving benefits."[17]

[2] Excluded Plans

Not all employee benefit "plans" are subject to ERISA. Rather, ERISA expressly exempts some specific types of plans from some[18] or all[19] of ERISA's provisions. In addition, the Department of Labor's regulations exempt certain types of plans from ERISA.

Example

The Labor regulations exempt "safe harbor" payroll practices, such as the payment of vacation benefits out of an employer's general assets.[20]

[3] Three-Step Inquiry

In determining whether a particular arrangement is plan subject to ERISA, courts typically apply a three-step inquiry.[21]

First, is the arrangement expressly exempt from ERISA under the terms of the statute or under the regulatory "safe harbors."[22]

---

[15] *Id.*

[16] *Id.* at 1372–73.

[17] *Id.* at 1373.

[18] For example, ERISA § 201(1) exempts all welfare benefit plans from ERISA's participation and vesting rules.

[19] For example, ERISA § 4(b)(3) exempts from coverage plans "maintained solely for the purpose of complying with applicable workmen's compensation laws or unemployment compensation or disability insurance laws."

[20] 29 C.F.R. § 2510.3-1(b)(3)(i).

[21] *See* Langley v. DaimlerChrysler Corp., 502 F.3d 475, 479 (6th Cir. 2007). Some courts collapse the first and third prongs. *See, e.g.,* Gahn v. Allstate Life Ins. Co., 926 F.2d 1449, 1452 (5th Cir. 1991).

[22] The regulatory safe harbor exemptions for pension plans are set forth in 29 C.F.R. 2510.3-2 while the regulatory safe harbor exemptions for welfare plans are set forth in 29 C.F.R. § 2510.3-1.

Second, if the arrangement is not expressly exempt, does it satisfy the four-part *Donovan* test; that is, are there (1) intended benefits, (2) intended beneficiaries, (3) a source of financing, and (4) a procedure to apply for and collect benefits.

Finally, if the *Donovan* test has been satisfied, has the employer "established or maintained" the plan with the intent of providing benefits. Something more than a mere promise to extend benefits is required to satisfy the final element.[23]

§ 3.03 INTRODUCTION TO EMPLOYMENT-BASED HEALTH CARE PLANS

The United States is unique in its approach to health care.[24] Unlike other advanced industrial countries, which provide health care through a mandatory universal national health care system, the United States relies principally on voluntary employment-based health insurance.[25]

Most workers consider their health care benefits their most important employee benefit.[26]

[A] Brief History of Employment-Based Health Care Plans

The current system of employment-based health insurance is often described as the result of a historical accident.[27] Prior to World War II, only about 3% of the U.S. population had employment-based health care coverage.[28] Employment-based health insurance began to grow rapidly during World War II and is now the principal source of health insurance for most individuals.

In 2012, 59% of the U.S. population under the age of 65 was covered by employment-based health insurance.[29]

---

[23] *Cf.* Guilbert v. Gardner, 480 F.3d 140 (2d Cir. 2007) (holding that district court did not err in granting summary judgment in favor of employer where employee's evidence of establishment of pension plan consisted of testimony regarding the employer's promise to establish a plan, the employer's writing of terms of plan on a legal pad and promising to file it in the company's record, employer's oral assurances that a plan was established, testimony from other employees that employee was owed money other than his salary, and evidence of tax returns that showed employer took tax deductions for "employee benefit programs").

[24] Pierre-Louis Bras & Didier Tabuteau, Les Assurances Maladie 19–20 (2010) (describing the American system as unique).

[25] Jacob S. Hacker, *Review Article: Dismantling the Health Care State? Political Institutions, Public Policies and the Comparative Policies of Health Reform*, 34 Brit. J. Pol. Sci. 693, 697 (2004) (noting that the United States is the only advanced industrial state to rely principally on voluntary employment-based health insurance).

[26] *See* Paul Fronstin & Ruth Helman, *Views on the Value of Workplace Benefits: Findings from the 2013 Health and Voluntary Workplace Benefits Survey*, 34 EBRI No. 11, at 14 (Nov. 2013).

[27] *See, e.g.*, David A. Hyman & Mark Hall, *Two Cheers for Employment-Based Health Insurance*, 2 Yale J. Health Pol'y L & Ethics 23, 25 (2001).

[28] *See id.*

[29] Paul Fronstin, *Sources of Health Insurance and Characteristics of the Uninsured: Analysis of the March 2013 Current Population Survey*, EBRI Issue Brief No. 390, at 4 & 5 Figure 1 (Sept. 2013).

[B]   Reasons for Employment-Based Health Care

Commentators often attribute the growth of employment-based health insurance to two principal factors:

(1)   wage and price controls instituted during World War II, and

(2)   the favorable income tax treatment accorded employment-based health insurance.[30]

[1]   Wage and Price Controls

During World War II, the Office of Price Administration instituted wage and price controls in an attempt to deal with inflation.[31] Excluded from the definition of wages, however, were fringe benefits, such as employer contributions to health insurance and pension plans.[32] As a result, employers sought to compete for scarce labor by enhancing their fringe benefits and offering employees health insurance and pension benefits.[33]

[2]   Favorable Income Tax Treatment[34]

Section 106(a) of the Internal Revenue Code generally excludes employer contributions to fund health care plans from income. In addition, section 105 of the Internal Revenue Code generally excludes from income benefits received under employer-provided accident and health plans. Thus, generally employees are never taxed on the value of the health care benefits they receive from their employers.

Although contributions to and benefits from employer-provided health plans are generally excludable from employees' income, the employer is generally entitled to deduct the cost of the health care benefits it provides its employees as an ordinary and necessary business expense.

According to the Joint Committee on Taxation, the tax exclusion for employer contributions for health care, health insurance premiums, and long-term care insurance premiums represents the single largest tax expenditure for the years 2014 through 2018.[35]

---

[30] Some commentators also credit other factors, such as unions and the military's return to civilian life. *See* Kathryn L. Moore, *The Future of Employment-Based Health Insurance After the Patient Protection and Affordable Care Act*, 89 NEB. L. REV. 885, 891–92 & 888 n.12 (2011).

[31] *See* Hyman & Hall, 2 YALE J. HEALTH POL'Y L & ETHICS, at 25.

[32] The Stabilization Act of 1942, Pub. L. No. 77-729 § 10, 56 Stat. 765, 768. Although fringe benefits were exempted from the wage and price controls, the exemption was limited; employers could only raise fringe benefits up to 5% of total payroll. *See* KIP SULLIVAN, THE HEALTH CARE MESS: HOW WE GOT INTO IT AND HOW WE'LL GET OUT OF IT 15 (2006).

[33] *See* Hyman & Hall, 2 YALE J. HEALTH POL'Y L & ETHICS, at 25.

[34] For a discussion of the history of the favorable income tax treatment accorded health care benefits, see Moore, *The Future of Employment-Based Health Insurance*, 89 NEB. L. REV., at 889–90.

[35] Joint Committee on Taxation, *Estimates of Federal Tax Expenditures for Fiscal Years 2014–2018*, at 2 (Aug. 5, 2014).

The favorable tax treatment accorded employer-provided health care benefits is discussed in more detail in §§ 3.08[A] and [B].

[C] Types of Employment-Based Health Care Plans[36]

Employers may offer one or more[37] of five different types of health care plans:

(1) conventional health insurance,

(2) Health Maintenance Organizations (HMOs),

(3) Preferred Provider Organization (PPO) plans,

(4) Point of Service (POS) plans, and

(5) Consumer-Driven Health Plans.[38]

[1] Conventional Health Insurance

Conventional health insurance predates the other forms of health insurance now available. Although it is uncommon today,[39] it was quite common when ERISA was enacted.[40] Thus, understanding conventional insurance helps to put the other types of insurance into perspective.

Often referred to as indemnity or comprehensive insurance, conventional health insurance covers a wide range of services but does not provide first-dollar coverage;[41] that is, covered individuals must first meet an annual deductible[42] before the insurer begins to pay for benefits. Once the annual deductible is met, the insurer begins to pay for benefits, but the covered individual must still pay a portion of the costs, referred to as co-insurance.[43]

---

[36] The following overview of the different types of health insurance is based, in large part, on the overview provided in Amy B. Monahan, *The Promise and Peril of Ownership Society Health Care Policy*, 80 Tul. L. Rev. 777, 787–91 (2006).

[37] Most employers (87%) offer only one type of health insurance plan; large employers are more likely than small employers to offer more than one type of plan. Kaiser Family Foundation and Health Research & Educational Trust, Employer Health Benefits: 2014 Annual Survey, at 58, *available at* http://kff.org/private-insurance/report/2014-employer-health-benefits/.

[38] *Id.* at 2.

[39] *Id.* (reporting that less than 1% of workers covered by conventional health insurance plans).

[40] Conventional insurance was introduced in 1949. *See* Monahan, *Ownership Society Health Care Policy*, 80 Tul. L. Rev., at 787. For a history of health insurance before the enactment of ERISA, see, for example, D. White, *Market Forces, Competitve Strategies, and Health Care Regulation*, 2004 U. Ill. L. Rev. 137, 145; Laura A. Scofea, *The Development and Growth of Employer-provided Health Insurance*, 117 Monthly Lab. Rev. 3, 4 (Mar. 1994).

[41] Under first-dollar coverage, an individual is not required to make any payments for care before insurance benefits are available. Scofea, 117 Monthly Lab. Rev., at 4 (Mar. 1994).

[42] A deductible is a specified amount of medical expenses that an insured individual must pay for before the insurer begins to help cover the cost of expenses. *Id.*

[43] *Id.*

Example

Employer provides its employees with conventional health insurance. The health insurance plan has a $500 deductible and 30-70 coinsurance. Employee incurs $700 in covered expenses. Employee must pay the first $500 of covered expenses out of pocket until the $500 deductible is reached. Once the $500 deductible is satisfied, Employee must pay for 30% of the remaining costs and the insurance company will pay the remaining 70% of the costs. Thus, Employee must pay the $500 deductible plus coinsurance of $60 (30% x ($700 - $500 = $200) = $60) for a total cost of $560 while the insurance company will pay the remaining 70% of the costs that exceed the deductible (70% x ($700 - $500 = $200) = $140).

Conventional health insurance pays medical care providers directly for their services based on their costs.[44] Thus, the more services doctors and hospitals provide, the more money they make, and medical care providers have no incentive to ration their care or rein in their costs.

Unlike medical providers who have no incentive to limit their "supply" of health care, that is, how much health care they provide, insured individuals under conventional health have some incentive to temper their "demand" for medical services because they must pay an annual deductible and co-insurance.

[2]   Health Maintenance Organizations (HMOs)

Despite the "demand-side" incentives to limit medical care and thus medical costs, conventional insurance led to escalating medical costs in the 1970s and 1980s.[45] As a result, Health Maintenance Organizations (HMOs) were introduced to create "supply-side incentives" to reduce medical costs, that is, incentives to encourage medical providers to limit the amount, and thus cost, of medical care they provide.

More common than conventional health insurance,[46] HMOs differ fundamentally from conventional health insurance in a number of ways.[47] First, HMOs do more than finance health care; they directly provide or contract with affiliated doctors, hospitals, and other health care providers to provide health care.[48] Insured individuals are covered if, but only if, they see one of the affiliated health care providers. Insured individuals are assigned a "primary care physician" and must

---

[44] See SARA ROSENBAUM ET AL., LAW AND THE AMERICAN HEALTH CARE SYSTEM 199 (2d ed. 2012) (noting that this arrangement is sometimes referred to as "fee-for-service").

[45] See William D. White, *Market Forces, Competitve Strategies, and Health Care Regulation*, 2004 U. ILL. L. REV. 137, 145.

[46] Kaiser Family Foundation and Health Research & Educational Trust, *Employer Health Benefits: 2014 Annual Survey*, at 2 (reporting that 13% of workers were enrolled in an HMO compared with less than 1% in conventional health insurance plans).

[47] For a detailed overview of HMOs, see Jason S. Lee, *Managed Health Care: A Primer*, CRS Report for Congress 97-913 EPW (Sept. 30, 1997).

[48] See The Henry J. Kaiser Family Foundation, *How Private Health Care Coverage Works: A Primer* 2 (2008 Update) (explaining that "HMOs operate as insurers (meaning they spread health care costs among people enrolled in the HMO) and as health care providers (meaning they directly provide or arrange for the necessary health care")).

get approval from their primary care physician before receiving any specialized care.

Second, rather than pay doctors and other health care providers on a fee-for-service basis, HMOs typically pay health care providers a set fee per insured individual. Thus, HMOs share financial risk with health care providers. Paying health care providers on a per patient basis rather than a per service basis is intended to provide a supply side incentive to ration or reduce health care costs.

Third, HMOs focus on preventive care and preventing illness rather than treating illness. Thus, they remove financial barriers to health care, such as high deductibles[49] and substantial co-pays,[50] to encourage insured individuals to get annual physicals and visit their primary care doctors to prevent illness. On the other hand, insured individuals' options are more constrained when they become ill. They must obtain approval before receiving specialized care, and services are only covered if the specialized care is provided by an affiliated health care provider. In addition, HMOs often exclude some types of treatments to reduce costs.

[3] Preferred Provider Organization (PPO) and Point of Service (POS) Plans

Despite their promise, HMOs proved to be unpopular. Insured individuals were unhappy because they had little control over their medical care and they were concerned that doctors and plan administrators were denying them care in order to receive higher compensation or profits.[51] As result, two new types of managed care plans[52] were introduced, Preferred Provider Organization (PPO) and Point of Service (POS) plans.

Like HMOs, PPO and POS plans contract with a number of health care providers to provide insured individuals with services at a discounted rate.[53] Insured individuals in PPO and POS plans, however, have a greater choice in care providers. PPO and POS plans cover services from providers who have not contracted with the plans; such services are simply subject to higher deductibles and co-insurance.[54]

---

[49] Just under 60% of workers covered by an employer-sponsored HMO have no general deductible. Kaiser Family Foundation, *2014 Employer Health Benefits Annual Survey*, at 119.

[50] Whether or not workers have a general deductible, most workers covered by an employer-sponsored HMO have separate cost sharing for hospital admissions and outpatient surgery. *Id.* at 116.

[51] Bernadette Fernandez, *Health Insurance: A Primer*, Congressional Research Service RL32237, at 16 (Feb. 16, 2012).

[52] "Managed care organizations integrate the financing and delivery of care, institute cost controls, share financial risk with providers, and manage service utilization." Lee, CRS Report for Congress 97-913 EPW, at CRS-2.

[53] *See* Kaiser Family Foundation, *How Private Health Care Coverage Works*, at 4 (explaining that "PPOs are networks composed of physicians and other health care providers that agree to provide services at discounted rates and/or pursuant to certain utilization protocols to people enrolled in health coverage offered by a health coverage provider").

[54] *See id.* at 2 (stating that "[t]ypically enrollees in [PPOs] are given financial incentives — such as lower copayments — to use network providers").

The principal difference between PPO and POS plans is that individuals in PPO plans can visit any doctor without a referral while individuals in POS plans may be required to receive a referral before specialized services and/or out-of-network care is covered.[55]

Preferred Provider Organization (PPO) plans are the most common type of employer-sponsored health insurance plan today.[56]

[4] Consumer-Driven Health Plans

Although PPO and POS plans are more popular than HMOs, they have proven to be very costly.[57] As result, a new form of health care plan has emerged, the "consumer-driven health plan," which adds a new demand-side incentive to control medical care costs.[58]

First introduced in 2001,[59] consumer-driven health plans combine a tax favored health savings account or health reimbursement account with a high deductible health insurance plan.[60] They are sometimes referred to as "High Deductible Health Plans with a Savings Option" or HDHP/SO.

Under a consumer-driven health plan, the insured individual first uses the money in the health savings account or health reimbursement account to pay for health care. Once the balance in the account has been exhausted, the insured individual pays for any medical care the individual receives until a high deductible has been met. Once the high deductible has been reached, the insurance kicks in and the insurance pays the covered individual's health care costs.

The theory behind consumer-driven health plans is that by giving individuals more control over the funds set aside for health care services, individuals will spend the money more responsibly, especially once they become more aware of the actual

---

[55] *Compare* Monahan, *Ownership Society Health Care Policy*, 80 Tul. L. Rev., at 790 (stating that under POS plan, covered individual must receive referral before receiving specialized in-network care) *with* HealthCare.gov, *Different Kinds of Health Insurance Plans*, *available at* https://www.healthcare.gov/what-are-the-different-types-of-health-insurance/ (stating that under POS plan, covered individuals can visit any in-network doctor without referral but need referral to visit out-of-network provider).

[56] Kaiser Family Foundation, *2014 Employer Health Benefits Annual Survey*, at 4 (showing that 58% of workers are covered by PPO plans and 8% of workers are covered by POS plans).

[57] For a discussion of the reasons why managed care plans have not managed to control costs, see Rosenbaum et al., Law and the American Health Care System, at 213–15.

[58] Fernandez, Congressional Research Service RL32237, at 17 (stating that "[c]onsumer-driven health care refers to a broad spectrum of coverage arrangements that give incentives to consumers to control their use of health services and/or ration their own health benefits"). Whether consumer-driven health plans will survive or thrive following the Affordable Care Act is subject to debate. *See, e.g.*, Merrill Matthews, *Health Savings Accounts Will Survive ObamaCare — At Least for Now*, Forbes (Mar. 27, 2013), *available at* http://www.forbes.com/sites/merrillmatthews/2013/03/27/health-savings-accounts-will-survive-obamacare-at-least-for-now/#; Whitney R. Johnson, *The Impact of the Affordable Care Act on HSAs*, Benefits Quarterly 45 (Third Quarter 2011).

[59] *See* Paul Fronstin, *Health Savings Accounts and Health Reimbursement Arrangements: Assets, Account Balances and Rollovers, 2006–2013*, EBRI Issue Brief No. 395, at 4 (Jan. 2014) (noting that employers first started to offer HRAs in 2001 and HSAs in 2004).

[60] For a more detailed discussion of health savings accounts and health reimbursement accounts, see § 3.08[B].

price of health services.[61] Thus, consumer-driven health plans[62] are intended to sensitize individuals to the cost of their health care while protecting them from catastrophic medical expenses.[63]

[D]   Employers' Methods of Financing Employment-Based Health Plans and the Implications of the Financing Methods

Employers may finance their health plans in one of two fundamentally different ways:

(1)   through the purchase of health insurance from an insurance company (so-called "fully-insured" plans), or

(2)   by directly paying for health care claims (so-called "self-funded" plans or "self-insured" plans).[64]

Whether a plan is fully-insured or self-funded may have significant implications under both ERISA and the Affordable Care Act. The distinction between fully-insured and self-funded plans, however, is not as clear and sharp as the law suggests. Many employers with self-funded plans purchase stop-loss insurance which blurs the distinction between the two methods of financing health care benefits.

[1]   Fully-Insured Plans

Under a fully-insured plan, the employer enters into a contract with an insurance company, pays a premium to the company, and the insurer assumes financial responsibility for the costs of the covered employees' (and their dependents') medical claims.[65] In a fully-insured plan, the insurer is said to bear the full risk for any covered claims made by the employees and their dependents.[66]

In 2014, about 40% of covered workers were in a fully-insured plan.[67] Small employers were much more likely to provide coverage through a fully-insured plan

---

[61]   Fronstin, *Health Savings Accounts and Health Reimbursement Arrangements*, EBRI Issue Brief No. 395, at 4.

[62]   About 20% of workers are covered by consumer-driven health plans. Kaiser Family Foundation, *2014 Employer Health Benefits Annual Survey*, at 4.

[63]   For a critique of consumer-driven health plans, see Russell Korobkin, *Comparative Effectiveness Research as Choice Architecture: The Behavioral Law and Economics Solution to the Health Care Cost Crisis*, 112 Mich. L. Rev. 523, 529–40 (2014).

[64]   Paul Fronstin, *Capping the Tax Exclusion for Employment-Based Health Coverage: Implications for Employers and Workers*, EBRI Issue Brief No. 325 6 (Jan. 2009).

[65]   Kaiser Family Foundation, 2014 Employer Health Benefits Annual Survey, at 174; Fronstin, *Capping the Tax Exclusion for Employment-Based Health Coverage*, EBRI Issue Brief No. 325, at 6.

[66]   Amaila R. Miller, et al., *Financing of Employer Sponsored Health Insurance Plans Before and After Health Reform: What Consumers Don't Know Won't Hurt Them?*, 36 Int'l Rev. L. & Econ. 36, 36–37 (2013).

[67]   Kaiser Family Foundation, *2014 Employer Health Benefits Annual Survey*, at 174.

than were larger employers.[68]

Example

Employer pays premiums totaling $100,000 to Acme Insurance Company to cover its workforce in Year One. Employer's employees and their dependents submit claims for covered expenses totaling $120,000 in Year One. Acme Insurance Company pays the $120,000 in claims even though it only received $100,000 in premiums.

Employer may require its employees to pay a share of the premiums it pays to Acme Insurance Company. Whether Employer or Employer and its employees pay the premiums, Acme Insurance Company must pay the $120,000 in claims submitted in Year One.

[2]   Self-Funded or Self-Insured Plans

Under a self-funded or self-insured plan, the employer acts as its own insurer and assumes direct financial responsibility for the costs of the covered individuals' medical claims.[69] In essence, under a self-funded plan, rather than paying premiums to an insurance company, the employer directly pays the cost of health care claims to providers[70] and bears the risk of unexpectedly large claims.[71]

In 2014, about 61% of covered workers were in a self-funded plan.[72] Large employers were much more likely to provide coverage through a self-funded plan than were small employers.[73]

Example

Company maintains a self-funded health plan in Year One. Company's employees and their dependents submit claims for covered expenses totaling $120,000 in Year One. Company must pay the $120,000 in claims out of its current revenues.

Just as an employer with a fully insured plan may require its employees to pay a share of the premiums it pays to its insurer, an employer with a self-funded plan may require its employees to pay a share of the cost of coverage. Thus, for example, Company could require its employees to contribute $30,000 toward the cost of coverage. If Company's employees and their dependents submitted $120,000 in

---

[68] *Id.* Exhibit 10.2, at 176 (showing that 15% of covered workers in small firms (3–199 workers) were covered by self-funded plan compared with 81% of covered workers in large firms (200 or more workers)).

[69] *Id.* at 174; Fronstin, *Capping the Tax Exclusion for Employment-Based Health Coverage*, EBRI ISSUE BRIEF No. 325, at 6.

[70] Fronstin, *Capping the Tax Exclusion for Employment-Based Health Coverage*, EBRI ISSUE BRIEF No. 325, at 6–7.

[71] CHRISTINE EIBNER, ET AL., EMPLOYER SELF-INSURANCE DECISIONS AND IMPLICATIONS OF THE PATIENT PROTECTION AND AFFORDABLE CARE ACT MODIFIED BY THE HEALTH CARE AND EDUCATION RECONCILIATION ACT OF 2010 (ACA) xi (RAND Corp. 2011).

[72] Kaiser Family Foundation, *2014 Employer Health Benefits Annual Survey*, at 176.

[73] *Id.* Exhibit 10.2, at 176.

covered claims, Company would be required to pay $90,000 of the cost out of its current revenues and the employees' $30,000 contributions would cover the remaining costs.

[3] Implications of Financing Methods under ERISA

Whether an employer-sponsored plan is fully-insured or self-insured has significant implications under ERISA.

Since its inception ERISA has imposed fiduciary and disclosure requirements on all employee benefits plans, including health care plans. When ERISA was originally enacted, however, it did not impose any additional substantive regulation on health care plans.[74] Instead, it left regulation of health care plans to the states through the so-called "saving clause."

The "saving clause" is an exception to ERISA's general express preemption provision, ERISA § 514(a).[75] Section 514(a) provides that ERISA preempts all state laws that "relate to" an employee benefit plan. Thus, under ERISA § 514(a), employee benefit plans are generally subject to regulation under ERISA and only ERISA. If a state law purports to regulate an employee benefit plan, that state law is preempted, that is, it does not apply.

Section 514(b)(2)(A) of ERISA provides an express exception to the general preemption provision. Specifically, it "saves" from preemption state laws that regulate insurance. Thus, if an employer purchases a fully-insured plan, state law continues to indirectly regulate the insured plan because the insurance company that insures the plan is subject to state insurance regulation. Since virtually all employer-provided health care benefits were provided through fully-insured plans when ERISA was enacted,[76] state law, rather than ERISA, effectively regulated employer-sponsored health care plans by regulating the plan's insurer. This was in keeping with the country's longstanding practice of state, rather than federal, regulation of insurance.[77]

Section 514(b)(2)(B) of ERISA, the so-called deemer clause, provides an express exception to the saving clause. The Supreme Court has interpreted the deemer clause to exempt self-funded plans from state laws that regulate insurance.[78] Thus, under this precedent, ERISA preempts state laws that regulate insurance insofar as they might apply to self-funded plans while insured plans are subject to indirect state insurance regulation because the insurance companies that insure the plans

---

[74] ERISA's civil enforcement provisions have also applied to health care plans since the enactment of ERISA.

[75] For a more detailed discussion of ERISA preemption, see Chapter 8, *infra.*

[76] *See* David Orentlicher, *A Restatement of Health Care Law,* 79 BROOK. L. REV. 435, 444 (2014) (stating that when ERISA was enacted only 4% of employees were covered by self-insured plans).

[77] *See* Timothy Stolzfus Jost and Mark Hall, *Self-Insurance for Small Employers under the Affordable Care Act: Federal and State Regulatory Options,* 68 N.Y.U. ANN. SURV. AM. L. 539, 552–53 (2013) (noting that in 1869 the Supreme Court held that Congress had no power to regulate insurance, and shortly after the Supreme Court reversed its position in 1944, Congress enacted the McCarran-Ferguson Act to cede back to the States primary responsibility for regulating insurance).

[78] FMC v. Holliday, 498 U.S. 52, 61 (1990).

are subject to state insurance regulation.

Because historically ERISA has imposed little substantive regulation on health care plans while states have extensively regulated health insurance, the insurance saving clause together with the deemer clause creates an incentive for employers to self-fund their employee benefit plans. As a result, more than half of employees with employer-provided health care are now covered by a self-funded plan.[79]

[4] Implication of Financing Method under the Affordable Care Act

In 2010, Congress enacted the Affordable Care Act, which substantially changes many aspects of health care regulation in this country. The Affordable Care Act, however, does not eliminate the distinction between insured and self-insured plans. Instead, in some instances, the Affordable Care Act applies different rules to self-funded plans than to insured plans. [80]

For example, the Affordable Care Act requires that health insurers in the small group market use standard "community ratings" to calculate premiums. Under community rating, everyone is charged the same premium and the premium reflects the cost of all individuals, including relatively sick individuals.[81] If a small employer purchases health insurance in the group market, the small employer will be required to pay a premium that reflects a share of the cost of all individuals in the market, not just the cost of the employer's employees. Self-insured employers, on the other hand, are only required to bear the cost of their employees. Thus, a small employer with a relatively healthy workforce may have lower health care costs if the employer self-insures than if it purchases an insurance policy. Moreover, if the small employer's workforce unexpectedly becomes unhealthy, the employer can abandon self-insurance and purchase insurance based on community ratings.[82]

In addition to the community ratings requirement, the Affordable Care Act imposes a number of consumer-protection regulations. For example, it requires that at least 80% or 85% of premium revenues be spent on medical benefits rather than on administrative costs or profits. Small employers can avoid many of these consumer-protection regulations by self-insuring.[83]

---

[79] Kaiser Family Foundation, *2014 Employer Health Benefits Annual Survey*, at 174.

[80] *See* Jost and Hall, 68 N.Y.U. Ann. Surv. Am. L., at 555 (noting that the Affordable Care Act "divides the world of health benefits coverage into two continents: state-regulated 'issuers' that cover groups and individuals, and other 'group health plans' covered by ERISA, which refers to self-funded employers"); Timothy Stoltzfus Jost, *Loopholes in the Affordable Care Act: Regulatory Gaps and Border Crossing Techniques and How to Address Them*, 5 Saint Louis U. J. of Health Law & Policy 27, 76–78 (2011) (discussing provisions of Affordable Care Act from which self-insured plans are exempt).

[81] Under the medically underwritten approach, in contrast, "groups and individuals are classified according to their expected morbidity levels and their premiums set accordingly." American Academy of Actuaries, *Fundamentals of Insurance: Implications for Health Coverage*, Issue Brief 6 (July 2008).

[82] Orentlicher, 79 Brook. L. Rev., at 444, 445; Miller et al., 36 Int'l Rev. L & Econ., at 40.

[83] Orentlicher, 79 Brook. L. Rev., at 444, 445; Jost, 5 Saint Louis U. J. of Health Law & Policy, at 76–78.

The Affordable Care Act's distinctions between insured and self-funded plans continue to provide an incentive for employers, particularly small employers with healthy workforces, to finance their health care benefits through self-insured plans.[84]

[5] Stop-Loss Insurance

Because ERISA and the Affordable Care Act create incentives for employers to self-fund their plans, many employers have self-funded plans. Not all employers, however, can afford to bear the risk associated with self-funded plans.

If an employer self-funds its health care plan, the plan must pay for the covered employees' (and their dependents') medical expenses either from a trust fund established for that purpose or from the employer's current revenues. If one or more employees suffer a catastrophic illness or injury in a given year, the employer, particularly if it is a small employer, could face a severe cash-flow problem or even insolvency.

Stop-loss insurance permits employers with self-funded plans to purchase stop-loss insurance, that is, "reinsurance," to cover the plan's losses.[85] Stop-loss insurance covers costs above a stated level, or "attachment point."

Attachment points can be either "specific" or "aggregate."

[a]   Specific Attachment Point

A specific attachment point applies to each individual employee and is typically a dollar amount. Thus, the stop-loss policy reimburses the employee benefit plan for any individual employee's claims that exceed the specific attachment point.[86]

Example

Employer with a self-funded health plan purchases a stop-loss policy with a specific attachment point of $10,000. Employer's employee, Andrew, submits claims of covered costs totaling $15,000. Employer must pay the first $10,000 in claims and the stop-loss insurer will cover the $5,000 of Andrew's claims that exceed the attachment point ($15,000 - $10,000 = $5,000).

[b]   Aggregate Attachment Point

An aggregate attachment point refers to the total claims made and typically is expressed as a percentage of the plan's actuarially determined expected annual cost. Thus, the stop-loss policy reimburses the plan if the total claims submitted exceed the attachment point.[87]

---

[84] Orentlicher, 79 Brook. L. Rev., at 444, 445.

[85] Jost and Hall, 68 N.Y.U. Ann. Surv. Am. L., at 541.

[86] Russell Korobkin, *The Battle over Self-Insured Health Plans, or "One Good Loophole Deserves Another,"* 5 Yale J. Health Pol'y & Ethics 89, 111 (2005).

[87] *Id.*

Example

Employer purchases a stop-loss policy with an aggregate attachment point of 125% of the plan's actuarially determined expected annual cost of $100,000 or $125,000 (125% x $100,000 = $125,000). A total of $140,000 in covered claims is submitted. Employer must pay the first $125,000 in claims and the stop-loss insurer will cover the $15,000 of claims that exceed the attachment point ($140,000 - $125,000 = $15,000).

In 2014, about 65% of employees in self-funded plans were in plans that had stop-loss coverage.[88]

[6] Stop-Loss Insurance and the Distinction between Fully-Insured and Self-Funded Plans

Stop-loss insurance blurs the distinction between fully-insured and self-funded plans.

Theoretically, in a fully-insured plan, the employer pays a premium to an insurance company and the insurance company bears the risk that the cost of the claims will exceed the income from the premiums while in a self-funded plan, the employer pays the claims and bears the risk that the cost of claims will be greater than estimated.[89] If, however, an employer purchases a stop-loss policy, the stop-loss insurer, rather than the employer, bears the risk that the cost of covered claims will exceed the attachment point.

Moreover, if the stop-loss policy's attachment point is low enough, the stop-loss policy will closely resemble a regular fully-insured high-deductible insurance plan. For example, there is little practical difference between a self-insured plan with a stop-loss policy with an individual attachment point of $10,000 and a traditional insurance plan with a high deductible of $10,000. Under either arrangement, the employer and/or employee is required to pay for the first $10,000 in covered costs while an insurer, either the stop-loss carrier or traditional insurer, bears the risk that the cost of covered claims will exceed $10,000.[90]

In addition, many employers with self-funded plans enter into Administrative Services Only (ASO) contracts with Third Party Administrators (TPAs), including insurance companies such as Humana or Anthem Blue Cross Blue Shield. Pursuant to these contracts, the TPA performs the functions typically performed by an insurance company in an insured arrangement, such as processing claims, resolving disputes, negotiating payment rates with health care providers, and contracting with health care provider networks.[91]

---

[88] Kaiser Family Foundation, *2014 Employer Health Benefits Annual Survey*, Exhibit 10.10, at 182. For additional data on self-funded plans with and without stop-loss insurance, see Hilda L. Solis, Secretary of Labor, *Annual Report to Congress on Self-Insured Group Health Plans* (Apr. 2012).

[89] Jost and Hall, 68 N.Y.U. ANN. SURV. AM. L., at 545–46.

[90] *Id.* at 546.

[91] *Id.*

Employees enrolled in a self-funded plan administered by an insurance company typically do not know that the plan is self-funded. In such a plan, the covered employees file their claims with the insurance company, and the insurance company pays or denies their claims, sends the employees an explanation of their benefits under the plan, and handles any appeals of denied claims.[92]

Commentators have recommended, and some states have enacted, laws to prevent employers from exploiting the legal distinction between self-funded and fully-insured plans. These laws may either ban the sale of stop-loss insurance or regulate stop-loss insurance policies.[93]

In a frequently cited case,[94] the Fourth Circuit invalidated a state regulation that deemed stop-loss insurance with low attachment points to be health insurance when sold to self-insured group plans.[95] The court held that the regulation was preempted by ERISA because its purpose and effect was to force state mandated health benefits on self-funded plans when they purchased stop-loss insurance policies with low attachment points.[96]

The state later enacted a law that simply prohibited insurers from selling stop-loss insurance with a specific attachment point of less than $10,000 or an aggregate attachment point of less than 115% of expected claims. [97] The Department of Labor has announced that, in its view, state laws that prohibit insurers from issuing stop-loss insurance policies with attachment points below specified levels would not be preempted by ERISA.[98]

§ 3.04 ERISA'S REGULATION OF EMPLOYER-SPONSORED HEALTH PLANS PRIOR TO THE AFFORDABLE CARE ACT

When ERISA was originally enacted, it did not impose any substantive regulation on health care plans. To the extent that it regulated health care plans, it was through ERISA's disclosure, fiduciary, and civil enforcement provisions. Over the years, Congress amended ERISA a number of times to impose some substantive rules on health care plans.

Two of the most significant amendments to ERISA were designed to address a specific problem arising from employer-provided health insurance: "job lock." Job

---

[92] *Id.*

[93] *See Id.* at 556–58.

[94] American Medical Security, Inc. v. Bartlett, 111 F.3d 358 (4th Cir. 1997), *cert. denied*, 524 U.S. 936 (1998). For a critique of the *Bartlett* decision, see Korobkin, *The Battle over Self-Insured Plans*, 5 YALE J. HEALTH POL'Y, L. & ETHICS, at 122–28.

[95] *Bartlett*, 111 F.3d at 360.

[96] *Id.*

[97] Md. Code Ann. Ins. § 15-129(d). In an unreported decision, *American Medical Security, Inc. v. Larsen* (D. Md. 1999), the district court declined to address whether the statute was preempted by ERISA. United States Dep't of Labor, *Guidance on State Regulation of Stop-Loss Insurance*, Tech. Release No. 2014-01 (Nov. 6, 2014).

[98] Dep't of Labor, *Guidance on State Regulation of Stop-Loss Insurance*, Tech. Release No. 2014-01.

lock refers to the phenomenon that employees often found it difficult to change jobs because changing jobs meant losing their health care coverage.[99]

Congress amended ERISA for the first time to address job lock in the Consolidated Omnibus Reconciliation Act of 1985,[100] commonly referred to as COBRA. Under COBRA, employers with health care plans are required to offer "qualified beneficiaries,"[101] who would otherwise lose coverage under a plan, the opportunity to continue coverage under the plan.[102] COBRA was intended to help employees with the transition between jobs by permitting employees and their covered dependents to continue coverage under their old employer's health insurance plan until they were eligible for health insurance under their new employer's plan.

Although COBRA helped to reduce job lock, it did not eliminate it. First, employers typically do not subsidize COBRA coverage;[103] thus, many employees cannot take advantage of COBRA coverage because they find the coverage prohibitively expensive. Second, even if employees can afford the premiums, COBRA only provides coverage for a limited period of time. Until 1996, employees could still be stuck in their old jobs if they (or their family members) had pre-existing health conditions because new employers could exclude health care coverage for such employees (or their family members) through the use of pre-existing condition exclusion provisions.

Generally, pre-existing conditions are health care problems that exist at the time the individual first purchases health insurance. Under a plan with a pre-existing condition exclusion, the health plan excludes, that is, does not provide coverage for pre-existing conditions.

Example

Employee has diabetes. Employee sees her doctor four times a year for care related to her diabetes and takes daily insulin shots. If Employee changes jobs, and her new employer's plan contains a pre-existing condition exclusion provision, the new plan may exclude, that is, not cover, diabetes and thus not pay for any health care costs arising from the treatment of Employee's diabetes.

---

[99] Uwe E. Reinhardt, *Employer-Based Health Insurance: A Balance* Sheet, 18 HEALTH AFFAIRS 124, 127 (1999) ("Because the employer-based system ties health insurance to a particular job, it can induce employees to remain indentured in a detested job simply because it is the sole source of affordable health coverage."). For a review of economics literature on job lock, see Jonathan Gruber & Brigitte C. Madrian, *Health Insurance, Labor Supply, and Job Mobility: Critical Review of the Literature, in* HEALTH POLICY AND THE UNINSURED 97 (Catherine G. McLaughlin ed., 2004).

[100] Consolidated Omnibus Budget Reconciliation Act of 1985, Pub. L. No. 99-272, 100 Stat. 82 (1985).

[101] Section 607 of ERISA defines a "qualified beneficiary" to include the covered employee, the covered employee's spouse, and the covered employee's dependent child.

[102] ERISA §§ 601–608.

[103] *Cf.* ERISA § 602(3) (permitting plan sponsor to charge beneficiary up to 102% of the applicable premium for the first 18 months of COBRA coverage and up to 150% thereafter).

In 1996, Congress enacted the Health Insurance Portability and Accountability Act of 1996 or HIPAA,[104] which among other things, amended ERISA to improve the portability of employer-based health insurance. HIPAA limits the length of time during which pre-existing health condition clauses can restrict coverage.[105]

Example

Employee has diabetes. Employee sees her doctor every four months for care related to her diabetes and takes daily insulin shots. Employee terminates her employment on January 1, 2007. She does not elect COBRA coverage and does not have any other health insurance for two years. Although Employee has no health care coverage, she continues to visit her doctor every four months for care related to her diabetes.

Two years later, on January 1, 2009, Employee begins to work for New Employer. If New Employer's plan has a preexisting condition exclusion provision, New Employer's plan may exclude coverage, that is, not provide coverage, for Employee's diabetes care for one year.[106] After one year, the plan must cover Employee's diabetes.

If Employee had had continuous health insurance during that two-year period through another plan, for example through her husband's employer's plan, New Employer's plan would not be able to impose any preexisting condition exclusion.[107]

In addition to addressing job lock, Congress amended ERISA on a number of other occasions to address discrete and specific health care concerns. For example, in 1996,[108] Congress enacted a provision requiring employer-sponsored health plans that offer maternity benefits to provide minimum hospital stays.[109]

§ 3.05   PROBLEMS WITH THE U.S. HEALTH CARE SYSTEM BEFORE THE ENACTMENT OF THE AFFORDABLE CARE ACT

Prior to the enactment of the Affordable Care Act in 2010, the U.S. health care system faced a number of long-term serious shortcomings.[110] Two of the most significant shortcomings were a sizeable number of uninsured individuals and high

---

[104] Health Insurance Portability and Accountability Act, Pub. L. No. 104-191, 110 Stat. 1936 (1996).

[105] ERISA §§ 701–702. For a detailed discussion of HIPAA, see Rebecca Lewin, *Job Lock: Will HIPAA Solve the Job Mobility Problem?*, 2 U. Pa. J. Lab. & Emp. L. 507 (2000); Colleen E. Medill, *HIPAA and Its Related Legislation: A New Role for ERISA in the Regulation of Health Care Plans?*, 65 Tenn. L. Rev. 485 (1998).

[106] *See* ERISA § 701(a)(2).

[107] *See* ERISA § 701(a)(3).

[108] Newborns' and Mothers' Health Protection Act of 1996, Pub. L. No. 104-204, 110 Stat. 2935.

[109] ERISA § 711(a).

[110] For critiques of the U.S. health care system prior to the enactment of the Affordable Care Act, see Rosenbaum et al., Law and the American Health Care System, at 450–65; Kip Sullivan, The Health Care Mess: How We Got Into It and How We'll Get Out of It (2006); Jacob S. Hacker, The Divided Welfare State: The Battle over Public and Private Social Benefits in the United States (2002).

costs. Another significant shortcoming was that the individual and small group insurance markets functioned poorly.

[A] Number of Uninsured Individuals

Virtually all industrialized countries have public health insurance that provides their citizens with universal (or nearly universal) health care coverage.[111] The United States, however, is an exception to that rule.

The United States does not have a single mandatory universal health care system. Rather, the nation has a few governmental health insurance programs, including Medicare[112] and Medicaid,[113] and programs for the military,[114] that cover a little over 30% of the U.S. population.[115] The remainder of the population must rely on private health insurance or is uninsured.[116]

In 2010, when the ACA was enacted, 55% of the total U.S. population was covered by an employer-provided health plan while 10% of the U.S. population purchased individual health insurance.[117] Most importantly, 16% of the U.S. population was uninsured.[118]

The vast majority of the uninsured were in working families.[119] Workers were typically uninsured for one of three reasons: (1) their employer did not offer health insurance, (2) although their employer offered health insurance, they were not eligible for coverage because they had not worked for their employer for a sufficiently long enough period of time, or (3) they declined coverage under their employer's plan because it was too expensive.[120]

---

[111] OECD, Health at a Glance 2013: OECD Indicators 138 & Table 6.1.1, at 139.

[112] Medicare is a social insurance program that provides health insurance coverage for the elderly. For an overview of Medicare, see Richard L. Kaplan, *Top Ten Myths of Medicare*, 20 ELDER L.J. 1 (2012); ROSENBAUM ET AL., LAW AND THE AMERICAN HEALTH CARE SYSTEM, at 450–65.

[113] Medicaid is a means tested welfare program that provides health insurance coverage principally to the "deserving" poor. For an overview of Medicaid and its history prior to the Affordable Care Act, see Nicole Huberfeld, et al., *Plunging into Endless Difficulties: Medicaid and Coercion in* National Federation of Independent Business v. Sebelius, 93 B.U.L. REV. 1, 13–24 (2013). *See also* ROSENBAUM ET AL., LAW AND THE AMERICAN HEALTH CARE SYSTEM, at 496–514 (providing an overview of Medicaid).

[114] Governmental programs for the military include TRICARE and CHAMPVA (Civilian Health and Medical Program of the Department of Veterans Affairs). Carmen DeNavas-Walt et al., U.S. Census Bureau, *Income, Poverty, and Health Insurance Income, Poverty, and Health Insurance Coverage in the United States: 2012*, at 67 table. C-1 n.1.

[115] *Id.* at 68 Table C-2.

[116] Some individuals have more than one type of health insurance.

[117] DeNavas-Walt et al., U.S. Census Bureau, *Income, Poverty, and Health Insurance Income*, at 68 Table C-2. Employer-sponsored coverage decreased from 64.1% in 1999 to 55.3% in 2010 while individual coverage decreased from 10.6% in 1999 to 9.9% in 2010. *Id.*

[118] *Id.* The percentage of the population that was uninsured increased from 13.6% in 1999 to 16.3% in 2010. *Id.*

[119] Paul Fronstin, *Sources of Health Insurance and Characteristics of the Uninsured: Analysis of the March 2013 Current Population Survey*, EBRI Issue Brief No. 390, at 12 Figure 10 (Sept. 2013) (stating that 80% of the uninsured were in working families).

[120] Paul Fronstin, *Tracking Health Insurance Coverage by Month: Trends in Employment-Based*

[B] High Costs

The United States spends more on health care costs than any other developed nation.[121] For example, the United States spent the equivalent of $8,508 per person for health care costs in 2011, which was more than twice the average of all OECD countries[122] and 50% more than the two next highest spending countries, Norway and Switzerland.[123] The United States' health care costs represent 17.7% of the nation's Gross Domestic Product (GDP),[124] again the highest of any developed nation.[125]

Not only is health care in this country costly, but health care spending has exceeded growth in the U.S. economy virtually every year for the last 30 years.[126] Indeed, the average total premium for employer-provided health insurance for a single individual increased from $2,196 in 1999 to $6,025 in 2014, and the average total premium for family coverage increased from $5,791 in 1999 to $16,834 in 2014.[127]

High cost plays an important role in the lack of health insurance in our country. The most common reason employers give for failing to offer health insurance is cost,[128] and the most common reason workers give for declining employment-based health insurance, when offered, is cost.[129]

Coverage Among Workers, and Access to Coverage Among Uninsured Workers, 1995–2012, 34 EBRI NOTES 2, 4 & 5 Figure 3 (No. 7 July 2013).

[121] OECD, Health at a Glance 2013: OECD Indicators 154. For a discussion of the reasons why health care costs are so high in the United States, see, for example, BARRY R. FURROW, ET AL., HEALTH LAW: CASES, MATERIALS, AND PROBLEMS 534–40 (7th ed. 2103) (discussing extent to which 10 different factors contribute to high cost of health care in the United States: (1) national wealth, (2) population aging, (3) waste, fraud, and abuse, (4) market structure, (5) administrative costs, (6) malpractice, (7) the changing nature of disease, (8) treating "hopeless cases," (9) higher prices, and (10) technology, and concluding that most health economists believe that technology is the primary reason why health care costs so much and why cost is increasing so rapidly); ROSENBAUM ET AL., LAW AND THE AMERICAN HEALTH CARE SYSTEM, at 178–84 (concluding that root cause of high cost of health care in this U.S. is "rapid diffusion of health care technologies (e.g., drugs, equipment, costly medical procedures), and the prices paid for these technologies, as well as the high price of physician, particularly specialist, care").

[122] There are 34 countries in the OECD. The OECD, or Organization for Economic Cooperation and Development, is an international economic organization founded in 1961 to stimulate economic progress and world trade.

[123] OECD, Health at a Glance 2013: OECD Indicators 154.

[124] *Id.*

[125] *Id.* The next highest spending group of countries, which includes Canada, France, Germany, the Netherlands, and Switzerland, spends about 11% of GDP on health care. *Id. See also* OECD, OECD Health Data 2013: How Does the United States Compare 1.

[126] National Institute for Health Care Management, *U.S. Health Care Spending: The Big Picture*, NIHCM FOUNDATION DATA BRIEF, at 3 (May 2012). The growth in health care costs has slowed since the enactment of the Affordable Care Act. *See* Council of Economic Advisers, *Trends in Health Care Costs and the Role of the Affordable Care Act* (Nov. 2013) (asserting that Affordable Care Act is contributing to slow down in rate of growth).

[127] Kaiser Family Foundation, *2014 Employer Health Benefits Annual Survey*, at 88.

[128] *Id.* at 40.

[129] Fronstin, *Tracking Health Insurance Coverage by Month*, 34 EBRI NOTES, at 4 & 5 Figure 3 (No. 7 July 2013).

[C]   Poorly Functioning Individual and Small Group Markets

Private health insurance in the United States is sold in three different markets: (1) the large-group market, (2) the small-group market, and (3) the individual market.[130]

Depending on its size, an employer may purchase health insurance for its employees through either the large-group market or the small-group market. For these purposes, large employers are generally defined as employers with at least 50 employees, and the large-group market is the market that serves these employers.[131] The small-group market is generally considered to be the market that serves employers with fewer than 50 employees. The individual market provides insurance to individuals who are unable to obtain insurance through their employer or a governmental program.

Prior to the enactment of the Affordable Care Act, the large-group health insurance market was thought to operate reasonably well with virtually all employers able to offer reasonable coverage to their employees.[132] The small-group and individual markets, in contrast, were thought to function poorly.[133]

The large-group market was able to function reasonably well due, in large part, to its ability to spread or pool risk. The very essence of insurance is to spread risk.[134] In a large group, an insurer can accurately determine the expected cost of claims because most health care claims are relatively stable and predictable.[135] If a single employee incurs a catastrophic loss, such as an automobile accident that results in a lengthy hospital stay and very large health care costs, that cost can be spread among a large number of employees and the cost of insurance remains

---

[130] Amy Monahan & Daniel Schwarcz, *Saving Small Employer Health Insurance*, 98 Iowa L. Rev., at 1938; Allison K. Hoffman, *Oil and Water: Mixing Individual Mandates, Fragmented Markets, and Health Reform*, 36 Am. J. L. and Med. 7, 18 (2010).

[131] *See* Monahan & Schwarcz, 98 Iowa L. Rev., at 1938 (describing small group market as serving employers with fewer than 50 full-time employees); Hoffman, 36 Am. J. L. and Med., at 18.

[132] In 2010, 95% of firms with 50 to 199 employees offered health insurance and 99% of firms with 200 or more employees offered health insurance. The Kaiser Family Foundation and Research & Educational Trust, *Employer Health Benefits 2010 Annual Survey*, Exhibit 2.2, at 33.

[133] *See* Monahan & Schwarcz, 98 Iowa L. Rev., at 1938; Tom Baker, *Health Insurance, Risk, and Responsibility After the Patient Protection and Affordable Care Act*, 159 U. Pa. L. Rev. 1577, 1580 (2011).

[134] *See* Kenneth S. Abraham, Distributing Risk: Insurance, Legal Theory, and Public Policy 1 (1986) (stating that "[i]nsurance is a method of managing risk by distributing it among large numbers of individuals or enterprises"). *See also* American Academy of Actuaries, *Fundamentals of Insurance: Implications for Health Coverage*, Issue Brief 2 (July 2008) (stating that "[i]nsurance is only possible when a sufficient number of insured pool their risk such that the few who have a loss can be financed by the many who do not").

[135] American Academy of Actuaries, *Fundamentals of Insurance:* Issue Brief, at 3 ("By pooling many individual losses, the insurer benefits from the increased predictability afforded by the law of large numbers. Not only can the insurer calculate the expected loss of the pool, but it may also calculate the statistical variation anticipated in these losses and other risk characteristics that enable it to establish a fair and visible premium.").

predictable and manageable.[136]

In a smaller group, and particularly in the individual market, it is much more difficult to spread risk.[137] A single employee with a high-cost medical condition has a much greater impact on a small employer's total health care costs because the employer cannot rely on the "law of large numbers" to spread the cost among a large number of individuals. Because the cost of health insurance in the small-group market and individual market was typically based on the expected costs of the small group or individual prior to the Affordable Care Act, the cost of health insurance in those markets was often prohibitively expensive.[138]

§ 3.06   THE AFFORDABLE CARE ACT

In 2010, Congress enacted the Affordable Care Act to address many of the challenges facing the American health care system.[139]

Running over 1,000 pages, the Affordable Care Act is a vast and ambitious piece of legislation. According to a leading insurance law expert, the Affordable Care Act "embodies a social contract of health care solidarity through private ownership, markets, choice, and individual responsibility."[140] According to other health insurance law experts, it is "the ultimate meshing of many themes in U.S health policy": (1) universal or near universal health care coverage; (2) preservation and strengthening of employment-based health insurance; (3) preservation of a strong role for states in the regulation of health insurance; (4) establishment of a viable individual market; (5) strengthening of Medicare and Medicaid; (6) emphasis on market-based

---

[136] Monahan & Schwarcz, 98 Iowa L. Rev., at 1943 ("Large employers can be insured at community-average rates because the law of large numbers tends to ensure that their employees' overall health care expenses are similar to those of the broader community.").

[137] The very division of health insurance into the three separate markets of large-group, small-group, and individual, makes it difficult to spread risk. *See* Hoffman, 36 Am. J. L. and Med., at 48–53 (discussing market fragmentation and its effects).

[138] For additional discussion of the problems with the individual and small-group markets prior to the enactment of the Affordable Care Act, see Jost and Hall, 68 N.Y.U. Ann. Surv. Am. L., at 541–42; Monahan & Schwarcz, 98 Iowa L. Rev., at 1942–44; Hoffman, 36 Am. J. L. and Med., at 48–57.

[139] *See* Robert B. Leflar, *Reform of the United States Health Care System: An Overview*, 10 U. of Tokyo J. of Law & Politics 44, 51–52 (2013) (stating that ACA "aims at improving all three dimensions of the health care system — access, cost, and quality"); David Gamage, *Perverse Incentives Arising from the Tax Provisions of Healthcare Reform: Why Further Reforms are Needed to Prevent Avoidable Costs for Low- and Moderate-Income Individuals*, 65 Tax L. Rev. 669, 713 (2012) ("[T]he ACA includes many provisions designed to slow the growth of health care costs, to expand health care coverage to the previously uninsured, and to achieve other laudable goals.").

[140] Baker, 159 U. Pa. L. Rev., at 1579. Professor Baker continues:

While some might regard this contract as the unnatural union of opposites — solidarity on the one hand and markets, choice, and individual responsibility on the other — those familiar with insurance history will recognize in the Act an effort to realize the dream of America's insurance evangelists: a "society united on the basis of mutual insurance." Public ownership and pure, tax-based financing are technically easier and almost certainly cheaper routes to health care solidarity, but they come at a cost to the status quo that Congress was not prepared to pay. *Id.* at 1579–80.

tools to contain costs; and (7) emphasis on individual responsibility.[141]

The Affordable Care Act does not create a single coherent health insurance system. Rather, it maintains and attempts to improve upon the mishmash of separate health insurance systems that existed prior to the enactment of the Affordable Care Act.

Thus, the Affordable Care Act does not eliminate the employment-based health care system. Rather, it builds upon, and arguably improves, the system.

The Affordable Care Act does not eliminate the division of the private health insurance market into three separate sectors consisting of large-group, small-group, and individual markets. Instead, it imposes different regulations on each of these sectors depending on the perceived need for additional regulation.

Finally, the Affordable Care Act does not repeal the separate governmental health insurance programs, such as Medicare and Medicaid. Instead, it simply attempts to improve upon those separate programs.

This section provides a broad overview of the Affordable Care Act. It begins with an explanation of how, specifically, the Affordable Care Act amends ERISA. It then describes each of the three key components of the Affordable Care Act:

(1) market reforms,

(2) individual and employer mandates, and

(3) health insurance exchanges.[142]

Because the Affordable Care Act does not create a single coherent uniform health insurance system but instead maintains and attempts to improve upon the mishmash of fragmented pre-existing systems, it may be described as "a wet blanket on a mud puddle."[143] It is necessarily complex and messy.

---

[141] ROSENBAUM ET AL., LAW AND THE AMERICAN HEALTH CARE SYSTEM, at 223–24.

[142] Some commentators describe the Affordable Care Act's expansion of Medicaid as a fourth key component or pillar. *See, e.g.*, Sarah Rosembaum, *Realigning the Social Order: The Patient Protection and Affordable Care Act and the U.S. Health Insurance System*, 7 J. HEALTH & BIOMED. L. 1, 11–16 (2011).

[143] Credit for this description of the Affordable Care Act goes to Professor Nicole Huberfeld.

[A] Broad Overview of the Affordable Care Act

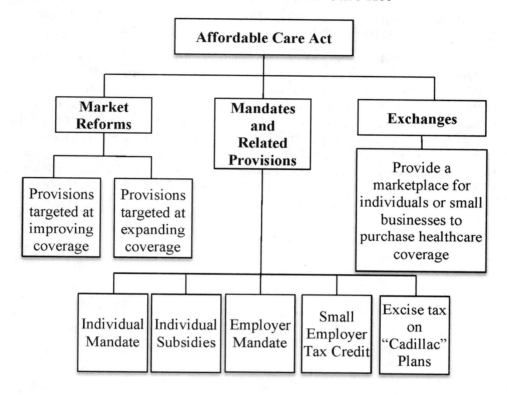

[B] ERISA's Incorporation of the Affordable Care Act's Provisions

Prior to the enactment of the Affordable Care Act, all of ERISA's substantive regulation of health care plans was specifically and separately codified in title 29 of the United States Code[144] so that there was a separate and specific provision in ERISA for all of the regulation.[145] This is no longer true. Rather than separately codify all of the Affordable Care Act's substantive regulation of employer-sponsored health care plans in title 29 of the United States Code, the Affordable Care Act simply added a single section to U.S.C. title 29 to incorporate sections 2701–2724 of the Public Health Service Act.[146] That section is referred to as

---

[144] Specifically, all of the substantive regulation of health care plans was contained in ERISA §§ 601–734, which was codified at 29 U.S.C. §§ 1161–1191c.

[145] Much of the regulation was also separately codified in separate provisions in the Internal Revenue Code, codified in title 26 of the United States Code, and the Public Health Service Act, codified in 42 U.S.C. § 201 et seq. For example, the COBRA continuing coverage requirements are found in ERISA §§ 601–608, 29 U.S.C. §§ 1161–1181, the Internal Revenue Code, 26 U.S.C. §§ 4980B(f) & (g), and the Public Health Service Act, PHSA §§ 2201–2208, 42 U.S.C. §§ 300bb-1–300bb-8.

[146] Specifically, ERISA § 715(a)(1) provides that "the provisions of part A of title XXVII of the Public Health Service Act (as amended by the Patient Protection and Affordable Care Act) shall apply to group

ERISA § 715 by ERISA practitioners.

Thus, one must now look not only at ERISA, but also the Public Health Service Act, to find the substantive regulation of employer-sponsored health care plans.

To add to the complexity, some of ERISA's provisions, such as its rules regarding the exclusion of preexisting conditions,[147] conflict with the Public Health Service Act, as amended by the Affordable Care Act.[148] Congress did not expressly repeal the inconsistent provisions of ERISA. Instead, it added ERISA § 715(b) to provide that the relevant provisions of the Public Health Service Act, as amended by the Affordable Care Act, govern over any conflicting provisions in ERISA.[149] Moreover, ERISA § 715(b) provides that sections 2716[150] and 2718[151] of the Public Health Service Act do not apply to self-insured health plans and that the provisions of ERISA shall continue to apply to such plans as if the Affordable Care Act had not amended the Public Health Service Act.

---

health plans, and health insurance issuers providing health insurance coverage in connection with group health plans, as if included in this subpart." Part A of title XXVII of the Public Health Service Act consists of sections 2701–2724 of the Public Health Service Act. Those sections are codified in 42 U.S.C. § 300gg–300gg-23. For a compilation of the Public Health Service Act immediately after the enactment of the Affordable Care Act, see housedocs.house.gov/energycommerce/phsa027.pdf.

[147] ERISA § 701 (permitting plans to impose limited preexisting condition exclusion under certain circumstances).

[148] PHSA § 2704(a), 42 U.S.C. § 300gg-4(a).

[149] ERISA § 715(a)(2).

[150] PHSA § 2716, 42 U.S.C. § 300gg-16 (prohibition on discrimination in favor of highly compensated individuals).

[151] PHSA § 2718, 42 U.S.C. § 300gg-18 (requiring rebates for certain plans).

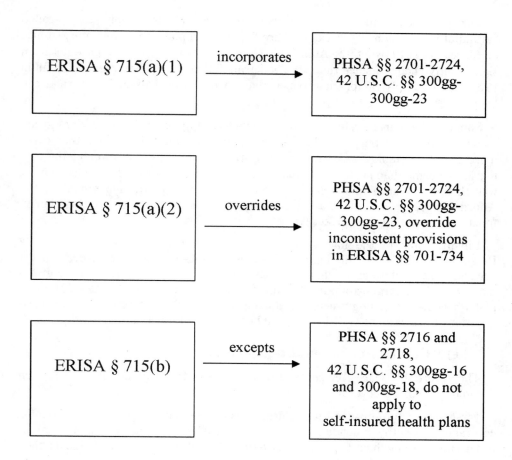

[C] Substantive Market Reforms

The Affordable Care Act introduced a host of substantive market reforms[152] that are designed to improve the current employer-provided health care system, ensure that individuals are not underinsured, and require the provision of preventive services to improve health.

Some of the reforms expand coverage, that is, who can or must be insured. Other reforms improve coverage, that is, the type of benefits must be provided.

Some of the market reforms apply to all employer-sponsored plans. Other reforms only apply to certain types of employer-sponsored plans.

---

[152] This section is designed to provide a broad overview of the ACA's market provisions. It is not intended to be a comprehensive discussion of all of its provisions.

For example, some of the market reforms do not apply to so-called "grandfathered" plans.[153] "Grandfathered" plans are plans that were in existence on March 23, 2010 (when the Affordable Care Act was enacted), and have not been significantly changed since then.[154] The "grandfather" rules are intended to fulfill President Obama's campaign promise that "people who like their coverage can keep it."[155]

Some of the market reforms apply to small-group plans but not to large group plans.[156] For these purposes, large-group plans are defined as plans that cover more than 100 employees.[157] Large-group plans are subject to fewer of the new market reforms than small-group plans because the large-group insurance market was thought to have functioned reasonably well prior to the enactment of the Affordable Care Act and was thus in need of less reform than the poorly-functioning small-group market.[158]

Finally, some of the market reforms do not apply to self-funded plans.[159] Presumably, Congress distinguished between self-funded and insured plans because, historically, self-funded plans have operated principally in the large-group market, and the large-group market functioned reasonably well.[160] As self-funded plans become increasingly common among small employers, commentators have questioned the wisdom of distinguishing between self-funded and insured plans.[161]

[1] Provisions Expanding Coverage

The Affordable Care Act contains two different types of provisions that are designed to expand coverage.

First, in order to ensure that health plans do not "cherry pick" and only offer coverage to healthy individuals, the Affordable Care Act imposes a number of provisions limiting health plans' ability to pick and choose the individuals they

---

[153] *See* 29 C.F.R. § 2590.715-1251(c)–(e) (identifying PHSA provisions which do and do not apply to grandfathered plans).

[154] Impermissible changes include (1) eliminating coverage for a condition, (2) increasing the employee co-insurance percentage, (3) increasing deductibles or co-payments beyond certain limits, and (4) increasing employee contribution rates by 5 or more percentage points. Temp. Treas. Reg. § 54.9815-1251T(g)(1). For a discussion of the limits applicable to grandfathered plans, see Elizabeth Weeks Leonard, *Can You Really Keep Your Health Plan? The Limits of Grandfathering Under the Affordable Care Act*, 36 J. CORP. L. 753 (2011).

[155] Alden J. Bianchi, *The Impact of Federal Health Care Reform on Employers and Employer-Sponsored Group Health Plans: An Overview and Retrospective*, 2010 N.Y.U. REV. OF EMP. BENEFITS AND EXEC. COMP., § 6.03[5].

[156] For an overview of the reforms that apply to the small-group market, see, Monahan & Schwarcz, 98 IOWA L. REV., at 1945–47; Baker, 159 U. PA. L. REV., at 1585–91.

[157] 42 U.S.C. § 18024(b)(1).

[158] *See* §3.05[C] (discussing problems with small-group market prior to the enactment of the Affordable Care Act).

[159] *See* § 3.03[D][2] (introducing self-funded plans).

[160] Jost and Hall, 68 N.Y.U. ANN. SURV. AM. L., at 552.

[161] *See, e.g., id.*

cover.[162]

Second, the Affordable Care Act contains a provision designed to expand coverage of young adults, a generally healthy group of individuals that was often uninsured prior to the enactment of the Affordable Care Act.[163]

[a]   Prohibitions on "Cherry Picking"

Prior to the enactment of the Affordable Care Act, insurers sought to keep down their costs by excluding from coverage (that is, not providing insurance for) individuals who were likely to incur large health care costs and thus be costly to insure.[164] The Affordable Care Act added a number of provisions designed to prevent this "cherry picking."

In the first of its cherry picking prohibitions, the Affordable Care Act requires insurers[165] to accept all applicants[166] and allow plans and individuals to renew their coverage.[167] These rules, sometimes referred to as guaranteed issue, mean that a health insurer must sell health insurance to anyone who wants it. Thus, an insurer must offer coverage to an individual and renew[168] that coverage even if the insurer expects the individual to submit substantial claims.

Second, health plans[169] are prohibited from rescinding[170] the plan or coverage with respect to an individual once the individual is covered under the plan, except

---

[162] Prior to the Affordable Care Act, insurers would limit their risks and thus their costs by "keeping bad risks out of the pool," that is, by not covering people who were likely to need to health care and thus be costly to cover. Insurers would keep out the bad risks by totally excluding them from coverage, imposing pre-existing condition exclusions, or rescinding, that is, cancelling their coverage. Rosenbaum et al., Law and the American Health Care System, at 218–19.

[163] *See* Carmen DeNavas-Walt et al., U.S. Census Bureau, *Income, Poverty, and Health Insurance Coverage in the United States: 2012* Figure 9 (showing that uninsured rate of individuals aged 19 to 25 exceeds that of any other age group but that it has decreased since 2010). *See also* Paul Fronstin, *Sources of Health Insurance and Characteristics of the Uninsured: Analysis of the March 2013 Current Population Survey*, EBRI Issue Brief No. 390, at 18 n.6 (Sept. 2013) (noting that young are less likely to be covered by health insurance and discussing reasons for this phenomenon).

[164] *See* Rosenbaum et al., Law and the American Health Care System, at 218–19 (discussing the "risk-shielding" behaviors insurers and self-funded plans engaged in to keep down their costs).

[165] This provision applies to all health insurance companies that offer health insurance in the individual or group market. It does not apply to self-insured group plans or grandfathered plans. *See* 42 U.S.C. § 300gg-91(2) (providing that "health insurance issuer" to which requirements apply does not include a group health plan); 29 C.F.R. § 2590.715-1251(c)(1) (providing that PHSA §§ 2702 and 2703 do not apply to grandfathered plans).

[166] PHSA § 2702, 42 U.S.C. § 300gg-1.

[167] PHSA § 2703, 42 U.S.C. § 300gg-2.

[168] Typically, insurance contracts are for a one-year period. If an insured individual or group wants coverage to continue after the end of the year, the insurance contract must be renewed.

[169] This provision applies to all employer-provided health plans, including large plans, small plans, grandfathered plans, and self-insured plans.

[170] In the health insurance context, the term rescission "generally refers to the cancellation of a policy by a carrier following the diagnosis of an expensive-to-treat condition or illness on the basis that the policyholder previously withheld information about a pre-existing condition." Bianchi, 2010 N.Y.U. Rev. of Emp. Benefits and Exec. Comp., at § 6.03[2][c].

in the case of fraud.[171] Thus, a plan may not rescind an individual's coverage even if the individual was healthy when she enrolled and later becomes sick and thus more expensive to insure.[172]

Third, health plans may not establish eligibility rules based on health status related factors.[173] Thus, a plan may not limit eligibility to individuals with normal blood pressure.

Finally, on a related note, plans must set premiums without regard to health status[174] and are constrained in their ability to vary premiums[175] (commonly referred to as "community rating"). In essence, community rating means that a health insurer cannot set the price of a health insurance policy based on how much it is likely to cost to cover that insured individual. Thus, an individual with high blood pressure may not be charged a higher premium than an individual with normal blood pressure.

[b] Coverage of Young Adults

Traditionally, many employer-sponsored health plans covered children through age 18 or 19, and permitted parents to extend coverage of their dependent children until age 24 so long as they were full-time students.[176] The Affordable Care Act enhances coverage of young adults by requiring health plans[177] to allow covered children to remain covered under their parents' health care plans until they reach age 26 without the imposition of eligibility requirements, such as financial dependency, residency, student status, or marital status.[178]

---

[171] PHSA § 2712, 42 U.S.C. § 300gg-12.

[172] Prior to the enactment of the Affordable Care Act, insurers in the individual market would often rescind coverage for innocent misrepresentations when an individual became high risk. *See* Baker, 159 U. PA. L. REV., at 1600–02.

[173] PHSA § 2705, 42 U.S.C. § 300gg-4. This provision does not apply to grandfathered plans. 29 C.F.R. § 2590.715-1251(c)(1).

[174] PHSA § 2705, 42 U.S.C. § 300gg-4. This provision does not apply to grandfathered plans. 29 C.F.R. § 2590.715-1251(c)(1).

[175] PHSA § 2701, 42 U.S.C. § 300gg-1. Insurers may only vary premiums based on four factors: (1) family size, (2) the geographic region which the applicant resides, (3) age, and (4) tobacco use. Even then, older individuals may be charged no more than three times the rates charged to younger individuals and tobacco users may be charged no more than 1 1/2 times the rate charged to nonsmokers. *Id.*

[176] *See* Kaiser Family Foundation, *2010 Employer Health Benefits Annual Survey*, 47 & 57–58, Exhibits 3.11 & 3.12

[177] This provision applies to all employer-provided health plans, including large plans, small plans, and grandfathered plans.

[178] PHSA § 2714, 42 U.S.C. § 300gg-14. The Affordable Care Act also amended IRC § 105(b) to extend favorable income tax treatment to employer-provided health insurance coverage for adult children under the age of 27. *See* Bianchi, 2010 N.Y.U. REV. OF EMP. BENEFITS AND EXEC. COMP., at § 6.03[1][a].

[2]   Provisions Improving Coverage

The Affordable Care Act has a number of provisions intended to improve coverage.[179]

[a]   Prohibition on Lifetime and Annual Dollar Limits on Benefits

Prior to the enactment of the Affordable Care Act, employers often tried to limit the cost of health insurance by imposing annual or lifetime caps on benefits.[180]

Example

Employer's plan limits benefits payable for HIV/AIDS-related claims to a lifetime limit of $5,000.[181] Ari, an employee covered by Employer's plan contracts HIV. Over his lifetime, Ari incurs $400,000 in medical expenses related to the cost of treating HIV and subsequently AIDS.[182] Employer's plan is not required to reimburse Ari for any of the medical expenses incurs over his lifetime to treat HIV/AIDS to the extent that the expenses exceed $5,000. This lifetime cap on benefits saves employer's plan $395,000.

Initially, the Affordable Care Act prohibited lifetime and annual limits only on "essential health benefits."[183] Effective for plan years beginning on or after January 1, 2014, the prohibition extends to all benefits.[184]

[b]   Prohibition on Preexisting Condition Exclusions

Traditionally, employers often controlled costs by imposing "preexisting condition exclusions," that is, by limiting or excluding coverage of conditions that were present prior to the time an individual enrolled in the health care plan.[185] Since the enactment of the Health Insurance Portability and Accountability Act of 1996 (HIPAA),[186] ERISA has strictly limited the types of pre-existing conditions

---

[179] The ACA's provisions improving coverage include a requirement that health insurers that offer health insurance coverage in the individual and small group market include an essential benefit package. PHSA § 2707, 42 U.S.C. § 300gg-6. The essential benefit package is discussed in § 3.06[E][2].

[180] *See* Kaiser Family Foundation and Health Research & Educational Trust, *Employer Health Benefits: 2009 Annual Survey*, at 184 (reporting that 59% of covered workers were in plans with a lifetime maximum on benefits).

[181] *See, e.g.*, McGann v. H & H Music Co., 946 F.2d 401 (5th Cir. 1991), *cert. denied*, 506 U.S. 981 (1992) (holding that imposition of $5,000 lifetime limit on AIDS-related claims did not violate ERISA § 510).

[182] According to the CDC, the estimated lifetime treatment cost of an HIV infection is $379,558 (in 2010 dollars). *See* http://www.cdc.gov/hiv/prevention/ongoing/costeffectiveness.

[183] PHSA § 2711, 42 U.S.C. § 42 U.S.C. § 300gg-11.

[184] *Id.*

[185] *See* Rebecca Lewin, *Job Lock: Will HIPAA Solve the Job Mobility Problem?*, 2 U. Pa. J. Lab. & Emp. L. 507, 518–20 (2000).

[186] Health Insurance Portability and Accountability Act of 1996, Pub. L. No. 104-191, 110 Stat. 1936 (1996).

that employer-sponsored health care plans can exclude and the length of time plans can impose such restrictions.[187]

The Affordable Care Act expands that protection by prohibiting all preexisting condition exclusions for all enrollees.[188] The regulations define a preexisting condition exclusion as a limitation or exclusion of benefits (including a denial of coverage) based on the fact that the condition was present before the effective date of coverage, whether or not any medical advice, diagnosis, care or treatment was recommended or received before that date.[189]

[c]   Preventive Care

In order to improve health, the Affordable Care Act requires that health plans provide coverage for a variety of preventive care items without imposing any cost-sharing requirements, such as deductibles or co-pays.[190]

The preventive care items include annual well child exams, certain immunizations, and breast cancer mammography screenings for women over 40 years of age.[191]

Example

Employer sponsors a health care plan. Anisa, a 45-year-old woman who is covered by the plan, has mammography screening at a local hospital. The hospital charges $100 for the screening. Employer's health plan must pay the hospital $100 for the screening. Anisa may not be charged anything for the screening.

---

[187] ERISA §§ 701–702. For a brief discussion of HIPAA, see § 3.04.

[188] PHSA § 2704, 42 U.S.C. § 300gg-3. It also expands the prohibition by imposing the limit on the individual market as well as employer-based plans.

[189] 29 C.F.R. § 2590.701-2.

[190] PHSA § 2713, 42 U.S.C. § 300gg-13. The provision does not apply to grandfathered health plans. 29 C.F.R. § 2590.715-1252(c)(2).

[191] Information about preventive services is available at http://www.healthcare.gov/news/factsheets/2010/07/preventive-services-list.html.

[3] Summary of Market Reforms

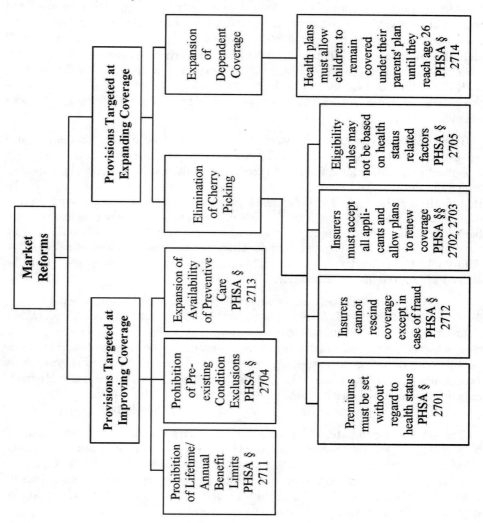

[D] Individual and Employer Mandates and Related Provisions

The Affordable Care Act's market reforms are backed up the second key component of the Affordable Care Act, individual and employer mandates.

As discussed above, prior to the enactment of the Affordable Care Act, insurers sought to keep down their costs by excluding from coverage (that is, not providing insurance for) individuals who were likely to incur large health care costs and thus be costly to insure. The Affordable Care Act rejects the notion that health care costs should be controlled by excluding the sick.[192] Thus, the Affordable Care Act includes market reform provisions that prohibit cherry picking, such as guaranteed issue and renewability provisions. If the Affordable Care Act only contained anti-cherry picking market reforms, it could cause an "adverse selection death spiral" as high-cost individuals (that is, ill individuals who are more likely to claim health care benefits) enter the market because it offers them a good deal while low-cost individuals (that is, healthier individuals who are less likely to claim benefits) leave the market as premiums rise to cover the cost of providing benefits for the sicker individuals.[193]

The Affordable Care Act addresses the risk of an adverse selection death spiral by providing an incentive for all individuals to purchase health insurance.[194] Specifically, the Affordable Care Act promotes "health care solidarity" by imposing individual and employer mandates. In essence, the mandates create incentives so that both healthy and sick individuals purchase health insurance, and healthy individuals will tend to pay more for health insurance than they are likely to get back in claims while sick individuals will tend to pay less for health insurance than they are likely to get back in claims. Thus, at its most fundamental level, the Affordable Care Act treats health care as a social good whose costs should be shared across the entire population.

The individual mandate is accompanied by federal subsidies and an expansion of Medicaid. The federal subsidies are intended to ensure that health care coverage is affordable for low- to middle-income taxpayers[195] while the Medicaid expansion was designed to extend health insurance coverage to the most vulnerable of the population, those with extremely low income. In *National Federation of Independent Businesses v. Sebelius*,[196] the Supreme Court held that the Medicaid expansion was an unconstitutionally coercive exercise of the Federal government's spending power and thus permits states to opt out of the Medicaid expansion.[197]

The employer mandate, which only applies to large employers, is accompanied by two other tax provisions: a tax credit for small employers, and a so-called "Cadillac tax" on employer plans that provide "excess benefits." The tax credit for small employers is designed to encourage small employers to offer health plans[198] while the "Cadillac tax" is "designed to sensitize employees to the costs of expensive medical coverage"[199] and thus reduce costs.

---

[192] Rosenbaum et al., Law and the American Health Care System, at 220 (stating that "[f]undamentally the Affordable Care Act rejects the notion that the way in which to keep health care costs down is to exclude the sick").

[193] *See* Gamage, 65 Tax L. Rev., at 676–77 (discussing "adverse selection death spiral").

[194] *Id.* at 684 (stating that "[i]n essence, the individual mandate is intended to incentivize healthier individuals to obtain insurance coverage so as to prevent adverse selection problems").

[195] 77 Fed. Reg. 73119–20 (Dec. 7, 2012) ("The section 36B credit is designed to make a qualified health plan affordable by reducing a taxpayer's out-of-pocket premium cost.").

[196] 132 S. Ct. 2566 (2012).

[197] For a critique of the Court's decision and its implications, see Huberfeld, et al., 93 B.U.L. Rev. 1.

[198] IRS News Release IR-2010-63 (May 17, 2010).

[199] Edward A. Zelinsky, *The Health-Related Tax Provisions of PPACA and HCERA: Contingent*,

[1] Overview of Individual and Employer Mandates and Related Provisions

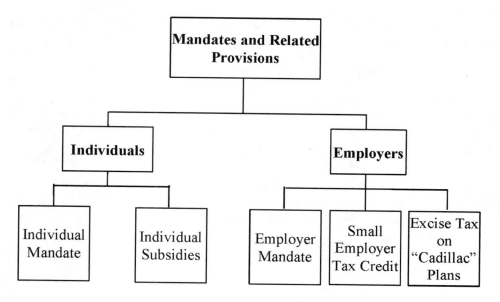

[2] Individual Mandate — IRC § 5000A

Section 5000A of the Internal Revenue Code, the Affordable Care Act's so-called individual mandate, does not actually mandate, that is, require, that individuals purchase health insurance. Rather, it provides an incentive for individuals to purchase health insurance. Specifically, it imposes a monetary penalty[200] on "applicable individuals" who fail to maintain "minimum essential coverage" for themselves and their dependents.[201]

[a]   "Applicable Individuals"

"Applicable individuals" are defined as all individuals unless they are expressly exempt from the requirement.[202]

Individuals are exempt from the mandate if they (1) qualify for a religious exemption,[203] (2) are not lawfully present in the United States,[204] or (3) are

---

Complex, Incremental and Lacking Cost Controls, 2010 N.Y.U. Rev. Emp. Benefits & Exec. Comp. § 7.02[1].

[200] Unlike other tax penalties, no criminal prosecution or penalty is imposed for failure to pay the penalty. IRC § 5000A(g)(2)(A). *See also* Edward A. Morse, *Lifting the Fog: Navigating Penalties in the Affordable Care Act,* 46 Creighton L. Rev. 207, 225–26 (2013) (discussing enforcement of the penalty).

[201] IRC § 5000A.

[202] IRC § 5000A(d)(1).

[203] IRC § 5000A(d)(2). *See also* Morse, *Navigating Penalties in the Affordable Care Act,* 46 Creighton L. Rev., at 226 (discussing the religious exemption).

incarcerated.[205] Additional exemptions are provided for (1) individuals who cannot afford coverage,[206] (2) certain low-income taxpayers,[207] (3) members of Indian tribes,[208] (4) individuals for months during which they have short coverage periods,[209] and (5) individuals who have suffered a hardship regarding the ability to obtain coverage.[210]

[b] "Minimum Essential Coverage"

"Minimum essential coverage" is simply health insurance coverage.[211] It may consist of health insurance coverage through an employer-sponsored plan,[212] an individual health insurance policy,[213] health insurance obtained through a federal program such as Medicare or Medicaid,[214] or other plans approved by the Secretary of Health and Human Services.[215]

Although the term "minimum essential coverage" sounds a lot like the term "essential health benefits," the two terms are not the same. "Essential health benefits" are specific types of health care benefits that certain plans must provide.[216]

---

[204] IRC § 5000A(d)(3).

[205] IRC § 5000A(d)(4).

[206] IRC § 5000A(e)(1). An individual is considered unable to afford coverage if the cost to the individual for individual coverage is more than 8% of annual household income. *Id.*

[207] IRC § 5000A(e)(2). Specifically, individuals with household income below the level required to file an income tax return are exempt. *Id.* In 2013, a single taxpayer with at least $10,000 in income was required to file an income tax return while a married taxpayer filing jointly was required to file an income tax return if household income was at least $20,000. IRS Publication 501, at 2 Table 1, 2013 Filing Requirements Chart.

[208] IRC § 5000A(e)(3). Indian tribes are eligible to purchase federal insurance for their employees under the Indian Health Care Improvement Act and individual tribe members may also be eligible to purchase insurance through the Act. Morse, *Navigating Penalties in the Affordable Care Act*, 46 CREIGHTON L. REV., at 227–28.

[209] IRC § 5000A(e)(4). Short gaps are generally periods of less than three months.

[210] IRC § 5000A(e)(5).

[211] If the insurance is limited, such as coverage solely for accident or disability income insurance, it does not qualify as minimum essential coverage. *See* IRC § 5000A(f)(3) (providing that minimum essential coverage does not include coverage of excepted benefits); PHSA § 2791(c), 42 U.S.C. § 300gg-91 (defining "excepted benefits").

[212] IRC § 5000A(f)(1)(B).

[213] IRC § 5000A(f)(1)(C).

[214] IRC § 5000A(f)(1)(A).

[215] IRC § 5000A(f)(1)(E).

[216] For a discussion of essential health benefits, see § 3.06[E][2].

[c]   Monetary Penalty

The monetary penalty for failing to maintain "minimum essential coverage" is generally the greater of a flat-dollar penalty or a percentage of income penalty.[217]

The flat dollar penalty was introduced at the rate of $95 per adult in 2014, increased to $325 per adult in 2015, and reaches $695 per adult in 2016.[218] After 2016, the cost of the flat dollar penalty is indexed to increases in the cost-of-living.[219]

The percentage of income[220] penalty was introduced at the rate of 1% beginning in 2014, increased to 2% in 2015, and reaches 2.5% in 2016 and thereafter.[221]

Both penalties are capped at the national average cost of minimum coverage under a Health Insurance Exchange[222] for individuals and dependents.[223]

[d]   Constitutionality of Individual Mandate

In *National Federation of Independent Businesses v. Sebelius*,[224] the Supreme Court, in a lengthy and divided opinion, upheld the constitutionality of the individual mandate. Specifically, the Court held that the individual mandate constituted a valid exercise of Congress' power to lay and collect taxes.[225]

[3] Individual Subsidies

The Affordable Care Act provides two federal subsidies to assist low- and moderate-income individuals and families to purchase health insurance through the Health Insurance Exchanges:

(1)   a refundable premium tax credit; and

(2)   a direct subsidy which covers a portion of the deductibles and copayments of individuals and families who qualify for coverage through the

---

[217] IRC § 5000A(c)(2).

[218] IRC § 5000A(c)(3). The penalty for children is one-half the penalty for adults, IRC § 5000A(c)(3)(C), and the penalty for families is capped at 3 times the adult rate, IRC § 5000A(c)(2)(A)(ii). Thus, for example, in 2016, the flat dollar penalty is $695 per adult, $347.50 per child under 18, and $2,085 per family.

[219] IRC § 5000A(c)(3)(D).

[220] The amount of income taken into account is the taxpayer's modified adjusted gross household income in excess of the amount of income required for an income tax return to be filed. IRC § 5000A(c)(2)(B).

[221] IRC § 5000A(c)(2)(B).

[222] For a discussion of the Health Exchanges, see § 3.06[E].

[223] IRC § 5000A(c)(1). For a critique of the penalty and its regressive traits, see Morse, *Navigating Penalties in the Affordable Care Act*, 46 CREIGHTON L. REV., at 228–31.

[224] 132 S. Ct. 2566 (2012).

[225] *Id.* at 2593–2601. The Court, however, rejected the government's claim that it constituted a valid exercise of Congress' power under the Commerce Clause. *Id.* at 2585–91. Whether the Court's rejection of the Commerce Clause claim is dicta or binding on lower courts is subject to considerable disagreement. *See* Liberty University, Inc. v. Lew, 733 F.3d 72, 92–93 n.6 (4th Cir. 2013).

Exchanges.[226]

[a]   Premium Tax Credit — IRC § 36B

Section 36B of the Internal Revenue Code provides a premium tax credit for eligible "applicable taxpayers."[227]

[i]   "Applicable Taxpayers"

"Applicable taxpayers" are defined as taxpayers with annual household income[228] between 100%[229] and 400% of the federal poverty line[230] based on the taxpayer's family size.[231]

"Applicable taxpayers" are eligible for a premium tax credit so long as (1) they are not eligible for "minimum essential coverage," such as governmental health insurance or an employer-sponsored health plan,[232] and (2) they purchase health insurance through a Health Insurance Exchange.[233]

The Treasury regulations provide that the refundable tax credit is available to taxpayers enrolled in a qualified health plan through any Exchange, including a Federal Exchange.[234] Focusing on IRC § 36B(c)(2)(A)(i)'s reference solely to "an exchange established by the state under section 1311," some commentators and litigants challenged that regulation and claimed that the credit is limited to health insurance purchased through a State Exchange.[235]

---

[226] For an explanation of the differences between a refundable tax credit and direct subsidy and an argument that the decision to use the two different methods is misguided, see Lawrence Zelenak, *Choosing Between Tax and Nontax Delivery Mechanisms for Health Insurance Subsidies*, 65 TAX L. REV. 723 (2012).

[227] IRC § 36B(a).

[228] Household income is defined as the modified adjusted gross income of all individuals included in the family size who are required to file an income tax return. IRC § 36B(d)(2).

[229] A taxpayer whose income is less than 100% of the federal poverty line may also receive the premium tax credit if the taxpayer is not eligible for Medicaid. IRC § 36B(c)(1)(B).

[230] In 2015, the federal poverty level is $11,770 for a 1-person household, $15,930 for a 2-person household, $20,090 for a 3-person household, and $24,250 for a 4-person household. Annual Update of the HHS Poverty Guidelines, 80 Fed Reg. 3236 (Jan. 22, 2015).

[231] IRC § 36B(c)(1). In addition, in order to be eligible, the taxpayer must not be claimed as a dependent by another taxpayer and must file a joint return if married. Prop. Treas. Reg. § 1.36B-2(b)(2)–(3).

[232] IRC § 36B(c)(2)(B). As discussed § 3.06[D][2][b], minimum essential coverage includes governmental health insurance, such as Medicaid and Medicare, and employer-sponsored health insurance. An employee with access to employer-provided health insurance will be eligible for a premium tax credit if the employer plan is not affordable or does not provide minimum value. For a discussion of affordability and minimum value, see § 3.06[4][d].

[233] IRC § 36B(c)(2)(A). For a discussion of Health Insurance Exchanges, see § 3.06[E].

[234] *See* Prop. Treas. Reg. §§ 1.36B-2(a)(1) & 1.36B-1(k).

[235] *See* Jonathan H. Adler & Michael F. Cannon, *Taxation Without Representation: The Illegal IRS Rule to Expand Tax Credits Under the PPACA*, 23 HEALTH MATRIX 119 (2013) (arguing that credit is limited to health insurance purchased through State Exchange); Jane Perkins & Dipti Singh, *ACA Implementation: The Court Challenges Continue*, 23 ANNALS HEALTH L. 200, 204–05 (Special Issue 2014) (citing cases).

In light of the fact that only 16 states (and the District of Columbia) have established state-based exchanges, limiting the availability of the credit to health insurance purchased through a State Exchange could substantially reduce its effectiveness and reach.[236] In *King v. Burwell*,[237] the Supreme Court held that the subsidy may be applied to health insurance purchased through a Federal Exchange.

[ii]   Amount of Tax Credit

The amount of the premium tax credit depends on the taxpayer's household income, the cost of health insurance premiums, and the number of eligible members in the taxpayer's family.[238] The lower the taxpayer's household income, the smaller the proportion of the health insurance premium the taxpayer is required to pay and thus, the greater the subsidy the taxpayer is entitled to receive.

For 2014, the percentage of premium contributions a taxpayer was required to pay was 2% of income for taxpayers with household income up to 133% of the federal poverty line and increased from 3% to 9.5% of income for taxpayers with household income between 133% and 400% of the federal poverty line.[239] After 2014, the percentages are indexed to changes in premium growth relative income growth.[240] Taxpayers with household income in excess of 400% of the federal poverty line are not eligible for a premium tax credit.

[iii]   Direct Payment to Insurer

Unlike most refundable tax credits, which are paid directly to the taxpayer,[241] the Affordable Care Act's refundable premium tax credit may be paid directly to the taxpayer's insurer.[242] The direct payment to the insurer is intended to ensure that illiquidity constraints, that is, lack of ready cash, will not prevent taxpayers from taking advantage of the credit.[243] If the premium were structured like most refundable tax credits, only taxpayers who had access to sufficient cash to pay

---

[236] *See* Huberfeld et al., 93 B.U.L. Rev. 1 (discussing impact of limiting credit to health insurance purchased through State exchanges and critiquing argument that it should be so limited).

[237] 135 S. Ct. 2480 (2015).

[238] For a detailed discussion of how the premium tax credit is calculated, see the preamble to the proposed Treasury regulations governing the premium tax credit. 76 Fed. Reg. 50931, 50933–34.

[239] IRC § 36B(c)(3)(A)(i).

[240] After 2014, the percentages are indexed to changes in premium growth relative to income growth. IRC § 36B(c)(3)(A)(ii). A study by the Tax Policy Center of the Urban Institute and Brookings Institution estimates that in 2016, the value of the premium tax credit for a family of four will range from $13,598 for a family at 100% of the federal poverty line to $4,570 for a family at 400% of the federal poverty line. Stephanie Rennane & C. Eugene Steurle, *Health Reform: A Two-Subsidy System*, at 3 table. 3 (Tax Pol'y Center 2010), *available at* http://www.taxpolicycenter.org/library/displayatab.cfm?Docid=2699.

[241] Morse, *Navigating Penalties in the Affordable Care Act*, 46 Creighton L. Rev., at 248.

[242] PHSA § 1412, 42 U.S.C. § 18082.

[243] Lawrence Zelanak, *Choosing Between Tax and Nontax Delivery Mechanisms for Health Insurance Subsidies*, 65 Tax L. Rev. 723, 725 (2012).

premiums in advance would be able to take advantage of the credit.[244]

[b] Cost-Sharing Subsidy — PHSA § 1402

Section 1402 of the Public Health Service Act[245] provides a direct subsidy to reduce the out-of-pocket costs for deductibles, co-insurance, copayments, and similar charges of "eligible insureds."

[i] "Eligible Insureds"

Like the premium tax credit, the cost-sharing subsidy is available to individuals with household income between 100% and 400% of the federal poverty line.[246] In addition, to be eligible, an individual must be enrolled in the "silver level" of coverage[247] in the individual market offered through an Exchange.[248]

[ii] Amount of Subsidy

The value of the cost-sharing subsidy depends on the taxpayer's household income as a percentage of the federal poverty line.[249] The lower the taxpayer's household income, the greater the cost-sharing subsidy the taxpayer is entitled to receive and thus, the smaller the share of out-of-pocket costs the taxpayer is required to bear.

The fraction by which the subsidy reduces the taxpayer's cost-sharing burden, that is, the fraction of the taxpayer's deductibles and copayments it reduces, ranges from 2/3 for taxpayers with household income between 100% and 200% of the federal poverty line to 1/3 for taxpayers with household income that is greater than 300% but no more than 400% of the federal poverty line.[250]

A study by the Tax Policy Center of the Urban Institute and Brookings Institution estimates that in 2016, the value of the cost-sharing subsidy for a family of four will range from $4,834 for a family at 100% of the federal poverty line to $604 for a family at 400% of the federal poverty line.[251]

---

[244] *Id.*

[245] 42 U.S.C. § 18071.

[246] PHSA § 1402(b)(2), 42 U.S.C. § 18071(b)(2).

[247] For a discussion of the levels of coverage available through the Exchanges, see § 3.06[E][2][c].

[248] PHSA § 1402(b)(1), 42 U.S.C. § 18071(b)(1).

[249] PHSA § 1402(b), 42 U.S.C. § 18071(b).

[250] PHSA § 1402(c)(1), 42 U.S.C. § 18071(c)(1). Additional reductions may apply in the case of taxpayers with household income equal to or less than 200% of the federal poverty line. PHSA § 1402(c)(2), 42 U.S.C. § 18071(c)(2).

[251] Rennane & Steurle, Health Reform: A Two-Subsidy System, at 3 table. 3. *See also* U.S. Government Accountability Office, Private Health Insurance: Expiration of the Health Coverage Tax Credit Will Affect Participants' Costs and Coverage Choices as Health Reform Provisions are Implemented, GAO Report 13-147, at 15 (Dec. 2012) (stating that had the cost-sharing subsidy been available in 2010, an individual with household income at 150% of the poverty level would have had an out-of-pocket maximum limit of about $1,981 rather than $5,950 for single coverage).

[iii]   Direct Payment to Insurer

The insurer is responsible for determining the taxpayer's share of deductibles and copayments, and the Department of Health and Human Services pays the subsidized share of costs directly to the insurer.[252]

[4]   Employer Mandate — IRC § 4980H

Just as the Affordable Care Act's so-called individual mandate does not actually mandate, that is, require, that individuals purchase health insurance, the Affordable Care Act's so-called employer mandate does not require that employers provide their employees with health insurance. Rather, it provides an incentive for employers to offer their employees affordable health care coverage.[253]

Specifically, section 4980H of the Internal Revenue Code imposes an excise tax on "applicable large employers" that fail to offer their employees the opportunity to enroll in affordable "minimum essential coverage" under an eligible employer-sponsored health care plan.

The IRC § 4980H excise tax is also sometimes referred to as a "pay-or-play penalty." Section 4980H imposes on "applicable large employers" two different penalties or excise taxes:

(1)   the IRC § 4980H(a) no offer penalty; and

(2)   the IRC § 4980H(b) unaffordable coverage penalty.

[a]   "Applicable Large Employers"

An "applicable large employer" is generally defined as an employer[254] that employed an average of at least fifty full-time employees during the preceding calendar year.[255]

Full-time employees are generally defined as employees who perform, on average, at least thirty hours of service per week.[256]

---

[252] PHSA §§ 1411, 1422, 42 U.S.C. § 18081, 18082.

[253] For a discussion of how effective IRC § 4980H is likely to be in encouraging employers to offer health insurance, see Moore, *The Future of Employment-Based Health Insurance*, 89 NEB. L. REV., at 906–12.

[254] In identifying the employer, the aggregation rules applicable to qualified plans apply. IRC § 4980H(c)(2)(C)(i). For an overview of the aggregation rules, see Chapter 9 § 9.04.

[255] IRC § 4980H(c)(2)(A).

[256] IRC § 4980H(c)(4)(A).

Solely for purposes of determining whether an employer qualifies as a "large" employer, full-time equivalents must be taken into account. IRC § 4980H(c)(2)(E). Full-time equivalents are calculated by adding the total hours worked in a month by employees, other than full-time employees, and dividing by 120. *Id.* For example, if 10 employees, who were not full-time employees work a total of 240 hours per month for the employer, the employer will be treated as having two full-time equivalents.

[b]   "Minimum Essential Coverage"

"Minimum essential coverage"[257] is an employer-sponsored group health plan offered in the large or small group market.[258]

[c]   IRC § 4980H(a) No Offer Penalty

Section 4980H(a) of the Internal Revenue Code imposes a no offer penalty on an "applicable large employer" if the employer does not offer its full-time employees and their dependents the opportunity to enroll in minimum essential coverage under an eligible employer-sponsored group health plan for a month and at least one full-time employee purchases subsidized coverage through a Health Insurance Exchange.[259]

An employer is treated as having offered coverage to its full-time employees and their dependents so long as it offers coverage to at least 95% of its employees and their dependents.[260]

The IRC § 4980H(a) no offer penalty is $2,000 per year (or 1/12 of $2,000 per month)[261] per full-time employee employed by the employer,[262] although 30 full-time employees may be excluded in calculating the penalty.[263] The no offer penalty is indexed to the rate of premium growth after 2014.[264]

Example

Employer has 100 full-time employees and does not offer its full-time employees and their dependents coverage under an eligible employer-sponsored group health plan. In 2016, two employees purchase subsidized health insurance through a Health Insurance Exchange. Employer will be subject to a penalty of $140,000 ($2,000 x (100 - 30) = $2,000 x 70 = $140,000) in 2016.[265]

---

[257] Minimum essential coverage is not the same as "essential health benefits." Essential health benefits are specific types of benefits insurers selling insurance in the individual and small group markets must provide. PHSA § 2707, 42 U.S.C. § 300gg-6. Essential health benefits are discussed in § 3.06[E][2].

[258] *See* IRC §§ 4980H(a)(1) & 4980H(b)(1)(A) (cross-referencing IRC § 5000A(f)(2)); IRC § 5000A(f)(2) (defining eligible employer-sponsored plan). An employer-sponsored plan also includes a grandfathered plan. IRC § 5000A(f)(2).

Limited coverage, such as coverage solely for accident or disability income insurance, does not qualify as minimum essential coverage. *See* IRC § 5000A(f)(3) (providing that minimum essential coverage does not include coverage of excepted benefits); PHSA § 2791(c), 42 U.S.C. § 300gg-91 (defining "excepted benefits").

[259] Subsidized coverage is only available to individuals with annual household income between 100% and 400% of the poverty line. *See* § 3.06[D][3] (discussing eligibility for premium tax credit and cost-sharing subsidy).

[260] Treas. Reg. § 54.4980H-4(a).

[261] IRC § 4980H(c)(1).

[262] IRC § 4980H(a).

[263] IRC § 4980H(c)(2)(D)(i)(I).

[264] IRC § 4980H(c)(5).

[265] This example does not take into account indexing under IRC § 4980H(c)(5).

[d]   IRC § 4980H(b) Unaffordable Coverage Penalty

Section 4980H(b) of the Internal Revenue Code imposes an unaffordable coverage penalty on an "applicable large employer" if the employer offers its full-time employees and their dependents the opportunity to enroll in minimum essential coverage under an eligible employer-sponsored group health plan for a month, and at least one full-time employee purchases subsidized coverage through a Health Insurance Exchange.[266]

An employee whose employer offers a health plan will only be able to purchase subsidized coverage through an Exchange if the employer's coverage is either

(1)   unaffordable or

(2)   does not provide minimum value.

[i]   Unaffordable

Coverage under an employer's plan is unaffordable if the premium required to be paid exceeds 9.5% of the employee's household income.[267]

After the enactment of the Affordable Care Act, there was some question whether affordability in the case of employees with dependents was to be based on the premium for individual or family coverage.[268] Family coverage is typically much more expensive than individual coverage, and employers typically require employees to pay more for family coverage than for individual coverage. For example, in 2014, the average annual worker contribution to premiums for single coverage was $1,081 while the average annual worker contribution to premiums for family coverage was $4,823.[269]

The IRS and Treasury Department have clarified that for purposes of the IRC § 4980H(b) unaffordable coverage penalty, affordability is based on the employee's share of the premium for individual, or self-only, coverage and not family coverage.[270]

---

[266] An employee whose employer offers health insurance is only eligible to purchase subsidized health insurance through a Health Insurance Exchange if the employee's household income is between 100% and 400% of the poverty line and the coverage either is unaffordable or does not provide minimum value. *See* 3.06[D][3] (discussing eligibility for premium tax credit and cost-sharing subsidy).

[267] IRC § 36B(c)(2)(C)(i).

[268] *See* Kathryn L. Moore, *The Pay or Play Penalty under the Affordable Care Act: Emerging Issues*, 47 Creighton L. Rev. 611, 617–18 (2014).

[269] Kaiser Family Foundation, *2010 Employer Health Benefits Annual Survey*, Exhibits 6.3 & 6.4, at 77–78.

[270] IRS Notice 2011-73; Shared Responsibility for Employers Regarding Health Coverage, 79 Fed. Reg. 8544, 8546 (Feb. 12, 2014) (stating that affordability is based on cost of self-only coverage). Similarly, for purposes of eligibility for the premium tax credit for dependent coverage, affordability is based on the cost of self-only, not family, coverage. Treas. Reg. § 1.36B-2(c)(3)(v)(A)(2). For purposes of the individual mandate, however, affordability is based on the cost of family coverage. Treas. Reg. § 1.5000A-3(e)(3)(ii)(B).

Example

In November 2015, Alexander, a married employee with two children, is eligible to enroll in his Employer's health care plan for the calendar year 2016. Alexander's cost for self-only coverage is $1,000 while his cost for family coverage is $5,000. Alexander's household income for 2016 is $50,000. For purposes of the unaffordable coverage penalty, Employer's plan offers Alexander affordable coverage because the cost of self-only coverage, $1,000, is less than 9.5% of Alexander's household income ($1,000/$50,000 = 2%) even though the cost of family coverage exceeds 9.5% of Alexander's household income ($5,000/$50,000 = 10%).

[ii]   Minimum Value

A plan does not provide minimum value if the plan's share of the total allowed cost of benefits is less than 60%.[271] In addition, a plan does not satisfy the minimum value requirement if it does not provide coverage for in-patient hospital services and physician services.[272]

"[T]he purpose of the minimum value rule is to ensure that employer-provided insurance must have some real content in order the protect the employer-mandate penalties of § 4980H and in order to disqualify employees from receiving the premium tax credits."[273]

According to a November 2011 report issued by the Department of Health and Human Services, 98% of individuals enrolled in employer-sponsored health plans were in plans that satisfied the minimum value requirement.[274]

[iii]   Amount of Penalty

The unaffordable coverage penalty under IRC § 4980H(b) is $3,000 per year (or 1/12 of $3,000 per month) for each full-time employee receiving a premium tax credit,[275] up to the maximum penalty that could be imposed under IRC § 4980H(a)[276] (or $2,000 per year (or 1/12 of $2,000 per month) times the employer's entire full-time workforce minus 30 workers.)[277] Like the no offer penalty, the unaffordable coverage penalty is indexed to the rate of premium growth after 2014.[278]

---

[271] IRC § 36B(c)(2)(C)(ii).

[272] IRS Notice 2014-69.

[273] Gamage, 65 Tax L. Rev., at 688 n.100.

[274] Minimum Value of an Employer-Sponsored Health Plan, IRS Notice 2012-31, at 4 (citing Actuarial Value and Employer-Sponsored Insurance, ASPE Research Brief, U.S. Dep't of Health and Human Services (Nov. 2011)).

[275] IRC § 4980H(b)(1).

[276] IRC § 4980H(b)(2).

[277] IRC § 4980H(c)(2)(D)(i)(II).

[278] IRC § 4980H(c)(5).

Example

Employer has 100 full-time employees and offers all 100 of its full-time employees and their dependents coverage under an employer-sponsored group health plan. In 2016, the employee's share of the premium for single coverage is $5,000. Two unrelated employees, Arthur and Bess, have annual household incomes of $40,000. Because Employer's insurance is unaffordable for them ($5,000/$40,000 = 12.5%), Arthur and Bess can and do purchase subsidized health insurance on a Health Insurance Exchange. Employer is subject to an unaffordable coverage penalty of $6,000 ($3,000 x 2 = $6,000) in 2016.[279]

[e]   Effective Date

Section 4980H was scheduled to go into effect beginning in 2014. In July 2013, the Treasury Department announced that it would delay enforcement of the penalty until 2015.[280] In February 2014, the Treasury Department extended the delay until 2016 for employers with 50 to 99 workers and provided a transitional rule for employers with 100 or more employees.[281]

---

[279] This example does not take into account indexing under IRC § 4980H(c)(5).

[280] IRS Notice 2013-45 (July 9, 2013).

[281] Shared Responsibility for Employers Regarding Health Coverage XV.D.6 & 7, 79 Fed. Reg. 8544, 8574–76 (Feb. 12, 2014).

[f]   Summary of Employer Mandate

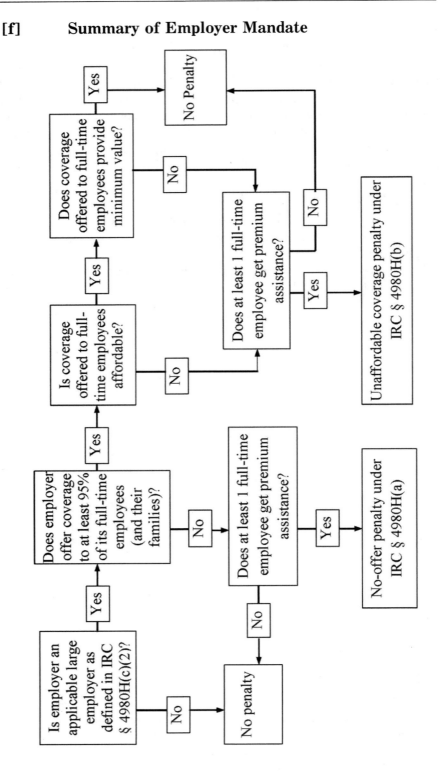

Pay-or-Play Penalty under IRC § 4980H

[5] Tax Credit for Small Employers — IRC § 45R

While the Affordable Care Act uses a "stick" approach to encourage large employers to offer health care coverage to their employees, it employs a "carrot" method to encourage small employers with low- and moderate-income employees to provide their employees with health care coverage. Specifically, the Affordable Care Act creates a small employer tax credit, codified at IRC § 45R, "to encourage small employers to offer health insurance coverage for the first time or maintain coverage they already have."[282]

In order to qualify for the IRC § 45R tax credit, small employers must satisfy four requirements:

(1) The employer must have fewer than 25 full-time equivalent employees (FTEs) for the taxable year.[283]

(2) The average annual wages of the employees for the year must be less than $50,000, adjusted for inflation, per FTE.[284]

(3) The employer must maintain a "qualifying arrangement" under which the employer pays a uniform percentage of at least 50% of the premium cost of the health coverage for employees covered under the employer-provided insurance.[285]

(4) The insurance must be provided through a Health Insurance Exchange.[286]

Small employers are eligible for a tax credit of up to 50%[287] for two years.[288] Employers with 10 or fewer FTEs with average taxable wages of $25,000 or less are eligible for the full credit. The credit is phased out as the number of FTEs increases from 10 to 25,[289] and annual average compensation increases from $25,000 to $50,000, adjusted for inflation.[290]

Eligible small employers may take the credit in the form of a general business credit[291] and must reduce their income tax deduction for the premiums they pay by the amount of the credit.[292]

---

[282] IRS News Release IR-2010-63 (May 17, 2010).

[283] IRC § 45R(d)(1)(A). The number of FTEs is determined by dividing the total number of hours of service for which wages were paid by the employer to employees during the taxable year by 2080. IRC § 45R(d)(2)(A).

[284] IRC § 45R(d)(1)(B), (d)(3)(B).

[285] IRC § 45R(d)(1)(C), (d)(4).

[286] IRC § 45R(d)(1)(C), (d)(4).

[287] IRC § 45R(b). The credit is 35% for tax-exempt employers.

[288] IRC § 45R(a), (e)(2).

[289] IRC § 45R(c)(1).

[290] IRC § 45R(c)(2).

[291] IRC § 38(b)(36).

[292] IRC § 280C(h).

[6] Excise Tax on "Cadillac" Health Plans — IRC § 4980I

The Affordable Care Act does not eliminate the favorable income tax treatment long accorded employer-sponsored health plans. It does, however, impose a 40% excise tax on employer-sponsored "Cadillac" health plans,[293] that is, high-cost employer-sponsored health care plans.

The excise tax on "Cadillac" health plans is one of the most controversial provisions of the Affordable Care Act.[294] It has three goals: (1) slow the rate of growth of health care costs; (2) provide revenues to finance the Affordable Care Act's expansion of health care coverage; and (3) address the inequalities created by the favorable income tax treatment granted employer-sponsored health plans.[295]

The 40% excise tax, codified at IRC § 4980I, applies to any "excess benefit" provided under "applicable employer-sponsored coverage."[296] The tax is imposed on the "coverage provider."[297]

[a]   "Applicable Employer-Sponsored Coverage"

Generally, a health plan qualifies as "applicable employer-sponsored coverage" if the value of coverage is excludable from the employee's income under section 106 of the Internal Revenue Code.[298] Employer-sponsored coverage includes coverage in the form of reimbursements under a health Flexible Spending Account (FSA)[299] and contributions to a Health Savings Account (HSA).[300]

[b]   "Excess Benefit"

An "excess benefit" arises if the annual cost of coverage exceeds $10,200 (in the case of individual coverage) or $27,500 (in the case of family coverage).[301]

These threshold dollar amounts are subject to three different adjustments.

---

[293] Named after the signature American luxury car, "Cadillac" health plans have the highest premiums and usually offer the most generous level of benefits. Robert Woods Johnson Foundation Health Affairs, *Excise Tax on "Cadillac" Plans. To slow growing costs and finance expanded coverage, the ACA imposes an excise tax on high-cost health plans to take effect in 2018*, HEALTH POLICY BRIEF 2 (Sept. 12, 2013).

[294] *See id.* at 1; Reed Abelson, *Bearing Down on Health Costs*, N.Y. TIMES, at B1 (May 28, 2013).

[295] Robert Woods Johnson Foundation Health Affairs, HEALTH POLICY BRIEF, at 3; Zelinsky, 2010 N.Y.U. Rev. Emp. Benefits & Exec. Comp., at § 7.02[1]; American Academy of Actuaries and Society of Actuaries, *Federal Health Care Reform: Excise Tax on High-Cost Employer Plans* 9 (Technical Paper Jan. 2010). For a critique of the excise tax, see Amy B. Monahan, *Why Tax High-Cost Employer Health Plans*, 65 TAX L. REV. 749 (2012).

[296] *See* IRC § 4980I(a).

[297] *See* IRC § 4980I(c).

[298] IRC § 4980I(d)(1)(A).

[299] For a discussion of flexible spending accounts, see § 3.08[D][2].

[300] IRC § 4980I(d)(2)(B) & (C) (providing rules for calculating cost of coverage under flexible spending account and health saving account). For a discussion of health savings accounts, see § 3.08[B][1].

[301] Coverage under a collectively bargained multiemployer plan is deemed to be family coverage and thus always eligible for the higher limit. IRC § 4980I(b)(3)(B)(ii).

First, if health care costs increase by more than 55% between 2010 (when the Affordable Care Act was enacted) and 2018 (when the excise tax is scheduled to go into effect), new threshold dollar amounts will apply based on the actual increase in health care costs.[302] Second, beginning in 2019, the threshold dollar amounts will be adjusted annually to reflect increases in the cost of living.[303] Finally, the threshold dollar amounts are adjusted for age and gender[304] and are increased for retirees and plans that cover mostly employees in high-risk professions[305] or employees who repair or install electrical or telecommunications lines.[306]

[c] "Coverage Provider"

The excise tax is imposed on the "coverage provider."[307] In the case of a group health plan, the coverage provider is the health insurance issuer.[308] In the case of HSA[309] and MSA[310] contributions, the employer is the coverage provider.[311] In all other instances, the coverage provider is the person that administers the plan,[312] which will often be the employer.[313]

Example

Employer purchases a health insurance plan for its employees from Insurance Company. The plan's total value exceeds the applicable annual limits by $1,500. Insurance Company must pay an excise tax on the excess value equal to $600 ($1,500 x .40 = $600.)

Many employers are expected to scale back their coverage in order to avoid the "Cadillac tax."[314]

---

[302] IRC § 4980I(b). Specifically, a "health cost adjustment percentage" increases the dollar limits to the extent that the 2018 per employee cost under the Blue Cross/Blue Shield standard option under the Federal Employees Health Benefits Plan exceeds the 2010 cost by more than 55%.

[303] IRC § 4980I(b)(3)(C)(v). Initially, the limits will increase at 1% over increases in the Consumer Price Index. After 2020, increases will be limited to increases in the Consumer Price Index. *See* IRC § 4980I(b)(3)(c)(v).

[304] *See* IRC § 4980I(b)(3)(C)(iii).

[305] High-risk professions are defined broadly to include law enforcement, fire protection, longshoremen, EMT, construction, mining, agriculture, forestry, and fishing industries. IRC § 4980I(f)(3).

[306] *See* IRC § 4980I(b)(3)(C)(iv).

[307] *See* IRC § 4980I(c).

[308] *See* IRC § 4980I(c)(2)(A).

[309] An HSA is a health savings account authorized by Section 223 of the Internal Revenue Code. For an overview of HSAs, see § 3.08[B][1].

[310] An MSA is an Archer medical savings account authorized by Section 220 of the Internal Revenue Code. Archer MSAs are functionally similar to HSAs but may only be established by self-employed individuals and small employers. *See* Amy Monahan, *Ownership Society Health Care Policy*, 80 Tul. L. Rev., at 799 n.131.

[311] *See* IRC § 4980I(c)(2)(B).

[312] *See* IRC § 4980I(c)(2)(C).

[313] *See* Zelinsky, 2010 N.Y.U. Rev. Emp. Benefits & Exec. Comp., at § 7.02[1].

[314] Robert Woods Johnson Foundation Health Affairs, Health Policy Brief, at 3; Moore, *The Future of Employment-Based Health Insurance*, 89 Neb. L. Rev., at 891–92 & 918–19.

[7] Summary of Mandates and Related Provisions

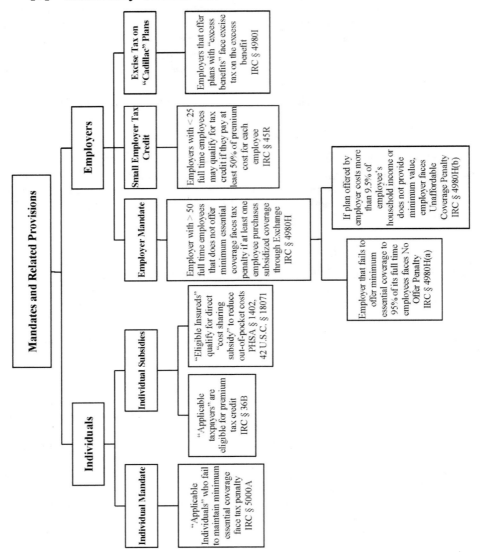

[E] Health Insurance Exchanges or Health Insurance Marketplaces

The third key component of the Affordable Care Act is the Health Insurance Exchanges, often referred to as the Health Insurance Marketplaces. The Exchanges or Marketplaces are not insurers; they do not issue insurance. Rather, they are structured marketplaces for the sale and purchase of health insurance;[315]

---

[315] Bernadette Fernandez and Annie L. Mach, *Health Insurance Exchanges Under the Patient*

they are like a "shopping mall where individuals evaluate and select appropriate health care plans for themselves and their families."[316] They are designed to bring together buyers and sellers of insurance to increase access to insurance.[317] They assist individuals and small businesses to comparison shop and provide them with ready access to pricing and coverage information.[318]

The Affordable Care Act directed the states to establish Exchanges by January 1, 2014.[319] The Department of Health and Human Services was directed to establish and operate an Exchange in any state that did not establish an Exchange.[320] Some, but not all, of the states established Exchanges or Marketplaces. Specifically, in 2015, there are 14 state-based Marketplaces, three Federally-supported Marketplaces, seven State-Partnership Marketplaces, and 27 Federally-facilitated Marketplaces.[321]

[1]   Types of Exchanges or Marketplaces

There are two basic types of Health Insurance Exchanges or Marketplaces:

(1) The American Health Benefit (AHB) Exchange, and

(2) The Small Business Health Options Program (SHOP).[322]

[a]   American Health Benefit (AHB) Exchange

The American Health Benefit (AHB) Exchange provides a marketplace where individuals can purchase "qualified health plans."[323] In addition, the AHB Exchange assists low- and moderate-income individuals to obtain tax subsidies and cost-sharing assistance.[324]

Protection and Affordable Care Act (ACA), CRS R42663, at 7 & 8 (Jan. 2013) ("The exchange concept was included in [the Affordable Care Act] as a means to increase access to health insurance.").

[316] *See* Erin M. Sweeney, *What Employers Must Do (and Not Do) in 2013 to Get Ready for Health Care Reform*, CA Labor & Employment Bulletin 200, 200 (June 2013).

[317] Fernandez & Mach, Congressional Research Service R42663, at 7.

[318] Joel M. Hamme, *Health Insurance Exchanges under the Affordable Care Act: A Primer*, 6 J. HEALTH & LIFE SCI. L. 35, 44 (2013).

[319] PHSA § 1311(b)(1), 42 U.S.C. § 18031(b)(1).

[320] PHSA § 1321(c)(1), 42 U.S.C. § 18041(c)(1).

[321] The Henry J. Kaiser Family Foundation, State Health Insurance Marketplace Types, 2015, *available at* http://kff.org/health-reform/state-indicator/state-health-insurance-marketplace-types/.

[322] 42 U.S.C. § 18031(b). *See also* Hamme, 6 J. HEALTH & LIFE SCI. L., at 41. A state may, however, elect to merge the two into a single exchange. 42 U.S.C. § 18031(b)(2).

[323] Fernandez and Mach, Congressional Research Service R42663, at 9. For the definition of "qualified health plans," see 42 U.S.C. §18021.

[324] Fernandez and Mach, Congressional Research Service R42663, at 9. For a discussion of the responsibilities of individual exchanges, see *id.* at 13–24.

[b]   Small Business Health Options Program (SHOP)

The Small Business Health Options Program (SHOP) is intended to help small businesses and their employees purchase qualified health plans offered in the small group market.[325]

[2] Essential Health Benefits Package

The Affordable Care Act requires that all plans[326] available through an Exchange or Marketplace offer an "essential health benefits package."[327] Specifically, all plans must

(1) include "essential health benefits,"[328]

(2) limit annual cost-sharing, including deductibles and co-pays,[329] and

(3) meet one of four "actuarial value requirements."[330]

The essential health benefits package serves two principal purposes. First, it sets forth a floor of contract quality standards, that is, it sets forth minimum benefits that all insurers must provide. Second, it provides some degree of uniformity among health insurance products to assist individuals and small groups to compare plans that they purchase through the Exchanges.

[a]   Essential Health Benefits

The Affordable Care Act outlines 10 broad categories of "essential health benefits" that must be covered. The categories are: (1) ambulatory patient services, (2) emergency services, (3) hospitalization, (4) maternity and newborn care, (5) mental health and substance abuse disorder services, including behavioral health treatment, (6) prescription drugs, (7) rehabilitative and habilitative services and devices, (8) laboratory services, (9) preventive and wellness services and chronic disease management, and (10) pediatric services, including oral and vision care.[331] The specific list of essential health benefits is defined at the state level.

The Affordable Care Act's outline of essential health benefits is similar in scope

---

[325] *Id.* at 9. For a discussion of the responsibilities of SHOPs, see *id.* at 13–24.

[326] The requirement applies to all health insurance issuers that offer coverage in the individual or small group market whether offered inside or outside of the exchange, but not to grandfathered plans. 78 Fed. Reg. 12836.

[327] This package is sometimes referred to "minimum essential coverage requirements." *See, e.g.,* Baker, 159 U. Pa. L. Rev. 1577 ("The minimum essential coverage requirements set a floor of contract quality standards on the health plans that may be offered in the individual and small group market beginning in 2014.").

[328] 42 U.S.C. § 18022(b).

[329] 42 U.S.C. § 18022(c).

[330] 42 U.S.C. § 18022(d).

[331] PHSA § 2707, 42 U.S.C. § 300gg-6; PHSA § 1302, 42 U.S.C. § 18022.

to benefits typically provided by employer-provided health plans.[332] The Affordable Care Act, however, does not mandate that employer-sponsored health care plans provide essential benefits.[333] Small employer plans, however, may be indirectly subject to the requirement because it applies to insurers in the small group market and thus, insurers that offer insurance to small employers must provide essential health benefits.[334]

[b] Annual Cost-Sharing Limits

The Affordable Care Act limits annual cost sharing, that is, the share of costs that plan participants must bear in the form of deductibles, coinsurance, copayments, and the like.[335] The limit on cost sharing is linked to the amount authorized for Health Savings Accounts (HSAs).[336] In addition, the annual deductible for employer-sponsored plans in the small group market is limited to $2,000 for single coverage and $4,000 for any other coverage in 2014[337] and adjusted annually thereafter.[338]

[c] Actuarial Value Requirements

The Affordable Care Act requires that health plans offered through the Exchanges meet one of four levels of coverage based on actuarial value.[339] The actuarial value requirements are intended to help purchasers understand and compare the relative generosity of the available plans.[340]

Actuarial value is the total average costs for covered benefits that a plan will cover.[341] For example, if a plan has an actuarial value of 75%, an individual, on average, would be responsible for 25% of the costs of all covered benefits (100% -

---

[332] 78 Fed. Reg. 12835 ("The law directs that EHB [essential health benefits] be equal in scope to the benefits covered by a typical employer plan.").

[333] Although the terms are similar, "minimum essential coverage" does not mean "essential health benefits." Minimum essential coverage is required to satisfy the individual and employer mandate. Health insurance offered on an Exchange must offer essential health benefits.

[334] PHSA § 2707(a), 42 U.S.C. § 300gg-6. For a critique of the exclusion of large employer plans, see Amy Monahan, *The ACA, the Large Group Market, and Content Regulation: What's a State to Do?*, 5 St. Louis U. J. Health L & Pol'y 83 (2011).

[335] PHSA § 1302(c)(3)(A), 42 U.S.C. § 18022(c)(3)(A) (defining "cost-sharing"). Cost sharing does not include premiums or costs for non-covered services. 41 U.S.C. § 18022(c)(3)(B).

[336] Initially, the limit is set at the amount authorized for HSAs. In later years, the limit is indexed to the annual limit on HSAs for self-only coverage and double that amount for any other plan. PHSA § 1302(c)(1), 42 U.S.C. § 18022(c)(1).

[337] PHSA § 1302(c)(2)(A), 42 U.S.C. § 18022(c)(2)(A).

[338] PHSA § 1302(c)(2)(B), 42 U.S.C. § 18022(c)(2)(B).

[339] PHSA § 1302(d), 42 U.S.C. § 18022(d).

[340] Hamme, 6 J. Health & Life Sci. L. at 46.

[341] "Actuarial value (AV) is a summary measure of a plan's generosity, expressed as the percentage of medical expenses estimated to be paid by the issuer for a standard population and set of allowed charges. In other words, AV reflects the relative share of cost sharing that may be imposed. On average, the lower the AV, the greater the cost sharing." Fernandez & Mach, Congressional Research Service R42663, at 29.

75% = 25%). A particular individual's share of costs might actually be more or less than 25% of costs, depending on the individual's actual health care needs. On average, though, covered individuals would pay 25% of costs.

The Affordable Care Act designates each of the four levels of coverage with a precious metal. Specifically, it requires that all plans meet one of the four following actuarial values:

Level	Actuarial Value
Bronze	60%
Silver	70%
Gold	80%
Platinum	90%

[F] Summary of the Affordable Care Act

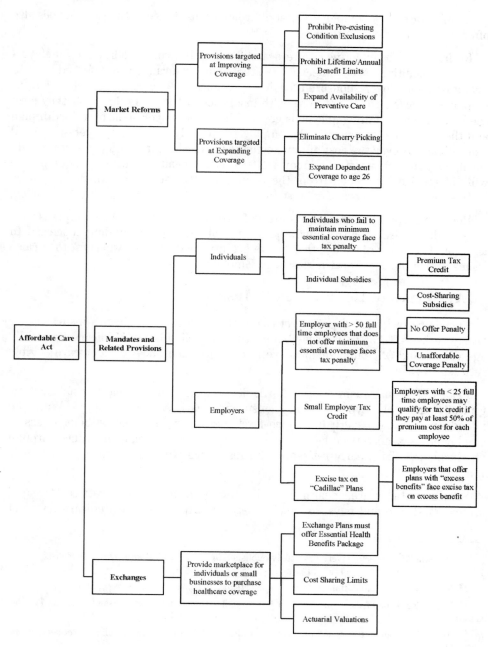

§ 3.07   RETIREE HEALTH INSURANCE[342]

About 25% of large employers that offer health insurance to their employees also offer health insurance to their retirees.[343]

Retiree health insurance differs fundamentally from traditional employer-sponsored health insurance because retiree health insurance is a deferred benefit. Traditional employer-sponsored health insurance is a current benefit, that is, employees receive the benefit of health insurance at the same time that they earn the benefit. Thus, if an employee is covered by an employer-sponsored health plan and the employee becomes ill, the employee may rely on the employer-sponsored health plan to cover the cost of any doctor's visits or hospitalization resulting from the illness. In contrast, if an employer offers retiree health insurance, the employee will not receive any benefit from the retiree health insurance until the employee retires, which will necessarily be some time in the future.

Because retiree health benefits are deferred benefits, they raise unique issues. Specifically, retiree health benefits raise special vesting and funding concerns. In addition, because retiree health benefits are provided to older workers, they raise issues under the Age Discrimination in Employment Act.

[A]   Types of Retiree Health Insurance

There are two basic types of retiree health insurance: (1) health insurance for "early retirees," that is, retirees before they are eligible for Medicare (generally age 65),[344] and (2) "supplemental" retiree health insurance for Medicare-eligible retirees.[345]

Prior to the enactment of the Affordable Care Act, retiree health insurance was typically the only type of health insurance early retirees had.[346] With the introduction of the Health Insurance Exchanges, early retirees without access to employment-based retiree health insurance may now purchase insurance through an Exchange. Thus, early retiree health insurance is not as important as it once was.[347]

Supplemental retiree health insurance for Medicare-eligible retirees "wraps" around Medicare and pays, to varying degrees, expenses that Medicare does not

---

[342] Portions of this section were previously published in Kathryn L. Moore, *The New Retiree Health VEBAs*, 2008 N.Y.U. REVIEW OF EMP. BENEFITS AND EXEC. COMP. 7-1, 7-2–7-3.

[343] Kaiser Family Foundation, *2014 Employer Health Benefits Annual Survey*, at 186.

[344] For a discussion of the structure of early retiree health care plans, see Susan Cancelosi, *The Bell is Tolling: Retiree Health Benefits Post Health Reform*, 19 ELDER L.J. 49, 57–59 (2011).

[345] For a discussion of the structure of retiree health care plans for Medicare-eligible retirees, see *id.* at 59–62.

[346] *See* Susan Cancelosi, *No Good News: Retiree Benefits One Year After Health Reform*, 21 ANNALS OF HEALTH LAW 89, 90–91 (2012).

[347] Of course, insurance purchased through an Exchange will not be subsidized by the retiree's former employer, and it may not be as comprehensive as employer-provided early retiree insurance. Thus, in some instances, a retiree may prefer retiree insurance to insurance purchased through an Exchange.

cover.[348] For example, Medicare has relatively high deductibles and cost-sharing requirements, does not limit out-of-pocket spending, and has (until 2020) a gap in prescription drug benefit coverage.[349] Supplemental retiree health insurance plans pay for at least a portion of these expenses not covered by Medicare.

Although the Affordable Care Act has a number of provisions that affect Medicare,[350] it does not change the fact that Medicare does not cover all medical expenses. Thus, supplemental retiree health insurance for Medicare-eligible retirees remains as important as ever to those individuals with access to it.[351]

[B] Vesting of Retiree Health Benefits

In enacting ERISA, Congress found that many employees who had worked for their employer for a long period of time had lost their anticipated retirement benefits because their employer's plan did not contain any vesting provisions.[352] In order to protect employees from losing their retirement benefits, Congress included detailed vesting rules in ERISA.[353] The vesting rules ensure that retirement benefits become nonforfeitable after an employee has worked for his employer for a set period of time.[354]

ERISA's vesting rules only apply to pension plans;[355] they do not apply to welfare benefit plans.[356] Indeed, the Supreme Court has repeatedly stated that "[e]mployers or other plan sponsors are generally free under ERISA, for any reason at any time, to adopt, modify, or terminate welfare plans."[357]

Congress' decision not to apply vesting rules to welfare benefit plans generally makes sense because welfare benefits are typically current benefits, that is, employees typically receive welfare benefits at the same time that they earn them. There is no great need to worry about losing a future welfare benefit.

Retiree health benefits, however, are an exception to that rule. Like pension benefits, retiree health benefits are deferred benefits. Employees earn retiree

---

[348] See Cancelosi, *Retiree Benefits One Year After Health Reform*, 21 ANN. HEALTH L., at 99.

[349] The Henry J. Kaiser Family Foundation, *Medicare at a Glance* (Nov. 14, 2012), *available at* http://kff.org/medicare/fact-sheet/medicare-at-a-glance-fact-sheet/. For an overview of Medicare and its deductibles, co-sharing and the like, see, for example, The Henry J. Kaiser Family Foundation, *Medicare: A Primer* 5–10 (Apr. 2010).

[350] For a discussion of how the Affordable Care Act has amended Medicare, see Eleanor D. Kinney, *The Affordable Care Act and the Medicare Program: The Engines of True Health Reform*, 13 YALE J. HEALTH POL'Y, L. & ETHICS 253 (2013).

[351] About one in three Medicare beneficiaries has retiree health coverage. *See* Kaiser Family Foundation, Medicare at a Glance.

[352] ERISA § 2(a).

[353] ERISA § 203.

[354] The vesting rules are discussed in Chapter 5 § 5.02[A].

[355] ERISA § 201.

[356] ERISA § 201(1).

[357] Lockheed Corp. v. Spink, 517 U.S. 882, 890 (1996); Curtiss-Wright Corp. v. Schoonejongen, 514 U.S. 73, 78 (1995).

health benefits while they are working, but do not receive the benefits until after they retire.

Although retiree health plans are different from most welfare benefit plans, ERISA treats them like any other welfare benefit plan and does not require that they be vested. Employers may, however, voluntarily provide for the vesting of retiree health benefits.

Whether an employer has voluntarily agreed to vest retiree health benefits has been frequently litigated.[358] Courts uniformly permit an employer to terminate retiree health benefits if the unambiguous terms of the agreement or plan document permit the employer to terminate the benefits.[359] On the other hand, if the terms of the agreement or plan document are ambiguous, courts will generally consider extrinsic evidence to determine whether the employer has the right to unilaterally modify or terminate benefits.[360]

In *M & G Polymers USA, LLC v. Tackett*,[361] the Supreme Court held that ordinary principles of contract law apply in interpreting the terms of a collective bargaining agreement to determine whether retiree health benefits survive the expiration of the agreement.

[C]   Retiree Health Benefits and the Accounting Rules

When retiree health benefits were first introduced in the late 1940s and early 1950s, they were considered an inexpensive benefit that was easily granted.[362] Employers financed them on a pay-as-you go basis from current operations, and few companies acknowledged the liabilities on their books or set money aside to fund the benefits.[363]

As health care costs soared through the 1980s and beyond, so too did the cost of retiree health benefits.[364] As costs skyrocketed, the issues of funding the benefits and acknowledging the liability for accounting purposes became important.

---

[358] *See, e.g.*, Stearns v. NCR Corp., 297 F.3d 706, 711–12 (8th Cir. 2002) (holding that unambiguous reservation of rights clause sufficient to defeat claims that retiree benefits vested); Sprague v. General Motors Corp., 133 F.3d 388 (6th Cir. 1998) (holding that employer had effectively retained right to modify or terminate retiree health benefits).

[359] Scott J. Macey & George F. O'Donnell, *Retiree Health Benefits — The Divergent Paths*, N.Y.U. Rev. of Emp. Benefits and Exec. Comp. 8-1, 8-15 (2003); In re Doskocil Cos., 130 B.R. 870, 873 (Bank. D. Kan. 1991) ("Absent proof of fraud, the Circuits have ruled unanimously that if the SPD is unambiguous in allowing modifications of welfare benefits, the employer will be permitted to make changes.").

[360] Douglas Sondgereth, *High Hopes: Why Courts Should Fulfill Expectations of Lifetime Retiree Health Benefits in Ambiguous Collective Bargaining Agreements*, 42 B.C. L. Rev. 1215, 1230 (2001).

[361] 135 S. Ct. 926 (2015).

[362] David A. Pratt, *The Past, Present, and Future of Retiree Health Benefits*, 3 J. Health & Biomedical L. 103, 110 (2007).

[363] Selwyn Feinstein, *The Inevitable Happens: Making the Improbable Possible, in* An EBRI Special Report and Issue Brief No. 124: Retirement Security in a Post-FASB Environment, 4 (1992).

[364] Daniel Keating, *Why the Bankruptcy Reform Act Left Labor Legacy Costs Alone*, 71 Mo. L. Rev. 985, 987 (2006).

In 1990, the Financial Accounting Standards Board decided that pay-as-you go accounting for retiree health benefits "ignores the measurement and recognition of the financial effects of promising to provide these benefits, and of the service that employees are rendering in exchange for those benefits."[365] Accordingly, the Financial Accounting Standards Board issued Statement No. 106, *Employer's Accounting for Postretirement Benefits Other Than Pensions* (FAS 106), which requires employers to accrue the cost of anticipated future retiree health care obligations.[366] Later, the Financial Accounting Standards Board issued FAS 158, which requires companies to move their retiree health costs out of their footnotes and into their balance sheets.[367] In 2004, the Government Accounting Standards Board issued a similar rule, GASB Statement No. 45.[368]

When FAS 106 took effect, it permitted employers to either report their unfunded liability as a one-time nonrecurring charge or report through annual charges taken over a period of up to 20 years.[369] Many companies chose to recognize the expense immediately. For example, in 1992, Ford Motor Company reported a $7.5 billion charge against income, and General Motors reported a charge of $20.8 billion in order to comply with FAS 106.[370] Some estimate that implementation of FAS 106 resulted in total reductions in current income of American corporations of about $1.5 trillion.[371]

Not all employers were willing to report significant liabilities as required by FAS 106, and thus, some employers eliminated retiree health benefits in order to avoid reporting the expense. Indeed, according to one survey, the number of large employers offering retiree health insurance fell from 66% in 1988 to 36% in 1993,[372] the year FAS 106 went into effect.[373]

---

[365] Feinstein, EBRI Special Report and Issue Brief No. 124: Retirement Security in a Post-FASB Environment.

[366] *Id.*

[367] Kevin L. Bacher and David S. Hauptman, *New Solutions to Funding Retiree Medical Benefits*, 24 J. OF COMP. AND BENEFITS 5 (Jan./Feb. 2008).

[368] Harvey M. Katz, *Who Will Pay the Cost of Government Employer Retiree Health Benefits*, 59 LABOR L.J. 40 (2008).

[369] Feinstein, EBRI Special Report and Issue Brief No. 124: Retirement Security in a Post-FASB Environment.

[370] Marily J. Ward Ford, *Broken Promises: Implementation of Financial Accounting Standards Board Rule 106, ERISA, and Legal Challenges to Modification and Termination of Postretirement Health Care Benefit Plans*, 68 ST. JOHN'S L. REV. 427, 432 (1994).

[371] Gregory J. Ossi, Comment, *It Doesn't Add Up: The Broken Promises of Lifetime Health Benefits, Medicare, and Accounting Rule FAS 106 Do Not Equal Satisfactory Medical Coverage for Retirees*, 13 J. CONTEMP. HEALTH L. & POL'Y 233, 238 (1996).

[372] Kaiser Family Foundation, *2014 Employer Health Benefits Annual Survey*, at 187.

[373] For a more detailed discussion of the accounting rules and their impact on retiree health plans, see Pratt, 3 J. HEALTH & BIOMEDICAL L. 103; Susan E. Cancelosi, *VEBAs to the Rescue: Evaluating One Alternative for Public Sector Retiree Health Benefits*, 42 J. MARSHALL L. REV. 879 (2009).

[D] Retiree Health Benefits and the Age Discrimination in Employment Act

The Age Discrimination in Employment Act (ADEA)[374] protects workers age 40 and over.[375] It generally prohibits employers from providing fewer benefits for workers because of their age.

The Equal Employment Opportunity Commission's regulations provide a narrow exception from the general rule to permit employers to alter, reduce, or eliminate health benefits for retirees who are eligible for Medicare or a comparable state health benefit plan.[376] The regulation also permits employers to alter, reduce, or eliminate health benefits for spouses or dependents of Medicare-eligible retirees.[377] It does not, however, permit employers to coordinate benefits for active Medicare-eligible employees, nor does it permit employers to coordinate retiree health benefits with Medicaid eligibility.[378]

This rule is designed to permit employers to offer retiree health insurance to early retirees without incurring the prohibitive cost of providing identical benefits to Medicare-eligible retirees.[379]

§ 3.08 FEDERAL TAXATION OF WELFARE BENEFITS

Section 61 of the Internal Revenue Code defines the term "gross income" broadly to include "compensation for services, including fees, commissions, fringe benefits, and similar items" except to the extent otherwise provided.[380] Thus, unless specifically excluded, welfare benefits are generally includible in gross income.

The Internal Revenue Code specifically excludes a number of welfare benefits from employees' taxable income.[381] First, and most significantly, the Internal Revenue Code excludes from an employee's taxable income employer contributions to fund health insurance. On a related note, the Internal Revenue Code excludes from taxable income contributions to fund two different types of health care savings vehicles, Health Savings Accounts (HSAs) and Health Reimbursement Accounts (HRAs). HSAs and HRAs are part of the most recent innovation in employer-sponsored health care plans: consumer-driven health plans.

Income tax exclusion is not limited to benefits related to health care. The Internal Revenue Code also excludes from income other welfare benefits, such as

---

[374] Pub. L. No. 90-202, 81 Stat. 602 (1967), codified in 29 U.S.C. § 621 et seq.

[375] 29 U.S.C. § 631(a).

[376] 29 C.F.R. § 1625.32.

[377] 29 C.F.R. § 1625.32, APP. Q&A-4.

[378] 29 C.F.R. § 1625.32, APP. Q&A-7.

[379] 29 C.F.R. § 1625.32. APP. Q&A-1 EEOC, *Questions and Answers About the EEOC's Retiree Health Rule, available at* http://www.eeoc.gov/policy/docs/qanda_retireehealthrule.html. *See also* Comment, *Winning the Battle but Losing the War: Purported Age Discrimination May Discourage Employers from Providing Retiree Medical Benefits*, 35 J. Marshall L. Rev. 709 (2002).

[380] IRC § 61(a).

[381] For a discussion of tax exclusion and how it differs from tax deferral, see Chapter 1 § 1.07.

the cost of employer-provided group-term life insurance coverage up to $50,000.[382]

Section 125 of the Internal Revenue Code permits an employer to establish a "cafeteria plan" to offer employees the choice between cash and a variety of nontaxable benefits without subjecting the employees to taxation on the nontaxable benefits under the constructive receipt doctrine.

[A] Contributions to Fund Employer-Provided Health Insurance — IRC § 106

Section 106(a) of the Internal Revenue Code generally excludes from an employee's income employer contributions to fund health care benefits. In addition, if an employer establishes a cafeteria plan under IRC § 125,[383] the employee may also pay its required contributions for coverage with pre-tax income, that is, income that is not subject to income tax.

Although the employee is not taxed on the value of these contributions, the employer may generally deduct its share of contributions as an ordinary business expense.[384] In addition, both employer and employee contributions to fund health care benefits are exempt from Social Security taxes[385] and federal unemployment taxes.[386]

Example

Aidan has an employer-sponsored health care plan. In 2014, Aidan contributed $1,000 toward the cost of coverage while his employer contributed $5,000. Because Aidan's contributions were made through an IRC § 125 cafeteria plan, his $1,000 was made on a pre-tax basis; that is, he never paid any income tax on the $1,000 withheld from his salary to pay for the health insurance. In addition, his employer's $5,000 contribution was not includible in his taxable income, although his employer was permitted to deduct the contribution as an ordinary business expense. In addition, no social security or unemployment taxes were paid on the $6,000 contributed to the health care plan.

The Joint Committee on Taxation has identified the income tax exclusion for employer contributions for health care, health insurance premiums, and long-term care insurance premiums[387] as the largest tax expenditure[388] for the fiscal year

---

[382] The Internal Revenue Code also provides an income tax exclusion for educational assistance programs under IRC § 127, dependent care assistance programs under IRC § 129, incidental fringe benefits under IRC § 132, and adoption assistance programs under IRC § 137.

[383] IRC § 125 cafeteria plans are discussed in more detail in § 3.08[D].

[384] IRC § 162; Treas. Reg. § 1.162.10(a).

[385] IRC § 3121(a)(2).

[386] IRC § 3306(b)(2).

[387] The exclusion for employer-provided coverage under accident and health plans and the exclusion for benefits employees receive under employer-provided accident and health plans are viewed as a single tax expenditure. Staff of Joint Comm. on Taxation, Estimates of Federal Tax Expenditures for Fiscal Years 2014–2018, JCS-97-14, at 3 n.8.

[388] Tax expenditures are defined as "revenue losses attributable to provisions of the Federal tax laws

2014, with an estimated loss of $143 billion in tax revenue in 2014 alone.[389]

This tax preference has been subject to a great deal of criticism. Critics contend that it is inequitable because (1) individuals who do not have employment-based health insurance do not benefit from the tax exclusion,[390] and (2) the tax exclusion is more valuable for higher-income workers than it is for lower-income workers.[391] In addition, critics contend that the tax exclusion creates an incentive to purchase too much health insurance.[392]

The Affordable Care addresses two of these criticisms. First, it addresses the inability of individuals who do not have employment-based health insurance to benefit from favorable income tax treatment by creating subsidies to assist low- to moderate-income individuals, who do not have access to affordable employment-based health insurance, to purchase health insurance from the Exchanges.[393] Second, it addresses the criticism that the tax subsidy creates an incentive to purchase too much insurance by imposing an excise tax, effective 2018, on so-called Cadillac health care plans that provide "excess benefits."[394]

The Affordable Care Act does not change the fact that the favorable tax treatment accorded employment-based insurance is more valuable for higher-income workers than it is for lower-income workers. Indeed, the new subsidies create perverse incentives such that low- and moderate-income workers may

---

which allow a special exclusion, exemption, or deduction from gross income or which provide a special credit, a preferential rate of tax, or a deferral of tax liability." *Id.* at 2.

[389] *Id.* at 38. The tax expenditure for fiscal years 2014–2018 is estimated to be $785.1 billion. *Id.* Table I, at 19.

[390] To illustrate:

> [A]ssume that Taxpayer A and Taxpayer B desire the same insurance coverage, an individual policy that costs $3,750. Taxpayer A is offered her desired coverage through her employer, while Taxpayer B is not. Both taxpayers are in the 25% marginal rate bracket. Taxpayer A needs to earn only $3,750 in wages to purchase such coverage. Taxpayer B, however, must earn $5,000 in wages to have sufficient after-tax funds available for his purchase. If we take into account payroll taxes of 7.65% and an assumed state income tax rate of 5%, the amount of wages necessary to pay for a $3,750 policy rises to $5,162. Under these assumptions, Taxpayer A receives an effective subsidy of $1,412 to purchase her health insurance coverage, solely because her employer makes such coverage available to her, and regardless of whether her employer makes any contribution toward such coverage.

Amy B. Monahan, *The Complex Relationship Between Taxes and Health Insurance, in* BEYOND ECONOMIC EFFICIENCY IN UNITED STATES TAX LAW 137, 140 (David A. Brennen et al., eds., 2013).

[391] To illustrate:

Assume that Employer offers its two employees, Candece and Dirk, identical health insurance coverage. Candece and Dirk both pay $1,000 toward the cost of coverage while their Employer contributes $5,000 toward the cost of coverage. Candece is in the 33% marginal rate bracket while Dirk is in the 25% marginal rate bracket. Because Candece is in a higher marginal rate bracket, the tax exclusion is more valuable to Candece than to Dirk. Specifically, Candece receives a subsidy of $1,980 ($5,000 x .33 = $1,980) (that is, she avoids paying $1,980 in tax) while Dirk only receives a subsidy of $1,250 ($5,000 x .25 = $1,250).

[392] See Moore, *The Future of Employment-Based Health Insurance*, 89 NEB. L. REV., at 893–94 and authorities cited therein.

[393] For a discussion of the tax subsidies, see § 3.06[D][3].

[394] For a discussion of the Cadillac tax, see § 3.06[D][6].

sometimes be better off without access to affordable employment-based health insurance so that they can purchase subsidized insurance through the Exchanges.[395]

[B] Contributions to Consumer-Driven Health Care Plans

Consumer-driven health plans are the most recent innovation in employment-based health care plans.[396] Consumer-driven health plans combine a tax-favored Health Savings Account (HSA) or Health Reimbursement Account (HRA) with a high deductible health plan (HDHP).

[1] Health Savings Accounts (HSAs)

A Health Savings Account (HSA) is a tax-favored personal savings account that may be used to pay for medical expenses.[397] Both individuals and employers may contribute to an HSA. Individual contributions are tax deductible[398] while employer contributions made on behalf of eligible individuals are excludable from income.[399]

In order to be eligible for tax-free contributions to an HSA, an individual must be enrolled in a High Deductible Health Plan (HDHP) and must not be enrolled in another health plan that is not an HDHP that provides coverage for benefits that are provided under the HDHP.[400]

Earnings on money held in an HSA are not taxable,[401] and distributions from the account may be excluded from income so long as they are used to pay for qualified medical expenses.[402] Distributions from HSAs that are not used to reimburse qualified medical expenses are subject to income tax.[403] In addition, except in the case of death or disability or after an individual has reached the Medicare eligibility age (generally age 65), distributions that are not used to pay qualified medical expenses are subject to an additional 20% tax.[404]

Section 223(b) of the Internal Revenue Code limits annual contribution to HSAs. In 2015, the HSA contribution limit was $3,350 for an individual with coverage only for himself or herself and $6,650 for an individual with family coverage. The limits are adjusted for changes in the cost of living.[405] A catch-up contribution of $1,000 is

---

[395] See Gamage, 65 Tax L. Rev., at 688–92.

[396] For a discussion of the reasons why consumer-driven health plans were created, see § 3.03[C][4].

[397] IRC § 223(d). For a more detailed discussion of HSAs, see Edward A. Morse, *Health Accounts/ Arrangements: An Expanding Role Under the Affordable Care Act*, 2014 N.Y.U. Rev. of Emp. Benefits & Exec. Comp. 14-1.

[398] IRC § 223(a).

[399] IRC § 106(d).

[400] IRC § 223(c)(1)(A).

[401] IRC § 223(e).

[402] IRC § 223(f).

[403] IRC § 223(f).

[404] IRC § 223(f)(4).

[405] IRC § 223(g).

permitted for individuals who are age 55 or older.[406]

Contributions to an HSA may be made through a cafeteria plan.[407]

[2] Health Reimbursement Accounts (HRAs)

A Health Reimbursement Account (HRA) is an arrangement that is funded solely by employer contributions and reimburses employees for medical care expenses incurred by the employee, or the employee's spouse, dependents or children under the age of 27, up to a maximum dollar amount.[408] The reimbursement is excludable from the employee's income, and amounts that remain in the account at the end of the year can generally be used to reimburse medical expenses incurred in later years.

HRAs may not be used to purchase individual health insurance. Rather, employees must be enrolled in group health plans that satisfy the Affordable Care Act's requirements in order to participate in an HRA.[409]

[3] High Deductible Health Plans (HDHPs)

A High Deductible Health Plan (HDHP) is a health plan that has annual deductible and out-of-pocket limits that fall within specific limits set forth in IRC § 223(c)(2). In 2015, the annual deductible for individuals must be at least $1,300 for individual coverage and $2,600 for family coverage, and out-of-pocket expenses must be limited to no more than $6,450 for individuals and $12,900 for families. The limits are adjusted each year for changes in the cost of living.[410]

A plan will not fail to qualify as a HDHP simply because it does not impose a deductible on preventive care as required by the Affordable Care Act.[411]

[C] Group-Term Life Insurance — IRC § 79

Section 79 of the Internal Revenue Code excludes from an employee's income the cost of employer-provided group-term life insurance coverage of up to $50,000.

[1] Group-Term Life Insurance

As its name suggests, group-term life insurance is a type of life insurance. It provides beneficiaries with a lump sum payment upon a policyholder's death if the policyholder dies during the term of the policy. If the policyholder dies after the expiration of the term, no benefits are provided.

---

[406] IRC § 223(b)(3).

[407] Prop. Treas. Reg. § 1.125-2(c)(1).

[408] IRS Notice 2002-45; Rev. Ruling 2002-41.

[409] IRS Notice 2013-54. For a discussion of the Affordable Care Act's annual benefit limit prohibition and preventive care requirements, see § 3.06[C][2]. Prior to 2014, stand-alone HRAs were permitted; that is, prior to 2014, HRAs did not need to be combined with any other health plan.

[410] IRC § 223(g).

[411] IRC § 223(c)(2)(C); IRS Notice 2013-54.

Example 1

Employer provides its employees with group-term life insurance. Each employee receives coverage equal to twice the employee's salary.

In 2015, Employer provides Arnold, who earns $25,000, with $50,000 of coverage. Arnold names his wife, Anabeth, his sole beneficiary. Arnold dies on March 15, 2015. Anabeth receives a death benefit of $50,000.

Example 2

Employer provides its employees with group-term life insurance. Each employee receives coverage equal to twice the employee's salary.

In 2014, Employer provides Bernie, who earns $30,000, with $60,000 of coverage. Bernie names his son, Bueller, his sole beneficiary. Bernie terminates employment with Employer on March 30, 2014. When Bernie terminates his employment, Employer terminates Bernie's group-term life insurance coverage.

Bernie dies on June 5, 2015. Bueller does not receive any death benefit from Employer's group-term life insurance policy because Bernie's coverage was terminated when he terminated his employment with Employer, which was before Bernie died.

[2]   Exclusion for Group-Term Life Insurance

Section 79 of the Internal Revenue Code excludes from an employee's income the cost of group-term life insurance providing a death benefit for an employee of up to $50,000.[412] Although the employer's contribution is excludable from the employee's income, the employer generally may deduct its contributions to fund the benefit as an ordinary business expense.[413]

To the extent that an employer provides its employees with group-term life insurance with a death benefit that exceeds $50,000, the employee must include in income the cost of that insurance less any amount the employee paid for the insurance.[414] The cost of the insurance is based on the uniform premiums table set forth in the Treasury regulations,[415] rather than the actual premium paid by the employer.

Table — Uniform Premiums for $1,000 of Group-Term Life Insurance Protection

Age of Employee	Cost per $1,000 of protection for 1-month period
Under 25	$.05
25 to 29	$.06

---

[412] IRC § 79(a). The exclusion only applies to the cost of group term life insurance. If the insurance also provides a permanent benefit, the cost of the permanent benefit must also be included in income. Treas. Reg. § 1.79-1(d).

[413] IRC § 162; Treas. Reg. § 1.162.10(a).

[414] IRC § 79(a).

[415] IRC § 79(c); Treas. Reg. § 1.79-3(d).

Age of Employee	Cost per $1,000 of protection for 1-month period
30 to 34	$.08
35 to 39	$.09
40 to 44	$.10
45 to 49	$.15
50 to 54	$.23
55 to 59	$.43
60 to 64	$.66
65 to 69	$1.27
70 and above	$2.06

Example 1

Ann's employer provides her with group-term life insurance coverage of $50,000. Ann is 30 years old. Her employer pays the entire premium for the life insurance.

Because the group-term life insurance coverage does not exceed $50,000, Ann is not required to include any of the cost of the coverage in income.

Example 2

Bennett's employer provides him with group-term life insurance coverage of $100,000. Bennett is 45 years old. His employer pays the entire premium for the life insurance.

In determining how much Bennett must include in income, the $100,000 of insurance coverage is first reduced by $50,000. The yearly cost of the remaining $50,000 ($100,000 - $50,000 = $50,000) of coverage is determined by looking at the uniform table. Because Bennett is 45 years old, the cost is $90 ($.15 x 50 x 12 = $90). Because Bennett does not pay any portion of the premiums, Bennett must include in income $90 for the cost of group-term life insurance coverage that exceeds $50,000.

Example 3

Carol's employer provides her with term group-life insurance coverage of $150,000. Carol is 50 years old. Carol pays $48 toward the cost of insurance.

In determining how much Carol must include in income, the $150,000 of insurance coverage is first reduced by $50,000. The yearly cost of the remaining $100,000 ($150,000 - $50,000 = $100,000) of coverage is determined by looking at the uniform table. Because Carol is 50 years old, the cost is $276 ($.23 x 100 x 12 = $276). Because Carol pays $48 toward the cost of insurance, she is only required to include in income $228 ($276 - $48 = $228) for the cost of coverage that exceeds $50,000.

[D]   IRC § 125 Cafeteria Plans

Section 125 of the Internal Revenue Code permits employers to establish "cafeteria plans" to offer employees the choice between cash and a variety of nontaxable benefits without requiring employees to be subject to income taxation on the nontaxable benefits under the constructive receipt doctrine.[416]

In order to qualify for favorable tax treatment under IRC § 125, the employer must establish a separate written plan, all plan participants must be employees, and plan participants must be permitted to choose among at least one permitted taxable benefit (such as current cash compensation) and at least one "qualified benefit."[417] Qualified benefits are generally employer-provided benefits that are not includible in gross income, such as employer-provided health insurance coverage, group-term life insurance coverage not in excess of $50,000, and benefits under a dependent care assistance program.[418]

Cafeteria plans may take a variety of forms. The simplest and most common type of cafeteria plan is the Premium Only Plan (POP), sometimes referred to as a pretax conversion plan or a premium conversion plan.[419] The second most common type of plan is the flexible spending account. Finally, a third type of plan, the full flex plan, is more complex and less common.

[1]   Premium Only Plans

Most employer-sponsored health care plans require employees to contribute toward the cost of the plan.[420] For example, in 2014, workers with single coverage contributed, on average, $90 per month or $1,081 per year for employer-sponsored health care coverage while workers with family coverage contributed an average of $402 per month or $4,823 per year for employer-sponsored health care coverage.[421]

Absent a cafeteria plan, the employee contributions are typically paid with after-tax dollars because individuals are only entitled to deduct medical expenses to the extent that they exceed 10% of adjusted gross income,[422] and the employees' share of premiums typically does not exceed 10% of adjusted gross income. If, however, an employer establishes a premium only plan that satisfies the requirements of IRC § 125, the employees' contributions are converted from after-tax contributions to pretax contributions.

---

[416] IRC § 125(a), Treas. Reg. §§ 1.125-1, Q&A-1, 1.125-2, Q&A-s. For a discussion of the constructive receipt doctrine, see Chapter 2 § 2.04[B][2].

[417] IRC § 125(d)(1).

[418] IRC § 125(f)(1). Some benefits, such as scholarships, employer-provided meals and lodging, educational assistance, and fringe benefits, are expressly excepted and cannot be included in a cafeteria plan. *Id.*

[419] *See* Treas. Reg. §§ 1.125-1(a)(5) (defining "premium-only-plan"), 1.125(b)(4)(ii) (stating that a cafeteria plan may be a "premium-only-plan").

[420] Kaiser Family Foundation, 2014 Exhibit 6.16, at 110 (showing that in 2014 only 14% of workers made no contribution toward single coverage and 5% of workers made no contribution toward family coverage).

[421] *Id.* Exhibit 6.3 & 6.4, at 97–98.

[422] IRC § 213.

From a policy standpoint, it makes little sense to permit employees with employer-sponsored health care plans to use pre-tax dollars to pay their share of premiums if their employer establishes a premium conversion plan but require all other individuals to pay for health insurance premiums with after-tax dollars.[423] From an employee relations standpoint, however, employers would be well-advised to establish premium only plans. Such plans are relatively inexpensive to establish and administer[424] and can provide substantial tax benefits to the employer as well as the employee. Not only is the employee relieved of income tax liability with respect to the income used to pay the health insurance premiums, but that income is also exempt from social security and federal unemployment taxes.[425]

[2] Flexible Spending Accounts

A Flexible Spending Account (FSA), sometimes referred to as a flexible spending arrangement, is an employee benefit program that reimburses employees for the expenses they incur with respect to certain qualified benefits.[426] Specifically, FSAs may reimburse expenses for three types of qualified benefits: (1) medical care under IRC § 105(b), (2) dependent care under IRC § 129, and (3) adoption assistance under IRC § 137.[427] An employer may offer FSAs with respect to all three types of qualified benefits, but contributions made for one purpose, such as medical care expenses, cannot be used to reimburse a different type of expense, such as dependent care. [428]

FSAs are typically funded by employee contributions through a salary reduction agreement; that is, employees agree to accept a lower salary in return for an offsetting contribution to an FSA.[429] Generally, an employee decides how much the employee will contribute to the FSA before the beginning of the coverage period and funds in the FSA are used to reimburse the employee for any eligible expenses the employee incurs during the coverage period.[430] Because contributions made to an FSA are not taxable to the employee (so long as the plan meets the

---

[423] Arguably, the fact that premium payments under cafeteria plans must be substantiated, Treas. Reg. § 1.125-6, justifies the difference in treatment between premiums paid for employer-sponsored health care coverage and premiums for private individual health insurance. The substantiation requirement ensures that employees will only exclude from income premium payments. Such a justification, however, suggests that the tax exclusion should extend to premiums paid for health insurance purchased through the Exchanges because it should be relatively easy to ensure accurate reporting regarding an individual's share of premiums for health insurance purchased through an Exchange. Health insurance purchased through an Exchange, however, is not currently deductible.

[424] See, e.g., BenefitsWorkshop: Tools to Improve the Financial Health of Your Employees (stating that "Premium Conversion Plans from BenefitsWorkshop are only $300 per year."), available at http://benefitsworkshop.com/pcp.html.

[425] The income may also be free of state and local income tax.

[426] Prop. Treas. Reg. § 1.125-5(a).

[427] Prop. Treas. Reg. § 1.125-5(h).

[428] Prop. Treas. Reg. §§ 1.125-5(i)(3), (j)(3), (k)(1).

[429] Employers may also contribute to FSAs on behalf of their employees.

[430] Some FSA administrators provide employees with a credit card so that the expenses can be paid directly from the FSA and the employee does not need to first pay the expenses and wait to be reimbursed.

requirements of IRC § 125), the FSA, like the premium only plan, permits the employee to pay for qualified expenses on a pre-tax basis.

[a]   Use It or Lose It Rule

Section 125 generally prohibits cafeteria plans from deferring compensation.[431] The IRS has interpreted this requirement to prohibit amounts held by a cafeteria plan from being carried over into a subsequent year and to prohibit cafeteria plans from permitting participants to use contributions for one plan year to purchase benefits that will be provided in a subsequent plan year.[432] This prohibition, referred to as the "use it or lose it" rule, requires that any amounts in an FSA that are unused as of the end of the plan year be forfeited.[433]

Example

Arturo contributes $5,000 to a calendar year dependent care FSA in 2014, but only incurs $4,700 in dependent care expenses that year. The dependent care FSA may reimburse Arturo for the $4,700 in expenses incurred in 2014. Arturo must forfeit the remaining $300 in his dependent care FSA.

[b]   Modifications to the Use It or Lose It Rule for Health FSAs

The IRS has modified the "use it or lose it" rule applicable to health FSAs in two ways. Specifically, it permits:

(1)   a 2 1/2 month grace period or

(2)   a $500 carryover.

A health FSA may offer either a grace period or a carryover.[434] A plan may not include both a grace period and a carryover provision. [435]

[i]   2 1/2 Month Grace Period

Under IRS Notice 2005-42, health FSAs may allow for an additional period of time ("grace period") of up to 2 1/2 months following the end of the plan year for

---

[431]   IRC § 125(d)(2)(A).

[432]   Prop. Treas. Reg. § 1.125-5(c).

[433]   Prop. Treas. Reg. §§ 1.125-1(c)(7)(C), 1.125-1(o), 1.125-5(c). Forfeited amounts can revert to the employer or the employer can use the amounts to offset the plan's administrative expenses. Forfeited amounts can also be returned to employees on a "reasonable and uniform" basis or credited to the following year's accounts on a "reasonable and uniform" basis. Prop. Treas. Reg. § 1.125-5(o)(1).

[434]   IRS Notice 2013-71.

[435]   All plans, however, may include a run-out period. A run-out period is the period immediately after the end of plan year during which a participant may submit claims for reimbursement of expenses incurred for qualified benefits during the plan year. Prop. Treas. Reg. §1.125-1(f). Thus, for example, a calendar year plan may permit a participant to submit a claim on January 20, 2015, for medical expenses incurred on December 15, 2014. A plan may also provide for a run-out period for expenses incurred during the grace period. Notice 2005-42; Prop. Treas. Reg. § 1.125-1(e).

reimbursement of expenses before the "use it or lose it" rule applies.[436]

Example

Adrienne contributes $2,000 to a health FSA for the 2014 calendar year but only incurs $1,800 in health care expenses in 2014. If Adrienne's employer elects to adopt a 2 1/2 month grace period, the health FSA may use contributions made in 2014 to reimburse Adrienne for up to $200 ($2,000 - $1,800 = $200) in medical expenses incurred between January 1, 2015, and March 15, 2015. If Adrienne only incurs $150 in medical expenses between January 1, 2014, and March 15, 2014, she must forfeit the remaining $50 ($200 - $150 = $50).

[ii] $500 Carryover

Under IRS Notice 2013-71, a cafeteria plan may permit up to $500 in an employee's health FSA remaining at the end of a plan year to be carried over and used to reimburse medical expenses incurred at any time during the following plan year.[437]

Example

Bob contributes $2,000 to a health FSA for the 2015 calendar year but only incurs $1,300 in health care expenses in 2015. If Bob's employer elects to adopt a carryover provision, the health FSA may carry over $500 of the $700 in unused contributions to reimburse Bob for health care expenses incurred in 2016. Bob must forfeit the remaining $200 ($700 - $500 = $200) in unused contributions.[438]

[c]   Uniform Coverage Rule for Health FSAs

The uniform coverage rule for health FSAs requires that the maximum amount of reimbursement from a health FSA be available at all times during the period of coverage.[439]

Example

Conrad elects to contribute $100 per month to a calendar year health FSA in 2014. Under the uniform coverage rule, the health FSA must make the entire $1,200 Conrad has elected to contribute to the health FSA over the course of the

---

[436] Prop. Treas. Reg. § 1.125-1(e) (authorizing grace period). The grace period exception is justified by the fact that other areas of tax law do not treat certain arrangements as providing for deferred compensation if the compensation is paid no later than 2 1/2 months after the end of the taxable year in which the services were performed. *See, e.g.*, Treas. Reg. § 1.404(b)-1T, Q&A-2.

[437] Justifications for the carryover exception include "the difficulty for employees of predicting their future needs for medical expenditures, the desirability of minimizing incentives for unnecessary spending at the end of a year or grace period, the possibility that lower- and moderate-paid employees are more reluctant than others to participate because of aversion to even modest forfeitures of their salary reduction contributions, and the opportunity to ease and potentially simplify the administration of health FSAs." IRS Notice 2013-71.

[438] *Id.*

[439] Prop. Treas. Reg. § 1.125-5(d).

plan year available on the first day of the plan year. If Conrad has surgery on January 15, 2015, and incurs $1,200 in expenses for the surgery, the plan must reimburse Conrad for his entire $1,200 expense even though Conrad will not have contributed $1,200 to the FSA until the end of the year. If Conrad terminates employment on March 31, 2015, after having only contributed $300 to the health FSA, Conrad's employer must bear the loss and may not require Conrad to contribute the outstanding $900 to the plan.

The theory behind the uniform coverage rule is that health FSAs must function as insurance and thus must have an element of loss.[440]

The uniform coverage rule does not apply to dependent care or adoption assistance FSAs.[441]

[d]   Limits on Contributions to FSAs

Beginning in 2013, IRC § 125(i) limits annual contributions to health FSAs to $2,500, indexed for cost-of-living adjustments. Section 125 does not impose express limits on contributions to dependent care and adoption assistance FSAs. The Code provisions authorizing such programs, however, limit the exclusions for such programs.[442]

[e]   Special FSA Rules for Health Savings Accounts (HSAs)

Several of the FSA rules do not apply to Health Savings Accounts (HSAs).

First, the prohibition on benefits that defer compensation does not apply to HSAs.[443] Thus, the use it or lose rule does not apply to HSAs. Second, the uniform coverage requirement that the maximum amount of the reimbursement be available at all times throughout the year does not apply to HSAs. Finally, employees may change their prospective HSA contribution elections throughout the year.[444]

[3]   Full Flex Plans

In a full flex cafeteria plan, the employer contributes a specific amount to the cafeteria plan, and the employee can use the employer's contribution (typically referred to as credits) to purchase benefits from among a menu of options.[445] If the employer's contribution exceeds the cost of the benefits the employee has elected,

---

[440] Monahan, *Complex Relationship Between Taxes and Health Insurance,* in Beyond Economic Efficiency in United States Tax Law, at 141.

[441] Prop. Treas. Reg. § 1.125-5(d)(5).

[442] *See* IRC § 129(a)(2) (limiting exclusion for dependent care assistance programs to $5,000); IRC § 137(b)(1) & (f) (limiting exclusion for adoption assistance programs to $10,000, indexed for cost-of living adjustments).

[443] IRC § 125(d)(2)(D).

[444] Prop. Treas. Reg. § 1.125-2(c)(1).

[445] *See* Prop. Treas. Reg. §§ 1.125-1(b)(4)(iii), Example 3, 1.125-2(a)(3).

the employee may convert the credits to taxable compensation. If the cost of the employee's benefit elections exceeds the employer's contribution, the employee may pay for the difference with pre-tax salary contributions.

Large employers are more likely to offer full-flex cafeteria plans than are small employers. In addition, they are more common among employers that offer consumer driven-health plans and are most beneficial for employers with a diverse workforce that seek to meet their employees' diverse needs while limiting their employee benefit costs.

Chapter 4

PLAN OPERATION

§ 4.01 INTRODUCTION

ERISA does not require that employers create employee benefit plans. Rather, the decision of whether to create a plan is entirely voluntary.[1] If, however, an employer elects to create an employee benefit plan, then ERISA regulates the creation and day-to-day operation of the plan. In addition, depending on the type of plan, ERISA may regulate the termination of the plan.[2]

This chapter focuses on a number of ERISA's regulatory requirements with respect to the day-to-day operation of the plan. It first addresses the requirement that employee benefit plans be established and maintained pursuant to a written document. It then turns to the reporting and disclosure requirements. It then addresses plan amendments. Finally, it discusses ERISA § 510, which prohibits employers from interfering with employees' rights under ERISA.

This chapter does not address all of ERISA's provisions regulating the day-to-day operation of an employee benefit plan. Most significantly, it does not address ERISA's fiduciary provisions. Those requirements are discussed at length in Chapter 6.

§ 4.02 WRITING REQUIREMENT — ERISA § 402(a)(1)

ERISA requires that all employee benefit plans be established and maintained pursuant to a written instrument.[3] This written instrument is often referred to as the "plan document."[4]

---

[1] *See* Lockheed Corp. v. Spink, 517 U.S. 882, 887 (1996) ("Nothing in ERISA requires employers to establish employee benefit plans. Nor does ERISA mandate what kind of benefits employers must provide if they choose to have such a plan.").

On the other hand, the Internal Revenue Code encourages the creation of employee benefit plans by (1) providing favorable income tax treatment to most plans, and (2) imposing an excise tax on large employers that fail to offer employees the opportunity to enroll in "minimum essential coverage" under a eligible employer-sponsored health plan. *See* Chapter 1 § 1.07 (discussing favorable tax treatment); Chapter 3 § 3.06[D][4] (discussing employer mandate).

[2] For a discussion of plan termination, *see* Chapter 11.

[3] ERISA § 402(a)(1). A parallel writing requirement is imposed on qualified plans. *See* Treas. Reg. § 1.401-1(a)(2).

[4] T. David Cowart, *Through a Glass Darkly: Musings About* Cigna Corp. v. Amara *and* Pfeil v. State Street Bank and Trust Co., SU014 ALI-ABA 371 (Oct. 18, 2012).

[A]   Purpose of Writing Requirement

ERISA's legislative history makes it clear that the writing requirement was intended to protect plan participants.[5] Specifically, the House Report states that "[a] written plan is to be required in order that every employee may, on examining the plan documents, determine exactly what his rights and obligations are under the plan. Also, a written plan is required so that employees may know who is responsible for operating the plan."[6]

The writing requirement is not always interpreted to protect plan participants. Indeed, courts have frequently rejected plan participants' estoppel claims as inconsistent with the plan writing requirement.[7] Moreover, in *Heimeshoff v. Hartford Life & Accident Ins. Co.*,[8] the Supreme Court suggested that the writing requirement is also intended to protect plan sponsors.

In *Heimeshoff*, a plan participant challenged a plan's denial of her benefit claim.[9] The plan administrator claimed that the participant's suit was time barred because the participant failed to bring suit within three years after "proof of loss" was due as required under the terms of the plan.[10] In upholding the plan's limitations provision, the Court announced that the principle that contractual limitations provisions should ordinarily be enforced as written was especially appropriate in the context of ERISA plans because "[t]he plan, in short, is at the center of ERISA."[11] According to the Court, once a plan is established, the plan administrator must ensure that the plan is maintained pursuant to the written document. "This focus on the written terms of the plan is the linchpin of 'a system that is [not] so complex that administrative costs or litigation expenses unduly discourage employers from offering [ERISA] plans in the first place.' "[12]

[B]   Required Elements of Written Plan Document

ERISA requires that every plan document provide for one or more named fiduciaries[13] who jointly or severally have the authority to control and manage the operation and administration of the plan.[14] In addition, ERISA requires that plan documents contain four specific features:

---

[5] Indeed, the requirement is set forth in ERISA § 402(a)(1) as part of ERISA's fiduciary provisions.

[6] H.R. Rep. No. 93-1280, 2d Sess., at 297 (1974), *reprinted in* 1974 U.S.C.C.A.N. 5038, 5077–78. *See also* Curtiss-Wright Corp. v. Schoonejongen, 514 U.S. 73, 83 (1995) (quoting House report and stating that "one of ERISA's central goals is to enable plan beneficiaries to learn their rights and obligations at any time" by examining the plan documents).

[7] *See* § 4.02[E].

[8] 134 S. Ct. 604 (2013).

[9] *Id.* at 609.

[10] *Id.*

[11] *Id.* at 612, *quoting*, U.S. Airways, Inc. v. McCutchen, 133 S. Ct. 1537, 1548 (2013).

[12] *Id.*, *quoting*, Varity Corp. v. Howe, 516 U.S. 489, 497 (1996).

[13] Named fiduciaries are discussed in Chapter 6 § 6.03[A].

[14] ERISA § 402(a)(1).

(1)   a procedure for establishing and carrying out a funding policy and method consistent with the plan;

(2)   a description of any plan procedure for allocating responsibilities for the operation and administration of the plan;

(3)   a procedure for amending the plan and identifying who has the authority to amend the plan; and

(4)   the basis on which payments are made to and from the plan.[15]

[C]   Satisfying the Writing Requirement

Pension plans tend to be lengthy, complex documents. The plan sponsor, that is, the employer, may hire an attorney or consultant to help draft an individualized pension plan document. Or, the employer may adopt a "prototype" pension plan,[16] in essence, a standardized pension plan developed by a service provider that individual employers can adopt at a relatively low cost.

Similarly, an employer may hire an attorney or consultant to draft an individualized welfare benefit plan document. Or, the employer may rely on a service provider, such as an insurance company, to provide the plan document. If the employer purchases insurance to fund a welfare plan, such as a health care plan, the plan document will often be the insurance contract.[17]

Plans must be reviewed and periodically updated to ensure that they continue to comply with applicable law and with the manner in which they operate. If a plan sponsor hires an attorney or consultant to draft an individual plan, the attorney or consultant will typically be responsible for maintaining and updating the plan document. If the plan sponsor adopts a prototype document, then the service provider typically is responsible for updating the document to be consistent with any changes in the law.

[D]   Effect of Failure to Satisfy Writing Requirement

Although ERISA requires that all employee plans be written, an employer may not avoid regulation under ERISA simply by failing to formalize its employee benefit plan in writing.[18] Instead, failure to satisfy the writing requirement constitutes a violation of ERISA.[19]

---

[15]   ERISA § 402(b).

[16]   For a discussion of the various types of pension plans that a service provider may establish and make available for employers to adopt, *see* IRS, Types of Pre-Approved Retirement Plans, *available at* http://www.irs.gov/Retirement-Plans/Preapproved-Retirement-Plans.

[17]   *See, e.g.*, Gonzales v. Unum Life Ins. Co., 861 F. Supp. 2d 1099, 1108 (S.D. Cal. 2012); Musto v. Am. Gen. Corp., 861 F.2d 897, 901 (6th Cir. 1988). Identifying the writings that constitute the "documents and instruments governing the plan" may give rise to practical uncertainties. *See* E. Thomas Veal, *Amara's World: The Past and Future of SPD Litigation*, 2011 NYU REVIEW OF EMPLOYEE BENEFITS § 7.01 n.20.

[18]   *See* Kenney v. Roland Parson Contracting Corp., 28 F.3d 1254, 1257 (D.C. Cir. 1994); Donovan v. Dillingham, 688 F.2d 1367, 1372 (11th Cir. 1982).

[19]   *See Donovan v. Dillingham*, 688 F.2d, at 1372.

[E] Oral Representations and Estoppel Claims

Plan participants and beneficiaries often file suit claiming benefits based on oral representations made to the participants or beneficiaries. For example, in *Plumb v. Fluid Pump Service, Inc.*,[20] a plan participant claimed that his employer's health insurance plan was estopped from denying coverage because a representative of the insurer had orally assured the participant that his son would be covered by the plan.[21]

In the first circuit court decision to address this issue,[22] the Eleventh Circuit held that enforcing oral modifications of the written terms of a plan would be contrary to ERISA § 402(a)(1)'s requirement that plans be maintained pursuant to a written instrument. The court explained:

> A central policy goal of ERISA is to protect the interests of employees and their beneficiaries in employee benefit plans. This goal would be undermined if we permitted oral modifications of ERISA plans because employees would be unable to rely on these plans if their expected retirement benefits could be radically affected by funds dispersed to other employees pursuant to oral agreements. This problem would be exacerbated by the fact that these oral agreements often would be made many years before any attempt to enforce them.[23]

Most courts have followed the Eleventh Circuit and refuse to grant estoppel[24] based on oral representations that are inconsistent with the unambiguous terms of a written plan.[25] Some courts, however, have been willing to enforce oral representations that constitute "interpretations" of ambiguous plan terms.[26]

---

[20] 124 F.3d 849 (7th Cir. 1997).

[21] *Id.* at 856.

[22] Nachwalter v. Christie, 805 F.2d 956, 960 (11th Cir. 1986).

[23] *Id.* at 960. For an argument that the Eleventh Circuit's approach is contrary to the purpose of ERISA's writing requirement, *see* Jay Conison, *Foundations of the Common Law of Plans*, 41 DePaul L. Rev. 575, 635 (1992) (contending that "[b]y prohibiting unwritten plans and oral plan provisions, ERISA seeks to prevent vague or unsystematic expectations that have a high risk of being defeated, and to promote clarity and definiteness in pension promises." To use this provision to defeat the expectations of employees is to defeat its purposes. While there may be good reasons to prohibit estoppel-based claims for benefits, the writing requirement is not one of them). For similar arguments, *see* Comment, Kimberly A. Kralowec, *Estoppel Claims Against ERISA Employee Benefit Plans*, 25 U.C. Davis L. Rev. 487, 535–42 (1992); *Note*, Loretta Rhodes Richard, *ERISA: Enforcing Oral Promises to Pay Employee Benefits*, 28 B.C. L. Rev. 723, 740–43 (1987).

[24] For a detailed discussion of estoppel claims under ERISA, *see* Robert E. Hoskins, *Equitable Estoppel as a Remedy Under ERISA*, 56 S.D. L. Rev. 456 (2011).

[25] *See, e.g.*, Livick v. Gillette Co., 524 F.3d 24, 31 (1st Cir. 2008); Curcio v. John Hancock Mut. Life Ins. Co., 33 F.3d 226, 236 n.17 (3d Cir. 1994); Coleman v. Nationwide Life Ins. Co., 969 F.2d 54, 58–59 (4th Cir. 1982); Mello v. Sara Lee Corp., 431 F.3d 440, 446–47 (5th Cir. 2005); Bowerman v. Wal-Mart Stores, Inc., 226 F.3d 574, 586 (7th Cir. 2000); Slice v. Sons of Norway, 34 F.3d 630, 634–35 (8th Cir. 1994); Callery v. U.S. Life Ins. Co., 392 F.3d 401, 407 (10th Cir. 2004).

[26] *See, e.g.*, Kane v. Aetna Life Ins., 893 F.2d 1283, 1286 n.4 (11th Cir. 1990); Greany v. Farm Bureau Life Ins. Co., 973 F.2d 812, 821–23 (9th Cir. 1980). *But see* Bonovich v. Knights of Columbus, 146 F.3d 57, 63 (2d Cir. 1998) (stating that *Kane* is not the law in the Second Circuit and suggesting that estoppel might be available even in the absence of ambiguous plan terms); Bloemker v. Laborers' Local 265

The Supreme Court has never addressed the issue of oral modifications of plan terms. In *CIGNA Corp. v. Amara*,[27] however, the Supreme Court announced, in *dicta*, that estoppel, a traditional equitable remedy, may be available when the written terms of a summary plan description conflict with the express terms of a plan.[28]

§ 4.03   REPORTING & DISCLOSURE REQUIREMENTS — ERISA §§ 101–111

ERISA imposes extensive express reporting and disclosure requirements.[29] Reporting refers to a plan's obligation to report required information to governmental agencies, such as the Department of Labor and the Pension Benefit Guaranty Corporation. Disclosure refers to a plan's obligation to disclose information to plan participants and beneficiaries.

ERISA's principle reporting and disclosure requirements are set forth in part one of ERISA's regulatory provisions, that is, sections 101 through 111 of ERISA. In addition, there are other reporting and disclosure requirements interspersed throughout ERISA[30] and the Internal Revenue Code.[31]

ERISA's reporting and disclosure requirements apply to all employee benefit plans subject to ERISA.[32] Specific requirements, however, vary depending on the type of plan.[33]

[A]   Purposes of Reporting and Disclosure Requirements

In enacting ERISA, Congress explained that the reporting and disclosure requirements are intended to protect plan participants and beneficiaries.[34] The plan disclosure requirements are designed to ensure that plan participants and

---

Pension Fund, 605 F.3d 436, 443 (6th Cir. 2010) (permitting estoppel even in case of unambiguous plan terms in extraordinary circumstances).

[27] 131 S. Ct. 1866 (2011).

[28] For a more detailed discussion of conflicts between the terms of a plan and SPD and the Court's *Amara* decision, *see* § 4.03[C].

[29] Courts have also found a common law duty to disclose under certain circumstances. For a discussion of the common law duty to disclose, *see* Clovis Trevino Bravo, *ERISA Misrepresentation and Nondisclosure Claims: Securities Litigation Under the Guise of ERISA?*, 26 Hofstra Lab. & Emp. L.J. 497 (2009); Daniel M. Nimtz, *ERISA Plan Changes*, 75 Denv. U. L. Rev. 891 (1998); Bryan L. Clobes, *In the Wake of* Varity Corp. v. Howe: *An Affirmative Duty to Disclose Under ERISA*, 9 DePaul Bus. L.J. 221 (1997); Edward E. Bintz, *Fiduciary Responsibility Under ERISA: Is There Ever a Fiduciary Duty to Disclose*, 54 U. Pitt. L. Rev. 979 (1993).

[30] *See, e.g.*, ERISA §§ 204(h), 205(c)(3), 503, 606, & 713.

[31] IRC §§ 402(f) & 417(a)(3).

[32] Certain plans, such as governmental plans, are exempt from ERISA and thus are not subject to ERISA's reporting and disclosure requirements. *See* ERISA § 4(b).

[33] For example, the notice of failure to meet the minimum funding requirements, ERISA § 101(d)(1), only applies to pension funds subject to the minimum funding requirements, and certain small welfare benefit plans are exempt from filing an annual report. 29 C.F.R. § 2520.104-20(b).

[34] In section 2(b) of ERISA, Congress declared that it is the policy of ERISA "to protect . . . the

beneficiaries are aware of their rights under the plan and have the necessary information to make informed decisions regarding their benefit options.[35] The plan reporting requirements are designed to ensure that the governmental agencies charged with overseeing and enforcing employee benefit plans have sufficient information to meet their obligations.[36]

[B] Specific Reporting and Disclosure Requirements[37]

ERISA and the Internal Revenue Code require that specific plan information be reported to governmental agencies, including the Department of Labor (DOL),[38] Department of Treasury (Treasury)[39], and the Pension Benefit and Guaranty Corporation (PBGC).[40] In order to ease plan administration,[41] the DOL, Treasury, and PBGC have worked together to develop a single reporting form, Form 5500,[42] that plans can use to satisfy the annual reporting requirement. In addition, ERISA and the Internal Revenue Code require that a variety of other forms of notice and material be provided to the three agencies.[43]

Generally, ERISA's disclosure obligations to plan participants and beneficiaries take one of three forms. First, plans are required to automatically furnish plan participants and beneficiaries with specific documents or notice at stated times or if certain events occur.[44] Second, plans are required to furnish participants and beneficiaries with a copy of certain documents if the participant or beneficiary requests.[45] Finally, plans are required to make certain documents available for

---

interests of plan participants and their beneficiaries by requiring disclosure and reporting of financial and other information."

[35] ABA Section of Labor and Employment Law Employee Benefits Law 4-3 (Jeffrey Lewis et al., eds., 3d ed. 2012).

[36] *Id.* at 4-4.

[37] For a more detailed overview of the basic disclosure requirements under ERISA, *see* Dep't of Labor, EBSA, Reporting and Disclosure Guide for Employee Benefit Plans (Aug. 2013), *available at* http://www.dol.gov/ebsa/pdf/rdguide.pdf; IRS, Retirement Plan Reporting and Disclosure Requirements (8/7/2014), *available at* http://www.irs.gov/pub/irs-tege/irs_reporting_disclosure_guide.pdf.

[38] ERISA § 103 (imposing obligation to report to DOL).

[39] IRC § 6058(a) (requiring tax-qualified pensions and other funded deferred compensation plans to file a return).

[40] ERISA § 4065 (requiring plans covered by termination insurance to file annual return with PBGC).

[41] Section 3004 of ERISA requires that the Departments of Labor and Treasury cooperate in order to prevent duplication of efforts. Section 4065 of ERISA requires that the PBGC cooperate with the Departments of Labor and Treasury as well.

[42] 29 C.F.R. §§ 2520.103-1(b), 2520.104a-5.

[43] For example, ERISA requires that, upon request, a plan administrator provide the Secretary of Labor with the latest summary plan description, summary of material modifications, and the bargaining agreement, trust agreement, contract or other instrument under which the plan is established or operated. ERISA § 104(a)(6).

[44] For example, ERISA requires that defined benefit plans and certain defined contribution plans provide plan participants with notice regarding survivor annuities within a certain period of time prior to making distributions from such plans. ERISA § 205(c); IRC § 417(a).

[45] ERISA § 104(b)(4). For a discussion of the litigation that has arisen regarding the documents that must be produced, *see* ABA Section of Labor and Employment Law, Employee Benefits Law, at 4-15–4-18.

inspection if a plan participant or beneficiary requests.[46]

Sections 101 through 111 of ERISA require three primary forms of disclosure to plan participants: (1) a summary plan description (SPD)[47] and summary of material modifications (SMM),[48] (2) a summary annual report,[49] and (3) individual benefits statements.[50] The SPD and SMM explain how the plan works and the benefits it promises. The summary annual report and individual benefits statements provide participants with the data necessary to determine whether the plan is working and providing the promised benefits.

In addition to these primary forms of disclosure, ERISA and the Internal Revenue Code impose a host of other disclosure requirements. For example, plan administrators of participant-directed individual account plans (most 401(k) plans) must disclose plan fees, expenses, and investment alternatives to plan participants and beneficiaries.[51]

[C]   Summary Plan Description

The "summary plan description" (SPD) is the "primary vehicle for informing participants and beneficiaries about their plan and how it operates."[52] ERISA requires that the plan administrator furnish each plan participant and beneficiary with an SPD within 90 days after the employee becomes a plan participant or the beneficiary begins receiving benefits under the plan.[53]

Section 102(b) of ERISA sets forth a lengthy list of information, such as the plan's eligibility requirements and source of financing, that must be included in the SPD.[54] In addition, ERISA requires that the SPD "be written in a manner calculated to be understood by the average plan participant"[55] and be "sufficiently accurate and comprehensive to reasonably apprise such participants and

---

[46]   ERISA § 104(b)(2).

[47]   ERISA § 104(b)(1) (requiring publication of SPD); ERISA § 102 (setting forth requirements for SPD).

[48]   ERISA § 104(b)(1) (requiring publication of SMM); ERISA § 102(a) (requiring that SMM be "written in a manner calculated to be understood by the average plan participant").

[49]   ERISA § 104(b)(1) (requiring publication of annual report); ERISA § 103 (setting out requirements for annual report).

[50]   ERISA § 105(a).

[51]   29 C.F.R. § 2550.404a-5.

[52]   Dep't of Labor, *Reporting and Disclosure Guide for Employee Benefit Plans* 2 (Oct. 2008). *See also* Curtiss-Wright Corp. v. Schoonejongen, 514 U.S. 73, 83 (1995) (stating that the purpose of the SPD is "to communicate to beneficiaries the essential information about the plan").

[53]   ERISA § 104(b)(1).

[54]   For a discussion of the information that must be included as well as regulatory citations, *see* David Pratt, *Summary Plan Descriptions After* Amara, 45 J. MARSHALL L. REV. 811, 816–21 (2011). *See also* Alison McMorran Sulentic, *Secrets, Lies & ERISA: The Social Ethics of Misrepresentation and Omissions in Summary Plan Descriptions*, 40 J. MARSHALL L. REV. 731, 739 (2007) (breaking down information that must be provided into six categories).

[55]   ERISA § 102(a).

beneficiaries of their rights and obligations under the plan."[56]

It is extremely difficult, if not impossible, to draft a SPD that is both accurate and understandable.[57] As a result, there has been a great deal of litigation regarding conflicts between SPDs and the terms of the plan.[58] Prior to the Supreme Court's decision in *CIGNA Corp. v. Amara*,[59] there was a split among the circuits as to when the terms of an SPD should control over the terms of the plan document in cases of conflict.[60] Some circuits held that the terms of a SPD would control over the terms of the plan if the plan participant could show detrimental reliance; other circuit courts required a showing of either reliance or prejudice before the terms of the SPD would control.[61] Moreover, a couple of circuits suggested *in dicta* that neither reliance nor prejudice was required for the terms of a SPD to control over the terms of a plan document.[62]

In *Amara*, the Supreme Court took a very different approach. In that case, the employer converted its traditional final average pay defined benefit (DB) plan into a cash balance plan.[63] The district court held that the SPD was deficient because it did not disclose the "wear away" phenomenon[64] arising from the conversion which caused some workers' expected retirement benefit not to grow for a period of time after the DB plan was converted into the cash balance plan.[65] The Second Circuit affirmed the district court's opinion.[66]

The Supreme Court described the lower court's decision as ordering relief in two steps: (1) ordering that the terms of the plan be reformed, and (2) ordering the plan administrator to enforce the terms of the plan as reformed.[67]

The Supreme Court declared that SPDs "provide communications with beneficiaries *about* the plan," but that SPDs themselves do not constitute terms of

---

[56] ERISA § 102(a).

[57] *See* Cowart, SU014 ALI-ABA 371 (Oct. 18, 2012); Pratt, 45 J. MARSHALL L. REV. at 811–12, 813. *Cf.* Sulentic, 45 J. MARSHALL L. REV. 731 (suggesting that uniform set of terms be adopted to increase understandability of SPDs); Colleen E. Medill et al., *How Readable are Summary Plan Descriptions for Health Care Plans?*, 27 EBRI Notes 2 (No. 10 Oct. 2006) (finding that readability level of SPDs higher than recommended level for technical material).

[58] Veal, 2011 NYU REVIEW OF EMPLOYEE BENEFITS, at § 7.06 (stating that "[i]n the nearly four decades since ERISA was enacted, courts have decided hundreds of cases in which errors or omissions in summary plan descriptions played a part").

[59] 131 S. Ct. 1866 (2011).

[60] For a discussion of the split in circuits on the issue, *see* Pratt, 45 J. MARSHALL L. REV. at 823–25; Veal, 2011 NYU REVIEW OF EMPLOYEE BENEFITS, at § 7.03. *See also* Burke v. Kodak Retirement Income Plan, 336 F.3d 103, 112 (2d Cir. 2003) (providing brief overview of circuit split).

[61] Pratt, 45 J. MARSHALL L. REV. at 824–25.

[62] *Id.*

[63] 131 S. Ct. at 1870. For an overview of cash balance plans, *see* Chapter 2 § 2.06[C].

[64] For a detailed explanation of cash balance plan conversions and the wear away phenomenon, *see* Jonathan Barry Forman and Amy Nixon, *Cash Balance Plan Conversions*, 25 OKLAHOMA CITY UNIV. L. REV. 379, 401–05 (2000). Wear away provisions are now prohibited. ERISA § 204(b)(5)(B)(ii) & (iii).

[65] 131 S. Ct. at 1875.

[66] *Id.* at 1876.

[67] *Id.* at 1876.

the plan.[68] Accordingly, the Court held that the district court did not have the power under ERISA § 502(a)(1)(B), which authorizes plan participants to bring suit "to recover benefits due . . . under the terms of the plan,"[69] to reform the terms of the plan to be consistent with the terms of the SPD.[70] In a significant break with its traditional ERISA remedy decisions, however, the Court left open the question what equitable remedy, if any, the court might impose under ERISA § 502(a)(3).[71]

The Court's holding that the terms of the plan document govern over the terms of the SPD is generally viewed as favorable toward plan sponsors.[72] It does, however, raise questions about "wrap plans."[73] Although the Court *Amara* assumed that SPDs are entirely distinct from plan documents, in many health and other welfare plans, SPDs are often either used as the plan documents or incorporated into the plan documents by reference under the terms of a "wrap plan." The Court's decision in *Amara* raises questions about the enforceability of such "wrap plans."[74]

§ 4.04   PLAN AMENDMENTS

Generally, employers are free to amend welfare benefit plans at any time.[75] In order to amend such plans, however, ERISA requires that welfare benefit plans provide a procedure for amending the plan.

Employers retain less flexibility to amend pension plans. Not only does ERISA require that pension plans set forth a plan amendment procedure, but ERISA also prohibits pension plan amendments that would reduce accrued benefits.

[A]   Plan Amendment Procedure — ERISA § 402(b)(3)

Section 402(b)(3) of ERISA requires that every employee benefit plan provide "a procedure for amending such plan, and for identifying the persons who have the authority to amend the plan." The requirement applies to both pension plans and welfare benefit plans.[76]

---

[68] *Id.* at 1878.

[69] *Id.* at 1876 (quoting ERISA § 502(a)(1)(B)). For a detailed discussion of ERISA § 502(a)(1)(B), *see* Chapter 7 § 7.08[A].

[70] 131 S. Ct. at 1878.

[71] *Id.* at 1878–82. For a detailed discussion of ERISA § 502(a)(3), *see* Chapter 7 § 7.08[C].

[72] The Court's suggestion that the plan participants might be entitled to equitable relief under ERISA § 502(a)(3), on the other hand, is much more favorable to plan participants.

[73] *Cf.* Cowart, SU014 ALI-ABA 371 (stating that "'[w]rap' documents so prevalent among welfare plans are not outlawed, but must be tied more tightly to the SPD/booklet around which they are wrapped").

[74] For a discussion of post-*Amara* SPD cases, *see* Robert N. Eccles, Amara *Turns Two*, 21 (no. 3) ERISA Litig. Rep. (Newsl.) 14 (2013); Pratt, 45 J. Marshall L. Rev. at 844–52; Robert N. Eccles and Theresa S. Gee, *A Year of* Amara, 20 (no. 3) ERISA Litig. Rep. (Newsl.) 14 (2012).

[75] Curtiss-Wright Corp. v. Schoonejongen, 514 U.S. 73, 78 (1995) (stating that "[e]mployers or other plan sponsors are generally free under ERISA, for any reason at any time, to adopt, modify, or terminate welfare plans").

[76] ERISA § 401(a).

In *Curtiss-Wright Corp. v. Schoonejongen,*[77] the Court declared that ERISA § 402(b)(3)'s primary purpose is "to ensure that every plan has a workable amendment procedure."[78] It explained that the requirement serves three laudable goals: (1) if the plan did not have such a procedure, it might be forever unamendable under standard trust law principles; (2) the requirement increases the likelihood that plan amendments are given the special consideration they deserve; and (3) having a procedure enables plan administrators to distinguish bona fide plan amendments from other types of corporate communications.[79]

In *Schoonejongen,* the welfare benefit plan stated that "The Company reserves the right at any time to amend the plan."[80] The Court held that this standard reservation of rights clause satisfied ERISA § 402(b)(3)'s requirement that the plan provide a procedure for amending the plan and identifying the person (the employer in this case) who has the authority to amend the plan.[81]

[B]   Anti-Cutback Rule for Pension Plans — ERISA § 204(g)

Section 204(g) of ERISA prohibits pension plan amendments[82] that would reduce accrued benefits.[83] The Internal Revenue Code imposes a parallel anti-cutback rule on qualified plans.[84]

[1]   Purpose of the Anti-Cutback Rule

The anti-cutback rule is designed to further ERISA's central objective of "protecting employees' justified expectations of receiving the benefits their employers promise them."[85]

---

[77] 514 U.S. 73 (1995).

[78] *Id.* at 82.

[79] *Id.*

[80] *Id.* at 75.

[81] *Id.* at 79.

[82] Neither ERISA nor the Internal Revenue Code define *plan amendment* for purposes of the anti-cutback rule. The Treasury Regulations provide that accrued benefits cannot be reduced or eliminated in plan mergers, spin-offs and any other transactions amending or having the effect of amending a plan or plans to transfer plan benefits. Treas. Reg. § 1.411(d)-4, Q&A-2(a)(3)(i).

[83] ERISA defines accrued benefit as
   (A)   in the case of a defined benefit plan, the individual's accrued benefit determined under the plan and, except as provided in section 204(c)(3), expressed in the form of an annual benefit commencing at normal retirement age, or
   (B)   in the case of a plan which is an individual account plan [defined contribution plan], the balance of the individual's account.

ERISA § 3(23).

[84] IRC § 411(d)(6). *See also* Treas. Reg. § 1.411(d)-3(a)(1) (stating that IRC § 411(d)(6) is a qualification requirement).

[85] Central Laborers' Pension Fund v. Heinz, 541 U.S 739, 743 (2004).

[2]   Accrued Versus Prospective Benefits

Section 204(g) only applies to accrued benefits, that is, benefits that have already been earned. It does not prohibit amendments that reduce benefits prospectively; that is, benefits that accrue after the effective date of the plan amendment.[86] Section 204(h), however, requires notice of amendments that provide for a significant reduction in the rate of future benefit accruals or that provide for the elimination or significant reduction of an early retirement benefit or retirement-type subsidy.[87]

Example

Jacob, age 50, begins to work for Employer on January 1, 2000. He is immediately eligible and begins to participate in Employer's defined benefit plan. In 2000, Employer's pension plan provides for an annual benefit (commencing at age 65) of a percentage of a participant's average compensation for the period of his final three years of compensation. The percentage is 1% for each of the first five years of participation, 1 1/4% for each of the next five years of participation, and 1 1/3% for each year of participation thereafter.

Effective January 1, 2010, Employer amends its plan's benefit formula to provide that with respect to benefits that accrue on or after January 1, 2010, the applicable percent is .5% for each of the first five years of participation, .575% for each of the next five years of participation, and .625% for each year of participation thereafter for up to 30 years of service.

Jacob retires on January 1, 2015, at age 65. The average of his final three years of compensation is $100,000. His benefit for his first ten years of employment (from 2000–2009) is based on the plan's benefit formula in effect when Jacob joined Employer, and his benefit for his final five years of employment (from 2010–2014) is based on the plan's amended benefit formula in effect beginning on January 1, 2010. Thus, Jacob's pension benefit is $14,375 (((1% x 5) + (1.25% x 5) + (.625% x 5)) x $100,000 or (5% + 6.25% + 3.125%) x $100,000 = $14,375).

[3]   Protected Benefits

The anti-cutback rule applies not only to basic accrued benefits, but also to early retirement benefits, retirement-type subsidies, and optional forms of benefits.[88] In addition, in *Central Laborers' Pension Fund v. Heinz*,[89] the Supreme Court held that ERISA § 204(g) also applies to conditions imposed on receiving those benefits.

In *Heinz*, a multiemployer defined benefit "service only" pension plan offered plan participants early retirement benefits. The plan prohibited beneficiaries from certain "disqualifying employment" after they retired. The plan provided that any beneficiary who accepted disqualifying employment after retirement would have his monthly benefit payments suspended, that is, stopped, until he ceased the prohib-

---

[86] Treas. Reg. § 1.411(d)-4 Q&A 2.

[87] The Internal Revenue Code imposes a similar notification requirement. IRC § 4980F.

[88] ERISA § 204(g)(2); IRC § 411(d)(6)(B). *See also* Treas. Reg. § 1.411(d)-3(g)(1) & (h) (defining these protected benefits and providing examples).

[89] 541 U.S. 739 (2004).

ited employment.[90] Once the plan participant was no longer engaged in the disqualifying employment, monthly benefit payments would resume. The participant, however, would never receive the suspended benefits. In other words, suspended benefits were forfeited.[91]

At the time that Heinz retired, the plan defined disqualifying employment as any job as "a union or non-union construction worker." It did not include employment in a supervisory category. Heinz retired and took a job as a construction supervisor, and the plan began to pay him his monthly retirement benefit.[92]

Two years later, the plan was amended to provide that "disqualifying employment" includes supervisory work. Heinz was warned that if he continued to work as a supervisor, his monthly pension benefit would be suspended. Heinz continued his employment as a supervisor and his monthly pension benefit was in fact suspended.[93]

Heinz filed suit to recover the suspended benefits on the basis that applying the amended definition of disqualifying employment to his retirement benefit violated ERISA § 204(g). The Seventh Circuit held that imposing new conditions on the rights to accrued benefits violated ERISA § 204(g), and the Supreme Court affirmed.[94]

Quoting the Seventh Circuit, the Supreme Court declared that as a matter of common sense, "[a] participant's benefits cannot be understood without reference to the conditions imposed on receiving those benefits, and an amendment placing materially greater restriction on the receipt of the benefits 'reduces' the benefit just as surely as a decrease in the size of the monthly benefit payment."[95] The Court explained that it did not see how the amendment which undercut his right to supplement retirement income by certain employment "could not be viewed as

---

[90] *Id.* at 741–42.

[91] ERISA § 203(a)(3)(B) permits defined benefit plans to suspend the payment of benefits. Specifically, in the case of a single employer plan, the plan may suspend benefits so long as the participant continues to work for the employer that sponsors the plan. In the case of a multi-employer plan, benefits may be suspended so long as the participant works in the same industry, same trade or craft, and same geographic area covered by the plan. ERISA § 203(a)(3)(B).

If benefits are suspended, the plan does not need to pay the participant any benefits during the period of time during which benefits are suspended. In addition, the plan does not need to compensate the plan participant for the foregone benefits.

Thus, for example, suppose that a plan participant is entitled to a monthly benefit of $100. If the plan participant's benefits are suspended for eight months, he will not receive any benefit for eight months. Once benefits resume, the participant will once again receive $100 per month. The plan participant, however, will not be reimbursed for the $800 he did not receive while benefits were suspended.

If the participant was covered by the plan during the suspension period, he may accrue or earn additional benefits under the terms of plan. If the participant accrued additional benefits, his new benefit would be higher than the original $100 monthly benefit. Again, however, he will never be directly reimbursed for the monthly benefits that were suspended.

[92] 541 U.S. at 742.

[93] *Id.* at 742.

[94] *Id.* at 742–43.

[95] *Id.* at 744.

shrinking the value of Heinz's pension rights and reducing his promised benefits."[96]

§ 4.05   ERISA § 510

Section 510 of ERISA prohibits employers from interfering with employees' rights under ERISA. It sets forth four separate clauses or prohibitions:

(1) an "exercise clause" or "retaliation provision";

(2) an "interference clause";

(3) a "whistleblower provision"; and

(4) a multi-employer plan provision.

Section 510 applies to employees' rights under both pension and welfare benefit plans.[97] It is enforced through ERISA's general enforcement provision, ERISA § 502.[98]

[A]   Purpose of ERISA § 510

Congress[99] enacted section 510 of ERISA "primarily to prevent employers from discharging or harassing their employees in order to keep them from obtaining ERISA-protected benefits."[100] It was a "crucial part of ERISA because, without it, employers would be able to circumvent the provision of promised benefits."[101]

[B]   Section 510's Four Prohibitions

Section 510 of ERISA sets forth four separate prohibitions on interference with employees' rights under ERISA.

[1]   Exercise Clause or Retaliation Provision

The section 510 exercise clause provides that "[i]t shall be unlawful for any person to discharge, fine, suspend, expel, discipline, or discriminate against a participant or beneficiary for exercising any right to which he is entitled under the

---

[96] *Id.* at 745.

[97] Intermodal Rail Employees Association v. Atchison, Topeka and Santa Fe Railway Co., 520 U.S. 510, 515 (1997) (stating that "§ 510 draws no distinction between those rights that 'vest' under ERISA and those that do not" and holding that § 510 applies to welfare benefits).

[98] For a discussion of ERISA § 502 enforcement, *see* Chapter 7 § 7.08. *See also* Ronald Dean, *Section 510 The True Black Hole of ERISA Litigation* (ALI-CLE Course Materials Dec. 6–7, 2012) (noting that the only remedy for section 510 claims is section 502(a)(3) because it is neither a benefits claim under section 502(a)(1) nor a fiduciary breach claim under section 502(a)(2)).

[99] For a discussion of the legislative history of Section 510, see, for example, JAMES F. JORDEN, ET AL., HANDBOOK ON ERISA LITIGATION § 9.01[C] (3d ed. 2012); Dana M. Muir, *Plant Closings and ERISA's Noninterference Provision*, 36 B.C. L. REV. 201, 231–34 (1995).

[100] Kowalski v. L&F Prods., 82 F.3d 1283, 1287 (3d Cir. 1996). *See also* Tolle v. Carroll Touch, Inc., 977 F.2d 1129, 1133 (7th Cir. 1992) (stating that the purpose of section 510 is to "prevent persons and entities from taking actions that might cut off or interfere with a participant's ability to collect present or future benefits or which punish a participant for exercising his or her rights under an employee benefit plan").

[101] Ingersoll-Rand Co. v. McClendon, 498 U.S. 133, 143 (1990).

provisions of an employee benefit plan, [ERISA], or the Welfare and Pension Plans Disclosure Act."[102]

The exercise clause is aimed at preventing employers from retaliating against employees for having claimed benefits in the past. Because the exercise clause protects against retaliation by employers, claims under the clause are sometimes referred to as "retaliation" claims.[103]

Example 1

Arnold is covered by his employer's self-funded health plan. Arnold contracts AIDS and submits large medical claims to his employer's plan. Arnold's employer violates ERISA § 510's exercise clause if it terminates Arnold because he submitted large medical claims.[104]

Example 2

Benita is covered by her employer's disability plan. Benita becomes disabled and claims benefits under the plan. If Benita's employer terminates her because she claimed disability benefits, the employer violates ERISA § 510's exercise clause.[105]

[2]   Interference Clause

The section 510 interference clause provides that "[i]t shall be unlawful for any person to discharge, fine, suspend, expel, discipline, or discriminate against a participant or beneficiary for . . . the purpose of interfering with the attainment of any right to which such participant may become entitled under the plan, [ERISA], or the Welfare and Pension Plans Disclosure Act."[106]

The interference clause is aimed at employers' attempts to prevent employees from attaining future benefits.

Example

Employer's defined benefit plan contains a five year cliff vesting schedule; that is, employees will be fully vested after five years of service. Employer violates ERISA § 510's interference clause if it terminates Connor, who has just completed his fourth year of service, in order to prevent him from vesting in the plan.[107]

---

[102] ERISA § 510 (first clause of first sentence).

[103] *See, e.g.,* Hamilton v. Starcom Mediavest Group, Inc., 522 F.3d 623, 627–28 (6th Cir. 2008).

[104] *Cf.* McGann v. H&H Music Co., 946 F.2d 401, 404 (5th Cir. 1991) (suit by employee with AIDS claiming that employer violated exercise clause by amending health plan to reduce AIDS coverage), *cert. denied,* 506 U.S. 981 (1992).

[105] *See, e.g.,* Hamilton, 522 F.3d 623 (claiming employee was terminated for claiming disability benefits in violation of ERISA § 510).

[106] ERISA § 510 (second clause of first sentence).

[107] *Cf.* Gavalik v. Continental Can Co., 812 F.2d 834, 852–53 (3d Cir. 1987) (holding that employer who established program to identify and terminate employees just prior to vesting of benefits violated ERISA § 510).

The exercise and interference clauses are not mutually exclusive. Rather, the same behavior may give rise to a claim that both clauses were violated. For example, in *McGann v. H&H Music Co,*[108] an employee with AIDS claimed that his employer violated both the exercise clause and the interference clause when it amended its health care plan to limit benefits for AIDS-related claims after the employee had submitted claims for the treatment of AIDS.

[3] Whistleblower Provision

The section 510 "whistleblower provision," provides that "[i]t shall be unlawful for any person to discharge, fine, suspend, expel, or discriminate against any person because he has given information or has testified or is about to testify in any inquiry or proceeding relating to [ERISA] or the Welfare and Pension Disclosure Act."[109]

Whether this provision extends to an employee's unsolicited, internal complaints to her employer has given rise to considerable litigation and is one of the hot topics in ERISA litigation today.[110]

The Department of Labor has taken the position that the provision should be broadly construed to include informal, unsolicited complaints: "[b]roadly, but naturally construed, 'any inquiry or proceeding' encompasses plan participants' complaints to management or plan officials about wrongdoing, and the process by which that information is considered, however informal."[111]

The federal circuit courts are deeply divided on the issue.[112] Three circuit courts, the Fifth,[113] Seventh,[114] and Ninth,[115] have held that section 510 may encompass informal internal complaints. Four other circuit courts, the Second,[116] Third,[117]

---

[108] 946 F.2d 401, 404 (5th Cir. 1991), *cert. denied,* 506 U.S. 981 (1992).

[109] ERISA § 510 (second sentence).

[110] Ronald Dean, *Section 510 The True Black Hole of ERISA Litigation* (ALI-CLE Course Materials Dec. 6–7, 2012).

[111] Edwards v. A.H. Cornell and Son, Inc., 610 F.3d 217, 222–23 (3d Cir. 2010) (quoting Secretary of Labor's amicus brief).

[112] *See* Sexton v. Panel Processing, Inc., 912 F. Supp. 2d 457 (E.D. Mi. 2012) (providing a detailed discussion of the circuit split and decisions and concluding that neither the text of section 510 nor the appellate opinions support including informal complaints under ERISA § 510 whistleblower provision). For additional discussions of the circuit split, see Adam B. Gartner, Note, *Protecting the Whistleblower: The Reach of Section 510 of ERISA,* 80 FORDHAM L. REV. 235, 255–66 (2011); Malena Kinsman, *Can You Hear Me? Will the Diminishing Scope of ERISA's Anti-Retaliation Provision Drown the Cries of Whistleblowers?,* 115 PENN. ST. L. REV. 685, 688–97 (2011); Adam Reinke, Comment, *Reversing the Perversion: Interpreting ERISA to Protect Employees Who Report Violations of Federal Law to Their Managers,* 61 EMORY L.J. 1287, 1294–1309 (2012); Michael C. Ross, Comment, *Blow the Whistle at Your Own Risk: ERISA's Retaliation Provision and the Dilemma of the "Unsolicited Internal Complaint,"* 56 ST. LOUIS U. L.J. 331, 338–46 (2011).

[113] Anderson v. Electronic Data Systems Corp., 11 F.3d 1311 (5th Cir. 1994).

[114] George v. Junior Achievement of Central Indiana, Inc., 694 F.3d 812 (7th Cir. 2012).

[115] Hashimoto v. Bank of Hawaii, 999 F.2d 408 (9th Cir. 1993).

[116] Nicolaou v. Horizon Media, Inc., 402 F.3d 325 (2d Cir. 2005).

[117] Edwards v. A.H. Cornell and Son, Inc., 610 F.3d 217 (3d Cir. 2010).

Fourth,[118] and Sixth[119] have held that section 510 does not extend to informal internal complaints.

[4] Multiemployer Plan Provision

The final, section 510 multiemployer plan provision provides that "[i]n the case of a multiemployer plan, it shall be unlawful for the plan sponsor or any other person to discriminate against any contributing employer for exercising rights under [ERISA] or for giving information or testifying in any inquiry or proceeding relating to [ERISA] before Congress."[120]

This final provision was added to section 510 in 2006[121] as a result of a large multiemployer fund targeting some small trucking companies after a representative for the companies testified before Congress regarding multiemployer pension reforms.[122] The provision was designed to close a loophole under the existing law and provide protection for employers who contribute to multiemployer plans.[123]

Although claims under section 510 are common, claims under the final provision of section 510 are rare.[124]

[C] Individuals Protected by ERISA § 510

By their terms, the section 510 interference and anti-retaliation clauses prohibit an employer from taking adverse employment action against a "participant" or "beneficiary."

Section 3(7) of ERISA defines a participant as "any employee or former employee of an employer or any member or former member of an employee organization, who is or may become eligible to receive a benefit of any type from an employee benefit plan which covers employees of such employer or members of such organization, or whose beneficiaries may be eligible to receive any such benefit."[125] Section 3(8) of ERISA defines a beneficiary as a "person designated by a participant, or by the terms of an employee benefit plan, who is or may become entitled to a benefit thereunder."[126]

A number of cases have addressed the question of whether section 510 protection extends to former employees. In *Becker v. Mack Trucks,*[127] former

---

[118] King v. Marriott International, Inc., 337 F.3d 421 (4th Cir. 2003).

[119] Sexton v. Panel Processing, Inc., 754 F.3d 332 (6th Cir. 2014), *cert denied*, 135 S. Ct. 677.

[120] ERISA § 510 (third sentence).

[121] Pension Protection Act of 2006, Pub. L. No. 93-406 § 205, 120 Stat. 780, 889.

[122] 152 Cong. Rec. S8747-01 (daily ed. Aug. 3, 2006) (Statement of Sen. Enzi).

[123] *Id.*

[124] For a rare case of an employer raising a § 510 claim against a multi-employer plan, *see* Borntrager v. Central States Southeast and Southwest Areas Pension Fund, 577 F.3d 913 (8th Cir. 2009) (ERISA § 510 claim was dismissed under Rule 12(b)(6) motion).

[125] ERISA § 3(7).

[126] ERISA § 3(8).

[127] 281 F.3d 372 (3d Cir. 2002).

employees brought suit under section 510 challenging their former employer's refusal to rehire them because pension benefits for the former employees would be more costly than pension benefits for new hires who had never worked for the company. The Third Circuit held that the former employees with vested pension benefits had standing as "participants" under Section 510 but that the former employees whose pension benefits were not vested at the time that their employment was terminated did not have standing as participants under section 510.

The Third Circuit relied on the Supreme Court's decision in *Firestone Tire & Rubber Co. v. Bruch*[128] to distinguish between the former employees with and without vested benefits. In *Firestone*, the Court addressed the question of who is a participant for purposes of ERISA's disclosure rules and declared that "the term 'participant' is naturally read to mean either 'employees in, or reasonably expected to be in, currently covered employment,' or former employees who 'have . . . a reasonable expectation of returning to covered employment' or who have 'a colorable claim' to vested benefits."[129] The Court further announced that "[i]n order to establish that he or she 'may become eligible' for benefits, a claimant must have a colorable claim that (1) he or she will prevail in a suit for benefits, or that (2) eligibility requirements will be fulfilled in the future."[130]

The court in *Becker* held that the former employees with vested pension benefits had standing as "participants" under Section 510 because they satisfied the second element of the *Firestone* test that they have "a colorable claim" to vested benefits.[131]

With respect to the former employees whose pension benefits were not vested at the time that their employment was terminated, the court first found that the employees, who were covered by a collective bargaining agreement, did not satisfy the first element of the test, that they have a reasonable expectation of returning to covered employment, because their recall rights had expired or been waived.[132] The court then found that they did not satisfy the second, colorable claim to vested benefits, element because their past service gave rise to a "forfeitable benefit" and "such a contingent claim for future benefits does not satisfy the dictates of *Firestone*."[133] According to the court, "a legally unenforceable claim to *contingent* benefits cannot establish a colorable claim to *vested* benefits under *Firestone*."[134]

A strong argument can be made that standing under ERISA § 510 should not be limited to former employees with a colorable claim to *vested* benefits. As the

---

[128] 489 U.S. 101 (1989).

[129] *Id.* at 117 (citations omitted).

[130] *Id.* at 117–18 (citations omitted).

[131] *Id.* at 377. The court, however, rejected their claims on the merits because, according to the court, section 510 does not encompass the decision to hire or rehire. *Id.* at 379–83. For a critique of this aspect of the court's decision, *see* Becker v. Mack Trucks, Inc.: *Third Circuit Holds that Refusal to Rehire Participant Never Violates Section 510*, 10 No. 1 ERISA Litig. Rep. (Newsl.) 13 (Apr. 2002).

[132] 489 U.S. at 377–78.

[133] *Id.* at 378, *quoting*, Shawley v. Bethlehem Steel Corp., 989 F.2d 652, 657 (3d Cir. 1995).

[134] *Id.* at 379.

Supreme Court held in *Inter-Modal Rail Employees Association v. Atchison, Topeka and Santa Fe Railway Co.*,[135] section 510 protection is not limited to pension benefits.[136] Rather, it extends to welfare benefits as well. Thus, at least in the context of a welfare benefit claim, standing for former employees should not be limited to those who can establish a colorable claim to *vested* welfare benefits.[137] Instead, former employees who can establish a colorable claim to *any* welfare benefit[138] should have standing.[139]

Recognizing that the Supreme Court's definition of the term participant in *Firestone* "developed outside of the standing context,"[140] several circuit courts[141] have applied a "but-for" test to determine whether a former employee has standing under section 510.[142] Under this "but for" test, "a former employee has standing as a 'participant' where, but for the alleged misrepresentations or breaches of duty by fiduciaries, the employee 'would have been in a class eligible to become a member of the plan.' "[143]

---

[135] 520 U.S. 510 (1997).

[136] The court in *Becker* recognized that the Supreme Court had decided *Inter-Modal* after it first established its section 510 standing rule with respect to former employees. The court found the *Inter-Modal* decision distinguishable because it did not address the standing issue and did not concern vested pension benefits. *Id.* at 379.

[137] Indeed, the court in *Becker* left open the possibility that it might apply a different rule to section 510 claims with respect to welfare benefits when it distinguished *Intermodal* on the ground that it concerned welfare benefits that do not vest. *Becker*, at 379.

[138] *See* ERISA § 3(7) (defining participant as "any employee or former employee . . . who is or may become eligible to receive a benefit *of any type* from an employee benefit plan. . . . ") (emphasis added).

[139] The Court in *Inter-Modal* remanded the case for the lower court to address the employer's argument that when applied to welfare benefits that do not vest, section 510 "only protects an employee's right to cross the 'threshold of eligibility' for welfare benefits." *Id.* at 516.

[140] Shahid v. Ford Motor Company, 76 F.3d 1404, 1410 (6th Cir. 1996), *citing*, Swinney v. General Motors Corp., 46 F.3d 512 (6th Cir. 1995).

[141] *See* McBride v. PLM Int'l, Inc., 179 F.3d 737, 743 (9th Cir. 1999); *Shahid*, 76 F.3d at 1410; Christopher v. Mobil Oil, 950 F.2d 1209, 1221 (5th Cir. 1992). *See also* Jones v. Allen, 2014 U.S. Dist. LEXIS 132672 (S.D. Ohio Sept. 22, 2014) (applying but for test).

[142] Without deciding when, if ever, the "but for" test should apply, the court in *Becker* found that the former employees did not have standing under the "but for" test because "Mack's refusal to rehire former employees did not 'in and of itself' strip them of their employee status." *Becker*, at 378.

[143] *Shahid*, 76 F.3d at 1410, *quoting*, Swinney v. General Motors Corp., 46 F.3d 512, 519 (6th Cir. 1995).

[D] Proving an ERISA § 510 Claim — Shifting Burden of Proof

In order to recover under section 510, a plaintiff must demonstrate that the employer had "specific intent" to engage in an activity prohibited by section 510.[144] Because plaintiffs are rarely able to provide direct proof of specific intent,[145] courts typically apply a burden shifting framework, like the three-step *McDonnell Douglas Corp. v. Green*[146] burden shifting framework applied to Title VII claims, to determine whether there has been a violation of Section 510.[147]

[1] Plaintiff's Initial Burden of Proof

Under the three step process, the plaintiff must first establish a *prima facie* case under section 510.

In the context of an exercise clause or retaliation case, the Sixth Circuit[148] has held that in order to establish a *prima facie* case, the plaintiff must show that

(1) "she was engaged in activity that ERISA protects;

(2) she suffered an adverse employment action; and

(3) a causal link exists between her protected activity and the employer's adverse action."[149]

In the context of an interference clause case, the Sixth Circuit[150] has held that in order to establish a *prima facie* case, the plaintiff must show

(1) prohibited employer conduct

(2) taken for the purpose of interfering

(3) with the attainment of any right to which the employee may become entitled.[151]

---

[144] *See, e.g.*, Hamilton v. Starcom Mediavest Group, Inc., 522 F.3d 623, 628 (6th Cir. 2008); McGann v. H&H Music Co., 946 F.2d 401, 404 (5th Cir. 1991), *cert. denied*, 506 U.S. 981 (1992); Kimbro v. Atlantic Richfield Co., 889 F.2d 869, 881 (9th Cir. 1989), *cert. denied*, 498 U.S. 814 (1990); Gavalik v. Continental Can Co., 812 F.2d 834, 851 (3d Cir.), *cert. denied*, 484 U.S. 979 (1987).

[145] *See Gavalik*, at 852 (stating that "[i]n most cases, specific intent will not be demonstrated by 'smoking gun' evidence").

[146] 411 U.S. 792, 802–04 (1973).

[147] *See, e.g.*, Crawford v. TRW Automotive U.S. LLC, 560 F.3d 607, 613 (6th Cir. 2009); Dister v. Continental Grp., Inc. 859 F.2d 1108, 1111–12 (2d Cir. 1988); Gavalik v. Continental Can Co., 812 F.2d 834, 852–53 (3d Cir. 1987).

[148] Other circuits have adopted similar tests. *See, e.g.*, Kimbro v. Atlantic Richfield Co., 889 F.2d 869, 881 (9th Cir. 1989), *cert. denied*, 498 U.S. 814 (1990); Holtzclaw v. DSC Commc'ns Corp., 255 F.3d 254, 260–62 (5th Cir. 2001); Rath v. Selection Research, Inc., 978 F.2d 1087 (8th Cir. 1992).

[149] *Hamilton*, 522 F.3d at 628.

[150] Other circuits have applied similar tests. *See, e.g.*, Berger v. Edgewater Steel Co., 911 F.2d 911, 922 (3d Cir. 1990), *cert. denied*, 499 U.S. 920 (1991); Holtzclaw v. DSC Commc'ns Corp., 255 F.3d 254, 260–62 (5th Cir. 2001).

[151] Crawford v. TRW Automotive U.S. LLC, 560 F.3d 607 (6th Cir. 2009).

[2] Defendant's Burden of Proof

Once the plaintiff establishes her *prima facie* case, the burden shifts to the employer to produce evidence supporting a legitimate nondiscriminatory reasons for the action.[152] The employer need not prove, but simply must articulate, a legitimate nondiscriminatory reason for the adverse employment action.[153]

[3] Plaintiff's Final Burden of Proof

If the employer satisfies its burden, the burden shifts back to the plaintiff to show by a preponderance of the evidence that the proffered reason was a prextext.[154]

---

[152] *See, e.g., Hamilton*, 522 F.3d at 628.

[153] *See, e.g.*, Dister v. Continental Group, Inc., 859 F.2d 1108, 1115 (2d Cir. 1988); Humphreys v. Bellaire Corp., 966 F.2d 1037, 1043 (6th Cir. 1992).

[154] *See, e.g., Dister*, 859 F.2d at 1108; *Hamilton*, 522 F.3d at 628–30.

Chapter 5

REGULATION OF PENSION PLANS

§ 5.01 INTRODUCTION

ERISA contains some provisions that solely regulate pension plans. Specifically, Parts 2 and 3 of subtitle B of Title I of ERISA, that is, ERISA §§ 201–211 and ERISA §§ 301–307, solely regulate pension plans. As its title Participation and Vesting suggests, Part 2 imposes participation and vesting requirements, sometimes referred to as pension benefit security rules. In addition, Part 2 sets forth rules regarding the form pension plan distributions must take and imposes limits on the alienability of pension benefits while the benefits are held by the pension plan. As the title of Part 3, Funding, indicates, Part 3 sets forth minimum funding rules for defined benefit plans.

These rules are designed to protect plan participants and their spouses. The Internal Revenue Code imposes parallel requirements on pension plans as part of its qualification requirements.

§ 5.02 PENSION BENEFIT SECURITY RULES

In enacting ERISA, Congress found that "despite the enormous growth in [employee benefit plans] many employees with long years of employment are losing anticipated retirement benefits owing to the lack of vesting provisions in such plans."[1] In order to protect employees from the loss of their expected pension benefits, ERISA imposes detailed rules regarding vesting,[2] participation,[3] and benefit accrual.[4] These rules are contained in Title I of ERISA. The Internal Revenue Code imposes parallel rules as qualification requirements.[5] The rules only apply to pension plans; they do not apply to welfare benefit plans.[6]

---

[1] ERISA § 2(a).

[2] ERISA § 203.

[3] ERISA § 202.

[4] ERISA § 204.

[5] IRC §§ 410 & 411.

[6] ERISA § 201. The vesting rules apply to pension plans because pension plans promise future benefits and Congress wanted to ensure that the promised benefits would become nonforfeitable and thus available to retirees at retirement. Congress did not, however, see a need to require vesting of welfare benefits because welfare benefits, unlike pension benefits, are typically current benefits that are funded on a pay-as-you go basis or through the current purchase of insurance. Dana M. Muir, *Plant Closings and ERISA's Noninterference Provision*, 36 B.C. L. Rev. 201, 208 (1995).

The vesting rules require that benefits become vested, that is, nonforfeitable,[7] after the employee has completed a minimum number of years of service with the employer. Once a participant's benefits are vested, the participant is entitled to receive the vested portion of her benefit even if she leaves her job before retirement. The participation rules restrict the amount of time an employer can exclude an employee from participating in a plan. The benefit accrual rules regulate the rate at which benefits are earned by a plan participant.

Example

The Acme Pension Plan provides that employees may begin to participate in the plan after one year of service, that benefits will be fully vested after five years of service, and that participants will receive an annual benefit at normal retirement age equal to 3% per year of participation multiplied by the employee's average annual salary over the final three years of employment.

Anna, an Acme employee, joins Acme Company on January 2, 2012. She will be eligible to participate (and thus earn) benefits in the Acme Pension Plan on January 2, 2013. On January 2, 2017, after five years of service with Acme, she will be fully vested in the plan, and thus will have the right to receive her benefit at the normal retirement age, even if she quits Acme before then. On January 2, 2017, after having participated in the plan for four years, her annual accrued benefit (the amount receivable at normal retirement age) will equal 12% (3% per year x 4 years) multiplied by her average annual salary over the final three years of her employment.

This example illustrates why regulation of vesting also requires regulation of participation and benefit accrual. Suppose that ERISA only imposed a five-year vesting rule; that is, it required that benefits be nonforfeitable after five years of service. If ERISA did not also regulate participation and benefit accruals, an employer could evade the purpose of the vesting rules by providing that an employee could not participate in the plan until after the employee had 30 years of service with the employer or by providing that benefits would accrue at the rate of 0% per year for the first 29 years of service and 70% of the employee's average annual salary over the final three years of employment for the 30th year of service.

[A]   Vesting Requirements — ERISA § 203; IRC § 411

When private pensions were originally introduced in the United States, they were viewed as "gratuities," and the employer had no obligation to pay benefits to plan participants.[8] By 1974, 88% of pension plans provided for the vesting of

---

[7] *See also* ERISA § 3(19) (defining "[t]he term 'nonforfeitable' when used with respect to a pension benefit or right [as] a claim obtained by a participant or his beneficiary to that part of an immediate or deferred benefit under a pension plan which arises from the participant's service, which is unconditional, and which is legally enforceable against the plan").

[8] *See* McNevin v. Solvay Process Co., 32 A.D. 610 (N.Y. App. Div. 1898), *aff'd per curium*, 60 N.E. 1115 (N.Y. 1901) (holding employer had no obligation to pay pension benefit because pensions are a gift from the employer to the employee). *See also* Patricia E. Dilley, *The Evolution of Entitlement: Retirement Income and the Problem of Integrating Private Pensions and Social Security*, 30 Loy. L.A. L. Rev. 1063, 1114–15 (1997) (discussing gratuity theory of early pension promises).

benefits, but the vesting schedules ranged widely, with some plans imposing both age and lengthy service requirements.[9] According to one account, due to lengthy service requirements and numerous disqualifying events, fewer than 10% of plan participants ever attained benefit eligibility prior to the enactment of ERISA.[10]

ERISA dramatically altered this landscape by imposing minimum vesting requirements.[11] ERISA imposes different vesting requirements depending on the source of the contribution (employer versus employee) and type of plan (defined benefit plan versus defined contribution plan).[12] ERISA requires that benefits derived from an employee's own contributions be immediately fully vested,[13] and imposes a faster vesting schedule on employer contributions to defined contribution plans than to defined benefit plans.[14]

The vesting rules are based on years of service, not years of participation in the plan, although certain types of service may be excluded.[15] Neither ERISA nor the Internal Revenue Code prevent a plan from providing a more generous vesting schedule. The required vesting schedules are simply minimum requirements plans must meet.

[1] Vesting Requirements for Employee Contributions

Benefits attributable to employee contributions must be immediately 100% vested.[16]

---

[9] Investment Company Institute, *A Look at Private-Sector Retirement Income After ERISA*, 16 Res. Persp. 1, 11 (2010).

[10] Mary E. O'Connell, *On the Fringe: Rethinking the Link Between Wages and Benefits*, 67 Tul. L. Rev. 1422, 1454–55 (1993). *But see* Pamela D. Perdue, *Overview of ERISA's Legislative and Regulatory Scheme*, ST043 ALI-ABA 1 (May 16–18, 2012) (stating that "during the first half of the last century, only approximately 1/3 of workers participating in retirement plans were vested due to stringent vesting standards imposed by plans").

[11] As noted above, vested benefits are nonforfeitable, that is, once a participant's benefits are vested, the participant is entitled to receive the vested portion of his benefit even if he leaves his job before retirement.

[12] For a discussion of the differences between defined benefit and defined contribution plans, see Chapter 2 § 2.02.

[13] ERISA § 203(a)(1); IRC § 411(a)(1).

[14] Prior to the enactment of the Economic Growth and Tax Relief Reconciliation Act (EGTRRA), the same vesting rules that currently apply to employer contributions to defined benefit plans applied to all employer contributions. In 2001, EGTRRA imposed an accelerated vesting rule for employer matching contributions to defined contribution plans. Economic Growth and Tax Relief Reconciliation Act (EGTRRA), Pub. L. No. 107-16, § 633, 155 Stat. 38. This accelerated vesting schedule was intended to increase participation by lower- and middle-income employees. It was believed that shortening the time of vesting employer contributions would allow short-term workers to accumulate greater retirement savings. H.R. Rep. No. 107-51, pt. 1, at 74 (2001). The Pension Protection Act of 2006 unified the vesting rules applicable to defined contribution plans by extending the accelerated vesting schedule to all employer contributions to defined contribution plans. Pension Protection Act of 2006, Pub. L. No. 109-280, 120 Stat. 780 (2006).

[15] *See* ERISA § 203(b)(1); IRC § 411(a)(4).

[16] ERISA § 203(a)(1); IRC § 411(a)(1).

[2] Vesting Requirements for Employer Contributions to Defined Benefit Plans

Benefits attributable to employer contributions to defined benefit plans must satisfy one of two alternative vesting schedules:

(1) a cliff vesting schedule, or

(2) a graded vesting schedule.

[a] Five-Year Cliff Vesting Schedule

Under the first, so-called cliff vesting schedule, an employee must be fully vested in benefits attributable to employer contributions to defined benefit plans after five years of service.[17]

[b] Three- to Seven-Year Graded Vesting Schedule

Under the alternative, graded vesting schedule,[18] an employee's benefit attributable to employer contributions must begin to vest after three years of service and be fully vested after seven years of service according to the following schedule:

Defined Benefit Plan Graded Vesting Schedule

Years of Service	Nonforfeitable Percentage
3	20
4	40
5	60
6	80
7 or more	100

---

[17] ERISA § 203(a)(2)(A)(ii); IRC § 411(a)(2)(A)(ii).

[18] ERISA § 203(a)(2)(A)(iii); IRC § 411(a)(2)(A)(iii).

[3]   Vesting Requirements for Employer Contributions to Defined Contribution Plans

Like benefits attributable to employer contributions to defined benefit plans, benefits attributable to employer contributions to defined contribution plans must satisfy either

(1)   a cliff vesting schedule or

(2)   an alternative grading vesting schedule.[19]

The schedules for employer contributions to defined contribution plans are faster than those for defined benefit plans.

[a]   Three-Year Cliff Vesting Schedule

Under the cliff vesting schedule, an employee must be fully vested in benefits attributable to employer contributions to defined contribution plans after three years of service.[20]

[b]   Two- to Six-Year Graded Vesting Schedule

Under the alternative, graded vesting schedule,[21] an employee's benefit attributable to employer contributions to defined contribution plans must begin to vest after two years of service and be fully vested after six years of service according to the following schedule:

---

[19] Employer contributions to safe harbor 401(k) plans are subject to faster vesting schedules. *See* Chapter 9 § 9.09[D] (discussing safe harbor 401(k) plans).

[20] ERISA § 203(a)(2)(B)(ii); IRC § 411(a)(2)(B)(ii).

[21] ERISA § 203(a)(2)(B)(iii); IRC § 411(a)(2)(B)(iii).

Defined Contribution Plan
Graded Vesting Schedule

Years of Service	Nonforfeitable Percentage
2	20
3	40
4	60
5	80
6 or more	100

[4]   Summary of Vesting Schedules

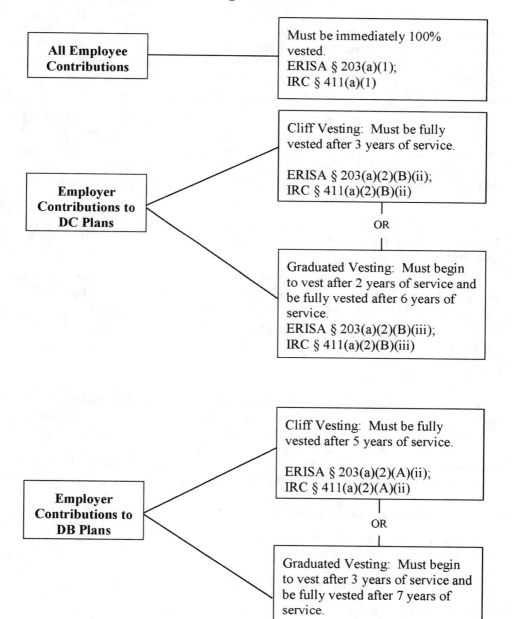

All Employee Contributions — Must be immediately 100% vested.
ERISA § 203(a)(1);
IRC § 411(a)(1)

Employer Contributions to DC Plans

Cliff Vesting: Must be fully vested after 3 years of service.

ERISA § 203(a)(2)(B)(ii);
IRC § 411(a)(2)(B)(ii)

OR

Graduated Vesting: Must begin to vest after 2 years of service and be fully vested after 6 years of service.
ERISA § 203(a)(2)(B)(iii);
IRC § 411(a)(2)(B)(iii)

Employer Contributions to DB Plans

Cliff Vesting: Must be fully vested after 5 years of service.

ERISA § 203(a)(2)(A)(ii);
IRC § 411(a)(2)(A)(ii)

OR

Graduated Vesting: Must begin to vest after 3 years of service and be fully vested after 7 years of service.

ERISA § 203(a)(2)(A)(iii);
IRC § 411(a)(2)(A)(iii)

Example

Acme Company has a profit-sharing plan with a 401(k) feature. The profit-sharing plan provides that Acme Company will contribute 3% of pay on behalf of each participant each year. In addition, the plan authorizes employees to contribute up to an additional 5% of pay each year and provides for employer matching contributions equal to 100% of each employee's elective contribution. The plan uses a three-year cliff vesting schedule for employer contributions.

Aaron joins the Acme workforce on January 2, 2014, and becomes eligible to participate in the plan on January 2, 2015. In 2015, Aaron earns $50,000 and elects to contribute 5% of his pay (or $2,500) to the plan. Aaron will be credited with a total of $6,500 for the year (a 3% or $1,500 regular employer contribution, a 5% or $2,500 employee elective contribution, and a 5% or $2,500 employer matching contribution).

Aaron's $2,500 elective contribution will be immediately fully vested. Acme Company's $1,500 regular contribution and $2,500 matching contribution will be fully vested after three years.

If Aaron resigns from Acme on January 2, 2016, after two years of service, he will not lose his $2,500 elective contribution, but he will forfeit the $4,000 Acme contributed on his behalf. If he leaves in 2017 or later (when he will have at least three years of service), he will be entitled to the entire $6,500 contribution made on his behalf in 2015.

[5] Forfeitures

In the case of defined contribution plans, forfeitures may be used to reduce future employer contributions or administrative expenses or may be reallocated to the account balances of the remaining plan participants to increase their benefits. In the case of qualified defined benefit plans, forfeitures may only be used to reduce future employer contributions or administrative expenses. They may not be used to increase the benefits of remaining participants in defined benefit plans.[22]

[6] Special Vesting Rules

In addition to the basic vesting rules, ERISA and the Internal Revenue Code impose three special vesting rules.

[a] Vesting upon Normal Retirement Age

ERISA and the Internal Revenue Code require that pension plans provide that an employee's right to his normal retirement benefit be nonforfeitable upon the attainment of the Normal Retirement Age (NRA).[23]

Normal retirement age is defined as the earlier of

---

[22] IRC § 401(a)(8).

[23] ERISA § 203(a); IRC § 411(a).

(1)   the time when the employee attains normal retirement age as defined in the plan or

(2)   the later of

   (A)   age 65 or

   (B)   five years after the participant begins to participate in the plan.[24]

Example

Employer's Pension Plan has a normal retirement age of 65. Joey, age 65, has worked for Employer for two years. Joey's benefit must be fully vested even though he has worked for Employer for less than five years.

[b]   Vesting upon Plan Termination

Section 411(d)(3) of the Internal Revenue Code imposes a special vesting requirement on qualified plans.[25] It requires that upon plan termination, all employees become fully vested in their plan benefits, "to the extent funded." This special rule also applies in the event that there is a "partial termination" of a qualified plan. The rule that plan benefits be fully vested upon plan termination is discussed in Chapter 11 § 11.02[A].

[c]   Vesting of Top Heavy Plans — IRC § 416

Section 416 of the Internal Revenue Code imposes accelerated vesting requirements, like the vesting schedules applicable to defined contribution plans, on top-heavy plans.[26] Top-heavy plans are plans for which 60% or more of benefits or contributions are held for the benefit of key employees.[27] Key employees are defined as: (1) officers with compensation in excess of $130,000, adjusted for inflation, (2) 5% owners, and (3) 1% owners who receive compensation in excess of $150,000.[28]

[B]   Minimum Age and Service Requirements — ERISA § 202; IRC § 410

ERISA does not require that a pension plan impose eligibility requirements; that is, an employer may draft its plan to provide that all employees are eligible to participate in the plan as soon as they begin to work for the employer. In order to ease administration and reduce benefit costs, however, most pension plans impose minimum age and/or service requirements.[29] ERISA limits the minimum age and

---

[24]   ERISA § 3(24); IRC § 411(a)(8).

[25]   For an overview of qualified plans, see Chapter 2 § 2.04.

[26]   IRC § 416(b)(1).

[27]   IRC § 416(g)(1)(A).

[28]   IRC § 416(i)(1)(A).

[29]   *See, e.g.*, Bureau of Labor Statistics, *National Compensation Survey: Employee Benefits in Private Industry in the United States, 2010*, Table 29 (showing that 69% of defined benefit plans open to new employees impose minimum age or service requirements); Bureau of Labor Statistics, *National*

service requirements that plans may impose.

Generally, ERISA requires that a pension plan permit an employee to participate in the plan once the employee has reached age 21 or completed one year of service, whichever occurs later.[30] There are two exceptions to this rule:

(1) a tax-exempt educational institution may set age 26 as the minimum participation age if the plan provides for immediate, full vesting,[31] and

(2) for any plan other than a 401(k) plan, an employer may impose a 2-year service requirement so long as employees are fully vested in their benefits once they enter the plan.[32]

A year of service is generally a calendar year during which a participant has completed at least 1,000 hours of service.[33] The Department of Labor regulations contain lengthy rules explaining how hours of service are to be calculated and credited and how breaks in service are to be treated.[34]

For administrative ease, ERISA permits an employer to delay the employee's "entry date," that is, the day on which the employee begins to participate in the plan, until the earlier of the first day of the plan year beginning after the employee satisfies the minimum age and service requirements or six months after the employee satisfies these requirements.[35]

ERISA also prohibits plans from establishing a maximum age for participation.[36]

[C]   Benefit Accrual Rules — ERISA § 204; IRC § 410

Once an employee is eligible to participate in a pension plan, the employee may begin to accrue or earn benefits under the plan.[37] Through its benefit accrual rules, ERISA regulates the rate at which employees may accrue or earn pension benefits. Because defined contribution plans provide benefits in a fundamentally different way than do defined benefit plans, the benefit accrual rules as applied to defined contribution plans are quite different from the rules as applicable to defined benefit

---

Compensation Survey: Employee Benefits in Private Industry in the United States, 2009, Table 29 (showing that 70% of savings and thrift plans impose minimum age or service requirements); Bureau of Labor Statistics, *National Compensation Survey: Employee Benefits in Private Industry in the United States, 2002–2003*, Tables 67, 97, 102 (showing that about 80% of pension plans impose minimum age and/or service requirements).

[30] ERISA § 202(a)(1)(A); IRC § 410(a)(1)(A).

[31] ERISA § 202(a)(1)(B)(ii); IRC § 410(a)(1)(B)(ii).

[32] ERISA § 202(a)(1)(B)(i); IRC § 410(a)(1)(B)(i).

[33] ERISA § 202(a)(3)(A); IRC § 410(a)(3)(A).

[34] 29 CFR §§ 2530.200b-1–200b-4.

[35] ERISA § 203(a)(4); IRC § 410(a)(3)(A).

[36] ERISA § 203(a)(2); IRC § 410(a)(2).

[37] "Accrual of benefits describes how an employee earns increased pension benefits over time." Muir, *Plant Closings*, 36 B.C. L. Rev., at 206.

plans.[38]

[1] Defined Contribution Plans

ERISA's benefit accrual rules with respect to defined contribution plans are quite simple. In a defined contribution plan, a participant's accrued benefit is the balance of the participant's individual account.[39] This balance consists of the employee and/or employer's contributions to the plan plus any earnings or losses on those contributions. The plan must separately account for each employee's accrued benefit[40] and contributions to the employee's individual account must not be reduced or eliminated because of the attainment of any age.[41]

[2] Defined Benefit Plans

The benefit accrual rules with respect to defined benefit plans are more complex.[42] In a defined benefit plan, the accrued benefit is the amount that the plan participant would receive annually as a life annuity beginning at the plan's normal retirement age.[43] A participant's accrued benefit is determined by the plan's benefit formula. Specifically, the accrued benefit is equal to the normal retirement benefit (as defined by the plan) multiplied by the applicable accrual rate.

A plan may explicitly specify a method for determining the accrual rate.

Example 1

Delta's Pension Plan provides that an employee's accrued benefit is equal to the normal retirement benefit under the terms of the plan multiplied by a fraction, the numerator of which is the number of years of participation completed by the participant and the denominator of which is the number of years of participation the employee would have had if he had continued to work for the employer until the normal retirement age.

In the alternative, the accrual rate may be incorporated into the plan's benefit formula.

---

[38] For a discussion of the difference between defined benefit and defined contribution plans, see Chapter 2 § 2.02.

[39] ERISA § 3(23)(B); IRC § 411(a)(7)(A)(ii).

[40] ERISA § 204(b)(3)(B); IRC § 411(b)(3)(B). The separate accounting requirement is simply a bookkeeping requirement and does not require that the funds be otherwise separated from any other plan accounts.

[41] ERISA § 204(b)(2)(A); IRC § 411(b)(2)(A).

[42] The rules are intended to address perceived abuses aimed at benefiting company insiders. Muir, *Plant Closings*, 36 B.C. L. Rev., at 207 n.53.

[43] ERISA § 3(23)(A); IRC § 411(a)(7)(A)(i). A participant's "normal retirement age" is defined as the earlier of (1) the time specified in the plan or (2) the later of (a) age 65 or (b) the 5th anniversary of the time a participant commenced participation under the plan. ERISA § 3(24); IRC § 411(a)(8).

Example 2

Company's Pension Plan provides that an employee's benefit is determined by multiplying a unit benefit ($200 per year) by the number of years of service completed by the employee.

In essence, a participant's accrued benefit is the portion of the participant's ultimate normal retirement benefit that has been earned as of the date of the determination.

An employee need not be fully vested in his accrued benefit.[44]

ERISA requires that defined benefit plans satisfy one of three alternative benefit accrual schedules:

(1)   the 3% method,

(2)   the 133 1/3% method, or

(3)   the fractional share method.[45]

The rules have the effect of requiring a plan to give participants accrual credit for their initial years of plan participation. In essence, the rules prevent excessive backloading of benefits,[46] that is, providing for lower benefit accruals in the early years of participation and much higher benefit accruals in the later years of participation.[47]

[a]   3% Method

The 3% method measures the accrual of benefits for a plan participant against the maximum accrual that the participant might expect if she continued to participate in the plan until the actual retirement age. The underlying assumption is that the participant will continue to participate in the plan and earn the maximum benefit available under the plan.

The 3% method requires that the accrued benefit be no less than 3% of the pension the employee would receive at normal retirement age if the participant joined the plan at the youngest possible age and remained in covered service until the earlier of age 65 or the normal retirement age multiplied by the employee's

---

[44] For example, a defined benefit plan's benefit formula might provide that "each participant will receive a benefit payable at normal retirement age equal to 2% of average annual compensation for each year of credited service up to a maximum of 30 years of credited service." If the plan permits employees to immediately join the plan, an employee who has worked for the company for two years will have an accrued benefit equal to 4% of the employee's annual average compensation beginning at the plan's normal retirement age. If the plan follows a five-year cliff vesting schedule, the employee will not be vested in any of his accrued benefit. Thus, if the employee leaves with less than five years of service, the employee will have accrued a benefit but will forfeit that benefit because the benefit was not vested.

[45] ERISA § 204(b)(1); IRC § 411(b)(1).

[46] For a discussion of how benefits under a defined benefit plan are inherently backloaded, see Chapter 2 §§ 2.02[C][6]&[7].

[47] The rules are driven, at least in part, by a perception that backloaded benefits may discriminate in favor of highly-compensated employees because lower-wage employees tend to have more rapid turnover than do highly compensated employees. Pamela D. Perdue, Qualified Pension and Profit-Sharing Plans ¶ 13.01[1] (2015).

actual years of participation in the plan, but not to exceed 33 1/3.[48]

To apply the 3% method,

(1) Determine the amount a participant could theoretically earn if the participant entered the plan at the earliest possible entry date[49] and remained in the plan until the earlier of age 65 or the normal retirement age.

(2) Once the theoretical maximum accrued benefit is determined, calculate 3% of that benefit.

(3) Compare that 3% figure with the benefit, at any given time, to which the participant is entitled.

With limited exceptions, a participant must, at any given time, have an accrued benefit equal to at least the 3% figure times the participant's years of service.

Example 1

The Delta defined benefit plan provides an annual retirement benefit commencing at age 65 equal to $500 for each year of participation, imposes a minimum age requirement of 25, and provides for no limit on the number of years of credited service.

To determine whether the plan satisfies the 3% method for plan participant Joshua, age 45, who has participated in the plan for 10 years, first determine the maximum amount Joshua could theoretically accrue under the plan if he entered on the earliest possible entry date (age 25) and remained until the plan's normal retirement age of 65, which is $500 x (65 - 25), or $20,000. Then calculate 3% of that theoretical maximum benefit, which is 3% x $20,000, or $600. Finally, compare the 3% figure with the benefit which Joshua has accrued.

Since Joshua's benefit of $5,000 (10 x $500 = $5,000) is less than the 3% figure times Joshua's years of service or $6,000 (10 x $600), the plan does not satisfy the 3% method.[50]

Example 2

The Beta defined benefit plan provides an annual retirement benefit commencing at age 65 equal to $500 for each year of participation, imposes a minimum age requirement of 25, and limits the number of years of credited service to the first 30 years of participation.

To determine whether the plan satisfies the 3% method for plan participant Jusmina, who like Joshua, is age 45 and has participated in the plan for 10 years, first determine the maximum amount Jusmina could theoretically accrue under the plan if she entered on the earliest possible entry date (age 25) and remained until the plan's normal retirement age of 65 is $500 x 30 or $15,000. Then calculate 3% of

---

[48] ERISA § 204(b)(1)(A); IRC § 411(b)(1)(A).

[49] If the plan has no minimum age or service requirement, the earliest possible entry age is 0. Treas. Reg. § 1.411(b)-1(b)(1)(iii) Ex. 3.

[50] *Cf. Id.* Ex. 1.

that theoretical maximum benefit, which is 3% x $15,000, or $450. Finally, compare the 3% figure with the benefit which Jusmina has accrued.

Since Jusmina's benefit (10 x $500) or $5,000 is more than the 3% figure times Jusmina's years of service (10 x $450) or $4,500, the plan satisfies the 3% method.[51]

[b]   133 1/3% Method

The 133 1/3% method measures a plan's benefit accrual rate in a given year against the benefit accrual rate for all subsequent years. A plan must satisfy two requirements to satisfy the 133 1/3% method:

(1)   the plan's accrued benefit at normal retirement age must be equal to the plan's normal retirement benefit, and

(2)   the annual rate at which any individual who is, or could be, a participant can accrue the retirement benefit payable at normal retirement age must be no more than 133 1/3% of the annual rate at which the participant can accrue benefits in any prior plan year.[52]

The method is used by plans using a unit benefit formula and by cash balance plans.[53]

Example 1

Plan A provides for an annual benefit (commencing at age 65) of a percentage of a participant's average compensation for the period of his final three years of participation. The percentage is 1% for each of the first five years of participation, 1 1/3% for each of the next five years of participation, and 1 3/4% for each year of participation thereafter.

Although no single rate of accrual under the plan exceeds 133 1/3% of the immediately preceding accrual rate, Plan A does not satisfy the 133 1/3% method because the rate of accrual for all years of participation in excess of 10 (1 3/4%) exceeds the rate of accrual for any of the first five years of participation (1%) by more than 133 1/3%.[54]

Example 2

Plan B provides for an annual benefit (commencing at age 65) of a percentage of a participant's average compensation for the period of his final three years of participation. The percentage is 1 3/4% for each of the first five years of participation, 1 1/3% for each of the next five years of participation, and 1% for each year of participation thereafter.

Plan B satisfies the 133 1/3% method because no rate of accrual exceeds a prior year's rate of accrual by more than 133 1/3%.

---

[51] *Cf. Id.* Ex. 2.

[52] ERISA § 204(b)(1)(B); IRC § 411(b)(1)(B).

[53] Perdue, Qualified Pension and Profit-Sharing Plans, at ¶ 13.03[3].

[54] *Cf.* Treas. Reg. § 1.411(b)-1(b)(2)(iii) Ex. 2.

Although the accrual rate for the first five years of participation (1 3/4%) exceeds the accrual rate for all years of participation in excess of 10 (1%) by more than 133 1/3%, the 133 1/3% method only limits increases in accrual rates in later years. It does not prohibit subsequent accrual rate reductions.[55]

[c]   Fractional Method

The fractional method requires that the accrued benefit to which a participant is entitled if the participant separates from service before reaching the plan's normal retirement age be not less than a fraction of the annual benefit beginning at the normal retirement age. The fraction, which cannot exceed one, has a numerator equal to the participant's total years of participation in the plan as of the date of separation and a denominator equal to the total number of years of participation the individual would have if the participant separated from service at the normal retirement age.

Thus, under the fractional method the participant's accrued benefit must be a ratable portion of the normal retirement benefit payable at the normal retirement age. For purposes of the calculation, the participant's compensation is deemed to remain constant.[56]

Example

Employer's defined benefit plan provides an annual retirement benefit beginning at age 65 equal to 30% of a participant's average compensation for his highest three consecutive years of compensation. If a participant separates from service prior to normal retirement age, Employer's plan provides a benefit equal to an amount which bears the same ratio to 30% of such average compensation as the participant's actual number of years of participation in the plan bears to the number of years the participant would have participated in the plan if the participant had separated from service at age 65. The normal retirement age under the plan is 65.

Toby, age 55, is a participant in Employer's plan for the current year and has 15 years of participation in Employer's plan. As of the current year, Toby's average compensation for his highest three years of compensation is $20,000. Employer's plan satisfies the fractional method requirement because if Toby separates from service in the current year, he will be entitled to an annual benefit of $3,600 beginning at age 65 (0.3 x $20,000 x 15/25).[57]

---

[55] *Cf. Id.* Ex. 1.

[56] ERISA § 204(b)(1)(C); IRC § 411(b)(1)(C).

[57] *Cf.* Treas. Reg. § 1.411(b)-1(b)(3)(iii) Ex. 1.

§ 5.03 QUALIFIED JOINT AND SURVIVOR ANNUITY (QJSA) AND QUALIFIED PRERETIREMENT SPOUSAL ANNUITY (QPSA) RULES — ERISA § 205; IRC § 417

Section 205 of ERISA[58] requires that all defined benefit plans[59] (and certain defined contribution plans)[60] provide benefits to married participants and their spouses in the form of a qualified joint and survivor annuity (QJSA) or a qualified preretirement spousal annuity (QPSA) unless the participant, with the consent of the participant's spouse, elects otherwise. Sections 401(a)(11) and 417 of the Internal Revenue Code impose parallel requirements on qualified plans.

[A] Brief Introduction to Annuities

An annuity is a contractual commitment to provide periodic payments for an agreed-upon period of time. There are many different types of annuities. The most common type of annuity is a nominal annuity that provides a fixed dollar amount per month.[61]

Example 1

Adam purchases an annuity that promises to pay Adam $500 per month for 10 years.

A life annuity is a contractual commitment to provide periodic payments to an individual for the life of the individual.

Example 2

Tess purchases a life annuity that promises to pay Tess $1,000 per month for as long as Tess lives.

A joint and survivor annuity is a contractual commitment to provide periodic payments for as long as the individual and his or her surviving spouse is alive.

Example 3

John and Jann purchase a joint and survivor annuity that promises to pay $1,000 per month to John so long as John lives, and upon John's death to pay $500 per month to Jann, his surviving spouse, so long as Jann is alive. If Jann predeceases John, payments will cease upon John's death.

---

[58] *See also* IRC § 401(a)(11).

[59] ERISA 205(b)(1)(A); IRC § 401(a)(11)(B)(i).

[60] Defined contribution plans that are subject to the minimum funding standards, that is, money purchase and target benefit plans, are subject to the same annuity rules as defined benefit plans. ERISA 205(b)(1)(B); IRC § 401(a)(11)(B)(ii). All other defined contribution plans are exempt from the rules if they satisfy the requirements set forth in ERISA 205(b)(1)(C); IRC § 401(a)(11)(B)(iii). The exemption is discussed in more detail in § 5.03[E].

[61] Steven A. Sass, *Should You Buy an Annuity from Social Security?*, CENTER FOR RETIREMENT RESEARCH AT BOSTON COLLEGE ISSUE IN BRIEF No. 12-10, at 2 (May 2012).

The principal advantage of a fixed, immediate lifetime joint and survivor annuity is that it guarantees the individual and his or her surviving spouse a steady stream of income for the rest of their lives. In other words, it eliminates longevity risk, that is, the risk that the couple will outlive their financial resources.[62]

[B]   Purpose of Qualified Joint and Survivor Annuity and Qualified Preretirement Survivor Annuity Rules

The qualified joint and survivor annuity (QJSA) and qualified preretirement survivor annuity (QPSA) rules were enacted in order to protect surviving spouses and ensure that they have a steady stream of retirement income after the death of their spouses.[63] In essence, the rules protect the spouses of plan participants by requiring that distributions from defined benefit plans (and certain defined contribution plans) be in the form of an annuity that provides for payments that continue for the lifetime of the participant's spouse in the event that the participant's spouse outlives the plan participant. The requirements may be waived if the participant elects with the spouse's consent, to another form of benefit payment.

[C]   Qualified Joint and Survivor Annuities

A joint and survivor annuity is an annuity for the life of an individual with a survivor annuity for the life of the individual's spouse. In the case of a QJSA, the individual is the plan participant and the spouse is the plan participant's spouse. In order to qualify as a QJSA, the survivor annuity must not be less than 50%, nor greater than 100%, of the amount of the annuity which is payable during the joint lives of the participant and spouse and must be the actuarial equivalent of a single life annuity for the life of the participant.[64]

---

[62] Julie R. Agnew, et al., *The Annuity Puzzle and Negative Framing*, Center for Retirement Research at Boston College Issue in Brief No. 8-10, at 1 (July 2008).

[63] Boggs v. Boggs, 520 U.S. 833, 843 (1997) ("The statutory object of the qualified joint and survivor annuity provisions, along with the rest of § 1055, is to ensure a stream of income to surviving spouses."). *See also* Internal Revenue Manual, Qualified Joint and Survivor Annuity Requirements 4.72.9.1.1 (4/01/2006) ("The legislative history of [the Retirement Equity Act of 1984 which introduced mandatory spousal rights in pension plans] reflects that Congress viewed the marriage relationship as a partnership, and the retirement benefit resulting from that partnership as derived from the contributions of both partners.").

[64] ERISA § 205(d); IRC § 417(b).

In essence, actuarial equivalence means of equal value.

For example, a single life annuity of $1,000 per month for a 65-year-old man may be the actuarially equivalent of a life with 10-year certain annuity of $900 per month for a 65-year-old man.

The two annuities are not identical. The single life annuity will pay the man $1,000 per month for as long as he lives. If he lives for 20 years, he will be paid $1,000 per month for 20 years. On the other hand, if he dies two years after the annuity begins, he will only receive $1,000 per month for two years. The life with 10-year certain annuity will pay the man $900 per month for at least 10 years regardless of how long he lives. If he dies two years after the annuity payments begin, his beneficiary will receive $900 per month for eight years. If he lives for 20 years, he will be paid $900 per month for 20 years. If the man lives more than 10 years, he will receive more from the single life annuity than from the 10-year certain annuity. On the other hand, if he dies less than 10 years after the commencement of the annuity, the

Plans that offer a QJSA must also offer a qualified optional survivor annuity (QOSA) to participants who elect to waive the QJSA.[65] A QOSA is an annuity benefit with a different survivor benefit percentage than that offered by a QJSA.[66] If the survivor annuity of the QJSA is less than 75%, the survivor annuity of the QOSA must be 75% of the amount of the annuity which is payable during the joint lives of the participant and spouse.[67] If the survivor annuity of the QJSA is 75% or more, the QOSA percentage must be 50%.[68] Like the QJSA, the QOSA must be actuarially equivalent to a single life annuity for the life of the participant.[69]

[D] Qualified Preretirement Survivor Annuities

A preretirement survivor annuity is a life annuity for the life of the surviving spouse of a vested participant if the participant dies before the distribution of benefits has begun. In essence, in order to qualify as a QPSA, the annuity must provide the surviving spouse with the same benefit the surviving spouse would have received had the participant retired immediately prior to death and received a joint and survivor annuity under the terms of the plan.

[1] Participant's Death After Normal Retirement Age

If the participant dies after normal retirement age (or early retirement age, if available) but before the payment of benefits has commenced, the QPSA is determined as if the participant had separated from service on the day before the participant's death, elected a QJSA, and then died.[70]

Example

Martin, a fully vested participant in the Acme pension plan, dies at age 67, survived by his wife, Glenda. The normal retirement age under the plan is age 65.

Glenda is entitled to a survivor annuity at the time of Martin's death.

[2] Participant's Death on or Before Normal Retirement Age

If the participant dies on or before normal retirement age (or early retirement age, if available), the QPSA is determined as if the participant had

---

10-year certain annuity will likely pay more. When he purchases the annuity no one knows for certain how long he will live. Thus, no one knows which annuity will actually pay him more. Only time will tell.

Although the two annuities are not identical, they may be worth the same amount. A lower payment of $900 per month for life that is guaranteed for 10 years may be worth the same as a higher payment of $1,000 per month for life that is not guaranteed for 10 years. *See Troyan, Inc., Learning Tools: Actuarial Equivalence, available at* http://www.troyaninc.com/QDRO/Learning-Tools.aspx.

[65] ERISA § 205(c)(1)(A)(ii); IRC § 417(a)(1)(A)(ii).

[66] ERISA § 205(d)(2)(A)(i); IRC § 417(g)(1)(A).

[67] ERISA § 205(d)(2)(B)(i); IRC § 417(g)(2)(A)(i).

[68] ERISA § 205(d)(2)(B)(ii); IRC § 417(g)(2)(A)(ii).

[69] ERISA § 205(d)(2)(A)(ii); IRC § 417(g)(1)(B).

[70] ERISA § 205(e)(1)(A)(i); IRC § 417(c)(1)(A)(i).

    (1)   separated from service (that is, terminated employment) on the date of death,

    (2)   survived until the earliest retirement age,

    (3)   retired with an immediate QJSA at the earliest retirement age, and

    (4)   died on the day after the day on which the participant would have attained the earliest retirement age.[71]

Example

Nicholas, a fully vested participant in the Arrow pension plan, dies at age 55, survived by his wife, Wendy. The normal retirement age under the plan is 65. Wendy will be entitled to a survivor annuity 10 years after Nicholas died, when he would have reached the normal retirement age of 65 under the terms of the plan. If the Arrow pension plan permitted participants to elect reduced retirement benefits at age 60, Wendy would be entitled to receive a survivor annuity benefit five years after Nicholas died, when he would have reached the earliest eligibility age of 60.[72]

[3] Value of Qualified Preretirement Survivor Annuity from Defined Contribution Plan

If the plan is a defined contribution plan, the value of the QPSA payments must not be less than the actuarial equivalent of 50% of the participant's vested account balance.[73]

[E] Plans and Benefits Exempt from the Qualified Joint and Survivor Annuity and Qualified Preretirement Survivor Annuity Rules

The QJSA and QPSA rules apply to defined contribution plans that are subject to the minimum funding standards, that is, money purchase and target benefit plans.[74] In addition, the rules apply to all other defined contribution plans unless the plan satisfies three requirements:

    (1)   the plan provides that the participant's entire vested benefit is payable in full, on the death of the plan participant to the participant's surviving spouse, unless the surviving spouse consents to the designation of another beneficiary;

    (2)   the participant does not elect benefits in the form of a life annuity; and

    (3)   with respect to the participant, the plan is not a direct or indirect transferee of a plan which is subject to the mandatory QJSA/QPSA

---

[71] ERISA § 205(e)(1)(A)(ii); IRC § 417(c)(1)(A)(ii).

[72] A defined benefit plan must permit the surviving spouse to begin receiving the QPSA payments no later than the month in which the participant would have reached the earliest retirement age under the plan. ERISA § 205(e)(1)(B); IRC § 417(c)(1)(B).

[73] ERISA § 205(e)(2); IRC § 417(c)(2).

[74] ERISA 205(b)(1)(B); IRC § 401(a)(11)(B)(ii).

rules.[75]

A plan may provide that benefits will be paid in the form of a lump sum, without the option of a QJSA or QPSA, if the present value of the participant's vested accrued benefit does not exceed $5,000.[76]

[F] Waiver with Spousal Consent

A participant may elect, with the written consent of his or her spouse, to waive distribution in the form of a QJSA, QOSA, or QPSA.[77] In order to be valid, the spouse of the participant must consent in writing, the participant must designate an alternative beneficiary or form of benefit that may not be changed without spousal consent,[78] and the spouse's consent must acknowledge the effect of the election and be witnessed by a plan representative or notary public.[79] Prenuptial agreements do not satisfy the spousal consent requirements.[80]

[G] Marriage Requirement

A plan may limit eligibility for survivor benefits to participants who have been married for at least one year as of the earlier of the annuity starting date or the participant's death.[81] If the participant marries less than one year before the annuity starting date and remains married for at least one year ending on the participant's death, the participant must be treated as having satisfied the one year marriage requirement.[82] If a participant is married on the date of death, QJSA or QPSA payments to the surviving spouse must continue even if the surviving spouse remarries.[83]

§ 5.04 ANTI-ALIENATION PROVISION — ERISA § 206(d); IRC § 401(a)(13)

Section 206(d) of ERISA prohibits pension plans from assigning or alienating benefits.[84] Section 401(a)(13) of the Internal Revenue Code imposes a parallel prohibition on qualified retirement plans. Referred to an "anti-alienation" or

---

[75] ERISA § 205(b)(1)(C); IRC § 401(a)(11)(B)(iii).

[76] ERISA § 205(g)(1); IRC § 417(e)(1).

[77] ERISA § 205(c)(1)&(2); IRC § 417(a)(1)&(2).

[78] The spousal consent may expressly permit the participant to change beneficiary designations without any requirement of further consent. ERISA § 205(c)(2)(A)(ii); IRC § 417(a)(2)(A)(ii).

[79] ERISA § 205(c)(2)(A); IRC § 417(a)(2)(A).

[80] Treas. Reg. § 1.401(a)-20, Q&A-28.

[81] ERISA § 205(f)(1); IRC § 417(d)(1). For a critique of the length of marriage requirement, see Camilla E. Watson, *Broken Promises Revisited: The Window of Vulnerability for Surviving Spouses under ERISA*, 76 Iowa L. Rev. 431, 493–500 (1991).

[82] ERISA § 205(f)(2); IRC § 417(d)&(2).

[83] Treas. Reg. § 1.401(a)-20, Q&A-25(b)(1).

[84] ERISA § 206(d).

"spendthrift" provision,[85] the provision prevents plan participants from bargaining away benefits or having them subject to creditors' claims prior to retirement. The provision only applies to pension plans; it does not apply to welfare benefit plans.[86]

Section 206(d) of ERISA regulates pension benefits while they are held by pension plans. It does not address what happens to pension benefits once they are distributed to beneficiaries. Most circuit courts have held that ERISA § 206(d) does not prevent creditors from attaching or garnishing pension benefits once they have been paid to retirees.[87]

[A]   Purpose of the Anti-Alienation Provision

ERISA's legislative history[88] explains that the anti-alienation provision is intended to ensure that employees' "accrued benefits are actually available for retirement purposes."[89] The Supreme Court has described ERISA's anti-alienation provision as "much like a spendthrift trust provision barring assignment or alienation of a benefit"[90] that "reflects a considered congressional policy choice, a decision to safeguard a stream of income for pensioners (and their dependents, who may be, and perhaps usually are, blameless) even if that decision prevents others from securing relief for the wrongs done [to] them."[91]

[B]   Definition of "Assign" or "Alienate"

Neither ERISA nor the Internal Revenue Code define the terms "assign" or "alienate." In *Kennedy v. Plan Administrator for DuPont Savings and Investment Plan*,[92] the Supreme Court declared that the two terms have "histories of legal

---

[85] *See, e.g.*, Alan K. Ragan, *Balancing ERISA's Anti-Alienation Provisions Against Garnishment of a Convicted Criminal's Retirement Funds: Unscrambling the Approaches to Protecting the Retirement Nest Egg*, 39 U. Balt. L. Rev. 63, 64 (2009). *See also* Kennedy v. Plan Administrator for DuPont Savings and Investment Plan, 555 U.S. 285, 294 (2009) (describing ERISA § 206(d) as "much like a spendthrift trust provision barring assignment or alienation of a benefit").

[86] *See* ERISA § 201(1).

[87] *See* NLRB v. HH3 Trucking, Inc., 2014 U.S. App. LEXIS 10998, at *6 (7th Cir. June 13, 2014); Hoult v. Hoult, 373 F.3d 47, 53–55 (1st Cir. 2004), *cert. denied*, 527 U.S. 1022 (1999); Central States Pension Fund v. Howell, 227 F.3d 672, 678–79 (6th Cir. 2000); Wright v. Riveland, 219 F.3d 905, 919–21 (9th Cir. 2000); Robbins v. DeBuono, 218 F.3d 197, 203 (2d Cir. 2000), *cert. denied*, 531 U.S. 1071 (2001) (abrogated by Wojchowski v. Daines, 498 F.3d 99 (2d Cir. 2007) but on a separate point of law); Trucking Employees of North Jersey Welfare Fund, Inc. v. Colville, 16 F.3d 52, 54–56 (3d Cir. 1994). *But see* United States v. Smith, 47 F.3d 681, 683–84 (4th Cir. 1995) (holding that ERISA § 206(d) shields pensions from creditors even after they have been distributed).

[88] The legislative history of the anti-alienation rules and their exceptions is sparse. The rules and their limited exceptions are only mentioned three times in the six extensive committee reports prepared during congressional consideration of ERISA. *See* Commercial Mortgage Ins., Inc. v. Citizens Nat'l Bank of Dallas, 526 F. Supp. 510, 516–17 (N.D. Tex. 1981) (discussing legislative history).

[89] H.R. Rep. No. 93-807, at 68 (1974), *reprinted in* 1974 U.S.C.A.A.N. 4670, 4734.

[90] Kennedy v. Plan Administrator for DuPont Savings and Investment Plan, 555 U.S. 285, 294 (2009).

[91] Guidry v. Sheet Metal Workers Nat'l Pension Fund, 493 U.S. 365, 376 (1990).

[92] 555 U.S. 285 (2009).

meaning."[93] Specifically, assign means "[t]o transfer; as to assign property, or some interest therein," while alienate means "[t]o convey; to transfer the title to the property."[94] The Court held that a spouse's waiver of her husband's pension during a divorce proceeding did not constitute an assignment of the benefit to her husband or his estate and thus did not violate ERISA's anti-alienation provision.[95]

The Treasury Regulations define the terms assign and alienate to include two types of arrangements:

(1) any arrangement that provides for the payment to the employer of the participant's benefits which would otherwise be due to the plan participant;[96] and

(2) any arrangement, direct or indirect, pursuant to which a third party acquires from a participant or beneficiary an enforceable right or interest against the plan in all or part of the benefit payment which is, or may become, payable to the participant or beneficiary.[97]

[C] Exceptions to the Anti-Alienation Provision

ERISA contains four express statutory exceptions to the anti-alienation provision:

(1) loans to plan participants;[98]

(2) 10% exception for benefits in pay status;[99]

(3) Qualified Domestic Relations Orders (QDROs);[100] and

(4) claims for fiduciary breaches with respect to the plan.[101]

In addition, the Treasury Regulations and lower courts have found a few other exceptions to the alienation provision.

For example, the Treasury Regulations provide that the anti-alienation provision does not preclude the federal government from enforcing a federal tax levy or collecting a judgment arising from unpaid taxes,[102] and lower courts have held that the anti-alienation provision does not apply to criminal restitutions

---

[93] *Id.* at 292.

[94] *Id.* (citing Black's Law Dictionary).

[95] *Id.* at 292. Although the Court held that the participant's ex-spouse's waiver did not violate ERISA's anti-alienation provision, the Court did not give effect to the waiver because the plan participant failed to change his beneficiary designation pursuant to the plan documents. *Id.* at 304.

[96] Treas. Reg. § 1.401(a)-13(c)(1)(i).

[97] Treas. Reg. § 1.401(a)-13(c)(1)(ii).

[98] ERISA § 206(d)(2); IRC § 401(a)(13)(A).

[99] ERISA § 206(d)(2); IRC § 401(a)(13)(A).

[100] ERISA § 206(d)(3); IRC § 401(a)(13)(B).

[101] ERISA § 206(d)(4); IRC § 401(a)(13)(C).

[102] Treas. Reg. 1.401(a)-13(b)(2). *See also* Ragan, 39 U. Balt. L. Rev., at 85–87 (stating that "[i]t is generally accepted that ERISA does not hinder the government's rights to levy a delinquent taxpayer's interest in her pension benefits" and discussing authority).

ordered under the federal Mandatory Victim Restitution Act.[103]

[1]   Loans to Plan Participants

Prior to the enactment of ERISA, the IRC prohibited transaction rules authorized plan participants to borrow from their plans under certain circumstances. When Congress enacted ERISA, it included an express exception from the anti-alienation provisions for loans to plan participants[104] that

(1)   are secured by the participant's accrued vested benefit and

(2)   satisfy the prohibited transaction rules.[105]

ERISA's legislative history explains that the exception for plan loans was intended to retain the pre-ERISA practice of permitting plan loans.[106]

At first blush, permitting plan loans clearly appears to be contrary to underlying purpose of the anti-alienation provisions — ensuring that accrued benefits are available for retirement purposes. Upon closer reflection, however, permitting plan loans may arguably increase the availability of benefits at retirement because the availability of loans may encourage employees (particularly nonhighly compensated employees) to participate in retirement programs because they know that they may be able to borrow from their plans if necessary.[107]

[2]   10% Exception for Benefits in Pay Status

When ERISA was originally enacted, it contained a second express exception to the anti-alienation provisions to permit participants in pay status (that is, participants currently receiving benefits) to assign up to 10% of their benefit payments so long as the assignment is voluntary and revocable and is not used to defray plan administration costs.[108] An assignment is not considered voluntary if it is pursuant

---

[103] *See, e.g.*, United States v. Novak, 476 F.3d 1041, 1049 (9th Cir. 2009) (holding that federal Mandatory Victims Restitution Act (MVRA) overrides ERISA's anti-alienation rule and permits attachment of retirement benefits for purposes of satisfying restitution order); United States v. Irving, 452 F.3d 110, 126 (2d Cir. 2006) (same). *See also* Ragan, 39 U. Balt. L. Rev., at 89–94 (noting that courts have generally interpreted the MVRA as an exception to the anti-alienation provision and discussing *Novak* and its arguments in favor and against applying MVRA to enforce restitution orders against pension plan benefits).

[104] For a discussion of the tax rules applicable to plan loans, see Chapter 10 § 10.04[E][2][c].

[105] ERISA § 206(d)(2). *See* also IRC § 401(a)(13)(A). For a discussion of the prohibited transaction rules, see Chapter 6 § 6.06.

[106] H. Rep. 807, 93d Cong., 2d Sess. 69 (1974) ("[A] plan will be permitted to provide for voluntary and revocable assignments (not to exceed 10% of any benefit payment). This provision is not intended to interfere with the current practice in many plans of using vested benefits as collateral for reasonable loans from the plans, where the 'prohibited transactions' provisions of present law ([then] sec. 503 of the Code) and other fiduciary requirements are not violated."). For a discussion of plan loans, see Chapter 10 § 10.04[E].

[107] *Cf.* Joint Comm. On Taxation, General Explanation of Revenue Provisions of the Tax Equity and Fiscal Responsibility Act of 1982, H.R. Doc. 97-4691, at 294–95 (1982) (recognizing that blanket prohibition against plan loans may deter nonhighly compensated employees from participating in retirement savings programs).

[108] ERISA § 206(d)(2). *See also* IRC § 401(a)(13)(A); Treas. Reg. § 1.401(a)-13(d)(1).

to an attachment, levy, garnishment, or other form of legal or equitable process.[109]

ERISA's legislative history does not explain the reason for this exception.[110] Professor Sharon Reece has speculated that the exception may be intended "to allow some freedom to the pensioner while restricting the pensioner and other possible third party claimants from pouncing on the payments at a time when the retiree needs it most."[111]

[3]   Qualified Domestic Relations Orders (QDROs)[112]

Retirement benefits often represent a major marital asset of divorcing couples.[113] When ERISA was originally enacted, there was no exception from the anti-alienation provision for child support or alimony payments. The courts were split as to whether ERISA preempted state domestic relations law such that the anti-alienation provision applied to family support obligations.[114] In light of this uncertainty and "taking into account changes in work patterns, the status of marriage as an economic partnership, and the substantial contribution to that partnership [made by] spouses who work . . . in and outside the home,"[115] Congress amended ERISA in 1984 to create an express exception from the anti-alienation provision for "qualified domestic relations orders" (QDROs).[116]

A QDRO is a domestic relations order (DRO) that creates or recognizes the existence of an alternate payee's right to, or assigns to an alternate payee the right to, receive all or a portion of the benefits payable with respect to a participant under a qualified retirement plan that complies with special requirements.[117] An alternate payee can be a spouse, former spouse, child, or other dependent of a participant.[118]

---

[109] ERISA § 206(d)(2). *See also* IRC § 401(a)(13)(A); Treas. Reg. § 1.401(a)-13(d)(1).

[110] The few references to the exception simply state the rule without explaining the reason for the exception. *See* Commercial Mortgage Ins. Inc. v. Citizens Nat'l Bank of Dallas, 526 F. Supp. 510, 516–17 (N.D. Tex. 1981) ("Thus far, the Labor Department has apparently not issued any regulations interpreting Sections 1056(d) or 1144(a), although it has such authority under ERISA . . . . The legislative history is similarly cryptic with only three references to the sections in all the six committee reports prepared during congressional consideration of the statute.").

[111] Sharon Reece, *The Gilded Gates of Pension Protection: Amending the Anti-Alienation Provision of ERISA Section 206(d)*, 80 OR. L. REV. 379, 392 (2001).

[112] For an overview of QDROs, see Dep't of Labor: QDROs: The Division of Retirement through Qualified Domestic Relations Orders, *available at* http://www.dol.gov/ebsa/publications/qdros.html.

[113] *See* Aaron Klein, *Divorce, Death, and Posthumous QDROs: When is it Too Late for a Divorcee to Claim Pension Benefits under ERISA?*, 26 CARDOZO L. REV. 1651, 1657 n.36 (2005) ("Pension rights are usually a divorcing couple's largest or second largest asset (the other being family home) and are usually a major source of alimony and child support payments.").

[114] *See* Terrence Cain, *A Primer on the History and Proper Drafting of Qualified Domestic-Relations Orders*, 28 T.M. COOLEY L. REV. 417, 453 (2011); Ragan, 39 U. BALT. L. REV., at 81–82.

[115] S. Rep. No. 98-575 (1984), at 1 *reprinted in* 1984 U.S.C.A.A.N. 2547.

[116] Retirement Equity Act of 1984, Pub. L. No. 98-397 § 104, 98 Stat. 1426, 1433–36, reprinted in 1984 U.S.C.A.A.N. 2547, 2549 (adding ERISA § 206(d)(3); IRC § 401(a)(13)).

[117] ERISA § 206(d)(3)(B)(i); IRC § 414(p)(1)(A).

[118] ERISA § 206(d)(3)(K); IRC § 414(p)(8).

A DRO is a judgment, decree, or order (including the approval of a property settlement) that is made pursuant to state domestic relations law (including community property law) and that relates to the provision of child support, alimony payments, or marital property rights for the benefit of a spouse, former spouse, child, or other dependent of a participant.[119]

In order for a DRO to qualify as a QDRO, it must contain the following information:

    (1)   the name and last known mailing address of the participant and each alternate payee;

    (2)   the name of each plan to which the order applies;

    (3)   the dollar amount or percentage (or the method of determining the amount or percentage) of the benefit to be paid to the alternate payee; and

    (4)   the number of payments or time period to which the order applies.[120]

Plans must establish reasonable procedures for determining whether a DRO is a QDRO and for administering distributions pursuant to QDROs.[121]

The plan administrator is the individual or entity initially responsible for determining whether a DRO is a QDRO. The plan administrator must promptly notify the participant and alternate payee(s) when a DRO is received and provide them with the plan's procedures for determining whether a DRO is a QDRO.[122] Within a reasonable time after receiving the DRO, the plan administrator must determine whether the DRO is qualified and must notify the participant and alternate payee(s) of its determination.[123]

In *Kennedy v. Plan Administrator for DuPont Savings and Investment Plan*,[124] the Supreme Court made clear that a QDRO cannot be used simply to waive the right to a pension in divorce.[125] Rather, it must be used to create an alternate payee's interest in a pension.[126]

The IRS has issued guidance, including draft language, to assist attorneys, employees, spouses, former spouses, and plan administrators in drafting and reviewing QDROs.[127]

[4]   Fiduciary Breaches with Respect to the Plan

When ERISA was originally enacted, it did not contain an exception for criminal misconduct.

---

[119] ERISA § 206(d)(3)(B)(ii); IRC § 414(p)(1)(B).

[120] ERISA § 206(d)(3)(C)(i)–(v); IRC § 414(p)(2)(A)–(D).

[121] ERISA § 206(d)(3)(G)(ii); IRC § 414(p)(6)(B).

[122] ERISA § 206(d)(3)(G)(i)(I); IRC § 414(p)(6)(A)(i).

[123] ERISA § 206(d)(3)(G)(i)(II); IRC § 414(p)(6)(A)(ii).

[124] 555 U.S. 285 (2009).

[125] *Id.* at 296.

[126] *Id.* at 296–97.

[127] IRS 1997-1 C.B. 379, Notice 97-11.

In *Guidry v. Sheet Metal Workers National Pension Fund*,[128] the Supreme Court declined to approve a generalized equitable exception to the anti-alienation rule for employee malfeasance or criminal misconduct.[129] The Court declared that "Section 206(d) reflects a considered congressional policy choice, a decision to safeguard a stream of income for pensioners (and their dependents, who may be, and perhaps usually are, blameless), even if that decision prevents others from securing relief for the wrongs done [to] them." The Court noted that ERISA's anti-alienation provision can only be defended on the ground that certain broad social policies sometimes take precedence over equity between the particular parties.[130] It would make little sense to create such a policy and then refuse to enforce it whenever enforcement appears inequitable.[131] In the Court's view, Congress, and only Congress, should undertake the task of creating exceptions from the anti-alienation rule.[132]

Seven years after the Court decided *Guidry*, Congress added an express exception to the anti-alienation provision for claims against a pension plan for fiduciary breaches with respect to the plan.[133] Specifically, the exception permits recovery from the plan for crimes involving the plan,[134] civil judgments for fiduciary breach claims,[135] and settlements between the participant and Secretary of Labor or PBGC for fiduciary breaches.[136] The exception does not extend to crimes against the employer that do not involve the plan.[137]

[D] The Anti-alienation Provision and the Bankruptcy Estate

In *Patterson v. Shumate*,[138] the Supreme Court, addressed the interaction between ERISA's anti-alienation provision, and the federal Bankruptcy Code. In a unanimous opinion, the Court held that section 541(c)(2) of the Bankruptcy Code

---

[128] 493 U.S. 365 (1990).

[129] *Id.* at 376.

[130] *Id.* at 376.

[131] *Id.* at 376–77.

[132] *Id.* at 376. For an argument that lower court's decisions holding that the federal Mandatory Victims Restitution Act creates an exception to the antialienation provision is inconsistent with *Guidry*, see Ragan, 39 U. BALT. L. REV., at 95 & 100–01.

[133] Taxpayer Relief Act of 1997, Pub. L. No. 105-34, § 1502, 111 Stat. 788, 1058–61 (adding ERISA § 206(d)(4); IRC § 401(a)(13)(C)).

[134] ERISA § 206(d)(4)(A)(i); IRC § 401(a)(13)(C)(i)(I).

[135] ERISA § 206(d)(4)(A)(ii); IRC § 401(a)(13)(C)(i)(II).

[136] ERISA § 206(d)(4)(A)(iii); IRC § 401(a)(13)(C)(i)(III).

[137] *See, e.g.*, Thomas v. Bostwick, 2013 U.S. Dist. LEXIS 134370, at *11–12 (N. D. Ca. Sept. 19, 2013). For arguments that an express statutory exception should be extended for general criminal misconduct and against tortfeasors generally, see Ragan, 39 U. BALT. L. REV. 63 (arguing that Congress should amend ERISA to incorporate an exception to the anti-alienation provision for qualified criminal restitution orders); Reece, 80 OR. L. REV., at 392 (arguing that ERISA should be amended to extend exception to alienation provision to adjudicated crimes and torts no matter against whom the crime or tort is perpetrated).

[138] 504 U.S. 753 (1992).

excludes from a debtor's bankruptcy estate the assets of an "ERISA-qualified" pension plan[139] because such a plan must contain an anti-alienation provision.

In 2005, Congress amended the Bankruptcy Code to clarify and expand the type of plans that may be excluded from bankruptcy estates.[140] Specifically, it permits debtors to exclude from the bankruptcy estate retirement funds or accounts that are exempt from tax under IRC §§ 401, 403, 408A, 414, 547, or 501(a).[141]

The Bankruptcy Act imposes a $1 million cap on the amount of a debtor's interest in a traditional or Roth IRA that may be claimed as exempt. The $1 million cap may be increased if the "interests of justice so require."[142] Assets that were "rolled over" to the IRA from a qualified plan or another IRA are disregarded for purposes of this $1 million limit.[143]

In *Clark v. Rameker*,[144] the Supreme Court held that funds in an inherited IRA are not "retirement funds" for purposes of the bankruptcy exemption.

§ 5.05   MINIMUM FUNDING STANDARDS — ERISA §§ 301–305; IRC §§ 412, 430–432

Both ERISA[145] and the Internal Revenue Code[146] impose minimum funding standards on defined benefit pension plans.[147] The minimum funding standards are quite complex,[148] and actuaries, rather than lawyers, are generally responsible for applying the standards. Nevertheless, attorneys should have a basic understanding of the standards and how they affect plan sponsors and their ability to modify plan benefits.

[A]   Funding Basics

Funding refers to the process by which an employer[149] sets aside funds in advance to pay for pension benefits before the benefits must be paid.[150]

---

[139] For a discussion of the meaning of "ERISA-qualified plan," see Chapter 2 § 2.05.

[140] Bankruptcy Abuse Prevention and Consumer Protection Act, Pub. L. No. 109-8 § 323, 119 Stat. 23, 62–65 (2005) (amending Bankruptcy Code § 522, 11 U.S.C. § 522(b)(3)(C), (d)(12)).

[141] 11 U.S.C. § 522(b)(3)(C).

[142] 11 U.S.C. § 522(n).

[143] *Id.*

[144] 134 S. Ct. 2242 (2014).

[145] ERISA §§ 301–305.

[146] IRC §§ 412, 430, 431, 432.

[147] Technically, the minimum funding standards also apply to money purchase plans and target benefit plans. Satisfaction of the requirement as applied to defined contribution plans, however, is quite straightforward. *See* § 5.05[A][1].

[148] Kathryn J. Kennedy, *The Demise of Defined Benefit Plans for Private Employers*, 121 Tax Notes 179, 181 (Oct. 13, 2008).

[149] The employee may also set aside funds in advance if the plan calls for employee contributions.

[150] McGill et al., Fundamentals of Private Pensions 616 (9th ed. 2010).

In theory, there are three different methods of funding a defined benefit plan: (1) on a pay-as-you-go

[1] Funding Defined Contribution Plans

Funding a defined contribution plan is quite straightforward. The employer[151] simply sets aside the amount called for under the terms of the plan.

Example

Employer's money purchase plan requires Employer to make an annual contribution equal to 2% of each participant's eligible compensation. The total eligible compensation under the plan is $1,000,000. Employer must contribute $20,000 to the plan that year (.02 x $1,000,000 = $20,000).

[2] Funding Defined Benefit Plans

Funding a defined benefit plan involves a much more complex process.

Unlike in a defined contribution plan, an employer does not promise to contribute a specific amount to a defined benefit plan. Instead, the employer promises to provide employees with a specified benefit as determined under the terms of the plan.[152] The ultimate cost of the promised benefit depends on a variety of factors, such as life expectancy, future compensation levels, employee turnover, and investment earnings on plan assets. Thus, determining how much should be set aside in advance to fund a defined benefit plan necessarily requires complex actuarial calculations that take into account those factors.

[B] Pre-ERISA Funding of Defined Benefit Plans

Prior to the enactment of ERISA, no state or federal law required that employee benefit plans be funded.[153] Because pre-ERISA law did not impose funding rules, many pension plans were underfunded, that is, the plans did not have sufficient assets set aside to pay for the promised benefits.[154] When the

---

basis, (2) on a terminal basis, or (3) on a prefunded basis. In a plan funded on a pay-as-you go basis, an employer does not set aside funds in advance to pay for plan benefits. Instead, the employer pays benefits from current assets as the benefits become due. Under the terminal funding method, an employer sets aside a lump sum of money to fund a retiree's benefit when the employee retirees. Finally, under a prefunded system, an employer sets aside funds during an employee's working life to fund the employee's retirement. ERISA requires that defined benefit plans be prefunded and thus, this section will only discus this method of funding.

[151] (and employee if the plan provides for employee contributions).

[152] For a more detailed discussion of the difference between defined benefit and defined contribution plans, see Chapter 2 § 2.02.

[153] Dana M. Muir, *Fiduciary Status As an Employer's Shield: The Perversity of ERISA Fiduciary Law*, 2 U. PA. J. LAB. & EMP. L. 391, 401–02 (2000). For a survey of pension funding prior to the enactment of ERISA, see James Wooten, *The Most Glorious Failure in the Business: The Studebaker-Packard Corporation and the Origins of ERISA*, 49 BUFFALO L. REV. 683, 697–704 (2001).

[154] As Patrick Purcell and Jennifer Staman of the Congressional Research Service have explained:

Determining whether a pension is adequately funded requires converting the future stream of pension payments into the amount that would be needed today to pay off those liabilities all at once. This amount — the "present value" of the plan's liabilities — is then compared with the value of the plan's assets. An underfunded plan is one in which the value of the plan's assets falls short of the present value of its liabilities. Converting a future stream

underfunded plans terminated, many plan participants did not receive the benefits they had been promised.[155] In the most famous example, almost 7,000 Studebaker employees lost most or all of their promised benefits when the Studebaker automobile plant terminated its underfunded plan in 1963.[156]

[C] Purpose of Minimum Funding Standards

Congress introduced minimum funding standards in ERISA in order to ensure that defined benefit plans have adequate funds to pay employees and their beneficiaries their promised benefits.[157] Thus, the primary purpose of the minimum funding standards is to protect plan participants and enhance the security of their promised benefits.[158]

The minimum funding standards also serve a second purpose, protecting the Pension Benefit Guaranty Corporation (PBGC) program from abuse.[159] As discussed in Chapter 11 § 11.03, ERISA established the PBGC to guarantee that vested participants receive their promised benefits up to certain limits. By requiring that employers adequately fund their pension plans, the minimum funding standards reduce the risk that the PBGC will be required to pay pension benefits in the event of plan termination.[160]

---

of payments (or income) into a present value requires the future payments (or income) to be discounted using an appropriate interest rate. Other things being equal, the *higher* the interest rate, the *smaller* the present value of the future payments (or income), and vice versa.

Patrick Purcell & Jennifer Staman, *Summary of the Retirement Income Security Act*, CRS Report for Congress RL34443 18–19 (May 12, 2009).

[155] *Cf.* Cong. Rec. 4279 (1974) (statement of Rep. Brademas) (noting that according to a Department of Treasury and Labor study, in 1972 alone, more than 15,000 pension plan participants lost their retirement benefits because their pension plans terminated without sufficient assets to meet all of their obligations).

[156] *See* Wooten, 49 Buffalo L. Rev., at 683–84. *See also* Chapter 1 § 1.04[B].

[157] *See* ERISA § 2 ("owing to the inadequacy of current minimum standards, the soundness and stability of plans with respect to adequate funds to pay promised benefits may be endangered; that owing to the termination of plans before requisite funds have been accumulated, employees and their beneficiaries have been deprived of anticipated benefits . . . it is therefore desirable . . . that minimum standards be provided assuring the equitable character of such plans and their financial soundness"). *See also* Perdue, Qualified Pension & Profit Sharing Plans, at ¶ 13.04[1] ("Both ERISA and the Code set forth requirements, discussed below, that must be satisfied in order to ensure adequate funding of these costs.").

[158] *Cf.* McGill et al., Fundamentals of Private Pensions, at 616.

[159] *Cf. id. See also* Kennedy, *The Demise of Defined Benefit Plans*, 121 Tax Notes, at 181 (discussing PBGC's efforts to reduce its liability through amendments to the minimum funding standards).

[160] *Cf.* Bender's Federal Income Taxation of Retirement Plans 10-6 (Alvin D. Lurie, ed., 2008) (stating that under the Pension Protection Act of 2006, "[t]he ideal is for every plan always to be fully funded, on a termination basis, for all accrued benefits. To the extent that that goal is achieved, the PBGC will be like a fire insurance company in terrain saturated by water."). For an argument that the minimum funding standards do not adequately reduce the PBGC's risk and should be replaced with a full funding standard, see Eric D. Chason, *Outlawing Pension-Funding Shortfalls*, 26 Va. Tax Rev. 519 (2007).

[D] Minimum Funding Standards Prior to the Pension Protection Act of 2006

Prior to the Pension Protection Act of 2006, the minimum funding standards afforded employers considerable flexibility in the funding of their plans.[161] For example, ERISA initially authorized six different actuarial cost methods,[162] and ERISA permitted actuaries discretion in setting actuarial assumptions, including the interest rate and mortality table (estimating life expectancy).[163]

Overall, the rules took a long-term approach to funding, similar to the approach taken by homeowners to the funding of their long-term home mortgages.[164] In essence, the rules assumed that employers would maintain their defined benefit plans for the indefinite future and permitted employers to make relatively level or even annual contributions to fund their plans.[165]

[E] Minimum Funding Standards Under the Pension Protection Act of 2006

For a variety of reasons, the minimum funding standards proved to be inadequate.[166] In the Pension Protection Act of 2006,[167] Congress repealed the old minimum funding standards and replaced them with new, tighter, less flexible standards.[168] The new rules significantly speed up the prefunding of pension costs[169] and impose greater benefit restrictions on underfunded plans.[170]

---

[161] For a brief overview of key elements in the traditional funding standards, see McGill et al., Fundamentals of Private Pensions, at 619–25; Kennedy, *The Demise of Defined Benefit Plans*, 121 Tax Notes 179, 181–83 (Oct. 13, 2008). For a detailed discussion of the minimum funding standards in effect prior to the enactment of the Pension Protection Act of 2006, see Kathryn J. Kennedy, *Pension Funding Reform: It's Time to Get the Rules Right (Part 1)*, 108 Tax Notes 907 (Aug. 22, 2005).

[162] ERISA § 3(31). A funding or cost method is a recognized actuarial technique used to establish the amount and incidence of the annual actuarial cost of pension benefits and expenses. Funding methods are designed to amortize (spread over time) three general types of plan costs: (1) normal cost, (2) accrued liability, and (3) experience gains and losses. Generally, normal cost reflects the present value of future benefits, accrued liability reflects the present value of benefits attributable to a prior year, and experience gains or losses reflect the difference between the plan's expected earnings and actual earnings or losses. Perdue, Qualified Pension & Profit Sharing Plans, at ¶ 13.05. *See also* Kennedy, *The Demise of Defined Benefit Plans*, 121 Tax Notes 179, 182 (noting that "[o]ver the years, Congress grew weary of the variety of cost methods, viewing them not as effective accounting schemes for the assignment of costs to appropriate plan years, but more as manipulation to forestall proper funding of the plan").

[163] Kennedy, *The Demise of Defined Benefit Plans*, 121 Tax Notes, at 182.

[164] *Id.* at 181.

[165] *Id.* For a detailed discussion of the minimum funding standards in effect prior to the enactment of the Pension Protection Act of 2006, see Kathryn J. Kennedy, *Pension Funding Reform: (Part 1)*, 108 Tax Notes 907.

[166] For a discussion of the inadequacy of the rules, see *id.*

[167] Pub. L. No. 109-280, 120 Stat. 780 (2006).

[168] Kennedy, *The Demise of Defined Benefit Plans*, 121 Tax Notes, at 180.

[169] ERISA § 303; IRC § 430.

[170] ERISA § 206(g); IRC § 436.

Nevertheless, the new minimum funding standards do not entirely eliminate the risk of underfunded plans.[171]

The new rules differ from the old rules in their basic approach to pension plans. Unlike the old rules, which treated pension plans as ongoing entities with an indefinite future, the new rules treat plans as if they were terminating and require that benefits be funded as they are earned.[172] In addition, they reduce flexibility in a variety of ways. For example, the new funding standards no longer permit discretion with respect to the actuarial cost method to be used. Instead, the new rules only permit one actuarial cost method, the unit credit cost method.[173] Similarly, the new funding rules eliminate actuarial discretion with respect to interest rate[174] and mortality assumptions.

The new minimum funding standards only apply to single-employer plans.[175] Generally, multiemployer plans are subject to the same funding rules as were in effect under prior law.[176] This section focuses on the new single-employer plan rules.

[1] Minimum Required Contribution

Under the new minimum funding standards, the minimum required contribution is determined by comparing the value of the plan's assets (reduced by any prefunding balance[177] and funding standard carryover balance)[178] with the plan's funding target. The plan's funding target is the present value of all benefits accrued

---

[171] For a critique of the new minimum funding standards and argument that they should be replaced with a full funding standard, see Chason, 26 VA. TAX REV. 519.

[172] PERDUE, QUALIFIED PENSION & PROFIT SHARING PLANS, at ¶ 13.04.

[173] *See* Kennedy, *The Demise of Defined Benefit Plans*, 121 TAX NOTES, at 192–93.

[174] "The discount rate choice is crucial; a 1 percentage point change in discount rates usually changes the net present value, the amount of funds needed now, by 10–15%. A high discount rate allows companies to put in less money" while a low discount rate requires companies to contribute more to the plan. Douglas J. Elliott, *A Guide to the Pension Benefit Guaranty Corporation, in* INITIATIVE ON BUSINESS AND PUBLIC POLICY AT BROOKINGS 12 (May 20, 2009).

The new funding rules require future liabilities to be discounted using three different interest rates, depending on when the liability must be paid. A short-term interest rate is used in calculating the present value of liabilities that must be paid within five years. A mid-term interest rate is used in calculating the present value of liabilities that must be paid in five to 20 years. A long-term term interest rate is used in calculating the present value of liabilities that must be paid in more than 20 years. The interest rates are based upon the 24-month averages of high-quality corporate bond yields which fall within those periods. ERISA § 303(h); IRC § 430(h). For additional discussion of the new interest rate rules, see Purcell & Staman, CRS Report for Congress RL34443, at 19; Kennedy, *The Demise of Defined Benefit Plans*, 121 TAX NOTES, at 191–92.

[175] The minimum funding standards applicable to multiemployer plans are set forth in ERISA § 304, and IRC § 431.

[176] BENDER'S FEDERAL INCOME TAXATION OF RETIREMENT PLANS, at 10-48–10-49.

[177] A prefunding balance is a credit balance created after the enactment of the Pension Protection Act. ERISA § 303(f)(6)(B)(i); IRC § 430(f)(6)(B)(i).

[178] A funding standard carryover balance is a credit balance existing when the Pension Protection Act was enacted. ERISA § 303(f)(7); IRC § 430(f)(7).

or earned as of the beginning of the plan year.[179]

The plan's normal cost[180] is generally the present value of benefits expected to accrue (be earned) during the plan year.[181] The plan's normal cost includes any increase in benefits attributable to past service arising from an increase in salary during the plan year[182] as well as plan-related expenses to be paid from the trust.[183]

If a plan's assets (less any credit balances) are less than the funding target, the plan has a funding shortfall.[184] Generally, the funding shortfall, less any permissible credit balances, must be amortized (paid) in annual installments over seven years.[185]

If the value of plan assets (reduced by any credit balances) is less than the funding target, the minimum contribution due is equal to the sum of

(1) the target normal cost,

(2) the total of installments to amortize any shortfall, and

(3) any waiver amortization charges for a plan that has obtained a funding waiver.[186]

If the value of plan assets (reduced by any credit balances) is equal to or greater than the funding target, the minimum contribution due is

(1) the target normal cost minus

(2) the amount by which the assets exceed the funding target, but not less than zero.[187]

[2] Benefit Restrictions

If a plan is underfunded by more than a specified percentage, the provision of certain benefits may be limited:

(1) Employers are prohibited from making plan amendments that would increase benefits, provide new benefits, or alter the benefit accrual rate if the plan is less than 80% funded taking into account the plan amend-

---

[179] ERISA § 303(d)(1); IRC § 430(d)(1).

[180] Broadly defined, normal cost reflects the present value of future benefits. PERDUE, QUALIFIED PENSION & PROFIT SHARING PLANS, at ¶ 13.05.

[181] When ERISA was enacted, it permitted six different actuarial cost methods. ERISA § 3(31). The current minimum funding rules only permit one type of cost method, the unit credit cost method. Kennedy, *The Demise of Defined Benefit Plans*, 121 TAX NOTES, at 181.

[182] Thus, for example, if an employee earns a benefit for each year of service, up to 30 years of service, equal to 3% of the employee's average salary, and the employee's salary increases, the employee's earned benefit will increase in two ways. First, the employee will earn a benefit of 3% of salary, plus the employee's benefit will be based on a higher average salary.

[183] ERISA § 303(b); IRC § 430(b). MCGILL ET AL., FUNDAMENTALS OF PRIVATE PENSIONS, at 629.

[184] ERISA § 303(c)(4); IRC § 430(c)(4).

[185] ERISA § 303(c); IRC § 430(c).

[186] ERISA § 303(a)(1); IRC § 430(a)(1).

[187] ERISA § 303(a)(2); IRC § 430(a)(2).

ment.[188]

(2) Plant shutdown[189] or other contingent event benefits are prohibited if the plan is less than 60% funded or would be less than 60% funded taking into account the occurrence of the event.[190]

(3) No lump sum distributions are permitted if the funding target is less than 100% of the plan assets and the employer sponsor is bankrupt.[191]

(4) Benefit accruals must cease if the plan is less than 60% funded unless the employer contributes an amount sufficient to increase funding to 60% in addition to the minimum required contribution for the year.[192]

[3] At-Risk Plans

"At-risk" plans are subject to additional funding requirements.

A plan is at-risk if

(1) the plan assets (generally reduced by credit balances) are less than 80% of the plan's funding target, computed using the generally applicable actuarial assumptions, and

(2) the plan's assets (generally reduced by credit balances) are less than 70% of the plan's funding target, computed using the special at-risk actuarial assumptions.[193]

If the plan is determined to be at-risk, the at-risk actuarial assumptions must be used to calculate the plan's funding target for purposes of determining the amount of the funding shortfall,[194] which increases the shortfall and accelerates funding.

[4] Funding Waivers

The Secretary of Labor is authorized to grant a funding waiver if an employer is unable to satisfy the minimum funding requirements without incurring a temporary substantial business hardship and applying the requirements would be adverse to the interests of the plan participants in the aggregate.[195] If a waiver is granted, the amount of the minimum required contribution will be reduced by the waived amount, and the amount of the waived funding deficiency must be amortized over

---

[188] ERISA 206(g)(2)(A); IRC 436(c)(3).

[189] Shutdown benefits are typically negotiated between labor unions and employers and provide payments to employees if a factory or plant is shut down. Typically, shutdown benefits are not prefunded. *See* Purcell & Staman, CRS Report for Congress RL34443, at 21.

[190] ERISA § 206(g)(1); IRC § 436(b).

[191] ERISA § 206(g)(3)(B); IRC § 436(d)(2).

[192] ERISA § 206(g)(4); IRC § 436(e).

[193] ERISA § 303(i)(4)(A); IRC § 430(i)(4)(A). Under the at-risk, "worst case scenario," actuarial assumptions, retirees are assumed to retire at the earliest possible date and take the most expensive form of benefit. ERISA § 303(i)(1)(B); IRC § 430(i)(1)(B).

[194] ERISA § 303(i)(1)(A); IRC § 430(i)(1)(A).

[195] IRC § 412(c)(1)(A).

five years.[196] Generally, a waiver must not be granted with respect to a plan for more than three of any 15 consecutive plan years.[197]

A funding waiver may only be granted if the business hardship is temporary. The following factors are taken into account in determining whether there is a temporary substantial business hardship:

(1) the employer is operating at an economic loss;

(2) there is substantial unemployment or underemployment in the trade or business and in the industry;

(3) the sales and profits of the industry are depressed or declining; and

(4) it is reasonable to expect that the plan will only continue if the waiver is granted.[198]

[5] Effect of Failure to Satisfy Minimum Funding Standards

Failure to satisfy the minimum standards results in a two-tier excise tax.[199]

---

[196] IRC §§ 412(c)(1)(B), 430(e)(1).

[197] IRC § 412(c)(1).

[198] IRC § 412(c)(2).

[199] IRC § 4971.

Chapter 6

FIDUCIARY STANDARDS

§ 6.01 INTRODUCTION

Prior to the enactment of ERISA, "kickbacks, embezzlement, outrageous administrative costs, and excessive investments in the securities of plan sponsors/employers"[1] were a serious problem in many employee benefit plans. In order to address this problem,[2] Congress established explicit fiduciary "standards of conduct, responsibility, and obligations"[3] in enacting ERISA. The fiduciary standards apply to virtually all employee benefit plans, including both pension plans and welfare benefit plans.[4]

ERISA's fiduciary standards are set forth in sections 401 through 414 of ERISA. ERISA's "fiduciary package" also includes ERISA's disclosure rules, principally ERISA §§ 101–105, which require the disclosure of information upon which fiduciary entitlement rests,[5] and ERISA's administration and enforcement provisions, ERISA §§ 501–514, which supply the remedial and enforcement structure for vindicating rights.[6]

ERISA's fiduciary standards are set forth solely in ERISA. The Internal Revenue Code, however, imposes similar requirements in some instances. For example, both ERISA and the Internal Revenue Code set forth prohibited transaction provisions.[7] In addition, IRC § 401(a)(2) imposes on qualified plans an exclusive benefit requirement that is similar to the exclusive purpose requirement imposed under ERISA § 404(a)(1)(A).

This chapter focuses on the fiduciary standards set forth in ERISA §§ 401 through 414.

---

[1] Elaine McClatchey Darroch, Mertens v. Hewitt Associates: *The Supreme Court's Dismantling of Civil Enforcement Under ERISA*, 1994 DET. CL REV. 1089, 1092 (1994).

[2] *See* Conf. Rep. No. 93-1280, 93d Cong., 2d Sess. 303, 306–309 (1974) (explaining that one of the motivations for enactment of ERISA was to protect employee benefit funds from being exploited for the benefit of employers who maintain them); S. Rep. No. 93-383, 93d Cong., 1st Sess. 100 (1973) (same).

[3] ERISA § 2(b).

[4] ERISA § 401(a).

[5] ERISA's disclosure rules are addressed in Chapter 4 § 4.03.

[6] ERISA's administrative and enforcement provisions are discussed in Chapter 7.

[7] ERISA's prohibited transaction provisions are set forth in ERISA § 406–408, while the Internal Revenue Code's prohibited transaction rules are set forth in IRC § 4975.

§ 6.02   OVERVIEW OF FIDUCIARY RESPONSIBILITY UNDER ERISA

Part 4 of Subtitle B of Title of I of ERISA is entitled "Fiduciary Responsibility." It consists of 14 separate sections, ERISA § 401–414.

The first section, ERISA § 401, sets forth the coverage rules for ERISA's fiduciary responsibility provisions. Pursuant to that section, ERISA's fiduciary rules apply to virtually all employees benefit plans subject to ERISA.[8] Thus, they apply to pension plans as well as welfare plans, and they apply to funded plans as well as unfunded plans.[9]

Section 402(a) of ERISA requires that every employee benefit plan be established and maintained pursuant to a written document and that the written document identify one or more "named fiduciaries" who have the authority to control and manage the operation and administration of the plan. Section 402(b) requires that every plan describe the structure of the plan and the manner in which it is to be administered.

Section 403 of ERISA requires that all plan assets, other than assets that take the form of insurance, be held in trust. Although ERISA requires that all plan assets be held in trust, ERISA plans differ from other trusts in that they originate from a contract, specifically an employment contract, rather than a trust. Thus, a recurrent issue that arises in applying the ERISA fiduciary rules is how to disentangle the overlap between trust law and contract law and how to determine which law should govern.

Section 404 of ERISA sets forth the substantive fiduciary duties. For the most part, it codifies the duties imposed on trustees under trust common law. Specifically, ERISA § 404(a) sets forth four basic fiduciary rules:

(1)   the exclusive purpose rule,

(2)   the prudent person rule,

(3)   the diversification rule, and

(4)   the requirement that plan documents be followed unless they conflict with ERISA's requirements.

Section 405 of ERISA sets forth the rules for determining when one fiduciary will be liable for the breach of another fiduciary. Because ERISA, unlike traditional trust law, contemplates multiple fiduciaries with limited liability, section 405 determines the scope of each fiduciary's liability with respect to the actions or inactions of its co-fiduciaries.

---

[8]   ERISA § 4(b) exempts certain plans, such as governmental and church plans, from ERISA. ERISA § 4(b). The fiduciary rules do not apply to plans that are exempt from ERISA.

[9]   Section 401(a) of ERISA sets forth two narrow exceptions to its broad coverage. First, it excepts from coverage unfunded "top hat" plans, that is, plans that are both unfunded and maintained by an employer primarily for the purpose of providing deferred compensation to a select group of management or highly compensated employees. ERISA § 401(a)(1). Second, it excepts any agreement under IRC § 736 which provides payments to a retired or deceased partner or to a deceased partner's successor in interest. ERISA § 401(a)(2).

Sections 406 through 408 of ERISA supplement Section 404's express fiduciary duties with a "prohibited transaction" regime. Sections 406 and 407 categorically bar or limit transactions that are likely to injure employee benefit plans. Section 408 of ERISA tempers the broad reach of sections 406 and 407 by statutorily exempting certain transactions that would otherwise be prohibited and authorizing the Secretary of Labor to grant additional class and individual exemptions from the prohibited transaction rules.

ERISA § 409 imposes personal liability on a fiduciary for breach of a fiduciary duty. The provision is enforced through ERISA § 502(a)(2).

ERISA § 410 prohibits a plan from relieving a fiduciary from its fiduciary duties or liability for any breaches of its fiduciary duties. It does, however, expressly permit a fiduciary to be insured against any such liability.

ERISA § 411 prohibits individuals who have been convicted of certain crimes from serving as a plan fiduciary.

ERISA § 412 imposes bonding requirements on plan officials.

ERISA § 413 sets forth a statute of limitations on fiduciary claims.

ERISA § 414 sets forth the effective date for ERISA's fiduciary rules. All of the fiduciary rules are currently effective.

FIDUCIARY
RESPONSIBILITY

Part 4 of Subtitle B of
Title I of ERISA

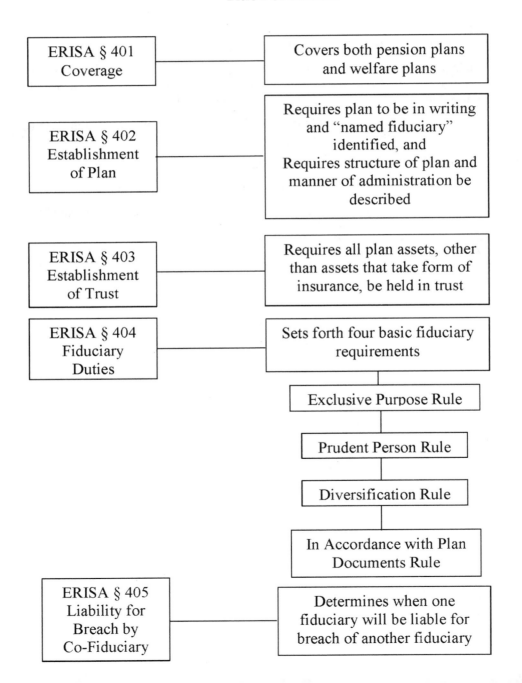

| ERISA § 401 Coverage | Covers both pension plans and welfare plans |

| ERISA § 402 Establishment of Plan | Requires plan to be in writing and "named fiduciary" identified, and Requires structure of plan and manner of administration be described |

| ERISA § 403 Establishment of Trust | Requires all plan assets, other than assets that take form of insurance, be held in trust |

| ERISA § 404 Fiduciary Duties | Sets forth four basic fiduciary requirements |

Exclusive Purpose Rule

Prudent Person Rule

Diversification Rule

In Accordance with Plan Documents Rule

| ERISA § 405 Liability for Breach by Co-Fiduciary | Determines when one fiduciary will be liable for breach of another fiduciary |

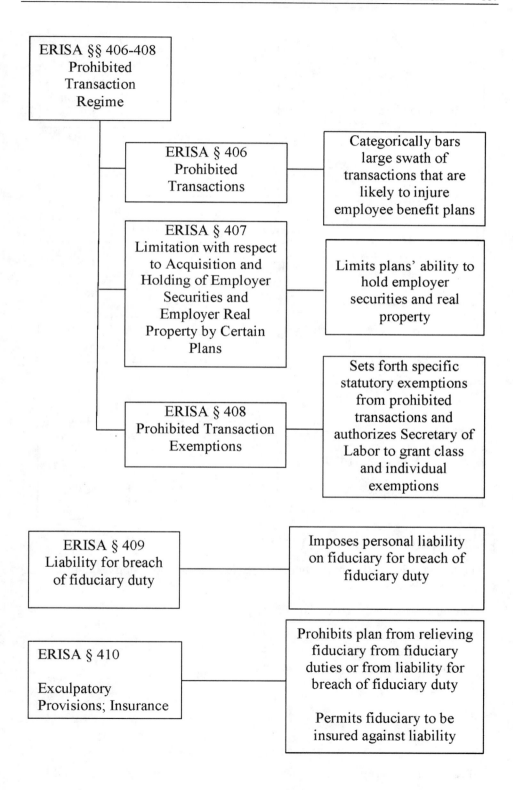

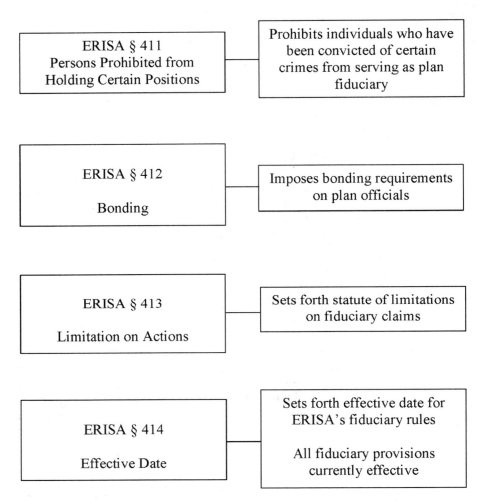

§ 6.03　WHO IS A FIDUCIARY?

The threshold question in applying ERISA's fiduciary provisions is determining who is a fiduciary.[10]

Fiduciary status may arise in one of two ways:

(1)　one may be named a fiduciary under the plan document, or

(2)　one may qualify as a fiduciary under ERISA § 3(21)(A)'s functional definition of a fiduciary.

---

[10]　Pegram v. Herdrich, 530 U.S. 211, 226 (2000).

[A]   Named Fiduciary — ERISA § 402(a)

ERISA requires that every employee benefit plan provide for one or more "named fiduciaries"[11] who jointly or severally have authority to control and manage the operation and administration of the employee benefit plan.[12] A "named fiduciary" must be either specifically named in the plan instrument or identified pursuant to a procedure specified in the plan.[13]

The named fiduciary may be an individual, a specifically identified corporate officer, such as treasurer, one or more committees made up of the employers' employees, or the employer itself.[14] Because the named fiduciary often does not have the time or expertise to properly control and manage all aspects of the operation and administration of an employee benefit plan, ERISA permits named fiduciaries to delegate most of their fiduciary functions to other service providers.[15]

---

[11] ERISA's terminology in this area is not a model of clarity. Presumably, ERISA § 402(a) means that every plan must name one or more "administrators" who are fiduciaries with respect to the plan. That, however, is not the terminology used by ERISA.

Instead, ERISA § 402(a)(1) provides that every employee benefit plan "shall provide for one or more named fiduciaries who jointly or severally shall have authority to control and manage the operation and administration of the plan." ERISA § 3(16)(A)(i) then defines the term "administrator" as "the person specifically so designated by the terms of the instrument under which the plan is operated," and ERISA § 3(21) defines a person as a "fiduciary" "with respect to a plan to the extent (i) he exercises any discretionary authority or discretionary control respecting management of such plan . . . or (iii) he has any discretionary authority or discretionary responsibility in the administration of such plan."

As one commentator has explained:

There is actually no objective reason a plan document must be drafted to name anyone as the "named fiduciary." What is mandatory is that the plan document name at least one fiduciary. Virtually every document, as a practical matter, names two – the trustee and the administrator – because ERISA requires a plan to have both. To name a third "named fiduciary" is superfluous, and in point of fact one of the most-used documents in the industry, the Relius volume submitter, does not designate a separate "named fiduciary" anywhere in the adoption agreement – instead there is simply mention in the basic document language stating that the administrator is also the named fiduciary for purposes of being the "go to" person for interested parties.

. . . Many documents specifically identify a "named fiduciary" and the adoption agreement, unlike the Relius document, has a fill-in-the-blank spot for a person's name to be inserted. ("Person" is used here in the legal sense, which can include a corporation or a human or "natural" person.) In nearly 100% of plans in existence today that bother naming a separate "named fiduciary" the plan sponsor is listed in this role. This begs the question – what is the "named fiduciary" in such a document actually responsible for? Short answer – not much. The trustee and administrator do all the work.

Pete Swisher, *15 Misconceptions About the Three Principal Fiduciary Roles in a Retirement Plan,* Pentegra Retirement Services, *available at* http://www.pentegra.com/expertise/articles-and-whitepapers.

[12] ERISA § 402(a)(1). Plan documents often specify more than one fiduciary. T. David Cowart, *Through a Glass Darkly: Musings About* Cigna Corp. v. Amara *and* Pfeil v. State Street Bank and Trust Co., SU014 ALI-ABA 371 (Oct. 28, 2012).

[13] ERISA §402(a)(2).

[14] Dana M. Muir and Cindy A. Schiapani, *New Standards of Director Loyalty and Care in the Post-Enron Era: Are Some Shareholders More Equal Than Others?*, 8 N.Y.U. J. Legis. & Pub. Pol'y 279, 315 (2004–2005).

[15] ERISA § 405(c).

To the extent that named fiduciaries delegate their duties, they may be relieved of much of their fiduciary responsibility. Named fiduciaries, however, remain liable for their selection of service providers and for providing ongoing oversight of the service provider's actions.[16]

[B]   Functional Fiduciary — ERISA § 3(21)(A)

ERISA § 3(21)(A) defines a fiduciary as a person[17] who exercises discretion or control with respect to the plan or its assets.[18]

Specifically, ERISA § 3(21)(A) identifies four ways in which a person may become a fiduciary. A person is a "fiduciary" to the extent that the person

(1) exercises any *discretionary authority or discretionary control* with respect to the *management of the plan*;[19]

(2) exercises *any authority or control* with respect to the *management or disposition of the plan's assets*;[20]

(3) renders *investment advice* for a fee or other compensation, whether direct or indirect, with respect to any plan assets, or has the authority or responsibility to do so;[21] or

(4) has *any discretionary authority or discretionary responsibility* in the *administration* of the plan.[22]

ERISA's functional definition of a fiduciary is noteworthy in a couple of ways. First, it casts a wide net[23] such that a plan may have many fiduciaries. Second, a person's fiduciary status is generally limited "to the extent"[24] that the person exercises discretion or control.[25] Unlike in traditional trust law,[26] ERISA

---

[16] ERISA § 405(c)(2)(A).

[17] ERISA defines a "person" as "an individual, partnership, joint venture, corporation, mutual company, joint-stock company, trust, estate, unincorporated organization, association, or employee organization." ERISA § 3(9).

[18] *In re* Luna, 406 F.3d 1192, 1201 (10th Cir. 2005) ("In addition to these so-called 'named fiduciaries,' individuals may acquire fiduciary status if they exercise the fiduciary functions set forth in ERISA § 3(21)(A).").

[19] ERISA § 3(21)(A)(i).

[20] ERISA § 3(21)(A)(i).

[21] ERISA § 3(21)(A)(ii).

[22] ERISA § 3(21)(A)(iii).

[23] *Cf.* John Hancock Mutual Life Ins. Co. v. Harris Trust and Savings Bank, 510 U.S. 86, 96 (1993) ("To help fulfill ERISA's broadly protective purposes, Congress commodiously imposed fiduciary standards on persons whose actions affect the amount of benefits retirement plan participants will receive.").

[24] ERISA § 3(21)(A).

[25] A person may, however, be found liable as a co-fiduciary for participating in, concealing, or failing to attempt to remedy fiduciary breaches committed by other plan fiduciaries. *See* ERISA § 405.

[26] *Cf.* Pegram v. Herdrich, 530 U.S. 211, 225 (2000) ("the trustee at common law characteristically wears only his fiduciary hat when he takes action to affect a beneficiary, whereas the trustee under ERISA may wear many hats").

contemplates many fiduciaries, each of whom has limited responsibilities.[27] Moreover, unlike in traditional trust law, ERISA permits fiduciaries to hold positions that create conflicts of interest with the participants and beneficiaries of employee benefit plans.[28]

Generally, ERISA's functional definition of a fiduciary requires that a person exercise discretion with respect to the plan in order to qualify as a fiduciary.

No discretion, however, is required in two instances:

(1) a person is a fiduciary to the extent that he "exercises any authority or control respecting management or disposition of [the plan's] assets,"[29] and

(2) a person is a fiduciary to the extent that "he renders investment advice for a fee or other compensation, direct or indirect, with respect to any moneys or other property of [the] plan, or has any authority or responsibility to do so."[30]

---

[27] *See* Dana M. Muir, *Fiduciary Status As an Employer's Shield: The Perversity of ERISA Fiduciary Law*, 2 U. Pa. J. Lab. & Emp. L. 391, 395 (2000)

[28] Pegram, 530 U.S., at 225; Varity Corp. v. Howe, 516 U.S. 489, 498 (1995).

[29] ERISA § 3(21)(A)(i).

[30] ERISA § 3(21)(A)(ii).

[C] Summary of Named and Functional Fiduciaries

Who is a Fiduciary?

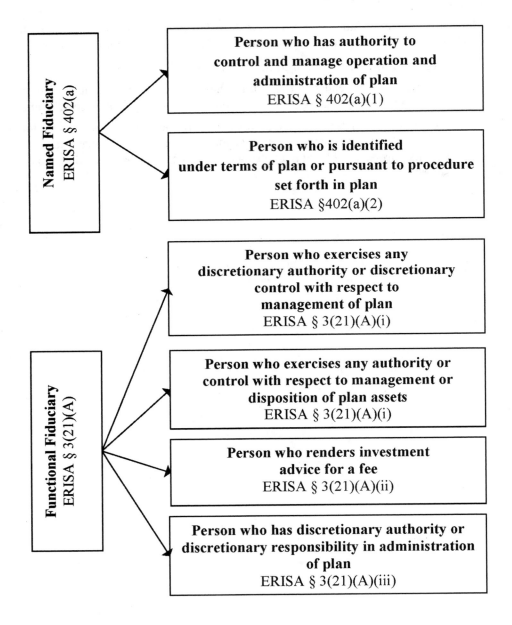

[D]   Determining when a Person is acting as a Functional Fiduciary

ERISA's fiduciary provisions only apply to the extent that a person is acting as a fiduciary. Sometimes it is easy to determine when a person is acting as a fiduciary. For example, a person is clearly acting as a fiduciary when (1) appointing other plan fiduciaries,[31] (2) selecting and monitoring plan investment vehicles,[32] (3) selecting and monitoring third party service providers,[33] (4) interpreting plan provisions,[34] and (5) exercising discretion in the approval or denial of benefit claims.[35]

Determining whether a person is acting as a fiduciary is less clear in other instances. Indeed, determining whether a person is acting as a fiduciary is one of the most frequently litigated issues in ERISA.

Fiduciary status is frequently litigated for two principal reasons. First, the stakes are quite high. A fiduciary may be held personally liable for a breach of fiduciary duty.[36] Second, determining whether a person is a fiduciary is a factually intensive inquiry.[37]

This section discusses a number of common scenarios and issues that arise in determining whether a particular individual or entity is acting as a fiduciary. [38]

[1]   Employers

ERISA permits an employer to wear "two hats" with respect to a plan:[39]

   (1)   that of "settlor,"[40] and

   (2)   that of "fiduciary."[41]

---

[31] *See, e.g., In re* Masters, Mates and Pilot Pension Plan, 11 E.B.C. 2629 (S.D.N.Y. 1990) (selecting investment manager).

[32] *See, e.g.,* Brock v. Berman, 673 F. Supp. 634, 637 n.3 (D. Mass. 1987).

[33] *See, e.g.,* Leigh v. Engle, 727 F.2d 113, 134–35 (7th Cir. 1984); 29 C.F.R. §§ 2509.75-8, FR-14, 2509.96-1(e).

[34] Firestone Tire & Rubber Co. v. Bruch, 489 U.S. 101, 106 (1989).

[35] *Cf.* Aetna Health Inc. v. Davila, 542 U.S. 200, 219 (2004) (stating that benefit determination is "part and parcel" of ordinary fiduciary responsibilities).

[36] *See* ERISA § 409.

[37] Jose Martin Jara, *What is the Correct Standard of Prudence in Employer Stock Cases?*, 45 J. Marshall L. Rev. 541, 553 (2012).

[38] For a more detailed discussion of who is a fiduciary under ERISA, see Jayne Zanglein and Susan Stabile, *Who are Enumerated Parties?*, 2008 N.Y.U. Rev. of Employee Benefits and Exec. Comp. 17-1, 17-11–17-29.

[39] *Pegram*, 530 U.S., at 225. Jara, 45 J. Marshall L. Rev., at 556 (discussing "two hats" doctrine).

[40] A settlor is the person who establishes a trust. Restatement (Third) of Trusts § 3(1) (2003).

[41] For a critique of the settlor/fiduciary doctrine, see Dana M. Muir & Norman Stein, *Two Hats, One Head, No Heart: The Anatomy of ERISA of the Settlor/Fiduciary Distinction*, 93 N.C. L. Rev. 459 (2015).

When an employer acts as a settlor, the employer is free from ERISA's fiduciary constraints. When an employer acts as a fiduciary, it is subject to ERISA's fiduciary rules.

[a]   Employer as Settlor

An employer acts as a settlor, not a plan fiduciary, when it establishes an employee benefit plan, selects its benefit formula and decides whom to cover under the terms of the plan.[42] In addition, an employer acts as a settlor, rather than a plan fiduciary, when it amends or terminates a plan[43] even if the plan amendment or termination benefits the employer.[44]

[b]   Employer as Fiduciary

ERISA permits, but does not require, an employer to serve as a fiduciary with respect to a plan.[45] For example, ERISA permits an employer to serve as the plan administrator[46] which is, by definition,[47] a plan fiduciary because plan administrators must necessarily exercise discretion when administering the plan.[48]

[c]   Distinguishing Employer as Settlor from Employer as Fiduciary

It is not always easy to determine whether, in a particular situation, an employer is acting as the settlor of the plan or as a plan fiduciary. Determining whether an employer is acting as a settlor or as a plan fiduciary depends on the specific facts of the particular case.

---

[42] *See* Hughes Aircraft Co. v. Jacobson, 525 U.S. 432, 444 (1999) (stating that "ERISA's fiduciary requirement simply is not implicated where Hughes, acting as the Plan's settlor, makes a decision regarding the form or structure of the Plan such as who is entitled to receive Plan benefits and in what amounts, or how such benefits are calculated"); Curtiss-Wright Corp. v. Schoonejongen, 514 U.S. 73, 78 (1995) (stating that "[e]mployers are generally free under ERISA, for any reason at any time, to adopt, modify, or terminate welfare plans").

[43] *See* Lockheed Corp. v. Spink, 517 U.S. 882, 890 (1996) (holding that employer acted as settlor when it amended terms of pension plan); Curtiss-Wright Corp. v. Schoonejongen, 514 U.S. 73, 78 (1995) (holding that employer was not acting as a fiduciary when it decided to terminate its welfare benefit plan).

[44] *See* Beck v. PACE International Union, 551 U.S. 96 (2007) (holding that employer was acting as settlor free from fiduciary constraints when it decided to terminate overfunded pension plan by purchasing annuities rather than merging plan with another union-sponsored plan when plan termination resulted in distribution of surplus plan assets to employer); Lockheed Corp. v. Spink, 517 U.S. 882 (1996) (holding that employer acted as settlor when it amended its pension plan to provide enhanced retirement benefits and required that employees sign a release of employment-related claims against the employer before receiving enhanced benefits).

[45] 29 C.F.R. § 2509.75-5, Q&A FR-3 (stating that an employee benefit plan covering a corporation's employees may designate the corporation as a "named fiduciary").

[46] Indeed, under certain circumstances, the employer may be the default plan administrator. *See* ERISA 3(16)(A)(ii).

[47] 29 C.F.R. §§ 2509.75-8, Q&A D-3.

[48] *See* ERISA § 3(21) (defining person as fiduciary to the extent that "(iii) he has any discretionary authority or discretionary responsibility in the administration of such plan").

The Supreme Court addressed the issue of whether an employer was acting as a fiduciary or settlor in one case: *Varity Corp. v. Howe.*[49] In that case, the Court held that the employer was acting as a plan fiduciary when it encouraged its employees to transfer from one corporate division to another.

In *Varity*, Massey-Ferguson, a wholly-owned subsidiary of Varity, was facing financial difficulties. Varity adopted a business plan, "Project Sunshine," to address the company's financial concerns. Project Sunshine placed many of Massey-Ferguson's money-losing divisions and various debts into a new subsidiary, Massey Combines. Varity anticipated that Massey Combines might fail, but viewed failure as a success because it would also eliminate the debts that were transferred to Massey Combines.[50]

Among the debts that Varity sought to transfer to Massey Combines was Massey Ferguson's obligation to pay welfare benefits to employees in Massey Ferguson's money-losing divisions. Varity could have eliminated its obligation to pay the benefits simply by terminating the welfare benefit plans; ERISA neither requires an employer to establish a welfare benefit plan nor prevents an employer from terminating a welfare benefit plan.[51] Had Varity elected to eliminate those obligations by terminating the plans, it would have been exercising a settlor function and would have not been subject to ERISA's fiduciary provisions.[52]

Instead, Varity sought to indirectly eliminate the benefit obligations by encouraging employees of Massy Ferguson's money-losing divisions to voluntarily transfer to Massey Combines. Varity held a special meeting in which it talked to the employees about Massey Combines' future business outlook, financial viability, and benefit security.[53] At the meeting, Varity essentially assured the workers that their benefits would remain secure if they transferred to Massey Combines even though Varity knew that Massey Combines' financial outlook was bleak.[54]

Following the meeting, about 1,500 Massey-Ferguson voluntarily agreed to transfer to Massey Combines. Two years later, Massey Combines was in receivership and the employees lost their welfare benefits. Many of the employees brought suit seeking the benefits to which they would have been entitled under the Massey-Ferguson plan had they not transferred to Massey Combines.[55]

After trial, the district court found that Varity had been acting as an ERISA fiduciary when it advised the employees about their benefits and Massey Combines' future financial outlook. The Supreme Court held that the district court's factual findings supported its decision that Varity was exercising its

---

[49] 516 U.S. 489 (1996).

[50] *Id.* at 492–93.

[51] *See* Curtiss-Wright Corp. v. Schoonejongen, 514 U.S. 73, 78 (1995). If, however, an employer elects to vest welfare benefits, an employer may restrained in its ability to terminate welfare benefits. *See* Chapter 3 § 3.07[B].

[52] 516 U.S. at 505.

[53] For a detailed discussion of the representations made at the meeting, see *id.* at 499–501.

[54] *Id.* at 493–94.

[55] *Id.*

discretionary authority regarding the management or administration of the plan when it misrepresented Massey Combine's future prospects and the security of its benefits. According to the Court, "the factual context in which the statements were made, combined with the plan-related nature of the activity, engaged in by those who had plan-related authority to do so, together provide sufficient support for the District Court's legal conclusion that Varity was acting as a fiduciary."[56]

[2]　Corporate Officers and Directors

A corporate officer or director may be a plan fiduciary if the plan document identifies the officer or director as the "named fiduciary."[57] In addition, a corporate officer or director may be a plan fiduciary if the officer or director exercises discretion or control over the plan or its assets under ERISA's functional definition of fiduciary.[58]

When the plan document designates the corporation or a committee as the "named fiduciary," courts are split as to whether the corporate officers or directors, as individuals, are fiduciaries when they act on behalf of the corporation.[59] According to the Third Circuit, corporate officers are not fiduciaries solely by reason of holding office; corporate officers will only be treated as fiduciaries if the "officers have *individual* discretionary roles as to plan administration."[60] The Ninth Circuit, however, has rejected the Third Circuit's position and held that if "a committee or entity is named as the plan fiduciary, the corporate officers or trustees who carry out the fiduciary functions are themselves fiduciaries and cannot be shielded from liability by the company."[61]

[3]　Third Party Administrators

Plan sponsors often hire third parties to administer employee benefit plans.[62] Whether the Third Party Administrator (TPA) qualifies as a plan fiduciary typically depends on the level of discretion granted to the TPA.[63] TPAs that simply perform ministerial tasks or process or pay claims without exercising any discretionary

---

[56] *Id.* at 503.

[57] *See, e.g.*, Yeseta v. Baima, 837 F.2d 380, 384 (9th Cir. 1988) (owners of close corporation "named fiduciaries").

[58] *See, e.g.*, LoPresti v. Terwilliger, 126 F.3d 34, 40 (2d Cir. 1997) (officer's use of plan assets for corporate purposes rendered him plan fiduciary).

[59] For a critique of the cases, see Muir and Schiapani, 8 N.Y.U. J. Legis. & Pub. Pol'y, at 315–19.

[60] Confer v. Custom Eng'g Co., 952 F.2d 34, 37 (3d Cir. 1991).

[61] Stewart v. Thorpe Holding Co. Profit Sharing Plan, 207 F.3d 1143, 1156 (9th Cir. 2000). *See also* Kayes v. Pacific Lumber Co., 51 F.3d 1449, 1459 (9th Cir. 1995) (rejecting Third Circuit's holding that individual officers' or directors' liability is extinguished unless the fiduciary duties are officially delegated to them); Musmeci v. Schwegmann Giant Super Mkts., Inc., 332 F.3d 339, 350–51 (5th Cir. 2003) (citing and following *Kayes*).

[62] According to Professor Dana Muir, plan administration should be unpacked into two separate elements, benefit administration and asset administration, each of which gives rises to different concerns. Muir, *Fiduciary Status As an Employer's Shield*, 2 U. Pa. J. Lab. & Empl. L., at 399.

[63] Under ERISA § 3(21)(A)(iii), a plan administrator is a fiduciary to the extent that the individual "has any discretionary authority or discretionary responsibility in the administration of such plan."

authority are not fiduciaries.[64] In contrast, TPAs that exercise discretion in investigating and deciding claims are fiduciaries.[65]

If a TPA has the authority to control, manage, or dispose of plan assets, fiduciary status does not depend on discretion. Under ERISA § 3(21)(A)(i), a person is a fiduciary to the extent that he "exercises any authority or control respecting management or disposition of [the plan's] assets." If a TPA exercises authority and control over the management of plan assets, the TPA will be a fiduciary[66] even if the control is unauthorized.[67]

[4] Investment Advice

Section 3(21)(A)(ii) of ERISA defines a fiduciary as someone who "render[s] investment advice for a fee or other compensation, direct or indirect, with respect to any moneys or other property of [a] plan."

[a]   Investment Advice and Defined Benefit Plans

When Congress enacted ERISA, defined benefit plans were the most common form of pension plan, and plan sponsors typically hired professional investment managers to invest their plan's assets.

Shortly after ERISA was enacted, the Department of Labor issued a regulation[68] to clarify the applicability of fiduciary status to persons who render investment advice to defined benefit plans and to persons who execute securities transactions on behalf of such plans.[69] The regulation creates a five-part test for determining when an adviser who does not have discretionary authority or control with respect to the purchase or sale of securities or other property for the plan will be rendering investment advice.

Under the five-factor test, an advisor will be deemed to have provided "investment advice" if

(1) the advice concerns the value of investments or property;

(2) the advice is provided on a regular basis;

(3) the advice is given pursuant to a mutual agreement with respect to a plan or plan fiduciary;

---

[64] DOL Interpretive Bulletin 75-8, 29 C.F.R. § 2509.75-8, at D-2; Lampen v. Albert Trostel & Sons Employee Welfare Plan, 832 F. Supp. 1287, 1291 (E.D. Wis. 1993); Confer v. Custom Eng'g Co., 952 F.2d 34, 39 (3d Cir. 1991).

[65] *See, e.g.*, Reich v. Lancaster, 55 F.3d 1034, 1047 (5th Cir. 1995); Pacificare Inc. v. Martin, 34 F.3d 834, 837 (9th Cir. 1994).

[66] Board of Trustees of Bricklayers v. Wettlin Assoc., 237 F.3d 270, 272–73 (3d Cir. 2001); IT Corp. v. General Am. Life Ins. Co., 107 F.3d 1415, 1420 (9th Cir. 1997).

[67] *In re* G.S. Consulting, Inc., 414 B.R. 454, 459–60 (N.D. Ind. 2009).

[68] Definition of the Term "Fiduciary," 40 Fed. Reg. 50, 843 (Oct. 31, 1975) (adding 29 C.F.R. § 2510.3-21(c)).

[69] Definitions and Coverage Under the Employee Retirement Income Security Act of 1974, 40 Fed. Reg. 33, 561, 33,562 (Aug. 8, 1975) (introducing proposed investment advice regulation).

(4)   the advice serves as the primary basis for investment decisions; and

(5)   the advice is individualized with respect to the particular needs of the plan.[70]

[b]   Investment Advice and Defined Contribution Plans

The pension plan landscape and financial marketplace have changed considerably since the enactment of ERISA and the promulgation of the investment advice regulation. Under a self-directed 401(k) plan, the most common type of retirement plan today, each plan participant must decide how to invest the assets held in his or her individual account, and each plan participant's benefit is based on the contributions made to the plan and the earnings and/or losses on the investment of the contributions. Thus, today, there is a much greater need for investment advice individualized to the needs of each plan participant. In addition, "the types and complexity of investment products and services available to plans have increased"[71] since the promulgation of the investment advice regulation.

In light of these changes, the Department of Labor proposed in 2010 to revise its investment regulation and broaden the definition of investment advice "to better ensure that persons, in fact, providing investment advice to plan fiduciaries and/or plan participants and beneficiaries are subject to ERISA's standards of fiduciary conduct."[72] Under the proposed regulation, investment advice would include advice, appraisals or fairness opinions concerning the value of securities, recommendations regarding investing, and recommendations regarding the management of securities.[73]

The Department of Labor's proposed regulation was met with considerable resistance and controversy,[74] and the Department of Labor decided to re-propose the regulation.[75] In April 2015, the Department of Labor issued a new proposed regulation.[76]

---

[70] 29 C.F.R. § 2510.3-21(c)(1)(ii)(B). The regulation has been subject to considerable litigation. *See,* *e.g.,* Farm King Integrated Supply, Inc. Integrated Profit-Sharing Plan & Trust v. Edward D. Jones & Co., 884 F.2d 288 (7th Cir. 1989); Thomas, Head & Greisen Emps. Trust v. Buster, 24 F.3d 1114 (9th Cir. 1994); Consolidated Beef Indus., Inc. v. New York Life Ins. Co., 949 F.2d 960 (8th Cir.), *cert. denied,* 503 U.S. 985 (1992).

[71] Definition of the Term "Fiduciary," 75 Fed. Reg. 65,263, 65,265 (Oct. 22, 2010) (proposing new investment advice regulation).

[72] *Id.* (75 Fed. Reg., at 65,265).

[73] *Id.* at 65,277 (proposing revised § 2510.3-21(c)(1)(i)(A)).

[74] For a critique of the proposal and discussion of the controversy, *see* Scott Mayland, Note, *Racheting up the Duty: The Department of Labor's Misguided Attempt to Impose a Paternalistic Model upon Defined Contribution Plans Through ERISA,* 75 OHIO ST. L.J. 645 (2014).

[75] U.S. Dep't of Labor, News Release, *U.S. Labor Department's EBSA to re-propose rule on definition of a fiduciary* (Sept. 19, 2011), *available at* http://www.dol.gov/opa/media/press/ebsa/EBSA20111382.htm.

[76] *Definition of the Term "Fiduciary"; Conflict of Interest Rule—Retirement Investment Advice,* 80 Fed. Reg. 21,928 (April 20, 2015).

[E] Trustees

Section 403 of ERISA requires that all plan assets, other than assets held in the form of insurance,[77] be held in trust.[78] The plan sponsor may serve as trustee, or the plan sponsor can appoint a separate entity, such as a bank, trust company, or affiliate of a mutual fund or stock brokerage company to serve as the plan's trustee.

Normally, the trustee has "exclusive authority and discretion to manage and control the assets of the plan,"[79] and thus is necessarily a fiduciary.[80] ERISA, however, recognizes two exceptions to the general rule that trustees have exclusive authority and control over plan assets:

(1) ERISA permits a plan to provide that a trustee shall be subject to the direction of a named fiduciary who is not a trustee,[81] and

(2) ERISA permits the named fiduciary to delegate the power to manage plan assets to an "investment manager."[82]

[1] Directed Trustees

ERISA recognizes that a trustee will have limited authority or discretion when "the plan expressly provides that the trustee or trustees are subject to the direction of a named fiduciary who is not a trustee."[83] In such a case, section 403(a)(1) of ERISA requires that the "directed trustee" follow the "proper" directions of the named fiduciary so long as the directions are "made in accordance with the terms of the plan" and are "not contrary to" ERISA.

ERISA does not specify what is "proper direction." Nor does it define the lengths to which a directed trustee must go to ensure that the direction is in accordance with the terms of the plan and ERISA.[84] Virtually all courts[85] and the Department of Labor[86] agree that directed trustees remain fiduciaries. They disagree, however, as to the scope of a directed trustee's fiduciary responsibility, and the scope of a

---

[77] ERISA § 403(b) also provides a few other exceptions to the general rule that all plan assets be held in trust.

[78] ERISA § 403(a).

[79] ERISA § 403(a) (stating that unless particular exception applies, "trustee or trustees shall have exclusive authority and discretion to manage and control the assets of the plan").

[80] 29 C.F.R. § 2509.75-8, Q&A D-3.

[81] ERISA § 403(a)(1).

[82] ERISA § 402(c)(3).

[83] ERISA § 403(a)(1).

[84] According to ERISA's legislative history, a directed trustee may rely on directions "unless it is clear on their face that the actions to be taken under those directions would be prohibited by the fiduciary responsibility rules of the bill [that is, ERISA] or would be contrary to the terms of the plan or trust." H.R. Rep. No. 93-1280, 2d Sess., at 298 (1974), reprinted in 1974 U.S.C.C.A.N. 5038, 5079.

[85] ABA Section of Labor and Employment Law, Employee Benefits Law 10-48–10-49 n.306 (Jeffrey Lewis et al., eds., 3d ed. 2012) (discussing cases and citing few cases holding that directed trustees were not fiduciaries).

[86] DOL Field Assistance Bulletin 2004-03 (stating that "section 403(a)(1) does not remove a directed trustee from section 3(21)'s purview").

directed trustee's fiduciary duty has been frequently litigated.[87]

[2] Investment Managers

"Because of the perceived importance of professional investment advice,"[88] section 402(c)(3) of ERISA permits the named fiduciary to delegate the power to manage plan assets to an "investment manager."

Section 3(38) of ERISA defines an investment manager as any fiduciary (other than a trustee or named fiduciary) who

(1) has the power to manage, acquire, or dispose of any plan asset,

(2) is registered as an investment adviser, is a bank, or is an insurance company qualified to do business in more than one state, and

(3) acknowledges in writing that he or she is a fiduciary.

Investment managers are, by definition, fiduciaries. Trustees, on the other hand, are not fiduciaries with respect to the assets which are invested or otherwise managed by the investment adviser.[89]

§ 6.04   ERISA'S FIDUCIARY STANDARDS — ERISA § 404(a)

Section 404(a) of ERISA sets forth the general standards of behavior that are applicable to all fiduciaries. It begins with the overarching principle[90] that a fiduciary must discharge his duties "solely in the interest of the participants and beneficiaries,"[91] sometimes referred to as the duty of loyalty.

ERISA § 404(a) then sets forth four specific fiduciary duties:

(1) the duty to act for the exclusive purpose of providing benefits to plan participants,[92] sometimes referred to as the exclusive purpose rule;

---

[87] According to three practitioners, "the degree of fiduciary responsibility owed by directed trustees has been the subject of much litigation . . . because they are often perceived to have deep pockets and are therefore attractive targets to plaintiffs." William J. Kilberg et al., *A Measured Approach to Employment and Labor Law During the George W. Bush Years*, 32 Harv. J. L. & Pub. Pol. 997, 1006–07 (2009). For a discussion of some of the cases, see Colleen E. Medill, *The Law of Directed Trustees Under ERISA: A Proposed Blueprint for the Federal Courts*, 61 Mo. L. Rev. 824, 836–47 (1996).

[88] Dana M. Muir, *The Dichotomy Between Investment Advice and Investment Education: Is No Advice Really the Answer?*, 23 Berkeley J. Emp. & Lab. L. 1, 9 (2002).

[89] *See, e.g.*, Beddall v. State St. Bank & Trust Co., 137 F.3d 12, 20 (1st Cir. 1998) (holding that trustee was not fiduciary where investment manager had sole discretion over investment decisions). There is, however, a continuing fiduciary duty to monitor the investment manager's performance. Muir, *The Dichotomy Between Investment Advice and Investment Education*, 23 Berkeley J. Emp. & Lab. L., at 9. *See, e.g.*, Brock v. Berman, 673 F. Supp. 634, 637 n.3 (D. Mass. 1987).

[90] Susan J. Stabile, *Breach of ERISA Fiduciary Responsibilities: Who's Liable Anyway?*, 5 Empl. Rts. & Employ. Pol'y J. 135, 138 (2001).

[91] ERISA § 404(a)(1).

[92] ERISA § 404(a)(1)(A).

(2) the duty to act with the care, skill, prudence and diligence of the prudent person,[93] also known as the duty of prudence or prudent person rule;

(3) the duty to diversify plan assets so as to minimize risks,[94] also known as the duty to diversify; and

(4) the duty to act in accordance with plan documents and instruments.[95]

ERISA's fiduciary standards, based in trust law, have been described as "the highest known to law."[96]

---

[93] ERISA § 404(a)(1)(B).

[94] ERISA § 404(a)(1)(C).

[95] ERISA § 404(a)(1)(D).

[96] Donovan v. Bierwirth, 680 F.2d 263, 272 n.8 (2d Cir.), *cert. denied,* 459 U.S. 1069 (1982).

[A]   Overview of ERISA § 404(a) Fiduciary Standards

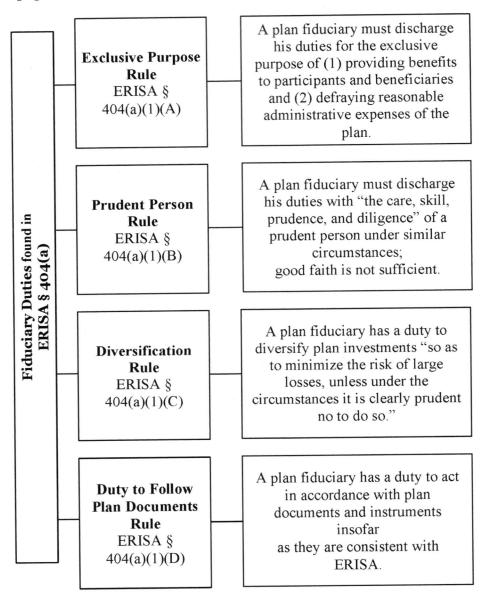

Fiduciary Duties found in ERISA § 404(a)

Exclusive Purpose Rule ERISA § 404(a)(1)(A)	A plan fiduciary must discharge his duties for the exclusive purpose of (1) providing benefits to participants and beneficiaries and (2) defraying reasonable administrative expenses of the plan.
Prudent Person Rule ERISA § 404(a)(1)(B)	A plan fiduciary must discharge his duties with "the care, skill, prudence, and diligence" of a prudent person under similar circumstances; good faith is not sufficient.
Diversification Rule ERISA § 404(a)(1)(C)	A plan fiduciary has a duty to diversify plan investments "so as to minimize the risk of large losses, unless under the circumstances it is clearly prudent no to do so."
Duty to Follow Plan Documents Rule ERISA § 404(a)(1)(D)	A plan fiduciary has a duty to act in accordance with plan documents and instruments insofar as they are consistent with ERISA.

[B]   Duty of Loyalty — ERISA § 404(a)(1)

ERISA § 404(a)(1) requires a fiduciary to discharge his duties "solely in the interest of participants and beneficiaries." The requirement that a plan fiduciary act solely in the interest of plan participants and beneficiaries is the most fundamental of ERISA's fiduciary standards. It is derived from the trustee's duty of loyalty[97] and requires that trustees make decisions "with an eye single to the interests of the participants and beneficiaries."[98]

Sometimes it is quite clear when a fiduciary has breached this fundamental duty. For example, if an employer, facing financial difficulties, does not deposit money withheld from an employee's paycheck into the employee's 401(k) account, the employer has clearly breached its fiduciary duties under ERISA.[99]

Other times it is less clear when the duty of loyalty has been breached. Because ERISA, unlike trust law,[100] permits conflicted fiduciaries,[101] application of the duty of loyalty is much more complex under ERISA than under traditional trust law. The biggest challenge under ERISA's fiduciary duty of loyalty is navigating the inevitable conflicts that arise when the plan sponsor's interests diverge from those of the plan beneficiaries.[102]

Recognizing that employers establish employee benefit plans for a variety of self-interested reasons, such as decreasing employee turnover and attracting high-quality workers,[103] courts have found that ERISA's duty of loyalty does not prevent fiduciaries from taking actions that provide "incidental" benefits to the employer.[104] Distinguishing between "incidental" benefits and impermissible benefits, however, is not always easy, and conflicted fiduciaries have been advised to exercise caution to ensure that their actions and decisions are made solely in the interest of plan participants and beneficiaries.[105]

On a number of occasions, lower courts have suggested that the best course of action for conflicted fiduciaries is to step down in favor of a disinterested fiduciary,[106] or at least consult with an independent adviser.[107] That is not to

---

[97] Varity Corp. v. Howe, 516 U.S. 489, 506 (1996).

[98] *Id.* at 271.

[99] *See* George v. Junior Achievement of Central Indiana, Inc., 694 F.3d 812 (7th Cir. 2012).

[100] RESTATEMENT (THIRD) OF TRUSTS § 78 (2007) (imposing on trustees undivided duty of loyalty to beneficiaries). *See also* 2A AUSTIN W. SCOTT & WILLIAM F. FRATCHER, THE LAW OF TRUSTS § 170 (4th ed. 1988) (discussing undivided duty of loyalty).

[101] *See, e.g.,* ERISA § 408(c)(3) (permitting employees who work for plan sponsor to serve as plan fiduciaries); ERISA § 408(c)(1) (permitting fiduciaries to be plan participants or beneficiaries so long as benefits are consistent with those received by all other participants and beneficiaries).

[102] *Cf.* Siskind v. Sperry Ret. Prog., Unisys, 47 F.3d 498, 500 (2d Cir. 1993) (recognizing that plan trustees who are also corporate officers "are obliged to act, on the one hand, for the plan's members, so as to secure and make certain that benefits will be available to them and, on the other hand, for the employer, so as to safeguard the business entity's profits").

[103] Muir and Schiapani, 8 N.Y.U. J. LEGIS. & PUB. POL'Y, at 327; Frank P. Vanderploeg, *Role-Playing Under ERISA: The Company as "Employer" and "Fiduciary,"* 9 DEPAUL BUS. L.J. 259, 271–72 (1997).

[104] Donovan v. Bierworth, 680 F.2d 263, 271 (2d Cir. 1982). *See also* Lockheed Corp. v. Spink, 517 U.S. 882, 893 (1996).

[105] Deak v. Masters, Mates & Pilots Pension Plan, 821 F.2d 572, 580 (11th Cir. 1987), *cert. denied,* 484 U.S. 1005 (1988).

[106] *See, e.g.,* McMahon v. McDowell, 794 F.2d 100, 110 (3d Cir. 1986), *cert. denied,* 479 U.S. 971 (1986); Sommers Drug Store Co. Employee Profit Sharing Trust v. Corrigan Enters. Inc., 793 F.2d 1456, 1468–69 (5th Cir. 1986), *cert. denied,* 479 U.S. 1089 (1987); Leigh v. Engle, 727 F.2d 113, 132 (7th Cir. 1984), *cert. denied,* 489 U.S. 1078 (1989). *See also* Jara, 45 J. MARSHALL L. REV., at 562–64 (noting that

suggest, however, that conflicted fiduciaries readily take such advice.

The Supreme Court expressly addressed the ERISA § 404(a)(1) duty of loyalty of a conflicted fiduciary in *Varity Corp. v. Howe*.[108] In *Varity*, discussed in more detail in § 6.03[D][1][c], the plan sponsor also served as the plan administrator. The Court held the plan sponsor, acting as plan administrator, violated the duty of loyalty when it misled plan participants about the security of their welfare benefits.[109]

[C] Exclusive Purpose Rule — ERISA § 404(a)(1)(A)

Section 404(a)(1)(A) directs a plan fiduciary to act on behalf of a plan for the sole purpose of

(1) providing benefits to participants and beneficiaries, and

(2) defraying reasonable administrative expenses of the plan.

The exclusive purpose rule "embodies both a fundamental principle of what it means to operate in a fiduciary capacity as well as the purpose of . . . ERISA . . . as a whole to ensure that the benefits promised to employees are safeguarded from employer malfeasance."[110]

The exclusive purpose rule is an extension of the duty of loyalty.[111] Indeed, some commentators and courts do not differentiate between the ERISA § 404(a)(1)(A) exclusive purpose requirement and the ERISA § 404(a)(1) overarching principle that a plan fiduciary act in the sole interest of plan participants and beneficiaries. Instead, these authorities simply refer to ERISA § 404(a)(1)(A) as imposing a duty of loyalty.[112]

Plan sponsors who are fiduciaries often find themselves facing a conflict of interest where the interests of the plan participants are different from those of the plan sponsor.[113] If the plan sponsor, as a fiduciary, acts in a manner that places the

---

lower courts have held that the duty of loyalty requires a fiduciary to resign if it "cannot ignore its self-interest" in making a fiduciary decision).

[107] Martin v. Feilen, 965 F.2d 660, 670 (8th Cir. 1992), *cert. denied*, 506 U.S. 1054 (1993).

[108] 516 U.S. 489 (1996).

[109] *Id.* at 506.

[110] Maria O'Brien Hylton, *Disclosure to the Rescue: A Conceptual Framework for Retained Asset Accounts*, 80 TENN. L. REV. 69, 81 (2012). For an argument that the exclusive purpose rule denies the essential nature of employee benefit plans as arrangements in which plan sponsors and plan participants share the plan's beneficial interest as well as the settlement of the vehicle, see Daniel Fischel & John H. Langbein, *ERISA's Fundamental Contradiction: The Exclusive Benefit Rule*, 55 U. CHI. L. REV. 1105, 1118 (1988).

[111] HANDBOOK ON ERISA LITIGATION § 4.03[A][3], at 4-69 (James F. Jorden et al., 3d ed. 2012 supp.).

[112] *See, e.g.*, Metzler v. Graham, 112 F.3d 207, 212–13 (5th Cir. 1997); Jara, 45 J. MARSHALL L. REV., at 561–64; Muir and Schiapani, 8 N.Y.U. J. LEGIS. & PUB. POL'Y, at 326. *Cf.* Fischel & Langbein, 55 U. CHI. L. REV., at 1108 (stating that "[i]n ERISA argot this 'sole interest/exclusive-purpose-of-benefitting' language of section 404(a)(1)(A) is compressed as the 'sole interest/exclusive purpose' or sometimes simply the 'exclusive benefit' rule").

[113] Felicia A. Finston and J. B. Friedman, Jr., *Are Your Service Providers Fiduciaries of Your 401(k) Plan?*, BENEFITS MAGAZINE 32, 34 (July 2014).

interest of the plan sponsor (that is, the employer) above the interest of the plan participants and beneficiaries, it breaches its fiduciary duty.[114]

For example, in the leading case of *Donovan v. Bierwirth*,[115] pension plan trustees, who were also corporate officers,[116] were faced with a hostile takeover attempt. They elected not to tender the plan's employer stock, but instead chose to purchase additional shares of employer stock to stave off the takeover attempt.[117] The court held that the trustees violated ERISA § 404(a)(1)(A) by failing to consult independent counsel or carefully investigate the facts.[118] The court recognized a plan fiduciary may make a decision that incidentally benefits the plan sponsor or even the plan fiduciary, but only if careful and impartial investigation leads to the conclusion that such a course of action best promotes the interests of the plan participants and beneficiaries. [119]

[D]   The Duty of Prudence — ERISA § 404(a)(1)(B)

ERISA § 404(a)(1)(B) requires that a plan fiduciary discharge his duties with "the care, skill, prudence, and diligence" of a prudent person under similar circumstances. Good faith will not insulate a fiduciary from liability for breach of the duty of prudence;[120] "a pure heart and an empty head are not enough."[121]

If the employer is not acting as a fiduciary, the exclusive purpose rule does not apply. Thus, if an employer, acting as plan settlor rather than plan fiduciary, decides to terminate an overfunded defined benefit plan, the decision to terminate is not a fiduciary decision and the reversion of excess plan assets to the employer does not breach the exclusive purpose rule. *See* ERISA § 4044(d) (permitting distribution of surplus assets to employer upon plan termination) *See also* Beck v. PACE International Union, 551 U.S. 96 (2007) (holding that employer was acting as settlor free from fiduciary constraints when it decided to terminate overfunded pension plan which resulted in reversion of $5 million in surplus assets to employer).

[114] Craig C. Martin et al., *What's Up on Stock-Drops? Moench Revisited*, 39 J. Marshall L. Rev. 605, 608 (2006) (stating that "[t]he paradigmatic example of fiduciary breach of the duty of loyalty is where the interests of the employer and the beneficiaries of the plan are at odds, and the fiduciary – having responsibilities with respect to both entities – acts in a manner that places the employer's interest above the beneficiaries").

[115] 680 F.2d 263 (2d Cir. 1982).

[116] *Id.* at 267.

[117] *Id.* at 268–69.

[118] *Id.* at 272–74

[119] *Id.* at 271.

[120] *See, e.g.*, Reich v. King, 867 F. Supp. 341, 343 (D. Md. 1994).

[121] Donovan v. Cunningham, 716 F.2d 1455, 1467 (5th Cir. 1983), *cert. denied*, 467 U.S. 1251 (1984). *But see* Muir & Schiapani, 8 N.Y.U. J. Legis. & Pub. Pol'y, at 328 (noting that some courts follow the traditional trust standard of negligence rather than strict liability in applying the duty of loyalty and concluding "[w]hether the courts settle on the threshold for ERISA fiduciary intent as a negligence or strict liability standard, it almost certainly will be a lower standard than corporate law's gross negligence standard").

[1] General Duty of Prudence

Courts use an objective standard to measure prudence.[122] Actions are judged based on how a "prudent man acting in a like capacity and familiar with such matters" would[123] act under the circumstances.[124]

Courts focus on process rather than results in evaluating whether fiduciaries have satisfied their duty of prudence.[125] Thus, prudence is based on whether the right questions were asked, whether expert assistance was sought, and whether the fiduciary was diligent in making inquiries.[126]

Some courts have found prudent process to encompass both substantive and procedural aspects.[127] According to this view, procedural prudence requires that the fiduciary obtain the relevant information needed to make a prudent decision[128] while substantive prudence requires that the fiduciary use the relevant information to make a reasoned decision.[129]

The Department of Labor regulations provide that, when making investment decisions, prudence requires that the fiduciary give "appropriate consideration" to the facts and circumstances that the fiduciary knows or should know are relevant to a particular investment or investment strategy, including the role that the investment (or strategy) will play in the plan's portfolio, and the fiduciary must act in accordance with the conclusions that were reached after that appropriate consideration has been undertaken.[130]

---

[122] Debra A. Davis, *How Much is Enough? Giving Fiduciaries and Participants Adequate Information About Plan Expenses*, 41 J. MARSHALL L. REV. 1005, 1010 (2008). *See, e.g.*, Tussey v. ABB, Inc., 746 F.3d 327, 335 (8th Cir.), *cert. denied*, 135 S. Ct. 477 (2014); Katsaros v. Cody, 744 F.2d 270, 279 (2d Cir. 1984), *cert. denied*, 469 U.S. 1072 (1984).

[123] In the face of a strongly worded dissent, the Fourth Circuit in *Tatum v. RJR Pension Inv. Comm.*, 761 F.3d 346 (4th Cir. 2014), *cert. denied*, 135 S. Ct. 2887 (2015), held that the district court applied the wrong standard when it held that the plan fiduciaries did not breach the duty of prudence because a prudent fiduciary "could have" made the same decision. Explaining that the difference between "could have" and "would have" is the difference between merely possible and probable, the Fourth Circuit remanded the case to the district court to determine whether a prudent fiduciary "would have" made the same decision.

[124] Courts and commentators are divided as to whether prudence is measured by a prudent person or prudent expert standard. *See* Dana Muir, *Fiduciary Constraints: Correlating Obligation with Liability*, 42 WAKE FOREST L. REV. 697, 708–11 (2007) (discussing controversy).

[125] Davis, 41 J. MARSHALL L. REV., at 1010. *See, e.g.*, Tussey v. ABB, Inc., 746 F.3d 327, 335 (8th Cir.), *cert. denied*, 135 S. Ct. 477 (2014); *In re* Unisys Sav. Plan Litig., 74 F.3d 420, 434 (3d Cir. 1996), *cert. denied*, 519 U.S. 810 (1996) ("[I]f at the time an investment is made, it is an investment a prudent person would make, there is no liability if the investment later depreciates in value.").

[126] Felicia A. Finston and J. B. Friedman, Jr., *Are Your Service Providers Fiduciaries of Your 401(k) Plan?*, BENEFITS MAGAZINE 32, 34 (July 2014).

[127] Davis, 41 J. MARSHALL L. REV., at 1009.

[128] *Id.*

[129] *Id. citing*, Riley v. Murdock, 890 F. Supp. 444, 458 (E.D.N.C. 1995). *But see* ABA SECTION OF LABOR AND EMPLOYMENT LAW, EMPLOYEE BENEFITS LAW, at 10-62–10-63 (noting that some judicial opinions treat the issue of "whether a procedurally prudent fiduciary would have made the same decision — as an element of loss causation, rather than as an element of whether a breach occurred").

[130] 29 C.F.R. § 2550.404a-(1)(b)(1).

[2] Duty of Prudence and Investment in Employer Stock

ERISA permits pension plan assets to be invested in employer stock. Section 407(a)(2) of ERISA limits employer stock holdings of defined benefit plans to 10% of the plan's assets.[131] The 10% limitation does not apply to ESOPs, which are "designed to invest primarily in employer,"[132] or to other defined contribution plans, including 401(k) plans, that permit investments in employer stock.[133]

In a host of cases, referred to as "stock drop" cases, ESOP and 401(k) plan participants have brought suit against plan fiduciaries (and others) to recover from losses sustained when the employer stock they owned plummeted in value.[134] In these cases, the plan participants have argued, among other things, that the plan fiduciaries breached their fiduciary duty of prudence by permitting the participants to buy and hold employer stock when the fiduciaries knew or should have known that the investment in company stock was imprudent.[135]

[a]   *Moench* Presumption

In *Moench v. Robertson*,[136] the Third Circuit held that "an ESOP fiduciary who invests the [ESOP's] assets in employer stock is entitled to a presumption that it acted consistently with ERISA"[137] in making such investments. The Third Circuit later extended the "*Moench* presumption" to other self-directed individual account plans, such as 401(k) plans, that provide for investments in employer stock.[138] Six other circuit courts adopted the *Moench* presumption, although they differed with respect to the stage it applied and the proof necessary to overcome the presumption.[139]

In *Fifth Third Bancorp v. Dudenhoeffer*,[140] the Supreme Court rejected the *Moench* presumption.

---

[131] For a discussion of ERISA § 407, see § 6.06[E].

[132] ERISA § 407(d)(6).

[133] For an argument that self-directed 401(k) plans should be subject to the 10% limit, see Susan J. Stabile, *Pension Plan Investments in Employer Securities: More is Not Always Better*, 15 YALE J. ON REG. 61, 88 (1998).

[134] For a discussion of significant stock drop cases, see Craig C. Martin and Elizabeth L. Fine, *ERISA Stock Drop Cases: An Evolving Standard*, 38 J. MARSHALL L. REV. 889, 905–12 (2005).

[135] Most of the stock drop cases have settled, with settlements ranging from less than $1 million to over $100 million. Frederick A. Brodie, *Complex ERISA Litigation*, 8 BUS. & COM. LITIG. FED. CTS. § 95:43 (3d ed. updated through Nov. 2013).

[136] 62 F.3d 553 (3d Cir. 1995), *abrogated by* Fifth Third Bancorp v. Dudenhoeffer, 134 S. Ct. 2459 (2014).

[137] 62 F.3d at 571.

[138] Edgar v. Avaya, Inc., 503 F.3d 340, 347 (3d Cir. 2007), *abrogated by* Fifth Third Bancorp v. Dudenhoeffer, 134 S. Ct. 2459 (2014).

[139] *See* Peter J. Wiedenbeck, *Trust Variation and ERISA's "Presumption of Prudence,"* 142 TAX NOTES 1205 (2014) (citing cases in n.15 and arguing that trust doctrines do not support presumption); Frederick A. Brodie, *Complex ERISA Litigation*, 8 BUS. & COM. LITIG. FED. CTS. § 95:43 (3d ed. updated through Nov. 2013) (discussing cases and their various approaches).

[140] 134 S. Ct. 2459 (2014).

[b]   *Fifth Third Bancorp. v. Dudenhoeffer*

Dudenhoeffer was a classic stock drop case. The employer, Fifth Third Bancorp, maintained a 401(k) plan that provided for participant-directed investments. The plan offered 20 different investment options, including a company stock fund and mutual funds. Like many such plans, the employer stock fund was structured to qualify as an ESOP for purposes of ERISA and the Internal Revenue Code. The company matched 100% of the plan participants' elective deferrals up to 4% of compensation in employer stock, but permitted participants to reinvest the matching contributions in other investment options.[141]

Like many financial institutions, the price of Fifth Third's stock plummeted between July 2007 and September 2009, and the plan participants lost a large part of their retirement savings invested in the ESOP.[142] The plan participants brought suit claiming that the plan fiduciaries violated their duty of prudence by holding and purchasing shares of company stock long after it ceased to be prudent to do so.[143]

Applying the *Moench* presumption at the pleading stage, the district court dismissed the plaintiffs' complaint.[144] The Sixth Circuit reversed on the ground that the *Moench* presumption was an evidentiary rule that could not be used at the pleading stage to dismiss a case.[145]

The Supreme Court granted *certiorari* and rejected the *Moench* presumption at any stage. Focusing on the text of the statute,[146] the Court held that ESOP fiduciaries are subject to the same duty of prudence that applies to all ERISA fiduciaries, except that the ERISA § 404(a)(1)(C) duty to diversify does not apply.[147]

The Court's decision, however, was not a total victory for plan participants. Rather, the Court remanded the case to the Sixth Circuit to reconsider whether the complaint stated a claim upon which relief could be granted. The Court declared that the *Iqbal*[148] and *Twombly*[149] pleading standards[150] should apply and

---

[141] *Id.* at 2463–64.

[142] The price of the stock fell 74% between July 2007 and September 2009, although it had made a partial recovery to half its July 2007 price by the time the Court decided the case. *Id.* at 2464.

[143] The participants also claimed that the fiduciaries violated their duty of loyalty, but the Supreme Court only addressed their breach of prudence claim. *Id.* at 2464.

[144] *Id.* at 2464.

[145] *Id.* at 2465. Whether the *Moench* presumption applies at the pleading stage or at summary judgment was a technical question with significant consequences. If it applied at the pleading stage, plan participants would not be entitled to discovery, and litigation would be much less costly for defendants and much more difficult for plaintiffs to win.

[146] Specifically, the Court focused on ERISA § 404(a)(1) which imposes the fiduciary duties, and ERISA § 404(a)(2) which provides that an ESOP fiduciary is exempt from the ERISA § 404(a)(1)(C) diversification requirement and the ERISA § 404(a)(1)(B) duty of prudence, but *"only to the extent that it requires diversification."* *Id.* at 2467, *quoting* ERISA § 404(a)(2), emphasis added by Court.

[147] *Id.* at 2467.

[148] Ashcroft v. Iqbal, 556 U.S. 662, 677–80 (2009).

[149] Bell Atlantic Corp. v. Twombly, 550 U.S. 544, 554–63 (2007).

identified some considerations the Sixth Circuit should take into account in applying the pleading standards. The considerations recognize the inevitable complexities that arise when a plan fiduciary is a corporate insider subject to securities regulation as well as ERISA's fiduciary standards.

The Court made clear that a fiduciary is not required to violate securities law in order to satisfy its ERISA fiduciary obligations. Beyond that, however, the Court did not provide an easy answer to what exactly fiduciaries must — or cannot — do. Instead, it identified basic principles courts should apply and left it to the lower courts to apply the principles. Specifically, the Court identified the following considerations that should be taken into account:

(1) Absent special circumstances, claims that a fiduciary breached his fiduciary duty because he knew or should have known, based on *publicly available information*, that a publicly traded stock was overvalued are implausible and thus insufficient to state a claim for relief.[151]

(2) Claims that a fiduciary breached his fiduciary duty based on *inside information* must be informed by the following:

    (a) ERISA's duty of prudence never requires a fiduciary to break a law so a fiduciary cannot be imprudent for failing to buy or sell stock in violation of insider trading laws;[152]

    (b) Where a complaint alleges fiduciaries breached their duty by failing to decide, based on negative information, to refrain from making additional stock purchases or by failing to publicly disclose information so that the stock would no longer be overvalued, courts should consider the extent to which imposing an obligation to refrain from purchasing stock or requiring disclosure of inside information would conflict with corporate securities law governing insider trading and corporate disclosure requirements and the objectives of those laws;[153] and

    (c) Courts confronted with such claims should consider whether a complaint has plausibly alleged that a prudent fiduciary could not have concluded that refraining from purchasing stock or disclosing negative inside information could do more harm than good.[154]

---

[150] For an overview of the *Iqual* and *Twombly* pleading standards, see Joshua Douglas, *Election Law Pleading*, 81 Geo. Wash. L. Rev. 1966, 1971–84 (2013). For a detailed discussion of *Twombly*, see A. Benjamin Spencer, *Plausiblity Pleading*, 49 B.C. L. Rev. 431 (2008). For an application of the *Iqbal* and *Twombly* standards in the context of an ERISA claim, see Braden v. Wal-Mart Stores, Inc., 588 F.3d 585, 594–98 (8th Cir. 2009).

[151] 134 S. Ct. at 2471 ("In our view, where stock is publicly traded, allegations that a fiduciary should have recognized from publicly available information alone that the market was over- or undervaluing the stock are implausible as a general rule, at least in the absence of special circumstances.").

[152] *Id.* at 2472.

[153] *Id.* at 2473.

[154] *Id.*

[E]   The Duty to Diversify — ERISA § 404(a)(1)(C)

ERISA § 404(a)(1)(C) requires plan fiduciaries to diversify plan investments "so as to minimize the risk of large losses, unless under the circumstances it is clearly prudent not to do so." The duty to diversify is intended to prevent fiduciaries from concentrating plan investments in a single type of investment, geographic location, or industry.[155] Claims under ERISA § 404(a)(1)(C)'s duty to diversify are typically raised in conjunction with a claim under the ERISA § 404(a)(1)(B) duty of prudence and may be viewed as a subset of the duty of prudence.

ERISA does not set forth a specific percentage limit by which to evaluate whether the risk of loss has been adequately spread. Instead, a prudent fiduciary must consider the "facts and circumstances" of each case.[156] Relevant factors include:

(1)   the purpose of the plan;

(2)   the amount of plan assets;

(3)   financial and industrial conditions;

(4)   the types of investment;

(5)   the distribution of the geographic location of the investments;

(6)   the distribution of the investments among industrial sectors; and

(7)   the dates of maturity.[157]

In analyzing whether the duty to diversify has been breached, courts first determine whether the plan investments are diverse. The plaintiff challenging the investments bears the burden of proving that the investments are not diverse.[158] If the court finds that investments are not diverse, the burden then shifts to the defendant to show that the nondiverse investments were nevertheless "clearly prudent" under the circumstances.[159] "Prudence is evaluated at the time of the investment without the benefit of hindsight."[160]

Although courts describe the defendant's burden as a "heavy burden,"[161] courts rarely find a breach of the duty to diversify.[162] For example, in *Reich v. King*,[163] the court found that a fiduciary did not breach the duty to diversify when 70% of the

---

[155]   H.R. Rep. No. 93-1280, at 304 (1974) (Conf. Rep.), *reprinted in* 1974 U.S.C.C.A.N. 5038, 5084–85.

[156]   *See* Metzler v. Graham, 112 F.3d 207, 209 (5th Cir. 1997), *citing* H.R. Rep. No. 93-1280, 2d Sess., at 304 (1974), *reprinted in* 1974 U.S.C.C.A.N. 5038, 5084.

[157]   112 F.3d at 209. The factors incorporate Comment b to Restatement (Second) of Trusts § 228. *See* H.R. Rep. No. 93-1280, 2d Sess., at 304 (1974), *reprinted in* 1974 U.S.C.C.A.N. 5038, 5084–85

[158]   *See, e.g.*, Reich v. King, 867 F. Supp. 341, 343 (D. Md. 1984).

[159]   *Id.*

[160]   Metzler v. Graham, 112 F.3d 207, 209 (5th Cir. 1997).

[161]   *See, e.g.*, Reich v. King, 867 F. Supp. at 343.

[162]   ABA Section of Labor and Employment Law, Employee Benefits Law, at 10-65 (noting that "[w]here courts have found a diversification violation, defendants generally have failed to explain to the courts' satisfaction why nondiversification was clearly prudent under the circumstances").

[163]   867 F. Supp. 341 (D. Md. 1994).

plan's investments were secured by real estate in a single county. The court was persuaded by the fact that the loans were short-term (5 year "balloons") as well as the testimony of an expert witness who had analyzed the specific loans and was familiar with the real estate market at issue and opined that investments were clearly prudent under the circumstances.[164]

Section 404(a)(2) exempts ESOPs and other individual account plans from the duty to diversify with respect to the acquisition and holding of employer stock and real property.

[F] The Duty to Follow Plan Documents — ERISA § 404(a)(1)(D)

Section 404(a)(1)(D) of ERISA requires plan fiduciaries to act in accordance with plan documents and instruments insofar as they are consistent with ERISA.

[1] Plan Documents

Courts have interpreted the duty to follow plan documents to extend to documents that have a substantive effect on the plan, such as investment management agreements, collective bargaining agreements, and internal memoranda regarding the sale of plan assets.[165]

In *Kennedy v. Plan Administrator for DuPont Savings and Investment Plan*,[166] the Supreme Court held that the duty extends to a plan's beneficiary designation forms. In *Kennedy*, a plan participant signed a form designating his wife as beneficiary of his savings and investment plan, a pension plan subject to ERISA.[167] The form did not name a contingent beneficiary if she disclaimed her interest.[168] Later, the participant and his wife divorced, and the ex-wife waived all interest in her spouse's pension plans pursuant to the divorce decree.[169] The plan participant did not execute any documents removing his wife as beneficiary of his savings and investment plan, although he did execute a new beneficiary-designation form naming his daughter as beneficiary of a different ERISA-governed pension plan.[170] The Court held that the waiver was valid but that the plan administrator of the savings and investment plan was not required to give it effect because the ex-wife was the named beneficiary under the documents and instrument governing plan; that is, the plan's beneficiary designation form.[171]

---

[164] *Id.* at 344–45. *See also* Metzler v. Graham, 112 F.3d 207 (5th Cir. 1997) (finding no violation of the duty to diversify where 63% of plan's assets invested in a single tract of undeveloped real estate).

[165] *See* George A. Norwood, *Who is Entitled to Receive a Deceased Participant's ERISA Retirement Plan Benefits — an Ex-Spouse or Current Spouse?*, The Federal Circuits Have an Irreconcilable Conflict, 33 Gonz. L. Rev. 61, 75 (1998).

[166] 555 U.S. 285 (2009).

[167] *Id.* at 288–89.

[168] *Id.* at 289.

[169] *Id.*

[170] *Id.*

[171] *Id.* at 209–304.

The Court explained:

> [B]ly giving a plan participant a clear set of instructions for making his own instructions clear, ERISA forecloses any justification for enquiries into nice expressions of intent, in favor of the virtues of adhering to an uncomplicated rule: 'simple administration, avoid[ing] double liability, and ensur[ing] that beneficiaries get what's coming quickly, without the folderol essential under less-certain rules.[172]

[2] Conflict with ERISA

If a plan provision conflicts with ERISA, section 404(a)(1)(D) requires the plan fiduciary to ignore the plan provision. The Supreme Court has noted, "trust documents cannot excuse trustees from their duties under ERISA, and . . . trust documents must generally be construed in light of ERISA's policies."[173] By requiring that fiduciaries only follow plan documents insofar as they are consistent with ERISA, section 404(a)(1)(D) prevents employers from overreaching and abusing their power as settlors in drafting plan documents.[174]

§ 6.05 ERISA'S EXEMPTION FROM FIDUCIARY STANDARDS FOR CERTAIN SELF-DIRECTED PLANS — ERISA § 404(c)

Section 404(c) of ERISA provides an exception from the fiduciary provisions for plans in which plan participants exercise independent control over the investment of the assets in their individual accounts.

In the absence of ERISA § 404(c), a 401(k) plan participant who directs the investment of her individual account balance in her 401(k) plan would be a fiduciary because she exercises control over the plan assets in her individual account.[175] More importantly, in the absence of ERISA § 404(c), an employer could be a co-fiduciary liable for any loss caused by the participant's failure to satisfy ERISA's fiduciary duties in investing the assets in her individual account.[176]

In fact, ERISA § 404(c) provides an exception for self-directed plans. Specifically, under the ERISA § 404(c) exception, plan participants are not treated as plan fiduciaries,[177] and persons who would otherwise qualify as plan fiduciaries face no liability for any losses caused by the participant's exercise of control.[178] Thus,

---

[172] *Id.* at 301.

[173] Cent. States v. Cent. Transp., 472 U.S. 559, 568 (1985) (citing ERISA § 404(a)(1)(D)).

[174] Colleen E. Medill, *The Federal Common Law of Vicarious Fiduciary Liability under ERISA*, 44 U. MICH. J.L. REFORM 249, 276 (2011).

[175] ERISA § 3(21)(A)(i) (defining fiduciary as person who exercises any authority or control regarding management or disposition of plan assets). *See* § 6.03 (discussing definition of fiduciary).

[176] ERISA § 405(a) (imposing liability on co-fiduciaries). *See* § 6.07[B] (discussing co-fiduciary liability).

[177] ERISA § 404(c)(1)(a)(i).

[178] ERISA § 404(c)(1)(a)(ii).

ERISA § 404(c) relieves plan sponsors from any liability (directly or as a co-fiduciary) for losses caused by plan participants' investment decisions.

ERISA § 404(c) does not eliminate all fiduciary liability with respect to self-directed plans.[179] For example, plan sponsors retain fiduciary liability with respect to the selection of investment options they offer under a plan,[180] and persons who provide participants with investment advice remain fiduciaries subject to ERISA's fiduciary duties and prohibited transaction provisions.[181]

[A] Purpose of ERISA § 404(c) Exception

ERISA's legislative history does not provide a great deal of insight regarding Congress' intent with respect to ERISA § 404(c).[182] According to Frank Cummings, past Chief of Staff to Senator Jacobs, one of the principle sponsors of ERISA, section 404(c) was added in response to lobbying by John Lippman, Vice President of a California company that administered self-directed defined contribution plans. Lippman's unique plans permitted plan participants, who were typically dentists, to direct their investments without having their partners or nurses know how they were investing their funds.[183]

[B] Significance of ERISA § 404(c) Exception

The ERISA § 404(c) exception was relatively insignificant at the time that ERISA was enacted.[184] 401(k) plans did not exist,[185] and the thrift or savings plans that allowed for after-tax employee contributions through payroll deductions simply supplemented traditional defined benefit plans. Thus, Congress did not

---

[179] *Final Regulation Regarding Participant Directed Individual Account Plans*, 57 Fed. Reg. 46,906, 46,924 (Oct. 13, 1992).

[180] 29 C.F.R. 2550.404c-1(d)(2)(iv).

[181] *See* DOL Advisory Opinion 2005-23A (stating that an individual who, for a fee, advises a participant on how to invest the assets of a plan account or manage the plan account is a fiduciary, even if the individual has no other connection with or fiduciary responsibility to the plan).

[182] A brief explanation of the provision is provided in H. Rep. No. 1280, at 305 (1974), *reprinted in* 1974 U.S.C.C.A.N. 5038, 5086 (noting that "[t]he conferees expect that the regulations will provide more stringent standards with respect to determining whether there is an independent exercise of control where the investments may inure to the direct or indirect benefit of the plan sponsor since, in this case participants might be subject to pressure with respect to investment decisions"). *Cf.* Stefanie Kastrinsky, *ERISA Section 404(c) and Investment Advice: What is an Employer or Plan Sponsor to Do?*, 80 Chi.-Kent L. Rev. 903, 908 (2005) (noting that ERISA's legislative history does not provide any insights about Congress' intent with respect to the scope or application of ERISA § 404(c)).

[183] *Panel 4: ERISA and the Fiduciary, Symposium: ERISA at 40: What were They Thinking?*, 6 Drexel L. Rev. 359, 378 (2014). Susan J. Stabile, *Freedom to Choose Unwisely: Congress' Misguided Decision to Leave 401(k) Plan Participants to their Own Devices*, 11 Cornell J.L. & Pub. Pol'y 361, 368–73 (2000).

[184] Indeed, Frank Cummings has said, "I never thought that it [section 414(c)] would be used after DB [defined benefit] plans got slaughtered by DC [defined contribution] plans, that it would become such a big deal in 401(k)s because of course there was no 401(k) at the time and most of the plans were DB plans." *See Panel 4: ERISA and the Fiduciary*, 6 Drexel L. Rev., at 369.

[185] Congress authorized 401(k) plans in 1978. Revenue Act of 1978, Pub. L. No. 95-600, § 135, 92 Stat. 2763, 2785–86 (1978). They became effective in 1980. *Id.* § 135(c)(1), 92 Stat. 2787.

need to be particularly concerned about the consequences of individual participant investment decisions in those supplemental plans.[186]

Today, the ERISA § 404(c) exception is quite important. Most pension plans are now 401(k) plans, and most 401(k) plans authorize plan participants to direct their investments.[187]

[C] ERISA § 404(c) Regulations

The ERISA § 404(c) exception applies if plan participants "exercise control" over the assets in their individual accounts.[188] ERISA does not define control for purposes of ERISA § 404(c). Instead, it authorizes the Department of Labor to flesh out the concept through regulations.[189]

Under the Department of Labor's ERISA § 404(c) regulations,[190] in order to qualify for protection under ERISA § 404(c), a plan must:

(1) provide participants with an opportunity to exercise control over the assets in their individual accounts, and

(2) provide participants the opportunity to choose among a broad range of investment options.[191]

In addition, a plan participant must in fact exercise independent control over her account.[192]

[1] Opportunity to Exercise Control

In order to be treated as having the opportunity to exercise control, the participant

(1) must have a reasonable opportunity to give investment instructions to a plan fiduciary who is obligated to comply with those instructions,[193] and

---

[186] Stabile, *Freedom to Choose Unwisely: Congress' Misguided Decision to Leave 401(k) Plan Participants to their Own Devices*, 11 CORNELL J.L. & PUB. POL'Y at 362 n.11.

[187] *Id.* at 366 (noting that since the Labor Department promulgated its ERISA § 404(c) regulations in 2002, more employers have restructured their plans so as to fall within the ERISA § 404(c) exception). *See also* Colleen E Medill, *Stock Market Volatility and 401(k) Plans*, 34 U. MICH. J.L. REFORM 469, 478–79 (discussing changes in 401(k) plan environment following promulgation of final regulations).

[188] Colleen E. Medill, *The Individual Responsibility Model of Retirement Plans Today: Conforming ERISA Policy to Reality*, 49 EMORY L.J. 1, 33 (2000) (explaining that the key concept under ERISA § 404(c) is plan participant's exercise of independent control over investment decisions).

[189] ERISA § 404(c)(1)(A)(1)(A) ("if a participant or beneficiary exercises control over the assets in his account (as determined under regulations of the Secretary)"). The Department of Labor issued final regulations in 1992. Final Regulation Regarding Participant Directed Individual Account Plans, 57 Fed. Reg. 46,906 (Oct. 13, 1992) (codified at 29 C.F.R. § 2550.404c-1).

[190] For a more detailed discussion of the regulations, see Medill, *The Individual Responsibility Model of Retirement Plans Today*, 49 EMORY L.J., at 33–38.

[191] 29 C.F.R. § 2550.404c-1(b)(1)(i)-(ii).

[192] 29 C.F.R. § 2550.404c-1(c)(1). Whether a participant has actually exercised independent control depends on the specific facts and circumstances. 29 C.F.R. § 2550.404c-1(c)(2).

[193] 29 C.F.R. § 2550.404c-1(b)(2)(i)(A).

(2) must be provided or have the opportunity to obtain sufficient information to make informed decisions with respect to the investment alternatives available under the plan.[194]

[2] Broad Range of Investment Options

The opportunity to choose among a broad range of investment options requires that the participant be given the opportunity to diversify investments among at least three investment choices with materially different risk and return characteristics.[195]

This requirement will generally be satisfied if a plan offers at least three investment options, including

(1) a broad-based common stock fund,

(2) a diversified bond fund, and

(3) a money market fund.[196]

[D] Investment Education versus Investment Advice

ERISA § 404(c) only applies if a plan participant exercises independent control over her individual account and thus makes the investment decisions with respect to her individual account.

Most plan participants are not professional investors. Rather, most plan participants are regular people with regular jobs, and they tend to be poor investors.[197] Policymakers first sought to address the problem of plan participants making poor investment decisions by encouraging plans to provide participants with investment education. When investment education failed to resolve the problem,[198] policymakers began to encourage plans to provide participants with investment advice.

---

[194] 29 C.F.R. § 2550.404c-1(b)(2)(i)(B). A variety of disclosures, including participant fee disclosures, must be made available to plan participants.

For a discussion of the type of information that must be made available, see Stephanie Kastrinsky, *ERISA Section 404(c) and Investment Advice: What is an Employer or Plan Sponsor to Do?*, 80 Chi.-Kent L. Rev. 903, 900-10 (2005); Medill, *The Individual Responsibility Model of Retirement Plans Today*, 49 Emory L.J., at 35-36.

[195] 29 C.F.R. § 2550.404c-1(b)(3)(i)(B).

[196] According to one authority, on average, 401(k) plans offer 17 investment choices. Jill E. Fisch, *Rethinking the Regulation of Securities Intermediaries*, 158 U. Pa. L. Rev. 1961, 1985 (2010)

[197] *See, e.g.*, Muir, *The Dichotomy Between Investment Advice and Investment Education*, 23 Berkeley J. Emp. & Lab. L., at 18 (noting that "the relevant data and theoretical research indicate that plan investors often do not invest their retirement plan assets in ways that are consistent with current financial investment theory"); Medill, *The Individual Responsibility Model of Retirement Plans Today*, 49 Emory L.J., at 18–24 (describing studies); Susan J. Stabile, *The Behavior of Defined Contribution Plan Participants*, 77 N.Y.U. L. Rev. 71, 88 (2002).

[198] *See, e.g.*, Colleen E. Medill, *Challenging the Four "Truths" of Personal Social Security Accounts: Evidence from the World of 401(k) Plans*, 81 N.C. L. Rev. 901, 947–49 (2003) (discussing and citing studies); Medill, *The Individual Responsibility Model of Retirement Plans Today*, 49 Emory L.J., at 18–24 (describing studies).

Some commentators contend that neither investment education nor investment advice are the answer to poor investment decision-making by plan participants. Instead, they contend that self-directed 401(k) plans are fundamentally flawed and investment decisions should be made by investment experts rather than plan participants.[199] Indeed, Phyllis Borzi, Assistant Secretary of Labor, Employee Benefit Security Administration, has described section 404(c) as a "completely nonsensical provision"[200] that she wishes she had "the power to excise."[201]

[1] Investment Education

Investment education is essentially general information regarding investment theory and plan investment options.[202] The provision of investment education does not give rise to fiduciary liability. The Department of Labor encourages, indeed to some extent requires, plan sponsors to provide plan participants with investment education.[203]

[2] Investment Advice

Investment advice is much more specific than investment education.[204] It constitutes personalized advice tailored to a particular individual and his or her needs, such as advice regarding which investments to purchase and how much of a particular security to hold.[205]

Unlike investment education, investment advice gives rise to fiduciary liability.

---

[199] *See, e.g.,* Kathryn L. Moore, *Regulating Investment Advice for 401(k) Plan Participants: Is More Investment Advice the Answer?*, 2010 N.Y.U. Rev. of Employee Benefits & Exec. Comp. 5-1, 5-33; Stabile, *Freedom to Choose Unwisely*, 11 Cornell J. L. & Pub. Pol'y 361 (2002).

[200] As Ms. Borzi has explained:

If you think about the logic . . . people say, "Look, these poor small employers, they can't possibly be able to figure out this complicated asset management stuff, so if the entrepreneur who started the business is too stupid to figure this out, let's give it to the workers because they're a heck of a lot smarter."

Panel 4: ERISA and the Fiduciary, 6 Drexel L. Rev., at 370.

[201] *Id.*

[202] Department of Labor Interpretive Bulletin 96-1 (identifying four increasingly specific categories of investment education: (1) plan information, (2) general financial and investment information, (3) asset allocation models, and (4) interactive investment models). For a detailed discussion of investment education, see James A. Fanto, *We're All Capitalists Now: The Importance, Nature, Provision and Regulation of Investor Education*, 49 Case W. Res. L. Rev. 105 (1998).

[203] *See* 29 C.F.R. § 2550.404c-1(b)(2)(i)(B) (requiring plan participants to be provided or have opportunity to obtain sufficient information to make informed decisions with respect to investment alternatives under 404(c) plan).

[204] *But see* Medill, *The Individual Responsibility Model of Retirement Plans Today*, 49 Emory L.J., at 54–62 (showing how the distinction between investment education and investment advice is often unclear, particularly from the perspective of plan participants).

[205] *See* Dana M Muir, *ERISA and Investment Issues*, 65 Ohio St. L.J. 199, 236 (2004) (discussing difference between investment advice and investment education); Department of Labor Interpretive Bulletin 96-1 (issuing guidance that draws line between investment education and investment advice).

Investment advisers are, by definition, fiduciaries subject to ERISA's fiduciary provisions.[206] In addition, plan sponsors may be liable as co-fiduciaries for losses that arise as a result of plan participants following the investment advice they receive. Finally, the prohibited transaction rules[207] prohibit service providers, such as mutual funds that offer plan investments, from providing investment advice to plan participants for a fee.

In order to make it easier for plan sponsors to offer plan participants investment advice, Congress amended ERISA's prohibited transaction rules in 2006[208] to create an express statutory exemption for "eligible investment advice arrangements."[209] The exemption makes clear that the selection of the investment adviser is itself a fiduciary act, but that a plan sponsor is not subject to fiduciary liability for investment advice provided under the exemption so long as the employer enters into the arrangement with the fiduciary adviser, the terms of the arrangement require the fiduciary to comply with the rules, and the fiduciary adviser acknowledges that it is an ERISA fiduciary.[210]

Although ERISA § 408(b)(14) is intended to make it easier for plan sponsors to provide plan participants with investment advice, few plan sponsors have taken advantage of the provision.[211]

§ 6.06   PROHIBITED TRANSACTION REGIME — ERISA §§ 406–408

ERISA § 404(a)(1)'s general fiduciary standards are supplemented by a prohibited transaction regime set forth in ERISA §§ 406–408. The Internal Revenue Code contains a nearly parallel prohibited transaction regime that applies to qualified plans and other retirement plans that receive favorable income tax treatment.[212]

---

[206]   ERISA § 3(38).

[207]   The prohibited transaction rules are discussed in § 6.06.

[208]   Pension Protection Act of 2006, Pub. L. No. 109-280 § 601(a)(2), 120 Stat. 780, 953 (2006).

[209]   In essence, section 408(b)(14) of ERISA provides an express statutory exemption from the prohibited transaction rules to allow a fiduciary adviser that is a bank, insurance company, registered investment adviser or registered broker-dealer to provide investment advice for a fee provided that the advice (1) is based on an unbiased computer model certified by a third party, or (2) the advisor's compensation does not vary with investment option recommended. For a more detailed discussion of ERISA § 408(b)(14), see Moore, *Regulating Investment Advice for 401(k) Plan Participants: Is More Investment Advice the Answer?*, 2010 N.Y.U. REV. OF EMPLOYEE BENEFITS & EXEC. COMP., at 5-13–5-15.

[210]   ERISA § 408(g)(10).

[211]   Pete Swisher, *Compensation and Conflicts of Interest in ERISA Plans*, 20 J. OF PENS. BENEFITS 17, 20 (Winter 2013) (stating that "[a]s a practical matter no one is using the exemption").

[212]   IRC § 4975.

There are some differences between the IRC prohibited transaction rules and ERISA's prohibited transaction rules. For example, the IRC prohibited transaction rules do not contain restrictions relating to employer securities like those contained in ERISA § 407 and do not contain a prohibition like ERISA § 406(b)(2) which prohibits a fiduciary from acting in a transaction that involves a party whose interests are adverse to those of the plan. In addition, the IRC rules prohibit transactions with "disqualified persons" which are similar, though not identical, to "parties in interest" for purposes of ERISA's prohibited transaction rules. *Compare* IRC § 4975(e)(2) (defining disqualified person) *with* ERISA

ERISA's prohibited transaction regime categorically prohibits specified transactions that, on their face, give rise to an inference that the fiduciary is not acting in the plan participants and beneficiaries' best interest.[213] The prohibited transaction rules are intended "to make illegal per se the types of transactions that experience had shown to entail a high potential for abuse."[214] No finding is required to show that a particular transaction is, in fact, inappropriate or unfair to the plan.[215]

Section 406 of ERISA prohibits three broad categories of transactions:

(1) transactions between the plan and a party in interest,[216]

(2) fiduciary conflicts,[217] and

(3) the transfer of real or personal property to a plan by a party in interest if the property is subject to a mortgage or lien which the plan assumes.[218]

Section 407 of ERISA prohibits a plan from acquiring or holding

(1) any employer security which is not a "qualifying employer security," and

(2) any employer real property which is not "qualifying real property."[219]

The prohibitions are defined so broadly that it would be impossible to operate any employee benefit plan without exemptions.[220] For example, absent an exemption, the prohibited transaction rules would prohibit a plan from paying benefits to a participant or compensating service providers. In fact, the prohibited transaction provisions are so broad that, absent an exception, they would prohibit a service provider from providing services.[221]

---

§ 3(14)(defining party in interest). For a more detailed discussion of the similarities and differences between the ERISA and IRC prohibited transaction rules, see Bender's Federal Income Taxation of Retirement Plans, Chapter 20 (Alvin D. Lurie, ed. 2008).

[213] Stabile, *Breach of ERISA Fiduciary Responsibilities: Who's Liable Anyway?*, 5 Empl. Rts. & Employ. Pol'y J., at 139.

[214] Donovan v. Cunningham, 716 F.2d 1455, 1464–65 (5th Cir. 1983), *cert. denied*, 467 U.S. 1251 (1984). *See also* Lockheed Corp. v. Spink, 517 U.S. 882, 888 (1996) ("Congress enacted § 406 'to bar categorically a transaction that [is] likely to injure the pension plan.' ")

[215] David A. Pratt, *Nor Rhyme nor Reason: Simplifying Defined Contribution Plans*, 49 Buffalo L. Rev. 741, 813 (2001). *See, e.g.*, Amalgamated Clothing & Textile Workers Union v. Murdock, 861 F.2d 1406, 1418 (9th Cir. 1988) (finding prohibited transaction even though plan not harmed and benefits paid in full).

[216] ERISA § 406(a).

[217] ERISA § 406(b).

[218] ERISA § 406(a)(c).

[219] ERISA § 406(a)(2) prohibits a fiduciary from permitting a plan to hold employer securities or real property if the fiduciary knows or should know that that holding of the securities or property violates ERISA § 407(a).

[220] Pratt, 49 Buffalo L. Rev., at 813.

[221] *See* Swisher, *Compensation and Conflicts of Interest in ERISA Plans*, 20 J. of Pens. Benefits, at 18 (noting that ERISA's broad prohibited transaction regime "leads to some interesting and sometimes nonintuitive outcomes, such as the fact that the provision of services causes one to be prohibited from providing services. (That is, a service provider is a party in interest under ERISA Section 3(14)(b), and parties in interest are prohibited from providing services under ERISA Section 406(a)(1)(C)).").

In order to make the system workable, ERISA § 408 sets forth a number of statutory exemptions from ERISA's prohibited transaction rules.[222] For example, ERISA § 408(c)(1) permits plan participants to receive benefits, and ERISA § 408(c)(2) authorizes contracts for necessary services for reasonable compensation. In addition, ERISA § 408 grants the Department of Labor regulatory authority to issue both class and individual exemptions.[223]

Violations of the prohibited transaction provisions may result in an excise tax[224] or civil penalty,[225] and fiduciaries may be held personally liable for violations.[226]

---

[222] ERISA § 408.

[223] ERISA § 408(a).

[224] IRC § 4975.

[225] ERISA § 502(i).

[226] ERISA § 409.

[A]   Overview of ERISA's Prohibited Transaction Regime

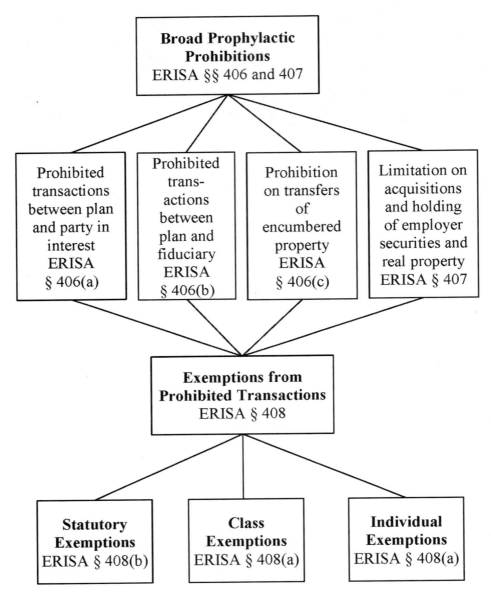

[B]   Section 406(a) Prohibited Transactions Between the Plan and a Party in Interest

ERISA § 406(a) prohibits a fiduciary from causing a plan to engage in a transaction if the fiduciary knows, or should know, that the transaction constitutes, directly or indirectly, a specifically identified transaction between a plan and a "party in interest."

Section 406(a) prohibited transactions do not necessarily involve any actual or potential conflict of interest. They do, however, always involve a transaction between a plan and a party in interest.

[1] Party in Interest — ERISA § 3(14)

"Congress defined 'party in interest' to encompass those entities that a fiduciary might be inclined to favor at the expense of the plan's beneficiaries."[227] Specifically, ERISA § 3(14)[228] defines the term "party in interest" to include nine categories of parties in interest.

The two most significant categories are

(1) fiduciaries,[229] and

(2) service providers.[230]

The other categories include

(1) any employer whose employees are covered by the plan;[231]

(2) any employee organization whose members are covered by the plan;[232]

(3) the officers, directors, employers, and majority owners of any employee organization or employer whose members or employees are covered by the plan;[233]

(4) relatives of a party in interest;[234] and

(5) certain majority-owned business entities of parties in interest.[235]

[2] ERISA § 406(a) Prohibited Transactions between the Plan and a Party in Interest

Section 406(a) prohibits five broad categories of transactions between a plan and a party in interest. Specifically, ERISA § 406(a) prohibits

(1) the sale, exchange, or leasing of property between a plan and a party in interest;[236]

---

[227] Harris Trust and Savings Bank v. Salomon Smith Barney Inc., 530 U.S. 238, 242 (2000).

[228] ERISA § 3(14).

[229] ERISA § 3(14)(A).

[230] ERISA § 3(14)(B).

[231] ERISA § 3(14)(C).

[232] ERISA § 3(14)(D).

[233] ERISA § 3(14)(E).

[234] ERISA § 3(14)(F).

[235] ERISA § 3(14)(G). Parties in interest also include employees, officers, directors, 10% shareholders, or 10% partners or joint venturers of parties in interest other than fiduciary and relative parties in interest. ERISA § 3(14)(H) & (I).

[236] ERISA § 406(a)(1)(A). In *Commissioner v. Keystone Consolidated Industries, Inc.*, 508 U.S. 152 (1993), discussed below, the Supreme Court held that an employer's contribution of unencumbered property to a defined benefit plan to satisfy the employer's funding obligation to the plan was a sale or

(2) the lending of money or extension of credit between a plan and a party in interest;[237]

(3) the furnishing of goods, services, or facilities between a plan and a party in interest;[238]

(4) the transfer to, or use by or for the benefit of, a party in interest, of the assets of the plan;[239] and

(5) the acquisition, on behalf of the plan, of any employer security or employer real property in violation of section 407(a).[240]

---

exchange within the meaning of the IRC's parallel prohibition on sales or exchanges, IRC § 4975(c)(1)(A), and thus was a prohibited transaction.

[237] ERISA § 406(a)(1)(B). *See, e.g.*, Brock v. Citizens Bank, 841 F.2d 344 (10th Cir. 1988) (holding that permitting bank's plan to borrow money from bank violated ERISA § 406(a)(1)(B)).

[238] ERISA § 406(a)(1)(C).

[239] ERISA § 406(a)(1)(D).

[240] ERISA § 406(a)(1)(E).

[3]   Overview of ERISA § 406(a) Party in Interest Prohibited Transactions

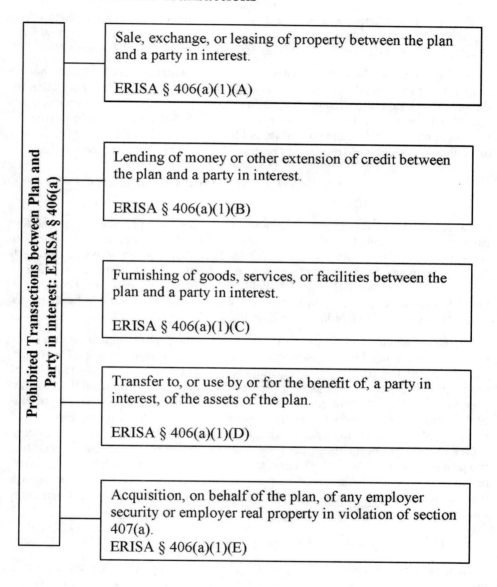

Prohibited Transactions between Plan and Party in interest: ERISA § 406(a)

Sale, exchange, or leasing of property between the plan and a party in interest.

ERISA § 406(a)(1)(A)

Lending of money or other extension of credit between the plan and a party in interest.

ERISA § 406(a)(1)(B)

Furnishing of goods, services, or facilities between the plan and a party in interest.

ERISA § 406(a)(1)(C)

Transfer to, or use by or for the benefit of, a party in interest, of the assets of the plan.

ERISA § 406(a)(1)(D)

Acquisition, on behalf of the plan, of any employer security or employer real property in violation of section 407(a).
ERISA § 406(a)(1)(E)

[4] Supreme Court Cases Interpreting ERISA § 406(a) Party In Interest Prohibited Transactions

The Supreme Court addressed the party in interest prohibited transaction provisions in three cases: *Commissioner v. Keystone Consolidated Industries, Inc.*,[241] *Lockheed Corp. v. Spink*,[242] and *Hughes Aircraft Co. v. Jacobson*.[243]

In *Keystone*, the Court held that an employer's contribution of unencumbered property[244] to a defined benefit plan to satisfy the employer's funding obligation to the plan was a sale or exchange in violation of the prohibition transaction rules. In *Spink*, the Court drew limits on the reach of ERISA § 406(a). In *Hughes Aircraft*, the Court cited *Spink* in support of its holding that ERISA's fiduciary provisions, including the prohibited transaction regime, do not apply to plan amendments.

[a] *Commissioner v. Keystone Consolidated Industries*

As noted above, the Internal Revenue Code contains prohibited transaction rules that are similar, though not identical, to the ERISA prohibited transaction rules. Like ERISA § 406(a)(1), IRC § 4975(c)(1)(A) prohibits any direct or indirect "sale or exchange, or leasing, of any property between a plan and a disqualified person." In *Keystone*, the Court held that an employer's contribution of unencumbered real property to satisfy the plan's minimum funding obligation was a sale or exchange in violation of IRC § 4975(c).

The Court noted that Congress' goal in enacting the prohibited transaction rules was to categorically bar transactions that are likely to injure plans. The Court explained that the transfer of unencumbered property as well as the transfer of property subject to a mortgage or lien could jeopardize a plan's ability to pay promised benefits. "Although the burden of an encumbrance is unique to the contribution of encumbered property, concerns about overvaluation, disposal of property, and the need to maintain an independent investment policy animate any contribution of property that satisfies a funding obligation, regardless of whether the property is encumbered."[245] Thus, the Court held that the prohibition on direct or indirect sales or exchanges of property between a plan and disqualified person includes an employer's transfer of unencumbered property to satisfy its minimum funding obligation.

[b] *Lockheed Corp. v. Spink*

Generally, the categories of transactions prohibited by ERISA § 406(a) are so broadly defined that it is fair to say that ERISA prohibits all transactions between a plan and a party in interest except transactions that are statutorily exempted

---

[241] 508 U.S. 152 (1993).

[242] 517 U.S. 882 (1996).

[243] 525 U.S. 432 (1999).

[244] "Encumbered" property is subject to a lien or mortgage. Unencumbered property is not.

[245] 508 U.S., at 160.

under ERISA § 408 or are exempted by the Department of Labor in class or individual exemptions through its exercise of rulemaking authority.[246] In *Lockheed Corp. v. Spink*,[247] the Supreme Court drew limits on the reach of ERISA § 406(a).

In *Spink*, an employee claimed that an employer's early retirement program that conditioned the receipt of early retirement benefits on an employee's release of employment-related claims violated ERISA § 406(a)(1)(D). As noted above, ERISA § 406(a)(1)(D) prohibits a fiduciary from causing a plan to engage in a transaction if the fiduciary knows or should know that the transaction constitutes a direct or indirect "transfer to, or use by or for the benefit of, a party in interest, of any assets of the plan."[248] The employee argued that the early retirement programs were prohibited because requiring the release of employment-related claims constituted a "significant benefit" to the employer.[249] The Court rejected the employee's argument and found that obtaining the waivers could not be distinguished from other legitimate "incidental" benefits that an employer may receive from a plan, such as attracting and retaining employees, and thus, the payment of benefits in exchange for the employee performing some condition is not a "transaction" within the meaning of ERISA § 406(a)(1)(D).[250]

[c]   *Hughes Aircraft Co. v. Jacobson*

In *Hughes Aircraft Co. v. Jacobson*,[251] a group of retirees filed suit claiming, among other things, that their former employer violated ERISA § 406(a)(1)(D) when it amended its defined benefit plan to provide for an early retirement program and a noncontributory benefit structure.[252] The Court rejected the retirees' claim. Citing *Spink*, the Court held that ERISA's fiduciary provisions (including its prohibited transaction regime) do not apply to plan amendments.[253]

[C]   Section 406(b) Prohibited Transactions Between the Plan and Fiduciary

Section 406(b) of ERISA prohibits transactions that involve actual or potential conflicts of interests or self-dealing by plan fiduciaries.

Specifically, ERISA § 406(b) prohibits three types of transactions between the plan and fiduciary:

---

[246] ERISA § 408(a). *See* Stabile, *Breach of ERISA Fiduciary Responsibilities: Who's Liable Anyway?*, 5 EMPL. RTS. & EMPLOY. POL'Y J., at 139 (stating that "[t]he categories of transactions that are prohibited are so broadly defined that it would not be hyperbole to say that all transactions between a plan and a party in interest are prohibited except for those specifically permitted by statute or DOL rulemaking").

[247] 517 U.S. 882 (1996).

[248] ERISA § 406(a)(1)(D).

[249] 517 U.S. at 893.

[250] *Id.* at 893–95.

[251] 525 U.S. 432 (1999).

[252] Prior to the plan amendment, the defined benefit plan required that employees contribute to the plan. Nevertheless, contributions had been suspended for several years because the plan had a surplus.

[253] 525 U.S. at 443-46.

(1) fiduciary "self-dealing" with respect to plan assets;[254]

(2) direct conflicts where the fiduciary represents the plan and an "adverse party" in the same transaction;[255] and

(3) a fiduciary's acceptance of compensation from a third party dealing with the plan,[256] sometimes referred to as the "anti-kickback provision."[257]

The section 406(b) prohibited transactions are derived from the common law trust principle that a fiduciary must have an undivided duty of loyalty to the trust on whose behalf it acts.[258] According to ERISA's legislative history, the ERISA § 406(b) prohibited transactions were designed to prevent "a fiduciary from being put in a position where he has dual loyalties, and, therefore, he cannot act exclusively for the benefit of a plan's participants and beneficiaries."[259]

Example of Prohibited Fiduciary Self-Dealing

An employer receives, for its business use, computer equipment from a bank because it maintains a minimum balance of plan assets in the bank's money market account.[260]

Example of Prohibited Conflict of Interest

A fiduciary represents both the lender and the borrower in a loan.[261]

Example of Prohibited Kickback

A fiduciary retains a person to provide services to a plan or invests a plan's assets in a specified investment in exchange for which the fiduciary receives money or other consideration.[262]

---

[254] ERISA § 406(b)(1). The prohibition against fiduciary self-dealing "was designed to protect the plan assets from being abused by the fiduciary to its own benefit at the expense of the beneficiaries." *Hylton*, 80 TENN. L. REV, at 81.

[255] ERISA § 406(b)(2).

[256] ERISA § 406(b)(3).

[257] *See, e.g.*, Swisher, *Compensation and Conflicts of Interest in ERISA Plans*, 20 J. OF PENS. BENEFITS, at 18.

[258] Medill, *The Individual Responsibility Model of Retirement Plans Today*, 49 EMORY L.J., at 39. *See* RESTATEMENT (THIRD) OF TRUSTS § 78 (2007) (imposing duty).

[259] H.R. Rep. No. 1280, at 309 (1974), reprinted in 1974 U.S.C.C.A.N. 5038, 5089.

[260] *See* Internal Revenue Manual, Prohibited Transactions 4.72.11.3.5.3, *available at* http://www.irs.gov/irm/part4/irm_04-072-011.html. *See also* Patelco Credit Union v. Sahni, 262 F.3d 897, 911 (9th Cir. 2001) (fiduciary violates ERISA § 406(b)(3) when he wrongfully deposits two checks payable to the company for the plan in his own account).

[261] *See* Martin v. National Bank of Alaska, 828 F. Supp. 1427 (D. Alaska 1992); Davidson v. Cook, 567 F. Supp. 225 (E.D. Va. 1983), *aff'd*, 734 F.2d 10 (4th Cir. 1983).

[262] *See* Internal Revenue Manual, Prohibited Transactions, at 4.72.11.3.6. *See also* Patelco Credit Union v. Sahni, 262 F.3d 897, 911 (9th Cir. 2001) (fiduciary violates ERISA § 406(b)(3) when he receives commissions from insurance company with whom he placed welfare benefit plan's coverage).

[D] ERISA § 406(c) Prohibition on Transfers of Encumbered Property

ERISA § 406(c) prohibits the transfer of real or personal property to a plan by a party in interest if:

(1) the property is subject to a mortgage or similar lien which the plan assumes, or

(2) the property is subject to a mortgage or lien placed on the property by a party-in-interest within 10 years of the transfer of the property.

[E] ERISA § 407(a) Limitation on Plan's Acquisition and Holding of Employer Securities and Real Property

As noted above, ERISA § 406(a)(1)(E) prohibits the acquisition, on behalf of the plan, of any employer security or employer real property in violation of section 407(a). ERISA § 407(a)(1) generally prohibits a plan from investing in the securities of an employer unless they are "qualifying employer securities"[263] and prohibits a plan from acquiring or holding employer real property unless it is "qualifying employer real property."[264]

Section 407(a)(2) expressly limits the amount of qualifying employer securities and employer real property that a plan may hold to 10% of the plan's assets. The section 407 requirements generally do not apply to defined contribution plans, such as 401(k) plans, that explicitly provide for investment in qualifying employer securities or qualifying employer property.[265] The exemption from the 10% rule, however, does not apply if the plan requires elective deferrals of more than 1% of compensation to be invested in qualifying employer securities or qualifying employer real property.[266]

---

[263] ERISA § 407(a)(1)(A). "Qualifying employer security" is defined as employer security which is (A) stock, (B) a marketable obligation, or (C) interest in an existing publicly traded partnership. ERISA § 407(d)(5).

[264] ERISA § 407(a)(1)(B). "Qualifying employer property" is defined as parcels of employer real property (1) if a substantial number of the parcels are dispersed geographically, (2) if each parcel of real property and the improvements thereon are suitable for more than one use, (3) even if all of the property is leased to a single lessee, and (4) if the acquisition and retention of the property complies with ERISA. ERISA § 407(d)(4).

[265] ERISA § 407(b)(1)(A). For an argument that the 10% limit should apply to self-directed plans, see Stabile, *Pension Plan Investments in Employer Securities: More is Not Always Better*, 15 YALE J. ON REGULATION, at 88.

[266] ERISA § 407(b)(2). Congress exempted individual account plans from the 10% limit in recognition of their "special purpose." Susan Stabile, *Another Look at 401(k) Investments in Employer Stock*, 35 J. MARSHALL L. REV. 539, 557 n.84 (2002).

[F]   Exemptions from ERISA's Prohibited Transaction Rules

ERISA § 408 sets forth a number of statutory exemptions from the prohibited transaction rules that permit customary business practices that are necessary for the operation of an employee benefit plan.[267] In addition, ERISA § 408 authorizes the DOL to grant administrative exemptions from the prohibited transaction provisions for classes of transactions or for individual transactions.

[1]   Statutory Exemptions

Section 408 of ERISA specifically exempts 20 transactions that would otherwise fall within the ERISA § 406 prohibited transaction rules.[268] Among the statutory exemptions are:

(1)   loans to plan participants or beneficiaries;[269]

(2)   contracts for the provision of services necessary for the operation of a plan for no more than reasonable compensation;[270]

(3)   loans to ESOPs;[271]

(4)   the investment of plan assets in a bank which is a fiduciary to the plan;[272] and

(5)   contracts for life insurance, health insurance, or annuities with one or more insurers.[273]

[2]   Administrative Exemptions

Section 408(a) of ERISA authorizes the Department of Labor (DOL) to grant a conditional or unconditional exemption for a transaction that would otherwise be prohibited under the prohibited transaction rules. In order to grant a Prohibited Transaction Exemption (PTE), the DOL must determine that the exemption is

(1)   administratively feasible,

(2)   in the interests of the plan and its participants and beneficiaries, and

(2)   protective of the rights of the plan participants and beneficiaries.[274]

Prior to granting an exemption, the DOL must publish a notice of proposed exemption in the Federal Register so that interested persons are given the

---

[267] United States Department of Labor Employee Benefits Security Administration, Exemption Procedures under Federal Pension Law, *available at* http://www.dol.gov/ebsa/publications/exemption_procedures.html.

[268] For a listing of the statutory exemptions, applicable Department of Labor advisory opinions, and conditions of exemption, see BENDER'S FEDERAL INCOME TAXATION OF RETIREMENT PLANS Chapter 22, at Table 22:1.

[269] ERISA § 408(b)(1).

[270] ERISA § 408(b)(2).

[271] ERISA § 408(b)(3).

[272] ERISA § 408(b)(4).

[273] ERISA § 408(b)(5).

[274] ERISA § 408(a).

opportunity to comment on the proposal.[275] If the proposal involves potential fiduciary self-dealing or conflicts of interest, the opportunity for a public hearing must be provided.[276]

There are two types of Prohibited Transaction Exemptions:

(1) class exemptions; and

(2) individual exemptions.

[a]   Class Exemptions

A class exemption provides relief from the prohibited transaction provisions to a class of entities or individuals who engage in the transaction or transactions described in the exemption and meet the conditions contained in the exemption. There are about 50 class exemptions covering a wide range of transactions.[277]

Examples of class exemptions include

(1) interest-free loans made to plans by their sponsoring employers,[278]

(2) transfers of individual life insurance contracts between plans and their participants,[279] and

(3) an employee benefit plan's purchase or sale of mutual fund shares when an investment broker for the fund, other than the plan sponsor, is also a plan fiduciary.[280]

[b]   Individual Exemptions

An individual exemption provides relief from the prohibited transaction provisions to the specific parties who request the exemption. In granting an individual exemption, the DOL must make a case-by-case determination as to whether the specific facts regarding a specific transaction support a finding that that requirements for relief from the prohibited transaction provisions have been

---

[275] ERISA § 408(a).

[276] ERISA § 408(a).

[277] United States Department of Labor Employee Benefits Security Administration, Exemption Procedures under Federal Pension Law, *available at* http://www.dol.gov/ebsa/publications/exemption_procedures.html. For a list of the DOL's class exemptions, see http://www.dol.gov/ebsa/regs/classexemptions/. For a synopsis of the major class exemptions, including the applicable conditions, see BENDER'S FEDERAL INCOME TAXATION OF RETIREMENT PLANS Chapter 22, at Table 22:3.

[278] PTE 80-26, Class Exemption for Certain Interest Free Loans to Employee Benefit Plans, 45 Fed. Reg. 28, 545 (Apr. 29, 1980).

[279] PTE 92-5, Amendment to Prohibited Transaction Exemption (PTE) 77-7 Involving the Transfer of Individual Life Insurance and Annuity Contracts to Employee Benefit Plans, 57 Fed. Reg. 5019 (Feb. 11, 1992); PTE 92-6, Amendment to Prohibited Transaction Exemption (PTE) 77-8 Involving the Transfer of Individual Life Insurance Contracts and Annuities from Employee Benefit Plans to Plan Participants, Certain Beneficiaries of Plan Participants, Employers and Other Employee Benefit Plans, 57 Fed. Reg. 5189 (Feb. 12, 1992).

[280] PTE 77-4, Class Exemption for Certain Transactions Between Investment Companies and Employee Benefit Plans, 45 Fed. Reg. 18,732 (Apr. 8, 1977).

satisfied.[281] The DOL granted 11 individual exemptions in 2014.[282]

[G] Sanctions and Remedies

Under the tax prohibited transaction rules, "disqualified persons"[283] who participate in a prohibited transaction with a qualified plan owe a tax for each year that the transaction remains uncorrected. The initial tax is 15% of the "amount involved" in the prohibited transaction.[284] If the prohibited transaction is not corrected by the end of the "taxable period," the disqualified persons owe an additional tax equal to 100% of the "amount involved" in the prohibited transaction.[285]

Under the ERISA prohibited transaction rules, a fiduciary may be held liable for any losses caused by the prohibited transaction[286] and is subject to all other remedies available under ERISA § 409(a).[287] In addition, ERISA § 502(i) authorizes the Secretary of Labor to assess a civil penalty on welfare plans.[288] The civil penalty is analogous to the excise tax described above which is only imposed on qualified plans.[289]

§ 6.07 FIDUCIARY LIABILITY

[A] Personal Liability of Fiduciary — ERISA § 409(a)

Section 409(a) of ERISA imposes personal liability on any fiduciary "who breaches any of the responsibilities, obligations, or duties" imposed upon fiduciaries under ERISA. Section 409(a) is enforced through ERISA § 502(a)(2), which authorizes participants, beneficiaries, fiduciaries, and the Secretary of Labor to bring a civil suit for appropriate relief under ERISA § 409(a). Such suits and

---

[281] United States Department of Labor Employee Benefits Security Administration, Exemption Procedures under Federal Pension Law, *available at* http://www.dol.gov/ebsa/publications/exemption_procedures.html.

[282] *See* http://www.dol.gov/ebsa/regs/ind_exemptionsmain.html (listing the DOL's most recent individual exemptions).

[283] "Disqualified persons" under the IRC are similar, though not identical, to "parties in interest" for purposes of ERISA's prohibited transaction rules. For example, ERISA § 3(14)(A), defines the term "party in interest" to include, among other categories, "any fiduciary (including, but limited to, any administrator, officer, trustee, or custodian), counsel, or employee of such employee benefit plan, while IRC § 4975(e)(2) limits that category of "disqualified persons" to "a fiduciary."

[284] IRC § 4975(a).

[285] IRC § 4975(b).

[286] Even if the prohibited transaction does not result in plan losses, the fiduciary may be required to disgorge any profits earned from the prohibited transaction. *See, e.g.*, Amalgamated Clothing & Textile Workers Union v. Murdock, 861 F.2d 1406, 1418 (9th Cir. 1988) (prohibiting fiduciary from retaining ill-gotten gains even though benefits paid in full).

[287] ERISA § 409 is discussed in § 6.07[A] & Chapter 7 § 7.08[B].

[288] In practice, the Department of Labor rarely assesses the ERISA § 502(i) penalty. ABA SECTION OF LABOR AND EMPLOYMENT LAW, EMPLOYEE BENEFITS LAW, at 10-140.

[289] The first tier civil penalty, however, is 5% rather than 15%. ERISA § 502(i).

remedies are discussed in Chapter 7 § 7.08[B].

[B] Co-Fiduciary Liability — ERISA § 405(a)

Section 405(a) of ERISA imposes "co-fiduciary liability" on a fiduciary ("co-fiduciary") who, although not directly engaged in a breach of fiduciary duty, participates in some way in a breach committed by another fiduciary ("breaching fiduciary").

Specifically, ERISA § 405(a) imposes co-fiduciary liability under the following three circumstances:

(1) if the co-fiduciary participates knowingly in, or knowingly undertakes to conceal, an act or omission of the breaching fiduciary, when the co-fiduciary knows that act or omission is a breach;

(2) if, by the co-fiduciary's failure to comply with the co-fiduciary's general fiduciary duties under ERISA § 404(a)(1) in his specific responsibilities which give rise to his status as a fiduciary, the co-fiduciary has enabled the breaching fiduciary to commit a breach;[290] or

(3) if the co-fiduciary has knowledge of a breach by the breaching fiduciary, unless the co-fiduciary makes reasonable efforts under the circumstances to remedy the breach.

According to Department of Labor guidance, a fiduciary must take all reasonable and legal steps to prevent or remedy a co-fiduciary breach. Reasonable steps include taking legal action against the co-fiduciary and informing the Department of Labor of the alleged breach. Resignation as a fiduciary, without more, does not constitute reasonable action.[291]

[C] Nonfiduciary Liability

Although ERISA explicitly imposes "co-fiduciary liability" on fiduciaries who participate in a fiduciary breach committed by another fiduciary, ERISA does not expressly address the liability of non-fiduciaries who participate in a breach of fiduciary duty or participate in a transaction prohibited under ERISA § 406.[292] Whether nonfiduciaries can be held liable in such cases has been the subject of considerable litigation.

The Supreme Court addressed liability of nonfiduciaries in two cases: *Mertens v. Hewitt*[293] and *Harris Trust v. Salomon Smith Barney, Inc.*[294] In *Mertens*, the

---

[290] This is the only circumstance in which co-fiduciary liability arises even if the co-fiduciary has no knowledge of the breaching fiduciary's breach.

[291] 29 C.F.R. 75-5, FR-10.

[292] ERISA does, however, authorize the Department of Labor to impose civil penalties on non-fiduciaries who engage in a prohibited transaction or participate in a fiduciary breach. ERISA § 502(i), (l).

[293] 508 U.S. 248 (1993).

[294] 530 U.S. 238 (2000). The Court also referred, in passing, to nonfiduciary liability in two cases decided between *Mertens* and *Harris Trust*. In *Central Bank of Denver v. First Interstate Bank of*

Court strongly suggested in *dicta* that a nonfiduciary could not be held liable under ERISA for participating in a breach of fiduciary duty. In *Harris Trust*, in contrast, the Court held that a nonfiduciary party in interest could be held liable for participating in a prohibited transaction.

The Court in *Harris Trust* did not decide whether a nonfiduciary could be held liable for participating in a breach of fiduciary duty. The Court's reasoning in the case, however, suggested that it can, and lower courts have applied the Court's reasoning in *Harris Trust* to hold that nonfiduciary liability extends to nonfiduciaries participating in a breach of fiduciary duty under ERISA § 404.

[1] *Mertens v. Hewitt*

The Supreme Court first addressed the issue of nonfiduciary liability in *Mertens v. Hewitt*.[295] In *Mertens*, the Court described the question before it as "whether a nonfiduciary who knowingly participates in the breach of a fiduciary duty imposed by [ERISA] is liable for losses that an employee benefit plan suffers as a result of the breach."[296] "[D]eciding [the] case on the narrow battlefield the parties have chosen,"[297] the Court dismissed the claim because "appropriate *equitable* relief" under ERISA § 502(a)(3)[298] does not include the monetary relief the plan participants sought in the case.

The Court in *Mertens* did not expressly decide whether nonfiduciaries can be held liable for participating in a breach of fiduciary duty. In *dicta*, however, the Court strongly suggested that ERISA would not allow such a suit. Specifically, the Court first noted that while ERISA § 405(a) explicitly imposes co-fiduciary liability on fiduciaries who knowingly participate in a fiduciary breach, it does not explicitly require that nonfiduciaries avoid participating in a fiduciary's breach of fiduciary duty. The Court then referred to its decision in *Russell* in which the Court expressed its unwillingness to infer causes of action in the ERISA context. Finally, the Court "acknowledged the oddity of resolving a dispute over remedies where it is unclear that a remediable wrong has been alleged"[299] before turning to decide the case on "the narrow battlefield the parties have chosen"[300] and expressly "reserved

---

Denver, 511 U.S. 164 (1994), the Court described its *Mertens* decision as rejecting the argument that a knowing participation cause of action should be available under ERISA. *Id.* at 175. Then, in a footnote in *Lockheed v. Spink*, 517 U.S. 882 (1996), the Court stated that the appellate court "was not necessarily wrong in saying that "a party interest who benefitted from an *impermissible* transaction can be held liable under ERISA." *Id.* at 889 n.3 (emphasis in original).

[295] 508 U.S. 248 (1993). In *Mertens*, pension plan beneficiaries brought suit against the plan's actuary claiming that the actuary knowingly participated in the plan fiduciaries' breach of fiduciary duty by, among other things, failing to adjust the plan's actuarial assumptions which caused the plan to be inadequately funded. For a critique of the Court's decision, see Susan J. Stabile, *The Role of Congressional Intent in Determining the Existence of Implied Private Rights of Action*, 71 Notre Dame L. Rev. 861, 908–12 (1996).

[296] 508 U.S. at 249–50.

[297] *Id.* at 255.

[298] *Id.* at 255 (emphasis in original).

[299] *Id.* at 254.

[300] *Id.* at 255.

decision of [the] antecedent question" of liability.[301]

[2]　*Harris Trust v. Salomon Smith Barney, Inc.*

The Court squarely addressed the issue of nonfiduciary liability in *Harris Trust v. Salomon Smith Barney, Inc.*[302] In *Harris Trust*, the Court assumed that Salomon, the plan's service provider and thus, a party in interest, entered into a prohibited transaction under ERISA § 406 when it sold several motel properties to the plan.[303] The Court rejected the Seventh Circuit's "conclusion, that absent a substantive provision under ERISA expressly imposing a duty upon a nonfiduciary party in interest, the nonfiduciary may not be held liable under § 502(a)(3)."[304] Instead, the Court expressly held that a nonfiduciary party in interest who participate in a prohibited transaction can be sued for "appropriate equitable relief" under ERISA § 502(a)(3).[305]

Although the Court did not expressly address nonfiduciary liability when a nonfiduciary participates in a breach of fiduciary duty under ERISA § 404, the Court's reasoning in *Harris Trust* suggests that its holding should extend liability to such a case. In *Harris Trust*, the Court declared that ERISA "§ 502(a)(3) itself imposes certain duties, and therefore that liability under that provision does not depend on whether ERISA's substantive provisions impose a specific duty on the party being sued."[306] In reaching that conclusion, the Court relied on two separate provisions of ERISA. First, it relied on ERISA § 502(a)(3)'s broad authorization of equitable relief to redress any violation or enforce any provision of ERISA without limiting the "universe of possible defendants."[307] Second, it relied on ERISA § 502(l), which imposes civil penalties upon parties for knowingly participating in fiduciary violations under part 4 of ERISA, and thus by implication supports the position that suit may be brought against non-fiduciaries under ERISA § 502(a).[308] Nothing in the Court's reasoning suggests that it should be limited to claims against nonfiduciary parties in interest who participate in prohibited transactions. Instead, it should apply equally to claims against nonfiduciary non-parties in interest who participate in prohibited transactions as well as to claims against nonfiduciaries who participate in breaches of fiduciary duty under ERISA § 404.[309]

Of course, extending liability to nonfiduciaries who participate in breaches of fiduciary duty under ERISA § 404 is inconsistent with the Court's *dicta* in *Mertens*. Unfortunately, the Court in *Harris Trust* did not expressly disavow its *dicta* in

---

[301]　*Id.*

[302]　530 U.S. 238 (2000).

[303]　*Id.* at 242–43.

[304]　*Id.* at 245.

[305]　*Id.* at 241. The Court's reasoning makes it clear that liability extends to claims brought by the Secretary of Labor under ERISA § 502(a)(5) as well. *Id.* at 248–49.

[306]　*Id.* at 245.

[307]　*Id.* at 246

[308]　*Id.* at 248–49.

[309]　For an exhaustive discussion of nonfiduciary liability, see Stabile, *Breach of ERISA Fiduciary Responsibilities: Who's Liable Anyway?*, 5 Empl. Rts. & Employ. Pol'y J. 135.

Mertens. Nor did it attempt to reconcile its decision with its *dicta* in *Mertens.* The Court simply noted that the Seventh Circuit saw no distinction between *Mertens* and *Harris Trust*[310] and then rejected the Seventh Circuit's decision without offering a distinction.[311]

[3] Extension of *Harris Trust* to Breach of Fiduciary Duty Cases

In light of the Court's reasoning in *Harris Trust*, lower courts have expressly rejected arguments that nonfiduciary liability should be limited to nonfiduciary parties in interest who participate in prohibited transactions.[312] Instead, lower courts have extended liability to nonfiduciary non-parties in interest who participate in prohibited transactions[313] as well as nonfiduciaries who participate in breaches of fiduciary duty under ERISA § 404.[314]

§ 6.08   FIDUCIARY LIABILITY AND 401(k) PLAN FEES

Employers that offer 401(k) plans typically hire service providers to administer their 401(k) plans,[315] and not surprisingly, the service providers charge fees for their services.[316] Those fees have been the subject of considerable scrutiny in recent years.[317]

The fees have been scrutinized because they can have a significant impact on retirement savings. In order to assist plan sponsors and plan participants in understanding and comparing plan fees, the Department of Labor has issued a series of regulations mandating fee disclosure. In addition, plan participants have

---

[310] 530 U.S. at 244.

[311] *Id.* at 245.

[312] *See, e.g.*, National Sec. Sys., Inc. v. Iola, 700 F.3d 65, 88–93 (3d Cir. 2012), *cert. denied*, 133 S. Ct. 1812 (2013). *Cf.* Longberger Co. v. Kolt, 586 F.3d 459, 468 n.7 (6th Cir. 2009) (declaring that reasoning in *Harris Trust* supports finding that participant's attorney, who is neither fiduciary nor party in interest, is proper defendant in ERISA § 502(a)(3) subrogation claim).

[313] *See, e.g.*, National Sec. Sys., Inc. v. Iola, 700 F.3d 65, 88–93 (3d Cir. 2012), *cert. denied*, 133 S. Ct. 1812 (2013).

[314] *See, e.g.*, Will v. General Dynamics Corp., 2009 U.S. Dist. LEXIS 105987, at *15–16 (S.D. Ill. Nov. 14, 2009); Chao v. Johnston, 2007 U.S. Dist. LEXIS 49921, at *22 (E.D. Tenn. July 9, 2007); *In re* Xerox Corp. ERISA Litig., 483 F. Supp.2d 206, 216 (D. Conn. 2007); Rudowski v. Sheet Metal Workers Int'l Ass'n, 24, 113 F. Supp. 2d 1176, 1180–81 (S.D. Ohio 2000).

[315] For a description of the services provided, see Investment Company Institute Research Perspective, *The Economics of Providing 401(k) Plans: Services, Fees, and Expenses, 2013* 3 (July 2014) (describing administrative services, participant-focused service, and regulatory and compliance services).

[316] For an overview of the structure of plan fees, see Richard W. Kopcke, *et. al.*, *The Structure of 401(k) Fees*, Center for Retirement Research at Boston College Issue in Brief 9-3, at 2–3 (Feb. 2009). *See also* Investment Company Institute Research Perspective, *The Economics of Providing 401(k) Plans: Services, Fees, and Expenses, 2013* 5 Figure 3 (July 2014) (diagraming the various arrangements that may be used to compensate service providers).

[317] For a discussion of the Department of Labor's initiatives on 401(k) plan fees beginning in the late 1990s, see Kathryn L. Moore, *401(k) Plan Fees: A Trifecta of Governmental Oversight*, 2009 N.Y.U. Review of Emp. Benes. & Exec. Comp. 17-1, 7-2–17-3.

filed a host of lawsuits challenging plan fees as excessive.

[A]   Plan Fees and their Impact on Retirement Savings

On average, fees and expenses for a small 401(k) plan were 1.46% in 2012.[318] Fees and expenses, however, range widely. For example, in 2012, fees for small plans ranged from a low of 0.38% to a high of 1.97%. Because fees and expenses are typically paid in large part by plan participants, they can have a significant impact on a plan participant's ultimate retirement benefit.

Example 1

Andrea, a 35 year-old employee plans to retire in 35 years at age 70. Andrea has a 401(k) account balance of $25,000, makes no additional contributions to the account, and the investment returns average 7% over the next 35 years. If Andrea pays 0.5% in fees and expenses each year, Andrea will have an account balance of $227,000 in 35 years. On the other hand, if Andrea pays 1.5% in fees and expenses each year, the account balance will only grow to $163,000 in 35 years.

A 1% increase in fees and expenses reduces Andrea's account balance by 28%.[319]

Example 2

Buford, a 401(k) plan participant, has an account balance of $100,000 earning a 7% annual return over 25 years. If Buford is charged 1.2% in annual fees, he will pay a total of $141,400 in fees. In contrast, if Buford is charged 0.3% in fees each year, Buford will only pay a total of $39,275 in fees.

The difference between fees of 1.2% and 0.3% over 25 years on a $100,000 account balance translates into a difference of just over $100,000 in fees.[320]

[B]   Fee Disclosure Regulations

Not only do plan fees and expenses range widely, but they are not charged in a uniform, straightforward manner. Rather, service providers are often compensated indirectly through revenue sharing agreements with mutual funds that offer investments in 401(k) plans.[321] Under a revenue sharing agreement, the mutual fund collects fees out of plan assets and disburses them to service providers. It can be difficult to determine exactly how much is paid in fees or who benefits from the fees under such an arrangement.

In order to ensure that plan participants and fiduciaries have the information necessary to understand and compare plan fees, the Department of Labor has

---

[318] Ashlea Ebeling, *401(k) Fees Still Widely Misunderstood*, Forbes (Mar. 11, 2013), *available at* http://www.forbes.com/sites/ashleaebeling/2013/03/11/401k-fees-still-widely-misunderstood/.

[319] *See* DOL EBSA, *A Look at 401(k) Plan Fees* 1–2 (Aug. 2013), *available at* http://www.dol.gov/ebsa/publications/401k_employee.html.

[320] Ian Salisbury, *The One Retirement Move You Must Get Right*, Money 45, 48 (July 2014).

[321] For a history of revenue sharing in 401(k) plans, see Dana M. Muir, *Revenue Sharing in 401(k) Plans: Employers as Monitors?*, 20 Conn. Ins. L.J. 485, 487–91 (2014)

mandated three different types of fee disclosures:

(1) Large plans, that is, plans with more than 100 participants, are required to identify in the annual reports they file with the Department of Labor all service providers who directly or indirectly receive more than $5,000 in compensation,[322]

(2) Plan service providers that receive at least $1,000 per year in plan-related compensation are required to disclose, among other things, their total compensation to plan fiduciaries,[323] and

(3) Plans must disclose to plan participants administrative fees and expenses.[324]

The effectiveness of these rules is subject to debate.[325] The reporting is undoubtedly complex,[326] and it is not clear how well plan sponsors or participants understand the disclosures[327] or how willing service providers are to make the disclosures understandable.[328]

[C] Excessive Plan Fee Litigation

Since 2006, more than 35 different lawsuits have been filed challenging 401(k) plan fees.[329] The facts vary in each case.

---

[322] Specifically, Schedule C to Form 5500 requires that plans with over 100 participants disclose (1) identifying information for all direct and indirect compensation over $5,000; (2) the types of services being provided; (3) the relationship of the service provider to the plan and any party in interest; (4) whether the indirect fees are "eligible" or "ineligible" indirect compensation; and (5) whether any service provider failed or refused to provide fee disclosure information necessary to complete Schedule C. Revision of Annual Information Return/Reports, 72 Fed. Reg. 64731, 64790–93 (Nov. 16, 2007).

[323] 29 C.F.R. § 2550.408b-2(c)(1)(iii) & (iv)(C).

[324] 29 C.F.R. § 2550.404a-5(c)(2) & (3).

[325] According to a survey by the Investment Company Institute, 401(k) plan fees have declined over the last decade. See 401(k) Mutual Fund Fees Continue Decline, ICI Says, 41 Pens. & Benefits Rep. (BNA) 1528 (July 22, 2014).

[326] Muir, Revenue Sharing in 401(k) Plans, 20 Conn. Ins. L.J., at 501 n.82 (noting that the preamble to the regulations mandating disclosure to plan participants exceeds 18 pages).

[327] See, e.g., U.S. Gov't Accountability Office (GAO), GAO-12-325, 401(k) Plans: Increased Educational Outreach and Broader Oversight May Help Reduce Plan Fees, 24–28 (2012) (discussing how some employers remain confused about plan fees even after disclosure requirements went into effect); EBRI Fast Facts, Many Haven't Noticed 401(k) Fee Disclosures, Most Haven't Made Changes (reporting that "[a]ccording to the 2013 Retirement Confidence Survey, about half (53%) of defined contribution plan participants report having noticed this information, and only 14% of those who noticed this information (7% of all plan participants) say they have made changes to their investments as a result of the expanded information about fees").

[328] Muir, Revenue Sharing in 401(k) Plans, 20 Conn. Ins. L.J., at 509 (stating that "experts in retirement system fees and the new disclosures explain that service providers are going to considerable lengths to make the mandated fee disclosures difficult for employers to comprehend and analyze").

[329] See Groom Law Group Chartered, 401(k) Fee Cases (Sept. 25, 2012), available at http://www.groom.com/resources-698.html. In addition, plan fees in welfare plans have been successfully challenged. See Hi Lex Controls, Inc. v. BC & BS Michigan, 2013 U.S. Dist. LEXIS 73043 (E.D. Mi. May 23, 2013) (holding plan entitled to reimbursement of hidden plan fees).

Generally, the complaints allege that plan fiduciaries breached their fiduciary duties by allowing or causing their plans to pay service providers excessive fees and expenses. The complaints tend to focus on revenue sharing arrangements and contend that these arrangements were not properly disclosed or accounted for in determining the compensation provided to service providers. Other practices have been challenged as well. For example, some complaints have claimed that plan fiduciaries have breached their fiduciary duties by selecting a more expensive class of shares when a less expensive one was available or by offering actively managed mutual funds rather than index funds (which are less expensive than actively managed funds).[330]

The plan fee cases have met with varying degrees of success. Some of have not survived a motion to dismiss[331] while others have been decided at the summary judgment stage.[332] A few have been decided after trial.[333]

Many of the cases have been decided in favor of the plan sponsors.[334] A few, however, have been decided in favor of plan participants.[335] In addition, a number have been settled for sizeable sums.[336]

The section discusses two of the plan fee cases:

   (1)   *Hecker v. Deere*,[337] and

   (2)   *Tussey v. ABB, Inc.*[338]

---

[330] *See* Andree M. St. Martin, *401(k) Fee Litigation*, PLI Pension Plan Investments 2008: Current Perspectives 118, 126 (May 1, 2008); Steven J. Sacher & Matthew A. Olson, *401(k) Sponsors become Targets: ERISA Actions Center on their Fee Arrangements with Retirement Plan Consultants*, NATIONAL L.J. (Jan. 8, 2007).

[331] *See, e.g.*, Renfro v. Unisys Corp., 671 F.3d 314 (3d Cir. 2011); Loomis v. Exelon Corp., 658 F.3d 667 (7th Cir. 2011); Hecker v. Deere, 556 F.3d 575 (7th Cir. 2009). *But see* Braden v. Wal-Mart Stores, Inc., 588 F.3d 585 (8th Cir. 2009) (holding district court erred in granting employer's motion to dismiss and remanding case to district court).

[332] *See, e.g.*, Taylor v. United Techs. Corp., 2009 U.S. App. LEXIS 26068 (D. Conn. Mar. 3, 2009), *aff'd*, 2009 U.S. App. LEXIS 26068 (2d Cir. Dec. 1, 2009). *But see* George v. Kraft Foods Global, Inc., 641 F.3d 786 (7th Cir. 2013) (affirming in part and reversing in part; reversing summary judgment in favor of plan fiduciaries).

[333] *See, e.g.*, Tussey v. ABB, Inc., 746 F.3d 327 (8th Cir. 2014); Tibble v. Edison, 729 F.3d 1110 (9th Cir. 2013).

[334] *See, e.g.*, Renfro v. Unisys Corp., 671 F.3d 314 (3d Cir. 2011); Loomis v. Exelon Corp., 658 F.3d 667 (7th Cir. 2011); Hecker v. Deere, 556 F.3d 575 (7th Cir. 2009); Taylor v. United Techs. Corp., 2009 U.S. Dist. LEXIS 19059 (D. Conn. Mar. 3, 2009), *aff'd*, 2009 U.S. App. LEXIS 26068 (2d Cir. Dec. 1, 2009).

[335] *See, e.g.*, Tussey v. ABB, Inc., 746 F.3d 327 (8th Cir.), *cert. denied*, 135 S. Ct. 477 (2014) (affirming $13.4 award in favor of plan participants for excessive record keeping fees); Tibble v. Edison International, 729 F.3d 1110 (9th Cir. 2013) (affirming judgment in favor of plan participants with respect to decision to include retail-class shares of three specific mutual funds), *vacated and remanded on other grounds*, 135 S. Ct. 1823 (2015).

[336] *See International Paper Agrees to Settle Excessive 401(k) Fee Lawsuit for $30M*, 40 BNA PENS. & BENES. RPTR. 2369 (Oct. 8, 2013) (discussing International Paper $30 million settlement as well as $35 million settlement with Cigna Corp. and $9.5 million Kraft plan settlement).

[337] 556 F.3d 575 (7th Cir. 2009), *cert. denied*, 558 U.S. 1148 (2010).

[338] 746 F.3d 327 (8th Cir. 2014).

The cases illustrate that resolution of the cases is highly dependent on the particular facts. In addition, they highlight the importance of plan fees and the need for plan sponsors to carefully consider fees when offering 401(k) plans.[339]

[1] *Hecker v. Deere*

In *Hecker v. Deere*,[340] three plan participants filed a class action suit against the plans' sponsor (Deere), recordkeeper and directed trustee (Fidelity Trust), and investment advisor for the mutual funds offered as investment options under the plans (Fidelity Research). The plaintiffs alleged that the defendants violated their fiduciary duties under ERISA in two separate ways:

(1) by providing investment options with excessive fees and costs; and

(2) by failing to disclose adequately the plans' fee structure to plan participants.[341]

The case involved a fairly typically 401(k) investment arrangement. Specifically, Fidelity Trust served as trustee to Deere's two 401(k) plans, advised Deere about the investments to include in its 401(k) plans, administered the participants' accounts, and maintained the plans' records. Each plan permitted participants to invest in 23 different Fidelity mutual funds, a Deere stock fund, two investment funds managed by Fidelity Trust, and a brokerage account option that permitted participants to invest in 2,500 non-Fidelity mutual funds. Plan participants made their own investment decisions.[342]

Fidelity Research served as the investment advisor for 23 of the 26 investment options under the plan. Each fund offered by the plans charged a fee, calculated as a percentage of assets held by the investor. All of the Fidelity funds were available on the open market for the same fee.[343]

The plan participants alleged that Fidelity Research shared the revenue it earned from the mutual fund fees with Fidelity Trust, and Fidelity Trust compensated itself through those fees rather than charging Deere a direct fee for its services. In their second amended complaint, the plan participants claimed that "the fees and expenses paid by the Plans, and thus borne by Plan participants, were and are unreasonable and excessive; not incurred solely for the benefit of the Plans and the Plans' participants; and undisclosed to participants. By subjecting the Plans and the participants to these excessive fees and expenses, and by other conduct set forth below, the Defendants violated their fiduciary obligations under ERISA."[344]

---

[339] For an argument that plan sponsors should not be subject to fiduciary liability for failure to adequately monitor plan fees, *see* Muir, *Revenue Sharing in 401(k) Plans*, 20 CONN. INS. L.J., at 506–15 (contending that plan sponsors are not the best-placed actors in 401(k) plan system to bear responsibility and liability for approving and monitoring plan fees and proposing a new type of investment product that would shift fiduciary responsibility to investment managers and fund directors).

[340] 556 F.3d 575 (7th Cir. 2009), *cert. denied*, 558 U.S. 1148 (2010).

[341] *Id.* at 578.

[342] *Id.*

[343] *Id.* at 578–79.

[344] *Id.* at 579.

The district court dismissed the plaintiffs' complaint for failure to state a claim and the defendants appealed.[345] In the first appellate decision to address the issue of revenue sharing, the Seventh Circuit affirmed. The first substantive issue the court reached was whether Fidelity Trust and Fidelity Research were functional fiduciaries with respect to the selection of investment options, the structure of fees, or the provision of information regarding the fee structure. The court held that they were not functional fiduciaries. The mere fact that they "played a role" in selecting the plans' investments did not transform them into functional fiduciaries.[346]

The court then rejected the plaintiffs' claim that Fidelity Research, and possibly Fidelity Trust, were fiduciaries because they exercised discretion over the disposition of the Plan's assets by determining how much revenue Fidelity Research would share with Fidelity Trust. The Court held that fees drawn from the assets of mutual funds are not plan assets.[347]

Turning then to the breach of fiduciary claims, the court first found that Deere satisfied its duty to disclose by disclosing the total fees for the funds and directing the participants to the prospectuses for information about fund level expenses. The court was not particularly troubled by the fact that the SPD supplements suggested that Deere was paying the administrative costs when the costs were in fact being paid by the participants through revenue sharing.[348]

The court then found that "no rational trier of fact could find, on the basis of the facts alleged in [the] Complaint, that Deere failed to satisfy" any duty it may have to furnish an acceptable array of investment vehicles. In so finding, the court emphasized the fact that the plans offered 26 investment options, including 23 retail mutual funds, as well as 2,500 non-Fidelity mutual funds through BrokerageLink.[349]

Finally, the court found that ERISA § 404(c) offered an alternative ground for dismissing the case. Without addressing the "abstract question" of whether the ERISA § 404(c) safe harbor applies to selection of investment options for a plan, the court emphasized the number of investment options offered and found that neither Deere nor Fidelity could be held liable for those choices under ERISA § 404(c).

Two aspects of the court's decision are worth noting. First, in rejecting the plaintiffs' claim that Deere violated its fiduciary duty by limiting the investment options to Fidelity Research funds, the court never mentioned process. The duty of prudence has long been measured by process.[350] To the extent that the court suggested that process is not relevant in determining whether a fiduciary has breached its duty of prudence, the court's "analysis stands 30 years of case law on

---

[345] *Id.* at 578.

[346] *Id.* at 583–84.

[347] *Id.* at 584.

[348] *Id.* at 585–86.

[349] *Id.* at 586.

[350] *See* § 6.04[D][1].

its head."[351]

Second, in declining to address the abstract question of whether the section 404(c) safe harbor applies to the selection of investment options for a plan, the court appeared to reject the Secretary of Labor's interpretation of her regulations. The 1992 preamble to the section 404(c) regulations states that "the act of designating investment alternatives" and "the ongoing determination that such alternatives and managers remain suitable and prudent investment alternatives for the plan" are fiduciary functions "to which the limitation on liability provided by section 404(c) is not applicable."[352] In a separate opinion denying a motion for rehearing, the Court made clear that it was not willing to grant *Chevron* deference to this position taken in a footnote to the preamble.[353]

In 2010, the Department of Labor codified its position so it now appears in the Code of Federal Regulations.[354]

[2] *Tussey v. ABB, Inc.*

Like *Hecker v. Deere, Tussey v. ABB, Inc.*[355] involved a fairly typically 401(k) arrangement. The employer offered self-directed 401(k) plans with Fidelity mutual funds as investment options, and Fidelity served as the plans' record keeper and directed trustee and received compensation through revenue sharing agreements.

The plan participants filed suit against the plans' sponsor and the committees and individual employees responsible for administering the plans and selecting and monitoring the plans' investment options (ABB fiduciaries). The participants claimed that the ABB fiduciaries breached their fiduciary duties

   (1) by permitting Fidelity to receive excessive revenue sharing payments, and

   (2) in their selection and retention of more expensive investment options.[356]

After a 16 day bench trial, the district court held that the ABB fiduciaries breached their fiduciary duties with respect to both claims.[357] The appellate court upheld the district court's decision with respect to excessive fees. The court explained that plan fee cases are inevitably fact intensive and found that the specific

---

[351] *ERISA Plan Fees Cases Face Uphill Battle After Seventh Circuit Ruling*, 36 PENS. & BENEFITS REP. (BNA) 589 (Mar. 10, 2009).

[352] *Final Regulation Regarding Participant-Directed Individual Account Plans*, 57 Fed. Reg. 46,906, 46,922 & 46,924 n.27 (Oct. 13, 1992).

[353] Hecker v. Deere, 569 F.3d 708 (7th Cir. 2009). The Seventh Circuit is not the only court to decline to defer to the Secretary's position set forth in the preamble to the regulations. *See, e.g.*, Langbecker v. Electronic Data Systems Corp., 476 F.3d 299, 310–13 (5th Cir. 2007). Other courts, however, have found that the Secretary's preamble position is entitled to deference. *See, e.g.*, Tibble v. Edison Int'l, 729 F.3d 1110 (9th Cir. 2013), *vacated and remanded on other grounds*, 135 S. Ct. 1823 (2015); *In re* Tyco Int'l Inc., 606 F. Supp. 2d 166 (D.N.H.).

[354] *See Fiduciary Requirements for Disclosure in Participant-Directed Individual Account Plans*, 75 Fed. Reg. 64,910, 64,946 (Oct. 20, 2010) (codified at 29 C.F.R. 2550.404c-1(d)(2)(iv)).

[355] 746 F.3d 327 (8th Cir. 2014).

[356] *Id.* at 332–33. The plan participants also claimed that Fidelity breached its fiduciary duty with respect to its use of "float income."

[357] *Id.* at 332–33.

facts of the case supported the trial court's finding that the ABB fiduciaries breached their fiduciary duties with respect to excessive fees and the court did not abuse its discretion in awarding $13.4 million in excessive recordkeeping fees.[358]

The appellate court vacated and remanded the court's decision with respect to the selection and retention of investment options. It found that the trial court did not afford proper deference to the plan administrators' interpretation of the plan documents and was improperly influenced by hindsight. The court emphasized that the prudent person standard is an objective rule that judges fiduciaries' actions as of the time of their decision rather than based on the results of their decision.[359]

---

[358] *Id.* at 336–37.
[359] *Id.* at 338.

Chapter 7

CIVIL ENFORCEMENT

§ 7.01 INTRODUCTION

ERISA's substantive rules are enforced principally through civil litigation.[1] Section 502 of ERISA, entitled "civil enforcement," grants federal courts jurisdiction over ERISA claims, identifies who may file suit, the causes of action plaintiffs may pursue, the remedies courts may award, and authorizes attorneys' fees.

This chapter focuses on ERISA § 502. It is not limited, however, to rules contained solely in the statute. Instead, it also addresses the "judicial glosses"[2] the Court has added to the statute. Although the Supreme Court has frequently described ERISA's civil enforcement provisions as "comprehensive and reticulated,"[3] its provisions are not as complete as the Court has suggested.[4] The Court has added judicial glosses to address issues such as the statute of limitations that apply to many claims, the standards that apply in awarding attorneys' fees, and the judicial standard of review that should govern ERISA cases.

In addition, this chapter discusses a few provisions other than ERISA § 502. Specifically, it discusses ERISA §§ 413 and 4301(f), which set forth statutes of limitations for certain claims under ERISA, and ERISA § 503 which sets forth a claims review procedure that courts have interpreted as imposing an exhaustion requirement.

Although the chapter addresses federal jurisdiction under ERISA § 502 and the complete preemption doctrine, it does not address express preemption under ERISA § 514. Express preemption is discussed in Chapter 8.

---

[1] ERISA also contains three criminal enforcement provisions. ERISA §§ 411, 501, and 511. ERISA, however, is enforced much less frequently under these provisions, which require willful and intentional misconduct, than under ERISA's civil enforcement provisions. Peter K. Stris & Victor A. O'Connell, *Enforcing ERISA*, 56 S. Dakota L. Rev. 515, 519 n.37 (2011).

[2] *See id.* at 515.

[3] *See, e.g.*, LaRue v. DeWolff, Boberg & Assocs., 552 U.S. 248, 258 (2008) (C.J. Roberts, concurring); Mass. Mutual Life Ins. Co. v. Russell, 473 U.S. 134, 147 (1985), *quoting* Nachman Corp. v. Pension Benefit Guar. Corp., 446 U.S. 359, 361 (1980).

[4] *See* Winstead v. J.C. Penney Co., 933 F.2d 576, 579–80 (7th Cir. 1991) (asserting that ERISA § 502(a) is not detailed because it is comprehensive, but rather it is detailed because it was intended to address a number of problems that were brought to Congress' attention; ERISA does not cover problems that were not brought to Congress' attention).

§ 7.02 ERISA § 502(a)'S CAUSES OF ACTION

Section 502(a) of ERISA contains 10 separate subsections identifying the causes of action that may be brought under ERISA.[5] Virtually all claims, however, are brought under the first three subsections:[6]

(1) ERISA § 502(a)(1)(B),

(2) ERISA § 502(a)(2), and

(3) ERISA § 502(a)(3).

[A] ERISA § 502(a)(1)(B)

Section 502(a)(1)(B) authorizes three types of suits:

(1) suits to recover benefits due under the terms of the plan,

(2) suits to enforce rights under the terms of the plan, and

(3) suits to clarify rights to future benefits under the terms of the plan.

[B] ERISA § 502(a)(2)

Section 502(a)(2) authorizes suits for appropriate relief under ERISA § 409. ERISA § 409, in turn, imposes personal liability on fiduciaries for breaching their fiduciary duties.

Section 409 authorizes four different classes of relief:

(1) reimbursement of plan asset losses;

(2) restoring to the plan profits earned by a fiduciary's use of plan assets;

(3) removal of a trustee who breaches his fiduciary duty; and

(4) "other equitable or remedial relief as the court may deem appropriate."

[C] ERISA § 502(a)(3)

Section 502(a)(3) authorizes:

(1) suits to enjoin any action which violates ERISA or the terms of the plan;

(2) suits to obtain other appropriate equitable relief to redress violations of ERISA or the terms of the plan, and

(3) suits to obtain other appropriate equitable relief to enforce any provisions of ERISA or the terms of the plan.[7]

---

[5] Two additional causes of action are authorized in ERISA §§ 502(k) and (m).

[6] John H. Langbein, *What ERISA Means by "Equitable": The Supreme Court's Trail of Error in Russell, Mertens, and Great West*, 103 COLUM. L. REV. 1317, 1334 (2003).

[7] Section 502(a)(5) is virtually identical to Section 502(a)(3) except (1) section 502(a)(5) gives standing to the Secretary of Labor to bring suits while section 502(a)(3) grants standing to participants, beneficiaries, and fiduciaries, and (2) equitable relief under section 502(a)(5) is limited to redressing violations of ERISA and enforcing ERISA's provisions while equitable relief under ERISA § 502(a)(3) extends to providing relief for violations of the plan and enforcing provisions of the plan.

[D] Summary of Principal Causes of Action Under ERISA § 502(a)

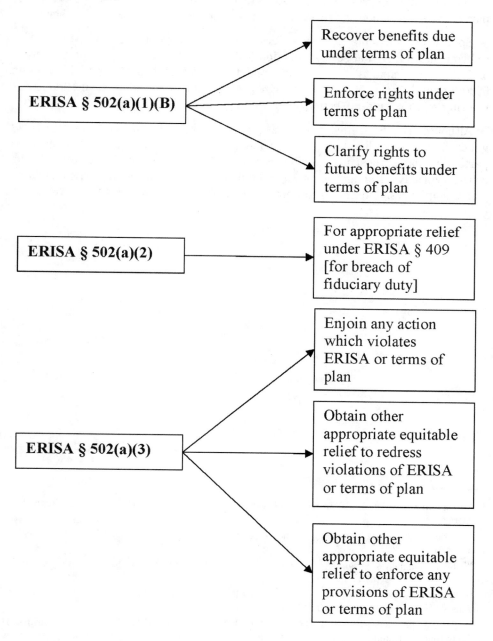

§ 7.03   STANDING — ERISA § 502(a)

Section 502(a) expressly authorizes four parties to bring suit under ERISA: (1) participants, (2) beneficiaries, (3) fiduciaries, and (4) the Secretary of Labor.[8]

Specifically, section 502(a)(1) confers standing on participants and beneficiaries to bring suit under that section. Section 502(a)(2) grants standing to the Secretary of Labor, participants, beneficiaries, and fiduciaries to bring suit under section 502(a)(2), and section 502(a)(3) authorizes participants, beneficiaries, and fiduciaries to bring suit under that section.[9]

Although the Supreme Court has never addressed the issue, lower courts generally limit standing to bring claims under section 502(a) to those "enumerated parties,"[10] that is, those parties who are specifically identified in the statute.[11] Thus, courts typically, although not always, hold that non-enumerated parties, such as plans, employers, and unions, do not have standing to bring suit under ERISA.[12]

---

[8] In addition, section 502(a)(7) authorizes a state to enforce compliance with a qualified medical support order.

[9] Section 502(a)(5) grants standing to the Secretary of Labor to file a suit that is similar to a claim under ERISA § 502(a)(3).

[10] Jayne Zanglein & Susan Stabile, *Who are Enumerated Parties?*, 2008 N.Y.U. REV. OF EMPLOYEE BENEFITS AND EXEC. COMP. 17-1, 17-5.

[11] "Courts refer to these parties as 'enumerated parties' because they are listed by number, or enumerated, in the statute." *Id.* at 17-2.

[12] *See, e.g.*, Local 159, 342, 343 & 444 v. Nor-Cal Plumbing, Inc., 185 F.3d 978, 983–85 (9th Cir. 1999) (holding that trust funds lack standing to sue under ERISA for unpaid employer contributions); Tuvia Convalescent Ctr., Inc. v. Nat'l Union of Hosp. & Health Care Emps., 717 F.2d 726, 730 (2d Cir. 1983) (holding employer lacks standing to sue); New Jersey State AFL-CIO v. New Jersey, 747 F.2d 891, 893 (3d Cir. 1984) (holding that labor union has no standing to sue). For a discussion of standing of non-enumerated parties, see ABA SECTION OF EMPLOYMENT AND LABOR LAW, EMPLOYEE BENEFITS LAW, 12-69–12-74 (Jeffrey Lewis et al., eds., 3d ed.); JAMES F. JORDEN, ET AL., HANDBOOK ON ERISA LITIGATION (3d ed. 2012 supp.) § 2.03[E][1].

Standing under ERISA § 502

Participant or Beneficiary

ERISA § 502(a)(1)(B) [typically claim for benefits]

ERISA § 502(a)(2) [claim for appropriate relief under ERISA § 409 for breach of fiduciary duty]

ERISA § 502(a)(3) [claim for injunction or appropriate equitable relief – (A) to enjoin any action which violates ERISA or terms of plan, or (B) to obtain other appropriate equitable relief (i) to redress violations of ERISA or terms of plan, or (ii) to enforce any provision of ERISA or terms of plan]

Secretary of Labor

ERISA § 502(a)(2) [claim for appropriate relief under ERISA § 409 for breach of fiduciary duty]

ERISA § 502(a)(5) [similar to claims under ERISA § 502(a)(3) except does not extend to violations of terms of plans or enforcement of terms of plan]

Fiduciary

ERISA §502(a)(2) [claim for appropriate relief under ERISA § 409 for breach of fiduciary duty]

ERISA § 502(a)(3) [claim for injunction or appropriate equitable relief – (A) to enjoin any action which violates ERISA or terms of plan, or (B) to obtain other appropriate equitable relief (i) to redress violations of ERISA or terms of plan, or (ii) to enforce any provision of ERISA or terms of plan]

ERISA expressly defines the terms participant,[13] beneficiary,[14] and fiduciary.[15] Nevertheless, it is not always clear when a person[16] qualifies as a participant, beneficiary, or fiduciary and thus is entitled to bring suit under ERISA § 502(a).[17]

[A] Participant

Section 3(7) of ERISA defines "participant" to include any employee or former employee who is or may become eligible to receive a benefit from an employee benefit plan.[18] Section 3(6) defines an "employee" as "any employee employed by an employer."[19]

In *Firestone Tire & Rubber Co. v. Bruch*,[20] the Supreme Court addressed the question of who is a participant for purposes of ERISA's disclosure rules. In that case, the Court declared that "the term 'participant' is naturally read to mean either 'employees in, or reasonably expected to be in, currently covered employment,' or former employees who 'have . . . a reasonable expectation of returning to covered employment' or who have 'a colorable claim' to vested benefits."[21] The Court further announced that "[i]n order to establish that he or she 'may become eligible' for benefits, a claimant must have a colorable claim that (1) he or she will prevail in a suit for benefits, or that (2) eligibility requirements will be fulfilled in the future."[22]

All of the circuit courts have applied the two-prong *Firestone* test to determine who is a participant for purposes of standing under ERISA § 502(a).[23]

---

[13] ERISA § 3(7).

[14] ERISA § 3(8).

[15] ERISA § 3(21).

[16] Section 3(9) of ERISA defines a "person" as "an individual, partnership, joint venture, corporation, mutual company, joint-stock company, trust, estate, unincorporated organization, association, or employee organization."

[17] Zanglein & Stabile, 2008 N.Y.U. REV. OF EMPLOYEE BENEFITS AND EXEC. COMP., at 17-2.

[18] For a discussion of standing of plan participants alleging a breach of fiduciary duty with respect to an overfunded defined benefit plan, see Dana M. Muir, *ERISA and Investment Issues*, 65 OHIO STATE L. J. 199, 206–30 (2004).

[19] ERISA § 3(6). In Nationwide Mutual Ins. Co. v. Darden, 503 U.S. 318 (1992), the Supreme Court adopted the common law definition of "employee" for purposes of applying ERISA § 3(6).

[20] 489 U.S. 101 (1989).

[21] *Id.* at 117 (citations omitted).

[22] *Id.* at 117–18 (citations omitted).

[23] Zanglein and Stabile, 2008 N.Y.U. REV. OF EMPLOYEE BENEFITS AND EXEC. COMP., at 17-9. Not all of the circuit courts, however, apply the two-prong *Firestone* test for determining standing for claims under ERISA § 510. See Chapter 4 § 4.05[C]. *See also* Kathryn L. Moore, *The Pay or Penalty Under the Affordable Care Act: Emerging Issues*, 47 CREIGHTON L. REV. 611, 625–29 (2014).

[B] Beneficiary

Section 3(8) of ERISA defines a beneficiary as "a person designated by a participant or by the terms of an employee benefit plan, who is or may become entitled to a benefit" under the plan. An alternate payee[24] under a Qualified Domestic Relations Order (QDRO)[25] is also considered a beneficiary for standing purposes. [26]

Litigation may arise when a spouse or other relative who was not explicitly identified as a beneficiary seeks benefits under the plan, or when a participant drops an individual as a beneficiary.[27] Some courts have held that if a former spouse, child, or other dependent is not named as a beneficiary, the individual does not have standing to bring a claim as a beneficiary.[28] Other courts, however, have granted an individual standing to bring suit if the individual claims that the individual should have been a beneficiary.[29]

[C] Fiduciary

Section 502 of ERISA requires every employee benefit plan to designate a "named fiduciary." Fiduciary status, however, is not limited to "named fiduciaries." Instead, persons who fall under ERISA § 3(21)(A)'s functional fiduciary definition may also qualify as fiduciaries. Determining who is a fiduciary is a frequently litigated issue that is discussed in Chapter 6 § 6.03.

§ 7.04   EXHAUSTION OF ERISA § 503 CLAIMS REVIEW PROCEDURE

Section 503 of ERISA requires that employee benefit plans (1) notify participants and beneficiaries in writing of any denial of a claim for benefits and (2) afford participants and beneficiaries the opportunity for "full and fair" review of adverse claim determinations.[30]

---

[24] ERISA § 206(d)(3)(K) (defining alternate payee).

[25] For a discussion of QDROs, see Chapter 5 § 5.04[3][c].

[26] ERISA § 206(d)(3)(J) (providing that alternate payee shall be considered a beneficiary under any provision of ERISA).

[27] For an overview of litigation regarding standing of beneficiaries, see ABA SECTION ON LABOR AND EMPLOYMENT LAW, EMPLOYEE BENEFITS LAW, at 12-66–12-68; Zanglein & Stabile, 2008 N .Y.U. REV. OF EMPLOYEE BENEFITS AND EXEC. COMP., at 17-11.

[28] *See, e.g.*, Cobb v. Cent. States Pension Fund, 461 F.3d 632, 636 (5th Cir. 2006), *cert. denied*, 549 U.S. 1180 (2007); Crawford v. Roane, 53 F.3d 750, 754–55 (6th Cir. 1995), *cert. denied*, 517 U.S. 1121 (1996); Keys v. Eastman Kodak Co., 739 F. Supp. 135, 138 (W.D.N.Y. 1990), *aff'd*, 923 F.2d 844 (2d Cir. 1990).

[29] *See, e.g.*, Riordan v. Commonwealth Edison Co., 128 F.3d 549, 551–52 (7th Cir. 1997); Sladek v. Bell Sys. Mgmt. Pension Plan, 880 F.2d 972 (7th Cir. 1989).

[30] The Department of Labor regulations set forth minimum requirements that must be met to satisfy section 503. 29 C.F.R. § 2560.503-1. For a discussion of changes to the regulations following the enactment of the Affordable Care Act, see Roy F. Harmon, *An Assessment of New Appeals and External Review Processes – ERISA Claimants Get "Some Kind of a Hearing,"* 56 S.D. L. REV. 408, 423–27 (2011). For a general discussion of claims procedure, see JAMES F. JORDEN, ET. AL., HANDBOOK ON ERISA LITIGATION 5-8–5-37 (3d ed. 2007).

[A] Exhaustion Requirement for Claims for Benefits Under ERISA § 502(a)(1)(B)

Although ERISA does not expressly link section 503's claims procedures with benefit claims under section 502(a)(1)(B), appellate courts have long required that plan participants and beneficiaries exhaust the plan's claims procedures before bringing suit claiming benefits under section 502(a)(1)(B).[31] Exhaustion of a plan's internal review procedures typically takes 15 to 16 months.[32]

The Supreme Court has never addressed an express challenge to the exhaustion requirement. In *Heimeshoff v. Hartford Life & Accident Insurance Co.*,[33] however, the Court indicated approval of such a requirement. In that case, a plan participant filed suit seeking review of a denied benefit claim under ERISA § 502(a)(1)(B). The court dismissed the complaint because it was barred by the plan's limitations period.[34] In its decision upholding the dismissal of the complaint, the Court noted that the courts of appeal have uniformly required that plan participants exhaust plan review procedures and declared that "[a] participant's cause of action accordingly does not accrue until the plan issues a final denial."[35]

[1] Reasons for Exhaustion Requirement

The most common reason courts offer for requiring that plan participants and beneficiaries exhaust the claims review procedure is that by requiring plans to offer claims review procedures under ERISA § 503, Congress must have intended that plan participants and beneficiaries be required to use them.[36] Additional justifications courts have offered for the exhaustion requirement include reducing the number of frivolous lawsuits, promoting the consistent treatment of claims, providing a non-adversarial method for settling claims, and reducing plan costs.[37] In his concurring opinion in *LaRue v. DeWolff, Boberg & Associates, Inc.*,[38] Chief Justice Roberts described the requirement as a "safeguard for plan administrators."[39]

---

[31] Brendan S. Maher, *Creating a Paternalistic Market for Legal Rules Affecting the Benefit Promise*, 2009 WISC. L. REV. 657, 674. *See, e.g.*, Drinkwater v. Metropolitan Life Ins. Co., 846 F.2d 821, 826 (1st Cir.), *cert. denied*, 488 U.S. 909 (1988); Barrowclough v. Kidder, Peabody & Co., 752 F.2d 923 (3d Cir. 1985). For additional cases, see Kathryn J. Kennedy, *The Perilous and Ever-Changing Procedural Rules of Pursuing an ERISA Claims Case*, 70 UMKC L. REV. 329, 358 n. 158 (2001).

[32] *See* Heimeshoff v. Hartford Life & Accident Ins. Co, 134 S. Ct. 604, 613 n.4 (2013) (noting that according to American Council of Life Insurers' recent study of ERISA § 502(a)(1)(B) cases exhaustion takes 15 to 16 months in a typical case).

[33] 134 S. Ct. 604, 610 (2013).

[34] The Court's decision is discussed in more detail in § 7.09[C][2].

[35] 134 S. Ct. at 610.

[36] Maher, *Creating a Paternalistic Market*, 2009 WISC. L. REV., at 674.

[37] Amato v. Bernard, 618 F.2d 559, 567 (9th Cir. 1980). *See also* Kennedy, *Procedural Rules of Pursuing an ERISA Claims Case*, 70 UMKC L. REV., at 358–60 (identifying the various justifications courts have offered for the exhaustion requirement).

[38] 552 U.S. 248 (2008).

[39] *Id.* at 258–59.

[2]   Criticisms of Exhaustion Requirement

A number of commentators have criticized the exhaustion requirement and the rationales offered in support of the requirement.[40] Among other things, they note that ERISA § 503 expressly requires that plans provide for a claims procedure, but does not mandate that plan participants use the procedure. Despite these objections, the courts have uniformly required plan participants and beneficiaries to exhaust the claims review procedure before bringing a claim under ERISA § 502(a)(1)(B).[41]

[3]   Exceptions to Exhaustion Requirement

There are generally four exceptions to the exhaustion requirement. First, if a plan does not provide a "reasonable" claims procedure,[42] the plan participant is deemed to have exhausted the administrative[43] remedies available under the plan.[44] Second, courts excuse the exhaustion requirement if resort to the plan's claims procedure would be futile.[45] Third, exhaustion is not required where the participant or beneficiary is denied meaningful access to the plan's administrative review procedures.[46] Finally, courts do not require plan participants and beneficiaries to exhaust administrative remedies if such a requirement would result in irreparable harm.[47]

---

[40] *See, e.g.*, Maher, *Creating a Paternalistic Market*, 2009 Wisc. L. Rev., at 674; Mark DeBofsky, *The Paradox of the Misuse of Administrative Law in ERISA Benefit Claims*, 37 J. Marshall L. Rev. 727, 730–32 (2004); Jay Conison, *Suits for Benefits Under ERISA*, 54 U. Pitt. L. Rev. 1, 21 (1992).

[41] *See* DeBofsky, 37 J. Marshall L. Rev., at 732 (noting that only court has come close to suggesting that the claims review procedure should be voluntary rather than mandatory).

[42] The regulations set forth five requirements that all plans must satisfy in order for their procedures to qualify as "reasonable." 29 C.F.R. § 2560.503-1(b)(1)–(5). Additional requirements apply to group health plans and plans that provide disability benefits. 29 C.F.R. § 2560.503–1(c) & (d).

[43] Critics contend that it is misleading to refer the requirement as exhaustion of "administrative" remedies because "[i]nternal review by plan fiduciaries bears little to no resemblance to genuine administrative review." Maher, *Creating a Paternalistic Market*, 2009 Wisc. L. Rev., at 674. n.56, *citing* Donald T. Bogan, *Reply to Judge Easterbrook: The Unsupported Delegation of Conflict Adjudication in ERISA Benefit Claims Under the Guise of Judicial Deference*, 57 Okla. L. Rev. 21, 27 (2004); DeBofsky, 37 J. Marshall L. Rev., at 729–31.

[44] 29 C.F.R. § 2560.503-1(e).

[45] *See, e.g.*, Dozier v. Sun Life Assurance Co., 466 F.3d 532, 536–37 (6th Cir. 2006); Ruttenberg v. United States Life Ins. Co., 413 F.3d 652, 663 (7th Cir. 2005); Dishman v. UNUM Life Ins. Co. of Am., 269 F.3d 974, 984–85 (9th Cir. 2001). For additional cases, see Kennedy, *Procedural Rules of Pursuing an ERISA Claims Case*, 70 UMKC L. Rev., at 364 & nn. 179–185.

[46] *See, e.g.* Lee v. California Butchers' Pension Trust Fund, 154 F.3d 1075, 1080 (9th Cir. 1998); Hall v. National Gypsum Co., 105 F.3d 225, 231–33 (5th Cir. 1997); Wilczynski v. Lumbermens Mut. Cas. Co., 93 F.3d 397, 402–04 (7th Cir. 1996). For additional cases, see Kennedy, *Procedural Rules of Pursuing an ERISA Claims Case*, 70 UMKC L. Rev., at 362–63 nn. 171–76.

[47] *See, e.g.*, Turner v. Fallon Cmty. Health Plan, 127 F.3d 196, 200 (1st Cir. 1997), *cert. denied*, 523 U.S. 1072 (1998); Henderson v. Bodine Aluminum, Inc., 70 F.3d 958, 961 (8th Cir. 1995); Watts v. Organogenesis, Inc., 30 F. Supp. 2d 101, 104 (D. Mass. 1998). For additional cases, see Kennedy, *Procedural Rules of Pursuing an ERISA Claims Case*, 70 UMKC L. Rev., at 365–66 & nn. 186 & 180.

[B]   Exhaustion Requirement for Claims Other than Under ERISA § 502(a)(1)(B)

Although the lower courts have uniformly held that the exhaustion requirement applies to claims for benefits under ERISA § 502(a)(1)(B), the lower courts are divided as to whether the exhaustion requirement applies to statute-based claims such as claims under ERISA § 502(a)(2) for breach of fiduciary duty.[48] In *LaRue v. DeWolff, Boberg & Associates, Inc.,*[49] the Supreme Court expressly left open the question whether the exhaustion requirement applies to breach of fiduciary claims under ERISA § 502(a)(2).[50]

§ 7.05   FEDERAL JURISDICTION UNDER ERISA § 502(e) AND REMOVAL

Section 502(e) of ERISA grants the federal courts jurisdiction over all civil actions brought under title I of ERISA.[51] Federal jurisdiction is exclusive with respect to all claims, except for claims brought under ERISA § 502(a)(1)(B). State and federal courts have concurrent jurisdiction over ERISA § 502(a)(1)(B) claims.[52] Thus, a plaintiff may file any claim arising under title I of ERISA in federal court. In addition, if a plaintiff so chooses, a plaintiff may file a section 502(a)(1)(B) claim in state court rather than federal court.

If a plaintiff chooses to file a section 502(a)(1)(B) claim in state court, the defendant may remove the action from state court to federal court. In addition, a defendant may remove from state court a complaint pleading only state law claims if the complaint is "completely preempted" by ERISA.

[A]   Removal of Express ERISA Claims

Federal law authorizes defendants to remove civil actions brought in state court to federal court if the federal court has original jurisdiction over the action.[53] Federal courts have original "federal question jurisdiction" in "all civil actions arising under the Constitution, law, or treaties of the United States."[54] ERISA claims arise under federal law. Thus, defendants have a right to remove to federal

---

[48] *See* ABA Section of Labor and Employment Law, Employee Benefits Law, at 12-94–12-95 & 15-84 (noting that Third, Fourth, Fifth, Sixth, Ninth, and Tenth Circuits have held that exhaustion of administrative remedies is not required for certain statute-based claims while Seventh and Eleventh Circuits have held that exhaustion requirement applies to statute-based claims and discussing exhaustion requirement as applied to section 510 claims).

[49] 552 U.S. 248 (2008).

[50] *Id.* at 253 n.3. Justice Roberts, in his concurring opinion, approved the Court's decision to leave the question open. *Id.* at 259 n*.

[51] ERISA § 502(e).

[52] State and federal courts also have concurrent jurisdiction over ERISA § 502(a)(7) claims to enforce qualified medical child support orders. ERISA § 502(e)(1).

[53] 28 U.S.C. § 1441.

[54] 28 U.S.C. § 1331. Federal courts also have original jurisdiction in other cases, such as "diversity of citizenship" cases, 28 U.S.C. § 1332, and admiralty, maritime, and prize cases, 28 U.S.C. § 1333.

court any civil actions alleging ERISA claims.

[B]   Removal Under Complete Preemption Doctrine

Under the well-pleaded complaint rule,[55] a cause of action "arises under" federal law and thus gives rise to federal question jurisdiction only if a plaintiff's properly pleaded complaint presents a federal question.[56] Thus, under the well-pleaded complaint rule, a defendant may not remove to federal court a civil action alleging only state law claims.[57] Moreover, a defendant may not remove a plaintiff's state law complaint to federal court even if section 514 of ERISA preempts the plaintiff's state law claim because ERISA § 514 is simply a federal defense that is insufficient to create federal question jurisdiction.[58]

Under the complete preemption doctrine, a "corollary" to the well-pleaded complaint rule,[59] defendants may remove certain state law claims to federal court. Specifically, under the complete preemption doctrine, "Congress may so completely pre-empt a particular area that any civil complaint raising this select group of claims is necessarily federal in character."[60] In few cases, the Supreme Court has considered the application of the complete preemption doctrine to ERISA.

[1]   Early Supreme Court Complete Preemption Cases

The Supreme Court first addressed the complete preemption doctrine in the context of ERISA[61] in *Franchise Tax Board v. Construction Laborers Vacation Trust*.[62] In that case, a state tax enforcement agency brought suit in state court against a multiemployer trust that was established to administer a collective bargaining agreement that provided construction workers with a yearly paid vacation. In addition to seeking money owed from tax levies, the state agency sought a declaratory judgment that ERISA's express preemption provision, ERISA § 514(a), did not preempt state enforcement of the levies against the trust. The trust removed the case to federal court, but the Supreme Court found that the federal courts had no removal jurisdiction over the case.

---

[55] For a history and overview of the well-pleaded complaint rule, see Karen A. Jordan, *The Complete Preemption Dilemma: A Legal Process Perspective*, 31 WAKE FOREST L. REV. 927, 939–50 (1996); Richard E. Levy, *Comment, Federal Preemption, Removal Jurisdiction, and the Well-Pleaded Complaint Rule*, 51 UNIV. OF CHICAGO L. REV. 634, 636–46 (1984).

[56] Metropolitan Life Ins. Co. v. Taylor, 481 U.S. 58, 63 (1987).

[57] Caterpillar, Inc. v. Williams, 482 U.S. 386, 392 (1987) (stating that the well pleaded complaint "rule makes the plaintiff the master of the claim, he or she may avoid federal jurisdiction by exclusive reliance on state law").

[58] *See* Chapter 8. For an argument that federal courts should have jurisdiction to decide whether state law claims are preempted under ERISA § 514, see Jordan, 31 WAKE FOREST L. REV., at 950–62.

[59] For a history of the complete preemption corollary to the well-pleaded complaint rule, see Jordan, 31 WAKE FOREST L. REV., at 939–50.

[60] Metropolitan Life Ins. Co. v. Taylor, 481 U.S. 58, 63–64 (1987).

[61] The Supreme Court first established the complete preemption doctrine in *Avco Corp. v. Aero Lodge No. 735, International Ass'n of Machinists*, 390 U.S. 557 (1968).

[62] 463 U.S. 1 (1983).

The Court held that express preemption under ERISA § 514(a) does not give rise to federal removal jurisdiction. The Court, however, suggested that federal removal jurisdiction may arise under ERISA if a state law claim falls within the scope of ERISA § 502(a).[63] Specifically, the Court declared that "[i]t may be that . . . any state action coming within the scope of § 502(a) of ERISA would be removable to federal district court, even if an otherwise adequate state cause of action were pleaded without reference to federal law." The Court found no federal removal jurisdiction under the complete preemption doctrine in that case because ERISA § 502(a) does not create a cause of action in favor of state governments to enforce tax levies.

Four years later, in *Metropolitan Life v. Taylor*,[64] the Court found federal removal jurisdiction in an ERISA case. In that case, a plan participant filed suit in state court claiming that the defendants' failure to pay the participant disability benefits violated state law.[65] Alleging federal question jurisdiction, the defendants removed the case to federal court.[66] The Court held that the plaintiff's common law contract and tort claims were preempted under ERISA § 514(a) and not saved under the saving clause.[67] The Court then characterized the plaintiffs' suit as a suit to recover benefits from a plan which falls directly under ERISA § 502(a)(1)(B).[68] The Court found that ERISA's legislative history made it clear that Congress intended causes of action that fall within the scope of ERISA § 502(a)'s remedial provisions to be removable to federal court.[69] Because the plaintiff's cause of action fell within the scope of ERISA § 502(a), the Court held that the defendants could remove the suit to federal court.[70]

[2] *Aetna Health Inc. v. Davila*

In *Aetna Health Inc. v. Davila*,[71] the most recent Supreme Court decision to address complete preemption, a plan participant and a plan beneficiary filed suit claiming that their HMOs violated the Texas Health Care Liability Act (THCLA) for failing to exercise ordinary care in handling their coverage decisions. The Court declared that

> if an individual brings suit complaining of a denial of coverage for medical care, where the individual is entitled to such coverage only because of the terms of an ERISA-regulated employee benefit plan and where no legal duty independent of ERISA or the plan's terms is violated, then the suit falls within the scope of ERISA § 502(a)(1)(B). In other words, if an individual, at some point in time, could have brought his claim under

---

[63] *Id.* at 24–25.

[64] 481 U.S. 58 (1987).

[65] *Id.* at 61.

[66] *Id.*

[67] *Id.* at 62.

[68] *Id.* at 62–63.

[69] *Id.* at 64–66.

[70] *Id.* at 66–67.

[71] 542 U.S. 200 (2004).

ERISA § 502(a)(1)(B), and where there is no other independent legal duty that is implicated by a defendant's actions, then the individual's cause of action is completely preempted by ERISA § 502(a)(1).[72]

The Court first examined the plaintiffs' complaints, the statute on which their claims were based, and the plan documents to determine whether the plaintiffs' claims were among the types of actions that fall within the scope of ERISA § 502(a)(1)(B). The Court found that that the plaintiffs could have brought their claims under ERISA § 502(a)(1)(B) because they "complain[ed] only about denials of coverage promised under the terms of ERISA-regulated employee benefit plans" and could have relied on ERISA remedies by filing a claim for benefits and/or seeking a preliminary injunction.[73]

The Court then found that, in the context of these individuals' complaints, the duties imposed by the Texas statute did not arise independently of ERISA or the plan terms.[74] Rather, the HMOs' potential liability under the THCLA was derived entirely from the rights and obligations established under the plans.[75] Accordingly, the Court held that the causes of action fell "within the scope of ERISA § 502(a)(1)(B) and were completely preempted."[76]

Since *Davila*, most of the federal appellate courts have recognized and applied the Supreme Court's two-part complete preemption test, which asks (1) whether the plaintiff could have brought its claim under ERISA § 502(a); and (2) whether any other legal duty supports the plaintiff's claim[77]

§ 7.06   RIGHT TO A JURY TRIAL

ERISA is silent as to whether plaintiffs have the right to a jury trial when pursuing claims under ERISA.[78] Because the statute is silent on the issue, the right to a jury trial turns on whether there is a right to a jury trial under the Seventh Amendment.[79]

The Seventh Amendment of the U.S. Constitution provides that "[i]n Suits at Common law, where the value in controversy shall exceed twenty dollars, the right of trial by jury shall be preserved."[80] The right to a jury trial is thus construed to

---

[72] *Id.* at 201.

[73] *Id.* at 211–12.

[74] *Id.* at 212.

[75] *Id.* at 213.

[76] *Id.* at 214.

[77] *See* Connecticut State Dental Ass'n v. Anthem Health Plans, Inc., 591 F.3d 1337 (11th Cir. 2009) (characterizing Davila as setting forth two-prong test and adopting and applying test and citing cases from six other circuits).

[78] *See* John H. Langbein, *What ERISA Means by "Equitable": The Supreme Court's Trail of Error in* Russell, Mertens, and Great West, 103 COLUM. L. REV. 1317, 1355 (2003) (stating that "ERISA's procedure and remedy sections are riddled with major omissions that the courts have had to fill in, such as whether jury trial pertains, and what statute of limitations to use").

[79] O'MALLEY ET AL., FEDERAL JURY PRACTICE AND INSTRUCTIONS § 1.02 (5th ed. 2000).

[80] U.S. CONST. amend. VII.

depend on the basic nature of the claim presented and the relief sought.[81] There is a right to a jury trial if the remedy sought is legal, but not if it is equitable in nature.[82]

Most courts hold that jury trials are not available in ERISA litigation because ERISA is grounded in trust law, and under the common law, trust disputes were resolved by courts of equity rather than courts of law.[83] There is, however, some contrary authority. For example, a few district courts have held that there is a right to a jury trial for a claim under ERISA § 502(a)(2) when the relief sought is legal rather than equitable in nature,[84] and some courts have afforded the right to a jury trial in ERISA § 510 claims.[85]

§ 7.07 JUDICIAL STANDARD OF REVIEW

The judicial standard of review refers to the degree of deference a court should give to the decision under review.[86] The standards range from *de novo* with no deference granted to the decision maker to complete deference with no judicial review whatsoever.[87] ERISA does not identify the standard of review that courts should apply. Thus, the appropriate standard of review is one of the many gaps in ERISA's civil enforcement provisions that courts have been required to fill.

The standard of review applicable to claims for benefits under ERISA § 502(a)(1)(B) is quite well-developed. Indeed, the Supreme Court has addressed the standard of review applicable to such claims in three separate cases.

The Supreme Court has not expressly addressed the standard of review for other ERISA claims. Circuit courts, however, have addressed the issue and have applied

---

[81] O'MALLEY ET AL., FEDERAL JURY PRACTICE AND INSTRUCTIONS, at § 1.02. *See, e.g.*, Stewart v. KHD Deut of Am. Corp., 75 F.3d 1522, 1525–27 (11th Cir.), *cert. denied*, 519 U.S. 930 (1996) (engaging in two step-process to find right to jury trial); Spinelli v. Gaughan, 12 F.3d 853, 856 (9th Cir. 1993) (examining nature of action and nature of remedy to find no right to jury trial for ERISA § 510 claim).

[82] Wooddell v. International Union of Electrical Workers, 502 U.S. 93, 97 (1991).

[83] *See* Brendan S. Maher, *The Affordable Care Act, Remedy, and Litigation Reform*, 63 AM. U. L. REV. 649, 660 (2014); Thomas P. Gies and Jane R. Foster, *Leaving Well Enough Alone: Reflections on the Current State of ERISA Remedial Law*, 26 HOFSTRA LAB. & EMP. L.J. 449, 472 n.159 (2009); George Lee Flint, Jr., *ERISA: Jury Trial Mandated for Benefit Claims Actions*, 25 LOY. L.A. L. REV. 361, 386–93 (1992). *See also* Deidre A. Grossman, *ERISA Claims for Relief*, ALI-ABA Course of Study, ST027 ALI-ABA 389 (2011) (citing cases).

[84] *See* Hellman v. Cataldo, 2013 U.S. Dist. LEXIS 117676, at *13 (E.D. Mo. Aug. 20, 2013); Kirse v. McCullough, 2005 U.S. Dist. LEXIS 17023, at *9 (W.D. Mo. May 12, 2005); Bona v. Barasch, 2003 U.S. Dist. LEXIS 4186, at *103 (S.D.N.Y. Mar. 20, 2003).

[85] *See, e.g.*, McDonald v. Artcraft Elec. Supply Co., 774 F. Supp. 29, 35 (D.D.C. 1991); Michaelis v. Deluxe Fin. Servs., 2006 U.S. Dist. LEXIS 265, at *11–12 (D. Kan. Jan. 5, 2006); Weber v. Jacobs Mfg. Co., 751 F. Supp. 21, 25–26 (D. Conn. 1990).

[86] Martha S. Davis, *A Basic Guide to Judicial Standards of Review*, 33 S.D. L. REV. 469, 469 (1988).

[87] *Id.* at 471. According to Professor Martha Davis, a leading authority on judicial standards of review, there are six basic standards of review: (1) *de novo* review, (2) clearly erroneous review, (3) reasonableness review, (4) arbitrary & capricious review, (5) abuse of discretion review, and (6) no review. *Id.* Professor Davis recognizes that arguably the sixth standard of review is not strictly speaking a standard of review. *Id.* at 471 n. 15. Nevertheless, it demonstrates the spectrum of deference reviewing courts will grant decisionmakers.

different standards of review.

[A] Standard of Review Applicable to Claims for Benefits Under ERISA § 502(a)(1)(B)

In a claim for benefits under ERISA § 502(a)(1)(B), if the plan does not grant a plan administrator discretion to interpret the terms of the plan, the default standard of judicial review is *de novo*. Most plans, however, grant the plan administrator discretion to interpret the terms of the plan, and courts apply a discretionary standard of review to the plan administrator's decision in such cases.

If a plan administrator is operating under a conflict of interest, the standard of review remains deferential, but courts must take the conflict of interest into account in reviewing claims for benefits. No specific weight is given to the conflict of interest, but the conflict should be of more importance when circumstances suggest that the conflict is likely to have affected the benefits decision, and the conflict should be of little to no importance when steps have been taken to increase accuracy and reduce bias.

If a court finds that a plan administrator's initial interpretation of the plan is arbitrary and capricious, courts should still defer to the plan administrator's subsequent plan interpretation if the first interpretation was a "single honest mistake."

[1] *De Novo* Default Standard

The Supreme Court first addressed the judicial standard of review to be applied to ERISA § 502(a)(1)(B) claims for benefits in *Firestone Tire & Rubber Co. v. Bruch*.[88] In that case, a plan administrator denied severance pay benefits to former *Firestone* employees who were rehired by Occidental when Firestone was sold to Occidental.[89] The former employees brought suit under ERISA § 502(a)(1)(B) challenging the denial of benefits.[90]

Recognizing that ERISA does not forth a standard of review,[91] the Supreme Court turned to principles of trust law for guidance in fashioning the appropriate standard.[92] The Court declared that consistent with trust principles, a benefits denial challenge under § 502(a)(1)(B) is to be reviewed under "a *de novo* standard unless the benefit plan gives the administrator or fiduciary discretionary authority

---

[88] 489 U.S. 101 (1989). For a discussion of the standard of review that applied to benefit denial claims prior to the enactment of ERISA, and after the enactment of ERISA but prior to *Firestone*, see Kathryn J. Kennedy, *Judicial Standard of Review in ERISA Benefit Claim Cases*, 50 Am. U. L. Rev. 1083, 1096–1110 (2001); Jay Conison, *Suits for Benefits Under ERISA*, 54 U. Pitt. L. Rev. 1, 35–49 (1992).

[89] 489 U.S. at 105–06.

[90] *Id.* at 106.

[91] *Id.* at 109.

[92] *Id.* at 111. For an argument that the Court's reliance on trust law was misplaced, see John H. Langbein, *Trust Law as Regulatory Law: The UNUM/Provident Scandal and Judicial Review of Benefit Denials Under ERISA*, 101 Nw. U. L. Rev. 1315, 1335–42 (2007).

to construe the terms of the plan."[93] Under the *de novo* standard, the court grants the plan administrator's decision no deference and instead substitutes its own judgment for that of the plan administrator.[94]

[2] Deferential Standard if Plan Administrator Granted Discretion

The Court in *Firestone* never explicitly identified the standard of review that should be applied if the plan grants the plan administrator discretion. Instead, it simply declared that "[t]rust principles make a deferential standard of review appropriate when a trustee exercises discretionary powers,"[95] and suggested that discretionary powers could be conferred through appropriate language in the plan document.[96] Since *Firestone*, most plans have been drafted — or amended — to afford the plan administrator discretion in interpreting the terms of the plan,[97] and lower courts have applied a deferential standard of review to such decisions.

Some courts have labeled the standard "abuse of discretion,"[98] others have called it "arbitrary and capricious."[99] Some courts have considered the two standards interchangeable[100] while others have considered the abuse of discretion standard less deferential than the arbitrary and capricious standard.[101] Despite these differences, lower courts have been uniform in applying a more deferential standard of review than *de novo* review when the plan provides the plan administrator with discretion to interpret the terms of the plan.[102]

---

[93] 489 U.S. at 115.

[94] Davis, 33 S.D. L. Rev., at 475–76.

[95] 489 U.S. at 111.

[96] *Id.* at 115 (stating that "[n]either general principles of trust law nor a concern for impartial decision making, however, forecloses parties from agreeing upon a narrower standard of review."). For a discussion of the case law construing the language necessary to confer discretion, see Kennedy, Judicial Standard of Review, 50 Am. U. L. Rev., at 1119–1130.

[97] In recent years, however, a number of states have prohibited insurers from including discretionary clauses in their insurance contracts. To the extent that an insured plan is subject to such a ban, the plan administrator may not be granted discretion, and thus the appropriate judicial standard of review under *Firestone* is *de novo* review. Not surprisingly, plans have argued that such bans are preempted by ERISA. To date, though, most courts that have addressed the issue have found that the bans are saved from ERISA preemption under the saving clause. See Radha A. Pathak, *Discretionary Clause Bans & ERISA Preemption*, 56 S.D. L. Rev. 500 (2011) (noting that 14 states have enacted laws prohibiting discretionary clauses in insurance contracts and arguing that such clauses should be saved from preemption under the saving clause); John Morrison & Jonathan McDonald, *Exorcising Discretion: The Death of Caprice in ERISA Claims Handling*, 56 S.D. L. Rev. 482 (2011) (discussing history and effect of discretionary clauses, states' imposition of bans on such clauses, and recent cases rejecting preemption challenges to such clauses).

[98] *See, e.g.*, Boyd v. Trs. of United Mine Workers Health & Ret. Funds, 873 F.2d 57, 59 (4th Cir. 1989).

[99] Nazay v. Miller, 949 F.2d 1323, 1335 (3d Cir. 1991); Batchelor v. Int'l Bhd. of Elec. Workers Local 861 Pension & Ret. Fund, 877 F.2d 441, 44 (5th Cir. 1989).

[100] Block v. Pitney Bowes Inc., 952 F.2d 1450, 1454 (D.C. Cir. 1992); Terry v. Bayer Corp., 145 F.3d 28, 37 n.6 (1st Cir. 1998).

[101] Booth v. Wal-Mart Stores, Inc. Assocs. Health & Welfare Plan, 201 F.3d 335, 341 (4th Cir. 2000).

[102] For a detailed discussion of the post-*Firestone* standards of review applied by circuit courts, see Kathryn J. Kennedy, *Conkright: A Conundrum for Future Courts, An Opportunity for Congress*, 2010

[3]   Standard of Review in Cases of Conflict

Unlike in most conventional trusts,[103] plan administrators in employee benefit plans often operate under a conflict of interest. For example, in *Firestone*, the employer acted as plan administrator and provided the sole source of funding for the unfunded welfare benefit plan at issue.[104] Thus, a decision by the employer-as-plan-administrator to grant benefits required a direct payment out of the pocket of the employer-as-employer. Such an arrangement is often referred to as a "structural" conflict of interest.[105]

The Court in *Firestone* cautioned that if a plan "administrator or fiduciary is operating under a conflict of interest, that conflict must be weighed as a 'factor in determining whether there is an abuse of discretion.' "[106] The Court did not, however, provide any additional guidance, and following *Firestone*, lower courts took varying views of what, specifically, constitutes a conflict of interest,[107] and the standard of review that should apply in the case of a conflict of interest.[108]

In *Metropolitan Life Insurance Co. v. Glenn*,[109] the Supreme Court revisited the issue of the appropriate standard of review to apply in ERISA § 502(a)(1)(B) claims involving a conflict of interest. In that case, a plan participant challenged the denial of disability benefits under her employer's disability insurance plan. With respect to the question of when a conflict of interest arises, the Court found there is clearly a conflict of interest when the employer administers a self-funded plan.[110] In such a case, "every dollar provided in benefits is a dollar spent by . . . the employer; and every dollar saved . . . is a dollar in [the employer's] pocket."[111] Although the Court characterized the answer as less clear when, as in that case, the plan administrator

---

N.Y.U. Rev. of Employee Benefits and Executive Compensation 16-1, 16-15–16-27; Christopher R. Stevenson, Abusing Abuse of Discretion: Judicial Review of ERISA Fiduciaries' Discretionary Decisions in Denial of Benefits Cases, 27 Hofstra Lab. & Emp. L.J. 105, 115–132 (2009).

[103] "Trust law presupposes that the trustee who administers a trust will be disinterested, in the sense of having no personal stake in the trust assets, although the trust terms can make a contrary provision." Langbein, *Trust Law as Regulatory Law*, 101 Nw. U. L. Rev., at 1326.

[104] 489 U.S. at 105.

[105] *See, e.g.*, Williams v. Metropolitan Life Ins. Co., 609 F.3d 622, 630 (4th Cir. 2010); Denmark v. Liberty Life Assur. Co. of Boston, 566 F.3d 1, 7 (1st Cir. 2009); Wachtel v. Health Net, Inc., 482 F.3d 225, 234 (3d Cir. 2007).

[106] 489 U.S. at 115, *quoting*, Restatement (Second) of Trusts § 187, Comment *d* (1959).

[107] *See* Kennedy, *Conkright*, 2010 N.Y.U. Rev. of Employee Benefits and Executive Compensation, at 16-18–16-19 (discussing approaches courts have taken to determining when a conflict of interest arises); Roy F. Harmon, *The Debate Over Deference in the ERISA Setting — Judicial Review of Decisions by Conflicted Fiduciaries*, 54 S.D. L. Rev. 1, 12 (2009) (same); Beverly Cohen, *Divided Loyalties: How the Metlife v. Glenn Standard Discounts ERISA Fiduciaries' Conflicts of Interest*, 2009 Utah L. Rev. 955, 960–66 (same); Stevenson, 27 Hofstra Lab. & Emp. L.J., at 115–132 (same).

[108] *See* Kennedy, *Conkright*, 2010 N.Y.U. Rev. of Employee Benefits and Executive Compensation, at 16-20–16-22 & 16-24–16-27 (discussing various standards of review courts applied to conflicts of interest); Cohen, 2009 Utah L. Rev., at 966-70 (same); Stevenson, 27 Hofstra Lab. & Emp. L.J., at 115–132 (same).

[109] 554 U.S. 105 (2008).

[110] *Id.* at 112.

[111] *Id.*

is an insurance company from whom the employer has purchased insurance,[112] the Court found such an arrangement also constitutes a structural conflict of interest for purposes of ERISA.[113]

Turning to the applicable standard of review, the Court reiterated the Court's statement in *Firestone* that the conflict should "be weighed as a 'factor in determining whether there is an abuse of discretion.' "[114] The Court announced that the standard should remain deferential[115] and that courts should not create special burden-of-proof rules or any other special procedural or evidentiary rules that focus on the administrator/payor conflict.[116]

The Court did not identify any specific weight that should be given to a conflict of interest. Instead, it simply said that a conflict of interest is one factor courts should take into account in reviewing claims for benefits. In cases involving several different, case-specific factors, "any one factor will act as a tiebreaker when the other factors are closely balanced, the degree of closeness necessary depending upon the tiebreaking factor's inherent or case-specific importance."[117]

To illustrate, the Court stated that a conflict of interest should prove to be of more importance where circumstances, such as a history of biased claims administration, suggest that the conflict is more likely to have affected the benefits decision.[118] In contrast, the conflict should prove to be of less importance (or even no importance) where the plan administrator has taken steps to increase accuracy and reduce bias, such as by walling off the plan administrator from employees who are interested in the company's finances.[119]

The Court recognized that its opinion did not provide courts with a "detailed set of instructions" on how to weigh conflicts of interest in reviewing challenges to benefit denials.[120] Thus, not surprisingly, lower courts continue to grapple with the appropriate standard of review to apply in benefit claim litigation and when to

---

[112] *Id.* at 114. The Court offered two arguments in support of the claim that an insurance company does not face a conflict of interest in such a case. First, the insurance company charges a fee that attempts to cover the costs of claims, and thus the payment does not come out of the company's own pocket. Second, the marketplace (and regulators) may punish an insurance company that is biased in its claims processing. *Id. But see* JAY M. FEINMAN, DENY, DELAY, DEFEND: WHY INSURANCE COMPANIES DON'T PAY CLAIMS AND WHAT YOU CAN DO ABOUT IT (2010) (arguing that the name of the game in the insurance industry market today is to delay and deny paying claims).

[113] *Id.* at 114. The Court found an inherent conflict because the employer's own conflict could extend to its selection of the insurance company to administer its plan, and ERISA imposes standards on insurers that exceed the marketplace's standards. *Id.* 114–15. The Court also noted that its rule offered courts flexibility to take into account the severity or significance of the conflict. *Id.* at 115.

[114] *Id.* at 115.

[115] *Id.*

[116] *Id.* at 116.

[117] *Id.* at 117.

[118] *Id.*

[119] *Id.*

[120] *Id.* at 119. Indeed, Justice Scalia, in dissent, described the Court's standard as "goobledygook." *Id.* at 130 n.3. According to Justice Scalia, a plan administrator's conflict of interest should only be taken into account if it actually and improperly motivated the plan administrator's decision. *Id.* at 128.

reduce deference to a plan administrator's decision,[121] and lower courts do not follow a uniform approach to such cases.[122]

[4] Standard of Review After Initial Plan Interpretation Rejected

Just two years after deciding *Glenn*, the Court returned to the standard of review applicable to ERISA § 502(a)(1)(B) claims in *Conkright v. Frommert*.[123] Unlike *Firestone* and *Glenn*, which involved welfare benefit plans, *Conkright* concerned a pension plan. The facts in *Conkright* were quite complex.[124] At the heart of the dispute was the manner in which the plan administrator calculated the retirement benefits of rehired employees who had previously received lump sum distributions from the plan.[125] The Ninth Circuit held that with respect to plan participants hired prior to 1998, the plan administrator's application of a "phantom account" offset mechanism to reduce the participants' benefits to account for the earlier lump sum distributions constituted a retroactive reduction of accrued benefits in violation of ERISA § 204(g).[126] The appellate court remanded the case to the district court to craft an appropriate remedy.[127]

---

[121] For an overview of the post-*Glenn*/pre-*Conkright* decisions, see Kennedy, *Conkright*, 2010 N.Y.U. REV. OF EMPLOYEE BENEFITS AND EXECUTIVE COMPENSATION, at 16-42–16-50. For an overview of post-*Conkright* decisions, see Rene E. Thorne, et al., *Conkright v. Frommert — One Year Later: Are Courts Getting It Right?*, 38 BNA PENSION & BENEFITS REPORTER 1008 (May 24, 2011).

[122] For example, the Fourth Circuit considers eight nonexclusive factors in determining the reasonableness of a plan administrator's decision. The plan administrator's motives and any conflict of interest it may have is one of the eight factors. *See, e.g.*, Vincent v. Lucent Technologies, Inc., 733 F. Supp. 2d 729, 733 (W.D.N.C. 2010), *citing* Booth v. WalMart Stores, Inc. Assoc. Health & Welfare Plan, 201 F.3d 335, 342 (4th Cir. 2000). The Fifth Circuit engages in a two step process in determining whether a conflicted plan administrator abused its discretion in interpreting a plan provision. First, it applies a three-factor test to determine whether the plan administrator's interpretation was legally correct. If the court finds that the interpretation was legally correct, then there is no abuse of discretion. If the court finds that the interpretation was not legally correct, then it considers whether the plan administrator operated under a conflict of interest. The Tenth Circuit applies a sliding scale approach to plan interpretation questions in the context of conflicts of interest. The court decreases the deference it accords plan administrators "in proportion to the seriousness of the conflict." *See* Kennedy, *Conkright*, 2010 N.Y.U. REV. OF EMPLOYEE BENEFITS AND EXECUTIVE COMPENSATION, at 16–47 (citing and discussing cases).

[123] 559 U.S. 506 (2010).

[124] The facts are set forth at length in the Ninth Circuit's first decision in this case. Frommert v. Conkright, 433 F.3d 254, 257–61 (2006). At oral argument, the Supreme Court justices spent a considerable amount of time trying to sort out the facts. *Focus of Xerox Pension Case Twists During Supreme Court Oral Arguments*, 37 BNA PENSION & BENEFITS REPORTER 214 (Jan. 26, 2010). In his dissenting opinion, Justice Breyer offered a simplified version of the facts. 559 U.S. at 523–26 and 538–41. The author of the majority opinion, Chief Justice Roberts, in contrast, devoted little attention to the specific facts at issue. *Id.* at 509 ("Fortunately, most of the factual details are unnecessary to the legal issues before us, so we cover them only in broad strokes.").

[125] Frommert v. Conkright, 433 F.3d 254, 257 (2006) ("The dispute in this case centers on the manner by which the rehired employees' previous distributions are factored into the calculation of their retirement benefits after returning to Xerox.").

[126] *Id.* at 268. The court also found that the plan was not properly amended pursuant to ERISA § 204(h) to apply the phantom account offset method to individuals rehired prior to 1998. *Id.* at 266–68.

[127] *Id.* at 268.

On remand, the district court directed the plan administrator to recalculate the participants' benefits by deducting the nominal value of the lump sum distributions that they had received and not providing for any adjustment for hypothetical investment gains or other adjustment to reflect the inflation-adjusted value of the prior lump sum distributions.[128] On appeal, the plan administrator argued, among other things, that the district court erred by failing to adopt the remedy the plan administrator proposed or at least remanding the case to the plan administrator to craft the appropriate remedy.[129] The appellate court held that the district court was not required to defer to the plan administrator's opinion when the plan administrator had previously construed the terms of the plan in violation of ERISA.[130]

The Supreme Court reversed. The Court held that a "single honest mistake" does not justify stripping a plan administrator of deference with respect to the plan administrator's subsequent related interpretations of the plan.[131] The Court looked to the three factors that had guided its decisions in *Firestone* and *Glenn:* the terms of the plan, trust law principles, and ERISA's purposes.[132] The Court first found that nothing in the terms of the plan suggested that discretion should be limited to the plan administrator's first efforts to interpret the plan.[133] The Court then found that trust law did not provide a clear answer to the question.[134] Finally, the Court found that continuing to grant the plan administrator deference after having made an honest mistake in plan interpretation was consistent with three guiding principles underlying ERISA; efficiency, predictability, and uniformity.[135]

---

[128] Frommert v. Conkright, 472 F. Supp. 2d 452, 457 (2007).

[129] Frommert v. Conkright, 535 F.3d 111, 118 (2008).

[130] *Id.* at 119.

[131] 559 U.S. at 509.

[132] *Id.* at 512.

[133] *Id.* at 513.

[134] *Id.* at 514–16. According to the dissent, in contrast, trust law authorizes a court to exercise its discretion rather than defer to a plan administrator after finding a plan administrator abused its discretion in the first instance. *Id.* at 528–34.

[135] *Id.* at 517. Commentators have harshly criticized the Court's decisions in *Firestone, Glenn,* and *Conkright. See, e.g.,* Andrew Stumpff, *Darkness at Noon: Judicial Interpretation May Have Made Things Worse for Benefit Plan Participants Under ERISA Than Had the Statute Never Been Enacted,* 23 St. Thomas L. Rev. 221, 232 (2011); Kennedy, *Conkright,* 2010 N.Y.U. Rev. of Employee Benefits and Executive Compensation, at 16-39–16-42 & 16-63–16-73; Maher, *Creating a Paternalistic Market,* 2009 Wisc. L. Rev., at 676–82; Donald T. Bogan, *ERISA: The Foundations Insufficiences for Deferential Review in Employee Benefit Claims — Metropolitan Life Ins. Co. v. Glenn,* 27 Hofstra Lab. & Emp. L.J. 147 (2009); Cohen, 2009 Utah L. Rev. 955; Langbein, *Trust Law as Regulatory Law,* 101 Nw. U. L. Rev. 1315; DeBofsky, 37 J. Marshall L. Rev. 727.

[5]   **Summary of Standard of Review Applicable to ERISA § 502(a)(1)(B) Claims**

Standard of Review
ERISA § 502(a)(1)(B)
Claims

Default Standard
(rarely applies)

De Novo Standard of Review

Firestone Tire & Rubber Co. v. Bruch, 489 U.S. 101 (1989)

Plan Grants Plan Administrator Discretion
(most plans)

No Conflict of Interest

Discretionary Standard of Review:

"abuse of discretion" or "arbitrary and capricious"

Firestone Tire & Rubber Co. v. Bruch, 489 U.S. 101 (1989)

Conflict of Interest

Conflict should be weighed as factor in determining whether there is abuse of discretion

Firestone Tire & Rubber Co. v. Bruch, 489 U.S. 101 (1989); *Metropolitan Life Insurance Co. v. Glenn*, 554 U.S. 105 (2008)

Second Interpretation

If court rejects plan administrator's first interpretation, standard of review remains discretionary

Conkright v. Frommert, 559 U.S. 506 (2010)

[B] Standard of Review Applicable to ERISA Claims Other than Claims Under ERISA § 502(a)(1)(B)

Although the Supreme Court has addressed the standard of review applicable to ERISA § 502(a)(1)(B) claims on several occasions, the Supreme Court has never expressly addressed the standard of review applicable to other ERISA claims. Several of the circuits, however, have addressed the issue and reached different results.

For example, in *John Blair Communications, Inc. Profit Sharing Plan v. Telemundo Group, Inc. Profit Sharing Plan*,[136] the Second Circuit declined to apply the arbitrary and capricious standard to a breach of fiduciary claim.[137] In that case, plan participants claimed that a plan fiduciary breached its fiduciary duty when it treated a plan surplus as an employer contribution.[138] In declining to apply an arbitrary and capricious standard, the court relied on a pre-*Firestone* Third Circuit decision[139] which distinguished between benefit denial claims in which the issue is "whether the trustees have correctly balanced the interests of present claimants against the interests of future claimants" and other fiduciary challenges in which the basis of the claim is that the trustees "have sacrificed the interests of the beneficiaries as a class in favor of some third party's interests."[140] The court declared "that decisions that improperly disregard the valid interests of beneficiaries in favor of third parties remain subject to the strict prudent person articulated in § 404 of ERISA."[141]

In *Tibble v. Edison International*,[142] the Ninth Circuit declined to follow the Second Circuit's decision and applied an arbitrary and capricious standard to an ERISA § 404(a)(1)(D) breach of fiduciary claim.[143] The court noted that *John Blair* involved the prudent person standard codified in ERISA § 404(a)(1)(B) while the case before it involved ERISA § 404(a)(1)(D) which "simply requires that actions be in line with the plan documents."[144] The court declared that issues of plan interpretation that do not implicate ERISA's statutory duties are subject to *Firestone*.[145]

The Ninth Circuit offered three justifications for applying the arbitrary and capricious standard to issues of plan interpretation outside the benefits context. First, the *Firestone* "rationale did not stem from an interpretive gloss on the welfare-benefits provision of ERISA."[146] Second, not applying deference could lead

---

[136] 26 F.3d 360 (2d Cir. 1994).

[137] *Id.* at 369–70.

[138] *Id.* at 368.

[139] Struble v. New Jersey Brewery Employees' Welfare Trust Fund, 732 F.2d 325 (3d Cir. 1984).

[140] 26 F.3d at 369.

[141] *Id.*

[142] 729 F.3d 1110 (9th Cir. 2013), *vacated and remanded on other grounds*, 135 S. Ct. 1823 (2015).

[143] *Id.* at 1128–30.

[144] *Id.* at 1129.

[145] *Id.*

[146] *Id.*

to "uniformity problems" with plans subject to different interpretations under ERISA § 502(a)(1)(B) benefits claim litigation and ERISA § 404(a)(1)(D) fiduciary breach litigation.[147] Finally, granting deference to plan administrators preserves ERISA's careful balancing by keeping administrative and litigation expenses under control.[148]

Other courts have gone further. For example, in *Tussey v. ABB, Inc.*,[149] the Eighth Circuit held that the arbitrary and capricious standard applies to all plan interpretations, even in the context of an ERISA § 404(a)(1)(B) breach of prudence claim.[150] Similarly, in *Moench v. Robertson*,[151] the Third Circuit declared that "we believe that after *Firestone*, trust law should guide the standard of review over claims, such as those here, not only under [ERISA § 502(a)(1)(B)] but over claims filed pursuant to [ERISA § 502(a)(2)] based on violations of" ERISA § 404 fiduciary duties.[152]

In *Fifth Third Bancorp v. Dudenhoeffer*,[153] the Supreme Court rejected the so-called *Moench* presumption, which presumed that an ESOP fiduciary who invested the ESOP's assets in employer stock acted consistently with ERISA.[154] The Court, however, did not expressly address the standard of review applicable in such a case and thus left open the question whether a plan fiduciary should be granted discretion if plan documents require that plan assets be invested in employer stock.[155]

§ 7.08 REMEDIES

Section 2(b) of ERISA declares that the policy of ERISA includes protecting the interests of plan participants and their beneficiaries "by providing for appropriate remedies, sanctions, and ready access to the Federal courts."[156] Section 502 of ERISA sets forth, among other things, the remedies available under ERISA.

---

[147] *Id.* at 1130.

[148] *Id.*

[149] 746 F.3d 327 (8th Cir.), *cert. denied*, 135 S. Ct. 477 (2014).

[150] *Id.* at 333–35. Although the court did not cite ERISA § 404(a)(1)(B), the court clearly applied the standard to a breach of prudence claim. *See id.* at 336–38 (holding that failure to afford discretion to plan administrator's interpretation with respect to recordkeeping and revenue sharing was harmless error and remanding claim with respect to selection of investment options and mapping).

[151] 62 F.3d 553 (3d Cir. 1995), *abrogated by* Fifth Third Bancorp v. Dudenhoeffer, 134 S. Ct. 2459 (2014).

[152] *Id.* at 565. *See also* Armstrong v. LaSalle Bank Nat'l Ass'n, 446 F.3d 728, 733 (7th Cir. 2006) (reviewing ESOP trustee's balancing decisions deferentially); Hunter v. Caliber Sys., Inc. 220 F.3d 702, 711 (6th Cir. 2000) (noting that case involves ERISA § 502(a)(1)(B) and finding no barrier to applying deferential standard to case "not involving typical review of denial of benefits").

[153] 134 S. Ct. 2459 (2014).

[154] For a discussion of the *Dudenhoeffer* decision, see Chapter 6 § 6.04[D][2][b].

[155] *See* Theresa S. Gee, *ERISA Litigation & Company Stock: Supreme Court's Decision in* Fifth Third Bancorp v. Dudenhoeffer (Aug. 11, 2014), available at http://www.americanbenefitscouncil.org/documents2014/presentation_blb_stockplans081114.pdf (asking question).

[156] ERISA § 2.

The vast majority of litigation under ERISA arises under three separate subsections of ERISA § 502:[157] (1) ERISA § 502(a)(1)(B), (2) ERISA § 502(a)(2), and (3) ERISA § 502(a)(3). Over the last twenty years or so, the Supreme Court has focused on the availability of remedies under these three provisions in eight separate cases.[158] In addition, the Supreme Court has referred to these provisions in a number of other cases.[159]

Historically, the Supreme Court has interpreted the remedies available under these provisions in a rather "cramped" fashion.[160] The Court's narrow construction of the remedial provisions combined with the expansive reach of ERISA preemption[161] has led to "betrayals without a remedy"[162] in a host of cases. That is, in a host of cases, plan participants have found themselves without an adequate remedy to redress a violation of ERISA or the terms of the plan.[163]

Thus, perhaps not surprisingly, the Supreme Court's remedial jurisprudence has been subject to considerable criticism. Critics have objected to it on a wide variety of grounds, ranging from claims that it has been inconsistent, to claims that it has misunderstood and/or misapplied trust law principles, to criticisms of its failure to provide plan participants with remedies.

---

[157] Peter K. Stris & Victor A. O'Connell, *Enforcing ERISA*, 56 S.D. L. Rev. 515, 519–20 (2011) (stating that substantive rules of ERISA are almost exclusively enforced through private civil actions brought under ERISA §§ 502(a)(1)(B), 502(a)(2), and 502(a)(3)); John H. Langbein, *What ERISA Means by "Equitable": The Supreme Court's Trail of Error in* Russell, Mertens, *and* Great-West, 103 Colum. L. Rev. 1317, 1334 (2003).

[158] U.S. Airways v. McCutchen, 133 S. Ct. 1537 (2013); CIGNA Corp. v. Amara, 131 S. Ct. 1866 (2011); LaRue v. DeWolff Boberg & Assocs., Inc., 552 U.S. 248 (2008); Sereboff v. MidAtlantic Medical Services, Inc., 547 U.S. 356 (2006); Great West Life & Annuity Ins. Co. v. Knudson, 534 U.S. 204 (2002); Varity Corp. v. Howe, 516 U.S. 489 (1996); Mertens v. Hewitt Associates, 508 U.S. 248 (1993); Massachusetts Mutual Life Ins. Co. v. Russell, 473 U.S. 134 (1985).

[159] *See, e.g.*, Ingersoll-Rand Co. v. McClendon, 498 U.S. 133, 145 (1990)(stating in *dicta* that "[t]here is no basis in section 502(a)'s language for limiting ERISA actions to only those which seek 'pension benefits.' It is clear that the relief requested here is well within the power of federal courts to provide."); Aetna Health Inc. v. Davila, 542 U.S. 200, 210 (2004) (describing available remedies under ERISA § 502(a)(1)(B)).

[160] Aetna Health Inc. v. Davila, 542 U.S. 200, 222 (2004) (Ginsburg, J., concurring) ("Because the [Supreme] Court has coupled an encompassing interpretation of ERISA's preemptive force with a cramped construction of the . . . relief[ ] allowable under [ERISA], a 'regulatory vacuum' exists: '[V]irtually all state law remedies are preempted but very few federal substitutes are provided.' "), *quoting*, DiFelice v Aetna U.S. Healthcare, 346 F.3d 442, 456 (3d Cir. 2003) (Becker, J., concurring)).

[161] For a discussion of ERISA preemption, see Chapter 8.

[162] *See* Allinder v. Inter-City Products Corp., 152 F.3d 544 (6th Cir. 1998), *cert. denied*, 525 U.S. 1178 (1999) (stating that "[m]any commentators have noted that the Supreme Court's 5-4 decision in Mertens has resulted in a 'betrayal without a remedy' for employees who pursue ERISA claims beyond the simple recovery of benefits").

[163] For cases in which plan participants have been left without a remedy, see, for example, Paul Secunda, *Sorry, No Remedy: Intersectionality and the Grand Irony of ERISA*, 26 Hofstra Lab. & Emp. L.J. 131, 155–58 (describing cases) (2009); Peter K. Stris, *ERISA Remedies, Welfare Benefits and Bad Faith: Losing Sight of the Cathedral*, 26 Hofstra Lab. & Emp. L.J. 387, 395 n. 47 (2009) (listing cases); Colleen E. Medill, *Resolving the Judicial Paradox of "Equitable" Relief Under ERISA Section 502(a)(3)*, 39 J. Marshall L. Rev. 827, 834–44 (2006) (describing four different categories of cases in which plan participants may be left without a remedy).

The Court's recent *dicta* in *CIGNA Corp. v. Amara*, [164] suggests that the Court may be willing, at least in some instances, to interpret ERISA's remedial provisions in a broader fashion.

[A] Claims for Benefits Under ERISA § 502(a)(1)(B)

Section 502(a)(1)(B) of ERISA provides that "[a] civil action may be brought by a participant or beneficiary . . . to recover benefits due to him under the terms of his plan, to enforce his rights under the terms of the plan, or to clarify his rights to future benefits under the terms of the plan."

Section 502(a)(1)(B) has been described as "the workhorse of ERISA remedy law."[165] Challenges to denials of claims for health care benefits are probably the most common type of § 502(a)(1)(B) claim.[166] Participants and beneficiaries may, however, file suit challenging denials of a wide variety of other benefits, such as severance benefits,[167] disability benefits,[168] and life insurance benefits.[169]

Benefit denial cases typically raise such questions as: (1) whether a proposed medical treatment is experimental and thus not covered by the plan; (2) whether a particular treatment is medically necessary; (3) whether a particular illness arises from a pre-existing condition and is thus precluded from coverage under the plan; and (4) whether an individual satisfies the plan's definition of disability.[170]

The Supreme Court has referred to available remedies under ERISA § 502(a)(1)(B) in a number of cases. In *Aetna Health Inc. v. Davila*,[171] the Court confirmed that, as the text of ERISA § 502(a)(1)(B) suggests, a plan participant can bring suit under section 502(a)(1)(B) to require the plan to provide benefits promised under the terms of the plan, or in the alternative, to seek reimbursement for the cost of benefits promised under the terms of the plan if the plan participant initially pays for the benefits. In *Massachusetts Mutual Life Insurance Co. v. Russell*,[172] the Supreme Court announced, in *dicta*, that "extracontractual"

---

[164] 131 S. Ct. 1866 (2011).

[165] Langbein, *What ERISA Means by "Equitable*," 103 COLUM. L. REV., at 1334. *See also* John Morrison & Jonathan McDonald, *Exorcising Discretion: The Death of Caprice in ERISA Claims Handling* 56 S.D. L. REV. 482, 483 (2011) (noting that according to insurance industry representatives, each year there are nearly 2 million benefit claims denials potentially subject to suit under ERISA § 502(1)(B)); Peter K. Stris, *ERISA Remedies, Welfare Benefits, and Bad Faith: Losing Sight of the Cathedral*, 26 HOFSTRA LAB. & EMP. L.J. 387, 392 (2009) (noting that "[e]ach year, there are millions of recorded disputes regarding the scope of coverage under employer-sponsored insurance arrangements").

[166] Maher, *Creating a Paternalistic Market*, 2009 WISC. L. REV., at 670 n.44.

[167] *See, e.g.*, Dabertin v. HCR Manor Care, Inc., 373 F.3d 822 (7th Cir. 2004).

[168] *See, e.g.*, Holmstrom v. Metro. Life Ins. Co., 615 F.3d 758 (7th Cir. 2010).

[169] *See, e.g.*, LaAsmar v. Phelps Dodge Corp. Life, Accidental Death & Dismemberment & Dependent Life Ins. Plan, 605 F.3d 789 (10th Cir. 2010); Critchlow v. First UNUM Life Ins. Co. of Am., 378 F.3d 246 (2d Cir. 2004).

[170] *See* Peter K. Stris, *ERISA Remedies, Welfare Benefits, and Bad Faith: Losing Sight of the Cathedral*, 26 HOFSTRA LAB. & EMP. L.J. 387, 392 (2009) (citing cases).

[171] 542 U.S. 200, 210 (2004).

[172] 473 U.S. 134 (1985).

damages are not available under ERISA § 502(a)(1)(B). Following *Russell,* lower courts have uniformly held that under *Russell* neither consequential nor punitive damages are available under ERISA § 502(a)(1)(B).

The Supreme Court has also addressed two other issues under ERISA § 502(a)(1)(B). First, in *CIGNA Corp. v. Amara,*[173] the Supreme Court held that for purposes of ERISA § 502(a)(1)(B), the "terms of the plan" are limited to the terms of the written plan document and do not include the terms of the summary plan description. In *Varity Corporation v. Howe,*[174] the Court suggested that if a remedy is available under section 502(a)(1)(B), remedies under ERISA § 502(a)'s other subsections may be foreclosed.

[1] Available Remedies Under ERISA § 502(a)(1)(B)

Section 502(a)(1)(B) authorizes plan participants and beneficiaries to challenge routine benefit denials. Thus, suppose, for example, a plan participant suffers from leukemia and his doctors recommend stem cell transplant therapy, but the plan denies the treatment because the plan excludes coverage for trial studies. If the plan participant believes that he should be provided the therapy under the terms of the plan, section 502(a)(1)(B) authorizes the plan participant to bring suit to seek provision of the therapy.[175] Or, in the alternative, if the plan participant has sufficient funds to pay out-of-pocket for the treatment, the participant may pay for the therapy and then bring suit under section 502(a)(1)(B) to seek reimbursement for the cost of the therapy.[176]

Suppose, however, that the participant is unable to pay for the cost of the therapy and suffers adverse consequences, perhaps even death, as a result of the plan's failure to cover the requested therapy.[177] Courts have consistently interpreted section 502(a)(1)(B) to deny consequential damages under such circumstances.[178] Instead, they have limited the remedy under section 502(a)(1)(B) to either an order directing the plan to provide the denied benefits, or reimbursement for the cost of the benefits if the participant or beneficiary paid for the benefits out of his own pocket.[179]

---

[173] 131 S. Ct. 1866 (2011).

[174] 516 U.S. 489 (1996).

[175] *See* Aetna Health Inc. v. Davila, 542 U.S. 200, 210 (2004) ("If a participant or beneficiary believes that benefits promised to him under the terms of the plan are not provided, he can bring suit seeking provision of those benefits.")

[176] *See id.* at 211 (noting that "respondents could have paid for the treatment themselves and then sought reimbursement through a § 502(a)(1)(B) action").

[177] *Cf.* Hamann v. Independence Blue Cross, 2013 U.S. App. LEXIS 19248 (5th Cir. Sept. 18, 2013)

[178] *See id.*; Bast v. Prudential Ins. Co. of Am., 150 F.3d 1003, 1009 (9th Cir. 1998), *cert. denied,* 528 U.S. 870 (1999); McRae v. Seafarers' Welfare Plan, 920 F.2d 819, 821–23 (11th Cir. 1991).

[179] Peter K. Stris, *ERISA Remedies, Welfare Benefits, and Bad Faith: Losing Sight of the Cathedral,* 26 Hofstra Lab. & Emp. L.J. 387, 393–94 (2009), *citing,* Richard A. Epstein & Alan O. Sykes, *The Assault on Managed Care: Vicarious Liability, ERISA Preemption, and Class Actions,* 30 J. Legal Stud. 625, 632 (2001); Dana M. Muir, *Fiduciary Status as an Employer's Shield: The Perversity of ERISA Fiduciary Law,* 2 U. Pa. J. Lab. & Empl. L. 391, 436 nn. 290 (2000) (citing cases).

The courts' unwillingness to provide consequential damages for the wrongful denial of benefits can be traced to the Supreme Court's first ERISA remedy decision, *Massachusetts Mutual Life Insurance Co. v. Russell*.[180] In that case, a plan participant claimed disability benefits under her employer's plan. The plan paid the participant benefits for about five months, and then terminated the benefits based on a doctor's report.[181] The participant requested an internal review of the decision terminating her benefits, and about five months later, the benefits were reinstated, and the participant received a retroactive payment of all of the benefits that had initially been withheld.[182]

The participant filed suit against the plan's fiduciaries under sections 502(a)(2) and 409(a) to recover for losses she allegedly incurred as a result of the interruption in benefit payments.[183] In *dicta*,[184] the Court stated:

> Significantly, the statutory provision explicitly authorizing a beneficiary to bring an action to enforce his rights under the plan — [section] 502(a)(1)(B) . . . says nothing about the recovery of extracontractual damages, or about the possible consequences of delay in the plan administrators' processing of a disputed claim. Thus, there really is nothing at all in the statutory text to support the conclusion that such a delay gives rise to a private right of action for compensatory or punitive relief.[185]

Although the term "extracontractual damages" does not appear in the text of ERISA, and is arguably ambiguous,[186] courts have consistently interpreted it to prohibit consequential and punitive damages under ERISA § 502(a)(1)(B).[187]

---

[180] 473 U.S. 134 (1985).

[181] *Id.* at 136.

[182] *Id.*

[183] *Id.* at 137.

[184] *Cf. id.* at 139 n.5 (noting that "[b]ecause respondent relies entirely on § 409(a) [which is enforced through § 502(a)(2)], and expressly disclaims reliance on § 502(a)(3), we have no occasion to consider whether any other provision of ERISA authorizes recovery of extracontractual damages").

[185] *Id.* at 144.

[186] *See* Richard Rouco, *Available Remedies Under ERISA Section 502(a)*, 45 ALA. L. REV. 631, 651 (1994) (noting that "[t]he line between contractual and extracontractual damages is not always easy to draw"); Muir, *Fiduciary Status*, 2 U. PA. J. LAB. & EMP. L., at 437–39 (discussing possible meanings of extracontractual damages); Robert A. Kamp, *The Argument for "Extra-Contractual" Damages Under ERISA*, 82 ILL. B.J. 70, 76 (1994) (noting that "the view that certain 'extra-contractual' damages are, in fact, contractual because they are foreseeable is not some novel or innovative concept; it dates back to the landmark case of *Hadley v. Baxendale*"). *See also* Langbein, *What ERISA Means by "Equitable,"* 103 COLUM. L. REV., at 1346 (contending that both parts of the word "extracontractual" are misleading — "extra" is inappropriate because it "suggests a bonus, something to which one is not entitled," and "contractual" "is a misemphasis on the setting of ERISA remedy law . . . . ERISA's central policy decision was to impose a regime of mandatory trusteeship and fiduciary law on pension and employee benefit plans").

[187] *See, e.g.*, Muir, *Fiduciary Status*, 2 U. PA. J. LAB. & EMP. L., at 436 (stating that "without exception, the benefits enforcement section has been construed to permit only the recovery of benefits due under a plan"). For criticisms of the Court's prohibition on extracontractual damages, see, for example, Maher, *Creating a Paternalistic Market*, 2009 WISC. L. REV., at 672–73; Muir, Fiduciary Status, 2 U . PA. J. LAB. & EMP. L., at 436–39. See also George Lee Flint, Jr., *ERISA: Extracontractual Damages Mandated for Benefit Claim Actions*, 36 ARIZ. L. REV. 611, 634–65 (1994) (arguing that the plain meaning

[2]   Terms of the Plan

Section 502(a)(1)(B) authorizes a plan participant to bring a civil action to, among other things, "recover benefits due to him under 'the terms of his plan.' " In *CIGNA Corporation v. Amara*,[188] the Supreme Court addressed the meaning of "the terms of [the] plan."

In *CIGNA*, plan participants filed suit challenging their employer's conversion of its traditional defined benefit plan to a cash balance plan. The plan participants claimed that the employer violated its disclosure obligations under ERISA because it failed to give them proper notice of the changes to their benefits. Relying on ERISA § 502(a)(1)(B), the district court reformed the plan and ordered the plan administrator (who was their employer) to pay them benefits that were consistent with the summary plan description provided to the plan participants rather than the lower benefits promised under the terms of the plan.[189]

The Supreme Court held that the district court did not have authority under ERISA § 502(a)(1)(B) to order this relief.[190] According to the Court, summary plan descriptions provide information *about* the plan but are not *part of* the plan itself.[191] Thus, the district court could not rely on the terms of the summary plan description to reform the terms of the plan under ERISA § 502(a)(1)(B).[192]

[3]   Availability of Other ERISA § 502(a) Remedies

Whether the availability of a claim under ERISA § 502(a)(1)(B) forecloses a claim under ERISA's other remedial provisions is an open question.[193]

In *Varity Corporation v. Howe*,[194] former plan participants brought suit under ERISA § 502(a)(3) for individual relief for a breach of fiduciary claim. *Amici* argued that permitting relief for individual breach of fiduciary claims would "complicate ordinary benefit claims by dressing them up in a 'fiduciary duty' clothing."[195] In rejecting this argument, the Court declared

> [ERISA § 502(a)(3)] authorizes "appropriate" equitable relief. We should expect that courts, in fashioning "appropriate" equitable relief, will keep in mind the "special nature and purpose of employee benefit plans," and will respect the "policy choices reflected in the inclusion of certain remedies and the exclusion of others." Thus, we should expect that where Congress

---

of the text as well as legislative history and policy considerations support finding that "benefits due under the terms of [the] plan" encompasses extracontractual damages and restitution).

[188]   131 S. Ct. 1866 (2011).

[189]   For a more detailed discussion of the facts of the case, see Chapter 4 § 4.03[C].

[190]   131 S. Ct. at 1878.

[191]   *Id.* at 1877.

[192]   *Id.* at 1878.

[193]   For an argument that the availability of a remedy under ERISA § 502(a)(1)(B) should not foreclose a claim under ERISA § 502(a)(3), see Medill, *"Equitable" Relief Under ERISA Section 502(a)(3)*, 39 J. MARSHALL L. REV., at 865–87.

[194]   516 U.S. 489 (1996).

[195]   *Id.* at 514.

elsewhere provided adequate relief for a beneficiary's injury, there will likely be no need for further equitable relief, in which case such relief normally would not be "appropriate."[196]

Following this *dicta*, many federal appellate courts have held if a claim may be brought under ERISA § 502(a)(1)(B), a remedy is foreclosed under the other subsections of ERISA § 502(a).[197] Not all courts, however, have so held.[198] In addition, some courts have recognized exceptions to the total bar on simultaneous ERISA § 502(a) claims when ERISA § 502(a)(1)(B) would not provide complete relief.[199]

In a concurring opinion in *LaRue v. DeWolff, Boberg & Associates, Inc,*[200] Chief Justice Roberts announced that if the plan participant may bring a claim under ERISA § 502(a)(1)(B), it is not clear whether he may also bring a claim under ERISA § 502(a)(2).[201] Chief Justice Roberts did not answer the question. He simply noted that "other courts in other cases remain free to consider what we have not – what effect the availability of relief under § 502(a)(1)(B) may have on a plan participant's ability to proceed under § 502(a)(2)."[202]

---

[196] *Id.* at 515 (citations omitted).

[197] *See, e.g.*, Larocca v. Borden, 276 F.3d 22, 28–29 (1st Cir. 2002) (declaring that "federal courts have uniformly concluded that, if a plaintiff can pursue benefits under the plan pursuant to Section (a)(1), there is an adequate remedy under the plan which bars a further remedy under Section (a)(3)" and citing cases from First, Fifth, Eighth, Ninth, and Eleventh Circuits). *See also* Coyne & Delany Co. v. Blue Cross & Blue Shield of Va., Inc., 102 F.3d 712 (4th Cir. 1996) (holding that fiduciary could not bring suit under ERISA § 502(a)(3) against another fiduciary for breaching its fiduciary duty by failing to provide benefits; only plan participants and beneficiaries can bring suit to recover benefits under ERISA § 502(a)(1)(B) and plan fiduciary cannot bring suit to recover benefits under ERISA § 502(a)(3) to recover what they do not have standing to recover under ERISA § 502(a)(1)(B)); Wilkins v. Baptist Healthcare Sys., Inc., 150 F.3d 609 (6th Cir. 1998) (holding that plan participant whose claim for disability benefits had been denied could not recover under ERISA § 502(a)(3) for breach of fiduciary duty; to hold otherwise would permit plan participant to characterize denial of benefits as breach of fiduciary claim).

[198] *See, e.g.*, Graden v. Conexant Systems, Inc., 496 F.3d 291, 301 (3d Cir. 2007), *cert. denied*, 552 U.S. 1243 (2008) (declaring that although former plan participant could demand full payment of benefit under ERISA § 502(a)(1)(B), participant not foreclosed from bringing suit for breach of fiduciary duty under ERISA § 502(a)(2)).

[199] *See, e.g.*, Hill v. Blue Cross and Blue Shield of Michigan, 409 F.3d 710, 718 (6th Cir. 2005) (permitting claim for breach of fiduciary duty under ERISA § 502(a)(3) seeking system-wide injunction against claims processing technique in addition to claim for benefits under ERISA § 502(a)(1)(B)); Gore v. El Paso Energy Corp. Long Term Disability Plan, 477 F.3d 833, 840-41 (holding that claims under both ERISA §§ 502(a)(1)(B) and 502(a)(3) permitted where each claim supported by different injury).

[200] 552 U.S. 248 (2008).

[201] *LaRue*, at 258.

[202] *Id.* at 260.

[4]   Summary of Remedies Under ERISA § 502(a)(1)(B)

ERISA § 502(a)(1)(B)

Authorizes suit seeking provision of benefits promised under terms of plan.

Aetna Health, Inc. v. Davila, 542 U.S. 200, 210 (2014) (dicta)

Authorizes suit seeking reimbursement for expenses paid for benefits promised under terms of plan.

Aetna Health, Inc. v. Davila, 542 U.S. 200, 211 (2014) (dicta)

"Extracontractual" damages, that is, consequential and punitive damages, prohibited.
Massachusetts Mutual Life Ins. Co. v. Russell, 473 U.S. 134, 144 (1985) (dicta)

Terms of plan limited to terms of plan document and do not include terms of summary plan description.

Cigna Corporation v. Amara, 131 S. Ct. 1866, 1877-78 (2011)

Availability of a claim under ERISA § 502(a)(1)(B) may foreclose a claim under ERISA's other remedial provisions.

Varity Corporation v. Howe, 516 U.S. 489 (1996); *LaRue v. DeWolff, Boberg & Associates, Inc.*, 552 U.S. 248, 258-60 (2008) (C.J. Roberts, concurring opinion)

[B] Claims for Breach of Fiduciary Duty Under ERISA § 502(a)(2)

Section 502(a)(2) of ERISA provides that "[a] civil action may be brought . . . by the Secretary [of Labor], or by a participant, beneficiary or fiduciary for appropriate relief under section 409." Section 409, in turn, imposes personality liability on plan fiduciaries for their fiduciary breaches and authorizes four different classes of relief: "(1) reimbursement of losses to plan assets; (2) payment of profits made by the fiduciary's use of plan assets; (3) removal of the breaching fiduciary; and (4) 'other equitable or remedial relief as the court may deem appropriate.' "[203]

The Supreme Court has addressed available remedies under ERISA § 502(a)(2) in two cases: *Massachusetts Mutual Life Insurance Co. v. Russell*,[204] and *LaRue v. DeWolff, Boberg & Associates, Inc.*[205] In *Russell*, the Court held that remedies under ERISA § 502(a)(2) run solely to the plan, and an individual may not recover for individual losses suffered as the result of a fiduciary breach. In *LaRue*, the Court held that even though ERISA § 502(a)(2) does not provide a remedy for individual injuries that are distinct from plan injuries, it does authorize recovery for breaches of fiduciary duty that impact the value of the plan assets in a plan participant's individual account.

[1] *Massachusetts Mutual Life Ins. Co. v. Russell*

In *Massachusetts Mutual Life Insurance Co. v. Russell*,[206] the Court's first ERISA remedy decision, a plan participant brought suit under ERISA §§ 502(a)(2) and 409(a) to recover losses she allegedly incurred as a result of the plan fiduciaries' alleged breach of their fiduciary duties when they interrupted the payment of her disability benefits. The Court rejected the participant's claim and held that § 409(a) only provides relief for harm to a plan, and not to an individual plan participant.[207]

In so holding, the Court first focused on the text of section 409(a). Section 409(a) provides in relevant part:

> Any person who is a fiduciary with respect to a plan who breaches any of the responsibilities, obligations, or duties imposed upon fiduciaries by this title shall be personally liable to make good to such plan any losses to the plan resulting from such breach, and to restore to such plan any profits of such fiduciary which have been made through use of assets of the plan by the fiduciary, and shall be subject to such other equitable or remedial relief as the court may deem appropriate, including removal of such fiduciary.

---

[203] *See* Eric D. Chason, *Redressing All ERISA Fiduciary Breaches under Section 409(a)*, 83 Temple L. Rev. 147, 157 (2010).

[204] 473 U.S. 134 (1985).

[205] 552 U.S. 248 (2008).

[206] 473 U.S. 134 (1985).

[207] *Id.* at 144. The Court left open the question whether a plan participant could rely on ERISA § 502(a)(3) under such circumstances. *Id.* at 139 n.5.

Although the clause upon which the plaintiff relied for relief simply subjects a fiduciary "to such other equitable or remedial relief as the court may deem appropriate" and does not expressly limit relief to plans, the Court found that the entire section read as whole emphasized the relationship between the fiduciary and the plan as an entity.

The Court declared that focusing solely on the clause at issue, that is, "to such other equitable or remedial relief as the court may deem appropriate," would render "superfluous" the preceding clauses that provide relief only to the plan, and would slight the language after the phrase "such other equitable or remedial relief."[208] In essence, the Court focused on the language as bolded below:

> Any person who is a fiduciary with respect to a plan who breaches any of the responsibilities, obligations, or duties imposed upon fiduciaries by this title shall be personally liable [1] to make good **to such plan** any losses to the plan resulting from such breach, and [2] to restore **to such plan** any profits of such fiduciary which have been made through use of assets of the plan by the fiduciary, and [3] shall be subject to such other equitable or remedial relief as the court may deem appropriate, **including removal of such fiduciary**.

According to the Court, "[a] fair contextual reading of the statute makes it abundantly clear that its draftsmen were primarily concerned with the possible misuse of plan assets, and with remedies that would protect the entire plan, rather than with the rights of an individual beneficiary."[209]

The Court then turned to the statutory obligations imposed on fiduciaries. The Court recognized that plan administrators have fiduciary obligations to serve the interests of plan participants and beneficiaries and provide them with benefits authorized by the plan. Nevertheless, the Court found that their principal fiduciary duties "relate to the proper management, administration, and investment of fund assets, the maintenance of proper records, the disclosure of specified information, and the avoidance of conflicts of interest."[210] Finally, the Court looked at ERISA's claims provision, ERISA § 503, and found that it simply provides plan participants with procedural rights. The Court concluded that "the entire text of § 409 persuades us that Congress did not intend that section to authorize any relief except for the plan itself."[211]

The Court rejected the plaintiff's claim that a private cause of action should be implied under *Cort v. Ash*.[212] Under *Cort v. Ash*,[213] four factors are relevant in determining whether a private right of action should be implied in a statute that

---

[208] 473 U.S. at 142.

[209] *Id.* For an argument that the Court erred in its interpretation of the text of ERISA § 409(a), see Chason, 83 TEMPLE L. REV., at 180–82 (arguing that Court applied wrong canon of construction in construing text of ERISA § 409(a)).

[210] 473 U.S. at 142–43.

[211] *Id.* at 144.

[212] *Id.* at 145–48.

[213] Cort v. Ash, 422 U.S. 66 (1975).

does not expressly provide for a remedy: (1) is the plaintiff a member of the class for whose benefit the statute was enacted; (2) is there any indication of legislative intent to create or deny a remedy; (3) is implying a remedy consistent with the underlying purposes of the legislative scheme; and (4) is the cause of action one which is traditionally relegated to state law.[214]

The Court recognized that two of the four *Cort* factors supported plaintiff's claim that a cause of action should be implied in favor of the plaintiff: (1) plaintiff was a member of the class for whose benefit ERISA was enacted, and (2) there was no state law impediment to implying a remedy in light of ERISA's preemption of state law.[215] Nevertheless, the Court found that the other two factors, legislative intent and consistency with the legislative scheme, counseled against implying a private cause of action.[216] The Court declared that 502(a)'s "six carefully integrated civil enforcement provisions . . . provide strong evidence that Congress did *not* intend to authorize other remedies that it simply forgot to incorporate expressly."[217] The Court declined to imply a private cause of action because it was "reluctant to tamper with an enforcement scheme crafted with such evident care as the one in ERISA."[218]

The Court's opinion in *Russell* has been harshly criticized.[219] For example, Professor John Langbein has argued that the Court's assertion in *Russell* that ERISA was meant to protect employee benefit plans, not plan participants, is "transparently wrong."[220]

Following *Russell*, it was often thought that fiduciaries would not be held liable for breaches of fiduciary duty causing harm to participants' individual accounts because such breaches would not harm the plan as a whole.[221] The Supreme Court reached a different result in *LaRue v. DeWolf Boberg & Associates, Inc.*

---

[214] 473 U.S. at 145 n.13.

[215] *Id.* at 145.

[216] *Id.* at 145.

[217] *Id.* at 146.

[218] *Id.* at 147.

[219] *See e.g.*, Chason, 83 TEMPLE L. REV., at 160 (criticizing *Russell* on a number of grounds).

[220] Langbein, *What ERISA Means by "Equitable,"* 103 COLUM. L. REV., at 1341. In support of this contention, he notes that ERISA's fiduciary standards begin with the overarching principle that fiduciaries are to discharge their duties "solely in the interest of the participants and beneficiaries," ERISA § 404(a), and ERISA's remedial provisions authorize plan participants to bring suit to recover benefits due under the terms of the plan and to sue for injunctive or other equitable relief, ERISA §§ 502(a)(1)(B) & 502(a)(3).

[221] *See, e.g.*, Coan v. Kaufman, 457 F.3d 250, 259–62 (2d Cir. 2006); Magin v. Monsanto Co., 420 F.3d 679, 687 (7th Cir. 2005); In re Schering-Plough Corp. ERISA Litigation, 420 F.3d 231, 240 (3d Cir. 2005); McDonald v. Provident Indem. Life Ins. Co., 60 F.3d 234, 237 (5th Cir. 1995), *cert. denied*, 516 U.S. 1174 (1996); Izzarelli v. Rexene Prods. Co., 24 F.3d 1506, 1523 (5th Cir. 1994). See Dana M. Muir, *ERISA Remedies in the Roberts Court: Consensus through Contextualization* (manuscript on file with author); Chason, 83 TEMPLE L. REV., at 160; Medill, *"Equitable" Relief Under ERISA Section 502(a)(3),* 39 J. Marshall L. Rev., at 834–44 (noting split in authority on issue and citing cases); Colleen E. Medill, *Stock Market Volatility and 401(k) Plans,* 34 Mich. J. L. Reform 469, 538 (2001).

[2] *LaRue v. DeWolff Boberg & Associates, Inc.*

In *LaRue v. DeWolff, Boberg & Associates, Inc*,[222] the Court returned to the question of remedies under ERISA § 502(a)(2). In that case, a 401(k) plan participant filed suit claiming that the plan administrator breached its fiduciary duty by failing to follow his investment directions, and that that breach caused a $150,000 loss in the value of his individual account.[223] Relying on *Russell*, the Fourth Circuit held that ERISA § 502(a)(2) only provides remedies for plans as a whole, and thus does not provide a remedy for an individual plan participant for losses to the participant's individual account.[224] The Supreme Court reversed and held that a participant in a defined contribution plan could assert a claim under ERISA § 502(a)(2) even though the alleged fiduciary breach only affected the value of his individual account.

The Court recognized that the language of its *Russell* opinion was consistent with the Fourth Circuit's position that an individual plan participant cannot recover under ERISA § 502(a)(2) for a breach of fiduciary causing harm to the participant's individual account.[225] Nevertheless, the Court declared that its rationale in *Russell* supported permitting a plan participant in a defined contribution plan to recover for losses in his individual account due to a fiduciary breach.[226]

The Court first distinguished the misconduct in *LaRue* from the misconduct in *Russell*. It described the misconduct in *LaRue* as falling squarely within the category of harm the fiduciary rules were meant to protect: " 'the proper management, administration, and investment of fund assets' with an eye toward ensuring that 'the benefits authorized by the plan' are ultimately paid to participants and beneficiaries."[227] The Court asserted that the misconduct in *Russell* fell outside this category because the plan participant was paid the benefits under the terms of the plan and sought consequential damages arising from the delay in the processing of her claim.[228]

The Court explained that the Court's focus on protecting the "entire plan" from fiduciary misconduct in *Russell* reflected "the landscape of employee benefit plans" at the time *Russell* was decided, and that that landscape has changed.[229] Specifically, the landscape has shifted from one dominated by traditional defined benefit plans to one dominated by defined contribution plans.[230]

In a world of defined benefit plans, fiduciary misconduct will not affect an individual's entitlement to a benefit unless it creates or enhances the risk that the

---

[222] 552 U.S. 248 (2008).

[223] *Id.* at 250–51.

[224] *Id.* at 250.

[225] *Id.* at 250.

[226] *Id.* at 250.

[227] *LaRue*, at 253, *quoting, Russell*, at 142.

[228] *Id.* at 254.

[229] *Id.* at 255.

[230] *Id.* at 255.

entire plan will default.[231] In a defined contribution plan, in contrast, fiduciary misconduct may reduce an individual participant's benefit without threatening the solvency of the entire plan.[232] According to the Court, "[w]hether a fiduciary breach diminishes plan assets payable to all participants and beneficiaries, or only persons tied to particular individual accounts, it creates the kind of harms that concerned the draftsmen of § 409."[233]

The Court held that although ERISA § 502(a)(2) does not provide a remedy for individual injuries that are distinct from plan injuries, it does authorize recovery for breaches of fiduciary duty that impact the value of the plan assets in a plan participant's individual account.[234] If ERISA § 502(a)(2) did not provide such a remedy, fiduciaries would never have any liability for losses in individual accounts.[235]

[3]   Summary of Remedies Under ERISA § 502(a)(2)

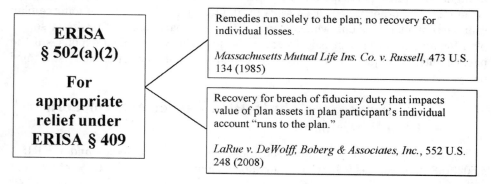

ERISA § 502(a)(2)

For appropriate relief under ERISA § 409

Remedies run solely to the plan; no recovery for individual losses.

Massachusetts Mutual Life Ins. Co. v. Russell, 473 U.S. 134 (1985)

Recovery for breach of fiduciary duty that impacts value of plan assets in plan participant's individual account "runs to the plan."

LaRue v. DeWolff, Boberg & Associates, Inc., 552 U.S. 248 (2008)

[C]   Claims Under the ERISA § 502(a)(3) "Safety Net"

Section 502(a)(3) of ERISA authorizes a plan participant, beneficiary, or fiduciary to bring suit "(A) to enjoin any act or practice which violates any provision of this subtitle or the terms of the plan, or (B) to obtain other appropriate equitable relief (i) to redress such violations or (ii) to enforce any provision of this

---

[231] If a fiduciary breach causes a plan to become underfunded and terminate, the PBGC guarantees plan participants' benefits, but the guarantee does not extend to all promised benefits. *See* Chapter 11 § 11.03[E]. Thus, a defined benefit plan participant may not receive all promised benefits if a fiduciary breach causes the plan to terminate in an underfunded status. *See, e.g.*, Mertens v. Hewitt Associates, 508 U.S. 248 (1993) (involving suit filed by participants of terminated underfunded plan whose PBGC guaranteed benefits were generally substantially lower than fully vested benefits promised under terms of plan).

[232] 552 U.S. at 255–56.

[233] *Id.* at 256.

[234] *Id.* at 256.

[235] For a suggestion that *LaRue* inappropriately expands remedies for plan participants, see Thomas P. Gies & Jane R. Foster, *Leaving Well Enough Alone: Reflections on the Current State of ERISA Remedial Law*, 26 HOFSTRA LAB. & EMP. L.J. 449, 470–71 (2009).

subtitle, or the terms of the plan."[236]

On its face, section 502(a)(3) appears to be a flexible mechanism pursuant to which courts may remedy problems concerning employee benefit plans.[237] Indeed, the Supreme Court has described section 502(a)(3) as a "catchall provision" or "safety net, offering appropriate equitable relief for injuries caused by violations that § 502 does not elsewhere adequately remedy."[238]

The Supreme Court, however, has not interpreted section 502(a)(3) to provide limitless flexibility to remedy problems arising from employee benefit plans. Instead, the Court has honed in on the term "equitable" and found the term to limit the breadth of equitable remedies, at least under certain circumstances.

The Supreme Court has addressed the meaning of "appropriate equitable relief" for purposes of ERISA § 502(a)(3) in six different cases. Three of the cases were brought by plan participants (or former participants) to challenge ERISA violations. The other three cases were brought by plan fiduciaries to enforce plan reimbursement provisions which required the plan participants to reimburse the plan for amounts the plan paid to cover the participants' medical expenses if the participants subsequently recovered on a claim in a liability action against a third party.

[1] Challenges Brought by Plan Participants (or Former Plan Participants)

The Supreme Court has addressed the availability of remedies under ERISA § 502(a)(3) in three cases in which a plan participant or former participant brought suit seeking a remedy for a violation of ERISA: *Mertens v. Hewitt Associates*,[239] *Varity Corporation v. Howe*,[240] and *CIGNA Corporation v. Amara*.[241] In *Mertens*, the Court held that "equitable" relief for purposes of ERISA § 502(a)(3) is limited to "those categories of relief that were *typically* available in equity (such as injunction, mandamus, and restitution, but not compensatory damages)."[242] In *Varity*, the Court held that "appropriate" equitable relief for purposes ERISA § 502(a)(3) encompasses individual equitable relief for a breach of fiduciary duty. Finally, in *Amara*, the Court announced in *dicta* that "equitable" relief for purposes of ERISA § 502(a)(3) in a suit brought by a beneficiary against a plan fiduciary about the terms of a plan includes reformation, estoppel, and surcharge, remedies that were available to courts of equity in breach of trust cases and thus were traditionally considered equitable remedies.

---

[236] For a discussion of the universe of claims that may be brought under ERISA 502(a)(3), see Medill, *"Equitable" Relief Under ERISA Section 502(a)(3)*, 39 J. Marshall L. Rev., at 889–917.

[237] *See id.* at 834.

[238] Varity Corp. v. Howe, 516 U.S. 489, 512 (1996).

[239] 508 U.S. 248 (1993).

[240] 516 U.S. 489 (1996)

[241] 131 S. Ct. 1866 (2011).

[242] 508 U.S. at 257.

[a] *Mertens v. Hewitt Associates*

The Supreme Court first addressed the availability of remedies under ERISA § 502(a)(3) in *Mertens v. Hewitt Associates*.[243] In that case, an underfunded defined benefit pension plan was terminated. As a result, the plan participants did not receive all of the benefits they had been promised under the terms of the plan but instead were limited to the benefits guaranteed by the Pension Benefit Guaranty Corporation.[244] A group of individuals who had been covered by the plan brought suit against the plan's actuary claiming that it was liable for their loss.[245] The Supreme Court granted *certiorari* to answer the question "whether ERISA authorizes suits for money damages against nonfiduciaries who knowingly participate in a fiduciary's breach of fiduciary duty."[246]

The Court suggested in *dicta* that the plan's actuary, as a non-fiduciary, could not be held liable for knowingly participating in a breach of fiduciary duty.[247] The Court did not, however, decide that issue. Instead, it focused on the meaning of the term "equitable relief" for purposes of ERISA § 502(a)(3) and held that that term did not encompass the remedy the former plan participants sought in the case.

The Court described the remedy the plan participants sought as "nothing other than compensatory *damages* — monetary relief for all loses their plan sustained as a result of the alleged breach of fiduciary duties."[248] The Court held that money damages, "the classic form of *legal* relief" are not "equitable" relief under ERISA § 502(a)(3).[249] Instead, the Court held that "equitable" relief for purposes of ERISA § 502(a)(3) is limited to "those categories of relief that were *typically* available in equity (such as injunction, mandamus, and restitution, but not compensatory damages)."[250]

Pointing to ERISA's roots in the common law of trusts, the Solicitor General asserted that the term equitable relief should encompass the type of relief the former plan participants sought because such relief traditionally could be obtained in a court of equity.[251] The Court acknowledged that courts of equity had virtually exclusive jurisdiction over trust claims and money damages were available against

---

[243] 508 U.S. 248 (1993).

[244] Many of the participants had elected to take early retirement, and their enhanced early benefit exceeded the PBGC guarantee. For example, the PBGC only guaranteed William Mertens a monthly benefit of $521 compared to an enhanced early retirement benefit of $2,016 under the plan. *See* Dana M. Muir, *ERISA Remedies: Chimera or Congressional Compromise?*, 81 Iowa L. Rev. 1, 27 (1995). For a more detailed discussion of benefits guaranteed by the PBGC, see Chapter 11 § 11.03[E].

[245] In the complaint, the former plan participants alleged that the actuary caused their loss by allowing their former employer to select the plan's actuarial assumptions, by failing to disclose that their former employer was one of its clients, and by failing to disclose the plan's funding shortfall. 508 U.S. at 250.

[246] *Id.* at 251.

[247] *Id.* at 253–55. This aspect of the Court's decision is discussed in Chapter 6 § 6.07[C][1].

[248] 508 U.S. at 255.

[249] *Id.* at 255.

[250] *Id.* at 257.

[251] *Id.* at 255–56.

trustees in these courts.[252] Nevertheless, the Court rejected the characterization of the term "equitable" as whatever relief a court of equity could provide in a breach of trust case because it would render the modifier "equitable" superfluous.[253] Courts of equity had the power to grant *all* forms of relief for breach of trust.[254]

The plan participants contended that the Court's narrow interpretation of the term "equitable" left them in a worse position than if ERISA had never been enacted because under state law the actuary would have been liable for knowing participation in a trustee's breach of fiduciary duty, and ERISA preempts such a state law claim.[255] Assuming, without deciding, that ERISA would preempt such a state law claim, the Court rejected the participants' claim that the term "equitable" relief should be interpreted more broadly in order to achieve ERISA's purpose of protecting plan participants and beneficiaries.[256] The Court stated that "vague notions" of the statute's "basic purpose" could not overcome the words of the text regarding the specific issue under consideration, especially in light of the fact that ERISA is "an enormously complex and detailed statute that resolved innumerable disputes between powerful competing interests — not all in favor of potential plaintiffs."[257]

Justice White filed a dissenting opinion in which three Justices concurred.[258] The dissenting Justices believed that in light of ERISA's fiduciary provisions' roots in the law of equity, it would be entirely reasonable to construe "equitable relief" for purposes of ERISA § 502(a)(3) as encompassing those remedies that were typically available in a court of equity for breach of trust, including a compensatory monetary award to make the plaintiff whole.[259] The dissenting opinion contended that this construction[260] of the term would not render the modifier "equitable" superfluous because it would not include all forms of relief; specifically, it would exclude punitive damages.[261] Moreover, it would be consistent with Congress' primary goal in enacting ERISA: protecting "beneficiaries' financial security against corrupt or inept plan mismanagement" and "avoid the perverse, and in this case entirely needless result of construing ERSIA so as to *deprive* beneficiaries of remedies they enjoyed prior to the statute's enactment."[262]

---

[252] *Id.* at 256.

[253] *Id,* at 257–58.

[254] *Id.* at 257.

[255] *Id.* at 261.

[256] *Id.* at 261.

[257] *Id.* at 261–62.

[258] *Id.* at 263. Chief Justice Rehnquist, Justice Stevens, and Justice O'Connor concurred in Justice White's dissenting opinion.

[259] *Id.* at 266.

[260] For a discussion of canons of statutory construction, Karl Llewellyn, *Remarks on the Theory of Appellate Decision and the Rules or Canons About How Statutes are to be Construed*, 3 VAND. L. REV. 395, 401–06 (1950).

[261] 508 U.S. at 270.

[262] *Id.* at 274.

The Supreme Court's opinion in *Mertens* has been harshly criticized,[263] and subsequent dicta in *Amara* has cut back on the breadth of its reach.

[b]   *Varity Corporation v. Howe*

Three years after deciding *Mertens*, the Court returned to the scope of "appropriate equitable relief" under section 502(a)(3) in *Varity Corporation v. Howe*.[264] In that case, former plan participants brought suit claiming that the plan administrator, who was also their former employer, breached its fiduciary duty when it made misrepresentations that caused them to voluntarily transfer to a new subsidiary that subsequently went bankrupt and resulted in the loss of their welfare benefits.[265] There was no question that the relief they sought, in essence reinstatement in their former employer's plan,[266] was "equitable." Instead, the question was whether equitable relief for breaches of fiduciary duty under ERISA § 502(a)(3) was "appropriate" or should be limited to relief under ERISA § 502(a)(2).

As discussed above, ERISA § 502(a)(2) authorizes suits for appropriate relief under ERISA § 409(a), which, in turn, imposes personal liability upon breaching fiduciaries for breaches of fiduciary duty. In *Massachusetts Mutual Life Insurance Co. v. Russell*, the Court held that section 409(a) only provides relief for harm to a plan, and not to an individual plan participant. Because the plan participants' request for reinstatement in *Varity* constituted individual relief, rather than relief for harm to the plan, it was not available under ERISA § 409(a) through ERISA § 502(a)(2).

Relying on *Russell*, Varity argued that the very relief excluded under ERISA § 502(a)(2), that is, individual relief, cannot be included as "appropriate" relief under ERISA § 502(a)(3).[267] The Court rejected Varity's argument and held that "appropriate" equitable relief under ERISA § 502(a)(3) includes individual

---

[263] *See, e.g.* Chason, 83 TEMPLE L. REV., at 162 (contending first that "Justice Scalia's enumeration of historical equitable relief (i.e., "injunction, mandamus, and restitution") is both unhelpful and wrong": injunction is plainly equitable but authorized by ERISA, mandamus was an extraordinary legal remedy, and "restitution is a modern invention, fusing legal and equitable remedies," and then asserting that Justice Scalia's real "bungle" in Mertens was his claim that "courts in equity granted legal relief in trust matters": trust law belonged to the exclusive jurisdiction of courts of equity and there were no legal remedies for breach of trust law); Langbein, *What ERISA Means by "Equitable*," 103 COLUM. L. REV., at 1351–55 (contending that Court erred (1) in its premise that pre-fusion equity courts did not award money damages to remedy equitable causes of action; (2) inventing the novel and unworkable category of "typically" equitable remedies; and (3) inferring that Congress intended to exclude money damages for consequential injury); Richard Rouco, *Available Remedies Under ERISA Section 502(a)*, 45 ALA. L. REV. 631, 660 (1994) (pointing to two flaws in *Mertens* decision: (1) assumption that courts of equity could award all forms of legal relief and (2) begs question as to whether equitable relief should be interpreted in context of trust common law).

[264] 516 U.S. 489 (1996).

[265] *Id.* at 492–95. The facts of *Varity* and the breach of fiduciary claim are discussed in Chapter 6 § 6.03[D][1][c].

[266] 516 U.S. at 492.

[267] *Id.* at 508–509.

equitable relief for breaches of fiduciary duty that is foreclosed under ERISA § 502(a)(2).

In rejecting Varity's argument, the Court began by noting that *Russell* addresses ERISA § 502(a)(2), not ERISA § 502(a)(3), and the language limiting relief to the plan is contained in ERISA § 409(a), which ERISA § 502(a)(2), but not ERISA § 502(a)(3), cross-references. The Court pointed out that the plaintiff expressly disavowed reliance on ERISA § 502(a)(3), and *Russell* involved a complicating factor not present in *Varity*. Specifically, ERISA § 502(a)(1)(B) offered specific relief for the sort of injury (wrongful denial of benefits) that the plaintiff in *Russell* had suffered but said nothing about the type of relief the plaintiff sought. The Court found those distinctions between *Russell* and *Varity* sufficient to conclude that *Russell* was not controlling.[268]

The Court then found ERISA § 502(a)(3)'s language broad enough to encompass individual relief for breaches of fiduciary duty.[269] The Court rejected Varity's claim that the canon of statutory construction, that the specific governs the general, means that the more specific, ERISA § 502(a)(2) fiduciary breach provision makes the third more general catchall provision, ERISA § 502(a)(3), inapplicable. The Court found no reason to believe that Congress intended the specific remedies in ERISA § 409 as a limitation on remedies available for breaches of fiduciary duty. Finally, the Court found that interpreting ERISA § 502(a)(3) to encompass individual relief for breaches of fiduciary duty was consistent with ERISA's basic purpose of protecting plan participants by providing for appropriate remedies.[270]

[c] *CIGNA Corporation v. Amara*

In *CIGNA Corporation v. Amara*,[271] plan participants filed suit challenging their employer's conversion of its traditional defined benefit plan to a cash balance plan. The plan participants claimed that their employer violated its disclosure obligations under ERISA because it failed to give them proper notice of the changes to their benefits. Relying on ERISA § 502(a)(1)(B), the district court reformed the plan and ordered the plan administrator (who was their employer) to pay them benefits that were consistent with the terms of the summary plan description provided to the plan participants rather than the lower benefits promised under the terms of the plan.

The Supreme Court held that the district court did not have authority under ERISA § 502(a)(1)(B) to order this relief.[272] The Court, however, did not end its opinion with that holding. Instead, it found that ERISA § 502(a)(3) authorized forms of relief that are similar to those entered by the district court. The Court pointed out that *Amara* concerned "a suit by a beneficiary against a plan fiduciary

---

[268] *Id.* at 509–10.

[269] *Id.* at 510. For an argument that remedies under ERISA § 409(a) should be interpreted more broadly, and all fiduciary breaches should be redressed under § 409(a), see Chason, 83 TEMPLE L. REV. 147.

[270] 516 U.S. at 513, *quoting,* ERISA § 2(b).

[271] 131 S. Ct. 1866 (2011).

[272] *Id.* at 1878.

(whom ERISA typically treats as a trustee) about the terms of a plan (which ERISA typically treats as a trust)."[273] The Court noted that historically such suits could only be brought in a court of equity and the remedies available to those courts of equity were traditionally viewed as equitable remedies.

The Court found that the relief provided by the district court resembled three traditional equitable remedies: reformation, estoppel, and surcharge. With respect to reformation, the Court noted that courts of equity have traditionally used their power to reform contracts to prevent fraud. The Court then described estoppel as "a traditional equitable remedy" which "operates to place the person entitled to its benefits in the same position he would have been in had the representation been true."[274] Finally, the Court found that the fact that the relief with respect to currently retired beneficiaries took the form of a money payment did not prevent it from being characterized as equitable. The Court explained that courts of equity had the power to provide monetary compensation for losses resulting from a trustee's breach of its duties or to prevent unjust enrichment to the trustee, and this type of relief, which was sometimes referred to as "surcharge,"[275] was an "exclusively equitable" remedy.[276]

The Supreme Court's discussion of remedies under ERISA § 502(a)(3) was *dicta*[277] and two Justices, Justice Scalia and Justice Thomas, did not join in the *dicta*.[278] Nevertheless, most lower courts have followed the Supreme Court's *dicta* so as to provide a remedy where a wrong has clearly occurred.[279] For example, the Fourth,[280] Fifth,[281] and Seventh[282] Circuits have all embraced the expanded remedy *dicta* of *Amara*. Lower courts, however, have limited the expansion of

---

[273] *Id.* at 1879.

[274] Estoppel "operates to place the person entitled to its benefit in the same position he would have been in had the representation been true." *Id.* at 1880, *quoting*, J. Eaton, Handbook of Equity Jurisprudence § 62, at 176 (1901).

[275] For a detailed discussion of the meaning of surcharge and the separate remedy of make-whole relief, see Susan Harthill, *A Square Peg in a Round Hole: Whether Traditional Trust Law "Make-Whole" Relief is Available under ERISA Section 502(a)(3)*, 61 Okla. L. Rev. 721, 751–82 (2008).

[276] 131 S. Ct. at 1880.

[277] *But see* Brendan S. Maher, *Thoughts on the Latest Battles over ERISA's Remedies*, 30 Hofstra Labor & Employment L.J. 339, 348–49 (contending that Court's discussion of cognizable remedies under ERISA § 502(a)(3) was not *dicta*).

[278] 131 S. Ct. at 1883.

[279] *See* Amanda N. Eastman, *ERISA Finally Makes Sense by Making Employees Whole: Can Make-Whole Remedies for American Workers Spur Transparency from Employee Benefit Plans?*, 22 Kan. J.L & Pub. Pol'y 412, 419.

[280] McCravy v. Metro. Life Ins. Co., 690 F.3d 176, 181 (4th Cir. 2012) (stating that "the portion of *Amara* in which the Supreme Court addressed Section [502](a)(3) stands for the proposition that remedies traditionally available in courts of equity, expressly including estoppel and surcharge, are indeed available to plaintiffs suing fiduciaries under Section [502](a)(3)").

[281] *See* Gearlds v. Entergy Servs., Inc., 709 F.3d 448 (5th Cir. 2013) (declaring that "based on the depth of the Court's treatment of the issue, we are persuaded to join the Fourth Circuit in concluding that *Amara's* pronouncements about surcharge as a potential remedy under § 502(a)(3) should be followed").

[282] *See* Kenseth v. Dean Health Plan, Inc., 722 F.3d 869 (7th Cir. 2013) (stating that following *Amara* "relief available for a breach of fiduciary duty under section [502](a)(3) is broader than we have

available remedies to situations expressly analogous to *Amara* where a plan participant is suing a plan fiduciary to recover due to a breach of a fiduciary duty.[283]

[2]   Claims Seeking Enforcement of Plan Reimbursement Provisions

The Supreme Court has considered the scope of relief available under ERISA § 502(a)(3) in three cases filed to enforce plan reimbursement provisions:[284] *Great West v. Knudson*,[285] *Sereboff v. Mid-Atlantic Medical Services, Inc.*,[286] and *U.S. Airways Inc. v. McCutchen*.[287] In *Great West*, the Court distinguished between equitable and legal restitution. The Court held that a plan could not sue a participant under ERISA § 502(a)(3) to enforce a plan's reimbursement provision when the settlement proceeds were held by a special needs trust rather than the plan participant because such a claim was a legal contractual claim rather than equitable in nature. In *Sereboff*, the Court held that a plan could enforce the provision as "an equitable lien by agreement" when the proceeds were distributed to the plan participant, and the Court further held that strict tracing rules do not apply to equitable liens by agreement. Finally, in *McCutchen*, the Court held the equitable doctrines of double recovery and common fund cannot override the express terms of a plan in a suit to enforce a reimbursement provision/equitable lien by agreement, but those equitable doctrines may serve as the appropriate default rule when the terms of a plan are silent, such as regarding the allocation of attorney's fees.

[a]   *Great West v. Knudson*

In *Great West v. Knudson*,[288] Great West, a self-funded health insurance plan's stop loss insurance provider, filed suit under ERISA § 502(a)(3) seeking to enforce the plan's reimbursement provision. The reimbursement provision provided the plan with "the right to recover from the [beneficiary] any payment for benefits" the plan paid that the beneficiary was entitled to recover from a third party.[289] The plan beneficiary, Knudson, rendered a quadriplegic by a car accident, filed a tort

---

previously held, and broader than the district court could have anticipated before the Supreme Court's decision in [*Amara*]").

[283] *Gearlds*, 709 F.3d at 452; Moon v. BWX Technologies, Inc., 956 F. Supp. 2d 711, 717 (W.D. Va., 2013) (holding that the plaintiff could not recover a surcharge because none of the defendants were actually fiduciaries).

[284] Such clauses are typically referred to as subrogation clauses. For a discussion of the history and prevalence of such clauses and an argument that the courts should develop federal common law prohibiting such clauses under ERISA, see Roger M. Baron & Anthony P. Lamb, *The Revictimization of Personal Injury Victims by ERISA Subrogation Claims*, 45 CREIGHTON L. REV. 325 (2012). *See also* Brendan S. Maher & Radha A. Pathak, *Understanding and Problematizing Contractual Tort Subrogation*, 40 LOY. UNIV. CHI. L.J. 49 (2008).

[285] 534 U.S. 204 (2002).

[286] 547 U.S. 356 (2006).

[287] 133 S. Ct. 1537 (2013).

[288] 534 U.S. 204 (2002).

[289] *Id.* at 207.

action seeking to recover for her losses due to the car accident. The parties to the tort action negotiated a $650,000 settlement which allocated $256,745.30 to a special needs trust to provide for Knudson's medical care, $373,426 to attorney's fees and costs, $5,000 to reimburse the California Medicaid program, and $13,828.70 to satisfy Great West's claim under the reimbursement provision of the plan. Great West, dissatisfied with the $14,000 or so allocated to it, filed suit seeking reimbursement of the $411,157.11 the plan had paid to cover the beneficiary's medical expenses. Great West claimed that it was entitled to relief under ERISA § 502(a)(3) because it sought restitution.[290]

Although the Supreme Court in *Mertens* suggested that restitution[291] is a form of equitable relief when it stated that "equitable" relief for purposes of ERISA § 502(a)(3) is limited to "those categories of relief that were *typically* available in equity (such as injunction, mandamus, and restitution, but not compensatory damages),"[292] restitution in fact is not a remedy known to historical courts of equity.[293] Rather, restitution is a modern invention, which fuses legal and equitable remedies.[294] It was largely created in 1937 when the Restatement of Restitution[295] was published, and brings together several equitable and legal doctrines.[296] Specifically, restitution encompasses "the legal remedy of quasi-contract[, and] the equitable remedies of constructive trust, equitable lien, accounting for profits, and subrogation."[297]

In *Great West*, the Court distinguished between equitable and legal restitution and held that the type of restitution[298] Great West sought was legal and thus not available under ERISA § 502(a)(3).[299] According to the Court, legal restitution concerns the imposition of personal liability while equitable restitution imposes a constructive trust or equitable lien on particular property.[300] Because the special needs trust, not Knudson, held the settlement proceeds, Great West's claim against Knudson was not that Knudson held "particular funds that, in good conscience" belonged to Great West, but that Great West was contractually entitled to some

---

[290] *Id.* at 212.

[291] Restitution is intended to "prevent unjust enrichment of the defendant by making him give up what he wrongfully obtained from the plaintiff." Chason, 83 TEMPLE L. REV., at 164, *quoting*, Dan B. Dobb, Law of Remedies: Damages — Equity — Restitution § 1.1, at 4 (2d ed. 1993).

[292] 508 U.S. at 257 (emphasis added).

[293] Chason, 83 TEMPLE L. REV., at 162.

[294] *Id.*

[295] RESTATEMENT (FIRST) OF RESTITUTION (1937).

[296] Chason, 83 TEMPLE L. REV., at 164.

[297] *Id.*

[298] *Cf.* Colleen P. Murphy, *Misclassifying Monetary Restitution*, 55 SMU L. REV. 1577, 1619 (2002) (noting that the Court assumed that Great West sought restitution but contending that it is arguable whether the remedy should have been characterized as restitution).

[299] 534 U.S. at 212–18. Before reaching the issue of restitution, the Court held that Great West could not seek an injunction or specific performance to "enforce a contractual obligation to pay money past due" because that type of relief was not typically available in equity. *Id.* at 210–211.

[300] *Id.* at 213.

funds.[301] The Court held that such a claim was legal rather than equitable in nature and thus not available under ERISA § 502(a)(3).

The Court in *Great West* recognized that its distinctions between equitable and legal remedies created challenges. Yet, it explained:

> It is easy to disparage the law-equity dichotomy as "an ancient classification," and an "obsolete distinctio[n]." Like it or not, however, that classification and distinction has been specified by the statute; and there is no way to give the specification meaning — indeed there is no way to render the unmistakable limitation of the statute a limitation at all — except by adverting to the differences between law and equity to which the statute refers.[302]

In dissent, Justice Ginsburg offered an alternative approach to interpreting the term equitable. According to Justice Ginsburg, courts should "look to the substance of the relief requested" and construe the term "equity" flexibly by taking into account the context and circumstances of the case.[303] The Court rejected Justice Ginsburg's alternative because its "rolling revision of the term" equity would "introduce a high degree of confusion into congressional use (and lawyers' understanding)" of the term.[304]

Like most of the Supreme Court's remedy decisions, the Court's decision in *Great West* has been subject to criticism.[305] For example, Professor Eric Chason has argued that by limiting restitution under ERISA § 502(a)(3) to equitable restitution, the Court "resurrected dead law and fissioned restitution, even though the field was the result of a deliberate fusion of law and equity that had occurred decades before ERISA was passed."[306]

---

[301] *Id.* at 214.

[302] *Id.* at 216–17.

[303] *Id.* at 233.

[304] *Id.* at 217.

[305] *See, e.g.,* Medill, *"Equitable" Relief Under ERISA Section 502(a)(3),* 39 J. MARSHALL L. REV., at 84–47 (describing *Great West* as paradoxal on several levels: (1) it creates daunting procedural and substantive barriers to reimbursement claims; and (2) while purporting to reaffirm *Mertens* it contradicts *Mertens* policy rationale of avoiding increased costs to plans); David L. Shapiro, *Justice Ginsburg's First Decade: Some Thoughts About Her Contributions in the Fields of Procedure and Jurisprudence,* 104 COLUM. L. REV. 21, 23 (2004) (expressing hope that Justice Ginsburg's view "— which emphasizes a sophisticated understanding of legislative purpose and the proper role of the Court in promoting that purpose — will ultimately prevail over the cramped, static and excessively literal approach of the majority"); Langbein, *What ERISA Means by "Equitable,"* 103 COLUM. L. REV., at 1351–55 (stating that Scalia's category of "typically equitable . . . was premised on two mistaken notions: (1) that when Congress enacted ERISA remedy law in 1974, it meant to revive the law/equity division that had caused such complexity before the Federal Rules fused the two systems in the 1930s; and (2) that in pre-fusion times there was a determinate category of remedies 'that were typically available in equity (such as injunction, mandamus, and restitution, but not compensatory damages)").

[306] Chason, 83 TEMPLE L. REV. 147, at 166.

[b]   *Sereboff v. Mid Atlantic Medical Services, Inc.*

In *Sereboff v. Mid Atlantic Medical Services, Inc.,*[307] a plan fiduciary again sought to enforce a plan's reimbursement provision. As in *Great West*, the plan beneficiaries were involved in a car accident and brought a tort action to recover for their losses. In addition, as in *Great West*, the plan in *Sereboff* covered the beneficiaries' medical expenses and contained a reimbursement provision. Unlike *Great West*, the proceeds from the tort settlement in *Sereboff* were distributed to the beneficiaries rather than held by a special needs trust, and the plan fiduciary sought a temporary restraining order and preliminary injunction requiring the beneficiaries to retain and set aside at least $74,869.37 of their settlement proceeds to cover the amount the plan had paid for the beneficiaries' medical expenses.

The Court in *Sereboff* held that the plan fiduciary had satisfied the requirement that recovery be sought from a particular fund. The Court then turned to the question whether the basis for Mid Atlantic's claim was equitable and found that it was equitable, specifically an equitable lien by agreement. The Court rejected the beneficiaries' argument that Mid Atlantic's claim did not satisfy the strict tracing rules applicable to equitable liens.[308] The Court explained that there are two types of equitable liens, equitable liens as a matter of restitution and equitable liens "by agreement," and the strict tracing rules do not apply to equitable liens by agreement.

In *Sereboff*, the plan fiduciary sought a temporary restraining order and preliminary injunction before the plan participants had an opportunity to spend the settlement funds. Thus, the Supreme Court did not decide what happens if suit is filed after the specific proceeds have been dissipated. The circuit courts are split as to whether a plan fiduciary may enforce a plan reimbursement provision under ERISA § 502(a)(3) if the funds have been dissipated.[309]

[c]   *U.S. Airways, Inc. v. McCutchen*

In *U.S. Airways, Inc. v. McCutchen,*[310] the Court addressed the question whether plan participants may raise certain equitable defenses in suits to enforce plan reimbursement provisions.[311] In that case, a plan participant, who had

---

[307] 547 U.S. 356 (2006).

[308] Under the strict tracing rules, if the defendant has exchanged the specific assets that the plaintiff claims be his, the plaintiff must be able to "trac[e] the asset into its products or substitutes," or "trace his money or property to some particular funds or assets." *Id.* at 364. Thus, in *Sereboff*, if strict tracing rules were to apply, the plan fiduciary would be required to trace or show exactly how the settlement proceeds were spent and could only collect the specific property or assets that were purchased with the settlement proceeds.

[309] *Compare* Thurber v. Aetna Life Ins. Co., 712 F.3d 654 (2d Cir. 2013), *cert. denied*, 134 S. Ct. 2723 (2014) (holding that equitable lien is enforceable under ERISA § 502(a)(3) even if specific funds have been dissipated) *with* Bilyeu v. Morgan Stanley Long Term Disability Plan 683 F.3d 1083 (9th Cir. 2012), *cert. denied*, 133 S. Ct. 1242 (2013) (holding that equitable lien not enforceable under ERISA § 502(a)(3) when specific funds have been dissipated).

[310] 133 S. Ct. 1537 (2013).

[311] For a discussion of the circuit split on this issue before *McCutchen*, see Dana M. Muir, *ERISA Remedies in the Roberts Court: Consensus Through Contextualization* (manuscript on file with author).

suffered serious injuries in a car accident, recovered $110,000 from the driver and the participant's own automobile insurance carrier. The plan administrator filed suit under ERISA § 502(a)(3) against the plan participant to recover the $66,866 the plan had paid to cover medical expenses arising from the accident under the plan's reimbursement provision.[312] The plan participant, who had paid $44,000 to cover attorney's fees and costs and thus only received $66,000 after deducting for the lawyer's fee, raised two equitable defenses against the claim.

The plan participant first raised the equitable doctrine that limits reimbursement to the amount of an insured's "double recovery." The plan participant's accident-related damages were estimated to exceed $1 million, but the plan participant settled for substantially less because the driver responsible for the accident had limited insurance coverage.[313] Under the double recovery doctrine, the plan participant sought to limit the plan's reimbursement to the share of the participant's settlement attributable to medical expenses.[314]

The plan participant's second equitable defense was the common-fund doctrine.[315] Under the common-fund doctrine, "a litigant or a lawyer who recovers a common fund for the benefit of persons other than himself or his client is entitled to a reasonable attorney's fee from the fund as a whole."[316] The plan participant argued that the common-fund doctrine permitted him to pass on a share of the attorney's fees to the plan.[317]

The Court noted that these two equitable defenses are derived from principles of unjust enrichment[318] while the plan administrator sought "to enforce the modern-day equivalent of an 'equitable lien by agreement.' "[319] The Court found that because an equitable lien by agreement arises from and serves to carry out the provisions of a contract, the plan participant could not rely on equitable

---

[312] The summary plan description (SPD) provided:

> If [US Airways] pays benefits for any claim you incur as the result of negligence, willful misconduct, or other actions of a third party, . . . [y]ou will be required to reimburse [US Airways] for amounts paid for claims out of any monies recovered from [the] third party, including, but not limited to, your own insurance company as the result of judgment, settlement, or otherwise.

133 S. Ct.. at 1543 n.1.

Because the parties and lower courts based the decision on the language in the SPD rather than the plan document itself, the Court treated the language as if it came from the plan document rather than the SPD. *Id.* at 1543.

[313] The plan participant settled for $10,000 with the driver and recovered an additional $100,000 from his own automobile insurance policy. *Id.* at 1543.

[314] *Id.* at 1545. Under the double recovery doctrine, the plan participant would be entitled to keep the portion of the settlement attributable to the loss of future earnings and pain and suffering. *Id.*

[315] For a discussion of the common-fund doctrine as applied to employee benefit plans prior to *McCutchen*, see E. Farish Percy, *Applying the Common Fund Doctrine to ERISA-Governed Employee Benefit Plan's Claim for Subrogation or Reimbursement*, 61 FLA. L. REV. 55 (2009).

[316] 133 S. Ct. at 1545, *quoting*, Boeing Co. v. Van Gemert, 444 U.S. 472, 478 (1980).

[317] The plan participant paid a 40% contingency fee and thus sought reduce the plan's reimbursement by 40% to cover the plan's share of the contingency fee. *Id.* at 1543–44.

[318] *Id.* at 1542.

[319] *Id.* at 1546.

principles to override the express terms of the plan. According to the Court, such principles are "beside the point" in a suit to enforce the terms of the agreement.[320] The plan is at the center of ERISA, and precluding equitable defenses from overriding the express terms of the plan helps the plan to remain at the center of ERISA.[321] The Court did not, however, entirely reject the equitable defenses. The Court held that even though the equitable doctrines cannot override the express terms of the plan, they can nevertheless aid in properly construing the plan.[322]

The Court rejected the plan participant's double recovery defense because it was contrary to the express terms of the plan which gave the plan "first claim on the whole third-party recovery."[323] With respect to the participant's common-fund defense, the Court found that because the plan was silent regarding the allocation of attorney's fees, the plan should be read as retaining the common-fund doctrine as the appropriate default rule.[324]

Following *McCutchen*, attorneys have recommended that plans be drafted or amended to expressly address the recovery of attorney's fees under the terms of plan.[325] While employers may wish to draft their plans to limit the plan's share of attorney's fees, employers risk discouraging plan participants from filing suit to recover from third parties if they draft their plans to require plan participants to bear the entire cost of the litigation. Indeed, if the Court had not applied the common fund doctrine in *McCutchen*, the cost of litigation would have exceeded the plan participant's recovery and the plan participant would have been required to "pay for the privilege of serving as [the plan's] collection agent."[326]

---

[320] *Id.*

[321] *Id.* at 1548.

[322] *Id.*

[323] *Id.* at 1545.

[324] *Id.* at 1548. Justice Scalia filed an opinion in which Chief Justice Roberts, Justice Thomas, and Justice Alito joined, dissenting from the Court's holding that the common-fund doctrine should be retained as the default rule. According to the dissent, the Court granted *certiorari* on the presumption that the terms of the plan unambiguously gave the plan "an absolute right to full reimbursement" and thus, the Court should not have considered an argument that was neither preserved nor fairly included within the question presented. *Id.* at 1551.

[325] *See, e.g.* Law 360 *U.S. Airways v. McCutchen Spurs Revision of Plans* (Apr. 16, 2013), *available at* http://www.law360.com/articles/435335/us-airways-v-mccutchen-spurs-revision-of-erisa-plans.

[326] 133 S. Ct. at 1550.

[3]   Summary of Remedies Under ERISA § 502(a)(3)

ERISA § 502(a)(3)

Plan participant seeking remedy

- Equitable relief for purposes of ERISA § 502(a)(3) limited to "those categories of relief that were *typically* available in equity (such as injunction, mandamus, and restitution and not compensatory damages)." *Mertens*, at 257

- Appropriate equitable relief for purposes of ERISA § 502(a)(3) encompasses individual equitable relief for breach of fiduciary duty. *Varity*

- Equitable relief in suit brought by beneficiary against plan fiduciary about terms of plan includes reformation, estoppel, and surcharge, remedies that were available to courts of equity in breach of trust cases. *Amara*

Plan seeking enforcement of reimbursement provision

- There is a distinction between equitable and legal restitution. A plan cannot sue a participant under ERISA § 502(a)(3) to enforce a reimbursement provision when settlement proceeds were not distributed to plan participant. Such a claim is legal, not equitable, restitution. *Great West*

- A plan can enforce reimbursement provision as equitable lien by agreement when settlement proceeds distributed to plan participant. Strict tracing rules do not apply to such liens. *Sereboff*

- Equitable doctrines of double recovery and common fund cannot override express terms of plan in suit to enforce reimbursement provision (that is, equitable lien by agreement). Equitable doctrines may serve as default rule where terms of plan silent on issue. *McCutchen*

[D] Making Sense of the Supreme Court's Remedy Decisions

The Supreme Court's remedy decisions have been frequently and harshly criticized. For example, lower courts[327] and commentators[328] have frequently criticized the Court's pre-*Amara* decisions for their narrow interpretations of ERISA's remedy provisions which leave plan participants in a worse position than if ERISA had never been enacted. Others have criticized the Court for misunderstanding the law. For example, commentators have argued that the Court's decisions reflect a basic misunderstanding of trust law and historical equitable relief.[329]

Without a doubt, the Supreme Courts' remedy decisions can be, at least superficially, difficult to understand and reconcile.[330] For example, in *Mertens*, the Court rejected the Solicitor General's argument that equitable relief should be whatever relief a court of equity could provide in a breach of trust case because a court of equity could provide all relief for a breach of trust claim and interpreting equitable relief as whatever relief a court of equity could order in a breach of trust case would render the modifier "equitable" superfluous.[331] The Court held that equitable relief for purposes of ERISA § 502(a)(3) is limited to "those categories of relief that were *typically* available in equity (such as injunction, mandamus, and restitution, but not compensatory damages)."[332] In *Amara*, in contrast, the Court declared in *dicta* that equitable relief in that case was any type of remedy that a court of equity could order in a breach of trust case "because remedies available to those courts of equity were traditionally considered equitable remedies."[333] Thus, according to the Court in *Amara* equitable relief in that case could encompass reformation, equitable estoppel, and surcharge.[334]

Professor Dana Muir has offered an approach to bring consistency and make sense of the Court's seemingly irreconcilable remedy decisions.[335] Specifically, she

---

[327] *See* Medill, *"Equitable" Relief Under ERISA Section 502(a)(3)*, 39 J. MARSHALL L. REV., at 848–52 (citing and describing cases in which courts have expressed their frustration with Supreme Court's remedy decisions).

[328] *See, e.g.*, Susan Harthill, *A Square Peg in a Round Hole: Whether Traditional Trust Law "Make-Whole" Relief is Available Under ERISA Section 502(a)(3)*, 61 OKLA. L. REV. 721 (2008); Paul Secunda, *Sorry, No Remedy: Intersectionality and the Grand Irony of ERISA*, 26 HOFSTRA LAB. & EMP. L.J. 131, 155–58 (2009); Dana M Muir, *Fiduciary Status as an Employer's Shield: The Perversity of ERISA Fiduciary Law*, 2 U . PA. J. LAB. & EMP. L. 391, 461 (2000). Brendan S. Maher, *The Benefits of Opt-In Federalism*, 52 B .C. L. REV. 1733, 1764–65 (2011).

[329] *See, e.g.*, Dana M. Muir, *ERISA Remedies in the Roberts Court: Consensus Through Contextualization* (manuscript on file with author); Chason, 83 TEMPLE L. REV., at 162; Harthill, 61 OKLA. L. REV., at 751–83; Langbein, *What ERISA Means by "Equitable,"* 103 COLUM. L. REV., at 1351–55.

[330] *Cf.* Chason, 83 TEMPLE L. REV., at 149 (noting that "[t]he Supreme Court has consistently narrowed ERISA remedies, but has used inconsistent methods of statutory interpretation to do so").

[331] 508 U.S. at 257–58.

[332] *Id.* at 257.

[333] 131 S Ct. at 1879.

[334] *Id.* at 1879–80.

[335] Dana M. Muir, *ERISA Remedies in the Roberts Court: Consensus through Contextualization* (manuscript on file with author).

contends that since Chief Justice Roberts joined the Court, the Court has considered the role the parties play in the benefit plan at issue, the nature of the claim, and the type of the benefit plan when rendering its remedy decisions.[336]

Under Professor Muir's approach, *Mertens* and *Amara* can be reconciled by considering the context in which the cases were decided. As the Court in *Amara* pointed out, the defendant in *Mertens* was not a plan fiduciary; rather it was a nonfiduciary actuary that provided services to the plan administrator. Thus, the defendant in *Amara* was not analogous to a trustee. In *Amara*, in contrast, the plan participants filed suit against the plan administrator, a plan fiduciary, who was analogous to a trustee. Thus, in *Amara*, the Court found that in a suit that is analogous to a breach of trust claim, equitable relief under ERISA § 502(a)(3) consists of all types of relief that a court of equity could apply in such a case, including surcharge, a form of monetary relief.

Similarly, *Russell* and *LaRue* may appear superficially inconsistent. In *Russell*, the Court held that an individual may not recover under ERISA § 502(a)(2) because it only permits relief that runs to the "entire plan." Arguably, in the case of a breach of fiduciary duty with respect to an individual account, relief to an individual account does not accrue to the "entire plan" because it benefits an individual plan participant rather than the entire plan. In *LaRue*, however, the Court took context into account to hold that in the case of a defined contribution plan relief to an individual account for a breach of fiduciary duty runs to the plan.

§ 7.09   STATUTE OF LIMITATIONS

ERISA sets forth two explicit statutes of limitations.[337] Specifically, ERISA § 413 sets forth a statute of limitations for breach of fiduciary claims,[338] and ERISA § 4301(f) provides a statute of limitations for disputes under the multiemployer provisions of Title IV of ERISA.[339]

ERISA, however, is silent with respect to the statute of limitations applicable to other claims under ERISA.[340] When is ERISA is silent, courts typically apply the most closely analogous state statute of limitations[341] or limitations period written

---

[336] According to Professor Muir, this nuanced "contextualized approach" is consistent with ERISA's statutory framework and intent. *Id.*

[337] ERISA also contains a few other explicit statutes of limitation. *See* ERISA § 4003(e)(6), ERISA § 4003(f)(5), ERISA § 4068(d)(2), ERISA § 4070(f).

[338] JORDEN, ET AL., HANDBOOK ON ERISA LITIGATION, at § 4.06[A]; George Lee Flint, Jr., *ERISA: Fumbling the Limitations Period*, 84 NEBRASKA L. REV. 313, 318 (2005).

[339] *See* ABA SECTION OF LABOR AND EMPLOYMENT LAW, EMPLOYEE BENEFITS LAW, at 17–83 (noting that ERISA § 4301(f) applies "to all disputes arising under the multiemployer plan provisions of Title IV."). *See also* Bay Area Laundry & Dry Cleaning Pension Trust Fund v. Ferbar Corp., 522 U.S. 192 (1997) (describing types of actions to which ERISA § 4301(f) applies).

[340] *See* Langbein, *What ERISA Means by "Equitable,"* 103 COLUM. L. REV., at 1355 (stating that "ERISA's procedure and remedy sections are riddled with major omissions that the courts have had to fill in, such as whether jury trial pertains, and what statute of limitations to use").

[341] JORDEN, ET AL., HANDBOOK ON ERISA LITIGATION, at § 4.06[A]; Flint, *ERISA: Fumbling the Limitations Period*, 84 NEBRASKA L. REV., at 319.

into the plan, so long as the period is "reasonable."[342]

[A] Statute of Limitations Applicable to Breach of Fiduciary Claims — ERISA § 413

Section 413 of ERISA provides that

No action may be commenced under [ERISA] with respect to a fiduciary's breach of any responsibility, duty, or obligation under [sections 401 through 414 of ERISA], or with respect to a violation of [ERISA §§ 401–414], after the earlier of —

> (1) Six years after
>
> > (A) the date of the last action which constituted a part of the breach or violation, or
> >
> > (B) in the case of an omission, the latest date on which the fiduciary could have cured the breach or violation; or
>
> (2) three years after the earliest date on which the plaintiff had actual knowledge of the breach or violation

except that in the case of fraud or concealment, such action may be commenced not later than six years after the date of discovery of such breach or violation.

Thus, ERISA § 413 contains three separate statutes of limitations:[343]

> (1) a general six year limitations period that begins to run on the date of the last action which constituted a part of the breach or violation (or in the case of omission on the latest date on which the fiduciary could have cured the breach or violation);
>
> (2) in the event that the plaintiff has actual knowledge of the breach, a three year limitations period that begins to run when the plaintiff acquires acknowledge of the breach or violation; and
>
> (3) in the event of fraud or concealment, a six year limitations period that begins to run when the breach or violation is discovered.

Application of the statutes of limitations under ERISA § 413 may give rise to a three-part inquiry. First, did the plaintiffs have "actual knowledge" of the breach? If so, did the plaintiffs file suit within three years of acquiring such knowledge as

---

[342] William E. Altman and Danielle C. Lester, *Demystifying the Complexities of ERISA Claims Litigation*, 92 MICH. B.J. 29, 32 (2013); Andrew Stumpff, *Darkness at Noon: Judicial Interpretation May Have Made Things Worse for Plan Participants Under ERISA Than Had the Statute Never Been Enacted*, 23 ST. THOMAS L. REV. 221, 234 (2011).

[343] The ERISA § 413(2) three-year limitations period is a traditional statute of limitations while the ERISA § 413(1) six year limitations period is a statute of repose. Aaron A. Reuter, *Do You Know What It Means to Know? Actual Knowledge and ERISA Section 413*, PROSKAUER ERISA LITIGATION NEWSLETTER 6, (Aug. 2011). *See also* David v. Alphin, 704 F.3d 327 (4th Cir. 2013) (describing ERISA § 413(1) six year limitations period as a statute of repose). For a discussion of the differences between traditional statutes of limitations and statutes of repose, see Adam Bain, *Determining the Preemptive Effect of Federal Law on State Statutes of Repose*, 43 U. BALT. L. REV. 119, 125–32 (2014).

required by ERISA § 413(2)? Second, if the plaintiffs did not have earlier "actual knowledge" of the breach, did they file suit within six years of the final action constituting the breach under ERISA § 413(1)? Third, if suit was not filed within six years of the breach, or within three year of acquiring actual knowledge of the breach, if applicable, did the defendants engage in fraud or concealment? If so, did the plaintiffs file suit within six years of discovering the breach?[344]

---

[344] *See* ABA SECTION OF LABOR AND EMPLOYMENT LAW, EMPLOYEE BENEFITS LAW, at 10–177–78 (laying out three-part inquiry).

ERISA § 413 STATUTE OF LIMITATIONS FOR BREACH OF FIDUCIARY DUTY

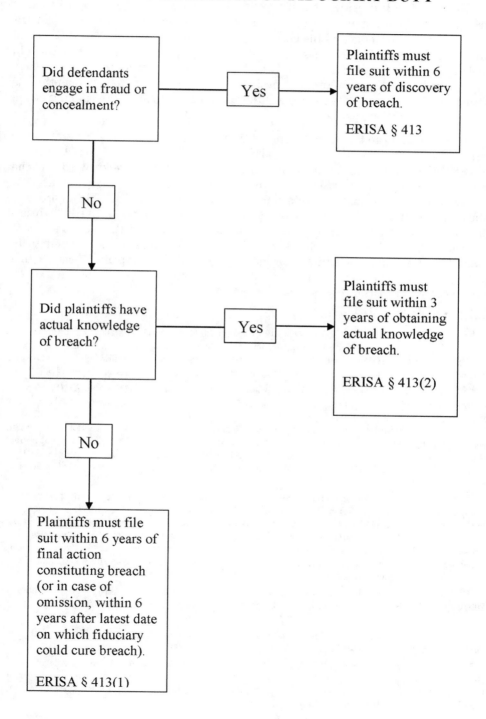

[1]　ERISA § 413(2) Three Year Actual Knowledge Limitations Period

ERISA § 413(2) provides that if a plaintiff has actual knowledge of a fiduciary breach, the plaintiff must file suit no later than three years after the plaintiff acquires such knowledge. As the statute states, "actual knowledge" must be actual knowledge, not constructive knowledge.[345] The courts, however, are not uniform in their approach to what constitutes "actual knowledge." Instead, the courts generally apply one of three different approaches to determining when a plaintiff has actual knowledge of the alleged breach that is sufficient to start the running of the three year limitations period.[346]

Under the first approach,[347] the plaintiff must know not only the facts that give rise to the alleged violation, but must also know that the facts constitute a violation of ERISA.[348] Under the second approach, the plaintiff must have knowledge of the relevant facts of a transaction or actions that give rise to a fiduciary breach, but need not understand that the facts support a legal claim under ERISA in order to start the running of the three year statute of limitations.[349] The third, "hybrid," approach is flexible and permits the court to take into account the factual scenario at issue. Under this approach, "knowledge of *facts* cannot be attributed to [a plaintiff] who [has] no actual knowledge of them," but a plaintiff has actual knowledge of a violation when he or she knows the "essential facts of the transaction or the conduct constituting the violation."[350]

---

[345] *See* Meyer v. Berkshire Life Ins. Co., 128 F. Supp. 2d 831, 838 (D. Md. 2001) (stating that the courts are adamant that ERISA § 413 requires actual, not constructive knowledge). *See also* Jorden, et al., ERISA Litigation Handbook, at § 4.06[D] (stating that "courts have almost uniformly held that *actual* and not constructive knowledge is necessary to trigger the running of the three year period").

[346] Aaron A. Reuter, *Do You Know What It Means to Know? Actual Knowledge and ERISA Section 413*, Proskauer ERISA Litigation Newsletter 6, 6 (Aug. 2011). *Cf.* ABA Section of Labor and Employment Law, Employee Benefits Law, at 10-177–78 (categorizing two, rather than three, different approaches – one requiring actual knowledge of the legal consequences of the transaction and one not requiring that the plaintiff understand that the facts would establish a claim under ERISA — but noting that its categorization should not be considered rigid or absolute). *See also* Jorden, et al., ERISA Litigation Handbook, at § 4.06[D] Table 4-4 (identifying ERISA § 413(2) statute of limitations accrual standards by circuit).

[347] Interestingly, this approach has been referred to as both the "strictest" and "permissive." *Compare* Fish v. GreatBanc Trust Co., 749 F.3d 671 (7th Cir. 2014) (describing approach as "strictest") *with* Aaron A. Reuter, *Do You Know What It Means to Know? Actual Knowledge and ERISA Section 413*, Proskauer ERISA Litigation Newsletter 6, 6 (Aug. 2011) (describing approach as "permissive"). Presumably, whether the approach is strict or permissive depends on your perspective. From the standpoint of the defendant, this is the strictest, most difficult to satisfy. From the standpoint of the plaintiff, this is the most favorable interpretation of the statute.

[348] *See, e.g.*, Koert v. GE Grp. Life Assurance Co., 2007 U.S. App. LEXIS 4715, 7 (3d Cir. Feb. 27, 2007); Babcock v. Hartmarx Corp., 182 F.3d 336, 339 (5th Cir. 1999); International Union v. Murata Erie N. Am., 980 F.2d 889, 900 (3d Cir. 1992).

[349] *See, e.g.*, Brown v. Owens Corning Investment Review Committee, 622 F.3d 564, 570 (6th Cir. 2010); Rush v. Martin Petersen Col, 83 F.3d 894, 896 (7th Cir. 1996).

[350] Edes v. Verizon Commc'ns, Inc., 417 F.3d 133, 142 (1st Cir. 2005). *See also* Browning v. Tiger's Eye Benefits Consulting, 2009 U.S. App. LEXIS 3927, 11 (4th Cir. Feb. 26, 2009) (applying similar standard); Caputo v. Pfizer, Inc., 267 F.3d 181, 193 (2d Cir. 2001) (adopting hybrid standard); Brown v. American Life Holdings, Inc., 190 F.3d 856, 859 (8th Cir. 1999).

[2]   ERISA § 413(1) General Six Year Limitations Period

ERISA § 413(1) sets forth a general limitations period that applies so long as the plaintiff has no actual knowledge of the breach and the defendant did not engage in fraud or concealment. Under this provision, no action may be brought more than six years after "the date of the last action which constituted a part of the breach or violation."

In *Tibble v. Edison International*,[351] the Supreme Court addressed the question whether a plan fiduciary's allegedly imprudent retention of an investment is an "action" or "omission" for purposes of ERISA § 413(1)'s general six year limitations period. In that case, plan participants claimed that the plan fiduciaries' selection of retail-class mutual funds violated their fiduciary duties. The initial selection of some of the funds occurred more than six years before the participants filed suit, and the plan fiduciaries argued that the claims were time barred under the ERISA § 413(1) general six year limitations period.

The Supreme Court rejected the plan administrators' view that the date of the last action for purposes of the six year statute of limitations is the date that the investments were selected. The Court noted that fiduciary duty under ERISA is "derived from the common law of trusts,"[352] and "[u]nder trust law, a trustee has a continuing duty to monitor trust investments and remove imprudent ones."[353] The Court expressed no view of the scope of the plan fiduciaries' duty. Instead, the Court remanded the case to the Ninth Circuit to determine whether the fiduciaries "breached their duties within the relevant 6-year period under [ERISA § 413(1)], recognizing the importance of analogous trust law."[354]

[3]   ERISA § 413 Six Year Fraud or Concealment Limitations Period

Under the ERISA § 413 fraud or concealment exception, an action may not be commenced more than six years after the date of discovery of the alleged breach or violation in the case of fraud or concealment.

Most circuit courts have held that the six year "fraud or concealment" limitations period incorporates the common law "fraudulent concealment doctrine,"[355] which delays the beginning of the limitations period until the date the injury is discovered.[356] Under this approach, the exception applies when the defendant has

---

[351]   135 S. Ct. 1823 (2015).

[352]   *Id.* at 1828, *quoting*, Central States, Southeast & Southwest Areas Pension Fund v. Central Transport, Inc., 472 U.S. 559, 570 (1985).

[353]   135 S. Ct. at 1828.

[354]   Id. at 1829.

[355]   The fraudulent concealment doctrine was first created by the Supreme Court in *Bailey v. Glover*, 88 U.S. 342 (1875). For a discussion of the doctrine, see Richard L. Marcus, *Fraudulent Concealment in Federal Court: Toward a More Disparate Standard?*, 71 Geo. L.J. 829 (1983).

[356]   ABA Section of Labor and Employment Law, Employee Benefits Law, at 10-183 (citing cases from 1st, 3d, 7th, 8th, 9th, and D.C. circuits).

committed either (1) a self-concealing act,[357] that is, an act committed during the course of the breach that has the effect of concealing the breach from the plaintiff, or (2) active concealment,[358] that is, an act that is distinct from the breach that is intended to conceal the breach.[359]

The Second Circuit, however, has rejected the view that the term "fraud or concealment" should be fused into a single "fraudulent concealment." Instead, the Second Circuit holds the fraud or concealment exception should apply to cases in which the fiduciary either "(1) breached its duty by making a knowing misrepresentation or omission of a material fact to induce an employee/beneficiary to act to his detriment; or (2) engaged in acts to hinder the discovery of a breach of fiduciary duty."[360]

[B] Statute of Limitations Applicable to Disputes Under the Multiemployer Plan Provisions of Title IV of ERISA — ERISA § 4301(f)

Section 4301(f) of ERISA provides that

An action under this section may not be brought after the later of —

(1) 6 years after the date on which the cause of action arose, or

(2) 3 years after the earliest date on which the plaintiff acquired or should have acquired actual knowledge of the existence of such cause of action;

except that in the case of fraud or concealment, such action may be brought not later than six years after the date of discovery of the existence of such cause of action.

Thus, like ERISA § 413, ERISA § 4301(f) contains three separate limitations periods: (1) a six year limitations period that begins to run on the date on which the cause of action arose; (2) a three year limitations period that begins to run when the plaintiff acquired or should have acquired actual knowledge of the existence of the cause of action; and (3) in the event of fraud or concealment, a three year limitations period that begins to run when the existence of the cause of action is discovered. ERISA § 4301(f) differs fundamentally from ERISA § 413 in that in cases other than cases of fraud or concealment, the statute of limitations expires upon the later, rather than the earlier, of six years after the cause of action arose or three years after the plaintiff acquires or should acquire actual knowledge of the existence of the cause of action. ERISA § 4301(f)(2) also differs significantly from ERISA

---

[357] *See, e.g.,* Wolin v. Smith Barney, Inc. 83 F.3d 847, 852 (7th Cir. 1996); J. Geils Band Employee Benefit Plan v. Smith Barney Shearson, Inc., 76 F.3d 1245, 1259 (1st Cir.), *cert. denied,* 519 U.S. 823 (1996); Martin v. Consultants & Adm'rs, Inc., 966 F.2d 1078, 1095 (7th Cir. 1992).

[358] Ranke v. Sanofi-Synthelabo Inc., 436 F.3d 197, 204 (3d Cir. 2006); Martin v. Consultants & Adm'rs, Inc., 966 F.2d 1078, 1095 (7th Cir. 1992).

[359] Caputo v. Pfizer, 267 F.3d 181, 189 (2d Cir. 2001). *Cf.* ABA Section of Labor and Employment Law, Employee Benefits Law, at 10-183 (stating that courts disagree as to whether "fraudulent concealment" requires that defendant have taken steps to conceal the breach that are independent of the breach itself).

[360] Caputo, 267 F.3d, at 190.

§ 413(2) in that it does not require actual knowledge. Instead, the three year statute of limitations begins to run when the plaintiff has or should have actual knowledge of the existence of the cause of action.

In *Bay Area Laundry & Dry Cleaning Pension Trust Fund v. Ferbar Corp,*[361] the Supreme Court addressed the question of when the six-year statute of limitations begins to run on a pension fund's action to collect unpaid withdrawal liability under the Multiemployer Pension Plan Amendments Act of 1980,[362] set forth in ERISA §§ 4201–4261. The Multiemployer Pension Plan Amendments Act of 1980 requires that employers who withdraw from underfunded multiemployer pension plans pay a "withdrawal liability."[363] Employers may satisfy their obligation by making a series of periodic payments according to a schedule established by the pension's trustees[364] or by paying the entire debt at any time.[365]

In *Ferbrar,* the fund filed suit more than six years after the employer's first payment was due, but less than six years after the second and all remaining periodic payments were due.[366] The Court held that a separate statute of limitations applies with respect to each payment due.[367] Thus, the statute of limitations had expired with respect to the first missed periodic payment, but not with respect to the remaining payments.[368]

[C] Statute of Limitations Applicable to Other ERISA Claims

ERISA is silent with respect to the statute of limitations applicable to most claims under ERISA. Thus, for example, ERISA does not provide an explicit statute of limitations for benefit due claims under ERISA § 502(a)(1)(B), to employer retaliation claims under ERISA § 510, or to claims for delinquent employer contributions under ERISA § 515.

ERISA is not the only federal statute not to contain an express statute of limitations applicable to causes of action created by the statute.[369] As a result, a common law practice has developed to fill in the gap in such cases.[370] Under this

---

[361] 522 U.S. 192 (1997).

[362] Multiemployer Pension Plan Amendments Act of 1980, Pub. L. No. 96-364, 94 Stat. 1208.

[363] ERISA § 29 U.S.C. § 1381(a).

[364] ERISA § 29 U.S.C. § 1399(c)(1).

[365] ERISA § 29 U.S.C. § 1399(c)(4).

[366] 522 U.S., at 206.

[367] *Id.* at 208.

[368] *Id.* at 210.

[369] *See* Michael R. Keefe, Comment, *Getting Past the "Fallback Rule of Thumb": Towards a Uniform ERISA Benefits-Due Statute of Limitations,* 78 U. Cin. L. Rev. 735, 739 nn. 38 & 39 (2009) (identifying several non-ERISA federal causes of action without express statutes of limitations).

[370] In 1990, Congress enacted a statute which establishes a blanket four-year statute of limitations for federal causes of action that are not otherwise subject to an express statute of limitations. The law, however, does not apply retroactively and thus does not apply to ERISA claims because ERISA was enacted in 1974. *See id.* at 745.

practice, courts generally apply the most analogous state statute of limitations.[371] If, however, an employee benefit plan contains an express limitations period, courts will apply the limitations period set forth in the plan as long as the period provided in the plan is reasonable.

[1] Analogous State Statutes of Limitation

In the absence of an express applicable limitations period under ERISA, courts apply the most analogous state statute of limitations.[372] Application of this rule has led to considerable litigation and lack of uniformity because different courts analogize similar ERISA claims to different types of state law claims, and state statutes of limitations for similar state law claims vary considerably.

Applying the most analogous state statute of limitations to an ERISA claim requires consideration of three separate issues. First, the court must decide which state law to apply.[373] Most, though not all, courts apply the state law of the forum state, that is, the state in which the suit was filed.[374] Because, as discussed below, state statutes of limitations vary considerably, litigants may forum shop to choose the federal court located in the state with the most favorable state statute of limitations.[375] Indeed, practitioners have suggested that failure to select a forum with a favorable limitations period may be a violation of a lawyer's professional responsibility.[376]

Second, the court must "characterize the essence of the [ERISA] claim in state law terms."[377] The character of the essence of an ERISA claim depends on the specific claim filed. ERISA authorizes a variety of claims for which there is no express statute of limitations. The most common is a claim for benefits due under ERISA § 502(a)(1)(B). Another common claim is a claim filed under ERISA § 502(a)(3) for impermissible retaliation and/or discrimination in violation of ERISA § 510. Most courts characterize benefits-due claims as written contract claims[378]

---

[371] *See* Reed v. United Transportation Union, 488 U.S. 319, 323 (1989). *See also* Keefe, 78 U. CIN. L. REV., at 739–40 (discussing this "Fallback Rule of Thumb" and exceptions to the general rule).

[372] Flint, *ERISA: Fumbling the Limitations Period*, 84 NEBRASKA L. REV., at 319.

[373] *Id.*

[374] *See* ABA SECTION OF LABOR AND EMPLOYMENT LAW, EMPLOYEE BENEFITS LAW, at 12–23 (citing cases).

[375] *See, e.g.*, Held v. Mfrs. Hanover Leasing Corp., 912 F.2d 1197, 1202–03 (10th Cir. 1990) (discussing choice of law rules applied in various circuits and applying New York law to ERISA claim filed in Colorado). *Cf.* Gluck v. Unisys Corp. 960 F.2d 1168, 1179 (3d Cir. 1992) (applying Pennsylvania statute of limitations to ERISA action filed by Pennsylvania residents to plan with Michigan choice of law provision).

[376] *See* Gregory C. Braden, et al., *What's New in Employee Benefits in 2010: A Summary of Significant Case Law Developments Since Spring 2010 Including What's New in Employee Benefits: A Summary of Current Case and Other Developments*, SS011 ABA-ALI 1 (Oct. 7–9, 2010) (stating that "[c]hoosing a jurisdiction in which an action is time-barred when the applicable statute of limitations has not run in another viable jurisdiction may raise issues of professional responsibility").

[377] ABA SECTION OF LABOR AND EMPLOYMENT LAW, EMPLOYEE BENEFITS LAW, at 12-12. *See also* Harrison v. Digital Health Plan, 183 F.3d 1235, 1239 (11th Cir. 1999) (stating that "court must first characterize the essential nature of the plaintiff's claim").

[378] Flint, *ERISA: Fumbling the Limitations Period*, 84 NEBRASKA L. REV., at 320 (stating that most circuit courts have settled on the statute of limitations for written contracts as the most analogous

while most courts characterize ERISA § 510 claims as wrongful termination claims.[379] The courts, however, are not entirely uniform in such characterizations. For example, courts have characterized benefits-due claims as claims for recovery of wages,[380] and courts have characterized ERISA § 510 claims as employment discrimination or breach of contract claims.[381]

Finally, once the court has characterized the "essence" of the claim, the court must select the most analogous state law statute of limitations.[382] Again, application of the most analogous state law statute of limitations leads to considerable diversity in limitations periods because (1) the statute of limitations with respect to particular claims vary widely from state to state, and (2) states may have multiple statutes of limitations of varying lengths with respect to particular types of claim.[383] For example, in actions to recover benefits due under ERISA § 502(a)(1)(B), courts have applied a four year Texas statute of limitations governing suits grounded in contract,[384] a six year Georgia statute of limitations for actions on simple contracts,[385] a 10 year Indiana statute of limitations on written contracts,[386] and a 15 year Ohio statute of limitations for contract actions.[387]

Commentators have criticized the lack of uniformity that results from courts' current practice of applying the most analogous state statute of limitations and have argued in favor of a uniform federal statute of limitations. For example, one commentator has argued that the ERISA § 413 breach of fiduciary statute of limitations should apply to virtually all ERISA claims[388] while another commentator has argued that Congress should amend ERISA to provide a uniform statute of limitations for benefits-due claims under ERISA § 502(a)(1)(B).[389]

---

statute of limitations"); ABA SECTION OF LABOR AND EMPLOYMENT LAW, EMPLOYEE BENEFITS LAW, at 12-21 (stating that "most court adopt the state statute of limitations that governs written contract actions" in claims for benefits under ERISA § 502(a)(2) and citing cases).

[379] ABA SECTION OF LABOR AND EMPLOYMENT LAW, EMPLOYEE BENEFITS LAW, at 15-84–15-85; Flint, *ERISA: Fumbling the Limitations Period*, 84 NEBRASKA L. REV., at 323.

[380] ABA SECTION OF LABOR AND EMPLOYMENT LAW, EMPLOYEE BENEFITS LAW, at 12-21–12-22. *See also* Keefe, 78 U. CIN. L. REV., at 745–750 (discussing various approaches to benefits-due claims).

[381] ABA SECTION OF LABOR AND EMPLOYMENT LAW, EMPLOYEE BENEFITS LAW, at 15-85. For a discussion of state statutes of limitations applied to informational penalty lawsuits, equitable remedy lawsuits to enforce plan provisions, and delinquent employer contributions, see Flint, *ERISA: Fumbling the Limitations Period*, 84 NEBRASKA L. REV., at 319–20, 322–23, and 325–27; ABA SECTION OF LABOR AND EMPLOYMENT LAW, EMPLOYEE BENEFITS LAW, at 12-12, 12-39–12-40.

[382] ABA SECTION OF LABOR AND EMPLOYMENT LAW, EMPLOYEE BENEFITS LAW, at 12–12. Harrison v. Digital Health Plan, 183 F.3d 1235, 1239 (11th Cir. 1999) (stating that "after characterizing the essential nature of the claim, the court must borrow the limitations period for the most analogous state law claim").

[383] Flint, *ERISA: Fumbling the Limitations Period*, 84 NEBRASKA L. REV., at 320–22 & 323–25; Keefe, 78 U. CIN. L. REV., at 745–750.

[384] *See* Hogan v. Kraft Foods, 969 F.2d 142, 145 (5th Cir. 1992).

[385] *See* Harrison v. Digital Health Plan, 183 F.3d 1235, 1239–40 (11th Cir. 1999).

[386] *See* Arena v. ABB Power T & D Co., Inc., 2003 U.S. Dist. LEXIS 13164, at *28 (S.D. Ind. July 21, 2003).

[387] *See* Meade v. Pension Appeals & Review Comm., 966 F.2d 190, 194–95 (6th Cir. 1992).

[388] Flint, *ERISA: Fumbling the Limitations Period*, 84 NEBRASKA L. REV., at 352–64

[389] *See* Keefe, 78 U. Cin. L. Rev., at 756–57.

[2] "Reasonable" Limitations Periods Set Forth in Plan

In the absence of an express limitations period under ERISA, courts will enforce a limitations period set forth in a plan so long as that period is reasonable.[390] Plans frequently include three-year limitations periods, and courts regularly uphold such periods.[391] Moreover, lower courts have upheld limitations periods as short as 45 days[392] and 90 days,[393] and the Supreme Court has found reasonable a limitations period that was effectively one year.[394]

In *Heimeshoff v. Hartford Life & Accident Insurance Co.*,[395] a plan participant challenged a plan's three-year limitations period that began when to run when the proof of loss was due, which was before the participant had exhausted the plan's internal review process. The Supreme Court began by observing that the cause of action for a section 502(a)(1)(B) claim does not accrue until the plan issues a final denial.[396] It then recognized that statutes of limitations typically begin to run when the cause of action accrues, but declared that such a rule is not an inexorable requirement.[397] Instead, just as the parties to a contract may agree to a particular limitations period, so too may the parties agree to when the limitations period begins to run so long as the period is reasonable.[398] The Court found that the period in *Heimeshoff* was reasonable as applied because the plan participant had about year after the plan issued its final denial to file suit.[399]

---

[390] *See* Flint, *ERISA: Fumbling the Limitations Period*, 84 Nebraska L. Rev., at 327–29; ABA Section of Labor and Employment Law, Employee Benefits Law, at 12-23.

[391] *See, e.g.*, Wilkins v. Hartford Life & Accident Ins. Co., 299 F.3d 945, 948–49 (8th Cir. 2002); Doe v. Blue Cross & Blue Shield United of Wisconsin, 112 F.3d 869, 875 (7th Cir. 1997). *See also* Flint, *ERISA: Fumbling the Limitations Period*, 84 Nebraska L. Rev., at 327–29 (citing cases); ABA Section of Labor and Employment Law, Employee Benefits Law, at 12–23 n.87 (same); Jim Greiner, Note, *Federal Common Law and Gaps in Federal Statutes: The Case of ERISA Plan Limitation Periods for Section 502(a)(1)(B) Actions*, 93 Mich. L Rev. 382 (1994) (discussing borrowing doctrine and arguing that states should adopt a uniform national rule upholding reasonable plan limitations periods).

[392] *See* Davidson v. Wal-Mart Assocs. Health & Welfare Plan, 305 F. Supp. 2d 1059, 1074–75 (S.D. Iowa 2004).

[393] *See* Northlake Reg'l Med. Ctr. v. Waffle House Sys. Emp. Benefit Plan, 160 F.3d 1301, 1303–04 (11th Cir. 1998).

[394] Heimeshoff v. Hartford Life & Accident Ins. Co., 134 S. Ct. 604, 612 (2013).

[395] 134 S. Ct. 604 (2013).

[396] *Id.* at 601.

[397] *Id.*

[398] *Id.* at 611.

[399] *Id.* at 612–13. The plan participant filed a claim for long-term disability benefits on August 22, 2005, and the plan required that proof of loss be submitted within 90 days of the start of benefits. The plan issued its final denial on November 26, 2007. The plaintiff did not file suit until November 18, 2010. *Id.* at 608–609.

§ 7.10   ATTORNEY'S FEES — ERISA § 502(g)(1)

The American rule in litigation provides that unless there is a statutory exception, each party in a lawsuit is responsible for his or her own attorney's fees.[400] ERISA contains such a statutory exception. Specifically, ERISA § 502(g)(1) provides that "[i]n any action under [Title I of ERISA (other than an action for delinquent contributions under ERISA § 515)],[401] by a participant, beneficiary, or fiduciary, the court in its discretion may allow a reasonable attorney's fee and costs of action to either party."[402]

In *Hardt v. Reliance Standard Life Ins. Co.*,[403] the Supreme Court held that a court may "in its discretion" award attorney's fees and costs "to either party" under ERISA § 502(g)(1) so long as the party claiming fees has achieved "some degree of success on the merits."[404]

In that case, a plan participant filed suit under ERISA § 502(a)(1)(B) challenging the denial of disability benefits. The district court awarded the plan participant attorney's fees and the Court of Appeals vacated the district court's order because, in the Court of Appeals' view, the plan participant had failed to establish that she was a "prevailing party." The Supreme Court granted *certiorari* to address a split among the Circuit Courts as to whether a party must be a "prevailing party" before attorney's fees may be awarded under ERISA § 502(g)(1).[405]

Relying on ERISA § 502(g)(1)'s express language, which authorizes an award to "either party," the Court held that a fee claimant does not have to be a "prevailing party" in order to be eligible for an attorney's fee award under ERISA § 502(g)(1).[406] Then, relying on *Ruckleshaus v. Sierra Club*,[407] the Court's "principal" precedent on interpreting statutes that do not limit awards of attorney's fees to the "prevailing party," the Court declared that before a court may award attorney's fees under ERISA § 502(g)(1), the fee claimant must show "some degree of success on the merits."[408] Quoting *Ruckleshaus*, the Court declared that "trivial success on the merits or a "purely procedural victor[y]" does not satisfy the

---

[400] Ruckelshaus v. Sierra Club, 463 U.S. 680, 683–84 (1983); Alyeska Pipeline Service Co. v. Wilderness Society, 421 U.S. 240, 247 (1975). Congress generally enacts fee-shifting statutes to encourage individuals who have been wronged to see judicial relief. Robert L Rossi, Attorneys' Fees § 10:2 (3d ed. updated through 2014).

[401] ERISA § 502(g)(2) contains a separate rule for attorney's fees for ERISA § 515 claims.

[402] ERISA § 502(g)(1).

[403] 130 S. Ct. 2149 (2010).

[404] *Id.* at 2152.

[405] *Id.* at 2155. For a discussion of the Circuit split, see Matthew D. Gimovsky, Note & Comment, Hardt v. Reliance Standard Insurance Co.: *Attorney's Fee Awards Under ERISA and the "Some Degree of Success Standard*," 14 J. of Health Care L. & Policy 177, 187–195 (2011). *See* Tiffany R. Timmerman, Student Article, Hardt v. Reliance Standard Ins. Co.: *Breathing New Life into Claimants' Ability to Obtain Attorney's Fees Under ERISA's Civil Enforcement Provision*, 56 S.D. L. Rev. 549, 567–71 (2011) (discussing various courts' approaches to fee shifting under ERISA § 502(g)(1) before *Hardt*).

[406] 130 S. Ct. at 2156.

[407] 463 U.S. 680 (1983).

[408] 130 S. Ct. at 2158, *quoting Ruckelshaus*, at 694. Justice Stephens did not join in the Court's reliance on *Ruckelshaus*. *Id.* at 2159 (stating that "I do not believe that our mistaken interpretation of

requirement, but a fee claimant does satisfy the requirement "if the court can fairly call the outcome of the litigation some success on the merits without conducting a 'lengthy inquir[y] into the question whether a particular party's success was 'substantial' or occurred on a 'central issue.' "[409]

In *Hardt*, the district court found that "the plan administrator ha[d] failed to comply with the ERISA guidelines" and "that [the plan participant] did not get the kind of review to which she was entitled under applicable law."[410] The court found "compelling evidence that [the plan participant was] totally disabled due to her neuropathy" and announced that it was "inclined to rule in [her] favor," but declined to grant her motion for summary judgment before "first giving [the plan administrator] the chance to address the deficiencies in its" statutorily mandated "full and fair review" of her claim.[411] The court issued an order instructing the plan administrator "to act on [the participant's] application by adequately considering all the evidence" within 30 days or judgment would be issued in the participant's favor.[412] The administrator conducted the court-ordered review, reversed its earlier decision, and awarded the participant the benefits she sought.[413]

The Supreme Court found that these facts showed that participant had achieved much more than "trivial success on the merits" or a "purely procedural victory."[414] Instead, she had achieved "some success on the merits," and thus the district court was properly within its discretion in awarding her attorney's fees.[415] The Court declined to rule on the question whether a remand order, without more, constitutes "some success on the merits" so as to make a party eligible for an award of attorney's fees under ERISA § 502(g)(1).[416]

Before the Supreme Court decided *Hardt*, almost all lower courts, including the district court in *Hardt*, applied a five-factor test to determine whether attorney's fees should be awarded.[417] Those factors were: (1) the relative bad faith or culpability of the opposing party; (2) the ability of the opposing party to satisfy an attorney's fee award; (3) Whether an award of attorney's fee would serve as a deterrent; (4) the extent to which the party seeking attorney's fees sought to benefit all plan participants and beneficiaries or sought to resolve a significant issue under ERISA; and (5) the relative merits of each of the parties' positions.[418]

---

§ 307 of the Clean Air Act in [*Ruckleshaus*] should be given any special weight in the interpretation of this-or any other-different statutory provision").

[409] *Id.*, *quoting Ruckelshaus*, at 688.

[410] *Id.* at 2158, *quoting* record.

[411] *Id.*

[412] *Id.* at 2159.

[413] *Id.*

[414] *Id.*

[415] *Id.*

[416] *Id.* For a discussion of how the lower courts have applied *Hardt's* "some degree of success on the merits" standard, see W. Bard Brockman, *Revisiting Hardt: The Developing Law on Recovery of Attorneys' Fees Under ERISA § 502(g)(1)*, 20 J. OF PENS. BENEFITS 33 (Winter 2013).

[417] ABA SECTION OF LABOR AND EMPLOYMENT LAW, EMPLOYEE BENEFITS LAW, at 12-99–12-100.

[418] *See id.* at 12-101 n.581 (citing cases from every circuit applying variations of this five-factor test).

The Court in *Hardt* announced that its decision did not foreclose the possibility that once a fee claimant shows "some degree of success on the merits," and thus is eligible for an award of attorney's fees under ERISA § 502(g)(1), that a court may consider those five factors in determining whether to award attorney's fees.[419]

---

[419] 130 S. Ct. at 2158 n.8.

Chapter 8

ERISA PREEMPTION

§ 8.01 INTRODUCTION

ERISA preemption is one of the most litigated aspects of ERISA.[1] It "has generated a huge volume of confusing and conflicting judicial opinions and a large body of critical commentary from judges, practitioners, and scholars."[2]

The fact that ERISA preemption has generated so much controversy and litigation is due, in part, to the stakes involved. If a court finds that ERISA preempts a plaintiff's state law claim, then the state law claim must be dismissed and the plaintiff will be without a remedy under state law. In addition, even though ERISA preempts a plaintiff's state law claim, ERISA may not provide a cause of action for the alleged wrong. Moreover, even if ERISA does provide the plaintiff with a cause of action, the law under ERISA may be less favorable than the state law that was preempted. For example, if ERISA rather than state law applies, the plaintiff may lose the right to a jury trial,[3] the court may apply a less favorable standard of review in reviewing a plan participant's challenge to a claim denial,[4] and, in some instances, the plaintiff may be without any remedy under ERISA.[5]

ERISA preemption is not alone in generating a considerable amount of uncertainty and litigation. The "[p]reemption doctrine is muddled in general, not just as applied to discrete areas."[6]

This chapter begins with a general introduction to preemption. It then provides an overview of ERISA's express preemption provision, ERISA § 514.

---

[1] *See* ABA Section of Labor and Employment Law, Employee Benefits Law 11-3 (Jeffrey Lewis et al., eds., 3d ed. 2012) (stating that "[n]o substantive provision of the Employee Retirement Income Security Act (ERISA) has generated as much controversy or as many reported appellate and Supreme Court decisions as ERISA's preemption provision").

[2] James A. Wooten, *A Legislative and Political History of ERISA Preemption, Part 1*, J. of Pension Benefits 31 (2006). *See, e.g.*, Aetna Health Inc. v. Davila, 542 U.S. 200, 222 (2004) (Ginsberg, J.) (writing separate opinion to join "the rising judicial chorus urging that Congress and [the] Court revisit what is an unjust increasingly tangled ERISA regime"), *quoting*, DiFelice v. Aetna U.S. Healthcare, 346 F.3d 442, 453 (3d Cir. 2003) (Becker, J., concurring).

[3] For a discussion of the right to a jury trial under ERISA, see Chapter 7 § 7.06.

[4] For a discussion of judicial standards of review under ERISA, see Chapter 7. § 7.07

[5] For a discussion of remedies under ERISA, see Chapter 7 § 7.08.

[6] Caleb Nelson, *Preemption*, 86 Va. L. Rev. 225, 233 (2000). For a critique of the Supreme Court's recent preemption decisions, see Daniel J. Meltzer, *Preemption and Textualism*, 112 Mich. L. Rev. 1 (2013).

§ 8.02   GENERAL INTRODUCTION TO PREEMPTION

The Supremacy Clause, Section 2 of Article VI of the U.S. Constitution, provides that the "Constitution, and the Laws of the United States . . . shall be the supreme Law of the Land."[7] To determine whether federal law is supreme, and thus preempts state law, the Supreme Court has declared that "[t]he purpose of Congress is the ultimate touchstone."[8]

The Supreme Court has recognized that congressional intent "may be 'explicitly stated in the statute's language or implicitly contained in its structure and purpose.'"[9] According to the Court, "[i]n the absence of express congressional command, state law is pre-empted if that law actually conflicts with federal law, or if federal law so thoroughly occupies a legislative field 'as to make reasonable the inference that Congress left no room for the States to supplement it.'"[10]

[A]   Basic Types of Preemption

The Supreme Court has recognized two basic types of preemption: (1) express preemption and (2) implied preemption.[11]

[1]   Express Preemption

Express preemption arises when a federal statute contains a preemption clause that explicitly preempts state law.[12] Section 514 of ERISA expressly "supersedes" all state laws that relate to an employee benefit plan. Thus, ERISA contains an express preemption provision: ERISA § 514.

[2]   Implied Preemption

Typically, implied preemption only arises when a federal statute does not contain an express preemption provision.[13] The Supreme Court, however, has referred to implied preemption principles in a number of ERISA preemption cases.[14]

---

[7] U.S. Const. art. VI, cl. 2 ("This Constitution, and the Laws of the United States which shall be made in Pursuance thereof; . . . shall be the supreme Law of the Land; and the Judges in every State shall be bound thereby, any Thing in the Constitution or Laws of any state to the Contrary notwithstanding.").

[8] Malone v. White Motor Corp., 435 U.S. 497, 504 (1978).

[9] Cipollone v. Liggett Grp., Inc., 505 U.S. 504, 516 (1992) (citing Jones v. Rather Packing Co., 430 U.S. 519, 525 (1977)).

[10] Id. at 516 (citing Fidelity Fed. Sav. & Loan Ass'n v. De la Cuesta, 458 U.S. 141, 153 (1982)).

[11] Preemption may also arise in a third situation: state taxation or regulation of federal activities. Erwin Chemerinsky, Constitutional Law: Principles And Policies 405 (4th ed. 2011). ERISA claims do not give rise to this type of preemption, which is arguably another form of conflict preemption.

[12] Gade v. National Solid Waste Management Assn., 505 U.S. 88, 98 (1992).

[13] But see Catherine L. Fisk, The Article about the Language of ERISA Preemption? A Case Study of the Failure of Textualism, 33 Harv. J. On Legis. 35, 45 (1996) (contending that "interpreting an express preemption provision like ERISA's . . . does not differ dramatically from the task of interpreting the preemptive effect of a statute without an express preemption provision").

[14] See, e.g., Boggs v. Boggs, 520 U.S. 833, 841 (1997) (holding that state law preempted under

The Supreme Court has recognized two different types of implied preemption: (1) field preemption and (2) conflict preemption.[15]

[a]　Field Preemption

Field preemption arises when the Court finds that a federal statute so wholly occupies a particular field that there is no room left for state action.[16] If field preemption applies, then all state laws related to that area of law are preempted.[17] Because of the breadth of the doctrine, implied field preemption is sometimes referred to as "complete preemption."[18]

[b]　Conflict Preemption

Conflict preemption arises under two different circumstances.[19] First, state law is preempted when it "actually conflicts" with a federal law so that "compliance with both federal and state regulations is a physical impossibility."[20] Second, state law is preempted when state law "stands as an obstacle to the accomplishment and execution of the full purposes and objectives of Congress."[21]

[3]　Effect of Preemption

Both express and implied preemption are substantive federal defenses to state law claims.[22] They do not give a federal court jurisdiction over a complaint filed in state court.[23] They simply provide the defendant with a federal defense to a state

---

conventional conflict principles and thus Court need not determine whether "statutory 'relate to' provides further and additional support for the pre-emption claim"); Egelhoff v. Egelhoff, 532 U.S. 141, 153 (Scalia, J., concurring) ("persist[ing] in the view that we can bring some coherence to this area and can give the statute both a plausible and precise content, only by interpreting the 'relate to' clause as a reference to our ordinary pre-emption jurisprudence"); Egelhoff v. Egelhoff, 532 U.S. 141, 153 (Breyer, J., dissenting) (stating that Court "should apply normal conflict pre-emption and field pre-emption principles where, as here, a state statute covers ERISA and non-ERISA documents alike").

[15] Gade v. National Solid Waste Management Assn., 505 U.S. 88, 98 (1992).

[16] See, e.g., Florida Lime & Avocado Growers, Inc. v. Paul, 373 U.S. 132, 142 (1963).

[17] CHEMERINSKY, CONSTITUTIONAL LAW: PRINCIPLES AND POLICIES, at 413 ("Field preemption means that federal law is exclusive in the area and preempts state laws even if they serve the same purposes as the federal law or its implementation.").

[18] See, e.g., Boomer v. AT&T Corp., 309 F.3d 404, 417 (7th Cir. 2002). As discussed below, the term "complete preemption" may also be used in a completely different sense to refer to a federal court's jurisdiction over a plan participant's complaint alleging a state law claim.

[19] Boggs v. Boggs, 520 U.S. 833, 844 (1997).

[20] CHEMERINSKY, CONSTITUTIONAL LAW: PRINCIPLES AND POLICIES, at 404, quoting Florida Lime & Avocado Growers, Inc. v. Paul, 373 U.S. 132, 142-143 (1963).

[21] Id. at 404, quoting Hines v. Davidowtiz, 312 U.S. 52, 67 (1941). Professor Chemerinsky treats the two forms of conflict preemption as distinct categories of implied preemption. He recognizes, however, that, as a practical matter, there is considerable overlap among the categories. Id.

[22] Connecticut State Dental Ass'n v. Anthem Health Plans, Inc., 591 F.3d 1337, 1344 (11th Cir. 2009) (stating that "[c]onflict preemption, also known as defensive preemption, is a substantive defense to preempted state law claims").

[23] Id. (stating that "[b]ecause conflict preemption is merely a defense, it is not a basis for removal"). See also Metropolitan Life v. Taylor, 481 U.S. 58, 63 (1987) (noting that federal preemption is ordinarily

law claim. Thus, if a plaintiff files a complaint in state court in which the plaintiff alleges one or more violations of state law, the defendant may raise the federal defense of preemption. If the state court finds that the state law claim is preempted, then the plaintiff may not rely on state law to remedy the alleged wrong.[24] Another provision of ERISA may, or may not, provide a remedy for the alleged wrong. Neither ERISA § 514 nor implied preemption principles give plan participants any rights or remedies. They simply provide a defense against a state law claim. Moreover, they do not provide a federal court with jurisdiction to decide the case.[25] The state court must decide whether or not ERISA preempts the state law claim. If ERISA preempts the state law claim, then the state court must dismiss the state law cause of action regardless of whether ERISA provides the plaintiff with any remedy.

[4]   Complete Preemption for Jurisdictional Purposes

Separate and apart from express and implied preemption principles, the Supreme Court has held, on a few occasions, that ERISA completely preempts state law so as to give rise to federal jurisdiction over the plaintiff's complaint.[26] This doctrine, often referred to as "complete preemption," is distinct from implied field preemption. Implied field preemption is a federal defense to a state law claim. Complete preemption, in contrast, is a jurisdictional doctrine.[27] If complete preemption applies, then a federal court has removal jurisdiction over the complaint, and the defendant has a right to remove the complaint to federal court. If complete preemption applies, the federal court must dismiss the plaintiff's state law claims and the plaintiff will necessarily have a cause of action under section 502 of ERISA. The plaintiff may not, however, necessarily have a remedy under ERISA § 502.[28]

Complete preemption for jurisdictional purposes is discussed in Chapter 7 § 7.05[B].

---

a federal defense and does not authorize removal to federal court). As discussed below, however, a federal court may have jurisdiction over a plan participant's complaint under the jurisdictional complete preemption doctrine.

[24] *Cf.* Cmty. State Bank v. Strong, 651 F.3d 1241, 1261 n16 (11th Cir. 2011) (stating that conflict preemption "allows a defendant to defeat a plaintiff's state-law claim on the merits by asserting the supremacy of federal law as an affirmative defense").

[25] *See* Franchise Tax Board v. Construction Laborers Vacation Trust, 463 U.S. 1 (1983) (holding that federal court did not have federal question removal jurisdiction over declaratory judgment action filed in state court by California Franchise Tax Board seeking declaration that defendant was "legally bound and obligated to honor all future levies by the Board" despite the defendant's claim that California law was preempted under ERISA § 514(a)).

[26] *See, e.g.,* Aetna Health Inc. v. Davila, 542 U.S. 200 (2004); Metropolitan Life v. Taylor, 481 U.S. 58 (1987). This form of complete preemption has only been recognized in a few contexts outside of ERISA. *See* Connecticut State Dental Ass'n v. Anthem Health Plans, Inc., 591 F.3d 1337, 1343 n.3 (11th Cir. 2009).

[27] Franciscan Skemp Healthcare, Inc. v. Central States Joint Board Health and Welfare Trust Fund, 538 F.3d 594, 596 (7th Cir. 2008).

[28] For a discussion of remedies under ERISA § 502, see Chapter 7 § 7.08.

[B] Typical Procedural Posture of ERISA Preemption Claims

Procedurally, ERISA preemption decisions typically arise when a plaintiff files a motion to remand a complaint to state court.[29] Specifically, the suit typically begins when a plaintiff files a state law complaint in state court alleging that the defendant violated some state law, such as breach of contract under state law. The defendant then removes the case to federal court on the ground of ERISA preemption. The plaintiff then brings a motion to remand the case back to state court.

In deciding the motion to remand, the federal court must decide whether the state law claims are completely preempted by ERISA. If the federal court finds that ERISA completely preempts the plaintiff's state law claims, then the federal court has jurisdiction to decide the case. The federal court can then find that the plaintiff's state law claim is preempted by ERISA and determine whether the plaintiff has an affirmative cause of action and remedy under ERISA § 502.

If the federal court finds that the plaintiff's state law claims are not completely preempted by ERISA, then the federal court must remand the case to state court.[30] That, however, does not dispose of the defendant's ERISA preemption defense. Instead, the state court must decide whether the plaintiff's state law claim is preempted by section 514 of ERISA.[31] If the state law claim is preempted under ERISA § 514, then the plaintiff's state law cause of action must be dismissed. The plaintiff has no cause of action under ERISA and thus is left without a remedy for the alleged wrong.

As two litigators have explained:

> Much of the confusion about how ERISA preemption operates stems from a lack of understanding about the differences between "complete" preemption and "conflict" preemption (also known as "traditional" preemption).
>
> . . . .

---

[29] *See, e.g.*, United State v. Roberson, III, 591 F.3d 1337 (11th Cir. 2009); Marin General Hospital v. Modesto & Empire Traction Co., 581 F.3d 941 (9th Cir. 2009); Franciscan Skemp Health-Care Inc. v. Central States Joint Board Health and Welfare Trust Fund, 538 F.3d 594 (7th Cir. 2008); Wright v. General Motors Corp., 262 F.3d 610 (6th Cir. 2001).

[30] *See, e.g.*, Franciscan Skemp Health-Care Inc. v. Central States Joint Board Health and Welfare Trust Fund, 538 F.3d 594, 601 (7th Cir. 2008) (reversing district court and vacating order dismissing state law claims and stating that upon return to district court, case is to be remanded to state court); Wright v. General Motors Corp., 262 F.3d 610, 615 (6th Cir. 2001). (reversing district court and remanding to district court with instructions to remand to state court because plaintiff's complaint was not completely preempted by ERISA).

[31] *See, e.g.*, Franciscan Skemp Health-Care Inc. v. Central States Joint Board Health and Welfare Trust Fund, 538 F.3d 594, 601 (7th Cir. 2008) (stating that "[c]onflict preemption . . . is an issue left to the state court in this case, since conflict preemption does not provide an independent basis for federal jurisdiction/removal"); Wright v. General Motors Corp., 262 F.3d 610, 615 (6th Cir. 2001) (declining to decide whether state law complaint preempted by ERISA § 514 because state courts are competent to decide whether ERISA preempts the state law claims).

[I]t is very important that lawyers determine at the outset, before filing a claim for denial of benefits, whether a state law claim would be completely preempted or conflict preempted under ERISA. . . . A lawyer wastes both time and money when asserting a state law claim that is conflict preempted, because such claims cannot exist in either a federal or a state forum. A lawyer also should avoid the inefficient practice of bringing a state law claim that is completely preempted. If a court correctly applies the complete preemption doctrine, the claim will be re-characterized as a federal cause of action and will be removable to federal court. But if a court misunderstands complete preemption, and applies a conflict preemption analysis instead, the litigant runs the risk of incurring dismissal of a completely preempted claim that actually properly could be asserted in federal court.[32]

§ 8.03 OVERVIEW OF EXPRESS PREEMPTION UNDER ERISA § 514

Section 514 of ERISA contains a three-part express preemption provision.[33] First, section 514(a) expressly preempts any and all state laws that "relate to" employee benefit plans. Second, section 514(b)(2)(A) saves (or excepts) from preemption state laws that regulate insurance, banking, or securities. Finally, the section 514(b)(2)(B) "deemer clause" excepts from the savings clause exception state laws with respect to self-insured employee benefit plans. Thus, under the section 514(b)(2)(B) deemer clause, all state laws that relate to an employee benefit plan are preempted with respect to self-insured employee benefit plans even if the state laws regulate insurance.

An express preemption analysis under ERISA § 514 begins with the question whether a state law relates to an employee benefit plan. If it does, then the state law is preempted under ERISA's general preemption provision, ERISA § 514(a). If the state law is preempted under ERISA § 514(a), the question then arises whether the law regulates insurance, banking, or securities. If the state law regulates insurance, banking or securities, the law is "saved" and thus not preempted under ERISA § 514(b)(2)(A). Finally, if the state law regulates insurance, banking, or securities, the question arises whether the employee benefit plan at issue is self-funded. If the employee benefit plan is self-funded, then ERISA § 514(b)(2)(B)'s deemer clause provides an exception from the saving clause so that the state law is once again preempted.[34]

---

[32] John R. Richards & Howard S. Suskin, *Understanding Complete and Conflict Preemption Under ERISA: A Primer For Lawyers*, 6 MEALY'S LITIGATION REPORT 1, 1-2 (#4 August 2007).

[33] For a discussion of the legislative history of ERISA § 514, see James A. Wooten, *A Legislative and Political History of ERISA Preemption, Part 1*, 14 J. OF PENSION BENEFITS 31 (2006); James A. Wooten, *A Legislative and Political History of ERISA Preemption, Part 2*, 14 J. OF PENSION BENEFITS 5 (2006); James A. Wooten, *A Legislative and Political History of ERISA Preemption, Part 3*, 15 J. OF PENSION BENEFITS 15 (2006); Fisk, 33 HARV. J. ON LEGIS., at 52-57; David Gregory, *The Scope of ERISA Preemption of State Law: A Study in Effective Federalism*, 48 U. PITT. L. REV. 427 (1987).

[34] Section 514(b) also contains a number of other express exceptions to the ERISA § 514(a) general preemption provision. For example, ERISA § 514(b)(4) provides an exception for generally applicable

EXPRESS PREEMPTION
UNDER ERISA § 514

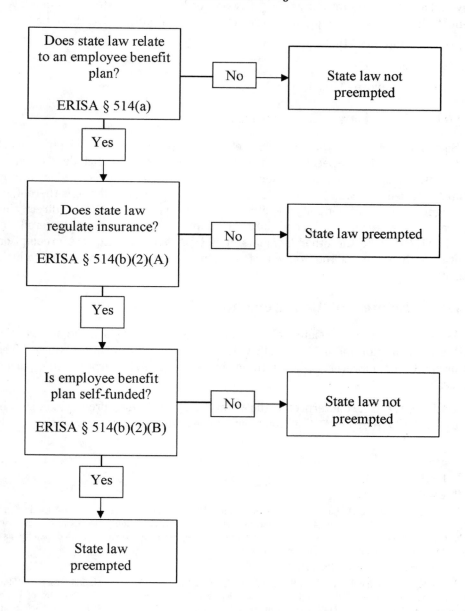

state criminal law. For a discussion of the state criminal law exception, see Albert Feuer, *When do State Laws Determine ERISA Plan Benefit Rights?*, 47 J. MARSHALL L. REV. 145, 299-306 (2013).

§ 8.04 ERISA § 514(a) AND ITS REQUIREMENTS

Section 514(a) of ERISA provides, in relevant part, that ERISA "shall supersede any and all State laws insofar as they may now or hereafter relate to any employee benefit plan." Thus, preemption under section 514(a) requires that there be

(1) a "state law" that

(2) "relates to"

(3) an "employee benefit plan."

[A] "State Law" Requirement

Section 514(c) defines the terms "State" and "State law" broadly for purposes of ERISA preemption. Specifically, it defines "state law" to include "all laws, decisions, rules, regulations or other State action having the effect of law, of any State."[35] It defines "State" to include "a State, any political subdivisions thereof, or any agency or instrumentality of either, which purports to regulate, directly or indirectly, the terms and conditions of employee benefit plans covered by [ERISA]."[36] Unlike the other elements of ERISA § 514(a)'s express preemption provision, the state law requirement is straightforward and has given rise to little litigation.[37]

[B] "Relates to" Requirement

Whether a State law "relates to" an employee benefit plan "is at the heart of the ERISA preemption inquiry."[38] ERISA does not define the term "relate to." The Supreme Court, however, has focused on the meaning of the term in ten separate cases.[39]

Initially, the Court interpreted the term "relate to" quite broadly. Indeed, in *Shaw v. Delta Airlines*,[40] the Court announced that Congress used the words

---

[35] ERISA § 514(c)(1).

[36] ERISA § 514(c)(2).

[37] *Cf.* ABA Section of Labor and Employment Law, Employee Benefits Law, at 11-5 (noting that courts have addressed the issue of what constitutes state law for preemption purposes in several cases involving governmental entities seeking to require private employers to provide specified benefits as a condition of doing business with the government).

[38] Gregory, 48 U. Pitt. L. Rev., at 457.

[39] *See* Egelhoff v. Egelhoff, 532 U.S. 141 (2001); UNUM Life Ins. Co. v. Ward, 526 U.S. 358 (1999); DeBuono v. NYSA-ILA Medical and Services Clinical Fund, 520 U.S. 806 (1997); Cal. Div. of Labor Standards Enforcement v. Dillingham Constr., N.A., Inc., 519 U.S. 316 (1997); New York State Conference of Blue Cross & Blue Shield Plans v. Travelers Insurance Co., 514 U.S. 645 (1995); Dist. of Columbia v. Greater Wash. Bd. of Trade, 506 U.S. 125 (1992); Ingersoll Rand v. McClendon, 498 U.S. 133 (1990); Mackey v. Lanier Collection Agency & Service, Inc., 486 U.S. 825 (1988); Shaw v. Delta Air Lines, Inc., 463 U.S. 85 (1983); Alessi v. Raybestos –Manhattan, Inc., 451 U.S. 504 (1981). The Court has also applied the "relate to" language in cases focusing on the saving and/or deemer clause. *See, e.g.*, FMC Corp. v. Holliday, 498 U.S. 52, 58-60 (1990).

[40] 463 U.S. 85 (1983).

"relate to" in section 514(a) of ERISA "in their broad sense."[41]

After more than a decade, the Supreme Court cut back on the reach of the term "relate to" in *New York State Conference of Blue Cross & Blue Shield Plans v. Travelers Insurance Co.*[42] The Court in *Travelers* recognized that its "prior attempt to construe the phrase 'relate to' [did] not give [the Court] much help drawing the line"[43] in determining whether a state law "relates to" an employee benefit plan for purposes of preemption under ERISA § 514(a). Thus, the Court declared that it "simply must go beyond the unhelpful text and the frustrating difficulty of defining its key term, and look instead to the objectives of the ERISA statute as a guide to the scope of the state law that Congress understood would survive."[44]

The Court, however, did not expressly repeal *Shaw* in *Travelers* or its progeny. Instead, the Court has continued to refer to *Shaw* and apply its two-prong test in determining whether a state law "relates to" an employee benefit plan and thus is preempted under ERISA § 514(a).

Despite — or arguably because of — this Supreme Court precedent,[45] the meaning of the term "relates to" remains uncertain and difficult to apply.[46] Indeed, whether a state law "relates to" an employee benefit plan remains one of the most litigated issues in ERISA.

[1] *Shaw* Two-Prong Test

In *Shaw v. Delta Air Lines*,[47] the Supreme Court's second ERISA preemption decision,[48] the Court declared, "A law 'relates to' an employee benefit plan, in the normal sense of the phrase, if it has a connection with or reference to such a plan."[49] Since then, the Court has treated the Shaw definition as a two-prong

---

[41] *Id.* at 98.

[42] 514 U.S. 645 (1995).

[43] *Id.* at 655.

[44] *Id.* at 656.

[45] *See* Egelhoff v. Egelhoff, 532 U.S. 141, 152-53 (Scalia, J., concurring).

[46] *Cf.* UNUM Life Ins. Co. v. Ward, 526 U.S. 358, 363 (1999) (stating that the key words "relate to" [and "regulates insurance"] "once again require interpretation for their meaning is not 'plain' ").

[47] 463 U.S. 85 (1983).

[48] The Court's first ERISA preemption case, *Alessi v. Raybestos-Manhattan, Inc.*, 451 U.S. 504 (1981), involved a relatively easy and straightforward application of the section 514(a) requirement that the state law "relate to" an employee benefit plan. In that case, retirees brought suit claiming that their employers' pension plans, which provided that pension benefits would be offset, that is, reduced, by an amount equal to workers' compensation benefits, violated New Jersey law. *Id.* at 507. The court held that the New Jersey statute "related to" pension plans because "it eliminate[d] one method for calculating pension benefits – integration – that is permitted by federal law." *Id.* at 524. The Court did not offer any guidance on how far "relate to" might extend. *Id.* at 525. The Court stated, "We need not determine the outer boundaries of ERISA's pre-emptive language to find this New Jersey provision an impermissible intrusion on the federal regulatory scheme."*Id.* The state law clearly conflicted with ERISA under traditional conflict preemption principles.

[49] 463 U.S. at 96–97.

inquiry for determining whether a law relates to an employee benefit plan.[50]

Under this so-called two-prong inquiry or test, a state law "relates to" an employee benefit plan if it has a

(1)   connection with or

(2)   reference to

such a plan.

[a]   "Reference to" Prong

Under the narrower "reference to" prong, the Court has found that a state law has an impermissible reference to an employee benefit plan if it acts immediately and exclusively on the plan or the existence of a plan is essential to the law's operation.[51] Three Supreme Court cases are often cited as applications of the "reference to" prong.[52]

In the first case, *Mackey v. Lanier Collection Agency & Service, Inc.*,[53] the Court considered a state law that provided that "[f]unds or benefits of a pension, retirement, or employee benefit plan or program subject to [ERISA] shall not be subject to the process of garnishment . . . unless such garnishment is based upon a judgment for alimony or for child support."[54] The Court held that the statute was preempted under the second, "reference to" prong because it impermissibly singled out employee benefit plans for different treatment under state garnishment procedures.[55] According to the Court, "[t]he state statute's express reference to ERISA plans suffices to bring it within the federal law's pre-emptive reach."[56]

In *Ingersoll-Rand Co. v. McClendon*,[57] the Court considered a state common law claim for wrongful discharge that arose when the plaintiff could establish that "the principal reason for his termination was the employer's desire to avoid contributing to or paying benefits under the employee's pension fund."[58] The Court held that the claim was preempted because the existence of a pension plan was a

---

[50] *See* Cal. Div. of Labor Standards Enforcement v. Dillingham Constr., N.A., Inc., 519 U.S. 316, 324 (1997), *quoting* Dist. of Columbia v. Greater Wash. Bd. of Trade, 506 U.S. 125, 129 (1992), *quoting* Shaw v. Delta Air Lines, Inc., 463 U.S. 85 (1983) ("Our efforts at applying the provision have yielded a two-part inquiry: A 'law 'relate[s] to' a covered employee benefit plan for purposes of § 514(a) 'if it [1] has a connection with or [2] reference to such a plan.' ").

[51] *See* Cal. Div. of Labor Standards Enforcement v. Dillingham Constr., N.A., Inc., 519 U.S. 316, 325 (1997), *citing* Dist. Of Columbia v. Greater Wash. Bd. of Trade, 506 U.S. 125 (1992), Mackey v. Lanier Collection Agency & Serv., Inc., 486 U.S. 825 (1988), and Ingersoll-Rand Co. v. McClendon, 498 U.S. 133 (1990).

[52] *Id.*

[53] 486 U.S. 825 (1988).

[54] *Id.* at 828 n.2

[55] *Id.* at 830.

[56] *Id.*

[57] 498 U.S. 133 (1990).

[58] *Id.* at 136.

critical factor in establishing liability and thus essential to the law's operation.[59]

In *District of Columbia v. Greater Washington Board of Trade*,[60] the Court addressed a preemption challenge to D.C. law that provided that "[a]ny employer who provides health insurance coverage for an employee shall provide health insurance coverage equivalent to the existing health insurance coverage of the employee while the employee receives or is eligible to receive workers' compensation benefits under this chapter."[61] The Court held that the law was preempted because it expressly referred to employee benefit plans – it required that benefits be set by reference to the terms of existing ERISA plans.[62]

[b]   "Connection with" Prong

The Court first applied the "connection with" prong of the *Shaw* two-prong test for determining when a state law "relates to" an employee benefit plan in *FMC v. Holliday*.[63] In that case, an employer sought to enforce an employee benefit plan's subrogation clause which required the plan participant to reimburse the plan for amounts the plan paid to cover the participant's medical expenses if the participant subsequently recovered on a claim in a liability action against a third party.[64] The plan participant claimed that the plan's subrogation claim was unenforceable because it violated a Pennsylvania law that prohibited subrogation from tort recoveries in actions arising out of the maintenance or use of a motor vehicle.[65]

The Court found that the Pennsylvania law had a "connection with" ERISA benefit plans.[66] It noted that the Court had not hesitated to apply ERISA preemption to "state laws that risk subjecting plan administrators to conflicting state regulations."[67] The Court declared that where a "patchwork scheme of regulation would introduce considerable inefficiencies in benefit program operation," the Court has applied the pre-emption clause "to ensure that benefit plans will be governed by only a single set of regulations."[68] The Court found the Pennsylvania statute violated this interest in national uniformity in administration because it would require "plan providers to calculate benefit levels in Pennsylvania based on expected liability conditions that differ from those in States that have not enacted similar antisubrogation legislation."[69]

---

[59] *Id.* at 139–40.

[60] 506 U.S. 125 (1992).

[61] *Id.* at 128.

[62] *Id.* at 130

[63] 498 U.S. 52 (1990).

[64] *Id.* at 54–55.

[65] *Id.* at 55.

[66] *Id.* at 59. The Court also found that it satisfied the first, "reference to," prong of the *Shaw* test. *Id.*

[67] *Id.*

[68] *Id.* at 60.

[69] *Id.* The Court then found that the statute was "saved" by the insurance saving clause because it regulated insurance but then preempted once again under the ERISA § 514(b)(2)(B) deemer clause because the plan at issue was self-funded.

In *New York State Conference of Blue Cross & Blue Shield Plans v. Travelers Insurance Co*,[70] the Supreme Court again considered the meaning of the "connection with" prong of the *Shaw* two-prong test for determining when a state law "relates to" an employee benefit plan.[71] The Court in that case diverged substantially from its earlier precedent and cut back on the breadth of the term "relate to" under ERISA § 514(a).[72] The Court did not, however, expressly repeal *Shaw* or explain how its new approach applies to the "reference to" prong of the *Shaw* two-prong test.[73]

Travelers involved a preemption challenge to a New York statute that (1) required hospitals to collect surcharges from patients covered by commercial insurers but not from patients insured by Blue Cross/Blue Shield, and (2) subjected certain HMOs to surcharges that varied with the number of Medicaid patients the HMOs enrolled.[74]

The Court began its preemption analysis by citing and discussing a number of traditional implied preemption cases.[75] The Court declared that it should begin its preemption analysis in this, ERISA, case, like in other areas of the law, with a presumption against preemption.[76]

The Court then criticized *Shaw* for failing to provide the Court with much guidance in drawing the line in applying the term "relate to" under ERISA 514(a).[77] The Court did not, however, repeal *Shaw* and its two-prong test. Instead, it announced that it must look "to the objectives of the ERISA statute as a guide to

---

[70] 514 U.S. 645 (1995).

[71] Before applying the "connection with" prong, the Court first addressed the "reference to" prong of the *Shaw* test. The Court found that the statute in that case clearly did not make reference to employee benefit plans because "[t]he surcharges [were] imposed upon patients and HMO's regardless of whether the commercial coverage or membership, respectively, [was] ultimately secured by an ERISA plan, private purchase, or otherwise." *Id.* at 656.

[72] *Cf.* Edward A. Zelinsky, *Maryland's Walmart Act: Policy and Preemption* 28 Cardozo L. Rev. 847 (2006) ("*Travelers* and its progeny represent an important effort by the Court to reform its overly-expansive Shaw-based approach to preemption").

[73] Commentators generally approve of the Court's new approach under *Travelers. See, e.g.,* John H. Langbein, *Destructive Federal Preemption of State Wealth Transfer Law in Beneficiary Designation Cases: Hillman Doubles Down on Egelhoff*, 67 Vand. L. Rev. 1665 (2014) (stating that "[a]fter a troubled early case law, the Supreme Court has come to interpret the 'relate to' standard as balancing the interests of state law with the purposes of ERISA"); Edward A. Zelinsky, *California Dreaming: The California Secure Choice Retirement Savings Trust Act*, 20 Conn. Ins. L.J. 547, 587 (2013) (contending that "as the Court's later and more persuasive interpretation of ERISA preemption, *Travelers* should prevail over *Shaw*"); Fisk, 33 Harv. J. On Legis., at 40 (describing Travelers as signaling "a long overdue and laudable reorientation in the Court's approach to ERISA preemption").

[74] 514 U.S. at 649.

[75] *Id.* at 654–55.

[76] *Id.* at 654–55.

[77] Specifically, the Court said, "If 'relate to' were taken to extend to the furthest stretch of its indeterminacy, then for all practical purposes pre-emption would never run its course, for '[r]eally, universally, relations stop nowhere.' . . . [W]e have to recognize that our prior attempt to construe the phrase 'relate to' does not give us much help drawing the line here." *Id.* at 655, *quoting* H. James, Roderick Hudson xli (New York ed., World's Classics 1980).

the scope of the state law that Congress understood would survive"[78] in applying the "connection with" prong.

After briefly reviewing the preemption clause's legislative history, the Court stated, "The basic thrust of the pre-emption clause, then, was to avoid a multiplicity of regulation in order to permit the nationally uniform administration of employee benefit plans."[79]

The Court distinguished the surcharge law from state laws that mandate employee benefit structures or their administration.[80] The Court recognized that the surcharges would make Blue Cross/Blue Shield more attractive to ERISA plans.[81] The Court, however, described their effect as "an indirect economic influence" that "does not bind plan administrators to any particular choice and thus function as a regulation of an ERISA plan itself."[82] According to the Court, "the indirect influence of the surcharges [does not] preclude uniform administrative practice or the provision of a uniform interstate benefit package if a plan wishes to provide one. It simply bears on the cost of benefits and the relative costs of competing insurance to provide them."[83]

The Court concluded that "cost uniformity was almost certainly not an object of pre-emption, just as laws with only an indirect economic effect on the relative costs of various health insurance packages in a given State are a far cry from those 'conflicting directives' from which Congress meant to insulate ERISA plans."[84] Thus, the Court held that the surcharges did not have an impermissible "connection with" employee benefit plans and were not preempted by ERISA.

Two years after the Court decided *Travelers*, the Court in *California Division of Labor Standards Enforcement v. Dillingham Construction, N.A., Inc,*[85] reaffirmed that in applying the "connection with" prong, the Court "look[s] both to 'the objectives of the ERISA statute as a guide to the scope of the state law that Congress understood would survive' as well as to the nature of the effect of the state law on ERISA plans."[86]

In *Dillingham*, a contractor and subcontractor challenged California's prevailing wage law that required payment of prevailing wages to employees in non-state-approved apprenticeship programs but permitted the payment of lower apprenticeship wages to employees participating in state-approved apprenticeship programs. The Court first noted that states have long regulated apprenticeship standards and wages paid for state public works.[87] The Court then found that

[78] 514 U.S. at 656.

[79] *Id.* at 657.

[80] *Id.* at 657–58.

[81] *Id.* at 659.

[82] *Id.*

[83] *Id.* at 660.

[84] *Id.* at 662.

[85] 519 U.S. 316 (1997).

[86] *Id.* at 325, *quoting Travelers*, at 658–59.

[87] *Id.* at 330.

wages for state public works and standards to be applied to apprenticeship programs are quite remote from the areas with which ERISA is expressly concerned: "reporting, disclosure, fiduciary responsibility, and the like."[88] The Court found that the apprenticeship portion of the statute, like the New York surcharge requirement, did not bind ERISA plans to anything.[89] Like the New York surcharges, "[t]he prevailing wage statute alters the incentives, but does not dictate the choices, facing ERISA plans."[90] Thus, the statute did not have a "connection with" employee benefit plans.

In *Egelhoff v. Egelhoff*,[91] the most recent Supreme Court decision to apply the "connection with" prong,[92] the Court held that ERISA preempted a state statute that upon divorce automatically revoked the designation of a spouse as a beneficiary of nonprobate assets.[93] The Court first found that the statute implicated "an area of core ERISA concern" because it regulated "the payment of benefits, a central matter of plan administration."[94] The Court then found that it interfered with one of the principal goals of ERISA: nationally uniform administration.[95] "Plan administrators cannot make payments simply by identifying the beneficiary specified by the plan documents. Instead, they must familiarize themselves with state statutes so that they can determine whether the

---

[88] *Id.* at 331, *quoting Travelers*, at 661.

[89] *Id.* at 332.

[90] *Id.* at 334.

[91] 532 U.S. 141 (2001).

[92] The Court interpreted the "relates to" prong in two additional cases decided after *Dillingham* but before *Egelhoff*: De Buono v. NYSA-ILA Medical and Clinical Services Fund, 520 U.S. 806 (1997), and UNUM Life Ins. Co. v. Ward, 526 U.S. 358 (1999). In neither case did the Court expressly apply the two-prong *Shaw* test to determine whether the state law "related to" an employee benefit plan.

In the first case, *De Buono*, the Court expressly reaffirmed *Dillingham* and held that a New York state tax on gross receipts of health care facilities operated by ERISA funds was not preempted. The Court held that the statute was "one of 'myriad state laws' of general applicability that impose some burdens on the administration of ERISA plans but nevertheless do not 'relate to' them within the meaning of the governing statute." *De Buono*, 520 U.S. at 815, *citing Travelers*, 514 U.S. at 668; *Dillingham*, at 333–34.

In the second case, *UNUM*, the Court held that a state common law agency "rule providing that "the employer is the agent of the insurer in performing the duties of administering group insurance policies," *UNUM*, 526 U.S. at 378, "related to" employee benefit plans and thus was preempted because it "would have a marked effect on plan administration. *Id.* at 379. Such a rule "would 'forc[e] the employer, as plan administrator, to assume a role, with attendant legal duties and consequences, that it has not undertaken voluntarily'; it would affect 'not merely the plan's bookkeeping obligations regarding to whom benefits checks must be sent, but [would] also regulat[e] the basic services that a plan may or must provide to its participants and beneficiaries." *Id.* at 379, *citing Brief* at 27.

[93] 532 U.S. at 143. Specifically, the statute provided

If a marriage is dissolved or invalidated, a provision made prior to that event that relates to the payment or transfer at death of the decedent's interest in a nonprobate asset in favor of or granting an interest or power to the decedent's former spouse is revoked. A provision affected by this section must be interpreted, and the nonprobate asset affected passes, as if the former spouse failed to survive the decedent, having died at the time of entry of the decress of dissolution or declaration of invalidity. *Id.* at 144, *quoting* Wash. Rev. Code. Sec. 11.07.010(2)(a) (1994).

[94] *Id.* at 147–148.

[95] 532 U.S. at 148.

named beneficiary's status has been 'revoked' by operation of law."[96]

[2] The Future of the Two-Prong *Shaw* Test

The future of the two-prong *Shaw* test is uncertain.

The Supreme Court has never expressly repealed the two-prong *Shaw* test. Indeed, in *Egelhof*, the Court expressly applied the second, "connection with," prong of the two-prong *Shaw* test in holding that a state statute that upon divorce automatically revoked the designation of a spouse as a beneficiary of nonprobate assets was preempted under ERISA § 514.[97]

The Court's decision, however, was not unanimous. First, Justice Scalia, joined by Justice Ginsburg, concurred in the Court's opinion because the state law "directly conflicts with ERISA's requirements that plans be administered, and benefits be paid, in accordance with plan documents."[98] Nevertheless, Justice Scalia made it clear that he believed traditional preemption principles should apply in interpreting the term "relate to" under ERISA § 514. Specifically, Justice Scalia declared:

> I remain unsure (as I think the lower courts and everyone else will be) as to what else triggers the "relate to" provision, which – if it is interpreted to be anything other than a reference to our established jurisprudence concerning conflict and field pre-emption – has no discernible content that would not pick up every ripple in the pond, producing a result "that no sensible person could have intended."[99]

In a dissenting opinion, Justice Breyer, with whom Justice Stevens joined, agreed with Justice Scalia that normal conflict and field pre-emption principles should apply. He expressed "fear that [the Court's] failure to endorse this 'new approach' explicitly will continue to produce an 'avalanche of litigation' as courts struggle to interpret a clause that lacks any 'discernible content' threatening results Congress could not have intended."[100] Nevertheless, he disagreed with Justice Scalia and believed that the state statute was not preempted under traditional preemption principles.

The majority declined to address the petitioner's argument that the state statute was preempted under traditional principles of conflict preemption. Instead, it found that the statute was expressly preempted under ERISA under the "connection with" prong of the two-prong *Shaw* test.[101]

---

[96] *Id.* at 148–149.

[97] 532 U.S. at 147.

[98] *Id.* at 152 (Scalia, J., concurring)

[99] *Id.* at 152–53, *quoting Dillingham,* at 335-36 (Scalia, J., concurring).

[100] *Id.* at 153–54 (Breyer, J., dissenting) (citations omitted).

[101] *Id.* at 146.

[3]   Final Thoughts on the "Relate to" Requirement

The "relate to" requirement poses challenges and difficulties, in part, because the Court has never expressly repealed *Shaw* and its sweeping approach to ERISA preemption. The challenges and difficulties are not, however, limited to the Court's failure to expressly repeal *Shaw*.

Under *Travelers*, and traditional preemption principles, federal preemption of state law turns on the objectives of federal law.[102] Determining the objectives of a federal law and whether they conflict with a particular state law, however, is not a straightforward objective inquiry. Rather, such inquiries necessarily involve discretion, and judges may disagree as to whether a particular state law is inconsistent with a federal law's objectives.[103]

To illustrate, in *Egelhoff*, seven justices believed that a state statute that automatically revoked the designation of a spouse as a beneficiary of nonprobate assets upon divorce interfered with one of ERISA's principal goals: nationally uniform administration. In contrast, Justice Breyer, joined by Justice Stevens, was of the opinion that no "plausible pre-emption principle . . . leads to a conclusion that ERISA pre-empts the statute at issue here."[104] Obviously, ERISA does not preempt the entire field of state law governing inheritance.[105] Moreover, there was no "direct conflict between the Washington statute and ERISA, for the one nowhere directly contradicts the other."[106] The state statute did not contradict ERISA's requirement that beneficiaries be paid "in accordance with the documents and instruments governing the plan."[107] Instead, it simply set forth "a default rule for interpreting documentary silence."[108]

Egelhoff illustrates that like in all preemption cases,[109] determining whether a state law "relates to" an employee benefit plan so as to be preempted under ERISA § 514(a) depends on the exercise of discretion and thus is fraught with uncertainty and subject to considerable litigation.

---

[102] For an overview of traditional preemption principles, see CHEMERINSKY, CONSTITUTIONAL LAW: PRINCIPLES AND POLICIES, at 411–27.

[103] *Cf. id.* at 423 (stating that "[a]s is the case throughout preemption law, this intent is rarely expressed or clear and court thus must make a judgment about how best to effectuate the policy behind a particular federal law."); Fisk, 33 HARV. J. ON LEGIS., at 44-45 (noting that "[j]udges complain . . . about implied preemption . . . for it is difficult to discern when Congress has occupied a field and what the scope of that field is, or when state law is an obstacle to some congressional goal").

[104] 532 U.S. at 154. *See also* Langbein, 67 VAND. L. REV., at 1677 (arguing that "[b]y treating ERISA as preempting the state-law solution to a traditional state-law issue, *Egglehoff* disrespects the longstanding allocation of responsibility between the two legal systems").

[105] 532 U.S. at 154.

[106] *Id.*

[107] *Id.*

[108] *Id.*

[109] For a general discussion of preemption and the difficulties that arise in applying both express preemption provisions and implied preemption principles, see CHEMERINSKY, CONSTITUTIONAL LAW: PRINCIPLES AND POLICIES, at 406–27.

[C] "Employee Benefit Plan" Requirement

Section 514 does not define the term "employee benefit plan" for purposes of ERISA preemption. The term, however, is defined in ERISA's general definition section, ERISA § 3. Specifically, ERISA § 3(3) defines the term "employee benefit plan" as "an employee welfare benefit plan or an employee pension benefit plan or a plan which is both a welfare plan and pension plan."[110] ERISA § 3(1), in turn, defines the term "welfare plan"[111] while ERISA § 3(2) defines the term "pension plan."[112] Although sections 3(1) and 3(2) do a good job of identifying particular types of welfare and pension *benefits*, they define the term "plan" in a rather circular fashion.[113] Specifically, both sections define "plan" as "any plan, fund, or program" established by an employer or employee organization, or both, for the purpose of providing specified benefits.

The Supreme Court has focused on the meaning of "plan" for purposes preemption under ERISA § 514(a) in two separate cases.[114] At the time that the

---

[110] The Department of Labor has issued a regulation clarifying that an employee benefit plan must cover at least one employee in order to qualify as an employee benefit plan under ERISA. 29 C.F.R. § 2510.3-3(b) ("For purposes of title I of the Act and this chapter, the term 'employee benefit plan' shall not include any plan, fund or program, other than an apprenticeship or other training program, under which no employees are participants covered under the plan, as defined in paragraph (d) of this section.").

[111] Specifically, ERISA § 3(1) defines a "welfare benefit plan" as "any plan, fund or program which . . . is established or maintained by an employer or an employee organization or both, to the extent that such plan, fund or program was established or is maintained for the purpose of providing for its participants or their beneficiaries, through the purchase of insurance or otherwise, medical, surgical or hospital care or benefits, or benefits in the event of sickness, accident disability, death or unemployment, or vacation benefits, apprenticeship or other training program, or day care centers, scholarship funds, or prepaid legal services."

The Department of Labor has issued a regulation clarifying the meaning of the term "welfare plan." As discussed *infra*, the regulation, among other things, excludes certain "payroll practices" from the definition of welfare plan. 29 C.F.R. § 2510.3-1.

[112] Specifically, ERISA § 3(2) defines a "pension plan" as "any plan, fund or program which . . . is established or maintained by an employer or by an employee organization or both, to the extent that by its express terms or as a result of surrounding circumstances such plan, fund or program provides retirement income to employees or results in a deferral of income by employees for periods extending to the termination of covered by employment or beyond, regardless of the method of calculating the contributions made to the plan, the method of calculating the benefits under plan or the method of distributing benefits from the plan."

The Department of Labor has issued a regulation clarifying the meaning of the term "pension plan." It identifies specific plans, funds, and programs, such as severance pay plans and individual retirement accounts, that do not constitute pension plans for purposes of ERISA. 29 C.F.R. § 2510.3-2.

[113] *Cf.* Fort Halifax Packing Co. v. Coyne, 482 U.S. 1, 8–9 (1987) ("Attention to purpose is particularly necessary in this case because the terms 'employee benefit plan' and 'plan' are defined only tautologically in the statute, each being described as 'an employee welfare benefit plan or employee pension benefit plan or a plan which is both an employee welfare benefit plan and an employee pension benefit plan.'"); Donovan v. Dillingham, 688 F.2d 1367 (11th Cir. 1982) ("Not so well defined are the first two prerequisites: 'plan, fund, or program' and 'established or maintained.' Commentators and courts define 'plan, fund, or program' by synonym — arrangement, scheme, unitary scheme, program of action, method of putting into effect an intention or proposal, design — but do not specify the prerequisites of a 'plan, fund, or program.' ").

[114] Massachusetts v. Morash, 490 U.S. 107 (1989); Fort Halifax Packing Co. v. Coyne, 482 U.S. 1 (1987).

Court decided these cases, the Court was interpreting ERISA's 514(a)'s "relate to" requirement in a very broad fashion.[115] Thus, the Court could, and did, cut back on ERISA 514(a)'s broad reach by interpreting "employee benefit plan" in a relatively narrow fashion in these cases.

In the first case, *Fort Halifax Packing Co. v. Coyne*,[116] the Court addressed the question whether ERISA § 514(a) preempted a Maine statute which required employers to provide a one-time severance payment to employees in the event of a plant closing. The Court held that ERISA § 514(a) did not preempt the statute because the statute neither established, nor required an employer to maintain, a welfare benefit "plan."[117] The Court looked at the purpose of ERISA preemption, to "eliminat[e] the threat of conflicting or inconsistent State and local regulation of employee benefit plans,"[118] and found that "Congress intended pre-emption to afford employers the advantages of a uniform set of regulations."[119] According to the Court, that concern only arises "with respect to benefits whose provision by nature requires an ongoing administrative program to meet the employer's obligation."[120] The Court held that because the Maine statute's "requirement of a one-time, lump-sum payment triggered by a single event require[d] no administrative scheme whatsoever to meet the employer's obligation,"[121] the statute neither established, nor required an employer to maintain, an employee benefit plan and was not preempted by ERISA § 514(a).

In the second case, *Massachusetts v. Morash*,[122] an employer was charged with criminal violations of a Massachusetts statute that required employers to pay discharged employees unused vacation time. The Court declared that "[i]n enacting ERISA, Congress' primary concern was with the mismanagement of funds accumulated to finance employee benefits and the failure to pay employee benefits from accumulated funds."[123] The Court found that the payment of ordinary vacation benefits out of the employer's general assets does not give rise to any of the risks that ERISA was intended to address.[124] Relying in part on a Department of Labor regulation that excludes from the definition of welfare plan "payroll practices," such as paying vacation benefits out of an employer's general assets rather than from a separate "trust fund,"[125] the Court held that the employer's policy of paying employees for unused vacation time did not constitute a welfare

---

[115] As discussed in the preceding section, the Court did not cut back on the breadth of the "relate to" requirement until its 1995 decision in *Travelers*.

[116] 482 U.S. 1 (1987).

[117] *Id.* at 6.

[118] *Id.* at 8, *quoting* Senator Williams, 120 Cong. Rec. 29933.

[119] *Id.* at 11.

[120] *Id.* at 11.

[121] *Id.* at 12.

[122] 490 U.S. 107 (1989).

[123] *Id.* at 115.

[124] *Id.*

[125] *Id.* at 117–18, *citing* 29 C.F.R. § 2510.3-1(b)(3).

benefit plan for purposes of ERISA preemption.[126] The Court noted that an "entirely different situation"[127] would be presented if a separate fund had been created to pay vacation benefits. In such a case, the separate fund would qualify as a welfare benefit plan and be subject to ERISA's reporting and disclosure requirements.[128]

In *California Division of Labor Standards Enforcement v. Dillingham,*[129] decided after the Court cut back on the breadth of the "relate to" requirement in *Travelers,* the Court reaffirmed *Massachusetts v. Morash.* Specifically, the Court in *Dillingham* found that an unfunded apprenticeship program was not an employee benefit plan for purposes of ERISA § 514(a).[130]

§ 8.05   ERISA § 514(b)(2)(A) SAVING CLAUSE

Section 514(b)(2)(A) of ERISA provides that "except as provided in [the 514(b)(2)(B) deemer clause], nothing in [ERISA] shall be construed to exempt or relieve any person from any law of any State which regulates insurance, banking or securities." Thus, if a state law regulates insurance, banking, or securities, the law will be "saved" from preemption under ERISA § 514(b)(2)(A) even though the law relates to an employee benefit plan within the meaning of ERISA's general preemption provision, ERISA § 514(a).

Whether a state law regulates banking or securities for purposes of the ERISA § 514(b)(2)(A) saving clause rarely arises.[131] Whether a state regulates insurance, on the other hand, is a frequently litigated issue.

ERISA does not define the term "regulates insurance" for purposes of the saving clause. The Supreme Court, however, has addressed the question whether a state law regulates insurance for purposes of the saving clause in five separate cases.[132]

[A]   Original Test Defining "Regulates Insurance"

The Court first addressed the question of whether a state law regulates insurance for purposes of the saving clause in *Metropolitan Life Insurance Company v. Massachusetts.*[133] That case involved a preemption challenge to a Massachusetts law that mandated that minimum mental health care benefits be

---

[126]   *Id.* at 114.

[127]   *Id.* at 120.

[128]   *Id. See also id.* at 114.

[129]   519 U.S. 316 (1996).

[130]   *Id.* at 325–28.

[131]   ABA Section of Labor and Employment Law, Employee Benefits Law, at 11-36.

[132]   *See* Kentucky Assoc. of Health Plans, Inc. v. Miller, 538 U.S. 329 (2003); Rush Prudential HMO, Inc. v. Moran, 536 U.S. 355 (2002); UNUM Life Ins. Co. v. Ward, 526 U.S. 358 (1999); Pilot Life Ins. Co. v. Dedeaux, 481 U.S. 41 (1987); Metropolitan Life Ins. Co. v. Mass., 471 U.S. 724 (1985). In a sixth case, FMC Corp. v. Holliday, 498 U.S. 52 (1990), the parties did not dispute that a Pennsylvania antisubrogation law fell within the insurance savings clause. Instead, the question was whether the deemer clause's exception to the savings clause applied.

[133]   471 U.S. 724 (1985).

provided to Massachusetts residents who were insured under a general insurance policy, an accident or sickness insurance policy, or an employee health care plan that covered hospital and surgical expenses.

The Court found that the state law at issue regulated insurance because it "regulate[d] the terms of certain insurance contracts."[134] The Court found that this "commonsense view of the matter" was reinforced by the deemer clause which states that an employee benefit plan shall not be deemed to be an insurance company for purposes of any law of state purporting to regulate, among other things, "insurance contracts."[135] In addition, the Court found that the case law interpreting the "business of insurance" for purposes of the McCarran Ferguson Act[136] also strongly supported the conclusion that the regulation fell within the meaning of "regulat[ing] insurance" for purposes of the saving clause.[137]

For almost 20 years, the Court generally applied the three factor McCarran-Ferguson test[138] to determine whether a state law regulates insurance for purposes of the saving clause.[139]

[B] Current Test Defining "Regulates Insurance"

In *Kentucky Association of Health Plans v. Miller*,[140] the Court made a "clean break"[141] from the McCarran-Ferguson factors and set forth a new two-prong test for determining whether a state law regulates insurance for purposes of the saving clause.

Under the *Miller* test, a state law regulates insurance if it: (1) is "specifically directed toward entities engaged in insurance"[142] and (2) "substantially affect[s] the risk pooling arrangement between the insurer and the insured."[143]

---

[134] *Id.* at 740.

[135] *Id.*

[136] Pub. L. No. 79-151, 59 Stat. 33, 34 (1945), codified at 15 U.S.C. §§ 1011–1015. Under the McCarran-Ferguson Act, Congress left regulation of the business of insurance to the states.

[137] 471 U.S. at 742–43.

[138] The three McCarran-Ferguson criteria are: (1) "whether the practice has the effect of transferring or spreading a policyholder's risk"; (2) whether the practice is an integral part of the policy relationship between the insurer and the insured"; and (3) "whether the practice is limited to entities within the insurance industry." 471 U.S. at 743.

[139] *See, e.g.*, Rush Prudential HMO, Inc. v. Moran, 536 U.S. 355, 373 (2002) (finding that McCarran-Ferguson factors confirmed conclusion that state law requiring HMOs to provide independent review regulated insurance where second and third McCarran-Ferguson factors clearly satisfied); UNUM Life Ins. Co. v. Ward, 526 U.S. 358, 374–75 (1999) (finding that California's notice-prejudice rule, which securely satisfied two of the three McCarran-Ferguson factors, regulated insurance); Pilot Life Ins. Co. v. Dedeaux, 481 U.S. 41, 50–51 (1987) (finding that common law of bad faith did not regulate insurance when law met at most one of the three McCarran-Ferguson factors).

[140] 538 U.S. 329 (2003).

[141] *Id.* at 341.

[142] *Id.* at 342.

[143] *Id.* at 342.

In *Miller*, several HMOs and a Kentucky-based HMO association challenged Kentucky's "Any Willing Provider" (AWP) statutes that (1) prohibited health insurers (including HMOs) from excluding any providers who were located within the geographic coverage area of the health benefit plan and were willing to meet the terms and conditions for participation, and (2) required health benefit plans with chiropractic benefits to permit any licensed chiropractor who agreed to abide by the terms and conditions of the plan to participate as a primary chiropractic provider.[144]

The Court found that the AWPs statutes satisfied both elements of the two-prong test and thus affirmed the Sixth Circuit's judgment that the Kentucky AWP statutes were saved by the ERISA § 514(b)(2)(A) saving clause.[145]

[1] First Prong of *Miller* Test — Specifically Directed Toward Entities Engaged in Insurance

With respect to the first prong of the *Miller* test, the HMOs argued that the AWP statutes were not "specifically directed toward" the insurance industry because not only did they regulate the insurance industry, but they also regulated doctors who sought to form limited provider networks with HMOs.[146] In rejecting this claim, the Court first noted that the statutes did not, by their express terms, impose any prohibitions or requirements on healthcare providers.[147] The Court then recognized that as a consequence of the AWP statutes, entities outside the insurance industry, including health care providers, would be unable to enter into certain agreements with Kentucky insurers.[148] The Court nevertheless concluded that "[r]egulations 'directed toward' certain entities will almost always disable other entities from doing, with the regulated entities, what the regulations forbid; this does not suffice to place such regulation outside the scope of ERISA's saving clause."[149]

---

[144] Most managed care organizations (including HMOs) oppose AWP statutes because they take away a powerful tool for containing health care costs. By selectively contracting with only certain doctors and other health care providers, the managed care organizations (MCOs) can force doctors and other providers to charge lower prices because the MCOs can guarantee a large quantity of business to the selected providers and the providers may worry that the MCOs will not contract with them at all if they do not offer lower prices. Russell Korobkin, *The Battle over Self-Insured Health Plans, or "One Good Loophole Deserves Another,* 5 Yale J. Health Pol'y & Ethics 89, 103 (2005).

[145] *Id.* at 342. For a discussion of the federal courts' application of the test, and an argument that the test should be read more broadly, see Beverly Cohen, *Saving the Savings Clause: Advocating a Broader Reading of the Miller Test to Enable States to Protect ERISA Health Plan Members by Regulating Insurance,* 18 Geo. Mason L. Rev. 125 (2010).

[146] *Id.* at 334.

[147] *Id.* at 335.

[148] *Id.*

[149] *Id.* at 335–36.

[2]   Second Prong of *Miller* Test — Substantially Affects the Risk Pooling Arrangement Between the Insurer and the Insured

With respect to the second prong of the *Miller* test, the Court held that the AWP statutes substantially affected the type of risk pooling arrangements that insurers could offer by increasing the number of health care providers from whom insured individuals could receive health services. "No longer may Kentucky insureds seek insurance from a closed network of health-care providers in exchange for a lower premium."[150]

§ 8.06   ERISA § 514(b)(2)(B) DEEMER CLAUSE

Section 514(b)(2)(B) of ERISA, the "deemer clause," provides that "neither an employee benefit plan . . . , nor any trust established under such a plan, shall be deemed to be an insurance company or other insurer, bank, trust company or investment company or to be engaged in the business of insurance or banking for purposes of any law of any State purporting to regulate insurance companies, insurance contracts, banks, trust companies, or investment companies."

[A]   Supreme Court's Interpretation of Deemer Clause

The Supreme Court has addressed the deemer clause in two cases. In the first insurance saving clause case, *Metropolitan Life Insurance Company v. Massachusetts*,[151] the Court noted in *dicta* that its decision results in a distinction between insured and uninsured plans with insured plans subject to indirect state insurance regulation while uninsured plans are free from such regulation.[152] In noting this distinction, the Court stated that it was "merely giv[ing] life to a distinction created by Congress in the deemer clause."[153]

In the second case, *FMC v. Holliday*,[154] the Court expressly applied the deemer clause to a self-funded employee benefit. The plan in that case contained a subrogation clause pursuant to which plan members agreed to reimburse the plan for benefits the plan paid if the members recovered on a claim in a liability action against a third party. A plan participant's daughter was seriously injured in an automobile accident, and the plan paid a portion of her medical expenses. The driver of the car in which the daughter was injured settled a suit brought against the driver, and the plan sought reimbursement under the subrogation clause for the amounts it had paid for the girl's medical expenses. The plan member argued that Pennsylvania's antisubrogation law prohibited the plan from enforcing the subrogation clause. The plan contended that ERISA preempted the Pennsylvania law.

---

[150] *Id.* at 339.

[151] 471 U.S. 724 (1985). *Metropolitan Life* is discussed in § 8.05[A].

[152] 471 U.S. at 747.

[153] *Id.*

[154] 498 U.S. 52 (1990).

The Court first found that the Pennsylvania antisubrogation law related to an employee benefit plan within the meaning of ERISA § 514(a)'s general preemption provision.[155] It then noted that the parties did not dispute that the law fell within the ERISA § 514(b)(2)(A) saving clause.[156] Finally, turning to the ERISA § 514(b)(2)(B) deemer clause, the Court announced, "We read the deemer clause to exempt self-funded ERISA plans from state laws that 'regulate insurance' within the meaning of the saving clause."[157] Thus, because the plan was self-funded, the antisubrogation law was not saved by the insurance saving clause but instead was preempted under ERISA's general preemption provision, ERISA § 514(a).

As in *Metropolitan Life*, the Court recognized that its decision created a dichotomy between insured and self-funded plans. Under its reading of the deemer clause, ERISA preempts state laws regulating insurance with respect to self-funded plans. Insured plans, in contrast, are subject to indirect state insurance regulation because the insurance companies that insure the employee benefit plans are subject to state insurance regulation.[158] Insured plans are "bound by state insurance regulations insofar as they apply to the plan's insurer."[159]

Justice Stevens, in dissent, criticized the Court for construing the statute to draw a "broad and illogical" distinction between self-funded and insured plans.[160] The Court, however, believed that its decision was consistent with both the plain language of the deemer clause as well Congress' intent.[161]

[B] Incentive to Self-Fund Under Deemer Clause and the Affordable Care Act

Together, the insurance saving and deemer clauses create an incentive for employers to self-fund or self-insure their employee health benefit plans. As discussed in Chapter 3, traditionally ERISA has provided little substantive regulation of employee health benefit plans. Instead, states have extensively regulated health insurance.[162] Thus, if an employer elected to self-fund its employee health benefit plan, the plan would be subject to little substantive regulation under ERISA. If, on the other hand, the employer purchased insurance, the plan would be indirectly subject to a multitude of state insurance mandates, such as a requirement to provide mental health care benefits,[163] as well as state

---

[155] *Id.* at 58–60.

[156] *Id.* at 60–61.

[157] *Id.* at 61.

[158] *Id.*

[159] *Id.*

[160] *Id.* at 65 (Stevens, J., dissenting). For an argument that the distinction between insured and self-funded plans is logically defensible, see Russell Korobkin, 5 YALE J. HEALTH POL'Y, L. & ETHICS, at 89.

[161] *Id.* at 63–65.

[162] *See id.* at 97 (noting that according to one researcher the number of state health insurance mandates rose from almost none in 1970 to 850 in 1991).

[163] State insurance mandates, like the law at issue in *Metropolitan Life*, require that the insurer provide specific benefits, such as mental health or in vitro fertilization benefits.

insurance policy regulations..[164]

The Affordable Care Act[165] (ACA) does not eliminate the incentive for employers to self-fund their health plan. Rather, the ACA itself may encourage some small firms to self-fund rather than purchase insurance from (or outside of) the ACA's Health Insurance Exchanges.[166]

[C] Role of Stop-Loss Insurance in Self-Funded Plans

While the insurance saving and deemer clauses (and the ACA) may encourage employers to self-fund their employee health benefit plans, it is stop-loss insurance that often actually permits employers, particularly smaller employers, to self-fund. Stop-loss insurance is discussed in Chapter 3 § 3.03[D][5].

The Supreme Court has never addressed the question whether the purchase of stop-loss insurance causes self-funded plans to lose their status as self-funded plans under the deemer clause. Most lower courts, however, have held that self-funded plans do not lose their status as self-insured simply because they purchase stop-loss insurance.[167] A few courts have suggested that a plan may lose its self-insured status if the stop-loss insurance has a low enough attachment point.[168]

[D] Prevalence of Self-Funded Plans

In light of the availability of stop-loss insurance, and the incentives created by the saving and deemer clauses and the Affordable Care Act, it is perhaps not surprising that more than half of private sector employees with employment-based health insurance are covered by a self-funded employee health benefit plan.[169] Many, though not all, of the self-funded plans have stop-loss insurance.[170]

---

[164] State insurance policy regulations include laws like the antisubrogration law at issue in *FMC* and the AWP statute at issue in *Miller*.

[165] Pub. L. No. 111-148, Stat. 119 (2010), as amended by Pub. L. No. 111-152, 124 Stat. 1029 (2010). The Affordable Care Act is discussed in Chapter 3 § 3.06.

[166] *See* Timothy Stoltzfus Jost, *Loopholes in the Affordable Care Act: Regulatory Gaps and Border Crossing Techniques and How to Address Them*, 5 SAINT LOUIS U. J. OF HEALTH LAW & POLICY 27, 76–81 (2011) (explaining why small employers may choose to self-fund and why that would threaten the health insurance exchanges and ACA in general). *See also* Chapter 3 § 3.06[c] (noting that some market reform provisions do not apply to self-funded plans).

[167] *See, e.g.*, Bill Gray Enters. v. Gourley, 248 F.3d 206, 209 (3d Cir. 2001); Thompson v. Talquin Bldg. Prods. Co., 928 F.2d 649, 653 (4th Cir. 1991); Lincoln Mut. Cas. Co. v. Lectron Prods., Inc., 970 F.2d 206, 210 (6th Cir. 1992); United Food & Commercial Workers v. Pacyga, 801 F.2d 1157, 1161 (9th Cir. 1986).

[168] Brown v. Granatelli, 897 F.2d 1351, 1354 (5th Cir. 1990); Bricklayers Local No. 1 Welfare Fund v. La. Health Ins. Ass'n, 771 F. Supp. 771, 774 (E.D. La. 1991); Associated Indus. v. Angoff, 937 S.W.2d 277, 283 (Mo. Ct. App. 1996). For a discussion and critique of the stop-loss cases, see Korobkin, 5 YALE J. HEALTH POL'Y, L. & ETHICS, at 112–15.

[169] *See* Kaiser Family Foundation and Health Research & Educational Trust, *Employer Health Benefits: 2014 Annual Survey*, Exhibit 10.1, at 174, *available at* http://ehbs.kff.org/pdf/2014/8225.pdf; Bernadette Fernandez, *Self-Insured Health Insurance Coverage*, CRS Report R41069, at 4 (2010).

[170] For data on self-funded plans with and without stop-loss insurance, see Hilda L. Solis, Secretary of Labor, *Annual Report to Congress on Self-Insured Group Health Plans* (Apr. 2012); Kaiser Family Foundation, *2014 Employer Health Benefits Annual Survey*, Exhibit 10.10, at 182.

Chapter 9

NONDISCRIMINATION RULES FOR QUALIFIED PLANS

§ 9.01 INTRODUCTION

In order to qualify for favorable income tax treatment, a qualified pension plan must not discriminate in favor of highly compensated employees[1] with respect to coverage,[2] amount of benefits,[3] and availability of benefits.[4] The nondiscrimination rules are solely tax requirements. They are not required by ERISA. If an employer is willing to forego the very substantial advantages of favorable income tax treatment,[5] the employer need not worry about the nondiscrimination requirements.

At their core, the nondiscrimination requirements are quite simple. They are designed to ensure that qualified plans give nonhighly compensated employees benefits that are roughly proportional to the benefits received by highly compensated employees. In addition, they can be quite simple to satisfy: if an employer establishes a single plan that covers all of its employees and provides all of its employees with identical benefits, the plan will satisfy the nondiscrimination rules.

Although the nondiscrimination requirements are quite simple in concept, they can, in fact, be exceedingly complex in application. This complexity arises in large part from the fact that the nondiscrimination requirements permit a limited amount of discrimination in favor of highly compensated employees. Plans are not required to cover all of an employer's employees, and all of an employer's employees need not receive identical benefits. This flexibility can lead to extraordinary complexity as employers try to maximize the benefits they provide to highly compensated employees while minimizing the benefits they provide to nonhighly compensated employees.

A second factor leading to the complexity in the rules is the complex nature of the corporate world today. A corporate entity can consist of a multiple separate corporations, and the separate corporations can all be engaged in a similar line of business or they may be engaged in a number of fundamentally different lines of business that compete in different markets. For example, General Electric owns

---

[1] The term "highly compensated" is defined in IRC § 414(q). *See* § 9.05 for a discussion of HCEs.

[2] IRC § 401(a)(3) (requiring qualified plan to satisfy the participation and coverage requirements of IRC § 410). *See* § 9.07 (discussing IRC § 410(b) coverage requirements).

[3] IRC § 401(a)(4). *See* § 9.08.

[4] *Id.*

[5] For a discussion of the tax advantages of qualified plans, see Chapter 2 § 2.04[B].

multiple subsidiaries that are involved in a wide variety of businesses and services ranging from the production of aircraft engines to washers and dryers, from commercial lending to healthcare products and services to mining.[6] This complexity can make it difficult to identify the relevant "employer" for purposes of the nondiscrimination requirements.

§ 9.02 PURPOSE OF THE NONDISCRIMINATION RULES

Based on the legislative history of the nondiscrimination rules, it appears that Congress' principal purpose in enacting the rules was to prevent tax avoidance.[7] Now, however, they are commonly viewed as a means of encouraging employers to provide retirement benefits to the lower paid as well as the highly compensated.[8] Indeed, the nondiscrimination rules have been described as a "stick" that forces employers to offer retirement benefits to nonhighly compensated employees while the favorable income tax treatment accorded to retirement plans is a "carrot" to entice employers to offer plans in the first place.[9]

The nondiscrimination rules have been the subject of considerable criticism. Indeed, a number of commentators have argued that the current system of voluntary retirement benefits should be replaced with mandatory pensions.[10] Despite the criticism, the nondiscrimination rules are unlikely to be repealed. They have been part of the "qualified plan paradigm" for more than 70 years.[11]

---

[6] For an overview of GE's products, see http://www.ge.com/products.

[7] *See* Madeline Lewis, *The Legislative History of the Nondiscrimination Provision of Qualified Retirement Plans*, 2014 N.Y.U. REV. OF EMP. BENEFITS AND EXEC. COMP. 7-1, 7-11–7-26; Joseph Bankman, *Tax Policy and Retirement Income: Are Pension Plan Anti-Discrimination Provisions Desirable?*, 55 U. CHI. L. REV. 790, 800–01 (1988).

[8] *See e.g.*, Joint Committee on Tax'n, *Present Law and Background Relating to the Tax Treatment of Retirement Savings*, JCX-44-11, at 22 (Sept. 13, 2011) (stating that "[t]he nondiscrimination require- ments are designed to help ensure that qualified retirement plans achieve the goal of retirement security for both lower and higher paid employees"). *See also* Daniel I. Halperin, *Special Tax Treatment for Employer-Based Retirement Programs: Is It "Still" Viable as a Means of Increasing Retirement Income? Should It Continue?*, 49 TAX L. REV. 1, 7 (1993); Peter J. Wiedenbeck, *Nondiscrimination in Employee Benefits: False Starts and Future Trends*, 52 TENN. L. REV. 167, 174 (1985); Bruce Wolk, *Discrimination Rules for Qualified Retirement Plans: Good Intentions Confront Economic Reality*, 70 VA. L. REV. 419, 420 (1984); Dana M. Muir, *From Yuppies to Guppies: Unfunded Mandates and Benefit Plan Regulation*, 34 Ga. L. Rev. 195, 232 (1999); Daniel Fischel & John H. Langbein, *ERISA's Fundamental Contradiction: The Exclusive Benefit Rule*, 55 U. CHI. L. REV. 1105, 1122–23 (1988).

[9] *See* Norman P. Stein and Patricia Dilley, *Leverage, Linkage, and Leakage: Problems with the Private Pension System and How They Should Inform the Social Security Reform Debate*, 58 Wash. and Lee L. Rev. 1369, 1375 (2001); Halperin, 49 TAX L. REV., at 7 (1993).

[10] *See, e.g.*, Halperin, 49 TAX L. REV., at 44–46; Bankman, 55 U. CHI. L. REV. 790 (1988).

[11] *See* Norman P. Stein, *Of Carrots and Sticks: The Paring Down of the Qualified-Plan Paradigm*, ALI-ABA COURSE OF STUDY: PENSION POLICY CONFERENCE AFTER 25 YEARS (1999) (stating that favorable tax treatment of qualified plans accompanied by nondiscrimination rules "has been the qualified-plan paradigm since the early 1940s"). *See also* Revenue Act of 1942 § 161, Pub. L. No. 77-753, 56 Stat. 798, 861 (1942) (enacting original nondiscrimination requirements).

§ 9.03   BROAD OVERVIEW OF THE NONDISCRIMINATION RULES

The nondiscrimination rules applicable to qualified plan are among the most complex and technical rules in all of tax law. This chapter does not provide a comprehensive discussion of the rules in all of their complexity. Rather, it provides a general overview of the rules. Even a general overview, however, is necessarily complex.

This section provides a broad overview of the rules and the steps that must be taken in applying the rules. The remainder of this chapter discusses the rules and their application in more detail.

[A]   Three Nondiscrimination Requirements

The Internal Revenue Code imposes three separate nondiscrimination requirements on qualified plans:

   (1)   the IRC § 401(a)(26) minimum participation requirement,

   (2)   the IRC § 410(b) minimum coverage requirement, and

   (3)   the IRC § 401(a)(4) nondiscrimination in contribution and benefits requirement.

[1]   Overview of IRC § 401(a)(26) Minimum Participation Requirement

The IRC § 401(a)(26) minimum participation requirement only applies to defined benefit plans. It is the easiest and most straightforward of the nondiscrimination requirements. As a general rule, it requires that every defined benefit plan benefit at least the lesser of 50 employees or 40% of all of the employees of the employer. A special rule applies to employers with fewer than five employees.

[2]   Overview of IRC § 410(b) Minimum Coverage Requirement

Section 401(a)(3) of the Internal Revenue Code requires that all qualified plans satisfy the requirements of IRC § 410. Section 410(b) of the Internal Revenue Code, in turn, requires that all qualified plans satisfy one of three alternative minimum coverage tests:

   (1)   a percentage test,

   (2)   a ratio percentage test, or

   (3)   an average benefit percentage test.

The percentage test is the most straightforward test. If a plan benefits at least 70% of the employer's nonhighly compensated workforce, the plan satisfies the percentage test. The percentage test is also the most difficult to satisfy. The second, ratio percentage test compares the percentage of nonhighly compensated employees (NHCEs) benefitting under the plan relative to the percentage of highly compensated employees (HCEs) benefitting under the plan. If the ratio percentage is at least 70%, the plan satisfies the ratio percentage test. The third, average benefit percentage test is the most complex of the three tests. It also provides employers with the most flexibility. The average benefits percentage test takes into account a variety of factors, such as the percentage of the employer's workforce that is nonhighly compensated and the specific benefits individual employees receive under the plan.

[3]   Overview of IRC § 401(a)(4) Nondiscrimination Requirement

Section 401(a)(4) of the Internal Revenue Codes requires that the contributions or benefits provided under a plan not discriminate in favor of HCEs in order to be eligible for favorable income tax treatment. The Treasury Department has issued lengthy regulations which provide the sole means for determining whether a plan satisfies this requirement.

The Treasury Regulations set forth three basic requirements:

(1)   a core "amounts rule," which requires that the amount of contributions or benefits not discriminate in favor of HCEs,

(2)   a requirement that other benefits, rights, and features not discriminate in favor of HCEs, and

(3)   a requirement that a plan not discriminate in favor of HCEs in special circumstances, such as plan amendments, including grants of past service credit, and plan terminations.

A plan may satisfy the core amounts rule by falling within one of the safe harbors set forth in the regulations. If the plan does not fall within a safe harbor, it is then subject to general testing, which divides the plan into rate groups and tests each rate group to see if it satisfies a slightly modified version of IRC § 410(b). If the plan fails to satisfy the general test, then flexibility features may be applied and the plan retested.

If an employer establishes a single plan that provides identical benefits for all employees, the plan will easily satisfy the IRC § 401(a)(4) amounts rule. On the other hand, if the employer wants to set up a number of different plans and provide different benefits to different employees, the plan may or may not satisfy the IRC § 401(a)(4) amounts rule — depending on the particular facts. The price the employer pays for flexibility and the ability to provide different benefits to different workers is complex testing.

The requirement that other benefits, rights, and features not discriminate focuses on optional benefit forms, such as retirement annuities and lump sum payments, ancillary benefits, such as disability benefits, and other rights and features, such as plan loans and investment options.

The final, special circumstances requirement ensures that plans are not amended in a way that appears facially neutral but actually discriminates in favor of HCEs in light of the composition of the workforce at the time the amendment takes effect.

[4]   Summary of the Three Nondiscrimination Requirements

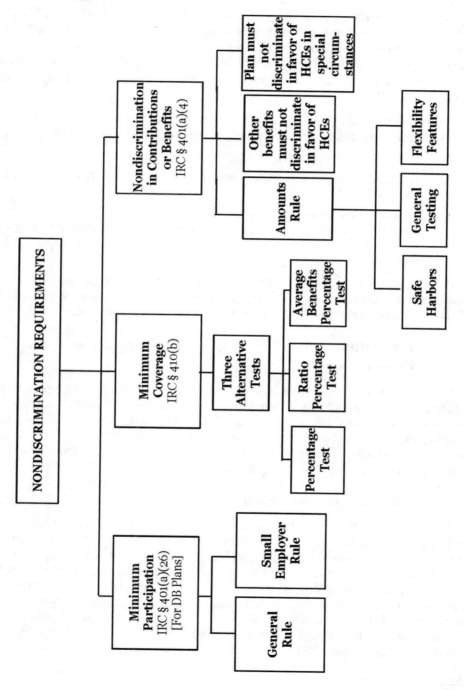

[5]   Special IRC § 401(a)(4) Amounts Rule for 401(k) Plans

A plan will be deemed to satisfy the IRC § 401(a)(4) amounts rule if it satisfies one of two alternative special nondiscrimination requirements set forth in IRC § 401(k)(3)(A)(ii). In essence, the two tests compare the percentage of income HCEs have elected to set aside in the 401(k) plan with the percentage of income NHCEs have elected to set aside. In order to satisfy the tests, the percentage of income set aside by HCEs must not be too much greater than the percentage of income set aside by the NHCEs.

If a plan fails to satisfy one of the two alternative special nondiscrimination tests, it will be disqualified unless it is corrected in one of three different ways:

(1)   by returning the excess contributions to the HCEs,

(2)   by recharacterizing the HCEs' excess contributions as after-tax contributions, or

(3)   by the employer making certain nonelective contributions to the plan. (Nonelective contributions are contributions made by the employer regardless of how much or even whether the employee elects to contribute to the plan.)

If the employer wishes to avoid the cost of testing and potentially correcting the plan each year, the employer may structure its plan so as to satisfy one of two sets of statutory safe harbors set forth in IRC §§ 401(k)(12) and 401(k)(13).

[B]   Preliminary Steps in Applying the Nondiscrimination Requirements

Before the nondiscrimination rules can be applied, a number of preliminary issues must be resolved. First, because the nondiscrimination rules apply on an employer-wide basis, the employer must be identified. Second, because the nondiscrimination rules prohibit discrimination in favor of HCEs, the HCEs must be identified. Finally, because the nondiscrimination rules mandate that a qualified plan not discriminate in favor of HCEs, the plan must be identified.

[1]   Identifying the Employer

Prior to the enactment of ERISA, the nondiscrimination rules applied separately with respect to each entity. Thus, an employer could circumvent the rules by structuring its business so that all of its HCEs were employed in a single, separate subsidiary and provide retirement benefits only to employees in that subsidiary. In enacting ERISA, Congress added sections 414(b) and 414(c) to the Internal Revenue Code in order to prevent employers from circumventing the nondiscrimination rules in this fashion.[12] These provisions require that "employers under common control" be aggregated, that is, combined, for purposes of applying the nondiscrimination rules.

---

[12]   *See* Garland v. Commissioner, 73 T.C. 5, 12 (1979) (quoting committee report's explanation for enacting IRC §§ 414(b) and (c)).

Sections 414(b) and 414(c) are straightforward objective tests for determining whether employers are under common control. Following the enactment of these provisions, creative taxpayers found new ways to restructure their businesses to get around the common control rules and thus avoid the nondiscrimination requirements. As a result, Congress enacted much more technical provisions, IRC §§ 414(m) and (n), to address the specific maneuvers employers had engaged in to get around IRC §§ 414(b) and (c). Finally, Congress enacted IRC § 414(o) to provide the Treasury Department with broader powers to address taxpayers' creative techniques of avoiding the nondiscrimination rules.

Separate and apart from IRC §§ 414(b), (c), (m), (n), and (o), which expand the definition of employer to address taxpayers' creative tax avoidance strategies, section 414(r) cuts back on the definition of employer to permit employers with genuinely separate lines of business to apply the nondiscrimination rules separately to each qualified separate line of business.

[2]   Identifying the Highly Compensated Employees

Section 414(q) of the Internal Revenue Code sets forth an objective, straightforward test to determine who is a highly compensated employee (HCE). It defines HCEs with respect to (1) ownership in the employer and (2) compensation. Generally, an individual is an HCE if the individual owns 5% or more of the employer and/or the individual earns in excess of $120,000 in 2015. IRC § 414(q) offers employers the opportunity to elect the limit the number of their HCEs based on compensation to the "top-paid group."

[3]   Identifying the Plan

The nondiscrimination rules require that a qualified "plan" not discriminate in coverage or in the provision of contributions or benefits. Thus, the final preliminary issue that must be resolved before applying the nondiscrimination requirements is identification of the "plan."

The Treasury regulations set forth detailed rules defining the term "plan" for purposes of the nondiscrimination requirements.[13] The regulations require that certain types of plans be disaggregated and tested separately. For example, the portion of a plan that is a 401(k) plan and the portion that is not a 401(k) plan must be treated as separate plans.[14] In addition, in some circumstances, the regulations permit employers to aggregate or combine two or more plans and treat the aggregated plans as a single plan for purposes of the nondiscrimination requirements.[15]

Typically, an employer will elect to aggregate plans when one plan, viewed alone, does not satisfy the nondiscrimination rules. If plans are aggregated for purposes of the IRC § 410(b) minimum coverage rules, however, they must also be aggregated for purposes of the IRC § 401(a)(4) nondiscrimination in contributions and

---

[13]   Treas. Reg. § 1.410(b)-7.

[14]   Treas. Reg. § 1.410(b)-7(c)(1).

[15]   Treas. Reg. § 1.410(b)-7(d).

benefits requirement.[16] Similarly, if plans are aggregated for purposes of the IRC § 401(a)(4) nondiscrimination in contributions and benefits requirement, they must also be aggregated for purposes of the IRC § 410(b) minimum coverage rules.[17]

If the plans being aggregated are all defined contribution plans, it is easy to determine the amount of contributions under the plan. Similarly, if all of the plans being aggregated are defined benefit plans, it is easy to determine the amount of benefits under the plan. If, however, the aggregated plans include both defined contribution plans and defined benefit plans, the contributions and benefits must be equated. The Treasury regulations provide a mechanism, called cross-testing, to do this.[18] Under the complex cross-testing rules, the amounts allocated to employees under a defined contribution plan are converted to equivalent benefits or the amounts accrued for employees under a defined benefit plan are converted to equivalent contributions.[19]

§ 9.04   A CLOSER LOOK AT EMPLOYERS

The nondiscrimination rules apply on an employer-wide basis. Thus, the employer must be identified before the nondiscrimination rules can be applied.

The Internal Revenue Code addresses the meaning of employer for purposes of the nondiscrimination rules in six different sections. Five of those section, IRC § 414(b), (c), (m), (n), and (o), expand the definition of employer. One section, IRC § 414(r), cuts back on the definition of employer.

---

[16] Treas. Reg. § 1.401(a)(4)-9(a); Treas. Reg. § 1.410(b)-7(d)(1).

[17] Treas. Reg. § 1.401(a)(4)-9(a); Treas. Reg. § 1.410(b)-7(d)(1).

[18] Treas. Reg. § 1.410(b)-8.

[19] For a discussion of the development of comparability testing, see Michael W. Melton, *Making the Nondiscrimination Rules of Tax-Qualified Retirement Plans More Effective*, 71 B.U. L. Rev. 47, 84–88 (1991).

[A]   Overview of Employer Rules

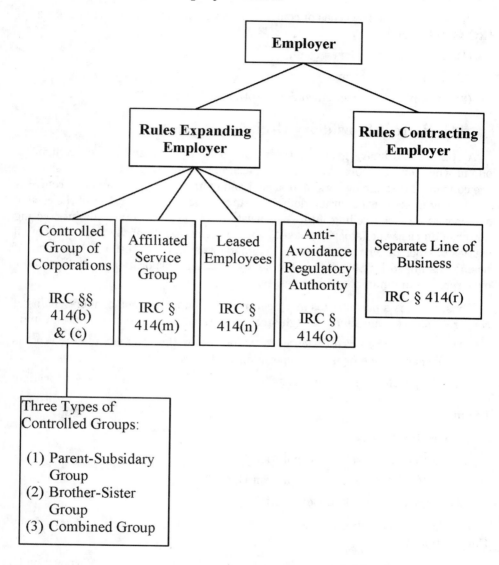

[B]   IRC §§ 414(b) and (c) Employers under Common Control

Section 414(b) of the Internal Revenue Code provides that employees of corporations who are members of a controlled group of corporations, as generally defined in IRC § 1563, will be treated as if employed by a single employer. Section 414(c) of the Internal Revenue Code establishes similar rules for employees of unincorporated trades or businesses under common control.[20]

There are three basic types of controlled groups of corporations for purposes of IRC §§ 414(b) and (c):

(1)   a parent-subsidiary group,

(2)   a brother-sister group, and

(3)   a combined parent-subsidiary/brother-sister group.[21]

[1]   Parent-Subsidiary Group

A "parent-subsidiary group of trades or businesses under common control" is one in which one or more chains of organizations conducting trades or businesses are connected through ownership of a controlling interest by a common parent.[22] A controlling interest is generally defined as an 80% or more interest.[23] In the case of a corporation, a controlling interest consists of 80% of the total combined voting power of all classes of stock entitled to vote, or at least 80% of the total value of all classes of stock of the corporation.[24] Common ownership can result from a chain of businesses linked by 80% ownership, or by a parent corporation with direct 80% ownership in any number of businesses.

Thus, there is a parent-subsidiary controlled group when one or more chains of corporations are connected through stock ownership with a common parent, and

(1)   80% of the stock of each corporation (other than the common parent) is owned by one or more corporation in the group; and

(2)   the parent corporation owns 80% or more of at least one other corporation.

Example 1

Corporation A owns

90% of the stock of Corporation B,

80% of the stock of Corporation C, and

50% of the stock of Corporation D.

Unrelated corporations own the remaining shares of stock not owned by Corporation A.

Because Corporation A owns 80% or more of Corporation B and Corporation C, Corporation A is the parent corporation of a parent-subsidiary group consisting of Corporations A, B, and C. Corporation D is not part of the parent-subsidiary group because Corporation A owns less than 80% of Corporation D.

---

[20]   For a discussion of the reasons why Congress enacted the controlled group rules, see § 9.03[B][1].

[21]   Treas. Reg. § 1.414(c)-2(a).

[22]   Treas. Reg. § 1.414(c)-2(b)(1).

[23]   Treas. Reg. § 1.414(c)-2(c)(1).

[24]   Treas. Reg. § 1.414(c)-2(c)(1)(A).

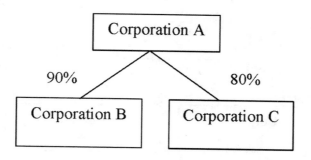

Example 2

Corporation E owns

    90% of the stock of Corporation F, and

    80% of the stock of Corporation G, and

Corporation F owns

    90% of the stock of Corporation H, and

Corporation H owns

    80% of the stock of Corporation I.

The five corporations are members of a parent-subsidiary group.

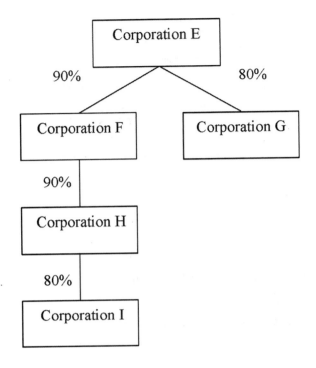

[2] Brother-Sister Group

A "brother-sister group of trades or businesses under common control"[25] consists of two or more trades or businesses which satisfy two requirements:

(1) the same five or fewer persons who are individuals, estates, or trusts, own a controlling interest in each organization,[26] and

(2) taking into account the ownership of each such person only to the extent that it is identical with respect to each such organization, such five or fewer persons are in "effective control of the organization.[27]

As discussed above, "controlling interest" generally means 80% or more ownership of the stock of each corporation (but only if each common owner owns stock in each corporation).

---

[25] In 2004, Congress amended IRC §1563(a) to eliminate the effective control requirement. Pub. L. No. 108-357 § 900(a), 118 Stat. 1418, 1650 (2004). The legislative history, however, makes clear that the amendment is not intended to apply to IRC §§ 414(b) and (c), H.R. Rep. No. 108-548, at 773 (2004) (Conf. Rep.), 2004 U.S.C.A.A.N. 1341, 1811, and the Treasury regulations continue to require effective control for a brother-sister controlled group, Treas. Reg. § 1.414(c)-2(c)(1).

[26] Treas. Reg. § 1.414(c)-2(c)(1).

[27] Treas. Reg. § 1.414(c)-2(c)(1).

"Effective control" is more than 50% interest or ownership.[28]

Example 1

Corporation A and Corporation B are owned by five shareholders in the following percentages:

Shareholder	Percentage of Ownership of Corporation A	Percentage of Ownership of Corporation B
A	20	25
B	30	10
C	10	20
D	20	30
E	20	15
Total	100	100

The controlling interest requirement is satisfied because the same five or fewer persons (A, B, C, D, and E) together own 80% or more of the stock of each corporation (specifically 100%).

The effective control requirement is satisfied because the same five or fewer common owners own more than 50% of each corporation (specifically 75%), taking into account the stock ownership of each person to the extent that the stock ownership is identical with respect to each corporation.

Shareholder	Percentage of Ownership of Corporation A	Percentage of Ownership of Corporation B	Effective Control Ownership
A	20	25	20
B	30	10	10
C	10	20	10
D	20	30	20
E	20	15	15
Total	100	100	75

Thus, Corporation A and Corporation B are members of a brother-sister controlled group of corporations.

Example 2

Corporation C and Corporation D are owned by three shareholders in the following percentages:

Shareholder	Percentage of Ownership of Corporation C	Percentage of Ownership of Corporation D
F	80	20
G	10	70

---

[28] Treas. Reg. § 1.414(c)-2(c)(2).

Shareholder	Percentage of Ownership of Corporation C	Percentage of Ownership of Corporation D
H	10	10
Total	100	100

The controlling interest requirement is satisfied because the same five or fewer persons (F, G, and H) together own 80% or more of the stock of each corporation (specifically 100%).

The effective control requirement, however, is not satisfied because the same five or fewer common owners own less than 50% of each corporation (specifically 40%), taking into account the stock ownership of each person to the extent that the stock ownership is identical with respect to each corporation.

Shareholder	Percentage of Ownership of Corporation C	Percentage of Ownership of Corporation D	Effective Control Ownership
F	80	20	20
G	10	70	10
H	10	10	10
Total	100	100	40

Thus, Corporation C and Corporation D are not members of a brother-sister controlled group of corporations.

Example 3

Corporation E, Corporation F, and Corporation G are owned by four shareholders in the following percentages:

Shareholder	Percentage of Ownership of Corporation E	Percentage of Ownership of Corporation F	Percentage of Ownership of Corporation G
I	35	10	30
J	25	30	15
K	40	40	20
L	0	20	35

To meet the controlling interest requirement, the same five or fewer common owners must own 80% or more of stock (or other interest) in all members of the controlled group. Each common owner must have some interest in each corporation in order to be taken into account.

Because L has no interest in Corporation E, only the ownership interests of I, J, and K may be taken into account in determining whether Corporation E, Corporation F, and Corporation G are a brother-sister controlled group of corporations. Thus, for purposes of determining whether the controlling interest is satisfied, I, J, and K hold ownership as follows:

Shareholder	Percentage of Ownership of Corporation E	Percentage of Ownership of Corporation F	Percentage of Ownership of Corporation G
I	35	10	30
J	25	30	15
K	40	40	20
Total	100	80	65

The controlling interest is not satisfied with respect to the three corporations because the three shareholders, I, J, and K, do not own 80% or more of all three corporations.

The controlling interest is, however, satisfied with respect to Corporation E and Corporation F because the three shareholders, I, J, and K, together own at least 80% of Corporation E and Corporation F. In addition, the effective control requirement is satisfied with respect to Corporation E and Corporation F because the same five or fewer owners (I, J, and K) own more than 50% (specifically 65%) of each corporation, taking into account the stock ownership of each person to the extent that the stock ownership is identical with respect to each corporation.

Shareholder	Percentage of Ownership of Corporation E	Percentage of Ownership of Corporation F	Effective Control Ownership
I	35	10	10
J	25	30	25
K	40	40	40
Total	100	80	75

Thus, Corporation E and Corporation F are members of a brother-sister controlled group of corporation.

In addition, Corporation F and Corporation G are members of a separate brother-sister group of trades or businesses under common control because (1) the same five or fewer persons (I, J, K, and L) own a controlling interest, that is at least 80% (in this case 100%) of Corporation F and Corporation G, and (2) taking into account the ownership of each such person only to the extent that it is identical with respect to each such organization, I, J, K, and L have effective control, that is more than a 50% ownership (65% in this case) of Corporation F and Corporation G.

Shareholder	Percentage of Ownership of Corporation F	Percentage of Ownership of Corporation G	Effective Control Ownership
I	10	30	10
J	30	15	15
K	40	20	20
L	20	35	20
Total	100	100	65

Because Corporation F is a member of two different controlled groups, both groups must be taken into account when testing Corporation F's plan to determine whether it satisfies the nondiscrimination requirements.[29]

[3] Combined Group

A "combined group of trades or businesses under common control" is a group of three or more organizations in which

(1) each organization is a member of either a parent-subsidiary group of trades or businesses under common control or a brother-sister group of trades or businesses under common control, and

(2) at least one organization is the common parent organization of a parent-subsidiary group of trades or businesses under common control and is also a member of a brother-sister group of trades or businesses under common control.[30]

Example

B and C each own

50% of Company D, and

50% of Company E.

Company D owns 100% of Corporation F.

Company D, Company E, and Corporation F are members of a combined group of trades or businesses under common control because

Company D is

the common parent of a parent-subsidiary group of trades or businesses under common control consisting of Company D and Corporation F, and

Company D is also a member of a brother-sister group of trades or businesses under common control consisting of Company D and Company E.

[4] Advantages and Limits of IRC §§ 414(b) and (c) Controlled Group Definition

IRC §§ 414(b) and (c) set forth a straightforward, objective test for determining whether a group of corporations or other affiliated entities constitutes a "controlled group of corporations."

The advantage of the test is that it provides a clear and certain rule that assists taxpayers in planning.[31] Employers know, in advance, which employees they must

---

[29] Treas. Reg. § 1.414(b)-1(a) ("For purposes of this section, if a corporation is a member of more than one controlled group of corporations, such corporation shall be treated as a member of each controlled group.").

[30] Treas. Reg. § 1.414(c)-2(d).

[31] For a discussion of the advantages and disadvantages of certain tax rules, see, for example, Emily

take into account in determining whether their pension plan satisfies the nondiscrimination requirements and thus qualifies for favorable income tax treatment.

The disadvantage of the clear, objective rule is that it permits employers to structure their businesses so as to comply with the letter, but not the spirit, of the controlled group requirements.[32]

[C]　Affiliated Service Groups

Following the enactment of the IRC §§ 414(c) and (d) controlled group rules, employers sought to get around the controlled group rules and thus circumvent the nondiscrimination requirements by placing their support staff into a separate entity from their professionals.

Garland v. Commissioner,[33] a Tax Court case decided in 1979, illustrates how employers structured their businesses so as to avoid the controlled group requirements. In 1980, Congress enacted the IRC § 414(m) affiliated service group rules to circumvent that strategy for avoiding the nondiscrimination rules.

[1]　*Garland v. Commissioner*

In *Garland,* Dr. Garland had practiced medicine in a partnership with another doctor, Dr. Dunn. He and Dr. Dunn then dissolved their partnership and formed a new partnership known as the Neurosurgical Unit, in which each partner owned a 50% interest in the profits. In addition, Dr. Garland formed a separate professional association (Association) in which he was the sole employee and shareholder. The Association adopted a pension plan which initially made contributions on behalf of Dr. Garland and the employees of the Neurosurgical Unit. The plan was then amended to cover only Dr. Garland. The Association sought a determination from the IRS that the exclusion of the Neurosurgical Unit employees would not adversely affect the pension plan's qualified status.[34]

There was no dispute that the Association and Neurosurgical Unit were not a controlled group of corporations under IRC § 414(c).[35] The Association and Neurosurgical Unit were not a parent-subsidiary group because the Association only owned a 50% interest in the Neurosurgical Unit, less than the 80% interest required for controlling interest. In addition, the Association and Neurosurgical Unit were not members of a brother-sister group. Because Dr. Dunn did not have any ownership interest in the Association, his ownership interest was disregarded, and Dr. Garland's 50% ownership interest in the Association met neither the 80%

Cauble, *Safe Harbors in Tax Law,* 47 CONN. L. REV. (forthcoming 2015) (Manuscript at 19–23), *available at* http://ssrn.com/abstract=2318438.

[32] For discussions of how taxpayers and their advisors use clear rules as a guide for arranging transactions that comply with the letter, but not the spirit, of the rules, see authorities cited in *id.* (Manuscript at 20).

[33] 73 T.C. 5 (1979).

[34] *Id.* at 6–7.

[35] *Id.* at 9.

controlling interest nor the more than 50% effective control requirement.[36]

The court held that the objective rules set forth in IRC §§ 414(b) and 414(c) were the exclusive test for determining whether affiliated organizations must be combined for purposes of applying the nondiscrimination requirements.[37] Because the Association and Neurosurgical Unit were not required to be combined under those provisions, the tax court held that the employees of the Neurological Unit did not need to be taken into account in determining whether the Association's pension plan was qualified and thus, Dr. Garland, a highly compensated individual, could be the sole beneficiary of the Association's qualified pension plan without running afoul of the nondiscrimination requirements.[38]

[2] IRC § 414(m) Affiliated Service Groups

In light of the tax court's decisions in *Garland* and *Kiddie*,[39] a case cited and reaffirmed in *Garland* and involving similar facts, many professionals avoided the nondiscrimination rules by placing their professionals and support staff into separate entities.[40] In 1980, Congress enacted the IRC § 414(m)[41] affiliated service group rules to prevent this method of circumventing the nondiscrimination requirements.[42]

Section 414(m) does not require that employers include all employees of an affiliated service group in the group's qualified plans. Rather, it requires that all of the employees of the affiliated service group be taken into account in determining whether any plan of the affiliated service group satisfies the nondiscrimination requirements.

An affiliated service group refers to two or more organizations that have a service relationship, and in some cases an ownership relationship, described in IRC § 414(m). There are three separate types of affiliated service groups:

(1) A-organization groups (A-orgs) which consist of an organization designated as a First Service Organization (FSO) and at least one "A Organization";[43]

(2) B-organization groups (B-orgs) which consists of an FSO and at least one "B Organization";[44] and

---

[36] *Id.* at 11 n.8.

[37] *Id.* at 13.

[38] *Id.* at 11.

[39] Thomas Kiddie, M.D., Inc. v. Commissioner, 69 T.C. 1055 (1978).

[40] Michael A. Laing, *Standards of Eligibility and Minimum Coverage*, ST043 ALI-ABA 81 (May 16–18, 2012).

[41] Miscellaneous Revenue Act of 1980, Pub. L. No. 96-605 201, 94 Stat. 3521, 3526–27.

[42] For a discussion of the reasons why IRC § 414(m) was enacted, see Philip S. Neal and Harry J. Conaway, *New Section 414(m) Limits Qualified Plan Abuse by Affiliated Service Organizations*, 54 J. Tax'n 258 (1981).

[43] IRC § 414(m)(2)(A).

[44] IRC § 414(m)(2)(B).

(3) Management groups.[45]

A FSO must be a "service organization." A service organization is defined as an organization the principal business of which is the performance of services.[46] The organization may be a corporation, partnership, or other organization.[47]

[a] IRC § 414(m)(2)(A) Organization

A two-part test applies to determine whether a group qualifies as an A-organization (A-org) under IRC § 414(m)(2)(A):

(1) an ownership test, and

(2) a working relationship test.[48]

The ownership test is satisfied if the organization is a shareholder or partner in the FSO.[49]

The working relationship test is satisfied if the organization regularly performs services for the FSO, or is regularly associated with the FSO in performing services for third parties.[50]

Example of an A-Org

The ABC Partnership is a partnership with offices throughout the country. ABC of Large City, P.C. is a corporation that is a partner in the law firm. ABC of Large City, P.C. provides paralegal and administrative services for the attorneys in the law firm. All of the employees of the corporation work directly for the corporation, and none of them work directly for any of the law firm's other offices.

The law firm is an FSO, and the corporation is an A-org because it is a partner in the FSO and is regularly associated with the law firm in performing services for third parties.

The corporation and the law firm together constitute an affiliated service group. Thus, the employees of ABC of Large City, P.C. and the employees of the law firm must be aggregated and treated as if they were employed by a single employer under IRC § 414(m).

[b] IRC § 414(m)(2)(B) Organization

An organization must satisfy three requirements in order to qualify as a B-organization under IRC § 414(m)(2)(B):

(1) a significant portion of the business of the organization must be the performance of services for an FSO, for one or more A-Orgs determined

---

[45] IRC § 414(m)(5).

[46] IRC § 414(m)(3).

[47] IRC § 414(m)(6)(A).

[48] IRC § 414(m)(2)(A).

[49] IRC § 414(m)(2)(A)(i).

[50] IRC § 414(m)(2)(A)(ii).

with respect to the FSO, or both;

(2)   the services must be of a type historically performed by employees in the service field of the FSO or the A-Orgs; and

(3)   10% or more of the interests in the organization must be held, in the aggregate, by HCEs of the FSO or A-Org.[51]

Example of a B-Org

A & Associates is a financial services organization that has 10 partners. Each partner in A & Associates owns 2% of the stock in Corporation B. Corporation B provides services of a type historically performed by employees in financial services field. A significant portion of Corporation B's business is the performance of services for A & Associates.

Considering A & Associates as a FSO, Corporation B is a B-Org because (1) a significant portion of its services is of a type historically performed by employees in the financial services field, and (2) more than 10% (in this case 20%) of the interests in Corporation B is held, in the aggregate, by the HCEs of the FSO.

A & Associates and Corporation B together constitute an affiliated services group. Thus, the employees of Corporation B and A & Associates must be aggregated and treated as if they were employed by a single employer under IRC § 414(m).

[c]   IRC § 414(m)(5) Management Organization

Section 414(m)(5) of the Internal Revenue provides that an affiliated service group includes certain organizations that perform management functions.

Specifically, management-type affiliated service group exists when

(1)   there is an organization that performs management services, and

(2)   the management organization's principal business is performing management services on a regular and continuing basis for another organization.[52]

No common ownership between the management organization and the organization for which it provides management services is required.[53]

Section 414(m)(5) was added to the Internal Revenue Code in 1982.[54]

---

[51]   IRC § 414(m)(2)(B).

[52]   IRC § 414(m)(5).

[53]   Larry Lawson & Jeff Nelson, *IRS Tax Exempt and Government Entities*, Chapter 7, Controlled and Affiliated Service Groups 7-72, *available at* http://www.irs.gov/pub/irs-tege/epchd704.pdf.

[54]   *See* Tax Equity and Fiscal Responsibility Act of 1982, Pub. L. 97-248 § 246, 96 Stat. 324, 525 (1982). Although *Achiro v. Commissioner*, 77 T.C. 881 (1981), was decided before IRC § 414(m)(5) was enacted, its facts illustrate the type of situation IRC § 414(m)(5) was intended to address. Lawson & Nelson, IRS Tax Exempt and Government Entities, Chapter 7, Controlled and Affiliated Service Groups, at 7-72.

[D] IRC § 414(n) Leased Employees

Following the enactment IRC § 414(m), professionals sought to avoid the affiliated service group rules by "leasing" their employees from a separate leasing company.[55]

In 1982, Congress enacted IRC § 414(n)[56] to prevent this method of circumventing the nondiscrimination requirements.[57] In essence, IRC § 414(n) treats the employees of certain leasing organizations as employed by the organization that leases their services for nondiscrimination purposes.

Section 414(n) does not require that employers include leased employees in their qualified plans. It only requires that leased employees be taken into account in determining whether the plan satisfies the nondiscrimination requirements. If a plan intends to exclude leased employees, it must explicitly state that they are excluded.[58]

Section 414(n) defines a leased employee as any person who performs services for a recipient if:

(1) the services are performed pursuant to an agreement between the recipient and any other person ("leasing organization");

(2) the person has performed such services on a substantially full-time basis for at least a year; and

(3) the services are performed under the direction or control of the recipient.[59]

Section 414(n)(5) provides a safe harbor if the leasing organization provides a plan covering the leased employees.

In order to satisfy the safe harbor, the plan must

(1) provide a nonintegrated minimum contribution of 10%;

(2) provide immediate and full vesting, and

(3) cover all of the employees who are leased out (except those whose total compensation is less than $1,000 for the current year and each of the preceding three years).[60]

---

[55] IRS Notice 84-11 provides guidance on the employee leasing provisions.

[56] Tax Equity and Fiscal Responsibility of 1982, Pub. L. No. 97-248, § 248, 96 Stat. 324, 526–27.

[57] For a discussion of the reasons why IRC § 414(n) was enacted, see Jeannette M. Arlin, *Pension Plans and the Employee Leasing Provision: A Proposal for Clarifying Change*, 53 GEO. WASH. L. REV. 852 (1985); Staff of the Joint Comm. on Taxation, 97th Cong., Explanation of the Revenue Provision of the Tax Equity and Fiscal Responsibity Act of 1982, 22-3, 37-8 (Comm. Print 1982).

[58] IRS Notice 84-11, Q&A-16.

[59] IRC § 414(n)(2).

[60] IRC § 414(n)(5).

[E] IRC § 414(o) Anti-Avoidance Rule

Apparently tired of enacting specific legislation to prohibit perceived abuses of the rules defining employer, Congress added section 414(o) to the Internal Revenue Code.[61]

Section 414(o) authorizes the Secretary of Treasury to issue regulations to prevent the circumvention of employee benefits requirements through the use of separate organizations, employee leasing, and other arrangements.

[F] IRC § 414(r) Separate Lines of Business

Sections 414(b), (c), (m), (n), and (o) of the Internal Revenue Code all expand the definition of employer and thus, the employees that must be taken into account in determining whether a plan satisfies the nondiscrimination requirements.

Section 414(r) of the Internal Revenue Code, in contrast, cuts back on the definition of employer and thus, employees that must be taken into account for nondiscrimination purposes.

Specifically, if an employer maintains separate lines of business that qualify under section 414(r), the separate lines of business are treated as separate employers for purposes of the nondiscrimination requirements.[62] Thus, in applying the nondiscrimination rules, employees of each qualified separate line of business are treated as if they were the only employees of the employer.

[1] Purpose of IRC § 414(r) Separate Lines of Business Rule

Congress enacted IRC § 414(r) in order to address competitive concerns.

Congress recognized that different industries may have different standards regarding the level of benefits they offer employees. Applying the nondiscrimination requirements[63] on an employer-wide basis to an employer operating separate lines of business that compete in fundamentally different markets could require the employer either (1) to offer benefits in one line of business that greatly exceed the benefits offered by competitors in that line of business or (2) to offer benefits in another line of business that are substantially below the level of benefits offered by competitors in that line of business. In either event, the employer would be placed at a competitive disadvantage.[64] Section 414(r) provides relief from this problem for employers that are genuinely engaged in different lines of business.

---

[61] Deficit Reduction Act of 1984, Pub. L. No. 98-369 § 526, 98 Stat. 494, 875.

[62] Specifically, the minimum coverage requirements of IRC § 410(b), including the nondiscrimination requirements of IRC § 401(a)(4), and the minimum participation requirements that apply to defined benefit plans, may be applied separately with respect to the employees each qualified separate line of business. *See* IRC §§ 414(r)(1), 401(a)(26)(F); Treas. Reg. § 1.414(r)-1(c)(2)(i).

[63] Specifically, the average benefits percentage test under IRC § 410(b)(2)(A)(ii). For a discussion of the average benefits percentage test under IRC § 410(b)(2)(A)(ii), see § 9.07[G].

[64] *Qualified Separate Lines of Business*, 56 Fed. Reg. 63420, 63421 (Dec. 4, 1991).

[2]   Treasury Regulations Implementing IRC § 414(r)

The Treasury Department has issued regulations implementing IRC § 414(r).[65] Running almost 50 pages, the regulations have been described as "mind-numbingly complex"[66] and difficult to satisfy.[67] Commentators have criticized the data collection and recordkeeping burden they impose on employers[68] as well as their separate management test which assumes a higher degree of decentralization among business segments than is likely to exist among most employers.[69]

The regulations set forth a three-part test to determine whether an employer satisfies the separate line of business rules:

(1)   The employer must be engaged in more than one "line of business;"

(2)   The lines of business must be "separate;" and

(3)   The separate lines of business must be "qualified."

[a]   Line of Business

The regulations define a "line of business" as a "portion of an employer that is identified by the property or services it provides to customers of the employer."[70] Employers are given a great deal of discretion in selecting their lines of business, so long as they are reasonable. For example, an employer may establish lines of business based upon geographic areas, levels of distribution (wholesale versus retail), or types of customers (governmental versus private).[71]

Once the employer identifies its "lines of business," it must show that they are organized and operated "separately" from one another.

[b]   Separate Lines of Business

Separate lines of business must satisfy four requirements:

(1)   each line of business must be formally organized by the employer as a separate unit in the corporation, such as a division;[72]

(2)   each line of business must have separate financial accountability;[73]

(3)   each line of business must have its own separate workforce; and

---

[65] For a detailed discussion of the regulations, see David A. Pratt & Charles Lockwood, *IRS Finalizes Separate Line of Business Regulations*, 21 J. PENSION PLANNING & COMPLIANCE 66 (1995).

[66] Michael J. Collins, *Reviving Defined Benefit Plans: Analysis and Suggestions for Reform*, 20 VA. TAX REV. 599, 620 (2001).

[67] David Pratt, *Nor Rhyme nor Reason: Simplifying Defined Contribution Plans*, 49 BUFFALO L. REV. 741, 785 n.198 (2001); Pratt & Lockwood, 21 J. PENSION PLANNING & COMPLIANCE 66.

[68] *See, e.g.*, Edward A. Zelinsky, *Qualified Plans and Identifying Tax Expenditures*, 9 AMERICAN J. OF TAX POL'Y 257, 279 (1991).

[69] Pratt & Lockwood, J. PENSION PLANNING & COMPLIANCE, at 72.

[70] Treas. Reg. § 1.414(r)-2(a).

[71] Treas. Reg. § 1.414(r)-2(b)(3)(iii).

[72] Treas. Reg. § 1.414(r)-3(b)(2).

[73] Treas. Reg. § 1.414(r)-3(b)(3).

(4)   each line of business must have its own separate management.

In order to satisfy the second requirement, that of separate financial accountability, each line of business must be a separate profit center or group of separate profit centers within the employer

With respect to the third requirement, a line of business has its own separate employee workforce if at least 90% of the employees who provide services to the line of business, and who are not substantial service employees with respect to any other line of business, are substantial service employees with respect to the line of business. An employee is a substantial service employee if at least 75% of the employee's services are provided to that line of business for a testing year.[74]

With respect to the fourth requirement, a line of business has its own separate management if at least 80% of the employees who are top-paid with respect to the line of business are substantial service employees with respect to the line of business.[75] Because vertically integrated lines of business typically cannot meet the separate workforce and separate management requirements, the regulations provide an optional rule to assist them to satisfy the separate lines of business requirements.[76]

Once an employer establishes that its lines of business are separate, it must show that the separate lines of business are "qualified."

[c]   Qualified Separate Lines of Business

In order to be a "qualified separate line of business,"

(1)   each line of business must have at least 50 employees,

(2)   the employer must give appropriate notice to the Internal Revenue Service, and

(3)   each line of must satisfy an "administrative scrutiny" requirement designed to ensure that the HCEs are not packed into a single unit.[77]

[i]   Statutory Safe Harbor

Section 414(r)(3) exempts from this "administrative scrutiny" requirement lines of business that satisfy a safe harbor percentage.

A separate line of business satisfies the statutory safe harbor if the percentage of highly compensated employees (HCEs) with respect to the line of business is at least 50%, but not more than 200%, of the HCE percentage for the employer as a whole.[78] If at least 10% of all HCEs of the employer perform services solely for a single line of business, that line of business is deemed to satisfy the 50%

---

[74] Treas. Reg. § 1.414(r)-3(b)(4).

[75] Treas. Reg. § 1.414(r)-3(b)(5).

[76] Treas. Reg. § 1.414(r)-3(d).

[77] IRC § 414(r)-2(A)-(C).

[78] IRC § 414(r)(3).

requirement, but still must satisfy the 200% requirement.[79]

Example

Corporation A has 400 employees, 40 of whom are highly compensated. Thirty of the employees, 10 of them highly compensated, work for a line of business.

10% of Corporation A's workforce is highly compensated (40/400 = 10%). In order to satisfy the statutory safe harbor, at least 5% (50% x 10% = 5%) but no more than 50% (25% x 200%) of the line of business' employees must be highly compensated.

In this case, 33.3% of the line of business' employees are highly compensated (10/30 = 33.3%). Thus, the line of business satisfies the statutory safe harbor.

[ii]   Regulatory Safe Harbors

The regulations set forth five regulatory safe harbors that satisfy the "administrative scrutiny" requirement:

(1)   industry category safe harbor,

(2)   mergers and acquisition safe harbor,

(3)   reportable business segments safe harbor,

(4)   average benefits safe harbor, and

(5)   minimum and maximum benefits safe harbor.[80]

[iii]   Individual Determination

If an employer's separate lines of business fail to satisfy the statutory safe harbor or one of the regulatory safe harbors, the employer may satisfy the "administrative scrutiny" requirement if it requests and receives an individual determination that the separate line of business satisfies administrative scrutiny.[81]

---

[79] IRC § 414(r)(3).

[80] Treas. Reg. § 1.414(r)-4(g).

[81] Treas. Reg. § 1.414(r)-6.

[d] **Summary of IRC § 414(r) Qualified Separate Lines of Business Requirements[82]**

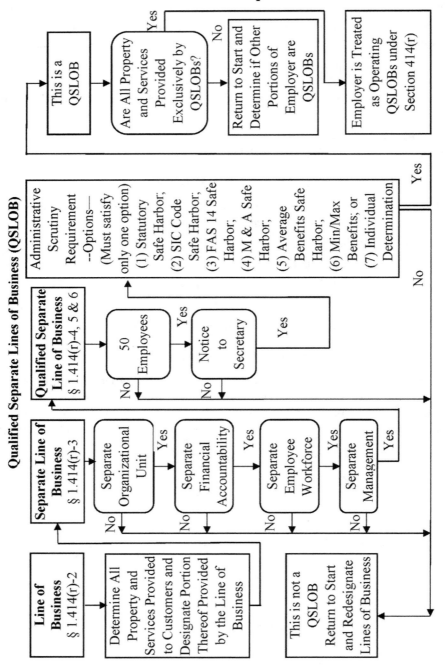

§ 9.05   A CLOSER LOOK AT HIGHLY COMPENSATED EMPLOYEES — IRC § 414(q)

Section 414(q) of the Internal Revenue Code sets forth an objective, straightforward test to determine who is a highly compensated employee (HCE).

It defines HCEs with respect to

(1)   ownership in the employer, and

(2)   compensation.

In addition, it offers employers the opportunity to elect the limit the number of their HCEs based on compensation to the "top-paid group."

[A]   Ownership Test

Section 414(q)(1)(A) defines an HCE as any employee who was a 5% owner during the current or preceding year. If an employee satisfies the ownership test; that is, the employee owned 5% or more of the employer during the current or preceding year, the employee will be deemed an "HCE" regardless of how much compensation the employee actually receives.

Example 1

Ana owned 5% of Corporation B in 2014. She is considered an HCE in 2014 and 2015 regardless of the level of her compensation.

Example 2

Benjamin purchased 5% of Corporation C in 2010 and sold it in 2012. Benjamin was an HCE in 2010, 2011, 2012, and 2013 based on his ownership of Corporation C between 2010 and 2012. He ceased to qualify as an HCE based on ownership in 2014.

Depending on Benjamin's compensation, he might, however, qualify as an HCE under the IRC § 414(q)(1)(B) compensation test.

[B]   Compensation Test

Section 414(q)(1)(B) of the Internal Revenue Code defines an HCE as any employee who had compensation from the employer in excess of $80,000, adjusted for the cost of living, in the preceding year. In 2015, the IRC § 414(q)(1)(B) limit, as adjusted for inflation, is $120,000.

Example 1

Chantel earned $150,000 in 2014. She is considered an HCE under IRC § 414(q)(1)(B).

Example 2

Dexter earned $90,000 in 2014 and expects to earn $150,000 in 2015. He is not considered an HCE in 2015 because status as an HCE depends on compensation in the prior year, not the current year, and Dexter earned less than $120,000 in 2014.

If he, in fact, earns $150,000 in 2015, he would be considered an HCE in 2016 based on his 2015 compensation.[83]

Determining whether an individual is an HCE based on compensation in the preceding year promotes administrative ease. It permits an employer to know at outset of the plan year who the HCEs are.

Example 3

Elliott earned $90,000 from Corporation D in 2014. In addition, he earned $35,000 from an unrelated employer, Company E, in 2014. Elliott is not considered an HCE in 2015 because only compensation "from the employer" is taken into account. If an employee has two separate, unrelated employers, compensation from each employer is considered separately.

Example 4

Fernando earned $80,000 from Corporation F in 2014. In addition, he earned $50,000 from Corporation F's wholly owned subsidiary, Corporation G. Because Corporation F and Corporation G are members of a parent-subsidiary controlled group of corporations,[84] Fernando's compensation from both Corporation F and Corporation G are aggregated (added together) and Fernando is considered an HCE in 2015 because he earned $130,000 ($80,000 + $50,000 = $130,000) from his employer (as defined in IRC § 414(b)) in 2014.

[C] Top-Paid Group Election

Section 414(q)(3) of the Internal Revenue Code permits, but does not require, an employer to elect to limit the number of its HCEs based on compensation to those who are in the "top-paid group."

The top-paid group consists of those employees who were among the highest paid 20% of the employer's workforce in the preceding year.[85] Once an employer makes a top-paid group election, it applies to all subsequent years unless the employer revokes the election.[86]

The top-paid group election does not apply to individuals who qualify as HCEs based on ownership rather than compensation.

Example

Company A has 30 employees, none of whom own any interest in Company A. If 10 of Company A's employees earned more than the $120,000 in 2014, then all 10 of those employees would qualify as HCEs in 2015 under IRC § 414(q)(1)(B).

---

[83] The 2016 limit, adjusted for inflation, may be higher than the 2015 limit of $120,000 but is unlikely to be higher than $150,000.

[84] *See* § 9.04[B] (discussing parent-subsidiary groups).

[85] IRC § 414(q)(3).

[86] IRS Notice 97-45, 1977-33 IRB 7.

Company A could, however, elect to limit its highly paid employees to those in the "top-paid group." Because Company A has 30 employees, the top-paid group would consist of six employees (20% x 30 = 6), Company A's six highest paid employees.

If Company A elected to limit its HCEs to its top-paid group, the 7th through 10th highest paid employees would not be considered HCEs in 2015 even though they earned more than $120,000 in 2014.

[D]   Implications of Objective Test

Section 414(q) is a straightforward, objective test.

Like all objective tests, it has the advantage of providing certainty.[87] An employer can be certain which of its employees are highly compensated.

The disadvantage of the objective test is that it may not always be fair. Sometimes it may be overinclusive. Other times, it may be underinclusive.[88]

Example 1

The law firm of Arnold & Donovan had five partners, each of whom earned in excess of $750,000, 15 associates who earned between $140,000 and $200,000, and five support staff who earned between $40,000 and $80,000 in 2014. Under IRC § 414(q)(1)(B), all five partners and 15 associates would qualify as HCEs in 2015 because their compensation exceeded $120,000 in 2014.

Because the nondiscrimination rules only protect against discrimination in favor of HCEs, the firm could establish a pension plan that only covered the partners and the support staff (and not the associates) without violating the nondiscrimination requirements.[89]

Arguably, the IRC § 414(q)(1)(B) definition of HCE is over inclusive in this case because the associates are not highly compensated relative to the partners and the firm would be discriminating against them if it excluded them.

Of course, the associates are highly compensated relative to the support staff, and the nondiscrimination rules protect against discrimination against the support staff.

---

[87] *See* Robert J. Misey, Jr., *Simplifying International Jurisdiction for United States Transfer Taxes: Retain Citizenship and Replace Domicile with the Green Card Test*, 76 Marq. L. Rev. 73, 100 (1992) (stating that "[T]he main advantage of an objective test is certainty. Objective tests provide certainty to taxpayers, planners, litigators, judges, and the IRS."). For a discussion of the relationship between certainty and complexity in the tax code, see John A. Miller, *Indeterminacy, Complexity, and Fairness: Justifying Rule Simplification in the Law of Taxation*, 68 Wash. L. Rev. 1 (1993).

[88] *See* Nancy J. Altman, *Rethinking Retirement Income Policies: Nondiscrimination, Integration, and the Quest for Worker Security*, 42 Tax L. Rev. 435, 466–68 (1987) (discussing inevitable problems of any definition of "highly compensated" employee).

[89] *See* §§ 9.07[E] & [F].

Example 2

In 2014, Employer had 40 employees, one of whom earned $130,000, two of whom earned $110,000, and the remainder of whom earned less than $35,000. Under IRC § 414(q)(1)(B), only the employee who earned $130,000 would be considered an HCE in 2015.

Arguably, the IRC § 414(q)(1)(B) definition of HCE is under inclusive in this case because the 2 employees who earned $110,000 are highly compensated relative to the 37 employees who earned less than $35,000.

Employer's plan would not satisfy the nondiscrimination requirements if it only covered the single HCE and the two employees who earned $110,000. Nevertheless, treating the two employees who earned $110,000 as NHCEs, rather than as HCEs, would permit Employer to exclude from the plan more of the other lower-paid employees than it would be permitted to exclude if the employees who earned $110,000 were treated as HCEs.[90]

§ 9.06   A CLOSER LOOK AT THE IRC § 401(a)(26) MINIMUM PARTICIPATION REQUIREMENT

Section 401(a)(26) of the Internal Revenue Code requires that a defined benefit plan satisfy a minimum participation requirement in order to qualify for favorable income tax treatment.

[A]   Purpose of IRC § 401(a)(26) Requirement

The minimum participation requirement is intended to address two concerns.

First, it is designed to limit the extent to which employers may create different benefit formulas for different groups of employees and thus maximize benefits in favor of HCEs.[91] Second, it limits the extent to which a defined benefit plan can operate as an individual account for a single employee, or a small group of employees.[92]

When the minimum participation requirement was originally enacted, it applied to all qualified plans.[93] In order to better target the rule, Congress amended section 401(a)(26)[94] to limit its application to defined benefit plans and impose the requirement that that plan benefit at least two employees (or only one employee if there is only one employee).[95]

---

[90] *See id.*

[91] *Minimum Participation Requirements*, 56 Fed. Reg. 63410, 63410–11 (Dec. 2, 1991).

[92] *Id.* at 63411.

[93] Tax Reform Act of 1986, Pub. L. No. 99-514 § 1112, 100 Stat. 2085, 2440–46.

[94] Small Business Job Protection Act of 1996, Pub. L. No. 104-188 § 1432, 110 Stat. 1755, 1803–04.

[95] H. Rep. 104-586, at 25 (1996).

[B]   Statutory Requirement

Section 401(a)(26) requires that a defined benefit plan benefit at least the lesser of

(1)   50 employees, or

(2)   40% of all of the employees of the employer.

A special rule applies to employers with fewer than five employees:

> If the employer has fewer than five, but more than one, employee, the plan must benefit at least two employees.[96]

> If the employer only has one employee, the plan need only benefit that employee.[97]

The minimum participation standards must be satisfied on each day of the plan year.[98] A plan, however, will be treated as having satisfied this requirement if it meets the test on any single day during the plan year, provided that that day is reasonably representative of the employer's workforce and the plan's coverage.[99]

If a plan only benefits NHCEs, it satisfies IRC § 401(a)(26) regardless of the number of employees it covers.[100]

Example 1

Employer A establishes a defined benefit plan that covers 25 of its 45 employees. The plan satisfies IRC § 401(a)(26) because it covers more than 40% of Employer A's employees (25/45 = 55.6%).

Example 2

Employer B establishes a defined benefit plan that covers 100 of its 500 employees. Even though the plan only covers 20% of Employer B's employees (100/500 = 20%), it satisfies IRC § 401(a)(26) because it covers at least 50 employees.

§ 9.07   A CLOSER LOOK AT THE IRC § 410(b) MINIMUM COVERAGE REQUIREMENT

Section 401(a)(3) of the Internal Revenue Code requires that a qualified plan satisfy the requirements of IRC § 410.

Section 410(b) requires that qualified plans satisfy minimum coverage requirements.[101]

---

[96]   IRC § 401(a)(26)(A)(ii)(II).

[97]   IRC § 401(a)(26)(A)(ii)(II).

[98]   IRC § 401(a)(26)(A).

[99]   Treas. Reg. § 1.401(a)(26)-7(b).

[100]   Treas. Reg. § 1.401(a)(26)-1(b)(1).

[101]   Section 410(a) of the Internal Revenue Code imposes a minimum age and service requirement. The minimum age and service requirement is discussed in Chapter 5 § 5.02[B].

While IRC § 401(a)(26) focuses on the absolute number of employees benefiting under a plan, the IRC § 410(b) minimum coverage rules focus on the mix of employees (that is, the number NHCEs relative to HCEs) benefiting under the plan.

[A] Plans that Automatically Satisfy IRC § 410(b)

Three types of plans are treated as automatically satisfying IRC § 410(b):

(1) Plans of employers that have only HCEs;[102]

(2) Plans that benefit no HCEs,[103] and

(3) Plans that benefit solely collectively bargained employees.[104]

There is nothing surprising about any of the exceptions. First, if there were not an exception for employers with only HCEs, then employers with only HCEs would never be able to satisfy the IRC § 410(b) coverage rules and they would never be able to have qualified plans. Second, plans that benefit no HCEs can never discriminate in favor in HCEs in violation of IRC § 410(b). Third, employees who are covered by a collective bargaining agreement may be excluded from IRC § 410(b) testing if retirement benefits were a subject of good faith. A plan that only covers employees who can be excluded from IRC § 410(b) testing should automatically satisfy IRC § 410(b).

[B] Meaning of "Benefit" Under the Plan

In the case of a traditional defined benefit plan, an employee is treated as benefiting under the plan if the employee's accrued benefit is increased for the plan year.[105]

In the case of most defined contribution plans, an employee is treated as benefiting under the plan if the employee receives an allocation of employer contributions for the plan year.[106]

In the case of a 401(k) plan, an employee is treated as benefiting under the plan if the employee is eligible to participate in the 401(k) plan even if the employee does not elect to make any contribution

---

[102] IRC § 410(b)(6)(F); Treas. Reg. § 1.410(b)-2(b)(5).

[103] Treas. Reg. § 1.410(b)-2(b)(6).

[104] Treas. Reg. § 1.410(b)-2(b)(7).

As discussed in § 9.07[C][3], employees may be excluded from IRC § 410(b) testing if they are covered by a collectively bargained agreement so long as retirement benefits were a subject of good faith bargaining. Since such employees may be excluded from IRC § 410(b) testing, it makes sense that a plan that only covers such excludable employees automatically satisfies IRC § 410(b).

[105] Treas. Reg. § 1.410(b)-3(a)(1).

[106] Treas. Reg. § 1.410(b)-3(a)(1).

[C]   Excludable Employees

Generally, all employees of the "employer"[107] must be counted in applying the IRC § 410(b) minimum coverage tests.

Certain employees, however, may be excluded. If an employee is considered excludable, then the employee is not counted for coverage and nondiscrimination purposes. In other words, these employees are "invisible" for testing purposes and considered in neither the numerator nor the denominator of the coverage tests as discussed below.[108]

Five categories of employees may be excluded in applying the IRC § 410(b) minimum coverage tests:

(1)   employees who do not satisfy the plan's minimum age and service requirements;

(2)   nonresident aliens;

(3)   employees covered by a collectively bargained agreement;

(4)   employees of qualified separate lines of business; and

(5)   certain terminating employees.

[1]   Employees Who Do Not Satisfy Minimum Age and Service Requirements

Section 410(b)(4)(A) of the Internal Revenue Code permits the exclusion of employees who do not meet the plan's minimum age and service requirements so long as the plan excludes all such employees.

Section 410(a) permits a plan to prescribe minimum age and service requirements which parallel the requirements set forth in ERISA § 203 and are discussed in Chapter 5 § 5.02[B]. In essence, the rules permit a pension plan to exclude employees who are younger than age 21 and/or have less than one year of service,[109] generally defined as less than 1,000 hours of service.[110]

Thus, if an employer so chooses, it may exclude employees who are younger than age 21 and new hires, that is, individuals who have worked for the employer for less than a year. In addition, it permits employers to exclude part-time employees who work less than 1,000 hours per year, the equivalent of a little less than 20 hours per week.[111]

The exclusion of workers who do not meet the minimum age and service requirements promotes administrative ease. It permits employers to exclude from their plans employees who are most likely to be short-term employees and least

---

[107]   For the definition of "employer," see § 9.04.

[108]   Terry Bates et al., *IRS Tax Exempt and Government Entities*, Chapter 10, Coverage and Nondiscrimination — Demo 6 10, *available at* http://www.irs.gov/pub/irs-tege/epchd1004.pdf.

[109]   IRC § 410(a)(1)(A).

[110]   IRC § 410(a)(3)(A).

[111]   (20 x 52 = 1,040).

likely to accrue large pensions.[112] The exclusion also helps to explain why part-time employees are much less likely to be covered by a pension plan than are full-time employees.[113]

[2] Nonresident Aliens

Section 410(b)(3)(C) of the Internal Revenue Code permits the exclusion of nonresident aliens who receive no U.S. source income.

Presumably, Congress permitted this exclusion because the U.S. government has little interest in ensuring retirement income security of nonresident aliens who receive no U.S. source income.[114]

[3] Employees Covered by Collective Bargained Agreements

Section 410(b)(3)(A) of the Internal Revenue Code permits the exclusion of employees who are covered by a collective bargaining agreement if retirement benefits were the subject of good faith bargaining.[115]

Congress enacted this exception because absent this exception, unionized employees could control the availability of pension benefits for nonunionized employees either by agreeing to no pension and thus preventing nonunionized employees from receiving a pension or using their ability to block nonunionized employees from having a pension to increase their power with respect to other bargaining issues.[116]

---

[112] *See* Altman, 42 Tax L. Rev., at 471–72 (contending that exclusion of workers younger than 21 and workers with less than a year of service does not raise concerns from a worker security perspective because they will eventually be eligible to participate and contending that administrative costs of including part-time workers with less than 1,000 hours of service per year may outweigh marginal worker security gains that would be achieved by requiring coverage of such workers).

[113] *See, e.g.,* Bureau of Labor Statistics, Economic News Release, *Retirement benefits: Access, participation, and take-up rates based on March 2014 National Compensation Survey,* available at http://www.bls.gov/mews.release/ebs2.t01.htm (reporting that among civilian workers, 78 percent of full-time workers compared to 37 percent of part-time workers have access to an employer-sponsored pension plan and 64 percent of full-time workers and 21 percent of part-time workers participate in such plans); Craig Copeland, *Employment-Based Retirement Plan Participation: Geographic Differences and Trends,* 2013, EBRI Issue Brief No. 405, at 35 fig. 26 (Oct. 2014) (showing that 54.5 percent of full-time full-year workers ages 21 to 64 participated in employment-based retirement plan in 2013 compared with 21.5 percent of part-time full-year workers ages 21 to 64).

[114] *See* Altman, 42 Tax L. Rev. at 471 (contending that excluding nonresident aliens with no U.S. source income does not raise any policy concerns because the U.S. government's interest in nonresident aliens with no U.S. source income is weak).

[115] In addition, IRC § 410(b)(3)(B) permits employers to exclude employees who are not covered by a collective bargaining agreement between air pilots and their employees. There is no apparent justification for this exclusion. It appears to merely be a special interest provision for air pilots. Altman, 42 Tax L. Rev. at 471 n.153.

[116] Altman, 42 Tax L. Rev. at 472 (explaining that Congress enacted this provision in response to the blocking problem illustrated in *Loevsky v. Commissioner,* 55 T.C. 1144 (1971), and contending that exclusion is justified from a taxpayer abuse perspective but not from a worker security perspective).

[4]   Employees of Qualified Separate Lines of Business

If an employer operates qualified separate lines of business under IRC § 414(r),[117] section 410(b)(5) permits the employer to apply the IRC § 410(b) coverage rules separately with respect to the employees in each qualified separate line of business.

This rule is consistent with the purpose of the separate line of business rules: to permit employers who operate separate lines of business in industries with different benefit standards to offer pension plans in each line of business that are consistent with the industry's standard.[118]

[5]   Certain Terminating Employees

Terminating employees may be excluded from the IRC § 410(b) coverage tests if they satisfy six requirements set forth in the Treasury regulations.[119]

[D]   Overview of the Three IRC § 410(b) Coverage Tests

Section 410(b) sets forth three alternative coverage tests:

(1)   the IRC § 410(b)(1)(A) percentage test,

(2)   the IRC § 410(b)(1)(B) ratio percentage test, and

(3)   the IRC § 410(b)(1)(C) average benefit percentage test.

---

[117] For a discussion of IRC § 414(r), see § 9.04[F].

[118] *See also* Altman, 42 Tax. L. Rev. at 473 (contending that exception to coverage rules should be permitted for conglomerate with two distinct product lines in order not to inappropriately constrain an employer's business choices).

[119] Those six requirements are: (1) the individual does not benefit under the plan for the plan year; (2) the employee was eligible to participate in the plan for the plan year; (3) the plan has a minimum period of service requirement or requirement that an individual be employed on the last day of the plan year in order for the individual to accrue a benefit in the case of a defined benefit plan or receive an allocation in the case of a defined contribution plan; (4) the individual fails to accrue a benefit or receive an allocation solely because the individual did not satisfy the minimum period of service or last-day requirement; (5) the individual terminates employment during the plan year with no more than 500 hours of service and is not an employee of the employer on the last day of the plan year; and (6) if this exclusion is applied with respect to one individual during the plan year, it is applied with respect to all similarly situated individuals with respect to the plan for the plan year. Treas. Reg. § 1.410(b)-6(f)(1)-(i)-(vi).

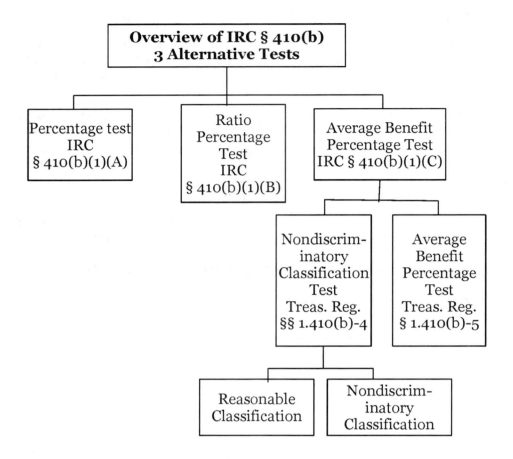

[E] IRC § 410(b)(1)(A) Percentage Test

In order to satisfy the IRC § 410(b)(1)(A) percentage test, the plan must benefit at least 70% of the employer's NHCEs.

IRC § 410(b)(1)(A) Percentage Test

$$\frac{\#\ \text{NHCEs benefiting under plan}}{\text{Total \# NHCEs}} \geq 70\%$$

If the plan benefits at least 70% of the employer's NHCEs, the plan satisfies IRC § 410(b) regardless of the number of the HCEs it benefits.

Because the IRC § 410(b)(1)(A) percentage test is the simplest and most straightforward of the three tests, and the IRC § 410(b)(1)(B) ratio percentage test and the IRC § 410(b)(1)(C) average benefit percentage test build on the IRC

§ 410(b)(1)(A) test, IRC § 410(b) testing should always begin with IRC § 410(b)(1)(A).

Example 1

Employer A has 25 HCEs and 75 NHCEs. Employer A's plan benefits 65 NHCEs. Because the plan benefits 87% (65/75 = 87%) of Employer A's NHCEs, it satisfies IRC § 410(b)(1)(A) regardless of how many of Employer A's HCEs benefit under the plan.

Example 2

Employer B has 200 NHCEs and 50 HCEs. Employer B's plan will satisfy IRC § 410(a)(1)(A) as long as the plan benefits at least 140 NHCEs (.70 x 200 = 140). As long as the plan benefits at least 140 NHCEs, it does not matter how many HCEs benefit under the plan.

Example 3

Recall Example 1 in § 9.05[D] in which the law firm of Arnold & Donovan had five partners, each of whom earned in excess of $750,000, 15 associates who earned between $140,000 and $200,000, and five support staff who earned between $40,000 and $80,000 in 2014. Under IRC § 414(q)(1)(B), all five partners and 15 associates qualified as HCEs in 2015 because their compensation exceeded $120,000 in 2014.

Because the 15 associates were considered HCEs and IRC § 410(b)(1)(A) focuses solely on the number of NHCEs benefiting under the plan, the law firm could exclude all 15 associates without violating IRC § 410(b)(1)(A).

In order to satisfy IRC § 410(b)(1)(A), the firm's plan would have to benefit at least four support staff (5 x .7 = 3.5). If the associates were considered NHCEs, then the plan would have to cover a total of 14 (.7 x 20 = 14) of the combined associates and support staff.

Example 4

Recall Example 2 in § 9.05[D] in which Employer had 40 employees, one of whom earned $130,000, two of whom earned $110,000, and the remainder of whom earned less than $35,000 in 2014. Under IRC § 414(q)(1)(B), only the employee who earned $130,000 would be considered an HCE in 2015.

Employer's plan would satisfy IRC § 410(b)(1)(A) as long as it covered at least 28 (39 x .7 = 27.3) of the 39 NHCEs (including the two employees who earned $110,000 in 2014). If the two employees who earned $110,000 were considered HCEs in 2014, then the Employer's plan would be required to benefit at least 26 (37 x .7 = 25.9) of the 37 employees who earned less than $35,000 in 2014 and 2015. The plan would not be able to take into account the two employees who earned $110,000 in 2014 in determining whether the plan satisfied IRC § 410(b)(1)(A) if those two employees were considered HCEs.

[F]   IRC § 410(b)(1)(B) Ratio Percentage Test

If a plan does not satisfy the IRC § 410(b)(1)(A) percentage test, then the plan should be tested under the IRC § 410(b)(1)(B) ratio percentage test.

Unlike the IRC § 410(b)(1)(A) percentage test, which focuses solely on the percentage of NHCEs benefiting under the plan, the IRC § 410(b)(1)(B) ratio percentage test compares the percentage of NHCEs benefiting under the plan with the percentage of HCEs benefiting under the plan. In order to satisfy the IRC § 410(b)(1)(B) ratio percentage test, the percentage of NHCEs benefiting under the plan must be at least 70% of the percentage of HCEs benefiting under the plan.

IRC § 410(b)(1)(B) Ratio Percentage Test

$$\frac{\dfrac{\text{\# NHCEs benefiting under plan}}{\text{total \# NHCEs}}}{\dfrac{\text{\#HCEs benefiting under plan}}{\text{total \# HCES}}} \geq 70\%$$

Example 1

The following employees work for Employer A and benefit under Employer A's plan

	# NHCEs	# HCEs
Employees Benefiting Under Plan	500	40
Total Nonexcludable Employees	1,250	80

Because only 40% of Employer A's NHCEs benefit under the plan (500/1,250 = 40%), the plan does not satisfy the IRC § 410(a)(1)(A) percentage test.

The plan does, however, satisfy the IRC § 410(a)(1)(B) ratio percentage test because the percentage of NHCEs benefiting under the plan is greater than 70% of the percentage of HCEs benefiting under the plan. Specifically, the percentage of the NHCEs under the plan is 40% (50/1,250 = 40%) while the percentage of HCEs benefiting under the plan is 50% (40/80 = 50%), and 40% is 80% of 50% (40%/50% = 80%).

Example 2

The following employees work for Employer B and benefit under Employer B's plan

	# NHCEs	# HCEs
Employees Benefiting Under Plan	60	9
Total Nonexcludable Employees	100	10

Because only 60% of Employer B's NHCEs benefit under the plan (60/100 = 60%), the plan does not satisfy the IRC § 410(a)(1)(A) percentage test.

In addition, the plan does not satisfy the IRC § 410(a)(1)(B) ratio percentage test because the percentage of NHCEs benefiting under the plan is less than 70% of the percentage of HCEs benefiting under the plan. Specifically, the percentage of NHCEs benefiting under the plan is 60% (60/100 = 60%) while the percentage of HCEs benefiting under the plan is 90% (9/10 = 90%), and 60% is 66.7% of 90% (60%/90% = 66.7%).

Example 3

Recall Example 1 in § 9.05[D] in which the law firm of Arnold & Donovan had five partners, each of whom earned in excess of $750,000, 15 associates who earned between $140,000 and $200,000, and five support staff who earned between $40,000 and $80,000 in 2014. Under IRC § 414(q)(1)(B), all five partners and 15 associates qualify as HCEs in 2015 because their compensation exceeded $120,000 in 2014.

If the law firm's plan excludes all 15 of the associates while all five of the partners benefit under the plan, the plan would benefit 25% of the law firm's HCEs (5/20 = 25%). If the law firm's plan benefits 25% of its HCEs, it would only need to benefit 17.25% (70% x 25% = 17.25%) or one member of its support staff (17.25% x 5 = .875) in order to satisfy the IRC § 410(b)(1)(B) ratio percentage test.

Example 4

Recall Example 2 in § 9.05[D] in which Employer had 40 employees, one of whom earned $130,000, two of whom earned $110,000, and the remainder of whom earned less than $35,000 in 2014. Under IRC § 414(q)(1)(B), only the employee who earned $130,000 would be considered an HCE in 2015.

If that HCE benefits under the plan, the plan would be required to benefit 70% of Employer's NHCEs in order to satisfy IRC § 410(b)(1)(B) ratio percentage test (70% x 100% = 70%) or 28 of its NHCEs (70% x 39 = 27.3).

As this example illustrates, the IRC § 410(b)(1)(B) ratio percentage test only permits the employer's plan to benefit less than 70% of the NHCEs (as required by the IRC § 410(b)(1)(A) percentage test) if the percentage of HCEs benefiting under the plan is less than 100%.

[G]   IRC § 410(b)(1)(C) Average Benefit Percentage Test

If a plan does not satisfy the IRC § 410(b)(1)(B) ratio percentage test, then the plan must satisfy the IRC § 410(b)(1)(C) average benefit percentage test in order to satisfy IRC § 410(b).

Unlike IRC §§ 401(b)(1)(A) and 401(b)(1)(B) which only consider who benefits under a plan, IRC § 410(b)(1)(C) also takes into account the amount of the benefits plan participants receive.

The IRC § 410(b)(1)(C) average benefit percentage test has two parts:

(1)   a classification test, and

(2)   an average benefit percentage test.

[1]   Classification Test

IRC § 410(b)(2)(A)(i) requires that a plan benefit such employees as qualify under a classification set up by the employer and found by the Secretary of Treasury not to be discriminatory in favor of HCEs.

The Treasury regulations set forth two parts to the classification test:

(1)   a reasonable classification test, and

(2)   a nondiscriminatory classification test.[120]

[a]   Reasonable Classification Test

The reasonable classification test is a facts and circumstances test that requires that the coverage classification established by the employer be reasonable and established under objective business criteria that identify the categories of employees who benefit under the plan.[121]

Reasonable classifications include specified job categories, nature of compensation (hourly versus salaried), and geographic location. Identifying employees by name or by other criteria that has the same effect as identifying them by name is not considered a reasonable classification.

Example

Employer A is a law firm with two offices: one in Washington, D.C. and one in Charleston, W. Va. The plan covers all of the employees in the Washington D.C. office and none of the employees in the Charleston, W. Va. Office. The plan satisfies the reasonable classification test.

[b]   Nondiscriminatory Classification Test

The nondiscriminatory classification test is a modified ratio percentage test which allows a plan to substitute a lower percentage for the 70% which is normally used in the ratio percentage test. Whether a plan satisfies the nondiscrimination classification test depends upon the employer's "NHCE concentration percentage" and whether the employer falls above or below a safe harbor percentage.

A plan satisfies the nondiscrimination classification test if the plan's ratio percentage (determined for purposes of IRC § 410(b)(1)(B)) is equal to or greater

---

[120]   Treas. Reg. § 1.410(b)-4(a).

[121]   Treas. Reg. § 1.410(b)-4(b).

than the employer's safe harbor percentage.[122]

If a plan does not fall within the safe harbor, the plan may still satisfy the nondiscrimination classification test if the plan's ratio percentage is greater than the unsafe harbor percentage and the plan satisfies a facts and circumstances test.

The plan's safe harbor percentage depends on the employer's NHCE concentration percentage.

[i]   Nonhighly Compensated Employee Concentration Percentage

The first step in applying the nondiscriminatory classification test is determining the employer's NHCE concentration percentage. An employer's NHCE concentration percentage is the percentage of all of the employer's nonexcludable employees who are not highly compensated.

Example

The following employees work for Employer B and benefit under Employer B's plan

	# NHCEs	# HCEs
Employees Benefiting Under Plan	200	250
Total Nonexcludable Employees	500	500

Employer B has 1,000 nonexcludable employees, of which 500 are nonhighly compensated. Employer B's NHCE concentration percentage is 50% (500/1,000 = 50%).

[ii]   Safe Harbor

An employer's safe harbor percentage is 50%, reduced by 3/4 of a percentage point for each percentage point by which the employer's non-HCE concentration percentage exceeds 60%.[123] A table in the Treasury regulations illustrates the percentages.[124]

If a plan's ratio percentage equals or exceeds the plan's safe harbor percentage, it satisfies the nondiscrimination classification test.

Example 1

The following employees work for Employer C and benefit under Employer C's plan

---

[122] Treas. Reg. § 1.410(b)-4(c)(2).

[123] Treas. Reg. § 1.410(b)-4(c)(4)(i).

[124] Treas. Reg. § 1.410(b)-4(c)(4)(iv). The chart is reproduced in Appendix C.

	# NHCEs	# HCEs
Employees Benefiting Under Plan	140	250
Total Nonexcludable Employees	500	500

Employer C's NHCE concentration percentage is 50% (500/1,000 = 50%).

Employer C's ratio percentage is 56%. (The percentage of NHCEs benefiting under the plan is 56% (140/500 = 28%) and the percentage of HCEs benefiting under the plan is 50% (250/500 = 50%). Thus, the ratio percentage is 56% (28%/50% = 56%).)

According to the table set forth in Treas. Reg. § 1.410(b)-4(c)(4)(iv), the safe harbor percentage for an employer with a NHCE concentration percentage of 50% is 50%. Because Employer C's ratio percentage of 56% exceeds the plan's safe harbor percentage of 50%, the plan satisfies the nondiscrimination classification test.

Example 2

The following employees work for Employer D and benefit under Employer D's plan

	# NHCEs	# HCEs
Employees Benefiting Under Plan	150	200
Total Nonexcludable Employees	750	250

Employer D's NHCE concentration percentage is 75% (750/1,000 = 75%).

Employer D's ratio percentage is 25%. (The percentage of NHCEs benefiting under the plan is 20% (150/750 = 20%) and the percentage of HCEs benefiting under the plan is 80% (200/250 = 80%). Thus, the ratio percentage is 25% (20%/80% = 25%).)

According to the table set forth in Treas. Reg. § 1.410(b)-4(c)(4)(iv), the safe harbor percentage for an employer with a NHCE concentration percentage of 75% is 38.75%. Because Employer D's ratio percentage of 25% is below the plan's safe harbor percentage of 38.75%, the plan does not satisfy the safe harbor of the nondiscrimination classification test.

[iii]   Facts and Circumstances Test

If a plan's ratio percentage falls below the plan's safe harbor percentage, it may still satisfy the nondiscrimination classification test if

(1) the plan's ratio percentage is equal to or greater than the plan's unsafe harbor, and

(2) the plan satisfies a facts and circumstances test.

The unsafe harbor equals 40%, reduced by 3/4 of a percentage point for each whole percentage point by which the NHCE concentration percentage exceeds 60%. In no case, however, is the unsafe harbor less than 20%.[125] A table in the Treasury regulations illustrates the percentages.[126]

A classification satisfies the facts and circumstances test if based on all the relevant facts and circumstances, the Commissioner of the IRS finds that the classification is nondiscriminatory.[127]

If a plan's ratio percentage is less than the plan's unsafe harbor percentage, it does not satisfy IRC § 410(b) and is not eligible for favorable income tax treatment.

Example 1

The following employees work for Employer E and benefit under Employer E's plan

	# NHCEs	# HCEs
Employees Benefiting Under Plan	80	120
Total Nonexcludable Employees	240	160

Employer E's NHCE concentration percentage is 60% (240/400 = 60%).

Employer E's percentage ratio age is 44.4%. (The percentage of NHCEs benefiting under the plan is 33.3% (80/240 = 33.3%) and the percentage of HCEs benefiting under the plan is 75% (120/160 = 75%). Thus, the ratio percentage is 44.4% (33.3%/75% = 44.4%).)

According to the table set forth in Treas. Reg. § 1.410(b)-4(c)(4)(iv), the safe harbor percentage for an employer with an NHCE concentration percentage of 60% is 50% and the unsafe harbor is 40%. Because Employer E's ratio percentage of 44.4% is below the plan's safe harbor percentage of 50% but above the unsafe percentage of 40%, the plan will satisfy the nondiscrimination classification test if the Commissioner of the IRS determines that the classification is nondiscriminatory after considering all the relevant facts and circumstances.

Example 2

The following employees work for Employer F and benefit under Employer F's plan

---

[125] Treas. Reg. § 1.410(b)-4(c)(4)(ii).

[126] Treas. Reg. § 1.410(b)-4(c)(4)(iv). The chart is reproduced in Appendix C.

[127] Treas. Reg. § 1.410(b)-4(c)(3). Relevant facts and circumstances include (1) business reasons, (2) percentage of employees benefiting under the plan, (3) representation of employees benefiting at various salary ranges, (4) the difference between the plan's ratio percentage and the employer's safe harbor percentage, and (5) the extent to which the plan's average benefit percentage exceeds 70%. *Id.*

	# NHCEs	# HCEs
Employees Benefiting Under Plan	40	72
Total Nonexcludable Employees	120	80

Employer F's NHCE concentration percentage is 60% (120/200 = 60%).

Employer F's plan's ratio percentage is 37.03%. (The percentage of NHCEs benefiting under the plan is 33.3% (40/120 = 33.3%) and the percentage of HCEs benefiting under the plan is 90% (72/80 = 90%). Thus, the ratio percentage is 37% (33.3%/90% = 37%).)

According to the table set forth in Treas. Reg. § 1.410(b)-4(c)(4)(iv), the safe harbor percentage for an employer with a NHCE concentration percentage of 60% is 50% and the unsafe harbor is 40%. Because Employer F's plan's ratio percentage of 37% is below the plan's unsafe harbor percentage of 40%, the plan does not satisfy IRC § 410(b).

[2]   Average Benefit Percentage Test

A plan satisfies the average benefit percentage test for a plan year if the average benefit percentage for NHCEs is at least 70% of the average benefit percentage for HCEs.

The average benefit percentage is the percentage determined by dividing the actual benefit percentage of the NHCEs in the employer's plan by the actual benefit percentage of the HCEs in the employer's plan.

The actual benefit percentage of a group of employees is the average of the employee benefit percentages, calculated separately with respect to each of the employees in the group. All nonexcludable employees of the employer are taken into account, even if they are not benefiting under any plan.

The testing group and "benefit percentage" are the same as would be used for purposes of applying the general nondiscrimination test for purposes of IRC § 401(a)(4), which is discussed in detail in the following section.

Example

Employer G's profit-sharing plan covered the following six employees with the following allocation rates.

Employee	Allocation
HCE 1	8%
HCE 2	6%
NHCE 1	8%
NHCE 2	7%
NHCE 3	6%
NHCE 4	6%

The average benefit percentage of the HCEs benefiting under Employer G's profit-sharing plan is 7% (8 + 6 = 14)/2 = 7). The average benefit percentage of the NHCEs benefiting under the plan is 6.75% (8 + 7 + 6 + 6 = 27)/4 = 6.75. Because the average benefit percentage of the NHCEs is 96% of the average benefit percentage of the highly compensated (6.75%/7% = 96%), the plan satisfies the average benefits percentage test.

[H] Summary of IRC § 410(b) Minimum Coverage Tests

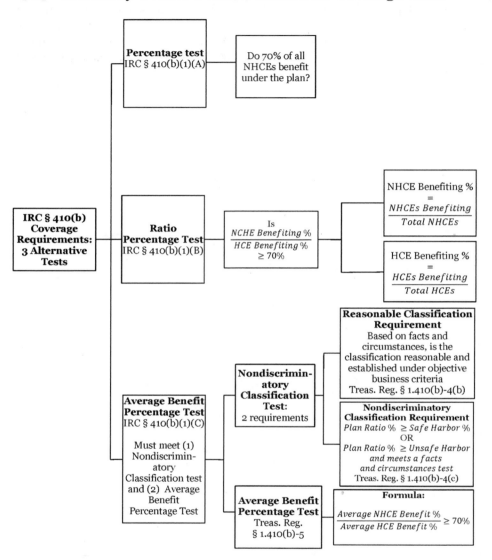

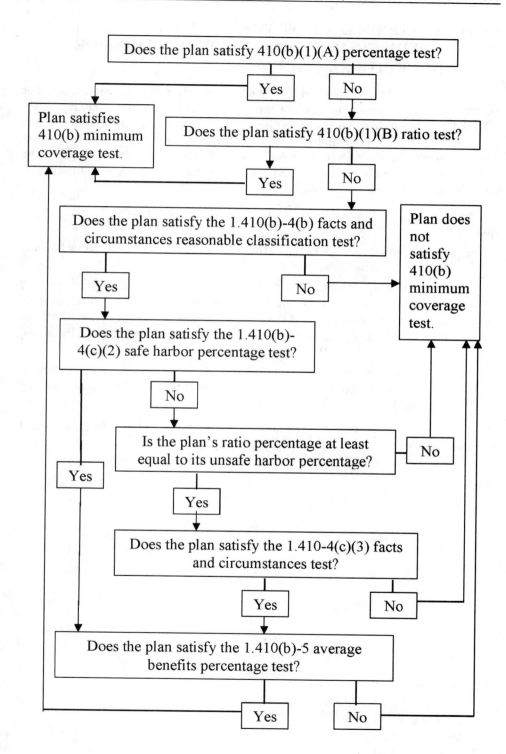

§ 9.08   A CLOSER LOOK AT THE IRC § 401(a)(4) NONDISCRIMINATION IN CONRIBUTIONS OR BENEFITS REQUIREMENT

Section 401(a)(4) of the Internal Revenue Code requires that the contributions or benefits provided under a qualified plan not discriminate in favor of HCEs. While IRC § 401(a)(26) focuses on the absolute number of employees benefiting under a plan and the IRC § 410(b) minimum coverage rules focus on the mix of employees (that is, the percentage of NHCEs relative to HCEs) benefiting under the plan, the IRC § 401(a)(4) nondiscrimination requirement focuses on the actual benefits or contributions provided by the plan.

The Treasury regulations implementing IRC § 401(a)(4) have three basic requirements:

(1)   A core "amounts" rule requires that the amount of contributions or benefits not discriminate in favor of HCEs.[128]

(2)   Other benefits, rights, and features must not discriminate in favor of HCEs.[129] Benefits, rights, and features include optional benefit forms, such as retirement annuities and lump sum payments, ancillary benefits, such as disability benefits, and other rights and features, such as plan loans and investment options.[130]

(3)   The plan must not discriminate in favor of HCEs in special circumstances, such as plan amendments, including grants of past service credit, and plan terminations.[131]

A plan must comply with the regulations in both form and in substance. Intent is irrelevant.[132]

---

[128]   Treas. Reg. § 1.401(a)(4)-1(b)(2).

[129]   Treas. Reg. § 1.401(a)(4)-1(b)(3).

[130]   Treas. Reg. § 1.401(a)(4)-4(a).

[131]   Treas. Reg. § 1.401(a)(4)-1(b)(4).

[132]   Treas. Reg. § 1.401(a)(4)-1(a).

[A]   Overview of IRC § 401(a)(4)

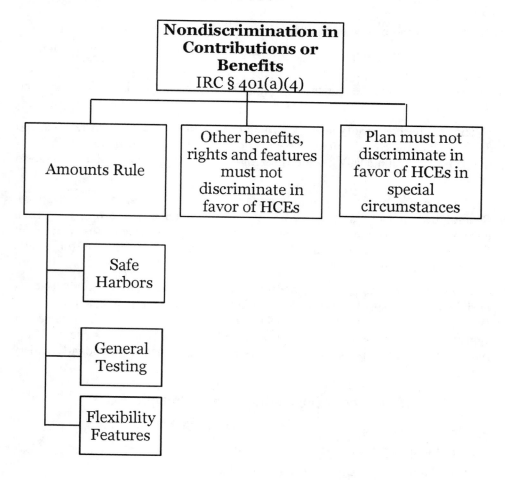

[B]   Amounts Rule

The Treasury regulations require that the "amount" of contributions or benefits provided by a qualified retirement plan not discriminate in favor of HCEs.

Typically, a defined contribution plan satisfies the nondiscriminatory amount requirement by showing that the contributions provided by the plan are not discriminatory in amount, while a defined benefit plan satisfies the requirement by showing that benefits provided under the plan are not discriminatory in amount. The regulations, however, permit a defined contribution plan to satisfy the requirement by showing that benefits are not discriminatory in amount while a defined benefit plan may satisfy the requirement by showing that contributions are not discriminatory in amount.[133]

---

[133] Treas. Reg. § 1.401(a)(4)-1(b)(2)(ii)(A) & (iii). An employer might elect to cross-test a defined

A three-step process applies to determine whether a plan satisfies the amounts rule.

(1)   Does the plan satisfy a "safe harbor?"

(2)   If the plan does not satisfy a safe harbor, does the plan pass "general testing?"

(3)   If the plan does not pass general testing, apply "flexibility features" and retest.

The safe harbors are typically based on the contribution or benefit formula and do not look at the contributions or benefits provided to each individual employee. If the plan falls within a safe harbor, it satisfies IRC § 401(a)(4) and there is no need to go further.

If a plan does not satisfy a safe harbor, the "general test" must be applied. General testing looks at the actual benefits or contributions provided to each employee to determine whether the plan, as a whole, discriminates in favor of HCEs. If the plan passes general testing, the plan satisfies IRC § 401(a)(4) and there is no need to go further.

If the plan does not satisfy general testing, the employer may use a variety of flexibility techniques to determine whether the plan discriminates in favor of HCEs. These flexibility features include restructuring the plan into halves or aggregating two plans and testing them together. If the plan is restructured, the restructured plan must satisfy IRC § 410(b) but not need independently satisfy IRC § 401(a)(26).

[1]   Safe Harbors for Defined Contribution Plans

There are two safe harbors for defined contribution plans:

(1)   the uniform allocation formula, and

(2)   the uniform points allocation formula.

The uniform allocation formula is the most common safe harbor. It is a design-based safe harbor. Thus, if a plan satisfies this safe harbor, it will always satisfy IRC § 401(a)(4) and does not need to be tested each year.

The uniform points allocation formula is not a design-based safe harbor. Thus, a plan falling within this safe harbor must be tested each year to ensure that the average allocation rate for the HCEs does not exceed the average allocation rate for the NHCEs.

---

benefit plan if the plan provides benefits that represent a larger proportion of compensation for HCEs than for NHCEs. For example, if the normal retirement benefit for a HCE were 50% of the final average compensation while the normal retirement benefit for a NHCE was 40% of final average compensation, the plan would not satisfy IRC § 401(a)(4) if the plan were tested based on the benefits provided by the plan. If, however, the HCEs were younger than the NHCEs, then the HCEss benefits would be funded over a longer period of time, and thus, the contributions necessary to fund their benefits might not be discriminatory in favor of the HCEs.

[a]   Uniform Allocation Formula

A defined contribution plan satisfies the uniform allocation formula if all employer contributions and forfeitures for the plan year are allocated or treated as allocated under a single formula that provides all employees with

(1)   the same percentage of plan year compensation,

(2)   the same dollar amount, or

(3)   the same dollar amount for each uniform unit of service (not to exceed one week) performed by the employee during the plan year.[134]

Both contributions and forfeitures must be allocated under a uniform formula for purposes of this safe harbor.

For purposes of this safe harbor, a plan can take into account permitted disparity under IRC § 401(l) if the plan follows IRC § 401(l) in form.[135]

Example 1

Under Employer A's profit-sharing plan, each eligible employee receives an allocation each plan year equal to 5% of compensation. In 2014, all of A's employees participated in and received an allocation under the plan. The plan satisfies the uniform allocation formula safe harbor and thus satisfies the Treasury regulation's IRC § 401(a)(4) amounts rule.

Example 2

Under Employer B's profit-sharing plan, each eligible employee receives an allocation each plan year equal to $1,000. In 2014, all of A's employees participated in and received an allocation under the plan. The plan satisfies the uniform allocation formula safe harbor and thus satisfies the Treasury regulation's IRC § 401(a)(4) amounts rule.

[b]   Uniform Points Allocation Formula

The uniform points allocation formula is available to all defined contribution plans, other than ESOPs.[136]

A plan satisfies the uniform points allocation formula if:

(1)   the plan allocates amounts under a uniform points allocation formula; and

(2)   for the plan year, the average of the allocation rates for the HCEs does not exceed the average allocation rates for the NHCEs.

Uniform points plans must allocate the employer's contributions to each employee's account by multiplying the total employer contribution by a fraction. The numerator of the fraction is the employee's number of points, and the

---

[134] Treas. Reg. § 1.401(a)(4)-2(b)(2).

[135] For a discussion of permitted disparity, see Kathryn L. Moore, *The Effects of Partial Privatization of Social Security upon Private Pensions*, 58 WASH. & LEE L. REV. 1255, 1257–72 (2001).

[136] Treas. Reg. § 1.401(a)(4)-2(b)(3).

denominator is the total number of points for all participants.

Points must be based on some combination of units of compensation, age, and service. The formula must award the same number of points for each year of service, year of age, and unit of compensation. Thus, a plan could not award one point for each year of service up to 15 and two points for each year of service in excess of 15. The plan, however, may cap the number of points for years of service. Compensation points must be awarded on the same basis for all employees, and such points must be based on increments of single dollar amounts, not to exceed $200.

Allocation rates are calculated in the same manner as in general testing, which is described in the following section, except that IRC § 401(l) permitted disparity may not be taken into account and the general testing allocation group rate method may not be used.

Example[137]

Employer C's plan has a single allocation formula that applies to all employees, under which an employee's allocation for the plan year equals the product of the total of all amounts taken into account for all employees for the plan year and a fraction, the numerator of which is the employee's points for the plan year and the denominator of which is the sum of the points of all employees for the plan year. The plan grants each employee 10 points for each year of service and one point for each $100 of plan year compensation.

For the 2014 plan year, the total allocations are $71,200 and the total points for all employees are 7,120. Each employee's allocation for the 2014 plan year is set forth in the table below.

Employee	Years of Service	Plan Year Compensation	Points	Amount of allocation	Allocation rate (percent)
HCE1	20	$150,000	1,700	$17,000	11.3
HCE2	10	$150,000	1,600	$1,6000	10.7
NHCE1	30	$100,000	1,300	$13,000	13.0
NHCE2	3	$100,000	1,030	$10,300	10.3
NHCE3	10	$40,000	500	$5,000	12.5
NHCE4	5	$35,000	400	$4,000	11.4
NHCE5	3	$30,000	330	$3,300	11.0
NHCE6	1	$25,000	260	$2,600	10.4
			7,120	$71,200	

For the 2014 plan year, Employer C's plan satisfies the uniform points allocation formula because (1) the plan allocates amounts under a uniform points allocation formula; and (2) for the 2014 plan year, the average of the allocation rates for the HCEs does not exceed the average allocation rates for the NHCEs. Specifically, the average allocation rate for the HCEs is 11 ((11.3 + 10.7 = 22)/2 = 11) while the

---

[137] Treas. Reg. § 1.401(a)(4)-2(b)(3)(ii) Example.

average allocation rate for the NHCEs is 11.43 ((13.0 + 10.3 + 12.5 + 11.4 + 11.0 + 10.4 = 68.6)/6 = 11.43).

[2]   General Testing of Defined Contribution Plans

If a defined contribution plan does not satisfy either of the safe harbors, then general testing must be applied to determine whether the plan satisfies IRC § 401(a)(4).

General testing of a defined contribution plan involves a two-step process:

(1)   The plan must be divided into rate groups; and

(2)   After the plan is divided into rate groups, each rate group must be tested to see if it satisfies IRC § 410(b).[138]

[a]   Dividing Plan into Rate Groups

A rate group exists under a plan for each HCE in the plan.[139]

Each rate group consists of that HCE and all other employees (both highly compensated and nonhighly compensated) who have an allocation rate that is greater than or equal to the HCE's allocation rate.[140]

An employee's allocation rate is based on the employer contributions and forfeitures that are allocated to the employee's account for the year.[141] The allocation rate does not include amounts attributable to earnings, expenses, gains, and losses.[142]

Example

Employer A's profit-sharing plan covered the following six employees with the following allocation rates.

Employee	Allocation
HCE 1	8%
HCE 2	7%
NHCE 1	8%
NHCE 2	7%
NHCE 3	6%
NHCE 4	6%

Employer A's plan has two rate group rates, one for each of the two HCEs.

Rate group 1 consists of HCE 1 and all employees with an allocation rate equal

---

[138] Treas. Reg. § 1.401(a)(4)-2(c).

[139] Treas. Reg. § 1.401(a)(4)-2(c)(1).

[140] Treas. Reg. § 1.401(a)(4)-2(c)(1).

[141] Treas. Reg. § 1.401(a)(4)-2(c)(2)(ii).

[142] Treas. Reg. § 1.401(a)(4)-2(c)(2)(iii).

to or greater than HCE 1's allocation rate. Thus, rate group 1 consists of HCE 1 and NHCE 1.

Rate group 2 consists of HCE 2 and all employees with an allocation rate equal to or greater than HCE 2's allocation rate. Thus, rate group 2 consists of HCE 1, HCE 2, NHCE 1, and NHCE 2.

[b]   Testing Each Rate Group

Once the rate groups are determined, each rate group must be tested to see if it satisfies IRC § 410(b).

The rules that apply in determining whether a rate group satisfies IRC § 410(b) are generally the same as those that apply in determining whether a plan satisfies IRC § 410(b). There are, however, some modifications to Treasury regulations governing IRC § 410(b) average benefits testing. First, the discretionary elements of the test are eliminated. Specifically, the reasonable classification test is not applied in testing a rate group, and a rate group is deemed to satisfy the Treas. Reg. § 1.410(b)-4 nondiscriminatory classification test if and only if the ratio percentage of the rate group is greater than or equal to the lesser of (A) the midpoint between the safe and the unsafe harbor percentages applicable to the plan, and (B) the ratio percentage of the plan.[143] In addition, if the plan as a whole satisfies the average benefits percentage test, each rate group is treated as satisfying the average benefits percentage test.[144]

Example

Again, Employer A's profit-sharing covered the following six employees with the following allocation rates:

Employee	Allocation
HCE 1	8%
HCE 2	7%
NHCE 1	8%
NHCE 2	7%
NHCE 3	6%
NHCE 4	6%

As discussed above, Employer A's profit-sharing plan has two rate groups. Rate group 1 consists of HCE 1 and NHCE 1. It excludes HCE 2, NHCE 2, NHCE 3, and NHCE 4. Rate group 2 consists of HCE 1, HCE 2, NHCE 1, and NHCE 2. It excludes NHCE 3 and NHCE 4.

Rate group 1:

The percentage of NHCEs benefiting in rate group 1 is 25%. (1/4 = 25%). Because the percentage of NHCEs benefiting in rate group 1 is less than 70%, rate

---

[143] Treas. Reg. § 1.401(a)(4)-2(c)(3)(ii).

[144] Treas. Reg. § 1.401(a)(4)-2(c)(3)(iii).

group 1 clearly does not satisfy IRC § 410(b)(1)(A).

The ratio percentage of rate group 1 is 50%. (The percentage of NHCEs benefiting is 25% and the percentage of HCEs benefiting is 50% (1/2 = 50%). Thus, the ratio percentage is 50% (25%/50% = 50%).) Because the ratio percentage of rate group 1 is less than 70%, rate group 1 clearly does not satisfy IRC § 410(b)(1)(B).

Finally, in order to determine whether rate group 1 satisfies IRC § 410(b)(1)(C), it is first necessary to determine the NHCE concentration percentage. The NHCE concentration percentage is 66.67% (4/6). The midpoint between the safe harbor (45.5%) and unsafe harbor (35.5%) for a NHCE concentration percentage of 66.67% is 40.5%. Because rate group 1's ratio percentage (50%) exceeds the midpoint between the applicable safe harbor and unsafe harbor, rate group 1 satisfies the nondiscriminatory classification test.

Once it is determined that rate group 1 satisfies the nondiscriminatory classification test, it must be determined whether the rate group satisfies the IRC § 410(b)(1)(C) average benefits percentage test. A rate group satisfies the average benefits percentage test if the plan of which it is a part satisfies the Treas. Reg. § 410(b)-5 average benefits percentage test. The average benefit percentage test is satisfied if the average benefit percentage of NHCEs divided by the average benefits percentage of HCEs is greater than or equal to 70%.

The average benefit percentage of the HCEs benefiting under Employer A's profit-sharing plan is 7.5% (8 + 7 = 15)/2 = 7.5%. The average benefit percentage of the NHCEs benefiting under the plan is 6.75% (8 + 7 + 6 + 6 = 27)/4 = 6.75%. Because the average benefit percentage of the NHCEs is 90% of the average benefit percentage of the highly compensated (6.75%/7.5% = 90%), the plan, and thus rate group 1 satisfies the average benefits percentage test.

Rate group 2:

The percentage of NHCEs benefiting in rate group 2 is 50%. (2/4 = 50%). Because the percentage of NHCEs benefiting in rate group 2 is less than 70%, rate group 2 clearly does not satisfy IRC § 410(b)(1)(A).

The ratio percentage of rate group 2 is 50%. (The percentage of NHCEs benefiting is 50% and the percentage of HCEs benefiting is 100%. (2/2 = 100%) Thus, the ratio percentage is 50% (50%/100% = 50%).) Because the ratio percentage of rate group 2 is less than 70%, rate group 2 clearly does not satisfy IRC § 410(b)(1)(B).

As discussed above, the NHCE concentration percentage for Employer A is 66.67% (4/6), and the midpoint between the safe harbor (45.5%) and unsafe harbor (35.5%) for a NHCE concentration percentage is 39%. Because rate group 2's ratio percentage (50%) exceeds the midpoint between the applicable safe harbor and unsafe harbor (40.5%), rate group 2 satisfies the nondiscriminatory classification test.

In addition, because, as discussed above, the average benefit percentage of the NHCEs is 90% of the average benefit percentage of the highly compensated, the plan, and thus rate group 2 satisfies the average benefits percentage test.

Because both rate groups satisfy IRC § 410(b), the plan satisfies IRC § 401(a)(4).

[3] Flexibility Features

If a defined contribution plan does not satisfy general testing, an employer may use a variety of flexibility techniques to try to satisfy the nondiscrimination amounts rule. These flexibility features may permit the employer to adjust the size of the plan or the rates.

There are four basic flexibility features:

(1) plan aggregation,

(2) plan restructuring,

(3) rate grouping, and

(4) "imputed" permitted disparity.

First, the Treasury regulations permit employers in some instances to aggregate or combine two or more plans and treat the aggregated plans as a single plan for purposes of the nondiscrimination rules.[145] Second, the Treasury regulations permit employers to restructure or divide a plan into separate component plans and test each component plan separately.[146] Third, the Treasury regulations permit employers to group or "round" rates so that employees with similar allocation or accrual rates may be treated as having the same rates for testing purposes.[147] Finally, the Treasury regulations permit employers to take into account permitted disparity in general testing; in essence, the permitted disparity rules permit an employer to take credit for Social Security benefits or contributions as if the employer provided them in determining whether a plan discriminates in favor of HCEs.[148]

---

[145] Treas. Reg. § 1.410(b)-7(d).

[146] Treas. Reg. § 1.401(a)(4)-9.

[147] Treas. Reg. § 1.401(a)(4)-2(c)(2)(V).

[148] Treas. Reg. § 1.401(a)(4)-7.

[4]   Summary of Amounts Rule as Applied to Defined Contribution Plans

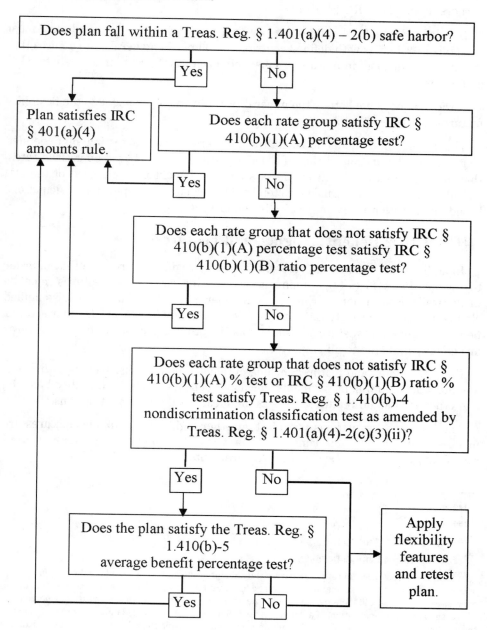

[5]   Testing of Defined Benefit Plans

The IRC § 401(a)(4) nondiscrimination rules apply to defined benefit plans in much the same manner as they apply to defined contribution plans.

Just as there are safe harbors for defined contribution plans, there are safe harbors for defined benefit plans.[149] If a defined benefit plan satisfies one of the safe harbors, it satisfies IRC § 401(a)(4).

If a defined benefit plan does not satisfy a safe harbor, the "general test" must be applied.[150] Just as with defined contribution plans, the general test requires that the plan be divided into rate groups and each rate group must satisfy IRC § 410(b).[151]

If the plan does not satisfy the general test, the employer may use the flexibility features and retest the plan.[152]

The testing of a defined benefit plan differs from the testing of a defined contribution plan in that testing of a defined benefit plan is based on accrual rates, that is, the increase in each employee's accrued benefit over a period of time.[153] Calculations based on accrual rates tend to be much more complex than calculations based on allocation rates and typically require actuarial calculations.

[C]   Other Benefits, Rights, and Features

In addition to the amounts rule, the Treasury regulations require that in order to satisfy IRC § 401(a)(4), a plan's other benefits, rights, and features must be made available in a nondiscriminatory manner.[154] A plan will not be disqualified simply because more HCEs than NHCEs take advantage of the plan's other benefits, rights, and features — so long as the other benefits, rights, and features are equally available to all employees.

Benefits, rights, and features include optional benefit forms, such as retirement annuities and lump sum payments, ancillary benefits, such as disability benefits, and other rights and features, such as plan loans and investment options.[155]

The Treasury regulations provide that other rights, benefits, and features are made available in a nondiscriminatory manner if, and only if, they satisfy current availability and effective availability requirements.[156]

---

[149] Treas. Reg. § 1.401(a)(4)-3(b).

[150] Treas. Reg. § 1.401(a)(4)-3(c).

[151] Treas. Reg. § 1.401(a)(4)-3(c).

[152] Treas. Reg. § 1.401(a)(4)-3(a)(2).

[153] An employee's accrual rate is generally the amount of the annual payments under the employee's accrued benefit payable at normal retirement age (or other testing age prescribed under the regulations) expressed as a straight life annuity divided by the employee's years of service, expressed as percentage of average annual compensation. If a defined benefit plan provides subsidized optional forms of benefits, the accrual rate for the most valuable benefit under the plan available to each employee is also calculated and tested. Joint Committee on Taxation, *Present Law and Background Relating to the Tax Treatment of Retirement Savings*, JCX-44-11, at 23 n.77 (Sept. 13, 2011). For the rules regarding the determination of accrual rates, see Treas. Reg. § 1.401(a)(4)-3(d).

[154] Treas. Reg. § 1.401(a)(4)-1(b)(3).

[155] Treas. Reg. § 1.401(a)(4)-4(e)(1).

[156] Treas. Reg. § 1.401(a)(4)-4(a).

In general, a benefit, right, or feature satisfies the current availability requirement if the group of employees to whom it is available satisfies IRC § 410(b) without regard to the Treas. Reg. § 1.410(b)-5 average benefits percentage test.[157] Current availability is based on the facts and circumstances relating to the employee (*e.g.*, current compensation, accrued benefit, position, or net worth).[158]

In general, based on all the facts and circumstances, the group of employees to whom a benefit, right, or feature is effectively available must not substantially favor HCEs.[159]

Example[160]

Employer A maintains a defined benefit plan that covers both of its HCEs and nine of its 12 NHCEs. The plan provides for a normal retirement benefit payable as an annuity based on a normal retirement age. In addition, the plan provides for an early retirement benefit payable upon termination in the form of an annuity to employees who terminate from service with the employer on or after 55 years of age with 30 or more years of service.

Both of Employer A's HCEs currently meet the age and service requirement or will have 30 years of service by the time they reach age 55. In contrast, all but two of the nine NHCEs covered by the plan were hired on or after age 35 and thus cannot qualify for the early retirement benefit.

The group of employees to whom the early retirement benefit is currently available satisfies IRC § 410(b) when age and service are disregarded. (9/12 = 75%). Nevertheless, absent other facts, the group of employees to whom the early retirement benefit is effectively available substantially favors HCEs.

[D]   Special Circumstances

In addition to the amounts rule and requirement that a plan's other benefits, rights and features not discriminate in favor of HCEs, the Treasury regulations require that the plan not discriminate in special circumstances in order for a plan to satisfy IRC § 401(a)(4).

Specifically, the Treasury regulations require that plan amendments, including grants of past service credit, and terminations not discriminate in favor of HCEs.[161] Whether a plan amendment discriminates is determined at the time the plan amendment first become effective based on all the facts and circumstances.[162]

Relevant facts and circumstances include the relative number of current and former HCEs and NHCEs affected by the plan amendment, the relative length of service of the current and former HCEs and NHCEs, the length of time the plan

---

[157] Treas. Reg. § 1.401(a)(4)-4(b)(1).

[158] Treas. Reg. § 1.401(a)(4)-4(b)(2)(i).

[159] Treas. Reg. § 1.401(a)(4)-4(c)(1).

[160] Treas. Reg. § 1.401(a)(4)-4(c)(2) Example 1.

[161] Treas. Reg. § 1.401(a)(4)-1(b)(4).

[162] Treas. Reg. § 1.401(a)(4)-5(a)(2).

or plan provision being amended has been in effect, and the turnover of employees prior to the plan amendment.[163]

This requirement is designed to prevent employers from taking advantage of changes in the composition of the employer's workforce to amend the plan so as to discriminate in favor of HCEs. If this requirement did not apply, then an employer might amend its plan to increase benefits just after a large number of NHCEs quit working for the employer. Or an employer might amend its plan to eliminate an optional form of benefit just after a number of HCEs took advantage of the benefit.

Example[164]

Employer A has a defined benefit plan that covered both HCEs and NHCEs during most of its existence. The employer is in the process of winding up its business. After all of the NHCEs have been terminated, when the plan covers only HCEs, Employer A amends the plan to increase benefits and then terminates the plan. The timing of this plan amendment has the effect of discriminating significantly in favor of HCEs.

§ 9.09   A CLOSER LOOK AT THE NONDISCRIMINATION RULES FOR 401(k) PLANS

Like all qualified plans, 401(k) plans are subject to nondiscrimination rules.

Because 401(k) plans must be defined contribution plans and not defined benefit plans,[165] they are not subject to the IRC § 401(a)(26) minimum participation requirement discussed in § 9.06. Like all other qualified plans, however, they must satisfy the IRC § 410(b) nondiscriminatory coverage requirement and the IRC § 401(a)(4) requirement that qualified plans not discriminate in contributions or benefits.

Generally, the regular IRC § 410(b) coverage rules apply to 401(k) plans.[166] An individual, however, will be treated as benefiting from a 401(k) plan for purposes of the IRC § 410(b) coverage requirement if the individual is eligible to participate in the plan even if the individual does not elect to participate.[167] The IRC § 410(b) coverage rules are discussed in detail in § 9.07.

A plan will be deemed to satisfy the IRC § 401(a)(4) core amounts rule discussed in § 9.08[B] if it satisfies one of two alternative special nondiscrimination require-

---

[163] Treas. Reg. § 1.401(a)(4)-5(a)(2). A safe harbor is provided for certain grants of benefits for past service. Treas. Reg. § 1.401(a)(4)-5(a)(3).

[164] Treas. Reg. § 1.401(a)(4)-5(a)(4) Example 1.

[165] Specifically, a 401(k) feature may be part of a profit-sharing plan, a stock bonus plan, a pre-ERISA money purchase plan, or a rural cooperative plan. IRC § 401(k)(1). Profit-sharing plans and stock bonus plans are traditional defined contribution plans. *See* Chapter 2 § 2.04[E]. In addition, pre-ERISA money purchase plans and rural cooperative plans must be defined contribution plans. *See* IRC §§ 401(k)(6)(A) & 401(k)(7)(A)(i).

[166] § 401(k)(3)(A)(i).

[167] Treas. Reg. § 1.410(b)-3(a)(2)(B).

ments set forth in IRC § 401(k)(3)(A)(ii).[168]

Generally, an employer must test its 401(k) plan each year to determine if it satisfies one of the IRC § 401(k)(3)(A)(ii) special nondiscrimination requirements. If a plan fails to satisfy at least one of the alternative special nondiscrimination tests, the plan may be corrected in one of three different ways: (1) by returning the excess contributions, (2) by recharacterizing the excess contributions as after-tax contributions, or (3) by the employer making certain nonelective contributions to the plan.[169]

If the employer wishes to avoid the cost of testing and potentially correcting the plan each year, the employer may structure its plan so as to satisfy one of two sets of statutory safe harbors set forth in IRC §§ 401(k)(12) and 401(k)(13).

---

[168] Treas. Reg. § 1.401(a)(4)-1(b)(2)(ii)(B). 401(k) plans are also subject to the other rights, benefits, and features requirement of the § 401(a)(4) Treasury regulations. Treas. Reg. § 1.401(k)-1(a)(iv)(B).

[169] Treas. Reg. § 1.401(k)-1(f).

[A]   Overview of IRC § 401(k) Special Nondiscrimination Testing

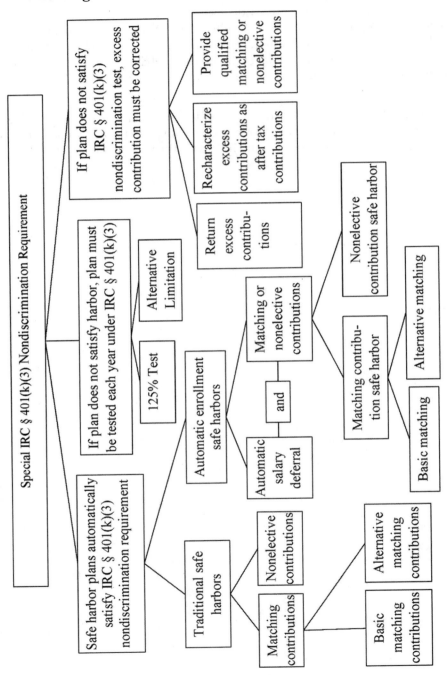

[B] Special IRC § 401(k)(3)(A)(ii) Nondiscrimination Tests

Section 401(k)(3)(A)(ii) of the Internal Revenue Code sets forth two alternative nondiscrimination tests that a 401(k) plan must satisfy in order to be eligible for favorable income tax treatment.

The tests compare the "actual deferral percentage" (ADP) of eligible HCEs with the ADP of eligible NHCEs.

[1] "Actual Deferral Percentage" (ADP)

The actual deferral percentage (ADP) is defined as the average of the ratios (calculated separately for each employee in the group) of the amount of the employer contributions[170] actually paid over to the trust on behalf of each employee for the plan year to the employee's compensation for the plan year.[171]

For administrative convenience, the NHCEs' ADP for the preceding year is normally taken into account in testing the plan.[172] If the employer elects, it may test the plan based on the ADP of the NHCEs for the current year rather than the preceding plan year.[173] If the employer makes such an election, however, it is generally binding for five years.[174]

Determining the ADP for the HCEs and the ADP for the NHCEs generally involves a three-step process.

(1) The HCEs must be identified.

(2) The actual deferral ratio (ADR) for the current plan year for each HCE must be calculated, and the actual deferral ratio for the preceding plan year for each NHCE must be calculated.

(3) The ADP for the HCEs for the current plan year must be calculated while the ADP for the preceding plan year for the NHCEs must be calculated.

In testing a plan for its first year, the ADP for the NHCEs "for the preceding plan year" is either 3% or, if the employer elects, the actual ADP for the NHCEs for the plan's first year.[175]

[a]   Highly Compensated Employees (HCEs)

HCEs are those employees who meet the IRC § 414(q) definition of HCE as discussed in § 9.05.

---

[170] For purposes of this test, elective contributions, that is, contributions that an employee elects to make to the 401(k) plan rather than receive as taxable income, are "employer contributions." *See* Treas. Reg. § 1.401(k)-6 (defining "elective contributions" as "employer contributions made to a plan pursuant to a cash or deferred election under a cash or deferred arrangement (whether or not the arrangement is a qualified cash or deferred arrangement under § 1.401(k)-1(a)(4))).

[171] IRC § 401(k)(3)(B).

[172] IRC § 401(k)(3)(A).

[173] IRC § 401(k)(3)(a)(ii).

[174] *Id.* Treas. Reg. § 1.410(k)-2(c)(1).

[175] IRC § 401(k)(3)(E).

[b]   Actual Deferral Ratio (ADR)

The actual deferral ratio is the ratio of the amount of contributions actually paid over to the 401(k) plan on behalf of an employee to the employee's compensation for the plan year.

Example 1

HCE 1 earns $200,000 in compensation. He elects to contribute $15,000 to his employer's 401(k) plan. HCE 1's ADR is 7.5% ($15,000/$200,000 = 7.5%).

Example 2

NHCE 1 earns $50,000 in compensation. She elects to contribute $5,000 to her employer's 401(k). NHCE 1's ADR is 10% ($5,000/$50,000 = 10%).

Example 3

HCE 2 earns $500,000 and elects to contribute $15,900 to his employer's 401(k) plan in 2015. Under IRC § 401(a)(17), as discussed in Chapter 10 § 10.2[A], the maximum amount of compensation that can be taken into account for qualified plan purposes is $265,000 in 2015. Thus, HCE 2's ADR is 6% ($15,900/$265,000 = 6%).

[c]   Actual Deferral Percentage

The actual deferral percentage is the average of the actual deferral ratios for each group.

Example

Employer A's 401(k) plan covers four employees, two HCEs, and two NHCEs. The compensation, elective deferrals, and ADRs for the HCEs for the current year and for the NHCEs for the preceding year are as follows:

Employee	Compensation	Contribution	ADR
HCE 1	$200,000	$15,000	7.5%
HCE 2	$150,000	$12,000	8%
NHCE 1	$70,000	$4,200	6%
NHCE 2	$35,000	$1,050	3%

The ADP for the HCEs is 7.75% ((7.5% + 8% = 15.5%)/2 = 7.75%)). The ADP for the NHCEs is 4.5% ((6% + 3% = 9%)/2 = 4.5%))

[2]   ADP Tests under IRC § 401(k)(3)(A)(ii)

Section 401(k)(3)(A)(ii) of the Internal Revenue Code requires that a 401(k) plan satisfy one of two alternative tests:

(1)   a "125% test" under IRC § 401(k)(3)(A)(ii)(I), or

(2)   an alternative limitation under IRC § 401(k)(3)(A)(ii)(II).

[a]   IRC § 401(k)(3)(A)(ii)(I) 125% Test

Under the first, "125% test," the ADP of eligible HCEs for the current plan year must be no more than the ADP of all other eligible employees for the preceding plan year multiplied by 1.25.[176]

IRC § 401(k)(3)(A)(ii)(I) 125% test

ADP of HCEs $\leq$ 1.25 x ADP of NHCEs

Example 1

Employer A has adopted a qualified profit-sharing plan with a 401(k) feature in which all four of its employees are eligible to participate. The plan permits employees to contribute up to the 402(g) limit, which is $18,000 in 2015.[177] Employer A has elected to include salary reduction amounts in the definition of compensation. This is the only plan provided by Employer A and no employees have any ownership interest in Employer A. The compensation, deferred amounts, ADRs, and ADPs for the HCEs for the current year and the NHCEs for the preceding year are as follows:

Employee	Compensation	Contribution	ADR	ADP
HCE 1	$150,000	$16,500	16,500/150,000 = 11%	ADP of HCEs = (11 + 10)/2 = 10.5%
HCE 2	$140,000	$14,000	14,000/140,000 = 10%	
NHCE 1	$75,000	$9,000	9,000/75,000 = 12%	ADP of NHCEs = (12 +9)/2 = 10.5%
NHCE 2	$65,000	$5,850	5,850/65,000 = 9%	

The plan satisfies the 125% test because the ADP of the HCEs (10.5%) is no greater than 125% of the ADP of the NHCEs (10.5% x 1.25 = 13.125%).

Example 2

Employer B has adopted a qualified profit-sharing plan with a 401(k) feature in which all six of its employees are eligible to participate. The plan permits employees to contribute up to 10% of their salary. Employer B has elected to include salary reduction amounts in the definition of compensation. This is the only

---

[176] IRC § 401(k)(3)(A)(ii)(I).

[177] IRC § 402(g) is discussed in Chapter 10 § 10.02[C].

plan provided by Employer B and no employees have any ownership interest in Employer B. The compensation, deferred amounts, ADRs, and ADPs for the HCEs for the current year and the NHCEs for the preceding year are as follows:

Employee	Compensation	Contribution	ADR	ADP
HCE 1	$175,000	$17,500	17,500/175,000 = 10%	ADP for HCEs = (10 + 5 = 15)/2 = 7.5%
HCE 2	$150,000	$7,500	7,500/150,000 = 5%	
NHCE 1	$70,000	$7,000	7,000/70,000 = 10%	ADP for NHCEs = (10 + 7 + 5 + 0 = 25)/ 4 = 5.5%
NHCE 2	$50,000	$3,500	3,500/50,000 = 7%	
NHCE 3	$40,000	$2,000	2,000/40,000 = 5%	
NHCE 4	$30,000	$0	0/30,000 = 0%	

The plan does not satisfy the 125% test because the ADP of the HCEs (7.5%) is greater than 125% of the ADPs of the NHCEs (5.5% x 1.25 = 6.875%).

Although the plan does not satisfy the 125% test, it may still satisfy the IRC § 401(k)(3)(A)(ii) nondiscrimination test if it satisfies the IRC § 401(k)(3)(A)(ii)(II) alternative limitation.

[b]   IRC § 401(k)(3)(A)(ii)(II) Alternative Limitation

Under the IRC § 401(k)(3)(A)(ii)(II) alternative limitation, a plan will satisfy the IRC § 401(k)(3)(A)(ii) nondiscrimination requirement if the ADP of the eligible HCEs for the current plan year is no more than

(1) 2 percentage points higher than the ADP of all other eligible employees for the preceding year, and

(2) no more than twice the ADP of all other eligible employees for the preceding plan year.

IRC § 401(k)(3)(ii)(II) Alternative Limitation

ADP of HCES $\leq$ ADP of NHCES + 2

and

ADP of HCES $\leq$ ADP of NHCES x 2

Example 1

Recall Example 2 above in which Employer B has adopted a qualified profit-sharing plan with a 401(k) feature in which all six of its employees are eligible to participate. The plan permits employees to contribute up to 10% of their salary. Employer B has elected to include salary reduction amounts in the definition of compensation. This is the only plan provided by Employer B and no employees have any ownership interest in Employer B. The compensation, deferred amounts, ADRs, and ADPs for the HCEs for the current year and the NHCEs for the preceding year are as follows:

Employee	Compensation	Contribution	ADR	ADP
HCE 1	$175,000	$17,500	17,500/175,000 = 10%	ADP for HCEs = (10 + 5 = 15)/2 = 7.5%
HCE 2	$150,000	$7,500	7,500/150,000 = 5%	
NHCE 1	$70,000	$7,000	7,000/70,000 = 10%	ADP for NHCEs = (10 + 7 + 5 + 0 = 25)/ 4 = 5.5%
NHCE 2	$50,000	$3,500	3,500/50,000 = 7%	
NHCE 3	$40,000	$2,000	2,000/40,000 = 5%	
NHCE 4	$30,000	$0	0/30,000 = 0%	

Although Employer B's plan does not satisfy the 125% test, it does satisfy the IRC § 401(k)(3)(A)(ii)(II) alternative limitation because the ADP of the HCEs (7.5%) is no more than 2 x the ADP of the NHCEs (5.5% x 2 = 11%) and no more than the ADP of the NHCEs + 2 (5.5% + 2 = 7.5%). Thus, Employer B's plan satisfies the IRC § 401(k)(3)(A)(ii) nondiscrimination requirement.

Example 2

Employer C has adopted a qualified profit-sharing plan with a 401(k) feature in which all six of its employees are eligible to participate. The plan permits employees to contribute up to 10% of their salary. Employer C has elected to include salary reduction amounts in the definition of compensation. This is the only plan provided by Employer C and no employees have any ownership interest in Employer C. The compensation, deferred amounts, ADRs, and ADPs for the HCEs for the current year and the NHCEs for the preceding year are as follows:

Employee	Compensation	Contribution	ADR	ADP
HCE 1	$190,000	$13,300	13,300/190,000 = 7%	ADP of HCEs = (7 + 10 + 10 = 27)/3 = 9%
HCE 2	$150,000	$15,000	15,000/150,000 = 10%	
HCE 3	$140,000	$14,000	14,000/140,000 = 10%	
NHCE 1	$70,000	$7,000	7,000/70,000 = 10%	ADP of NHCEs = (10 + 5 + 0 = 15)/3 = 5%
NHCE 2	$50,000	$2,500	2,500/50,000 = 5%	
NHCE 3	$30,000	$0	0/30,000 = 0%	

The plan does not satisfy the alternative limitation because the ADP for the HCEs for the current plan year (9%) exceeds the ADP for the NHCEs for the preceding plan year (5%) by more than two percentage points (5% + 2 = 7%). (Although the ADP for the HCEs for the current plan year is not more than twice the ADP for NHCEs for the preceding plan year, the plan must satisfy both parts of the alternative limitation in order to satisfy the requirement).

In addition, the plan does not satisfy the 125% test because the ADP of the HCEs for the current plan year (9%) is more than 125% of the ADP of NHCEs for the preceding plan year (5% x 1.25 = 6.25%).

Because the plan does not satisfy either of the special IRC §401(k)(3)(A)(ii) nondiscrimination tests, the plan will not be eligible for favorable income tax treatment unless the excess contributions are corrected.

[c]   Rule of Thumb

As shown in the examples above, a plan may not satisfy the IRC § 401(k)(3)(A)(ii)(I) 125% test but may satisfy the IRC §401(k)(3)(A)(ii)(II) alternative limitation. In the alternative, a plan may satisfy the IRC §401(k)(3)(A)(ii)(I) 125% test but may not satisfy the IRC § 401(k)(3)(A)(ii) alternative limitation.

A plan need not satisfy both tests. Rather, a plan need only satisfy the test that sets the higher limit.

If the NHCEs' ADP is less than or equal to eight percent, the IRC §401(k)(3)(A)(ii)(II) alternative limitation will permit a higher maximum ADP for the HCEs. If the NHCEs' ADP is greater than eight percent, the IRC § 401(k)(3)(A)(ii)(I) 125% test will permit a higher maximum ADP for HCEs as shown below.

If the ADP of the NHCEs is:	The maximum allowable ADP of the HCEs is:
< 2%	ADP of NHCEs x 2
Between 2% and 8%	ADP of NHCEs + 2
> 8%	ADP of NHCEs x 1.25

Example 1

If the ADP of the NHCEs for the preceding plan year was 1%, under the IRC § 401(k)(3)(A)(ii)(I) 125% test, the maximum ADP for the HCES for the current year is 1.25% (1% x 1.25 = 1.25%).

If the ADP of the NHCEs for the preceding plan year was 1%, under the IRC § 401(k)(3)(A)(ii)(II) alternative limitation, the maximum ADP for the HCES for the current year is 2% (The lesser of (1% x 2 = 2%) and (1% + 2 = 3%) is 2%).

Thus, if the ADP of the NHCEs for the preceding plan year was 1%, the maximum ADP for the HCEs for the current year is 1% x 2 or 2%.

Example 2

If the ADP of the NHCEs for the preceding plan year was 4%, under the IRC § 401(k)(3)(A)(ii)(I) 125% test, the maximum ADP for the HCES for the current year is 5% (4% x 1.25 = 5%).

If the ADP of the NHCEs for the preceding plan year was 4%, under the IRC § 401(k)(3)(A)(ii)(II) alternative limitation, the maximum ADP for the HCES for the current year is 6% (The lesser of (4% x 2 = 8%) and (4% + 2 = 6%) is 6%).

Thus, if the ADP of the NHCEs for the preceding plan year was 4%, the maximum ADP for the HCEs for the current year is 4% + 2 or 6%.

Example 3

If the ADP of the NHCEs for the preceding plan year was 9%, under the IRC § 401(k)(3)(A)(ii)(I) 125% test, the maximum ADP for the HCEs for the current year is 11.25% (9% x 1.25 = 11.25%).

If the ADP of the NHCEs for the preceding plan year was 9%, under the IRC § 401(k)(3)(A)(ii)(II) alternative limitation, the maximum ADP for the HCES for the current year is 11% (The lesser of (9% x 2 = 18%) and (9% + 2 = 11%) is 11%).

Thus, if the ADP of the NHCEs for the preceding plan year was 9%, the maximum ADP for the HCEs for the current year is 9% x 1.25 or 11.25%.

[C] Methods for Correcting Excess Contributions

If a 401(k) plan does not satisfy either of the special IRC § 401(k)(3)(A)(ii) nondiscrimination tests for a plan year, the plan may provide for the correction of excess contributions in one or a combination of three ways:

(1) the excess contributions plus income allocated to those contributions may be distributed from the plan before the close of the following plan year,

(2) the excess contributions may be characterized as after-tax contributions, or

(3) the employer can make qualified nonelective or qualified matching contributions.[178]

Generally, if the excess contributions are not corrected within 2 1/2 months after the end of the plan year, the employer will incur a 10% excise tax on the amount of the excess contribution not corrected at that time.[179] If the excess contributions are not corrected within 12 months, the plan will be disqualified for the plan year in which the excess contributions were made and all subsequent plan years during which the excess contributions remain in the trust.[180] Thus, all plans should be drafted to include a correction method.

[1] Distribution of Excess Contributions

If a plan so provides, a plan may correct excess contributions by distributing the excess contributions.[181]

Excess contributions are defined as the excess of the total amount of contributions actually paid to a 401(k) plan on behalf of HCEs for the plan year over the maximum amount of contributions permissible under the special IRC § 401(k)(3)(A)(ii) nondiscrimination tests.[182]

The Treasury regulations[183] establish a four-step process for distributing excess contributions:

(1) The plan must determine the total amount of excess contributions that must be distributed under the plan.

(2) The plan must apportion the total amount of excess contributions among the HCEs.

(3) The plan must determine the income allocable to the excess contributions.

(4) The plan must distribute the apportioned excess contributions and allocable income.

---

[178] Treas. Reg. § 1.401(k)-2(b)(1).

[179] IRC § 4979. Treas. Reg. § 1.401(k)-2(b)(5)(i). Plans with automatic contribution arrangements must be corrected within six months rather than within 2 1/2 months. Treas. Reg. § 1.401(k)-2(b)(5)(iii).

[180] Treas. Reg. § 1.401(k)-2(b)(5)(ii).

[181] IRC § 401(k)(8)(A)(i).

[182] IRC § 401(k)(8)(B).

[183] Treas. Reg. § 1.401(k)-2(b)(2).

[a]   Step One

In order to determine the total amount of excess contributions that must distributed, the dollar amount of the excess contributions for each affected HCE must be calculated.

The amount of excess contributions attributable to an HCE is the amount (if any) by which the HCE's contributions must be reduced for the HCE's ADR to equal the highest permitted ADR under the plan.[184]

To calculate the highest permitted ADR under a plan, the ADR of the HCE with the highest ADR is reduced by the amount required to cause that HCE's ADR to equal the ADR of the HCE with the next highest ADR. If a lesser reduction would enable the plan to satisfy the special IRC § 401(k)(3)(A)(ii) nondiscrimination tests, only the lesser reduction is used in determining the highest permitted ADR.[185]

This process is repeated until the maximum ADP for the HCEs is achieved.[186]

Example 1

Employer A has adopted a qualified profit-sharing plan with a 401(k) feature in which all four of its employees are eligible to participate. The plan permits employees to contribute up to 10% of their salary. Employer C has elected to include salary reduction amounts in the definition of compensation. This is the only plan provided by Employer A and no employees have any ownership interest in Employer A. The compensation, deferred amounts, ADRs, and ADPs for the HCEs for the current year and the NHCEs for the preceding year are as follows:

Employee	Compensation	Contribution	ADR	ADP
HCE	$200,000	$16,000	16,000/200,000 = 8%	ADP of HCEs = (8 + 10 = 18.75)/2 = 9%
HCE 2	$150,000	$15,000	15,000/150,000 = 10%	
NHCE 1	$80,000	$8,000	8,000/80,000 = 10%	ADP of NHCEs = (10 + 2.5 = 12.5)/2 = 6.25%
NHCE 2	$40,000	$1,000	1,000/40,000 = 2.5%	

Because the ADP of the NHCEs is 6.25%, the maximum allowable ADP for the HCEs is 8.25% (6.25% + 2% = 8.25%).[187] (The maximum allowable ADP for the HCEs is 8.25% which is the greater of 7.81% (6.25% x 1.25 = 7.81%) or 8.25% (the lesser of (6.25% + 2 = 8.25%)) or (6.25% x 2 = 12.50%)).

---

[184] Treas. Reg. § 1.401(k)-2(b)(2)(ii)(A).

[185] Treas. Reg. § 1.401(k)-2(b)(2)(ii)(A).

[186] Treas. Reg. § 1.401(k)-2(b)(2)(ii)(B).

[187] See § 9.09[B][2][c].

In this case, HCE 2 has the highest ADR. HCE 2's ADR of 10% does not need to be reduced all the way down to the level of HCE 1's ADR of 8% because the maximum permissible ADP is 8.25%. In order for the plan to have an ADP of 8.25%, HCE 2's contribution needs to be reduced by 1.5% to 8.5% ((HCE 1's ADR of 8 + HCE 2's ADR of 8.5 = 16.5)/2 = 8.25%).

The total amount of excess contributions that must be distributed under the plan is HCE 2's excess contribution of $2,250 (1.5% x $150,000 = $2,250).

Example 2

Employer B has adopted a qualified profit-sharing plan with a 401(k) feature in which all six of its employees are eligible to participate. The plan permits employees to contribute up to 10% of their salary. Employer B has elected to include salary reduction amounts in the definition of compensation. This is the only plan provided by Employer B and no employees have any ownership interest in Employer B. The compensation, deferred amounts, ADRs, and ADPs for the HCEs for the current year and the NHCEs for the preceding year are as follows:

Employee	Compensation	Elective Contribution	ADR	ADP
HCE 1	$190,000	$15,200	15,200/190,000 = 8%	ADP of HCEs = (8 + 10 + 9 = 27)/3 = 9%
HCE 2	$150,000	$15,000	15,000/150,000 = 10%	
HCE 3	$140,000	$12,600	12,600/140,000 = 9%	
NHCE 1	$70,000	$7,000	7,000/70,000 = 10%	ADP of NHCEs = (10 + 5 + 0 = 15)/3 = 5%
NHCE 2	$50,000	$2,500	2,500/50,000 = 5%	
NHCE 3	$30,000	$0	0/30,000 = 0%	

Because the ADP of the NHCEs is 5%, the maximum allowable ADP for the HCEs is 7% (5% + 2% = 7%).[188] (The maximum allowable ADP for the HCEs is 7% which is the greater of 6.25% (5% x 1.25 = 6.25%) or 7% (the lesser of (5% + 2 = 7%) or (5% x 2 = 10%))).

In this case, HCE 2 has the highest ADR. HCE 2's ADR of 10% must be reduced to the level of HCE 3's ADR of 9%. This process must be repeated because the plan's ADP still exceeds the maximum allowable ADP of 7% ((8% + 9% + 9% = 26%)/3 = 8.67%).

Since HCE 3 has the next highest ADR, the ADR of HCE 2 and HCE 3 must be

---

[188] *See id.*

reduced to the level of HCE 1's ADR of 8%. This process must be repeated because the plan's ADP still exceeds the maximum allowable ADP of 7% ((8% + 8% + 8% = 24%)/3 = 8%).

The ADR of HCE 1, HCE 2, and HCE 3 must be reduced until they reach 7%, the maximum allowable ADP.

Thus, the excess contribution for HCE 1 is $1,900 (ADR must be reduced by 1% from 8% to 7%, and 1% of $190,000 is $1,900 ($190,000 x .01 = $1,900)). The excess contribution for HCE 2 is $4,500 (ADR must be reduced by 3% from 10% to 7%, and 3% of $150,000 is $4,500 ($150,000 x .03 = $4,500)). The excess contribution for HCE 3 is $2,800 (ADR must be reduced by 2% from 9% to 7%, and 2% of $140,000 is $2,800 ($140,000 x .02 = $2,800)).

The total amount of excess contributions that must be distributed under the plan is $9,200 (HCE 1's excess contribution of $1,900, plus HCE 2's excess contribution of $4,500, plus HCE 3's excess contribution of $2,800 ($1,900 + $4,500 + $2,800 = $9,200)).

[b]   Step Two

The second step requires that the total amount of excess contributions be apportioned among the HCEs.[189]

Section 401(k)(8) of the Internal Revenue Code requires that the excess contributions be apportioned on the basis of the dollar amount of contributions rather than on the basis of the ADRs.[190]

Specifically, the elective contributions of the HCE with the highest dollar amount of elective contributions are reduced by the amount required to cause that HCE's elective contributions to equal the dollar amount of the elective contributions of the HCE with the next highest dollar amount. If a lesser apportionment to the HCE would enable the plan to apportion the total amount of excess contributions, only the lesser apportionment would apply.[191]

If the amount apportioned as described in the preceding paragraph is less than the total excess contributions, then the process described above is repeated until all the excess contributions are apportioned.[192]

---

[189] Treas. Reg. § 1.401(k)-2(b)(2)(iii).

[190] Presumably, section 401(k)(8) requires that excess contributions be distributed in order of dollar amount of elective contributions rather than in order of ADRs in order to benefit the lower paid of the highly compensated. By basing distributions on the dollar amount of the contributions rather than percentage of compensation, more distributions may be returned to the higher paid of the highly compensated. This appears to represent an extension of the nondiscrimination principle to discrimination as between HCEs and protects the relatively lower paid of the HCEs. Prior to the Small Business Jobs Protection Act, corrections were made in order of ADRs. The Small Business Jobs Protection Act of 1996, Pub. L. No. 104-188 §1433(e), 110 Stat. 1755, 1807 amended IRC § 401(k)(8) to require that corrections be distributed in order of dollar amount of contributions rather than in order of ADRs, but neither the Senate Report nor the House Conference Report explain the reason for this change.

[191] Treas. Reg. § 1.401(k)-2(b)(2)(iii)(A).

[192] Treas. Reg. § 1.401(k)-2(b)(2)(iii)(C).

Example 1

Recall Example 1 above in which Employer A has adopted a qualified profit-sharing plan with a 401(k) feature in which all four of its employees are eligible to participate. The compensation, deferred amounts, ADRs, and ADPs for the HCEs for the current year and the NHCEs for the preceding year are as follows:

Employee	Compensation	Elective Contribution	ADR	ADP
HCE 1	$200,000	$16,000	16,000/200,000 = 8%	ADP of HCEs = (8 + 10 = 18.75)/2 = 9%
HCE 2	$150,000	$15,000	15,000/150,000 = 10%	
NHCE 1	$80,000	$8,000	8,000/80,000 = 10%	ADP of NHCEs = (10 + 2.5 = 12.5)/2 = 6.25%
NHCE 2	$40,000	$1,000	1,000/40,000 = 2.5%	

As shown above, the total amount of excess contributions that must be distributed under the plan is HCE 2's excess contribution of $2,250 (1.5% x $150,000 = $2,250).

In this example, HCE 1 has the highest dollar of elective contributions. Thus, HCE 1's elective contributions are reduced by $1,000 so that HCE 1's elective contributions equal the dollar amount of the elective contributions of HCE 2 ($15,000).

Because the total amount apportioned ($1,000) is less than the total excess contributions ($2,250), elective contributions must continue to be apportioned. Because the dollar amount of the remaining elective contributions for HCE 1 and HCE 2 are equal, the remaining $1,250 ($2,250 - $1,000 = $1,250) of excess contributions is then apportioned equally with HCE 1 and HCE 2 each being allocated $625 ($1,250/2 = $625).

Thus, excess contributions of $1,625 ($1,000 + $625 = $1,625) are allocated to HCE 1 and excess contributions of $625 are allocated to HCE 2.

Example 2

Recall Example 2 above in which Employer B has adopted a qualified profit-sharing plan with a 401(k) feature in which all six of its employees are eligible to participate. The compensation, deferred amounts, ADRs, and ADPs for the HCEs for the current year and the NHCEs for the preceding year are as follows:

Employee	Compensation	Elective Contribution	ADR	ADP
HCE 1	$190,000	$15,200	15,200/190,000 = 8%	ADP of HCEs = (8 + 10 + 9 = 27)/3 = 9%
HCE 2	$150,000	$15,000	15,000/150,000 = 10%	
HCE 3	$140,000	$12,600	12,600/140,000 = 9%	
NHCE 1	$70,000	$7,000	7,000/70,000 = 10%	ADP of NHCEs = (10 + 5 + 0 = 15)/3 = 5%
NHCE 2	$50,000	$2,500	2,500/50,000 = 5%	
NHCE 3	$30,000	$0	0/30,000 = 0%	

As shown above, the total amount of excess contributions that must be distributed under the plan is $9,200 (HCE 1's excess contribution of $1,900, plus HCE 2's excess contribution of $4,500, plus HCE 3's excess contribution of $2,800 ($1,900 + $4,500 + $2,800 = $9,200)).

In this example, HCE 1 has the highest dollar of elective contributions. Thus, HCE 1's elective contributions are reduced by $200 so that HCE 1's elective contributions equal the dollar amount of the elective contributions of HCE 2 ($15,000).

Because the total amount apportioned ($200) is less than the total excess contributions ($9,200), elective contributions must continue to be apportioned. The elective contributions of HCE 1 and HCE 2 must be reduced by $2,400 each so that they equal the dollar amount of the elective contributions of HCE 3 ($12,600) ($15,000 - $2,400 = $12,600). Because the total apportioned ($5,000) ($200 + $2,400 = $5,000) is less than the total excess contributions ($9,200), elective contributions must continue to be apportioned. Because the dollar amount of the remaining elective contributions for HCE 1, HCE 2, and HCE 3 are equal, the remaining $4,200 ($9,200 - $5,000 = $4,200) of excess contributions is then apportioned equally with HCE 1, HCE 2, and HCE 3 each being allocated $1,400 ($4,200/3= $1,400).

Thus, excess contributions of $4,000 ($200 + $2,400 + $1,400 = $4,000) are allocated to HCE 1, excess contributions of $3,800 ($2,400 + $1,400 = $3,800) are allocated to HCE 2, and excess contributions of $1,400 are allocated to HCE 3.

[c]   Step Three

Under the third step, the plan must determine the income allocable to the excess contributions.[193]

The income allocable to excess contributions is equal to the allocable gain or loss through the end of the plan year.[194]

A plan may use any reasonable method for computing the income allocable to excess contributions so long as the method does not violate IRC § 401(a)(4), is used consistently for all participants and all corrective distributions, and is used by the plan for allocating income to the participants' accounts.[195]

[d]   Step Four

Under the fourth and final step, the plan must distribute to each HCE the excess contributions allocable to that employee as well as the allocable income.[196]

A corrective distribution of excess contributions (and allocable income) is includible in the employee's gross income for the year in which it is distributed.[197] The corrective distribution is not subject to an early distribution tax under IRC § 72(t).[198]

In addition, as noted above, if the excess contributions are not corrected within 2 1/2 months after the end of the plan year, the employer will incur a 10% excise tax on the amount of the excess contribution not corrected at that time.[199]

[2]   Recharacterization of Excess Contributions

If a plan so provides, it may correct excess contributions by recharacterizing the excess contributions as after-tax employee contributions.[200] Such recharacterizations must be made within 2 1/2 months after the end of the plan year.[201]

After-tax employee contributions must also meet a special nondiscrimination requirement that is similar to the special nondiscrimination tests under IRC § 1.401(k)(3)(A)(ii).[202]

---

[193] Treas. Reg. § 1.401(k)-2(b)(2)(iv).

[194] Treas. Reg. § 1.401(k)-2(b)(2)(iv)(A).

[195] Treas. Reg. § 1.401(k)-2(b)(2)(iv)(B). The regulations also authorize plans to use an alternative pro rata method to allocate income to excess contributions. Treas. Reg. § 1.401(k)-2(b)(2)(iv)(C).

[196] Treas. Reg. § 1.401(k)-2(b)(2)(v).

[197] IRC § 4979(f)(2); Treas. Reg. § 1.401(k)-2(b)(2)(vi).

[198] Treas. Reg. § 1.401(k)-2(b)(2)(vi). The IRC § 72(t) additional tax on early distributions is discussed in Chapter 10 § 10.04[D].

[199] IRC § 4979. Treas. Reg. § 1.401(k)-2(b)(5)(i). Plans with automatic contribution arrangements must be corrected within six months rather than within 2 1/2 months. Treas. Reg. § 1.401(k)-2(b)(5)(iii).

[200] IRC § 401(k)(8)(A)(ii).

[201] Treas. Reg. § 1.401(k)-2(b)(3)(iii)(A).

[202] IRC § 401(m)(2)(A).

Because HCEs typically make larger after-tax contributions than do NHCEs, recharacterizing excess contributions as after-tax contributions usually creates problems under IRC § 401(m) as it solves them under IRC § 401(k). Thus, recharacterizing excess contributions as after-tax employee contributions is often a more theoretical than practical solution to correcting excess contributions.

[3]   Qualified Matching or Nonelective Contributions

If a plan so provides, the employer may correct excess contributions by making qualified nonelective contributions or qualified matching contributions that are taken into account, with other contributions made to the plan, in determining whether the plan satisfies the special IRC § 401(k)(3)(A)(ii) nondiscrimination requirement.[203]

Qualified matching contributions (QMACs) are contributions made on behalf of an employee on account of a contribution made by the employee and which are fully and immediately vested and subject to the special IRC § 401(k)(B)(2) distribution limitations for elective contributions.[204]

Qualified nonelective contributions (QNECs) are employer contributions (other than matching contributions) with respect to which the employee may not elect to have the contribution paid to the employee in cash instead of being contributed to the plan and which are fully and immediately vested and subject to the special IRC § 401(k)(B)(2) distribution limitations for elective contributions.[205]

[D]   Safe Harbors

If an employer wants to avoid the cost and uncertainty of testing and correcting excess contributions, it may elect to draft its plan to satisfy one of the safe harbors set forth in IRC §§ 401(k)(12) and 401(k)(13).

Like the third method of correcting excess contributions discussed above, the safe harbors involve the use of matching or elective contributions. Nevertheless, they differ fundamentally from the correction methods.

If a plan satisfies a safe harbor, the plan does not need to be tested under the special IRC § 401(k)(3)(A)(ii) nondiscrimination tests. A safe harbor plan automatically satisfies the nondiscrimination requirement.

The plan correction method, in contrast, applies after a plan has been tested and failed to satisfy the special 401(k)(3)(A)(ii) nondiscrimination tests. Under the correction method, a plan can be retested with the matching or nonelective contributions treated as if they were elective contributions for purposes of the special nondiscrimination tests.

---

[203] Treas. Reg. § 1.401(k)-2(b)(1)(i)(A).

[204] IRC §§ 401(k)(3)(D)(ii)(I) & 401(m)(4)(A).

[205] IRC §§ 401(k)(3)(D)(ii)(II) & 401(m)(4)(C).

[1] IRC § 401(k)(12) Safe Harbors

Section 401(k)(12) provides that a plan will be treated as satisfying the special IRC § 401(k)(3)(A)(ii) nondiscrimination requirement if the plan satisfies either

(1) a matching contribution safe harbor or

(2) a nonelective contribution safe harbor.

In order to satisfy either safe harbor, the employer must provide each employee with timely, written notice describing her rights and obligations under the plan.[206] In addition, the matching or nonelective contributions must be fully vested at all times and satisfy the special IRC § 401(k)(B)(2) distribution limitations for elective contributions.[207]

[a]   IRC § 401(k)(12)(B) Matching Contribution Safe Harbor

Under the IRC § 401(k)(12)(B) general matching contribution safe harbor, a 401(k) plan will automatically satisfy the section IRC § 401(k)(3)(A)(ii) nondiscrimination requirement if the employer makes a matching contribution equal to 100% of each NHCE's elective contribution up to 3% of the employee's compensation plus 50% of the amount the employee contributes that is greater than 3% but does not exceed 5% of compensation.[208]

If an NHCE elects to contribute:	Employer match is:	Total (Elective Contribution and Matching Contribution) is:
1%	1%	2%
2%	2%	4%
3%	3%	6%
4%	3.5%	7.5%
5%	4%	9%
6%	4%	10%

A plan may, but is not required to, make matching contributions with respect to elective contributions of HCEs. Thus, a safe harbor plan may discriminate in favor of NHCEs.

On the other hand, a safe harbor plan may not discriminate in favor of HCEs. Thus, a plan will not satisfy the matching contribution safe harbor if the rate of

---

[206] IRC §§ 401(k)(12)(A)(ii) & 401(k)(13)(D).

[207] IRC § 401(k)(12)(E)(i). Section 401(k)(2)(B)(i) requires that contributions may not be distributable earlier than separation from service, death, disability, plan termination, or in the case of a profit-sharing or stock bonus plan the attainment of age 59 1/2 or hardship. In addition, special distribution rules apply to qualified reservist distributions. *See* IRC § 401(k)(2)(B)(i)(V).

[208] IRC § 401(k)(12)(B)(i). A plan will not satisfy the matching contribution if the rate of matching contribution with respect to any elective contribution of a HCE at any rate of elective contribution is greater than that with respect to an employee who is not an HCE.

matching contributions with respect to any elective contribution of an HCE at any rate of elective contribution is greater than that with respect to an employee who is not an HCE.[209]

In addition to the basic matching contribution safe harbor, IRC § 401(k)(12)(B) authorizes an alternative matching contribution safe harbor. The alternative option is satisfied if (1) the rate of an employer's matching contribution does not increase as an employee's rate of contribution increases, and (2) the aggregate amount of the matching contributions at each rate of elective contribution is at least equal to the aggregate amount of matching contributions which would be made if the contributions were made on the basis of the general rule.[210]

Example 1

Employer A establishes a 401(k) plan pursuant to which Employer A makes a matching contribution equal to 100% of each NHCE's elective contribution up to 5% of the employee's compensation.

If an NHCE elects to contribute:	Employer match is:	Total (Elective Contribution and Matching Contribution) is:
1%	1%	2%
2%	2%	4%
3%	3%	6%
4%	4% (100% match rather than 50% match)	8% (8% total contribution rather than 7.5%)
5%	5% (100% match rather than 50% match)	10% (10% total contribution rather than 9%)
6%	5%	11% (11% total contribution rather than 10%)

Employer A's plan satisfies the alternative matching contribution safe harbor because (1) the rate of the employer's matching contribution does not increase as an employee's rate of contribution increases, and (2) the aggregate amount of the matching contributions at each rate of elective contributions is at least equal to the aggregate amount of matching contributions which would be made if the contributions were made on the basis of the general rule.

Example 2

Employer B establishes a 401(k) plan pursuant to which Employer B makes a matching contribution equal to 100% of each NHCE's elective contribution up to 4% of the employee's compensation.

---

[209] IRC § 401(k)(12)(B)(ii).

[210] IRC § 401(k)(12)(B)(iii).

If an NHCE elects to contribute:	Employer match is:	Total (Elective Contribution and Matching Contribution) is:
1%	1%	2%
2%	2%	4%
3%	3%	6%
4%	4% (100% match rather than 50% match)	8% (8% total contribution rather than 7.5%)
5%	4% (0% match rather than 50% match)	9% (same total contribution)
6%	4%	10%

Employer B's plan satisfies the alternative matching contribution safe harbor because (1) the rate of the employer's matching contribution does not increase as an employee's rate of contribution increases, and (2) the aggregate amount of the matching contributions at each rate of elective contributions is at least equal to the aggregate amount of matching contributions which would be made if the contributions were made on the basis of the general rule.

Example 3

Employer C establishes a 401(k) plan pursuant to which Employer C makes a matching contribution equal to 50% of each NHCE's elective contribution up to 3% of the employee's compensation plus 100% of the amount the employee contributes that is greater than 3% but does not exceed 6% of compensation.

If an NHCE elects to contribute:	Employer match is:	Total (Elective Contribution and Matching Contribution) is:
1%	.5% (50% rather than 100%)	1.5% (1.5% total rather than 2%)
2%	1% (50% rather than 100%)	3% (3% total rather than 4%)
3%	1.5% (50% rather than 100%)	4.5% (4.5% total rather than 6%)
4%	2.5% (100% rather than 50%)	6.5% (6.5% total rather than 7.5%)
5%	3.5% (100% rather than 50%)	8.5% (8.5% total rather than 9%)
6%	4.5% (100% rather than 0%)	10.5% (10.5% total rather than 10%)

Employer C's plan does not satisfy the alternative matching contribution safe harbor because (1) the rate of the employer's matching contribution increases as an employee's rate of contribution increases, and (2) the aggregate amount of the matching contributions at each rate of elective contributions is not at least equal to the aggregate amount of matching contributions which would be made if the contributions were made on the basis of the general rule. Specifically, the aggregate amount of matching contributions is lower at every level of contribution until 6%.

[b] IRC § 401(k)(12)(C) Nonelective Contribution Safe Harbor

Under the IRC § 401(k)(12)(C) nonelective contribution safe harbor, a 401(k) plan will automatically satisfy the special IRC § 401(k)(3)(A)(ii) nondescrimination requirement if the employer makes a contribution on behalf of each NHCE eligible to participate in the plan equal to at least 3% of the NHCE's compensation regardless of whether the employee makes any contribution to the plan.

If employee elects to contribute:	Employer's Nonelective Contribution is:	Total (Elective and Nonelective Contribution) is:
0%	3%	3%
1%	3%	4%
2%	3%	5%
3%	3%	6%
4%	3%	7%
5%	3%	8%
6%	3%	9%

[2] IRC § 401(k)(13) Safe Harbors

Section 401(k)(13) provides that a plan will be treated as satisfying the special IRC § 401(k)(3)(A)(ii) nondiscrimination requirement if

(1) the plan provides for certain minimum automatic salary deferrals, and

(2) satisfies either

(a) a matching contribution safe harbor, or

(b) a nonelective contribution safe harbor.

In order to satisfy either safe harbor, the employer must provide each employee with timely, written notice describing her rights and obligations under the plan.[211] In addition, the matching or nonelective contributions must fully vest within two years and satisfy the special IRC § 401(k)(B)(2) distribution limitations for elective contributions.[212]

---

[211] IRC § 401(k)(13)(D).

[212] IRC § 401(k)(13)(D)(iii). Section 401(k)(2)(B)(i) requires that contributions may not be distributable earlier than separation from service, death, disability, plan termination, or in the case of a profit-sharing or stock bonus plan the attainment of age 59 1/2 or hardship. In addition, special distribution rules apply to qualified reservist distributions. *See* IRC § 401(k)(2)(B)(i)(V).

[a]   IRC § 401(k)(13) Automatic Salary Deferral Requirement

In order to satisfy the IRC § 401(k)(13) automatic salary deferral requirement, the plan must provide for minimum automatic salary deferrals equal to at least 3% during the first year of participation, 4% during the second year, 5% during the third year, and 6% thereafter.[213] The automatic salary deferrals may exceed these minimum amounts, but they must not exceed 10%.[214]

The automatic salary deferral amounts are simply a default option. Plan participants have the right to elect not to have any contributions made on their behalf or to specify the amount of contribution they would like to have. Thus, the automatic salary deferrals only apply if a plan participant does not elect either not to have contributions made or to have contributions made at a specified level,[215] and plan participants must be given notice of their right not to have automatic elections made or to have contributions made at a different level.[216]

Example 1

Employer A's plan provides:

During year of participation	Compensation automatically deferred
1	3%
2	4%
3	5%
4	6%
5	6%
6	6%
7	6%

Employer A's plan satisfies the IRC § 401(k)(13) automatic salary deferral requirement because it provides for the minimum automatic salary deferrals required under IRC § 401(k)(13)(C)(iii).

Example 2

Employer B's plan provides:

During year of participation	Compensation automatically deferred
1	3%
2	4%
3	5%
4	6%

---

[213] IRC § 401(k)(13)(C)(iii).

[214] IRC § 401(k)(13)(C)(iii).

[215] IRC § 401(k)(13)(C)(ii).

[216] IRC § 401(k)(13)(E)(ii).

During year of participation	Compensation automatically deferred
5	7%
6	8%
7	8%

Employer B's plan satisfies the IRC § 401(k)(13) automatic salary deferral requirement because it provides for at least the minimum automatic salary deferrals required under IRC § 40(1k)(13)(C)(iii) and does not exceed the maximum automatic salary deferral of 10%.

Example 3

Employer C's plan provides:

During year of participation	Compensation automatically deferred
1	5%
2	7%
3	9%
4	10%
5	10%
6	10%
7	10%

Employer C's plan satisfies the IRC § 401(k)(13) automatic salary deferral requirement because it provides for at least the minimum automatic salary deferrals required under IRC § 401(k)(13)(C)(iii) and does not exceed the maximum automatic salary deferral of 10%.

Example 4

Employer D's plan provides:

During year of participation	Compensation automatically deferred
1	1%
2	3%
3	5%
4	7%
5	7%
6	7%
7	7%

Employer D's plan does not satisfy the IRC § 401(k)(13) automatic salary deferral requirement because it does not provide for at least the minimum automatic salary deferrals required under IRC § 401(k)(13)(C)(iii) for the first and second years of participation.

[b]   IRC § 401(k)(13)(D)(i)(I) Matching Contribution Safe Harbor

Under the IRC § 401(k)(13)(D)(i)(I) matching contribution safe harbor, the plan must provide matching contributions equal to 100% of elective deferrals up to 1% of compensation, plus 50% of elective deferrals between 1% and 6% of compensation.

If an NHCE elects to contribute:	Employer match is:	Total (Elective Contribution and Matching Contribution) is:
1%	1%	2%
2%	1.5%	3.5%
3%	2%	5%
4%	2.5%	6.5%
5%	3%	8%
6%	3.5%	9.5%

Like a IRC § 401(k)(12) matching contribution safe harbor plan, a plan will not satisfy the IRC § 401(k)(13) matching contribution safe harbor if the rate of matching contributions with respect to any elective contribution of an HCE at any rate of elective contribution is greater than that with respect to an employee who is not an HCE.[217]

In addition, IRC § 401(k)(13) authorizes an alternative matching contribution option like the IRC § 401(k)(12) alternative matching contribution option.[218]

Thus, the IRC § 401(k)(13) alternative option is also satisfied if

(1)   the rate of an employer's matching contribution does not increase as an employee's rate of contribution increases, and

(2)   the aggregate amount of the matching contributions at each rate of elective contribution is at least equal to the aggregate amount of matching contributions which would be made if the contributions were made on the basis of the general rule.[219]

Example 1

Employer A's plan provides:

---

[217]   IRC § 401(k)(13)(D)(ii) (incorporating IRC § 401(k)(12)(B)(ii)).

[218]   IRC § 401(k)(13)(D)(ii) (incorporating IRC § 401(k)(12)(B)(iii)).

[219]   IRC § 401(k)(12)(B)(iii).

During year of participation	Compensation automatically deferred	Employer Matching Contribution	Total Contribution (Employee's Automatic Elective Deferral and Employer Matching Contribution)
1	3%	2% (100% of first 1% (1%) + 50% of second 1% (.5%) + 50% of third 1% (.5%) = 2%)	5%
2	4%	2.5% (100% of first 1% (1%) + 50% of second 1% (.5%) + 50% of third 1% (.5%) + 50% of fourth 1% (.5%) = 2.5%)	6.5%
3	5%	3% (100% of first 1% (1%) + 50% of second 1% (.5%) + 50% of third 1% (.5%) + 50% of fourth 1% (.5%) + 50% of fifth 1% (.5%) = 3%)	8%
4	6%	3.5% (100% of first 1% (1%) + 50% of second 1% (.5%) + 50% of third 1% (.5%) + 50% of fourth 1% (.5%) + 50% of fifth 1% (.5%) + 50% of sixth 1% (.5%) = 3.5%)	9.5%
5	6%	3.5% (same as above)	9.5%
6	6%	3.5% (same as above)	9.5%
7	6%	3.5% (same as above)	9.5%

Employer A's plan satisfies the IRC § 401(k)(13)(D) matching contribution safe harbor because the plan provides matching contributions equal to 100% of elective deferrals up to 1% of compensation, plus 50% of elective deferrals between 1% and 6% of compensation.

Example 2

Employer B's plan provides:

During year of participation	Compensation automatically deferred	Employer Matching Contribution	Total Contribution (Employee's Automatic Elective Deferral and Employer Matching Contribution)
1	3%	3% (100% of first 1% (1%) + 100% of second 1% (1%) + 100% of third 1% (1%) = 3%)	6%
2	4%	3.5% (100% of first 1% (1%) + 100% of second 1% (1%) + 100% of third 1% (1%) + 50% of fourth 1% (.5%) = 3.5%)	7.5%
3	5%	3.5% (same as above)	8.5%
4	6%	3.5% (same as above)	9.5%
5	6%	3.5% (same as above)	9.5%
6	6%	3.5% (same as above)	9.5%
7	6%	3.5% (same as above)	9.5%

Employer B's plan satisfies the IRC § 401(k)(13)(D) alternative matching contribution safe harbor because the plan provides matching contributions at least as generous as under the general matching contribution safe harbor.

Example 3

Employer C's plan provides:

During year of participation	Compensation automatically deferred	Employer Matching Contribution	Total Contribution (Employee's Automatic Elective Deferral and Employer Matching Contribution)
1	3%	2% (100% of first 1% (1%) + 50% of second 1% (.5%) + 50% of third 1% (.5%) = 2%)	5%
2	4%	2.5% (100% of first 1% (1%) + 50% of second 1% (.5%) + 50% of third 1% (.5%) + 50% of fourth 1% (.5%) = 2.5%)	6.5%
3	5%	3% (100% of first 1% (1%) + 50% of second 1% (.5%) + 50% of third 1% (.5%) + 50% of fourth 1% (.5%) + 50% of fifth 1% (.5%) = 3%)	8%
4	6%	3.5% (100% of first 1% (1%) + 50% of second 1% (.5%) + 50% of third 1% (.5%) + 50% of fourth 1% (.5%) + 50% of fifth 1% (.5%) + 50% of sixth 1% (.5%) = 3.5%)	9.5%
5	7%	3.5% (same as above)	10.5%
6	8%	3.5% (same as above)	11.5%
7	8%	3.5% (same as above)	11.5%

Employer C's plan satisfies the IRC § 401(k)(13)(D) matching contribution safe harbor because the plan provides matching contributions equal to 100% of elective deferrals up to 1% of compensation, plus 50% of elective deferrals between 1% and 6% of compensation.

[c]   IRC § 401(k)(13)(D)(i)(II) Nonelective Contribution Safe Harbor

Under the IRC § 401(k)(13)(D)(i)(II) nonelective contribution safe harbor, the plan must provide for an employer nonelective contribution of at least 3% of compensation of all NHCEs eligible to participate in the plan, regardless of whether the employee makes elective contributions.

If employee elects to contribute:	Employer's Nonelective Contribution is:	Total (Elective and Nonelective Contribution) is:
0%	3%	3%
1%	3%	4%
2%	3%	5%
3%	3%	6%
4%	3%	7%
5%	3%	8%
6%	3%	9%

Example

Employer A's plan provides:

During year of participation	Compensation automatically deferred	Employer Matching Contribution	Total Contribution (Employee's Automatic Elective Deferral and Employer Matching Contribution)
1	3%	3%	6%
2	4%	3%	7%
3	5%	3%	8%
4	6%	3%	9%
5	6%	3%	9%
6	6%	3%	9%
7	6%	3%	9%

Employer A's plan satisfies the IRC § 401(k)(13)(D)(i)(II) nonelective safe harbor because the plan provides for an employer nonelective contribution of at least 3% of compensation of all NHCEs eligible to participate in the plan, regardless of whether the employee makes an elective contribution.

[E]   Summary of IRC § 401(k) Special Nondiscrimination Requirement

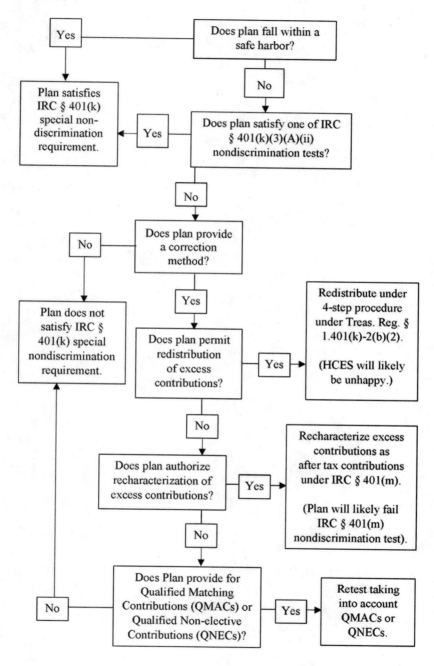

Chapter 10

TAX RULES GOVERNING PENSION PLANS

§ 10.01 INTRODUCTION

This chapter addresses a number of tax rules governing pension plans.

It begins by addressing a number of qualified plan requirements that are designed to limit and target the tax subsidy accorded qualified plans. Specifically, it addresses (1) the limit on annual compensation that may be taken into account for purposes of qualified plans; (2) the limit on benefits that may be provided by defined benefit plans and contributions that may be made to defined contribution plans; (3) the limit on the amount of elective contributions plan participants can make to 401(k) plans; and (4) the exception to the elective contribution limit for "catch-up contributions," that is, contributions by participants who are age 50 or older.

The chapter then turns to the rules governing the deductibility of employer contributions to pension plans.

Finally, the chapter addresses a number of tax rules governing distributions from qualified plans. It begins by addressing the general default tax rules governing plan distributions. It then turns to the rules governing distributions from Roth plans. It then addresses the rollover rules which permit plan participants to delay taxation on plan distributions if they roll plan distributions over into another qualified plan or IRA. The chapter then turns to the 10% excise tax imposed on early distributions and the rules governing plan loans. Finally, the chapter addresses the minimum required distribution rules which essentially require that plans begin to distribute benefits to plan participants after they reach age 70 1/2.

§ 10.02 TAX QUALIFICATION REQUIREMENTS

Section 401(a) of the Internal Revenue Code sets forth a list of about 30 requirements that plans must satisfy in order to qualify for favorable income tax treatment. The qualification requirements include two separate sets of rules and regulations. The first set of rules is designed to protect plan participants against employer fraud or misrepresentation. Those rules are generally duplicated in title I of ERISA and are addressed elsewhere in this book. The second set of rules is designed to limit and target the tax subsidy. They are contained solely in the Internal Revenue Code.

The tax qualification requirements that are designed to limit and target the tax subsidy include the nondiscrimination requirements. Chapter 9 addresses those rules. This section discusses four other qualification requirements that are designed to limit and target the tax subsidy. Specifically, it addresses

(1) the limit on annual compensation that may be taken into account for purposes of qualified plans;

(2) the limit on benefits that may be provided by defined benefit plans and contributions that may be made to defined contribution plans;

(3) the limit on the amount of elective contributions plan participants can make to 401(k) plans; and

(4) the exception to the elective contribution limit for "catch-up contributions," that is, contributions by participants who are age 50 or older.

Section 10.04, at the end of this chapter, addresses two other tax qualification requirements that are designed to limit and target the tax subsidy. Specifically, it addresses (1) the rollover requirement and (2) the minimum distribution rules. Because these two qualification requirements relate directly to plan distributions, they are discussed in the portion of this chapter which focuses on the tax rules governing plan distributions rather than this section.

[A]   IRC § 401(a)(17) Annual Compensation Limit

Section 401(a)(17) of the Internal Revenue Code limits the amount of compensation that may be taken into account for purposes of a qualified plan.[1]

The statutory limit is $200,000 for plan years beginning after December 31, 2001,[2] and is adjusted for increases in the cost-of-living in $5,000 increments.[3] In 2015, the IRC § 401(a)(17) limit, as adjusted, is $265,000.

Example 1

Alberto's employer's defined contribution plan provides for an employer contribution equal to 10% of compensation. Although Alberto earns $500,000 in 2015, his employer may only contribute $26,500 (10% x $265,000) on behalf Alberto's behalf. Alberto's compensation that exceeds $265,000 must be disregarded in determining the contribution made on his behalf.

Example 2

Bernice contributes $18,000 to her 401(k) plan in 2015. Although Bernice earns $550,000 in 2015, she will be treated as having contributed 6.8% ($18,000/$265,000) of her compensation in 2015 in determining whether the plan satisfies the IRC § 401(k)(3) nondiscrimination requirement. Bernice's compensation in excess of $265,000 must be disregarded in determining whether the plan satisfies the IRC § 401(k)(3) nondiscrimination requirement.

---

[1] Treas. Reg. § 1.401(a)(17)-1(a)(1).

"The purpose of the limitation is to ensure that reductions in the maximum contributions or benefits do not reduce the contributions or benefits of low- and middle-income employees." Joint Committee on Taxation, General Explanation of the Tax Reform Act of 1986, JCS 10-87 NO 14, at 102 (1987)

[2] IRC § 401(a)(17)(A).

[3] IRC § 401(a)(17)(B).

[B] IRC § 415 Limitation on Contributions and Benefits

Section 401(a)(16) of the Internal Revenue Code requires that qualified plans satisfy the limitations on contributions and benefits set forth in IRC § 415. Section 415(b) limits the annual benefit that defined benefit plans may provide while section 415(c) limits the contributions that may be made to defined contribution plans.[4] If an employer maintains both a defined benefit plan and a defined contribution plan, the limitations apply separately with respect to each plan.[5]

[1] Purpose of IRC § 415

Prior to the enactment of ERISA, the Internal Revenue Code did not impose any direct limitations on the amount of contributions or benefits a qualified plan could provide for an individual employee.[6] Accordingly, it was possible for an employer to fund very large benefits for a single employee so long as proportionate benefits were funded for other employees.[7]

Section 415 was enacted to limit qualified plan contributions and benefits "to levels that are proportionate 'to the reasonable needs of individuals for a dignified level of retirement income.' "[8] Benefits that exceed these levels are not eligible for favorable income tax treatment.

[2] IRC § 415(c) Limitation on Contributions

Section 415(c) limits the "annual additions" which may be made to a defined contribution plan to the lesser of

(1) $40,000, adjusted for increases in the cost-of-living, or

(2) 100% of the participant's compensation.[9]

Annual additions are defined as employer contributions, employee contributions, and forfeitures.[10] In 2015, the IRC § 415(c) limit, as adjusted for inflation, is $53,000.

---

[4] The section 415 limitations also apply to other retirement plans that receive favorable income tax treatment. Specifically, the limits also apply to section 413(a) annuity plans, section 403(b) annuity contracts, and section 408(k) simplified employee pensions (SEPs). IRC § 415(a)(2).

[5] Prior to 1996, section 415 imposed a separate limit if an employer maintained both a defined benefit plan and a defined contribution plan. *See* Norman P. Stein, *Simplification and IRC § 415*, 2 FLA. TAX REV. 69, 73–82 (1994) (describing the combined IRC § 415(e) and all of its complexity). The combined limit was repealed in 1996. Small Business Protection Act of 1996, Pub. L. 104-188 § 1452(a), 110 Stat. 1755, 1816.

[6] *See* Stein, 2 FLA. TAX REV., at 82.

[7] *See* JAMES A. WOOTEN, THE EMPLOYEE RETIREMENT INCOME SECURITY ACT OF 1974: A POLITICAL HISTORY 89 (2004).

[8] Stein, 2 FLA. TAX REV., at 82.

[9] IRC § 415(c)(1).

[10] IRC § 415(c)(2). Annual additions do not include rollover contributions. For a discussion of rollovers, see § 10.04[C].

Example 1

David makes $200,000 in 2015. The maximum contribution that can be made on David's behalf in 2015 is $53,000.

Example 2

Erin makes $45,000 in 2015. The maximum contribution that can be made on Erin's behalf in 2015 is $45,000.

If Erin elects to defer $5,000 of her $45,000 salary to a 401(k) plan, the maximum contribution that her employer can make on her behalf is $40,000, but the maximum total contribution, including both Erin's employer's contribution of $40,000 and Erin's elective deferral of $5,000, is $45,000 because compensation is defined to include elective deferrals.[11]

[3]   IRC § 415(b) Limitation on Benefits

Section 415(b) limits the annual benefit that a participant may receive under a defined benefit plan to the lesser of

(1) $160,000, adjusted for increases in the cost-of-living, or

(2) 100% of the participant's average compensation for the three consecutive years during which the participant had his or her highest compensation.

The limitation applies to benefits payable at age 62 in the form of a straight life annuity or in the form of a joint and survivor annuity for the lives of the employee and the employee's spouse.[12] The permissible level of benefits is actuarially reduced if the benefits begin before age 62 or are paid in a different form and are actuarially increased if the benefits begin later than age 65.[13]

In 2015, the IRC § 415(b)(1)(A) limit, as adjusted, is $210,000.

Example 1

Angela began to participate in her employer's pension plan on January 2, 2000, and her salary increased every year since she started working for Employer. For the last three years, she earned $130,000, $133,000, and $136,000. The maximum annual benefit that Employer's pension plan may provide for her this year is $133,000. (($130,000 + 133,000 + $136,000)/3 = $133,000)

Example 2

Like Angela, Brodie began to participate in his employer's pension plan on January 2, 2000, and his salary increased every year since he started working for his employer. Brodie earned $250,000 in 2013, $255,000 in 2014, and $260,000 in 2015. The maximum annual benefit that Employer's pension plan would be able to provide Brodie in 2015 is $210,000.

---

[11] IRC § 415(c)(3)(D).

[12] IRC § 415(b)(2)(B).

[13] IRC § 415(b)(2)(B)–(D).

[4] Phased in Limit

If an employee participates in a plan for less than 10 years, the maximum benefit limitations are reduced.[14]

Specifically, the IRC § 415(b)(1)(A) maximum benefit limitation is reduced by multiplying the dollar limitation by a fraction, the numerator of which is the employee's years of participation in the plan and denominator of which is 10.[15]

Example 1

Adele has participated in her Employer's plan for six years. She earned $300,000 in 2013, $315,000 in 2014, and $335,000 in 2015 (her highest three years' consecutive compensation). In 2015, the maximum accrued benefit Employer's pension plan can provide her is $126,000 ($210,000 x 6/10 = $126,000).

The IRC § 415(b)(1)(B) highest three years of compensation is also reduced by multiplying the limitation by a fraction, the numerator of which is the employee's years of service (rather than years of participation) and the denominator of which is 10.[16]

Example 2

Bennett has participated in his Employer's plan for six years. He earned $50,000 in 2013, $54,000 in 2014, and $58,000 in 2015 (his highest three years' consecutive compensation). In 2015, the maximum annual benefit Employer's pension plan can provide Bennett in 2015 is $32,400. (($50,000 + $54,000 + $58,000)/3 x 6/10 = 32,400).

[5] De Minimis Benefit

A defined benefit plan may provide an annual pension benefit of up to $10,000 without regard to the IRC § 415(b)(1)(B) highest three year of compensation limitation if the employer has never maintained a defined contribution plan in which the employer participated.[17]

The $10,000 de minimis allowance is also phased in over 10 years of service.[18]

Example

Conrad has worked for Employer for four years. His annual salary is $3,000. Employer may provide Conrad with a maximum annual benefit of $4,000 ($10,000 x 4/10).

---

[14] IRC § 415(b)(5)(A).

[15] IRC § 415(b)(5).

[16] IRC § 415(b)(5)(B).

[17] IRC § 415(b)(4).

[18] IRC § 415(b)(5)(B).

[C] IRC § 402(g) Limitation on Elective Deferrals

Section 401(a)(30) of the Internal Revenue Code requires that qualified plans that accept elective deferrals provide that the amount of elective deferrals under the plan and all other such plans[19] maintained by the employer not exceed the limit set forth in IRC § 402(g).

Elective deferrals include any elective contributions to a qualified 401(k) plan to the extent that the contributions are not taxed to the employee before applying the section 402(g) limit.[20]

Designated Roth contributions are treated like regular "elective contributions"[21] to 401(k) plans even though they are includible in income in the year of contribution.[22]

[1] Brief History and Purpose of the IRC § 402(g) Limitation

Prior to the Tax Reform Act of 1986, elective deferrals were only subject to the regular IRC § 415(c) limitations on contributions to defined contribution plans. The Tax Reform Act of 1986 added section 402(g) to the Internal Revenue Code.[23] According to the Joint Committee on Taxation, the provision was intended to limit employers' ability to use 401(k) plans instead of traditional employer-sponsored plans.

Specifically, the Joint Committee on Taxation explained,

Congress was concerned that the rules relating to qualified cash or deferred arrangements [401(k) plans] under prior law encouraged employers to shift too large a portion of the share of the cost of retirement savings to employees. . . . In particular, Congress believed that qualified cash or deferred arrangements should be supplementary retirement savings arrangements for employees; such arrangements should not be the primary employer-maintained retirement plan.[24]

---

[19] Elective deferrals may also be made to IRC § 408(k) simplified employee pensions (SEPs), IRC § 408(p) simple retirement accounts (SIMPLE plans), and through IRC § 403(b) tax-sheltered annuity agreements. IRC § 402(g)(3); Treas. Reg. § 1.402(g)-1(b).

[20] IRC § 402(g)(3)(A). Elective deferrals also include (1) any employer contribution to an IRC § 408(k) SEP made at the employee's election which is excluded from the employee's income, (2) any employer contribution under an IRC § 403(b) tax-sheltered annuity agreement, to the extent that the contribution is not included in the employee's gross income, and (3) any elective employer contribution to a section 408(p) SIMPLE plan. IRC § 402(g)(3)(B)–(D).

[21] Treas. Reg. § 1.402(g)-1(b)(5).

[22] Roth contributions are includible in the year of contribution but not in the year of distribution. IRC § 402A(a)(2).

[23] P. L. No. 99-514 § 1105, 100 Stat. 2085, 2417–20.

[24] Joint Comm. on Taxation, 100th Cong., General Explanation of the Tax Reform Act of 1986 634 (Comm. Print 1987).

[2] Basic IRC § 402(g) Limitation on Elective Deferrals

Section 402(g) limits the total amount of elective deferrals that an employee may make in a single year to $15,000,[25] as adjusted for increases in the cost-of-living.[26]

The IRC § 402(g) limit, as adjusted, is $18,000 in 2015.

The IRC § 402(g) limit applies on an employee, not employer, basis.

Example 1

Angelina works for two unrelated companies, Company A and Company B, during 2015. The maximum she can contribute to both plans is $18,000. If she contributes $10,000 to the Company A 401(k) plan in 2015, the maximum she can contribute to the Company B 401(k) plan in 2015 is $8,000.

[3] IRC § 401(a)(30) Qualification Requirement

If an employer, including employers treated as related employers under the controlled group rules,[27] maintains more than one plan, IRC § 401(a)(30) requires that all of the employer's plans together not accept elective deferrals that exceed the IRC § 402(g) limit.

Thus, the IRC § 401(a)(30) qualification requirement applies on an employer-wide basis.

Example 1

Anniston works for two related companies, Company A and Company B, in 2015. The maximum she can contribute to both plans is $18,000. If she contributes $10,000 to the Company A 401(k) plan in 2015, the maximum she can contribute to the Company B 401(k) plan in 2015 is $8,000. If both plans permit Anniston to contribute $18,000, for a total contribution of $36,000, the plans would be disqualified.[28]

The IRC § 401(a)(30) qualification requirement only applies on an employer-wide basis. Thus, if two unrelated employers maintain 401(k) plans, and an individual works for both employers, each plan will be considered separately to determine whether the IRC § 401(a)(30) requirement is satisfied.

Example 2

Bill works for Company C and Company D, two unrelated employers, in 2015. Bill contributes $18,000 to the Company C 401(k) plan and $18,000 to the Company D 401(k) plan in 2015. Because Company C and Company D are unrelated, each plan is only required to take into account elective deferrals made to that company's

---

[25] IRC § 402(g)(1)(B).

[26] IRC § 402(g)(4).

[27] For a discussion of the definition of employer, see Chapter 9 § 9.04.

[28] *See* Bryan E. Gates, Internal Revenue Manual — Abridged & Annotated § 4.72.2.7, 2A I.R.M. Abr. & Ann. § 4.72.2.7.

plan for qualification purposes. Thus, neither company's plan is disqualified because neither company's plan accepted elective deferrals that exceeded the IRC 402(g) limit of $18,000 in 2015.

Bill, however, will only be able to exclude from income $18,000 of the $36,000 he contributed to the two plans in 2015.

[4] Treatment of Excess Deferrals

If an individual's elective deferrals exceed the IRC § 402(g) limit, the excess deferrals must be included in the individual's gross income for that year.[29] In addition, if the excess deferrals (and income) for a taxable year are not distributed by April 15 of the following year, the amounts will be includible in gross income again when distributed from the plan.[30]

Example

Constance contributes $18,000 to the Company A plan and another $18,000 to the Company B plan in 2015. She is only able to exclude a total of $18,000 from income in 2015. Thus, she could, for example, exclude the $18,000 she contributed to the Company A 401(k) plan but she could not exclude the $18,000 she contributed to the Company B 401(k) plan. If the $18,000 contributed to the Company B 401(k) plan were not distributed by April 15, 2016, then the $18,000 would be includible in income again when it was later distributed from the Company B 401(k) plan.

[5] Correction of Excess Deferrals

A plan may provide for a correction method to avoid double taxation of excess deferrals.

Specifically, a plan may provide that excess deferrals may be distributed by the first April 15 following the close of the individual's taxable year in which the excess deferrals were included in income.[31]

In addition, a plan may provide that an individual who has excess deferrals for a taxable year may receive a corrective distribution of the excess deferrals during the same year provided that

(1) the individual designates the distribution as an excess deferral,

(2) the corrective distribution is made after the date on which the plan received the excess deferral, and

(3) the plan designates the distribution as a distribution of excess deferrals.[32]

A corrective distribution of excess deferrals made on or before April 15 of the year following the year of deferral is not includible in income for the year of

---

[29] IRC § 402(g)(1); Treas. Reg. § 1.402(g)-1(a).

[30] Treas. Reg. § 1.402(g)-1(e)(8)(iii).

[31] IRC § 402(g)(2)(A); Treas. Reg. § 1.402(g)-1(e)(2).

[32] Treas. Reg. § 1.402(g)-1(e)(3).

distribution but is includible in income for the year of deferral.[33] The income allocable to excess deferrals, however, is includible in the employee's income in the year in which the allocable income is distributed.[34] The corrective distribution of excess deferrals (and income) is not subject to the IRC § 72(t) early distribution tax.[35]

Even if distributed, excess deferrals must be treated as employer contributions for purposes of IRC §§ 401(a)(4), 401(k)(3), 404, 409, 411, 412, and 416. Excess deferrals of a nonhighly compensated employee, however, are not taken into account under the IRC § 401(k)(3) actual deferral percentage test to the extent the excess deferrals are prohibited under IRC § 401(a)(30). In addition, excess deferrals are treated as employer contributions for purposes of IRC § 415 unless distributed.[36]

Example

In 2015 Dwayne contributes $18,000 to the Company A 401(k) plan and $2,500 to the Company B 401(k) plan, and the terms of the Company A plan include a correction method for excess deferrals. If Dwayne advises the Company A 401(k) plan that he had an excess deferral of $2,500 in 2015, and the Company A 401(k) plan distributes the $2,500 of excess deferrals plus $25 in earnings on the excess deferral by April 15, 2016, then Dwayne would be required to include the $2,500 in excess deferrals in income in 2015 and the $25 of earnings on the excess deferrals in income for 2016. Neither the distribution of the excess deferrals nor the distribution of the $25 of earnings on the excess deferrals would be subject to the IRC § 72(t) early distribution tax.

[D]   IRC § 414(v) Catch Up Contributions

Section 414(v) of the Internal Revenue creates an exception to the IRC § 402(g) limit.

As discussed above, IRC § 401(a)(30) provides that in order for a 401(k) plan to qualify for tax favorable treatment, the amount of elective deferrals cannot exceed the IRC § 402(g) limit.

IRC § 414(v) provides an exception for catch-up contributions. Catch-up contributions are not taken into account for purposes of IRC § 402(g) and other statutory provisions.

An employer is not required to permit participants to make catch-up contributions. If, however, an employer elects to make catch-up contributions available, the plan must permit all eligible participants to make the same election with respect to catch-up contributions in order to satisfy the IRC § 401(a)(4)

---

[33] IRC § 402(g)(2)(C)(i); Treas. Reg. § 1.402(g)-1(e)(8).

[34] IRC § 402(g)(2)(C); Treas. Reg. § 1.402(g)-1(e)(8).

[35] IRC § 402(g)(2)(A); Treas. Reg. § 1.402(g)-1(e)(2).

[36] Treas. Reg. § 1.402(g)-1(e)(1)(ii).

nondiscrimination rules.[37]

Catch-up contributions are not subject to any other contribution limitations that would otherwise apply, such as IRC § 402(g), and are not taken into account in applying statutory limitations to other contributions or benefits under the plan.[38]

[1]   Purpose of IRC § 414(v) Catch-up Contributions

Catch-up contributions are intended to permit individuals who fail to save for retirement early in life to increase their contributions later in life to "catch up."[39]

Despite its purpose, section 414(v) does not distinguish between individuals who contributed little or nothing to their 401(k) plans early in their careers and those who contributed the maximum amount permitted throughout their careers. Thus, an individual who saved at the maximum contribution rate throughout his career could still make catch-up contributions beginning at age 50.

[2]   Application of IRC § 414(v) Catch-up Contributions

Section 414(v) of the Internal Revenue Code authorizes 401(k) plans[40] to permit individuals who are age 50 or over to make "catch-up contributions," that is, additional elective deferrals to their 401(k) plan.

Under IRC § 414(v), the plan may allow "eligible participants" to make catch-up contributions equal to the lesser of

(1)   the "applicable dollar amount" or

(2)   the participant's compensation for the year reduced by any other elective deferrals of the participant for the year.[41]

The "applicable dollar amount" was set at $5,000 in 2006 and is adjusted for increases in the cost-of-living.[42] In 2015, the IRC § 414(v)(2)(B)(i) limit, as adjusted, is $6,000.

"Eligible participants" are defined as individuals who are 50 or older and for whom no other elective deferrals (without regard to section 414(v)) may be made to the plan due to other statutory limitations under the Internal Revenue Code or due to limitations set forth under the terms of the plan.[43]

Catch-up contributions are thus made by reference to three limitations that would otherwise apply:

---

[37] IRC § 414(v)(4).

[38] IRC § 414(v)(3)(A).

[39] H. R. Rep. No. 107-51(I), at 69–70 (2001).

[40] Catch-up contributions may also be made to other plans that accept elective deferrals, specifically IRC § 408(p) SIMPLE IRA plans, IRC § 408(k) simplified employee pensions (SEPs), IRC § 403(b) plans or contracts, or IRC § 457 eligible governmental plans. Treas. Reg. § 1.414(v)-1(g)(1).

[41] IRC § 414(v)(1)(A).

[42] IRC § 414(v)(1)(B).

[43] IRC § 414(v)(5).

(1)   statutory limitations, that is, IRC § 401(a)(30)'s incorporation of the IRC § 402(g) limit;[44]

(2)   employer limitations set forth in the plan; and

(3)   the ADP (actual deferral percentage) limitation established when applying the IRC § 401(k)(3) nondiscrimination test to the 401(k) plan.[45]

Example of Statutory Limitation

Plan A does not limit elective deferrals except to comply with IRC § 401(a)(30) (which incorporates the IRC § 402(g) limit equal to $18,000 in 2015) and IRC § 415 (which limits contributions in 2015 to the lesser of $53,000 or 100% of compensation). Plan A also provides that a catch-up eligible participant is permitted to defer amounts in excess of the IRC § 401(a)(30) limit up to the applicable dollar catch-up limit for the year.

In 2015, Participant A, who is age 55 and earns $100,000, could elect to defer up to $24,000 to her 401(k) plan that year: (a) a regular contribution up to the 2015 IRC § 402(g) limit of $18,000, plus (b) a catch-up contribution up to the 2015 limit of $6,000.

If Participant A elects to defer $20,000 to her 401(k) plan, she is treated as having made a regular 401(k) contribution of $18,000 (the 402(g) limit) and a catch-up contribution of $2,000. Her $2,000 catch-up is not taken into account in determining her actual deferral ratio (ADR) for purposes of discrimination testing under IRC § 401(k)(3).[46]

Example of Plan Limitation

Plan B limits elective deferrals so as to comply with IRC § 401(a)(30) and IRC § 415. In addition, Plan B limits elective deferrals to 10% of compensation and authorizes catch-up contributions.

In 2015, Participant B, who is 55 and earns $100,000, could elect to defer up to $16,000 to his 401(k) plan that year: (a) a regular contribution up to $10,000 (or 10% of his compensation under the terms of the plan), plus (b) a catch-up contribution of up to the 2015 limit of $6,000.

If Participant B elects to defer $12,000 to his 401(k) plan that year, he would be treated as having made a regular 401(k) contribution of $10,000 (the plan limit of 10% of compensation) and a catch-up contribution of $2,000. His $2,000 catch-up contribution is not taken into account in determining his actual deferral ratio (ADR) for purposes of discrimination testing under IRC § 401(k)(3).

---

[44] Other plans, such as IRC § 408(p) SIMPLE IRA plans, are subject to statutory limitations set forth in other sections of the Internal Revenue Code. *See* Treas. Reg. § 1.414(v)-1(b)(i).

[45] Treas. Reg. § 1.414(v)-1(b).

[46] *Cf.* Treas. Reg. § 1.414(v)-1(h) Example 1.

Example of ADP Limitation

Plan C does not limit elective deferrals except to comply with IRC § 401(a)(30) and IRC § 415 and authorizes catch-up eligible contributions.

In 2015, highly compensated employee, Participant C, is age 55 and earns $175,000. After applying the IRC § 401(k)(3) nondiscrimination test, the maximum Participant C can contribute to the plan is 5% of compensation. Thus, the maximum Participant C can contribute in 2015 is $14,750: (a) a regular contribution of $8,750 (the IRC § 401(k)(3) limit of 5% of compensation), plus (b) a catch-up contribution of $6,000.

If Participant C elects to contribute $10,000 to her 401(k) plan in 2015, she would be treated as having made a regular 401(k) contribution of $8,750 and a catch-up contribution of $1,250. Her $1,250 catch-up contribution is not taken into account in determining her actual deferral ratio (ADR) for purposes of nondiscrimination testing under IRC § 401(k)(3).

§ 10.03   DEDUCTIBILITY OF EMPLOYER CONTRIBUTIONS

One of the principal advantages of a tax qualified plan is that an employer may deduct contributions to the plan when the contributions are made, regardless of when the employee includes those contributions in income. The Internal Revenue Code, however, limits the deductibility of those contributions.

In order for employer contributions to be deductible, they must satisfy two separate requirements. First, they must be ordinary, necessary, and reasonable business expenses under IRC §§ 162 or 212.[47] Second, they must satisfy the requirements of IRC § 404, which limits the amount of contributions an employer may deduct in a year.[48]

If an employer's contribution exceeds the IRC § 404 limitations, the excess contribution may be returned to the employer if the contribution was conditioned on its deductibility and the facts and circumstances indicate that a good faith mistake was made in determining the deductibility of the contribution.[49] If the employer's excess contribution is not returned, the employer may carry the excess over and deduct it in succeeding years.[50] Excess contributions, however, are subject to a 10% excise tax under IRC § 4972.

Section 404 limits the aggregate contribution an employer may deduct. Section 404 does not affect or otherwise restrict the maximum contribution or benefit which may be allocated to or accrued on behalf of any individual participant. Instead, as

---

[47] *See* Treas. Reg. § 1.404(a)-1(b).

[48] Section 404 is not limited to tax qualified plans. Rather, it governs the deductibility of contributions to all pension plans, profit-sharing plans, annuity plans, stock-bonus plans, and deferred compensation plans, regardless of whether they are tax qualified.

[49] Rev. Rul. 91-4, 1991-1 C.B. 57.

[50] IRC § 404(a)(3)(A)(ii).

discussed above, IRC § 415 limits the allocations or accruals for individual participants.

[A] Timing of Deductions

Under IRC § 404(a), contributions are generally deductible in the year paid.

Section 404(a)(6), however, permits a limited retroactive deduction. Contributions made after the close of the taxable year, but not later than the due date (including extensions) of the employer's tax return, are eligible for deduction in the preceding year.

In order to be eligible for a retroactive deduction,

(1) the contributions must be made to a qualified plan that was in existence by the end of the employer's taxable year, and

(2) the contributions must be attributable to compensation earned in the year of deduction.

Example 1

Corporation A's taxable year is the fiscal year beginning April 1 and ending the following March 31. Corporation A files for an extension so its tax return for fiscal year ending March 31, 2015, is due December 31, 2015.

If Corporation A establishes a qualified plan by March 31, 2015, and funds it by December 31, 2015, Corporation A may deduct the contributions it makes to the plan for its fiscal year ending March 31, 2015, so long as the contributions are attributable to compensation earned in the fiscal year ending March 31, 2015.[51]

Example 2

Corporation B's taxable year is the fiscal year beginning April 1 and ending the following March 31. It does not file for an extension so its tax return for the fiscal year ending March 31, 2015, is due June 30, 2015.

If Corporation B establishes a qualified plan by March 31, 2015, and funds it by June 30, 2015, Corporation B may deduct the contributions it makes to the plan for its fiscal year ending March 31, 2015, so long as the contributions are attributable to compensation earned in the fiscal year ending March 31, 2015. Any contributions made to the plan after the June 30, 2015, due date for its tax return are not deductible for the fiscal year ending March 31, 2015.

Example 3

Corporation C's taxable year is the fiscal year beginning April 1 and ending the following March 31. Corporation C files for an extension so its tax return for fiscal year ending March 31, 2015, is due December 31, 2015.

If Corporation C does not establish a qualified plan until after March 31, 2015, it may not deduct any contributions made to the plan after March 31, 2015, for its

---

[51] *See* Rev. Rul. 81-114, 1981-1 CB 207.

fiscal year ending March 31, 2015, regardless of the year in which the attributable compensation was earned.

Example 4

Corporation D maintains a 401(k) plan with a calendar plan year. Corporation D's taxable year is the fiscal year ending March 31. It files an extension so its tax return for the fiscal year ending March 31, 2015, is due December 31, 2015.

By the last day of Corporation D's 2015 calendar plan year, Corporation D has contributed $80,000 to the Corporation D 401(k) plan. The $80,000 consists of (a) $20,000 in elective deferral and matching contributions attributable to compensation earned by plan participants before the end of Corporation D's taxable year ending March 31, 2015 (Pre-Year End Contributions) and (b) $60,000 in elective deferral and matching contributions attributable to compensation earned by plan participants after the end of Corporation D's taxable year ending March 31, 2015 (Post-Year End Contributions).

Corporation D can deduct the $20,000 of Pre-Year End Contributions but not the $60,000 of Post-Year End Contributions for its taxable year ending March 31, 2015. Although the $60,000 of Post-Year End Contributions were made before the due date (including extensions) for Corporation D's taxable year ending March 31, 2015, the Post-Year End Contributions are not attributable to compensation earned in that tax year and thus, cannot be deducted in that year.

IRC § 404(a)(6) deems contributions made by the due date made by the end of the taxable year. It does not, however, permit contributions that are attributable to income earned after the end of the taxable year to be deductible in that year.[52]

[B] IRC § 404(a)(3) Deduction Limitations on Defined Contribution Plans

Section 404(a)(3) limits the deductible contribution with respect to defined contribution plans to 25% of aggregate participant compensation. If an employer maintains two or more defined contribution plans, they are considered as a single plan for purposes of the limitation.[53]

Example

The following employees with the following compensation in 2015 participate in Employer A's profit-sharing plan:

Employee	Compensation
A	$200,000
B	$175,000
C	$90,000
D	$75,000

---

[52] *See* Rev. Rul. 90-105, 1990-2 C.B. 69.

[53] A special rule applies to "SIMPLE" 401(k) plans. IRS §§ 401(k)(11) and 404(a)(3)(A)(i)(II).

Employee	Compensation
E	$60,000
F	$45,000

The maximum deductible contribution Employer A can make in 2015 is $161,250 (($200,000 + $175,000 + $90,000 + $75,000 + $60,000 + $45,000 = $645,000) x .25 = $161,250.)

[1] Compensation for Purposes of IRC § 404

In determining the 25% limit, only the compensation of employees who, in the relevant taxable year, are participants under the plan may be taken into account.[54]

An employee must actually participate in the allocation of the employer's contribution to the plan in the year for which the contribution is made in order for the employee's compensation to be taken account.[55] An employer may not include the compensation paid to an employee who terminates service during the plan year if the employee does not share in the allocation of the employer's contribution for the year.

Compensation for purposes of the IRC § 404(a) limitation means all compensation paid or accrued other than that for which a deduction is allowable under a qualified plan. [56] Thus, an employer's contribution to a qualified plan on behalf of an employee is not compensation for purposes of the deduction limit.

Example

Five employees participate in Employer B's profit-sharing plan. Employer B contributes 5% of compensation on behalf of each employee. The employee's compensation and employer contributions for 2015 are as follows:

Employee	Compensation	Employer Contribution	Cost to Employer for Compensation and Contribution	Compensation for purpose of IRC § 404(a) limitation
A	$175,000	$8,750	$183,750	$175,000
B	$90,000	$4,500	$94,500	$90,000
C	$60,000	$3,000	$63,000	$60,000
D	$50,000	$2,500	$52,500	$50,000
E	$35,000	$1,750	$36,750	$35,000

The maximum deductible contribution Employer B can make in 2015 is $102,500 (($175,000 + $90,000 + $60,000 + $50,000 + $35,000 = $410,000) x .25 = $102,500). Employer B's total contribution of $20,500 ($8,750 + $4,500 +$3,000 + $2,500 +

---

[54] Treas. Reg. § 1.404(a)-9(b).

[55] Rev. Rul. 65-295, 1965-2 CB 148.

[56] Treas. Reg. § 1.404(a)-9(b).

$1,750 = $20,500) clearly satisfies the IRC § 404(a) limit.

[2] Compensation and Elective Deferrals

Although an employer's contribution to a qualified plan on behalf of an employee does not constitute compensation for purposes of the IRC § 404(a)(3) limit, an employee's elective deferrals constitute compensation for purposes of the deduction limit.[57]

Example

Five employees participate in Employer C's profit-sharing plan with a 401(k) feature. Their compensation and elective deferrals for 2015 are as follows:

Employee	Compensation	Elective Deferral	Compensation after Elective Deferral
A	$175,000	$17,500	$157,500
B	$90,000	$9,000	$81,000
C	$60,000	$6,000	$54,000
D	$50,000	$5,000	$45,000
E	$35,000	$0	$35,000

The maximum deductible contribution Employer C can make in 2015 is $102,500 (($175,000 + $90,000 + $60,000 + $50,000 + $35,000 = $410,000) x .25 = $102,500.)

Elective deferrals are not taken into account in determining the IRC § 404(a)(3) limit.[58] Thus, the employees' elective deferrals of $37,500 ($17,500 + $9,000 + $6,000 + $5,000 = $37,500) do not count toward the $102,500 IRC § 404(a)(3) limit.

[3] IRC § 404(l) Limit on Compensation

Section 404(l) provides that compensation for purposes of IRC § 404 shall be limited to $200,000, as adjusted for increases in the cost-of-living under IRC § 401(a)(17).[59]

---

[57] IRC § 404(a)(12) (incorporating IRC § 415(c)(3)(D) definition of compensation which includes elective deferrals). Prior to 2002, compensation for purposes of the IRC § 404 limitations excluded elective deferrals. In 2001, Congress amended IRC § 404 to include elective deferrals in the definition of compensation. Economic Growth and Tax Relief Reconciliation Act of 2001, Pub. L. No. 107-16 § 616(b), 115 Stat. 38, 103. The House Report offers the following explanation for this change:

> Subjecting elective deferrals to the normally applicable deduction limits may cause employers to restrict the amount of elective deferrals an employee may make or to restrict employer contributions to the plan, thereby reducing participants' ultimate retirement benefits and their ability to save adequately for retirement. The Committee believes that the amount of elective deferrals otherwise allowable should not be further limited through application of deduction rules.

H.R. Rep. No. 51(I), 107th Cong., 1st Sess. 61 (2001).

[58] IRC § 404(n).

[59] For a discussion of the IRC § 401(a)(17) limit on compensation for qualified plan purposes, see § 10.02[A].

In 2015, the IRC § 401(a)(17) limit, as adjusted, is $265,000. Thus, in 2015, the maximum compensation that can be taken into account for any individual employee is $265,000.

Example

The following employees with the following compensation in 2014 participate in Employer D's profit-sharing plan:

Employee	Compensation	Compensation after IRC § 404(l) limit
A	$500,000	$265,000
B	$350,000	$265,000
C	$235,000	$235,000
D	$130,000	$130,000
E	$75,000	$75,000
F	$50,000	$50,000
G	$30,000	$30,000

The maximum deductible contribution Employer D can make in 2015 is $262,500 (($265,000 + $265,000 + $235,000 + $130,000 + $75,000 + $50,000 + $30,000 = $1,050,000) x .25 = $262,500).

[4] Interaction with IRC § 415 Limits

IRC § 404 does not affect or otherwise restrict the maximum contribution or benefit which may be allocated or accrued for any individual participant. Instead, as discussed above, IRC § 415 limits the allocations or accruals for individual participants.

Specifically, section 415(c) limits the "annual additions" which may be made to a defined contribution plan to the lesser of

(1) $40,000, adjusted for increases in the cost-of-living, or

(2)   100% of the participant's compensation.[60]

In 2015, the IRC § 415(c) limit, as adjusted for inflation, was $53,000.

Example 1

Seven employees participate in Employer E's profit-sharing plan. The following list provides their total compensation, the compensation that may be taken into account under IRC § 404 (and IRC § 401(a)(17)), and maximum "annual addition" or total contribution permitted for each employee under IRC § 415(c):

---

[60] IRC § 415(c)(1).

Employee	Compensation	Compensation after IRC § 404(l) Limit	Maximum Contribution Under IRC § 415(c)
A	$600,000	$265,000	$53,000
B	$450,000	$265,000	$53,000
C	$230,000	$230,000	$53,000
D	$150,000	$150,000	$53,000
E	$60,000	$60,000	$53,000
F	$40,000	$40,000	$40,000
G	$25,000	$25,000	$25,000

The maximum deductible contribution Employer E can make in 2015 is $258,750 (($265,000 + $265,000 + $230,000 + $150,000 + $60,000 + $40,000 + $25,000 = $1,035,000) x .25 = $258,750).

The total of the maximum contributions Employer E can make to a qualified profit-sharing plan on behalf of each of its seven employee under IRC § 415(c) is $330,000 ($53,000 + $53,000 + $53,000 + $53,000 + $53,000 + $40,000 + $25,000 = $330,000).

Although a total maximum contribution of $330,000 would be permissible under IRC § 415(c), it would not all be deductible under IRC § 404. Instead, the deduction would be limited to $258,750. Moreover, the excess $71,250 ($330,000 - $258,750 = $71,250) would be subject to a 10% excise tax under IRC 4972, as discussed below.

Example 2

Four employees participate in Employer F's profit-sharing plan. The following list provides their total compensation, the compensation that may be taken into account under IRC § 404 (and IRC § 401(a)(17)), and maximum "annual addition" or total contribution permitted for each employee under IRC § 415(c):

Employee	Compensation	Compensation after IRC § 404(l) limit	Maximum Contribution Under IRC § 415
A	$600,000	$265,000	$53,000
B	$500,000	$265,000	$53,000
C	$400,000	$265,000	$53,000
D	$100,000	$100,000	$53,000

The maximum deductible contribution Employer F can make in 2015 is $223,750 (($265,000 + $265,000 + $265,000 + $100,000 = $895,000) x .25 = $223,750).

The total of the maximum contributions Employer F can make to a qualified profit-sharing plan on behalf of each of its four employee is $212,000 ($53,000 + $53,000 + $53,000 + $53,000 = $212,000).

In this case, because Employer F's workforce consists of mostly very highly compensated employees, the IRC § 415 limit is lower than the IRC § 404 limit. If

Employer F wishes to contribute the maximum deductible contribution under IRC § 404, $11,750 ($223,750 - $212,000 = $11,750) of those contributions must be made to a nonqualified plan.

[C] IRC § 404(o) Deduction Limitations on Defined Benefit Plans

Section 404(o) of the Internal Revenue Code sets forth the deduction limit for defined benefit plans, other than multi-employer plans.

The limit ensures that, at a minimum, employers are permitted to deduct an amount equal to any contribution required under the minimum funding rules. (The minimum funding rules are discussed in Chapter 5 § 5.05.)

Specifically, section 404(o)(1) provides that the employer may deduct the greater of

(1) the excess (if any) of the sum of the plan's funding target, the plan's normal cost, and a cushion amount for the plan year over the plan assets, or

(2) the minimum required contribution for the plan year.

[D] IRC § 404(a)(7) Deduction Limitations on Combined Plans

Section 404(a)(7) of the Internal Revenue Code imposes an overall maximum limitation on the deductibility of contributions for employers that maintain both a defined contribution plan and a defined benefit plan.

If an employer maintains both a defined benefit plan and a defined contribution plan and at least one employee is covered by both plans, the maximum deducible contribution is equal to the greater of

(1) 25% of the aggregate compensation of all participants, or

(2) the amount necessary to meet the defined benefit plan's minimum funding standard.[61]

If no employee is covered by both plans, the regular deductible contribution limits apply.[62]

[E] IRC § 4972 Excise Tax on Excess Contributions

If an employer's contribution to a qualified plan[63] exceeds the deductible limit and the excess contribution is not returned to the employer prior to the employer's tax filing date, including extensions, IRC § 4972 imposes a 10% excise tax on the

---

[61] IRC § 404(a)(7)(A).

[62] IRC § 404(a)(7)(C).

[63] The IRC § 4972 excise tax only applies to excess contributions to qualified plans. Presumably, the purpose of the IRC § 4972 excise tax is to discourage employers from overfunding their qualified plans to take advantage of the tax-free build up in qualified plans. *See* Jt. Comm. on Tax'n, Description of the Revenue Provisions Contained in the President's Fiscal Year 2006 Budget Proposal, JCS-3-05 No. 6, at

nondeductible contribution. The excise tax applies regardless of whether or not the employer claimed a deduction with respect to the contribution.

The nondeductible contribution is generally equal to the sum of

    (1)   the nondeductible contributions made for the current year, and

    (2)   the nondeductible contributions from the preceding year.[64]

Section 4972 provides an ordering rule pursuant to which amounts allowable as a deductible contribution for any plan year are deemed to come first from carryforwards from prior taxable years with the oldest contributions being deducted first and then from current contributions.[65]

The effect of the rule is to subject the same nondeductible contribution to the excise tax until it is allowed as deduction pursuant to the carryover rules.

Example

Employer A establishes a qualified profit-sharing plan on January 1, 2011. The plan operates on a calendar year basis. The following chart sets forth for each year between 2011 and 2015, the total compensation of the employees who participate in the plan, the total deductible contribution under IRC § 404, Employer A's actual contributions, the amount Employer A can deduct, the amount that must be carried forward, and the applicable IRC § 4972 excise tax, if any.

Year	Total Compensation	Total Deductible Contribution Under IRC § 404	Employer A's Actual Contribution	Amount Deducted	Amount Carried Forward	IRC § 4972 Excise Tax
2011	$400,000	$100,000 ($400,000 x .25 = $100,000)	$150,000	$100,000	$50,000 ($150,000 — $100,000 = $50,000)	$5,000 ($50,000 x .10 = $5,000)
2012	$600,000	$150,000 ($600,000 x .25 = $125,000)	$175,000	$150,000 ($50,000 carryforward from 2011 plus $100,000 of $175,000 contributed in 2012)	$75,000 (the excess of the $175,000 2012 contribution that was not deducted in 2012 ($175,000 - $100,000 = $75,000))	$7,500 ($75,000 x .10 = $7,500)

28 (2005) (stating that the "excise tax on nondeductible contributions . . . [has] as a major objective preventing the use of defined benefit pension plans as a tax-favored funding mechanism for the business needs of the employer").

[64]   IRC § 4972(c)(1). Certain exceptions apply in determining the amount of nondeductible contributions for purposes of IRC § 4972. *See* § 4972(c)(6) & (7).

[65]   IRC § 4972(c)(2).

Year	Total Compensation	Total Deductible Contribution Under IRC § 404	Employer A's Actual Contribution	Amount Deducted	Amount Carried Forward	IRC § 4972 Excise Tax
2013	$800,000	$200,000 ($800,000 x .25 = $200,000)	$175,000	$200,000 ($75,000 carryforward from 2012 plus $125,000 of the $175,000 contributed in 2013)	$50,000 (the excess of the $175,000 2013 contribution that was not deducted in 2013 ($175,000 - $125,000 = $50,000))	$5,000 ($50,000 x .10 = $5,000)
2014	$600,000	$150,000 ($600,000 x .25 = $150,000)	$125,000	$150,000 ($50,000 carryforward from 2013 plus $100,000 of the $125,000 contributed in 2014)	$25,000 (the excess of the $125,000 2014 contribution that was not deducted in 2014 ($125,000 - $100,000 = $25,000))	$2,500
2015	$1,000,000	$250,000 ($1,000,000 x .25 = $250,000)	$200,000	$225,000 ($25,000 carryforward from 2014 plus entire $200,000 contributed in 2015)	0	0

[F]   Summary of Deduction Limitations

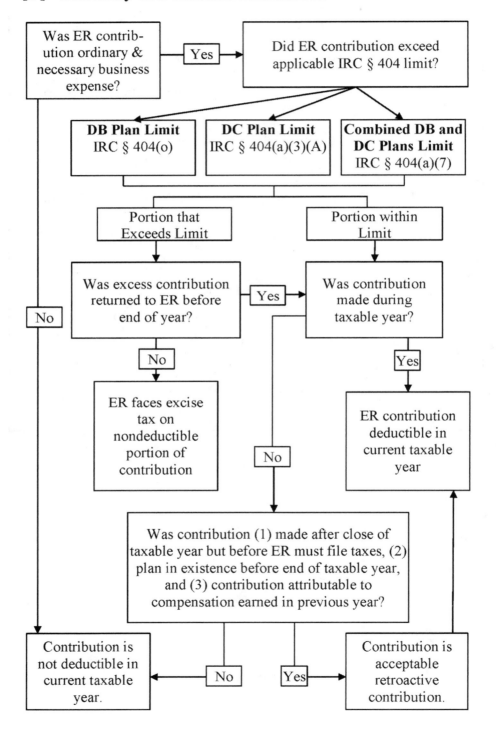

§ 10.04 PLAN DISTRIBUTIONS

This section addresses a few of the basic rules governing plan distributions.[66]

Specifically, it addresses:

(1) the IRC § 402(a)(1) rule that amounts distributed from qualified plans are generally taxable when distributed as ordinary income under IRC § 72,

(2) the IRC § 402A special rule which excludes from income most distributions from Roth accounts,

(3) the special exception from the general IRC § 402(a)(1) rule for rollover distributions which permits a continuing deferral of taxation of "eligible rollover distributions,"

(4) the IRC § 72(t) 10% additional tax on early distributions,

(5) the rules governing plan loans, particularly, IRC § 72(p), and

(6) the minimum distribution rules under IRC § 401(a)(9) which essentially require that qualified plans begin to make distributions to plan participants after they reach age 70 1/2.

[A] Taxation of Distributions under IRC § 72

One of the principle benefits of qualified plans is that contributions to qualified plans are not currently taxable to plan participants. As the old saying goes, though, "All good things must come to an end."[67] At some point, plan contributions must be distributed and become taxable income.

Section 402(a)(1) of the Internal Revenue Code provides that as a general rule any amount distributed from a qualified plan is taxable to the recipient under IRC § 72 in the taxable year distributed.[68]

---

[66] According to two commentators:

The rules governing distributions from tax-favored retirement arrangements are so complex that even tax practitioners who came of age with ERISA approach them with trepidation. Much of this complexity is attributable to the continued proliferation of different types of retirement plans, each with its own set of rules, and to the numerous special rules, most of which were enacted to achieve worthwhile goals, but many of which have outlived their original purpose and usefulness. David A. Pratt and Dianne Bennett, *Simplifying Retirement Plan Distributions*, New York University 57th Institute on Federal Taxation — Employee Benefits and Executive Compensation 5-3 (1999).

This section does not delve into all of the intricacies of the law governing plan distributions. Instead, it focuses on a few of the fundamental rules. For a more detailed discussion of the taxation of plan distributions, see, for example, PAMELA D. PERDUE, QUALIFIED PENSION AND PROFIT-SHARING PLANS Chapter 23 (2014).

[67] Michael L. Epstein, *Taxation of Qualified Plan Distributions and Required Minimum Distributions*, ALI-CLE Course Materials on the Fundamentals of Employee Benefits Law, SV034 ALI-ABA 243 (May 15–16, 2014).

[68] Specifically, section 402(a)(1) provides:

Except as otherwise provided in this section, any amount actually distributed to any distributee by an employees' trust described in section 401(a) which is exempt from tax under section 501(a) shall be taxable to the distribute, in the taxable year of the distribute in which

Section 72 is entitled "Annuities; Certain Proceeds of Endowment and Life Insurance Contracts," and was originally enacted to address the taxation of annuities.[69] Section 72, however, also applies to distributions from qualified plans.[70]

Under section 72, distributions from qualified plans are generally taxable as ordinary income in the year distributed. Thus, as a general rule, taxation under section 72 is quite simple. Distributions from qualified plans are taxable as ordinary income when received.

If, however, a plan participant has made nondeductible contributions to the plan and thus has a basis or "investment in the contract," the part of any distribution that represents the participant's basis, or investment in the contract, is not includible in income.

The basis recovery rules depend on whether or not the distribution is received as an annuity.

[1]   Amounts Received as an Annuity

[a]   Definition of Amount Received as an Annuity

A distribution constitutes an amount received as an annuity if

(1)   the distribution is received on or after the annuity starting date;[71]

(2)   the distribution is one of a series of periodic payments payable in periodic installments at regular intervals (such as annually, semiannually, quarterly, monthly, or weekly) over a period of more than one year; and

(3)   the total amount payable is determinable at the annuity starting date either directly under the terms of the contract, or indirectly by the use of mortality tables or compound interest calculations in accordance with sound actuarial theory.[72]

Example 1

Under Employer's plan, Arthur receives $500 per month for Arthur's life. This is a classic single life annuity. Each monthly $500 distribution Arthur receives constitutes an amount received as an annuity.

Example 2

Under Employer's plan, Bethany receives $500 per month for her life. If she predeceases her husband, Jarrod, Jarrod will receive $250 per month for his life.

---

distributed, under section 72 (relating to annuities).

[69] PERDUE, QUALIFIED PENSION AND PROFIT-SHARING PLANS, at ¶ 23.02.

[70] Section 72 also applies to distributions from IRC § 403(b) plans. IRC § 403(b)(1).

[71] The annuity starting date is the first day of the first period for which an amount is received as an annuity under the contract. IRC § 72(b)(4). *See* Treas. Reg. § 72-4(b) (defining annuity starting date).

[72] Treas. Reg. § 1.72-2(b)(2). There is an exception to this rule for periodic distributions from defined contribution plans that vary as a result of the fund's investment performance. *See* Treas. Reg. § 1.72-2(b)(3)(i).

This is a classic joint and survivor annuity. Each monthly distribution of $500 that Bethany receives, and any monthly $250 distribution that Jarrod receives after Bethany's death constitutes an amount received as an annuity.

[b] "Simplified Method of Taxation" under IRC § 72(d)

If a qualified plan participant has an investment in the contract and the participant receives distributions in the form of an annuity, IRC § 72(d) sets forth a mandatory "simplified method" to determine how the participant's basis or investment in the contract is to be recovered.[73] Generally, a plan participant has an investment in the contract if the plan participant has made after tax contributions to the plan.[74]

Under the IRC § 72(d) simplified method, the participant recovers the investment in the contract in level amounts over an expected number of monthly payments.[75] The anticipated number of payments depends on whether the payments are based on the life of a single individual or more than one individual.

If the annuity is payable over the life of a single individual, the number of anticipated payments is determined as follows:[76]

If the age of the annuitant on the annuity starting date is:	The number of anticipated payments is:
Not more than 55	360
More than 55 but not more than 60	310
More than 60 but not more than 65	260
More than 65 but not more than 70	210
More than 70	160

If the annuity is payable over the lives of more than one individual, the number of anticipated payments is determined as follows:[77]

If the combined ages of the annuitants are:	The number is:
Not more than 110	410

---

[73] If the annuity is over age 75 and there are five or more years of guaranteed payments under the annuity, the IRC § 72(d) simplified method does not apply. Instead, the IRC § 72(b)(2) general method applies. For a discussion of the general method, see PERDUE, QUALIFIED PENSION AND PROFIT-SHARING PLANS, at ¶ 23.02.

[74] A participant's investment in the contract is defined as the aggregate premiums or other consideration paid, reduced by any amounts received before the annuity starting date that were excluded from gross income. IRC §§ 72(c)(1) & (f). For a more detailed discussion regarding the calculation of the investment in the contract, see Treas. Reg. § 1.72-6.

[75] If periodic payments are made on other than a monthly basis, adjustments are made to reflect the different frequency of payments. IRC § 72(d)(1)(F).

[76] IRC § 72(d)(1)(B)(iii).

[77] IRC § 72(d)(1)(B)(iv).

If the combined ages of the annuitants are:	The number is:
More than 110 but not more than 120	360
More than 120 but not more than 130	310
More than 130 but not more than 140	260
More than 140	210

If the annuity does not depend in whole or in part on the life expectancy of one or more individuals, the expected number of payments is the number of monthly annuity payments under the contract.[78]

Example

Justin, age 65, began receiving retirement benefits in 2005 under a joint-and-survivor annuity. Justin's annuity starting date is January 1, 2005. The benefits are to be paid for the joint lives of Justin and his wife, Joan, age 62. Justin made after-tax contributions of $31,000 to the qualified plan and received no distributions before the annuity starting date. Justin is to receive a retirement benefit of $1,400 per month, and Joan is to receive a monthly survivor benefit of $700 on Justin's death.

Because Justin's annuity is payable over the lives of more than one individual, he must use his and Joan's combined ages to determine the anticipated number of payments. Because their combined ages are 127 (65 + 62 = 127), the number of anticipated payments is 310, and Justin's tax-free monthly amount is $100 ($31,000/310 = $100).

Thus, each month that Justin receives $1,400, he must treat $1,300 as taxable income and may exclude $100 from his taxable income.

Upon Justin's death, if Justin has not recovered the full $31,000 investment in the contract, Joan may also exclude from income $100 of the annuity payments she receives. Specifically, each month that she receives $700, she must treat $600 as taxable income and may exclude $100 from taxable income.

Any annuity payments received after the 310 monthly payments have been made will be fully includible in gross income. If Justin and Joan die before 310 payments have been made, a miscellaneous itemized deduction will be allowed for the unrecovered cost on the final income tax return of the last to die.

[2]   Amounts Not Received as an Annuity — IRC § 72(e)

If a plan participant receives a distribution and the distribution does not constitute an amount received as an annuity, IRC § 72(e) governs the tax treatment of the distribution, sometimes referred to as a nonperiodic payment.

---

[78] IRC § 72(d)(1)(B)(i)(II).

Example

If a plan participant takes out a plan loan, and the plan does not satisfy the requirements of IRC § 72(p), discussed in § 10.04[E][2][c], the loan will be treated as a taxable nonperiodic payment.[79]

If a participant receives a nonperiodic payment, and the participant has an investment in the contract,[80] taxation of the distribution depends on when the distribution is made in relation to the annuity starting date.

If the nonperiodic payment is made on or after the annuity starting date, then generally all of the payment is includible in gross income when received.[81]

If the nonperiodic payment is made before the annuity starting date, the participant can generally allocate part of the distribution to the cost basis and exclude from gross income that part of the nonperiodic payment allocable to the cost basis.[82] Generally, the portion of any distribution that is a recovery of the basis is determined by multiplying that amount of the distribution by the ratio of the participant's investment in the contract over the participant's entire account balance (or value of the accrued benefit in the case of a defined benefit plan).[83]

Example

James receives a distribution of $40,000 from his Employer's profit-sharing plan. James has an investment in the contract of $8,000 and James' account balance before the distribution was $80,000.

James can exclude from income $4,000 of the $40,000 distribution ($40,000 (amount received) x $8,000 (investment in contract)/$80,000 (account balance) = $4,000)

[B] Taxation of Qualified Distributions from Designated Roth Accounts — IRC § 402A(d)

IRC § 402A sets forth special tax rules with respect to distributions from designated Roth accounts.

Specifically, IRC § 402A(d) provides that qualified distributions from a designated Roth account shall not be includible in gross income. Thus, under IRC § 402A(d), a plan participant will never be taxed on the earnings on Roth

---

[79] Other common nonperiodic payments include (1) distributions of current earnings (dividends) other than dividends retained by the insurer to pay premiums or other consideration for the contract and (2) the value of annuity contracts transferred without adequate consideration. *See* Perdue, Qualified Pension and Profit-Sharing Plans, at ¶ 23.02.

[80] For these purposes, a participant's investment in the contract as of any date is the aggregate premiums or other consideration paid (generally, the aggregate amount of after-tax contributions made to the plan) before such date, reduced by the aggregate amounts received before such date to the extent that such amounts were excluded from gross income. IRC §§ 72(e)(6).

[81] IRC § 72(e)(2)(A).

[82] IRC § 72(e)(2)(B).

[83] IRC § 72(e)(8)(B).

contributions so long as the earnings are distributed in a qualified distribution.[84]

In order to constitute a qualified distribution, two requirements must be satisfied:

(1) the distribution must be after the end of a specified period, generally five years after the participant's first designated Roth contribution,[85] and

(2) the distribution must be

  (a) made on or after the date the employee attains age 59 1/2,

  (b) made on or after the date the employee dies, or

  (c) be attributable to the employee being disabled within the meaning of IRC § 72(m)(7).[86]

[C] Rollover Distributions — IRC § 402(c)

Section 402(c) of the Internal Revenue Code sets forth a significant exception to the general rule that distributions from qualified plans are generally taxable as ordinary income in the year distributed under IRC § 72.

Specifically, IRC § 402(c) provides than any participant who transfers all or any portion of an "eligible rollover distribution" to an "eligible retirement plan" may exclude the amount rolled over from gross income in the year distributed. The amount rolled over will not be included in the participant's income until it is distributed from the retirement plan into which it was rolled over.

[1] Purpose of the Exception for Rollover Distributions

The Internal Revenue Code provides favorable tax treatment for qualified plans in order to encourage retirement savings. The rollover rules are designed to further that purpose.

Specifically, the rollover rules are designed to encourage plan participants to roll over their plan distributions to retirement plans rather than consume their retirement plan distributions prior to retirement.[87]

[2] Eligible Rollover Distributions

IRC § 402(c)(4) defines an "eligible rollover distribution" as any distribution from a qualified plan to a participant with the exception of three specific types of distributions:

(1) periodic payments,

---

[84] Recall that Roth contributions, unlike traditional qualified plan contributions, are subject to taxation when made. *See* Chapter 2 § 2.04[D]. Like earnings on qualified plan contributions, earnings on Roth contributions are not taxable so long as held in the qualified plan. *See id.*

[85] IRC § 402A(d)(2)(B).

[86] IRC § 402A(d)(2)(A).

[87] *See* Perdue, Qualified Pension and Profit-Sharing Plans, at ¶ 23.03.

   (2)   distributions required under the IRC § 401(a)(9) minimum distribution rules, and

   (3)   hardship distributions.[88]

[a]   Periodic Payments

Periodic payments are defined as any distribution that is one of a series of substantially equal periodic payments, payable in installments no less often than annually, and made over the life or life expectancy of the employee or joint lives or joint life expectancies of the employee and his or her beneficiary or for a specified period of 10 years or more.[89] Periodic payments are similar, though not identical, to "amounts received as an annuity" under IRC § 72.[90]

Periodic payments are in essence regular pension payments that represent regular retirement income. Because periodic payments are essentially regular pension income, there is no reason to encourage the rollover of periodic payments. Accordingly, periodic payments may not be rolled over.

Instead, periodic payments are taxed as ordinary income when received under IRC § 72 as discussed in § 10.04[A].

Example 1

Jerome, age 70, terminates his employment with Employer. Employer's qualified pension plan distributes to Jerome $500 per month for Jerome's life. Each monthly $500 distribution Jerome receives is a periodic payment and does not qualify as an eligible rollover distribution. Instead, it is taxed as ordinary income when received under IRC § 72.

Example 2

Rosa, age 68, terminates her employment with Employer. Employer's qualified plan distributes to Rosa $1,000 per month for eight years. Because the payments to Rosa are only made for eight years, rather than for Rosa's life or for at least 10 years, they do not qualify as periodic payments. Nor are they minimum required distributions or hardship distributions. Thus, each payment is an eligible rollover distribution.

---

[88] IRC § 402(c)(4). The Treasury regulations also exclude certain other distributions, such as loans treated as deemed distributions under IRC § 72(p), from the definition of eligible rollover distribution. Treas. Reg. § 1.402(c)-2 Q&A-4.

[89] IRC § 402(c)(4)(A).

[90] The most significant difference is guaranteed payments for less than 10 years do not qualify as periodic payments under the IRC § 402(c) rollover rules but may qualify as amounts received as an annuity under IRC § 72. *Compare* 1.72-2(b)(2) (defining amounts received as an annuity) *with* IRC § 402(c)(4)(A) (defining periodic payments).

[b]   Minimum Required Distributions

As discussed in § 10.04[F], IRC § 401(a)(9) requires that qualified plans make minimum required distributions.

Essentially, the minimum distribution rules require that qualified plans begin to make distributions to plan participants after they reach age 70 1/2. The rules are designed to ensure that the funds in qualified plans are used for retirement purposes, not estate planning purposes.

Plan participants may not roll over minimum required distributions. Indeed, rolling over minimum required distribution would defeat the entire purpose of minimum required distributions.

Instead, minimum required distributions are taxed as ordinary income when received under IRC § 72.

[c]   Hardship Distributions

Many 401(k) plans authorize hardship distributions.[91]

A hardship distribution is a distribution made on account of an immediate and heavy financial need of an employee or his or her spouse or dependent and is necessary to satisfy that financial need.[92]

A distribution will be deemed to satisfy an immediate and heavy financial need if it is used for

(1) unreimbursed medical expenses that are deductible under IRC § 213(d);

(2) the purchase of a principal residence;

(3) tuition and related educational fees and room and board expenses for up to the next 12 months of post-secondary education;

(4) prevention of eviction from or foreclosure on the principal residence;

(5) funeral expenses; or

(6) expenses for the repair of a principal residence due to hurricane, flood, and other casualty deduction reasons.[93]

Plan participants may not roll over hardship distributions. Indeed, if a plan participant were able to roll over a hardship distribution, the plan participant would not be eligible for a hardship distribution because the hardship distribution would not be necessary to satisfy a financial need.

---

[91] *See* 401(k) Help Center, *Benchmark Your 401(k) Plan — 2015* (stating that hardship withdrawals are permitted in 83% of 401(k) plans but that only 4% of plan participants take hardship withdrawals when permitted), *available at* http://www.401khelpcenter.com/benchmarking.html. *See also* Profit Sharing/401k Council of America, 51st Annual Survey Reflecting 2007 Plan Experience 46 Table 80 (2008) (reporting that hardship withdrawals are permitted in 88.81% of 401(k) plans and 78.7% of combined profit sharing/401(k) plans).

[92] Reg. § 1.401(k)(1)-1(d)(3).

[93] Treas. Reg. § 1.401(7)-1(d)(3)(iii).

Hardship distributions are taxed as ordinary income when received under IRC § 72.

[3] Eligible Retirement Plans

IRC § 402(c)(8) identifies the types of retirement plans to which eligible rollover distributions may be rolled over.

Specifically, eligible retirement plans are defined as

    (1)   individual retirement accounts under IRC § 408(a),

    (2)   individual retirement annuities under IRC § 408(b),

    (3)   qualified plans under IRC § 401(a),

    (4)   annuity plans under IRC § 403(a),

    (5)   governmental plans under IRC § 457, and

    (6)   tax-sheltered annuities under IRC § 403(b).[94]

Although all six of these types of plans are "eligible" to receive rollovers, they are not required to accept rollover contributions.[95] Virtually all 401(k) plans accept rollover contributions.[96]

[4] Types of Rollovers

There are two basic types of rollovers:

    (1)   actual rollovers and

    (2)   direct rollovers.

In an actual rollover distribution, the plan administrator makes an eligible rollover distribution to a plan participant. The plan participant then rolls the distribution over to an eligible retirement plan within 60 days of receipt in order to avoid taxation on the distribution.

In a direct rollover distribution, the plan administrator transfers the eligible rollover distribution directly to the recipient retirement plan in a direct trustee-to-trustee transfer.

IRC § 401(a)(31) requires qualified plans to offer plan participants the option of a direct rollover. The Internal Revenue Code encourages participants to choose direct rollovers by subjecting any eligible rollover distribution that is not directly rolled over to a 20% withholding tax.[97]

---

[94] IRC § 402(c)(8)(B).

[95] Treas. Reg. § 1.401(a)(31)-1 Q&A-13.

[96] *See* Profit Sharing/401k Council of America, 51st Annual Survey, at 65 Table 106 (reporting that 98.2% of 401(k) plans, 97.4% of combined profit sharing/401(k) plans, and 50% of standalone profit sharing plans accept rollover contributions).

[97] IRC § 3405(c).

Example 1

Julie, age 40, terminates employment with Employer on March 1, 2015. She asks the plan administrator of Employer's 401(k) plan to transfer her entire $40,000 account balance directly to an individual retirement account (IRA) she has established at Vanguard. Because the distribution is an eligible rollover distribution and Julie elected to roll the entire distribution directly into an eligible retirement plan, no tax is required to be withheld from the distribution, and Julie will not be subject to tax on the distribution until it is distributed from her Vanguard IRA.

Example 2

Bob, age 57, terminates employment with Company A on March 1, 2015. He asks the plan administrator of Company A's 401(k) plan to distribute his entire $15,000 account balance to him. Because the distribution is an eligible rollover distribution, and Bob does not elect a direct rollover distribution, the plan administrator must withhold $3,000 ($15,000 x .20 = $3,000) from the distribution as federal income tax. Bob will receive a check for $12,000 ($15,000 - $3,000 = $12,000) from the plan.

Bob has 60 days to roll over the distribution to an eligible retirement plan. If Bob rolls over the distribution to the 401(k) plan of his new employer, Company B, within 60 days, he will not be subject to income tax on the distribution in 2015. Instead, he will be subject to tax on the distribution when it is distributed from the Company B 401(k) plan.

In order to avoid any tax on the distribution, Bob must contribute $15,000 to the Company B 401(k) plan within 60 days. Thus, not only must he contribute the $12,000 he received from the Company A 401(k) plan but he must also find $3,000 from another source to contribute to the Company B plan in order to avoid income tax on the distribution in 2015. If he only rolls over the $12,000 he received from the Company A 401(k) plan, he will be subject to income tax on the $3,000 withheld

When reporting his income for 2015, Bob will get credit for the $3,000 in taxes withheld, and he may be entitled to a refund of some or all of that $3,000, depending on his individual tax situation and income tax bracket.

[5] Rollovers of Property

If an eligible rollover distribution is made in the form of property, such as stock, the actual property distributed must be rolled over, or the property must be sold and the proceeds rolled over.[98] An employee cannot keep the distributed property and roll over cash or other property. If the distributed property is sold and the proceeds rolled over, no gain or loss is recognized on the sale.[99] The entire sale proceeds (including any portion representing an increase in value) is treated as part

---

[98] IRC §§ 401(c)(1)(C) & 401(c)(6)(A).

If an eligible rollover distribution is made in the form of property, the withholding requirement must still be satisfied. The plan administrator may permit the participant to satisfy the withholding requirement by providing sufficient cash to satisfy the requirement. Or the plan administrator may sell some or all of the property to satisfy the requirement. Treas. Reg. § 35.3405-1T f-2 Q&A

[99] IRC § 402(c)(6)(D).

of the distribution, and is not included in gross income.

Example 1

Plan distributes $10,000 in non-employer stock to Joseph and Joseph sells the stock for $10,300. Joseph rolls the full $10,300 to an IRA within 60 days. None of the proceeds of the sale of non-employer stock are includible in Joseph's income until it is withdrawn from the IRA. When withdrawn, the entire $10,300 is includible as ordinary income under section 72.

If only a portion of the proceeds is rolled over, the employee is taxed on the portion retained. The proceeds must be allocated between the part representing ordinary income from the distribution (its value upon distribution) and the part representing gain or loss from the sale (its change in value from the time of distribution until the time of sale).

Example 2

Plan distributes $10,000 in non-employer stock to Joseph and Joseph sells the stock for $10,300. Joseph rolls $8,000 of the proceeds into an IRA within 60 days. Joseph must include $2,300 ($10,300 - $8,000 = $2,300) in income in the year of the distribution. The income will be apportioned as follows: $67 as capital gain ($300/$10,300 x $2,300 = $67) and $2,233 as ordinary income ($10,000/10,300 x $2,300 = $2,233).

Example 3

Plan distributes $10,000 in non-employer stock to Joseph and Joseph sells the stock for $9,700. Joseph rolls $8,000 of the proceeds into an IRA within 60 days. Joseph must include $1,700 ($9,700 - $8,000 = $1,700) in income in the year of the distribution. The income will be apportioned as follows: $53 as capital loss ($300/$9,700 x $1,700 = $53) and $1,753 as ordinary income ($10,000/$9,700 x $1,700 = $1,753).

If an employee receives an eligible rollover distribution consisting of both cash and property and makes a rollover after selling part or all of the distributed property, the employee may designate the portions of such rollover to be treated as a contribution of sales proceeds and as cash received in the rollover distribution, respectively.[100]

[D]   IRC § 72(t) 10% Additional Tax on Early Distributions

The Internal Revenue Code provides favorable income tax treatment to qualified plans primarily to encourage individuals to save for retirement.[101] Thus, in order to ensure that funds in qualified plans are available for retirement purposes and are

---

[100]   IRC § 402(c)(6)(C).

[101]   Pratt & Bennett, N.Y.U. 57th Institute on Federal Taxation — Employee Benefits and Executive Compensation, at 5–9.

not taken too early, the Internal Revenue Code imposes restrictions on the timing of distributions from qualified plans.[102]

Specifically, IRC § 72(t) imposes a 10% additional tax on early distributions from qualified plans.

In theory, IRC § 72(t) could be quite simple. It could simply impose a 10% additional tax on distributions to an employee before the employee reaches a particular age, such as the age of 59 1/2.[103]

In fact, however, IRC § 72(t) is rather complex. It does not define "early distributions" from qualified plans as distributions before a particular age. Instead, section 72(t) provides that an additional tax applies to all distributions from qualified plans unless they fall within an express exception set forth in IRC § 72(t).[104] The first exception is for distributions after the employee reaches age 59 1/2.[105]

Section 72(t) is then riddled with additional exceptions. Some of those exceptions are consistent,[106] or reasonably consistent,[107] with IRC § 72(t)'s purpose of ensuring that funds in qualified plans are available for retirement purposes and are not taken too early. Other exceptions, in contrast, are entirely inconsistent with its purpose of ensuring that qualified plan funds are available for retirement purposes. Instead, those exceptions promote other policies such as covering the cost of certain medical expenses.[108]

Specifically, IRC § 72(t) excepts from the 10% additional tax distributions from qualified plan that are:

(1)   made on or after the employee attains the age 59 1/2;[109]

(2)   made to a beneficiary (or the estate of the employee) on or after the death of the employee;[110]

(3)   attributable to the employee being disabled;[111]

---

[102] Joint Committee on Taxation, Present Law and Background Relating to the Tax Treatment of Retirement Savings, JCX-44-11, at 28 (Sept. 13, 2011).

[103] Cf. IRC § 72(t)(2)(A)(i) (excepting from additional tax distributions to employee after employee reaches age 59 1/2).

[104] IRC § 72(t)(1) & (2).

[105] IRC § 72(t)(2)(A)(i).

[106] For example, IRC § 72(t)(2)(A)(v) excepts distributions made to an employee after the employee separates from service after age 55.

[107] For example, IRC § 72(t)(2)(A)(ii) excepts distributions made to a beneficiary (or estate of the employee) on or after the death of the employee. Once an employee dies, the employee does not need retirement income and thus, this exception appears reasonably consistent, or at least not inconsistent, with the purpose of the exception. Arguably, this exception should not apply if the individual dies leaving a spouse because the spouse will need retirement income. Drafting an exception to address that situation, however, could create unnecessary difficulties and thus, the exception is not unreasonable.

[108] IRC § 72(t)(2)(B).

[109] IRC § 72(t)(2)(A)(i).

[110] IRC § 72(t)(2)(A)(ii).

[111] IRC § 72(t)(2)(A)(iii).

(4)   part of a life annuity for the employee and his beneficiary;[112]

(5)   made to an employee after he separates from service (terminates employment with the employer) after age 55;[113]

(6)   stock dividends paid by ESOPs;[114]

(7)   made on account of a tax levy on the plan;[115]

(8)   made to an employee to cover certain medical expenses;[116]

(9)   made to alternate payees under qualified domestic relations orders (QDROs);[117] or

(10) made to a member of a reserve unit called to active duty for 180 days or longer.[118]

To add to the complexity of IRC § 72(t), the provision does not apply solely to distributions from qualified plans under IRC § 401(a). Instead, it also applies to other retirement savings arrangements eligible for favorable income tax treatment, such as IRAs,[119] and contains some exceptions that apply solely to IRAs and not to qualified plans.[120]

[E]   Plan Loans — IRC § 72(p)

Although qualified plans[121] are not required to offer loans to plan participants, most 401(k) plans do offer plan loans.[122] Overall, about 20% of 401(k) plan participants have outstanding plan loans at any one time.[123]

---

[112]   IRC § 72(t)(2)(A)(iv).

[113]   IRC § 72(t)(2)(A)(v). This exception only applies if the separation from service occurs after the individual reaches age 55. Notice 87-13, Q & A-20.

[114]   IRC § 72(t)(2)(A)(vi).

[115]   IRC § 72(t)(2)(A)(vii).

[116]   IRC § 72(t)(2)(B).

[117]   IRC § 72(t)(2)(C). For a discussion of QDROs, see Chapter 5 § 5.04[3][c].

[118]   IRC § 72(t)(2)(G).

[119]   IRC § 72(t) also applies to distributions from IRC § 403(a) annuity plans, IRC § 403(b) annuity contracts, IRC § 408(a) IRAs, and IRC § IRC § 408(b) individual retirement annuities. See IRC § 72(t)(1) (stating that tax applies to qualified retirement plans as defined in IRC § 4974(c)).

[120]   See, e.g., IRC § 72(t)(2)(E) (excepting distributions from IRAs for higher education expenses); IRC § 72(t)(2)(F) (excepting distributions from IRAs for certain first home purchases).

[121]   Other types of tax-favored retirement plans, such as 403(b) plans and governmental plans, may offer plan loans. Treas. Reg. § 72(p)(4); Treas. Reg. § 1.72(p)-1, Q&A-2. IRAs and IRA-based plans may not offer plan loans.

[122]   Jack VanDerhei et al., *401(k) Plan Asset Allocation, Account Balances, and Loan Activity in 2012*, EBRI Issue Brief No. 394, at 23 (Dec. 2013) (stating that 59% of the 401(k) plans in the 2012 EBRI/ICI 401(k) database for which loan data were available offered plan participants loans); Vanguard, *Diversity and Defined Contribution Plans: Loans and Hardship Withdrawals* 3 (Apr. 2012) (reporting that three-quarters of Vanguard-administered funds offered plan loans in 2010).

[123]   Jack VanDerhei et al., EBRI Issue Brief No. 394, at 23 (stating that at year-end 2012, 21% of 401(k) plan participants eligible for plan loans had outstanding loans). For additional statistics, see Vanguard, *Diversity and Defined Contribution Plans: Loans and Hardship Withdrawals* 6 (Apr. 2012); TIAA-CREF, *Borrowing Against Your Future Survey: Executive Summary* 1 (June 18, 2014); Timothy

[1]   Advantages and Disadvantages of Plan Loans

Plan loans have both advantages and disadvantages.

The availability of plan loans tends to encourage individuals, particularly lower-income individuals, to participate in, and/or contribute more to, 401(k) plans than they would in the absence of loan provisions.[124] In addition, from the standpoint of plan participants, plan loans tend to be quick and convenient with no credit check or long application form.[125] Moreover, interest rates on plan loans tend to be lower than interest rates charged by credit card companies,[126] and the interest is paid to the plan participant rather than a bank or credit card company.

On the other hand, plan loans create the risk that plan participants may have lower account balances at retirement than they would have had had they not taken out a loan.[127] Interest rates on plan loans tend to be lower than the rates of return on alternative 401(k) plan investments.[128] Thus, taking out a plan loan may cause a plan participant to have a lower account balance at retirement than if the participant had not taken out a loan.

It is not entirely clear whether plan loans do in fact cause reduced retirement savings. The availability of plan loans tends to increase plan participation and contribution rates. Whether plan loans in fact reduce plan participants' ultimate retirement savings depends on whether plan participants borrow money that they would not have otherwise contributed to a 401(k) plan or borrow money that they would have contributed to the plan even in the absence of a loan provision. There is no readily available answer to that empirical question.[129]

The risk of lower retirement savings is not the only disadvantage of plan loans. Plan participants may be subject to double taxation on the interest paid on plan loans. The plan participant must pay the interest with after-tax dollars, and the

---

(Jun) Lu, et al., *Borrowing from the Future: 401(k) Plan Loans and Loan Defaults*, Pension Research Council Working Paper 2014-01, at 7 (Feb. 2014).

[124] *See* GAO, *401(k) Pension Plans: Loan Provisions Enhance Participation but May Affect Income Security for Some*, GAO/HEHS-98-5, at 2 & 5–6 (reporting that participation rates in plans with loan provisions are about 6 percentage points higher than in plans with no loan provisions and that average annual employee contribution amounts are 35% higher in 401(k) plans with loan provisions than in plans without loan provisions); Lu, et al., Pension Research Council Working Paper 2014-01, at 7 (citing additional studies that show increased contributions rates in plans with loan provisions).

[125] *See* Amy B. Monhan, *Addressing the Problem of Impatients, Impulsives, and Other Imperfect Actors in 401(k) Plans*, 23 Va. Tax Rev. 471, 494 n.89 (2004).

[126] As discussed in § 10.04[E][2][b], the interest rate on plan loans must be "reasonable." *See also* Lu, et al., Pension Research Council Working Paper 2014-01, at 13 (noting that in a study of 882 different 401(k) or similar defined contribution plans, interest rates range from 1.8% to 11.5%).

[127] *See* Susan J. Stabile, *The Behavior of Defined Contribution Plan Participants*, 77 N.Y.U. L. Rev. 71, 85 (2002).

[128] GAO, GAO/HEHS-98-5, at 10–11 (Oct. 1997).

[129] *Cf. id.* at 2 & 5–6 (studying loan provisions, but data not clear whether most borrowing by participants who would not have participated in absence of loans or whether availability of loans causes participants who would otherwise have participated in plans to borrow). Lu, et al., Pension Research Council Working Paper 2014-01, at 2 (Feb. 2014) (finding that plan participants with lower-income and lower non-retirement wealth more likely to borrow from 401(k) plan while participants with higher incomes and higher non-retirement savings tend to borrow highest fraction of current 401(k) wealth).

participant is taxed on the interest when it is distributed from the plan. Moreover, from the standpoint of plan sponsors, plan loans may be burdensome because they are highly regulated under both ERISA and the Internal Revenue Code and thus create administrative and compliance burdens.

[2] Regulation of Plan Loans

Plan loans are subject to three distinct sets of rules:

(1) plan qualification rules,

(2) prohibited transaction rules, and

(3) taxable distribution rules.

If a plan fails to satisfy the plan qualification rules with respect to a plan loan, the plan may lose its qualification status and thus its favorable income tax treatment.

If the prohibited transaction rules are violated, the plan may be subject to an excise tax and/or the plan fiduciaries may be subject to personal liability.

If the tax rules are not satisfied, the loan may be treated as a taxable distribution.

[a] Plan Loans and the Plan Qualification Requirements

As discussed in Chapter 5 § 5.04, section 401(a)(13) of the Internal Revenue Code provides that a trust shall not be a qualified trust "unless the plan of which such trust is a part provides that benefits under the plan may not be assigned or alienated."[130] Section 401(a)(13) provides an express exception from the anti-alienation rule for a plan loan if the plan loan is secured by the plan participant's accrued nonforfeitable benefit and is exempt under the Internal Revenue Code's prohibited transaction provisions.[131]

[b] Plan Loans and the Prohibited Transaction Rules

Section 4975 of the Internal Revenue Code imposes an excise tax on prohibited transactions. Section 406 of ERISA sets forth prohibited transaction rules that are substantially similar to the prohibited transaction rules contained in the Internal Revenue Code.[132]

Generally, loans to plan participants or beneficiaries are prohibited transactions.[133] An exemption, however, is provided for such loans if the loans

---

[130] IRC § 401(a)(13)(A).

[131] IRC § 401(a)(13)(A). For a discussion of additional qualification requirements that apply to plan loans, see Michael A. Laing, *Participant Loans*, SV034 ALI-CLE 389 (May 15–16, 2014).

[132] The prohibited transaction rules are discussed in Chapter 6 § 6.06.

[133] IRC § 4975(c)(1)(B); ERISA § 406(a)(1)(B).

(1)   are available to all participants and beneficiaries on a reasonably equivalent basis;

(2)   are not made available to highly compensated employees in an amount greater than that made available to other employees;

(3)   are made in accordance with specific provisions set forth in the plan;

(4)   bear a reasonable rate of interest;[134] and

(5)   are adequately secured.[135]

[c]   Plan Loans and the Tax Distribution Rules — IRC § 72(p)

Under section 72(p) of the Internal Revenue Code, plan loans to participants or beneficiaries are treated as taxable distributions unless they meet three requirements:

(1)   a maximum loan amount;

(2)   a repayment period; and

(3)   an amortization requirement.

In addition, if a plan participant takes out multiple plan loans, a special maximum limit applies.

ERISA's prohibited transaction provisions apply to transactions between a plan and a party in interest, and a party in interest includes an employee. ERISA § 3(14)(H). Thus, for purposes of ERISA's prohibited transaction rules, a plan loan to a rank and file employee must satisfy the requirements for an exemption or the loan will be a prohibited transaction under ERISA.

The Internal Revenue Code's prohibited transaction rules apply to transactions between a plan and a "disqualified person," and an employee is not a "disqualified person" for purposes of the Internal Revenue Code's prohibited transaction rules. See IRC § 4975(e)(2)(H). Thus, a plan loan to a rank and file employee is not a per se prohibited transaction for purposes of the IRC excise tax.

Nevertheless, the Treasury regulations require that plan loans to participants and beneficiaries who are not disqualified persons satisfy the prohibited transaction exemption requirements in order for the plan not to be disqualified. Treas. Reg. § 1.401(a)-13(d)(2)(iii). Thus, a plan loan to a rank and file employee that would be a prohibited transaction but for the fact that the plan participant is a rank and file employee causes a plan to be disqualified even though no excise tax would apply under the IRC prohibited transaction provisions.

[134] In order to qualify as a reasonable rate of interest, the rate must be commensurate with the interest rate charged by persons in the business of lending money for loans under similar circumstances. 29 C.F.R. § 408b-1(e). In a telephone forum, the IRS referred to prime plus two percentage points as a reasonable rate of interest. See New IRS Position on Plan Loan Interest Rate, available at http://www.schwabe.com/showarticle.aspx?Show=12454;   http://www.irs.gov/pub/irs-tege/loans_phoneforum_transcript.pdf (setting forth transcript of phone forum).

[135] IRC § 4975(d)(1); ERISA § 408(b)(1). See also 29 C.F.R. § 408b-1 (interpreting five requirements and providing examples).

[i] General Maximum Loan Amount — IRC § 72(p)(2)(A)

Generally, the maximum amount that a plan participant may borrow from his plan is 50% of his vested account balance or $50,000, whichever is less.[136] Loans of up to $10,000 may exceed 50% of the plan participant's account balance.[137]

Maximum Loan Amounts[138]

Vested Accrued Benefit	Maximum Loan Amount[139]
$1–$10,000	100% of Vested Benefit
$10,001–$99,999	1/2 of Vested Benefit
$100,000 or more	$50,000

Example 1

Andrew has a vested account balance of $5,000. Because Andrew's vested account balance is less than $10,000, the maximum loan he may take out under IRC § 72(p)(2)(A) is $5,000, or 100% of his vested account balance.

Example 2

Bill has a vested account balance of $80,000. Because Bill's vested account balance is greater than $10,000 but less than $100,000, the maximum amount Bill may borrow under IRC § 72(p)(2)(A) is $40,000, or 50% of his account balance ($80,000 x .50 = $40,000).

Example 3

Connor has a vested account balance of $120,000. Because Connor's vested account balance is greater than $100,000, the maximum amount Connor may borrow under IRC § 72(p)(2)(A) is $50,000, the lesser of $50,000 or 50% of his account balance (.50 x $120,000 = $60,000).

If the principal amount of a plan loan exceeds the maximum permissible amount, the excess loan amount will be treated as a deemed distribution.

Example 4

Dylan has a vested account balance of $120,000. Dylan takes a loan of $60,000. Because Dylan's loan amount exceeds the maximum permissible limit of $50,000 (the lesser of $50,000 or 50% of Dylan's vested account balance of $120,000 (.50 x $120,000 = $60,000) by $10,000 ($60,000 - $50,000 = $10,000)), Dylan will have a deemed distribution of $10,000 when the loan is made.

---

[136] IRC § 72(p)(2)(A).

[137] IRC § 72(p)(2)(A)(ii).

[138] *See* Laing, SV034 ALI-CLE 389 (setting forth chart upon which this chart is based).

[139] A further reduction is made when a plan participant has taken out multiple loans. *See* § 10.04[E][2][c][iv].

[ii]   **Repayment Period — IRC § 72(p)(2)(B)**

Generally, plan participants must repay plan loans within five years.[140] If, however, the loan is used to purchase a primary residence, the five year limit does not apply.[141]

Example 1

Evan has a nonforfeitable account balance of $100,000 and borrows $50,000 from the plan. The loan is repayable in level quarterly installments over five years.

The loan is not a deemed distribution when made under IRC § 72(p)(2)(B) because the loan is payable over five years.

Example 2

Frances has a nonforfeitable account balance of $80,000 and borrows $40,000 from the plan. The loan is repayable in level quarterly installments over eight years. The loan is not used to purchase a primary residence.

The loan is a deemed distribution when made under IRC § 72(p)(2)(B) because the repayment period exceeds five years and the loan is not used to purchase a primary residence.

Example 3

Gina has a nonforfeitable account balance of $150,000 and borrows $50,000 from the plan. The loan is repayable in level quarterly installments over 15 years. The loan is used to purchase a primary residence for Gina.

Even though the repayment period exceeds five years, the loan is not a deemed distribution when made under IRC § 72(p)(2)(B) because the loan is used to purchase a primary residence.

[iii]   **Amortization Requirement — IRC § 72(p)(2)(C)**

Payments must be made in substantially equal payments that include principal and interest and must be paid at least quarterly.[142]

[iv]   **Special Maximum for Multiple Loans — IRC § 72(p)(2)(A)**

A plan participant may take out more than one loan from a plan, but a special maximum amount applies when multiple loans are taken out.

Specifically, the new loan, when added to the outstanding balance of all of the participant's loans from the plan cannot be more than the lesser of

---

[140] IRC § 72(p)(2)(B)(i).

[141] IRC § 72(p)(2)(B)(ii).

[142] IRC § 72(p)(2)(C); Treas. Reg. § 1.72(p)-1 Q&A-3.

(1) $50,000, reduced by the difference between the highest outstanding balance of all of the participant's loans during the 12-month period ending on the day before the new loan was made and the outstanding balance of the participant's loans from the plan on the date of the new loan, or

(2) The greater of $10,000 or 1/2 of the plan participant's vested account balance.[143]

The reduction in the $50,000 limit is intended to prevent a plan participant from having a constant outstanding balance of $50,000.[144]

Example 1

Haley, a plan participant, has a vested account balance of $80,000. She borrowed $27,000 and eight months later wants to take out a second loan. She still owes $18,000 on the first loan. The maximum amount Haley can borrow, when added to the outstanding balance of Haley's outstanding loan ($18,000), cannot exceed the lesser of:

$50,000 - ($27,000 - $18,000 or $9,000) = $41,000 (which is $50,000 minus the difference between the highest outstanding balance of all of Haley's loans during the 12-month period ending on the day before the new loan ($27,000) and the outstanding balance of Haley's loans from the plan on the date of the new loan ($18,000)), or

The greater of $10,000 or $40,000 (which is 1/2 of Haley's account balance).

Haley's total permissible balance is $40,000 (the lesser of $41,000 and $40,000). She has an outstanding loan balance of $18,000. Thus, the maximum new loan Haley may take out is $22,000 ($40,000 - $18,000 = $22,000).

Example 2

Ismaila has a vested account balance of $100,000 and took out a plan loan of $40,000 on January 1, 2014. On January 1, 2015, when the outstanding balance is $33,322, Ismaila would like to take out a second loan. The maximum amount Ismaila can borrow, when added to the outstanding balance of Ismaila's outstanding loan ($33,322), cannot exceed the lesser of

$50,000 - ($40,000 - $33,322) = $43,322 (which is $50,000 minus the difference between the highest outstanding balance of all of Ismaila's loans during the 12-month period ending on the day before the new loan ($40,000) and the outstanding balance of Ismaila's loans from the plan on the date of the new loan ($33,322)), or

The greater of $10,000 or $50,000 (which is 1/2 of Ismaila's account balance).

Ismaila's total permissible loan balance is $43,322 (the lesser of $43,322 and $50,000). He has an existing loan balance of $33,322. Thus, the maximum new loan

---

[143] IRC § 72(p)(2)(A).

[144] Staff of the Joint Comm. on Taxation, General Explanation of the Tax Reform Act of 1986, at 727–28 (1987).

Ismaila may take out is $10,000 ($43,322 - $33,322 = $10,000).

[F]   Minimum Required Distributions — IRC § 401(a)(9)

In order to ensure that funds in qualified plans are used for retirement purposes, and not for estate planning purposes, the Internal Revenue Code imposes minimum distribution requirements.[145]

The minimum distribution requirements, codified in section 401(a)(9) of the Internal Revenue Code, are a qualification requirement. Thus, plans must satisfy the rules in order to receive favorable income tax treatment.[146]

In addition, failure to satisfy the minimum distribution requirements may result in an excise tax equal to 50% of the amount of the underpayment.[147] The excise tax is imposed on the plan participant (or beneficiary who should have received the distribution if the plan participant is deceased).

In essence, the minimum required distribution rules generally require that qualified plans begin to distribute benefits after a plan participant reaches age 70 1/2.

Specifically, the minimum required distribution rules require that the distribution of benefits begin no later than the "required beginning date."[148]

[1]   Required Beginning Date

The required beginning date is generally defined as April 1st of the calendar year following the year in which the participant reaches age 70 1/2.[149] If the participant remains actively employed at age 70 1/2, the required beginning date is extended until April 1st of the calendar year following the participant's retirement date.[150]

Example 1

Audrey, a participant in Employer's profit-sharing plan, was born on June 30, 1943, and retired from Employer on June 30, 2011.

---

[145] Joint Committee on Taxation, Present Law and Background Relating to the Tax Treatment of Retirement Savings, JCX-44-11, at 29 (Sept. 13, 2011).

[146] Minimum distribution rules also apply to other tax-favored retirement savings arrangements, such as 403(a) annuity contracts, 403(b) annuity contracts and custodial accounts, IRAs, and certain deferred compensation plans for employees of tax-exempt organizations and state and local governments. Treas. Reg. § 1.401(a)(9)-1 Q&A-1.

[147] IRC § 4974. Individuals may request that the excise tax be waived if the underpayment was due to a reasonable error and reasonable steps are taken to remedy the shortfall. Treas. Reg. § 54.4974-2 Q&A-7(a).

[148] IRC § 401(a)(9)(A).

[149] IRC § 401(a)(9)(C)(i)(I).

[150] IRC § 401(a)(9)(C)(i)(II). If, however, the plan participant is a 5% owner, that is, owns 5% or more of the employer, the required beginning date remains April 1 of the calendar year following the year in which the participant reaches age 70 1/2 even if the participant has not retired. IRC § 401(a)(9)(C)(ii)(I).

Because Audrey reached 70 1/2 on December 30, 2013,[151] Audrey's required beginning date is April 1, 2014.

Example 2

Bruce, a participant in Employer's 401(k) plan, was born on July 1, 1943, and retired from Employer on December 31, 2012.

Because Bruce reached 70 1/2 on January 1, 2014, his required beginning date is April 1, 2015.

Example 3

Connie, a participant in Employer's 401(k) plan, was born on March 15, 1940, and retired from Employer on December 31, 2014.

Although Connie reached 70 1/2 on September 15, 2010, her required beginning date is April 1, 2015, because she did not retire until December 31, 2014.

[2] Distribution Period

The minimum distribution rules will be satisfied if a plan participant's entire interest is distributed no later than the required beginning date.

In the alternative, the minimum distribution rules will be satisfied if distributions begin no later than the required beginning date and are paid out in substantially equal periodic payments over

(1) the life of the participant,

(2) the joint lives of the participant and a designated beneficiary,

(3) a period not extending beyond the participant's life expectancy, or

(4) a period not extending beyond the joint and last survivor expectancy of the participant and a designated beneficiary.[152]

[3] Minimum Required Distributions from Defined Contribution Plans

The amount of the minimum required distribution is generally determined by dividing the participant's account balance by a life expectancy factor for the participant's age.

The account balance is determined as of the last valuation date in the calendar year immediately preceding the calendar year in which the distribution is required.[153]

---

[151] "An employee attains 70 1/2 as of the date six calendar months after the 70th anniversary of the employee's birth." Treas. Reg. § 1.401(a)(9)-2 Q&A-3.

[152] IRC § 401(a)(9)(A) & Treas. Reg. § 1.401(a)(9)-2 Q&A-1(a).

[153] The account balance is increased to reflect any contributions or forfeitures attributable to that year and decreased to reflect any distributions for that year. Treas. Reg. § 1.401(a)(9)-5 Q&A-3.

The life expectancy factor or distribution period is generally based on the uniform lifetime table set forth in the Treasury regulations.[154] If, however, the participant's sole designated beneficiary is the participant's spouse and the spouse is more than 10 years older than the participant, then the account balance is divided by a life expectancy factor determined using the joint and last survivor table set forth in the Treasury regulations.[155]

Example 1

Alfred, age 75, is a retired participant in Employer's 401(k) plan. Alfred has named his wife Winnie, age 70, his sole beneficiary. On December 31, 2014, Alfred's account balance in Employer's 401(k) plan was $300,000.

According to the Uniform Lifetime Table set forth in the Treasury regulations, the distribution period for a 75 year old is 22.9. Thus, Alfred's minimum required distribution in 2015 is $13,100 ($300,000/22.9 = $13,100).

Example 2

Bonnie, age 80, is a retired participant in Employer's 401(k) plan. Bonnie has named her husband, Harold, age 65, her sole beneficiary. On December 31, 2014, Bonnie's account balance in Employer's 401(k) plan is $200,000.

According the Joint and Last Survivor table set forth in the Treasury regulations, the life expectancy period for an 80 year old with 65 year old spouse is 22.1. Thus, Bonnie's minimum required distribution in 2015 is $9,050 ($200,000/22.1 = $9,050).

The first minimum required distribution must be paid by April 1st of the calendar year following the year in which the plan participant reaches age 70 1/2. All subsequent minimum required distributions must be paid by December 31st of the distribution year.

Thus, two distributions must be made the calendar year after the plan participant reaches 70 1/2. The first required minimum distribution must be made on or before April 1 of the first distribution calendar year. The second required minimum distribution must be made on or before December 31st of that distribution year.

[4] Minimum Required Distributions from Defined Benefit Plans

Distributions of a participant's entire interest in a defined benefit plan must generally be paid in the form of periodic annuity payments for the participant's life expectancy (or the joint lives of the participant and beneficiary) or over a fixed

---

[154] Treas. Reg. § 1.401(a)(9)-9 A-2 (setting forth Uniform Lifetime Table). The uniform lifetime table set forth in regulations represents the joint life expectancy of participant 70 or older and a hypothetical beneficiary who is 10 years younger than the participant. The preamble to the proposed regulations explains that the uniform table "reflects the fact that an employee's beneficiary is subject to change until the death of the employee and ultimately may be a beneficiary more than 10 years younger than the employee." *Required Distributions From Retirement Plans*, 67 Fed. Reg. 18988-01 (Apr. 17, 2002).

[155] Treas. Reg. § 1.401(a)(9)-9 A-3 (setting forth Joint and Last Survivor Table).

period of time that does not exceed the maximum length of the period determined under the uniform lifetime table for the calendar year containing the annuity starting date.[156]

Generally, distribution amounts may not increase.[157]

Example 1

Aiden, age 65, retires from Employer, and Employer's Pension Plan begins to pay Aiden a single life annuity of $5,000 per year. Employer's Pension Plan satisfies the minimum distribution requirement.

Example 2

Employer's Pension Plan provides monthly annuity payments of $500 per month for the life of unmarried participants with a 10-year period certain. (Thus, under the plan, if a plan participant lives for 10 years or more after benefits commence, the participant will receive $500 per month for life. If the plan participant dies less than 10 years after the benefits commence, the participant's beneficiary will continue to receive benefits until benefits have been paid for 10 years.)

Bernadette, an unmarried retired participant, reaches age 70 1/2 in 2014. In order to satisfy the minimum distribution requirement, Employer's Pension Plan must make Bernadette's first $500 payment on or before April 1, 2015, and must continue to make the $500 monthly payments thereafter for Bernadette's life, or for 10 years if Bernadette dies less than 10 years after the payments begin.

[5] Post-Death Distributions

[a] Death after Distributions Have Begun

If the plan participant dies on or after the date on which distributions have begun, the remaining portion of the participant's interest must be distributed at least as rapidly as under the method of distribution being used on the date of death.[158]

[b] Death before Distributions Have Begun

If a plan participant dies before distributions have begun, the participant's entire interest under the plan must be paid under either

(1)   a five-year rule,[159] or

(2)   a life expectancy rule.[160]

---

[156]   Treas. Reg. § 1.401(a)(9)-6 Q&A-1.

[157]   Treas. Reg. § 1.401(a)(9)-6 Q&A-14 (providing that increases in payments may be permitted under certain circumstances, including cost of living adjustments).

[158]   IRC § 1.401(a)(9)(B)(ii).

[159]   IRC § 401(a)(9)(B)(ii).

[160]   IRC § 401(a)(9)(B)(iii)&(iv).

Generally, a plan participant is considered not to have received any distributions until he reaches his required beginning date, even if benefit payments were made before that time.[161]

[i]   Five-Year Rule

Under the five-year rule, the plan participant's entire interest must be distributed by December 31st of the calendar year five years after the participant's death, regardless of who receives the distribution.[162]

Example

Aileen, age 65, is a participant in Employer's 401(k) plan and dies on January 1, 2010. Her entire interest must be distributed by December 31, 2015, in order to satisfy the five-year rule.

There is no yearly required minimum distribution under the five year rule. If the terms of the plan permit a lump sum distribution, the five-year rule may be satisfied if the entire death benefit is distributed in the form of a lump sum by December 31st of the year five years after the participant dies.

[ii]   Life Expectancy Rule

Under the life expectancy rule, the plan participant's entire interest must be distributed over the life expectancy of the beneficiary. Life expectancy is determined under the Single Life Table set forth in the Treasury regulations.[163] If more than one beneficiary is named, the life expectancy of the beneficiary with the shortest life expectancy is used to determine the distribution period.[164]

If the participant's surviving spouse is not the sole designated beneficiary, distributions to the designated beneficiary must begin by December 31st of the calendar year following the calendar year in which the participant died.

If the participant's surviving spouse is the sole designated beneficiary, distributions to the spouse must begin on or before the later of:

(1)   December 31st of the calendar year immediately following the calendar year in which the participant died, or

(2)   December 31st of the calendar year in which the participant would have reached age 70 1/2.[165]

---

[161] Treas. Reg. § 1.401(a)(9)-2 Q&A-6.

[162] Treas. Reg. § 1.401(a)(9)-3 Q&A-1(a).

[163] Treas. Reg. § 1.401(a)(9)-9 Q&A-1.

[164] Treas. Reg. § 1.401(a)(9)-5 Q&A-7.

[165] IRC § 1.401(a)(9)(B)(iv).

Chapter 11

PLAN TERMINATION

§ 11.01   INTRODUCTION

Generally, an employer or other plan sponsor is free under ERISA and the Internal Revenue Code to terminate a welfare benefit plan at any time for any reason.[1] ERISA and the Internal Revenue Code, however, impose restrictions on the termination of pension plans.

The Internal Revenue Code restricts the termination of pension plans in two principle ways. First, IRC § 411(d)(3) imposes a special vesting rule that applies upon the termination of both defined benefit plans and defined contribution plans. Second, the Internal Revenue Code imposes an excise on the reversion of plan assets upon the termination of defined benefit plans.

ERISA imposes much more extensive regulation on the termination of defined benefit plans. The termination rules are set forth in title IV of ERISA and discussed in § 11.03.

§ 11.02   REGULATION OF PENSION PLAN TERMINATION UNDER THE INTERNAL REVENUE CODE

In order to qualify for favorable income tax treatment, a pension plan must be established with the intent of continuing indefinitely.[2] That, however, does not mean that a qualified plan may never be terminated. Rather, an employer may terminate a qualified plan when the plan no longer serves the employer's business needs.[3]

The Internal Revenue Code imposes two noteworthy limits and restrictions on the termination of qualified plans:

(1)   a special vesting requirement upon plan termination, and

(2)   an excise tax on surplus assets that revert to an employer upon plan termination.

---

[1] Curtiss-Wright Corp. v. Schoonejongen, 514 U.S. 73, 78 (1995).

[2] Treas. Reg. § 1.401-1(b)(2) ("The term 'plan' implies a permanent as distinguished from a temporary program.").

[3] If an employer terminates a plan within a few years after establishing the plan, there may be a question as to whether the plan was ever a bona fide program for the exclusive benefit of employees and thus eligible for favorable income tax treatment. *See* Treas. Reg. § 1.401-1(b)(2).

[A]   Special Vesting Requirement — IRC § 411(d)(3)

Section 411(d)(3) of the Internal Revenue Code imposes a special vesting requirement on the termination or partial termination of a qualified plan.

The special vesting requirement applies to both defined benefit plans and defined contribution plans.

For defined benefit plans, it requires that plan participants become fully vested in their benefits to the extent that the benefits are funded at the time of plan termination.

For defined contribution plans, it requires that plan participants become vested in the amounts credited to their individual accounts at the time of plan termination.

The special vesting requirement is intended to prevent the forfeiture of unvested benefits of terminated employees and to prevent employers from receiving a windfall through a reversion of excess assets upon plan termination.[4] The requirement extends to partial terminations in order to prevent employers from circumventing the special vesting requirement by terminating employees or amending the plan before terminating the plan.[5]

The Internal Revenue Code does not define the term "partial termination." The regulations provide that the determination of whether (and when) a partial termination has occurred is to be made by the Commissioner based on all of the surrounding facts and circumstances.[6]

The regulations and courts recognize two different types of partial terminations:

(1)   "vertical partial terminations," and

(2)   "horizontal partial terminations."[7]

[1]   Vertical Partial Termination

A vertical partial termination occurs when employees are terminated and thus, there is a reduction in the number of employees covered by the plan.[8]

Determining whether a sufficient number or percentage of employees has been terminated is a factually intensive question that is subject to considerable litigation. The Internal Revenue Service has established a presumption of partial plan

---

[4] *In re* Gulf Pension Litigation, 764 F. Supp. 1149, 1162 (S.D. Tex. 1991), *aff'd sub. nom.*, Borst v. Chevron Corp., 36 F.3d 1308 (5th Cir. 1994).

[5] PAMELA D. PERDUE, QUALIFIED PENSION AND PROFIT-SHARING PLANS ¶ 21.05[4][c] (2014) ("These rules are designed to preclude an employer from allowing participation to dwindle substantially before formally declaring a plan termination, thus avoiding full vesting of all affected participants."); *In re Gulf Pension Litigation*, 764 F. Supp., at 1162 ("[a]t times, it is easier to devour an object with several bites than it is to attempt to swallow it in one gulp. So it is with a plan which is chopped down little by little until it becomes merely an empty shell.").

[6] Treas. Reg. § 1.411(d)-2(b)(1).

[7] *See, e.g.*, *In re Gulf Pension Litigation*, 764 F. Supp., at 1162.

[8] For a discussion of partial vertical terminations, see PERDUE, QUALIFIED PENSION AND PROFIT-SHARING PLANS, at ¶ 9.02[3][e][ii]–[v].

termination in the event of a turnover rate of 20% or more.[9]

[2] Horizontal Partial Termination

A horizontal partial termination occurs when a plan is amended in a manner that adversely affects the rights of participants under the plan.[10]

Two different types of plan amendments may adversely affect the rights of participants under the plan. First, a partial termination may occur if a plan amendment adversely affects the rights of plan participants to vest in the plan. Second, a partial termination may occur if a plan amendment reduces future benefit accruals.

[B] Tax on Reversions — IRC § 4980

Generally, all of the assets in a qualified plan must be used for the exclusive benefit of the plan participants and beneficiaries.[11] If, however, surplus assets remain upon the termination of a defined benefit plan[12] after all of the plan's liabilities have been satisfied, the surplus may revert to the employer.[13]

In order for an employer to be eligible for a plan reversion, the terms of the plan must specifically authorize the reversion, and the provision must have been in effect for at least five years.[14] In addition, the reversion must not contravene any other law.[15]

In order to discourage employers from terminating their plans in order to capture plan surpluses,[16] the Internal Revenue Code imposes an excise tax on plan reversions.

Specifically, IRC § 4980 imposes a 50% excise tax on any asset reversion unless the employer establishes a qualified replacement plan or provides specified required benefit increases.[17]

---

[9] Rev. Rul. 2007-43.

[10] For a discussion of partial horizontal terminations, see PERDUE, QUALIFIED PENSION AND PROFIT-SHARING PLANS, at ¶ 9.02[3][e][vi].

[11] ERISA §§ 401(a)(2) & ERISA § 403(c).

[12] Reversions of surplus assets from defined contribution plans are rare. They may occur under two conditions. First, if forfeitures have not been allocated and held in a suspense account because the allocation of the forfeitures would violate the IRC 415 contribution limits, the unallocated forfeitures may revert to the employer on plan termination. Second, an employer may receive a reversion of unused forfeitures where the forfeitures are to be used to offset future contributions under the terms of the plan. *See* PERDUE, QUALIFIED PENSION AND PROFIT-SHARING PLANS, at ¶ 21.06[3].

[13] Treas. Reg. § 1.401-2(b)(1); ERISA § 4044(d). For a discussion of the history of the tax treatment of asset reversions, see Norman P. Stein, *Reversions from Pension Plans: History, Policies, and Prospects*, 44 TAX L. REV. 259 (1989).

[14] ERISA § 4044(d)(2)(A).

[15] ERISA § 4044(d)(1)(B).

[16] H.R. Rep. No. 101-881 (2001).

[17] IRC § 4980(d)(1). The excise tax does not apply if the employer is in bankruptcy liquidation at the time of the termination or has always been a tax-exempt entity. IRC § 4980(c)(1), (d)(6).

If the employer establishes a qualified replacement plan or provides specified required benefit increases, the excise tax is reduced to 20%.[18]

[1] Qualified Replacement Plan

In order to fall within the exception for a qualified replacement plan, the employer must establish a replacement plan that covers at least 95% of the remaining active participants in the terminated plan, and 25% of the reversion otherwise payable to the employer must be transferred to the replacement plan or used to increase benefits in the terminated plan.[19]

[2] Benefit Increase Exception

In order to fall within the required benefit increase exception, the employer must provide pro rata benefit increases in the terminated plan with a present value of at least 20% of the maximum reversion.[20] Each qualified participant[21] must receive a pro rata share of the increase equal to the ratio of the participant's accrued benefit to the total present value of accrued benefits under the terminated plan.[22]

§ 11.03 REGULATION OF PENSION PLAN TERMINATION UNDER TITLE IV OF ERISA

Prior to the enactment of ERISA, the decision to terminate a pension plan was generally within the discretion of the plan sponsor.[23] If an employer terminated an underfunded defined benefit plan, the plan participants risked losing all or most of their benefits.[24] In the most famous instance, almost 7,000 employees lost all or most of their retirement benefits when the Studebaker-Packard Corporation closed its plant and terminated its underfunded defined benefit plan in 1963.[25]

---

[18] IRC § 4980(a).

[19] ERISA § 4044(d)(2). For a more detailed discussion of the qualified replacement plan exception, see PAUL M. HAMBURGER, P.C & JOSEPH S. ADAMS, II PENSION PLAN FIX-IT HANDBOOK, Plan Reversions ¶ 1040.

[20] ERISA § 4044(d)(3).

[21] Qualified participants entitled to share in the benefit increases include active participants, participants or beneficiaries in pay status as of the termination date, other participants who have vested rights to benefits under the plan as of the termination date and who terminated within three years of the plan termination, and beneficiaries of these participants. IRC § 4980(d)(5)(A).

[22] For a more detailed discussion of qualified participant and the required benefit increase exception, see HAMBURGER AND ADAMS, II PENSION PLAN FIX-IT HANDBOOK, Plan Reversions, at ¶ 1040.

[23] See ABA SECTION OF LABOR AND EMPLOYMENT LAW, EMPLOYEE BENEFITS LAW 9-3–9-6 (Jeffrey Lewis et al. eds. 2012) (discussing regulation of plan termination prior to enactment of ERISA).

[24] "Before ERISA, defined benefit plans routinely contained disclaimer clauses by which employers disclaimed any liability for unfunded benefits in the event of plan termination." Dan S. Brandenburg & Lincoln Weed, *Discontinuing Plans: Termination and Freezes, in* 2 BENDER'S FEDERAL INCOME TAXATION OF RETIREMENT PLANS 16-6 (Alvin D. Lurie, ed., 2008).

[25] For a detailed discussion of the role the failed Studebaker plan played in the enactment of ERISA, see James A. Wooten, *"The Most Glorious Story of Failure in the Business": The Studebaker-Packard Corporation and the Origins of ERISA*, 49 BUFFALO L. REV. 683 (2001).

Title IV of ERISA protects against this default risk by establishing the Pension Benefit Guaranty Corporation (PBGC)[26] to guarantee the payment of basic pension benefits in the event an underfunded defined benefit plan is terminated.[27] The PBGC administers ERISA's "pension plan termination insurance program"[28] and guarantees the payment of basic pension benefits for more than 41 million workers and retirees in almost 24,000 private-sector defined benefit plans.[29]

Title IV guarantees the pension benefits of defined benefit plans.[30] It does not cover defined contribution plans.[31]

[A]   Purposes of Title IV of ERISA — ERISA § 4002(a)

Title IV of ERISA has three express purposes:

(1)   to encourage the continuation and maintenance of voluntary private pension plans for the benefit of their participants,

(2)   to provide for the timely and uninterrupted payment of pension benefits to participants and beneficiaries under plans to which [Title IV] applies, and

(3)   to maintain premiums established by the [Pension Benefit Guaranty Corporation] under section 4006 at the lowest level consistent with carrying out its obligations under [Title IV].[32]

---

[26] ERISA § 4002.

[27] "The PBGC was established to protect employees against the possibility that a company would go bankrupt at a time when its pension fund did not have enough money to make all its future payments." Douglas J. Elliott, *A Guide to the Pension Benefit Guaranty Corporation*, Initiative on Business and Public Policy at Brookings 10 (May 20, 2009).

For a discussion of the other ways in which ERISA addresses default risk, see Chapter 1 § 1.05[D][1].

[28] Title IV of ERISA is titled "Plan Termination Insurance."

[29] PBGC, Annual Report 20 (Fiscal Year 2014).

[30] ERISA § 4021(a)(1).

Title IV only covers "qualified" defined benefit plans. For an overview of qualified plans, see Chapter 2 § 2.04. Specifically, a plan will only be covered by Title IV if (1) it has received a favorable determination letter from the IRS, that is, an official determination from the IRS that the plan satisfies the qualification requirements, or (2) it has satisfied the qualification requirements for the preceding five years. ERISA § 4021(a).

[31] ERISA § 4021(b)(1). As discussed in Chapter 2 § 2.02[B], a defined contribution plan does not promise plan participants a particular benefit. Rather, a plan participant is simply entitled to contributions to the plan and any earnings and losses on those contributions. Thus, Title IV does not apply to defined contribution plans. For an argument that the PBGC should guarantee defined contribution plans, see Regina Jefferson, *Rethinking the Risk of Defined Contribution Plans*, 4 FLA. TAX REV. 607 (2000).

[32] ERISA § 4002(a)(1)–(3).

[B] Pension Benefit Guaranty Corporation

Modeled to some extent after the Federal Deposit Insurance Corporation that rescued the banking system in the 1930s,[33] the Pension Benefit Guaranty Corporation (PBGC) is a wholly owned federal corporation.[34]

The PBGC is governed by a Board of Directors that consists of three members: (1) the Secretary of Labor, (2) the Secretary of Treasury, and (3) the Secretary of Commerce.[35] The PBGC's day-to-day operations are overseen by a Director who is appointed by the President with the advice and consent of Congress.[36]

The PBGC is financed from three principle sources:

(1)   insurance premiums that it receives from employers that sponsor insured pension plans,

(2)   assets it receives from terminated pension plans, and

(3)   investment income that it earns from those assets.[37]

The PBGC receives no funds from general tax revenues,[38] and the U.S. government is not liable for any obligations or liability incurred by the PBGC.[39]

[C] PBGC Insurance Programs

The PBGC operates two separate insurance programs:

(1)   the single-employer program, and

(2)   the multiemployer program.[40]

[1] Single-Employer Program

The single-employer program insures two different types of plans:

(1)   single-employer plans, that is, plans sponsored by a single employer, and

(2)   multiple employer plans, that is, plans sponsored by more than one unrelated employer if the plans are not maintained under a collective

---

[33] John H. Langbein, *What ERISA Means by "Equitable": The Supreme Court's Trail of Error in Russell, Mertens, and Great-West*, 103 Colum. L. Rev. 1317, 1322–23 (2003).

[34] PBGC v. LTV Corp., 496 U.S. 633, 636–37 (1990). For an overview of the PBGC's administrative structure, see John J. Topoleski, *Pension Benefit Guaranty Corporation (PBGC): A Primer*, Congressional Research Service Report 95-118, at 1 (Sept. 3, 2014).

[35] ERISA § 4002(d)(1).

[36] ERISA § 4002(a).

[37] United States Government Accountability Office, *Pension Benefit Guaranty Corporation: Redesigned Premium Structure Could Better Align Rates with Risk from Plan Sponsors*, GAO-13-58, at 6 (2012). A fourth source of funds is recoveries from companies that were formerly responsible for the plans. PBGC, Annual Report 20 (Fiscal Year 2014).

[38] PBGC, 2014 Annual Report, at 20.

[39] ERISA § 4002(g)(2).

[40] *See* Topoleski, Congressional Research Service Report 95-118, at 1 (Sept. 3, 2014).

bargaining agreement.[41]

The PBGC's single-employer program regulates the termination of pension plans. It provides the exclusive means by which plans may be terminated.

If an underfunded plan is terminated under the single-employer program, the PBGC takes over as statutory trustee of the plan and directly pays benefits due to the retirees (and future retirees) up to legal limits.

[2] Multiemployer Program

The PBGC's multiemployer program insures plans that are maintained under a collective bargaining agreement between one or more employee organizations and more than one employer.[42]

Under the multiemployer program, the PBGC does not directly pay benefits to retirees. Instead, the PBGC provides financial assistance to multiemployer plans which continue to pay benefits to retirees. Specifically, the PBGC provides loans to multiemployer plans under its multiemployer program.[43]

[D] PBGC Premiums — ERISA § 4006(a)(3)

Although the PBGC has a number of financing sources, premiums are the most reliable source of PBGC revenue.[44]

Single-employer plans may be subject to three different types of premiums:

(1) a per-participant flat-rate premium,

(2) a variable-rate premium, and

(3) a termination premium.

Multiemployer plans are subject to a single per-participant flat-rate premium.

---

[41] Technically, a single-employer plan is defined as "a plan which is not a multiemployer plan." ERISA § 3(41). In common parlance, however, a single-employer plan is a plan established and maintained by one employer (including related employers) for the benefit of its employees. PBGC, Glossary, *available at* http://www.pbgc.gov/about/pg/header/glossary.html. A multiple employer plan, in contrast, is a plan sponsored by more than one unrelated employer if the plan is not maintained under a collective bargaining agreement. ABA SECTION OF LABOR AND EMPLOYMENT LAW, EMPLOYEE BENEFITS LAW, at 9-54. Multiple employer plans are much less common than plans maintained by a single employer or multiemployer plans. Elliott, Initiative on Business and Public Policy at Brookings, at 14 (stating that there are several hundred multiple employer plans).

[42] ERISA § 3(37)(A) (defining multiemployer plan as "a plan maintained under a collective bargaining agreement between one or more employee organizations and more than one employer."). Multiemployer plans are established in industries, such as trucking, where employees commonly move from one employer to another. A multiemployer plan permits an employee to earn pension credits for working at any company participating in the plan.

[43] ERISA § 4261.

[44] *See* Topoleski, Congressional Research Service Report 95-118, at 1–2. The PBGC collected $1.8 billion in premiums in 2014. PBGC, 2014 Annual Report, at 11.

[1] Single-Employer Per-Participant Flat-Rate Premium — ERISA § 4006(a)(3)(A)(i)

All single-employer plans must pay a per-participant flat-rate premium.

The flat-rate premium is equal to $57 per participant in 2015.[45] The flat-rate premium is scheduled to increase to $64 per participant in 2016.[46] After 2016, the per-participant flat-rate premium is indexed for increases in average national wages.[47]

The flat-rate premium applies regardless of the plan's funding level, the employer's solvency, or the amount of benefits promised to plan participants.[48]

[2] Single-Employer Variable-Rate Premium — ERISA § 4006(a)(3)(E)

Single-employer plans with unfunded vested benefits are also subject to a variable-rate premium.[49]

In 2015, the variable-rate premium is equal to $24 per $1,000 of unfunded vested benefits.[50] In 2016, the variable-rate premium is scheduled to increase by $5 per $1,000 of unfunded vested benefits. In addition, the variable-rate premium is indexed for increases in average national wages.[51] Thus, in 2016, the variable-rate premium will be at least $29 per $1,000 of unfunded vested benefits, and it may be higher depending on the rate of inflation.[52]

Caps apply to the variable-rate premium.

Specifically, the variable-rate premium is capped at $418 per participant in 2015.[53] The cap is increased to $500 per participant beginning in 2016.[54] For employers with 25 or fewer employees, the variable-rate premium is capped at $5 per plan participant.[55]

Unlike the per-participant flat-rate premium, the variable-rate premium is tied to the plan's funding level. The variable-rate premium, however, is not tied to the employer's solvency or benefit level. A well-financed employer and an employer on

---

[45] ERISA § 4006(a)(3)(i)(IV).

[46] ERISA § 4006(a)(3)(i)(V).

[47] ERISA § 4006(a)(3)(G).

[48] Eric D. Chason, *Outlawing Pension-Funding Shortfalls*, 26 Va. Tax Rev. 519, 525–26 (2007).

[49] ERISA § 4006(a)(3)(E)(ii). Fully funded plans, plans without vested benefit liabilities, and insurance contract plans are exempt from the variable rate premium.

[50] ERISA § 4006(a)(8); PBGC, Premium Rates, *available at* http://www.pbgc.gov/prac/prem/premium-rates.html.

[51] ERISA § 4006(a)(8).

[52] PBGC, Premium Rates, *available at* http://www.pbgc.gov/prac/prem/premium-rates.html.

[53] ERISA §§ 4006(a)(3)(E)(i)(II) & 4006(a)(3)(K); PBGC, Premium Rates, *available at* http://www.pbgc.gov/prac/prem/premium-rates.html.

[54] ERISA § 4006(a)(3)(E)(i)(III).

[55] ERISA § 4006(a)(3)(I).

the brink of bankruptcy are subject to the same variable-rate premium.

[3]   Single-Employer Termination Premium — ERISA § 4006(a)(7)

If a single-employer plan terminates in a distress or involuntary termination,[56] a special "termination" premium may apply for a three-year period after the plan termination.[57]

Generally, the termination premium equals $1,250 multiplied by the number of individuals participating in the plan immediately before the termination date.[58]

[4]   Multiemployer Per-Participant Flat-Rate Premium — ERISA § 4006(a)(3)(A)(v)

Multiemployer plans are subject to a single per-participant flat-rate premium.

In 2015, the multiemployer premium is $26 per plan participant.[59] The premium is indexed for increases in average annual wages in 2016 and thereafter.[60]

Like the single-employer per-participant flat-rate premium, the multiemployer per-participant flat-rate applies regardless of the plan's funding level, the employer's solvency, or the amount of benefits promised to plan participants.

[5]   Critique of PBGC Premium Structure

The PBGC's current premium structure has been subject to considerable criticism because it does not reflect the risk that particular plan sponsors impose on the PBGC.[61]

The PBGC's flat-rate premiums require plan sponsors with larger plans, that is, plans with more plan participants, to pay more toward the cost of covering risk than plan sponsors with plans covering fewer plan participants, regardless of the ages of the participants, their average benefit levels, or other risk-related differences.[62] The variable-rate premium requires plan sponsors with more underfunded plans to pay more toward the cost of covering risk than plan sponsors with better funded plans regardless of the riskiness of the plan's assets or the financial soundness of the plan

---

[56] For a discussion of distress and involuntary terminations, see §§ 11.03[F][2] & [3].

[57] ERISA § 4006(a)(7). The premium, however, does not apply while a bankruptcy reorganization is pending. ERISA § 4006(a)(7)(B). For additional discussion of the termination premium and when it applies, see ABA Section of Labor and Employment Law, Employee Benefits Law, at 9-72–73.

[58] ERISA § 4006(a)(7)(A). In some instances, a higher premium applies. See 29 C.F.R. § 4006.

[59] ERISA § 4006(a)(3)(A)(v), as amended by the Multiemployer Pension Reform Act of 2014, Pub. L. No. 113-235, Division O. PBGC, Premium Rates, available at http://www.pbgc.gov/prac/prem/premium-rates.html.

[60] ERISA § 4006(a)(3)(H).

[61] See e.g., Chason, 26 Va. Tax Rev., at 524–27.

[62] See United States Government Accountability Office, Pension Benefit Guaranty Corporation: Redesigned Premium Structure Could Better Align Rates with Risk from Plan Sponsors, GAO-13-58, at 9 (2012).

sponsor.[63] Indeed, the system's heavy focus on flat-rate premiums tends to cause financially healthy plan sponsors to cover the risks imposed by less financially secure plan sponsors.[64]

Policymakers and commentators have introduced a number of proposals to change the PBGC's premium structure to better reflect the risks that the PBGC faces.[65]

[E] Guaranteed Benefits

At the heart of the PBGC's termination insurance program is the PBGC's benefit guarantee;[66] that is, the PBGC's guarantee of the pension benefits of terminated single-employer defined benefit plans.[67]

In order to be guaranteed,

(1) the benefits must be nonforfeitable (that is, generally, vested),[68]

(2) the benefits must be pension, not welfare, benefits,[69] and

(3) the plan participants and beneficiaries must be entitled to the benefits under the terms of the plan or under applicable law.[70]

In order keep PBGC premiums low and discourage employers from offering unreasonably large pension benefits, limits are imposed on guaranteed benefits.[71]

Specifically, benefits are only guaranteed up to a specific statutory dollar amount[72] and the guarantee is phased in[73] over five years (1) for plans that were created less than five years before termination, and (2) for benefits that were increased as the result of a plan amendment that went into effect less than five years before plan termination.[74]

---

[63] *Id.* at 9–10.

[64] *Id.* at 10.

[65] *Id.* at 13–49 (analyzing variety of possible premium structures and their costs and benefits).

[66] Israel Goldowitz, et al., *The PBGC Wins a Case Whenever the Debtor Keeps Its Pension Plan*, 1 MARQUETTE BENEFITS & SOCIAL WELFARE L. REV. (forthcoming 2015).

[67] For a discussion of how the guarantee for multiemployer plans differs from the guarantee for single-employer plans, see ABA SECTION OF LABOR AND EMPLOYMENT LAW, EMPLOYEE BENEFITS LAW, at 9-27–9-28.

[68] *See* ERISA § 4001(a)(8) (defining "nonforfeitable"); ABA SECTION OF LABOR AND EMPLOYMENT LAW, EMPLOYEE BENEFITS LAW, at 9-17–20 (discussing nonforfeitable benefits requirement).

[69] *See* 29 C.F.R. § 4022.2 (defining "pension benefit"); ABA SECTION OF LABOR AND EMPLOYMENT LAW, EMPLOYEE BENEFITS LAW, at 9-14–16 (discussing pension benefit requirement).

[70] 29 C.F.R. § 4022.3(a).

[71] Elliott, Initiative on Business and Public Policy at Brookings, at 7.

[72] ERISA § 4022(b)(3). This is sometimes referred to as the "maximum guaranteeable benefit." Goldowitz, et al., 1 MARQUETTE BENEFITS & SOCIAL WELFARE L. REV. (forthcoming 2015).

[73] This is sometimes referred to as the "phase-in limit." Goldowitz, et al., 1 MARQUETTE BENEFITS & SOCIAL WELFARE L. REV. (forthcoming 2015).

[74] ERISA § 4022(b)(1) & (b)(7).

For plans terminating in 2015, the maximum guaranteed benefit is $60,136 per year for employees who begin receiving payments from the PBGC beginning at age 65.[75]

The guaranteed amount is reduced for workers who begin to receive benefits before age 65 or receive benefits in the form of a joint and survivor annuity to reflect the fact that those beneficiaries are expected to receive benefits over a longer period of time.[76]

The guaranteed amount is increased for workers who begin to receive benefits after age 65 to reflect the fact that those beneficiaries are expected to receive benefits over a shorter period of time.

Despite the limits on the PBGC guarantee, the vast majority of retirees receiving benefits from the PBGC receive the full amount of their earned benefit.[77]

[F] Single-Employer Plan Terminations

Title IV of ERISA provides the exclusive means by which a plan sponsor may terminate a single-employer plan.[78]

Title IV authorizes three types of single-employer plan terminations:

(1) standard terminations,

(2) distress terminations, and

(3) involuntary terminations.

In a standard termination, the plan's assets are sufficient to cover the plan's liabilities. The vast majority of plan terminations are standard terminations.

Terminations of underfunded plans may be either voluntary distress terminations or involuntary terminations initiated by the PBGC if the plan sponsor is unable to fund its pension obligations. Historically, only about 3% of plan terminations have been terminations of underfunded plans.[79]

Because the PBGC's purpose is to ensure that plan participants receive a minimum guaranteed benefit, the PBGC's participation in the plan termination process is quite narrow. The PBC is focused solely on the sufficiency of plan asset; that is, the ability of the plan's assets to satisfy the plan's liabilities.[80]

---

[75] PBGC, Press Release: *PBGC Maximum Insurance Benefit Level for 2015, available at* http://www.pbgc.gov/news/press/releases/pr14-12.html.

[76] For example, in 2015, the maximum guaranteed benefit for an individual who begins to receive a single life annuity at age 60 is $39,089 per year, and the maximum guaranteed for a joint and 50% survivor annuity beginning at age 65 is $54,123 per year. PBGC, Press Release: *PBGC Maximum Insurance Benefit Level for 2015, available at* http://www.pbgc.gov/news/press/releases/pr14-12.html.

[77] *See id.* (stating that "according to a 2006 study, almost 85% of retirees receiving PBGC benefits at that time received the full amount of their earned benefit").

[78] ERISA § 4041(a)(1); Hughes Aircraft Co. v. Jacobson, 525 U.S. 432, 446 (1999).

[79] Topoleski, Congressional Research Service Report 95-118, at 6 (Sept. 3, 2014).

[80] Pamela D. Perdue, *Terminating the Single Employer Plan — Procedures and Issues,* ST043 ALI-CLE 575 (May 16–18, 2012).

[1] Voluntary Standard Termination — ERISA § 4041(b)

An employer may voluntarily terminate its plan in a standard termination if the plan's assets are sufficient to cover all of the plan's "benefit liabilities."[81]

Generally, benefit liabilities are equal to all benefits earned to date by plan participants, including both vested and nonvested benefits, and certain early retirement benefits and retirement-type subsidies.[82] Benefit liabilities may also include contingent benefits, such as "shutdown benefits," that is, additional benefits provided in the event of a plant or facility closure.[83]

Standard terminations entail three fundamental obligations:[84]

(1) the plan administrator must notify all plan participants, other affected parties,[85] and the PBGC of its intent to terminate the plan,[86]

(2) the plan assets must be distributed to the plan participants in the form of lump sum distributions[87] or annuities,[88] and

(3) the plan administrator must certify to the PBGC that all benefit liabilities have been paid.[89]

The selection of the annuity provider is subject to ERISA's fiduciary provisions.[90] If the annuity provider becomes insolvent, the plan administrator may be subject to liability for breaching its fiduciary duty in selecting the annuity provider.[91] The PBGC, however, does not guarantee the annuity contracts.[92]

---

[81] ERISA § 4041(b)(2)(D).

[82] ABA Section of Labor and Employment Law, Employee Benefits Law, at 9-30–31.

[83] Topoleski, Congressional Research Service Report 95-118, at 4 (Sept. 3, 2014). For a discussion of coverage of shutdown benefits, see Brandenburg and Weed, 2 Bender's Federal Income Taxation of Retirement Plans, at 16-21–16-22.

[84] Goldowitz, et al., 1 Marquette Benefits & Social Welfare L. Rev. (forthcoming 2015). For an overview of the standard termination process and the procedural requirements, see ABA Section of Labor and Employment Law, Employee Benefits Law, at 9-32–9-38; PBGC, *Standard Termination Filing Instructions 3, available at* http://www.pbgc.gov/documents/500-instructions.pdf.

[85] For the definition of "affected party," see ERISA § 4001(a)(21).

[86] ERISA § 4041(b)(1)(A). Technically, the PBGC is not required to receive notice of intent to terminate. Instead, the PBGC must receive certification by an enrolled actuary that the plan has sufficient assets to cover its benefit liabilities. ERISA § 4041(b)(2)(A).

[87] In a lump sum distribution, "the employee receives the value in today's dollars of what their lifetime payments would have been, based on expectations of how long they would be expected to live on average and using an interest rate defined by law." Elliott, Initiative on Business and Public Policy at Brookings, at 9. For a discussion of valuations of lump sum distributions for terminating plans, see Brandenburg & Weed, 2 Bender's Federal Income Taxation of Retirement Plans, at 16-23–16-24.

[88] ERISA § 4041(b)(3)(A); 29 C.F.R. § 4041.28. *See also* Beck v. PACE Int'l Union, 551 U.S. 96, 103 (2007) (noting that distributions most commonly are through the purchase of annuity contracts or lump sum payments).

[89] ERISA § 4041(b)(3)(B).

[90] *Cf.* ERISA 502(a)(9) (authorizing suit in event that the purchase of an annuity contract in connection with a plan termination violates part 4 of ERISA (ERISA's fiduciary provisions)).

[91] Bussian v. RJR Nabisco, Inc., 223 F.3d 286 (5th Cir. 2000).

[92] PBGC Op. Ltrs. 90-3, 91-1, 91-4; Beck v. PACE Int'l Union, 551 U.S. 96, 106 (2007) (noting that

If, upon plan termination, the plan retains surplus assets, the surplus assets may revert to the employer.[93] The reversion is subject to an excise tax under IRC § 4980.[94]

[2] Voluntary Distress Termination — ERISA § 4041(c)

If a plan's assets are not sufficient to cover all of its benefit liabilities, then the plan may seek a voluntary distress termination.[95]

Plan sponsors do not have a right to a distress termination. Rather, distress terminations are only available if the plan sponsor and each member of its "controlled group"[96] is facing severe financial hardship.[97]

In order to be eligible for a distress termination, the plan sponsor and each of its controlled group members must satisfy at least one of four tests:

(1) the "liquidation test,"

(2) the "reorganization test,"

(3) the "business continuation test," or

(4) the "pension costs test."[98]

The first two tests apply within a bankruptcy or similar insolvency proceeding. The second two tests apply outside of bankruptcy. As a practical matter, most distress terminations are sought in the context of a bankruptcy proceeding.[99]

The plan sponsor and each member of its controlled group must satisfy at least one of the four tests.[100] Each entity, however, does not have to meet the same test.[101]

---

when a plan terminates through the purchase of annuities, "[t]he assets of the plan are wholly removed from the ERISA system, and plan participants and beneficiaries must rely primarily (if not exclusively) on state-contract remedies if they do not receive proper payments or are otherwise denied access to their funds").

[93] ERISA § 4044(d)(1).

[94] *See* § 11.02[B] (discussing tax on reversions).

[95] Technically, a plan may seek a distress termination even if its assets are sufficient to cover all of its liabilities if it satisfies one of the distress tests. In fact, however, a plan that has sufficient assets to cover all of its liabilities would be well-advised to pursue a standard termination because the process is generally faster. Tax Advisors Planning System ¶ 24.14.02(D)(2).

[96] For a discussion of the meaning of controlled group, see Chapter 9 § 9.04[B].

[97] Goldowitz, et al., 1 Marquette Benefits & Social Welfare L. Rev. (forthcoming 2015).

[98] *Id.* For a more detailed discussion of each of the four tests, see Perdue, Qualified Pension and Profit-Sharing Plans, at ¶ 21.03[3][b][iii].

[99] Goldowitz, et al., 1 Marquette Benefits & Social Welfare L. Rev. (forthcoming 2015).

[100] ERISA § 4041(c)(2)(B).

[101] ABA Section of Labor and Employment Law, Employee Benefits Law, at 9-41. For a discussion of the procedural aspects of a distress termination, see *id.* at 9-40–9-44; Perdue, Qualified Pension and Profit-Sharing Plans, at ¶ 21.03[3][b][iii] (2010–2011).

[a]   Liquidation Test

Under the liquidation test, the plan sponsor must have filed, or have had filed against it, a petition to liquidate assets under the federal bankruptcy code or similar state law, and the case must not have been dismissed as of the plan termination date.[102]

[b]   Reorganization Test

Under the reorganization test, the plan sponsor must have filed, or have filed against it, a petition seeking reorganization under federal or state law, and the bankruptcy court or state court must determine that the entity will be unable to pay all its debts pursuant to a reorganization plan unless the plan is terminated.[103]

[c]   Business Continuation Test

Under the business continuation test, the PBGC must determine that the plan sponsor will be unable to pay its debts when due and will be unable to continue in business unless the pension plan is terminated.[104]

[d]   Pension Costs Test

Under the pension costs test, the PBGC must determine that the cost of providing pension coverage has become unreasonably burdensome solely because of a decline in the plan sponsor's workforce.[105]

[3]   Involuntary Termination — ERISA § 4042

Although most plan terminations are initiated by the plan sponsor, the PBGC has the power, in certain circumstances, to initiate a plan termination.

PBGC-initiated terminations may be mandatory or discretionary.

[a]   Mandatory Terminations

The PBGC must terminate a single-employer pension plan if the plan does not have sufficient assets available to pay benefits that are currently due under the terms of the plan.[106] In other words, "if the plan runs out of money to pay current retirees, [the] PBGC must terminate the plan."[107]

---

[102] ERISA § 4041(c)(2)(B)(i).

[103] ERISA § 4041(c)(2)(B)(ii). The standard is whether *any* reorganization plan is confirmable, not just the plan proposed by the debtor, absent plan termination. ABA SECTION OF LABOR AND EMPLOYMENT LAW, EMPLOYEE BENEFITS LAW, at 9-39.

[104] ERISA § 4041(c)(2)(B)(iii)(I).

[105] ERISA § 4041(c)(2)(B)(iii)(II).

[106] ERISA § 4042(a).

[107] Goldowitz, et al., 1 MARQUETTE BENEFITS & SOCIAL WELFARE L. REV. (forthcoming 2015).

[b]   Discretionary Terminations

The PBGC has the discretionary authority to terminate a plan under four circumstances:

(1) the plan has failed to satisfy the minimum funding standards,[108]

(2) the plan will be unable to pay benefits when due,[109]

(3) the plan has made a large distribution to a plan participant who is a substantial owner and the plan has unfunded vested benefits,[110] and

(4) the possible long-run loss to the PBGC "may reasonably be expected to increase unreasonably if the plan is not terminated."[111]

---

[108] ERISA § 4042(a)(1). The minimum funding standards are discussed in Chapter 5 § 5.05.

[109] ERISA § 4042(a)(2).

[110] ERISA § 4042(a)(3). Plans are rarely terminated under this provision. Goldowitz, et al., 1 MARQUETTE BENEFITS & SOCIAL WELFARE L. REV. (forthcoming 2015).

[111] ERISA § 4042(a)(4).

[4] Summary of Single-Employer Plan Terminations

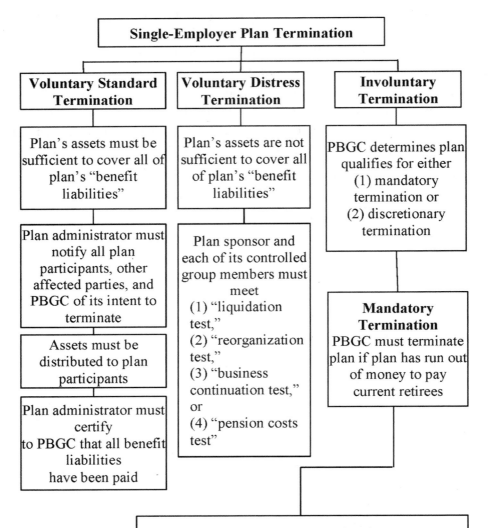

[G]   Liability to PGCG upon Plan Termination

In the event an underfunded pension plan is terminated, the PBGC may seek to collect four different types of liabilities from the plan sponsor and members of its controlled group:

   (1)   unfunded benefit liabilities;

   (2)   unpaid minimum funding contributions;

   (3)   unpaid annual premiums; and

   (4)   termination premiums.

Distress and PBGC-initiated terminations of underfunded plans most commonly arise in the context of a bankruptcy. Thus, these liabilities are often sought in the context of a bankruptcy proceeding, and the PBGC will enter into the bankruptcy proceedings as a member of the creditors' committee in order to protect its interest.

[1]   Unfunded Benefit Liabilities

Upon plan termination, the plan sponsor is generally liable to the PBGC "for the total amount of unfunded benefit liabilities (as of the termination date) to all plan participants and beneficiaries under the plan" plus interest from the termination date.[112]

The amount of the unfunded benefit liabilities is defined as the excess, if any, of the benefit liabilities under the plan over the current value of the plan assets.[113]

The PBGC often refers to the unfunded benefit liabilities as the underfunding on a termination basis.[114]

Unfunded benefit liabilities are typically the PBGC's largest claim.[115]

[2]   Unpaid Minimum Funding Contributions

The plan sponsor (and members of its controlled group) are liable to the plan for contributions necessary to satisfy the minimum funding requirements.[116] Upon plan termination, this liability is owed to the PBGC because the PBGC becomes the statutory trustee when the plan is terminated.[117]

Unpaid minimum funding contributions are typically the second largest claim the PBGC seeks to recover in bankruptcy proceedings.[118]

---

[112] ERISA § 4062(b)(1).

[113] ERISA § 4001(a)(18). PBGC regulations prescribe the interest rate and mortality assumptions to be used in calculating this liability. 29 C.F.R. §§ 4044.52–.53; 29 C.F.R.pt. 4044 App. B.

[114] Goldowitz, et al., 1 MARQUETTE BENEFITS & SOCIAL WELFARE L. REV. (forthcoming 2015).

[115] For a more detailed discussion of unfunded benefit liabilities claim in bankruptcy, see id.

[116] IRC § 402(b). For a discussion of the minimum funding requirements, see Chapter 5 § 5.05.

[117] ERISA § 4042(d)(1)(B)(ii).

[118] For a more detailed discussion of unpaid minimum funding contributions, see Goldowitz, et al., 1 MARQUETTE BENEFITS & SOCIAL WELFARE L. REV. (forthcoming 2015).

[3] Unpaid Annual Premiums

The plan sponsor (and members of its controlled group) are liable to the PBGC for any unpaid premiums, including both flat-rate and variable premiums, as well as interest, and penalties for failure to pay the premiums.[119]

Unpaid annual premiums are typically the PBGC's smallest claim in bankruptcy.[120]

[4] Termination Premiums

If a single-employer plan terminates in a distress or involuntary termination,[121] a special "termination" premium applies for a three-year period after the plan termination.[122]

Generally, the termination premium equals $1,250 multiplied by the number of individuals participating in the plan immediately before the termination date.[123]

[H] Distribution of Plan Assets upon Plan Termination

If an employer voluntarily terminates a plan pursuant to a standard termination under ERISA § 4041(b), the plan assets must be distributed to the plan participants in the form of lump sum distributions or annuities. If there are excess assets after all the plan's benefit liabilities have been satisfied, the surplus may revert to the employer, subject to an excise tax under IRC § 4980.

If a plan is terminated pursuant to a voluntary distress termination, and the plan has sufficient assets to pay all benefit liabilities, then the plan will be terminated and its assets distributed as in a standard termination. If a plan is terminated pursuant to a voluntary distress termination, and the plan has sufficient assets to pay all PBGC-guaranteed benefits, but not all benefit liabilities, then the plan will be terminated and its assets will be distributed to plan participants according to a six-tier priority hierarchy set forth in ERISA § 4044(a).

If a plan does not have sufficient assets to pay guaranteed benefits, the PBGC will take over the plan as trustee and pay the plan participants their guaranteed benefits. In addition, the PBGC may be able to pay plan participants a portion of their nonguaranteed benefits from recoveries from employers under ERISA § 4022(c) according to the priorities set forth in ERISA § 4044(a).

Section 4044(a) of ERISA sets forth a six-tier hierarchy for allocating assets among various categories of guaranteed and nonguaranteed benefits.

Specifically, it provides that plan assets are to be allocated to benefits in following priority categories:

---

[119] ERISA § 4007(e).

[120] Goldowitz, et al., 1 MARQUETTE BENEFITS & SOCIAL WELFARE L. REV. (forthcoming 2015).

[121] For a discussion of distress and involuntary terminations, see §§ 11.03[F][2] & [3].

[122] ERISA § 4006(a)(7). The premium, however, does not apply while a bankruptcy reorganization is pending. ERISA § 4006(a)(7)(B).

[123] ERISA § 4006(a)(7)(A). In some instances, a higher premium applies. See 29 C.F.R. § 4006.

(1)   benefits attributable to voluntary employee contributions;

(2)   benefits attributable to mandatory employee contributions;

(3)   annuity benefits in pay status (or eligible to be in pay status) for three years before plan termination limited to the lowest benefit payable under the terms of the plan in effect five years before plan termination;

(4)   PBGC-guaranteed benefits and benefits that would have been guaranteed absent limitations on guarantees for benefits of majority owners;

(5)   all other nonforfeitable benefits; and

(6)   all other benefits.

If assets are insufficient to fully fund a priority category, then assets are allocated pro rata within the category.[124] In category 4, assets are allocated first to PBGC-guaranteed benefits, then to nonguaranteed benefits of majority owners.[125]

---

[124] ERISA § 4044(b)(2).

[125] ERISA § 4044(b)(3).

Appendix A

ERISA

ERISA contains both labor law provisions and tax law provisions. The labor law provisions are codified in title 29 of the United States Code (U.S.C.) while the tax law provisions are codified in the Internal Revenue Code (IRC) in title 26 of the U.S.C.

The tax law provisions are referred to by their IRC number, which is identical to their section number in title 26 of the U.S.C. For example, IRC § 401(a), which is found at 26 U.S.C. § 401(a), sets forth the qualification requirements pension plans must satisfy to receive favorable income tax treatment.

ERISA practitioners refer to the labor law provision by their ERISA number. The ERISA number, however, is different from the section number in which it is codified in 29 U.S.C. For example, ERISA § 3 sets forth definitions for purposes of ERISA. It is codified in 29 U.S.C. § 1002. Courts sometimes refer to the labor law provisions by their ERISA section number. Other times, courts refer to the labor law section number in title 29 of the U.S.C. Moreover, courts sometimes provide parallel cites.

This table identifies each of the labor law sections of ERISA and the corresponding section number in 29 U.S.C.

ERISA §		**29 U.S.C. §**
1	Short title and table of contents	

ERISA Title I
Protection of Employee Benefit Rights
Subtitle A — General Provisions

2	Congressional findings and declaration of policy	1001
-	Additional congressional findings and declaration of policy	1001a
-	Findings and declaration of policy	1001b
3	Definitions	1002
4	Coverage	1003

Subtitle B — Regulatory Provisions
Part 1 — Reporting and Disclosure

101	Duty of disclosure and reporting	1021
102	Summary plan description	1022
103	Annual reports	1023
104	Filing and furnishing of information	1024

ERISA §		29 U.S.C. §
105	Reporting of participant's benefit rights	1025
106	Reports made public information	1026
107	Retention of records	1027
108	Reliance on administrative interpretations	1028
109	Forms	1029
110	Alternative methods of compliance	1030
111	Repeal and effective date	1031

Part 2 — Participation and Vesting

201	Coverage	1051
202	Minimum participation standards	1052
203	Minimum vesting standards	1053
204	Benefit accrual requirements	1054
205	Requirement of joint and survivor annuity and preretirement survivor annuity	1055
206	Form and payment of benefits	1056
207	Temporary variances from certain vesting requirements [Repealed]	1057
208	Mergers and consolidations of plans or transfers of plan assets	1058
209	Recordkeeping and reporting requirements	1059
210	Multiple employer plans and other special rules	1060
211	Effective dates	1061

Part 3 — Funding

301	Coverage	1081
302	Minimum funding standards	1082
303	Minimum funding standards for single-employer defined benefit pension plans	1083
303	Variance from minimum funding standard [Repealed]	1083
304	Minimum funding standards for multiemployer plans	1084
304	Extension of amortization periods [Repealed]	1084
305	Additional funding rules for multiemployer plans in endangered status or critical status	1085
305	Alternative minimum funding standard [Repealed]	1085
306	Security for waivers of minimum funding standard and extensions of amortization period [Repealed]	1085a
307	Security required upon adoption of plan amendment resulting in significant underfunding [Repealed]	1085b

ERISA §   **29 U.S.C. §**

308   Effective dates [Repealed]   1086

Part 4 — Fiduciary Responsibility

401	Coverage	1101
402	Establishment of plan	1102
403	Establishment of trust	1103
404	Fiduciary duties	1104
405	Liability for breach by co-fiduciary	1105
406	Prohibited transactions	1106
407	Limitation with respect to acquisition and holding of employer securities and employer real property by certain plans	1107
408	Exemptions from prohibited transactions	1108
409	Liability for breach of fiduciary duty	1109
410	Exculpatory provisions; insurance	1110
411	Persons prohibited from holding certain positions	1111
412	Bonding	1112
413	Limitation of actions	1113
414	Effective date	1114

Part 5 — Administration and Enforcement

501	Criminal penalties	1131
502	Civil enforcement	1132
503	Claims procedure	1133
504	Investigative authority	1134
505	Regulations	1135
506	Coordination and responsibility of agencies enforcing Employee Retirement Income Security Act and related federal laws	1136
507	Administration	1137
508	Appropriations	1138
509	Separability	1139
510	Interference with protected rights	1140
511	Coercive interference	1141
512	Advisory council on employee welfare and pension benefit plans	1142
513	Research, studies, and reports	1143
514	Other laws	1144
515	Delinquent contributions	1145
516	Outreach to promote retirement income savings	1146
517	National summit on retirement savings	1147

ERISA §		**29 U.S.C. §**
518	Authority to postpone certain deadlines by reason of Presidentially declared disaster or terroristic or military actions	1148
519	Prohibition on false statements of representations	1149
520	Applicability of State law to combat fraud and abuse	1150
521	Administrative summary cease and desist orders and summary seizure orders against multiple employer welfare arrangements in financially hazardous condition	1151

Part 6 — Continuation Coverage and Additional Standards for Group Health Plans

601	Plans must provide continuation coverage to certain individuals	1161
602	Continuation coverage	1162
603	Qualifying event	1163
604	Applicable premium	1164
605	Election	1165
606	Notice requirements	1166
607	Definitions and special rules	1167
608	Regulations	1168
609	Additional standards for group health plans	1169

Part 7 — Group Health Plan Requirements
Subpart A — Requirements Relating to Portability, Access, and Renewability

701	Increased portability through limitation on preexisting condition exclusions	1181
702	Prohibiting discrimination against individual participants And beneficiaries based on health status	1182
703	Guaranteed renewability in multiemployer plans and Multiple employer welfare arrangements	1183

Subpart B — Other Requirements

711	Standards relating to benefits for mothers and newborns	1185
712	Parity in mental health and substance use disorder benefits	1185a
713	Required coverage for reconstructive surgery following Mastectomies	1185b

ERISA §		29 U.S.C. §
714	Coverage of dependent students on medically necessary leave of absence	1185c
715	Additional market reforms	1185d

Subpart C — General Provisions

731	Preemption; State flexibility; construction	1191
732	Special rules relating to group health plans	1191a
733	Definitions	1191b
734	Regulations	1191c

Title III — Jurisdiction, Administration, Enforcement;
Joint Pension Task Force, etc.
Subtitle A — Jurisdiction, Administration, and Enforcement

3001	Procedures in connection with the issuance of certain determination letters by the Secretary of the Treasury covering qualifications under 26 USCS §§ 1 et seq.	1201
3002	Procedures with respect to continued compliance with Internal Revenue requirements relating to participation, Vesting, and funding standards	1202
3003	Procedures in connection with prohibited transactions	1203
3004	Coordination between the Department of the Treasury and the Department of Labor	1204

Subtitle B — Joint Pension, Profit-Sharing, and Employee
Stock Ownership Plan Task Force; Studies
Part 1 — Joint Pension, Profit-Sharing, and Employee Stock Ownership Plan Task Force

3021	Establishment	1221
3022	Duties	1222

Part 2 — Other Studies

3031	Congressional study	1231
3032	Protection for employees under Federal procurement, construction, and research contracts and grants	1232

ERISA §   **29 U.S.C. §**
Subtitle C — Enrollment of Actuaries

3041   Joint Board for the Enrollment of Actuaries   1241
3042   Enrollment by Board; standards and   1242
        qualifications; Suspension or termination of
        enrollment

Title IV — Plan Termination Insurance
Subtitle A — Pension Benefit Guaranty Corporation

4001   Definitions   1301
4002   Pension Benefit Guaranty Corporation   1302
4003   Operation of Corporation   1303
4004   [Repealed]   1304
4005   Pension benefit guaranty funds   1305
4006   Premium rates   1306
4007   Payment of premiums   1307
4008   Annual report by the Corporation   1308
4009   Portability assistance   1309
4010   Authority to require certain information   1310
4011   Notice to participants [Repealed]   1311

Subtitle B — Coverage

4021   Coverage   1321
4022   Single-employer plan benefits guaranteed   1322
4022A   Multiemployer plan benefits guaranteed   1322a
4022B   Aggregate limit on benefits guaranteed; criteria   1322b
        applicable
4023   Plan fiduciaries   1323

Subtitle C — Termination

4041   Termination of single-employer plans   1341
4041A   Termination of multiemployer plans   1341a
4042   Institution of termination proceedings by the   1342
        Corporation
4043   Reportable evens   1343
4044   Allocation of assets   1344
4045   Recapture of payments   1345
4046   Reports to trustee   1346
4047   Restoration of plans   1347
4048   Termination date   1348

ERISA §		29 U.S.C. §
4049	Distribution of participants and beneficiaries of liability payments to section 4049 trust [Repealed]	1349
4050	Missing participants	1350

Subtitle D — Liability

4061	Amounts payable by Corporation	1361
4062	Liability for termination of single-employer plans under a distress termination or a termination by Corporation	1362
4063	Liability of substantial employer for withdrawal from single- Employer plans under multiple controlled groups	1363
4064	Liability on termination of single-employer plans under multiple controlled groups	1364
4065	Annual report of plan administrator	1365
4066	Annual notification to substantial employers	1366
4067	Recovery of liability for plan termination	1367
4068	Lien for liability	1368
4069	Treatment of transactions to evade liability; effect of corporate reorganization	1369
4070	Enforcement authority relating to terminations of Single-employer plans	1370
4071	Penalty for failure to timely provide required information	1371

Subtitle E — Special Provisions for Multiemployer Plans
Part 1 — Employer Withdrawals

4201	Withdrawal liability established; criteria and definitions	1381
4202	Determination and collection of liability; notification of Employer	1382
4203	Complete withdrawal	1383
4204	Sale of assets	1384
4205	Partial withdrawals	1385
4206	Adjustment for partial withdrawal; determination of amount; reduction for partial withdrawal liability; procedures applicable	1386
4207	Reduction or waiver of complete withdrawal liability; procedures and standards applicable	1387
4208	Reduction of partial withdrawal liability	1388
4209	De minimis rule	1389

ERISA §		29 U.S.C. §
4210	Nonapplicability of withdrawal liability for certain temporary Contribution obligation periods; exception	1390
4211	Methods of computing withdrawal liability	1391
4212	Obligation to contribute	1392
4213	Actuarial assumptions	1393
4214	Application of plan amendments; exception	1394
4215	Plan notification to Corporation of potentially significant withdrawals	1395
4216	Special rules for plans under section 404(c) of Title 26	1396
4217	Application of Part in case of certain pre-1980 withdrawals; Adjustment of covered plan	1397
4218	Withdrawal not to occur merely because of change in business form or suspension of contributions during labor dispute	1398
4219	Notice, collection, etc., of withdrawal liability	1399
4220	Approval of amendments	1400
4221	Resolution of disputes	1401
4222	Reimbursements for uncollectible withdrawal liability	1402
4223	Withdrawal liability payment fund	1403
4224	Alternative method of withdrawal liability payments	1404
4225	Limitation on withdrawal liability	1405

Part 2 — Merger or Transfer of Plan Assets or Liabilities

4231	Mergers and transfers between multiemployer plans	1411
4232	Transfers between a multiemployer plan and a single-employer plan	1412
4233	Partition	1413
4234	Asset transfer rules	1414
4235	Transfers pursuant to change in bargaining representative	1415

Part 3 — Reorganization; Minimum Contribution Requirement for Multiemployer Plans

4241	Reorganization status	1421
4242	Notice of reorganization and funding requirements	1422
4243	Minimum contribution requirement	1423

ERISA §   **29 U.S.C. §**

4244   Overburden credit against minimum   1424
              contribution requirement

4244A   Adjustments is accrued benefits   1425

4245   Insolvent plans   1426

Part 4 — Financial Assistance

4261   Assistance by Corporation   1431

Part 5 — Benefits After Termination

4281   Benefits under certain terminated plans   1441

Part 6 — Enforcement

4301   Civil actions   1451

4302   Penalty for failure to provide notice   1452

4303   Election of plan status   1453

Subtitle F — Transition Rules and Effective Dates

4402   Effective date, special rules   1461

Appendix B

ECONOMIC EFFECT OF FAVORABLE TAX TREATMENT ACCORDED QUALIFIED PLANS

Favorable Tax Treatment Accorded Traditional Qualified Plans:

Essentially, the favorable tax treatment of traditional qualified plans consists of four elements:

(1) Employers may deduct contributions to qualified plans when the contributions are made;

(2) Employees do not need to include the contributions in income until the contributions are distributed to them;

(3) Earnings on contributions held by qualified plans are exempt from tax; and

(4) Participants can roll over distributions from a qualified plan to an individual retirement account (IRA) or another qualified plan and further delay taxation of benefits.

Favorable Tax Treatment Accorded Roth Contributions to Qualified Plans:

Unlike contributions to traditional qualified plans, Roth contributions to qualified plans are includible in taxable income when made. Like earnings on contributions to traditional qualified plans, earnings on Roth contributions held by qualified plans are exempt from income tax. In addition, unlike distributions from traditional qualified plans, distributions attributable to Roth contributions are exempt from income tax. Thus, earnings on Roth contributions are never subject to income tax.

Economic Equivalence of Favorable Tax Treatment Accorded Traditional Qualified Plans and Roth Contributions to Qualified Plans:

Assuming no change in tax rates, the tax treatment accorded traditional qualified plans is economically equivalent to the tax treatment accorded Roth contributions; that is, the earnings on contributions are never taxed.

Example

Suppose that Constance has $1,000 that she can save each year, is taxed at a 20% rate, and earns 10% interest on her contributions each year. If she contributes $1,000 to a regular savings account (which taxes both the contributions and earnings) each year, she will have $2,804.89 at the end of three years. In contrast, if she contributes it to a qualified plan, she will have $2,912.80 (after taxes at the end of three years). If she was taxed on the original contribution but never taxed on the earnings, she would again have $2,912.80.

Contributions to Regular Savings Account

(tax imposed on contributions and tax imposed on earnings)

Year One:

$1,000 x 20% = $200 — (tax imposed on $1,000)

$1,000 - $200 = $800 — (amount Constance has remaining after taxes to contribute)

$800 x .10 = $80 — (earnings on contribution based on 10% interest rate)

$80 x .20 = $16 — (tax on earnings)

$800 + ($80 - $16) = $864 — (amount at end of Year One after tax on contribution and earnings)

Year Two:

$864 + ($1,000 - $200) = $1,664 — (carryover contribution and earnings from Year One plus Year Two after tax contribution of $800)

$1,664 x .10 = $166.40 — (earnings on total contributions and past earnings based on 10% interest rate)

$166.40 x .20 = $33.28 — (tax on earnings)

$1,664 + ($166.40 - $33.28) = $1,797.12 — (amount at end of Year Two after tax on contributions and earnings)

Year Three:

$1,797.12 + ($1,000 - $200) = $2,597.12 — (carryover contributions and earnings from Years One and Two plus Year Three after tax contribution of $800)

$2,597.12 x .10 = $259.71 — (earnings on total contributions and past earnings based on 10% interest rate)

$259.71 x .20 = $51.94 — (tax on earnings)

$2,597.12 + ($259.71 - $51.94) = $2,804.89 — (amount at end of Year Three after tax on contributions and earnings)

Contributions to Qualified Retirement Plan

(tax deferral: no tax imposed on initial contributions or earnings; tax imposed on distributions)

Year One:

$1,000 — (no tax imposed when $1,000 contribution made)

$1,000 x .10 = $100 — (earnings on contribution based on 10% interest rate)

$1,000 + $100 = $1,100 — (amount at end of Year One — no tax on earnings or contribution)

Year Two:

$1,100 + $1,000 = $2,100	(carryover contribution and earnings from Year One plus Year Two contribution of $1,000)
$2,100 x .10 = $210	(earnings on total contributions and past earnings based on 10% interest rate)
$2,100 + $210 = $2,310	(amount at end of Year Two — no tax on earnings or contributions)

Year Three:

$2,310 + $1,000 = $3,310	(carryover contribution from Years One and Two plus Year Three after tax contribution of $800)
$3,310 x .10 = $331	(earnings on total contributions based on 10% interest rate)
$3,310 + $331 = $3,641	(amount at end of Year Three after tax on contributions and earnings)
$3,641 x .20 = $728.20	(tax on distribution of $3,641 after end of Year Three)
$3,641 - 728.20 = $2,912.80	(amount remaining after tax on distribution after Year Three)

Roth Contributions to Qualified Plan (Tax imposed on initial contributions; no tax imposed on earnings and no tax imposed on distributions)

Year One:

$1,000 x 20% = $200	(tax imposed on $1,000)
$1,000 - $200 = $800	(amount Constance has remaining after taxes to contribute)
$800 x .10 = $80	(earnings on contribution based on 10% interest rate)
$800 + $80 = $880	(amount at end of Year One after tax on contribution but no tax on earnings)

Year Two:

$880 + ($1,000 - $200) = $1,680	(carryover contribution and earnings from Year One plus Year Two after tax contribution of $800)
$1,680 x .10 = $168.00	(earnings on total contributions and past earnings based on 10% interest rate)
$1,680 + $168.00 = $1,848	(amount at end of Year Two after tax on contributions but no tax on earnings)

Year Three:

$1,848 + ($1,000 - $200) = $2,648

(carryover contributions and earnings from Years One and Two plus Year Three after tax contribution of $800)

$2,648 x .10 = $264.80

(earnings on total contributions and past earnings based on 10% interest rate)

$2,648 + $264.80 = $2,912.80

(amount at end of Year Three after tax on contributions but no tax on earnings)

$2,912.80

(non-taxable distribution available at end of Year Three)

Appendix C

SAFE AND UNSAFE HARBOR PERCENTAGES

Treas. Reg. § 1.410(b)-4(c)(4)(iv)
Safe and Unsafe Harbor Percentages

Non-highly compensated employee concentration percentage	Safe harbor percentage	Unsafe harbor percentage
0–60	50	40
61	49.25	39.25
62	48.5	38.5
63	47.75	37.75
64	47	37
65	46.25	36.25
66	45.5	35.5
67	44.75	34.75
68	44	34
69	43.25	33.25
70	42.5	32.5
71	41.75	31.75
72	41	31
73	40.25	30.25
74	39.5	29.5
75	38.75	28.75
76	38	28
77	37.25	27.25
78	36.5	26.5
79	37.75	25.75
80	35	25
81	34.25	24.25
82	33.5	23.5
83	32.75	22.75
84	32	22
85	31.25	21.25
86	30.5	20.5
87	29.75	20
88	29	20
89	28.25	20
90	27.5	20
91	26.75	20
92	26	20

Non-highly compensated employee concentration percentage	Safe harbor percentage	Unsafe harbor percentage
93	25.25	20
94	24.5	20
95	23.75	20
96	23	20
97	22.25	20
98	21.5	20
99	20.75	20

TABLE OF CASES

[References are to pages]

A

Achiro v. Commissioner, 77 T.C. 881 (1981). . .350

Aetna Health Inc. v. Davila, 542 U.S. 200 (2004). 193; 254; 266–268; 307; 310

Alessi, 451 U.S. 504 (1981). 314, 315

Allinder v. Inter-City Products Corp., 152 F.3d 544 (6th Cir. 1998). 266

Alyeska Pipeline Service Co. v. Wilderness Society, 421 U.S. 240 (1975). 303

Amalgamated Clothing & Textile Workers Union v. Murdock, 861 F.2d 1406 (9th Cir. 1988).218; 230

Amato v. Bernard, 618 F.2d 559 (9th Cir. 1980).250

American Flint Glass Workers Union v. Beaumont Glass Co., 62 F.3d 574 (3d Cir. 1995) 15

American Medical Security, Inc. v. Bartlett, 111 F.3d 358 (4th Cir. 1997). 73

Anderson v. Electronic Data Systems Corp., 11 F.3d 1311 (5th Cir. 1994). 143

Annual Update of the HHS Poverty Guidelines, 80 Fed Reg. 3236 (Jan. 22, 2015). 94

Arena v. ABB Power T & D Co., Inc., 2003 U.S. Dist. LEXIS 13164 (S.D. Ind. July 21, 2003). . . .301

Armstrong v. LaSalle Bank Nat'l Ass'n, 446 F.3d 728 (7th Cir. 2006) 265

Ashcroft v. Iqbal, 556 U.S. 662 (2009). 208

Associated Indus. v. Angoff, 937 S.W.2d 277 (Mo. Ct. App. 1996). 330

Avco Corp., 390 U.S. 557 (1968). 253

B

Babcock v. Hartmarx Corp., 182 F.3d 336 (5th Cir. 1999). 296

Bailey v. Glover, 88 U.S. 342 (1875). 297

Barrowclough v. Kidder, Peabody & Co., 752 F.2d 923 (3d Cir. 1985). 250

Bast v. Prudential Ins. Co. of Am., 150 F.3d 1003 (9th Cir. 1998). 268

Batchelor v. International Brotherhood of Electrical Workers Local 861 Pension & Retirement Fund, 877 F.2d 441 (5th Cir. 1989). 258

Bay Area Laundry & Dry Cleaning Pension Trust Fund v. Ferbar Corp., 522 U.S. 192 (1997). .292; 299

Beck v. PACE International Union, 551 U.S. 96 (2007). 194; 204; 478

Becker v. Mack Trucks, Inc., 281 F.3d 372 (3d Cir. 2002). 144

Beddall v. State St. Bank & Trust Co., 137 F.3d 12 (1st Cir. 1998). 200

Bell Atlantic Corp. v. Twombly, 550 U.S. 544 (2007). 208

Berger v. Edgewater Steel Co., 911 F.2d 911 (3d Cir. 1990). 147

Bill Gray Enters. v. Gourley, 248 F.3d 206 (3d Cir. 2001). 330

Bilyeu v. Morgan Stanley Long Term Disability Plan, 683 F.3d 1083 (9th Cir. 2012). 287

Block v. Pitney Bowes Inc., 952 F.2d 1450 (D.C. Cir. 1992). 258

Bloemker v. Laborers' Local 265 Pension Fund, 605 F.3d 436 (6th Cir. 2010). 132

Board of Trustees v. Wettlin Assocs., 237 F.3d 270 (3d Cir. 2001). .197

Boeing Co. v. Van Gemert, 444 U.S. 472 (1980).288

Boggs v. Boggs, 520 U.S. 833 (1997). .9; 165; 308, 309

Bona v. Barasch, 174 LRRM 2051 (S.D.N.Y. Mar. 20, 2003). 256

Bonovich v. Knights of Columbus, 146 F.3d 57 (2d Cir. 1998). 132

Boomer v. AT&T Corp., 309 F.3d 404 (7th Cir. 2002). 309

Booth v. Wal-Mart Stores, Inc. Assocs. Health & Welfare Plan, 201 F.3d 335 (4th Cir. 2000). .258; 261

Borntrager v. Central States Southeast and Southwest Areas Pension Fund, 577 F.3d 913 (8th Cir. 2009). 144

Borst v. Chevron Corp., 36 F.3d 1308 (5th Cir. 1994). 468

Bowerman v. Wal-Mart Stores, Inc., 226 F.3d 574 (7th Cir. 2000). .132

Boyd v. Trs. of United Mine Workers Health & Ret. Funds, 873 F.2d 57 (4th Cir. 1989) 258

Braden v. Wal-Mart Stores, Inc., 588 F.3d 585 (8th Cir. 2009). 208; 237

Bricklayers Local No. 1 Welfare Fund v. La. Health Ins. Ass'n, 771 F. Supp. 771 (E.D. La. 1991).330

Brock v. Berman, 673 F. Supp. 634 (D. Mass. 1987). 193; 200

Brock v. Citizens Bank, 841 F.2d 344 (10th Cir. 1988). 222

Brown v. American Life Holdings, Inc., 190 F.3d 856 (8th Cir. 1999). 296

Brown v. Granatelli, 897 F.2d 1351 (5th Cir. 1990). 330

Brown v. Owens Corning Investment Review Committee, 622 F.3d 564 (6th Cir. 2010). . . .296

Browning v. Tiger's Eye Benefits Consulting, 313 Fed. Appx. 656 (4th Cir. Feb. 26, 2009). . . .296

Burke v. Kodak Retirement Income Plan, 336 F.3d 103 (2d Cir. 2003). 136

Bussian v. RJR Nabisco, Inc., 223 F.3d 286 (5th Cir. 2000) 478

C

Cal. Div. of Labor Standards Enforcement v. Dillingham Constr., N.A., Inc., 519 U.S. 316 (1997). 314; 316; 319–322; 325

Callery v. U.S. Life Ins. Co., 392 F.3d 401 (10th Cir. 2004) 132

Caputo v. Pfizer, Inc., 267 F.3d 181 (2d Cir. 2001). 296; 298

Caterpillar, Inc. v. Williams, 482 U.S. 386 (1987). 253

Cent. States v. Cent. Transp., 472 U.S. 559 (1985). 212

Central Bank, N.A. v. First Interstate Bank, N.A., 511 U.S. 164 (1994). 231

Central Laborers' Pension Fund v. Heinz, 541 U.S 739 (2004). 138, 139

Central States Pension Fund v. Howell, 227 F.3d 672 (6th Cir. 2000) 169

Chao v. Johnston, 2007 U.S. Dist. LEXIS 49921 (E.D. Tenn. July 9, 2007). 234

Christopher v. Mobil Oil, 950 F.2d 1209 (5th Cir. 1992) 146

CIGNA Corp. v. Amara, 131 S. Ct. 1866 (2011) . 53; 133; 136; 266–268; 270; 278; 282

Cipollone v. Liggett Grp., Inc., 505 U.S. 504 (1992). 308

Citigroup Pension Plan ERISA Litigation, In re, 470 F. Supp. 2d 323 (S.D.N.Y. 2006). 53

Clark v. Rameker, 134 S. Ct. 2242 (2014) 175

Cmty. State Bank v. Strong, 651 F.3d 1241 (11th Cir. 2011) 310

Coan v. Kaufman, 457 F.3d 250 (2d Cir. 2006) . 275

Cobb v. Cent. States Pension Fund, 461 F.3d 632 (5th Cir. 2006). 249

Coleman v. Nationwide Life Ins. Co., 969 F.2d 54 (4th Cir. 1982). 132

Commercial Mortgage Ins., Inc. v. Citizens Nat'l Bank of Dallas, 526 F. Supp. 510 (N.D. Tex. 1981). 169; 172

Commissioner v. (see name of defendant)

Concha v. London, 62 F.3d 1493 (9th Cir. 1995) . 15

Confer v. Custom Eng'g Co., 952 F.2d 34 (3d Cir. 1991). 196, 197

Connecticut State Dental Ass'n v. Anthem Health Plans, Inc., 591 F.3d 1337 (11th Cir. 2009). .255; 309, 310

Consolidated Beef Indus., Inc. v. New York Life Ins. Co., 949 F.2d 960 (8th Cir.) 198

Cooper v. IBM Personal Pension Plan, 457 F.3d 636 (7th Cir. 2006) 53

Cooper Tire & Rubber Co. v. St. Paul Fire & Marine Ins. Co., 48 F.3d 365 (8th Cir. 1995). 15

Cort v. Ash, 422 U.S. 66 (1975). 274

Coyne & Delany Co. v. Blue Cross & Blue Shield of Va., Inc., 102 F.3d 712 (4th Cir. 1996) 271

Crawford v. Roane, 53 F.3d 750 (6th Cir. 1995) . 249

Crawford v. TRW Automotive U.S. LLC, 560 F.3d 607 (6th Cir. 2009). 147

Critchlow v. First UNUM Life Ins. Co. of Am., 378 F.3d 246 (2d Cir. 2004). 267

Curcio v. John Hancock Mut. Life Ins. Co., 33 F.3d 226 (3d Cir. 1994) 132

Curtiss-Wright Corp. v. Schoonejongen, 514 U.S. 73 (1995) . . 113; 130; 135; 137, 138; 194, 195; 467

D

Dabertin v. HCR Manor Care, Inc., 373 F.3d 822 (7th Cir. 2004). 267

David v. Alphin, 704 F.3d 327 (4th Cir. 2013). . .293

Davidson v. Cook, 567 F. Supp. 225 (E.D. Va. 1983) 226

Davidson v. Wal-Mart Assocs. Health & Welfare Plan, 305 F. Supp. 2d 1059 (S.D. Iowa 2004). 302

Davidson on behalf of Local 666 Ben. Trust Fund v. Cook, 734 F.2d 10 (4th Cir. 1983). 226

Deak v. Masters, Mates & Pilots Pension Plan, 821 F.2d 572 (11th Cir. 1987). 203

DeBuono v. NYSA-ILA Medical and Services Clinical Fund, 520 U.S. 806 (1997) . . .314; 320

Denmark v. Liberty Life Assur. Co. of Boston, 566 F.3d 1 (1st Cir. 2009). 259

DiFelice v. Aetna U.S. Healthcare, 346 F.3d 442 (3d Cir. 2003). 266; 307

Dishman v. UNUM Life Ins. Co. of Am., 269 F.3d 974 (9th Cir. 2001) 251

Dist. of Columbia v. Greater Wash. Bd. of Trade, 506 U.S. 125 (1992) 314; 316, 317

Dister v. Continental Grp., Inc., 859 F.2d 1108 (2d Cir. 1988). 147, 148

Doe v. Blue Cross & Blue Shield United of Wisconsin, 112 F.3d 869 (7th Cir. 1997). 302

Donovan v. Bierwirth, 680 F.2d 263 (2d Cir.). . .201; 203; 205

Donovan v. Cunningham, 716 F.2d 1455 (5th Cir. 1983) 51; 205; 218

Donovan v. Dillingham, 688 F.2d 1367 (11th Cir. 1982) 59; 131; 323

Doskocil Cos., In re, 130 B.R. 870 (Bank. D. Kan. 1991) 114

Dozier v. Sun Life Assurance Co., 466 F.3d 532 (6th Cir. 2006) 251

Drinkwater v. Metropolitan Life Ins. Co., 846 F.2d 821 (1st Cir.) .250

Drutis v. Rand McNally & Co., 499 F.3d 608 (6th Cir. 2007) 53

E

Edes v. Verizon Communs., 417 F.3d 133 (1st Cir. 2005) 296

Edgar v. Avaya, Inc., 503 F.3d 340 (3d Cir. 2007) 207

Edwards v. A.H. Cornell and Son, Inc., 610 F.3d 217 (3d Cir. 2010) 143

Egelhoff v. Egelhoff, 532 U.S. 141 . . 308; 314, 315; 320

F

Farm King Integrated Supply, Inc. Integrated Profit-Sharing Plan & Trust v. Edward D. Jones & Co., 884 F.2d 288 (7th Cir. 1989) 198

Fidelity Fed. Sav. & Loan Ass'n v. De la Cuesta, 458 U.S. 141 (1982) 308

Fifth Third Bancorp v. Dudenhoeffer, 134 S. Ct. 2459 (2014) 207; 209; 265

Firestone Tire & Rubber Co. v. Bruch, 489 U.S. 101 (1989) 145; 193; 248; 257

Fish v. Greatbanc Trust Co., 749 F.3d 671 (7th Cir. 2014) 296

Florida Lime & Avocado Growers, Inc. v. Paul, 373 U.S. 132 (1963) 309

FMC v. Holliday, 498 U.S. 52 (1990) . 69; 314; 317; 325; 328

Fort Halifax Packing Co. v. Coyne, 482 U.S. 1 (1987) 323, 324

Franchise Tax Bd. v. Construction Laborers Vacation Trust, 463 U.S. 1 (1983) 253; 310

Franciscan Skemp Healthcare, Inc. v. Central States Joint Board Health and Welfare Trust Fund, 538 F.3d 594 (7th Cir. 2008) 310, 311

Frommert v. Conkright, 433 F.3d 254 (2006) . .261

Frommert v. Conkright, 472 F. Supp. 2d 452 (2007) 262

Frommert v. Conkright, 535 F.3d 111 (2008) . .262

G

G.S. Consulting, Inc., In re, 414 B.R. 454 (N.D. Ind. 2009) 197

Gade v. National Solid Wastes Management Ass'n, 505 U.S. 88 (1992) 308, 309

Gahn v. Allstate Life Ins. Co., 926 F.2d 1449 (5th Cir. 1991) 60

Garland v. Commissioner, 73 T.C. 5 (1979) . . .336; 347, 348

Gavalik v. Continental Can Co., 812 F.2d 834 (3d Cir. 1987) 142; 147

Gearlds v. Entergy Servs., Inc., 709 F.3d 448 (5th Cir. 2013) 283, 284

George v. Junior Achievement of Central Indiana, Inc., 694 F.3d 812 (7th Cir. 2012) 143; 203

George v. Kraft Foods Global, Inc., 641 F.3d 786 (7th Cir. 2013) 237

Gluck v. Unisys Corp., 960 F.2d 1168 (3d Cir. 1992) 300

Gonzales v. Unum Life Ins. Co., 861 F. Supp. 2d 1099 (S.D. Cal. 2012) 131

Gore v. El Paso Energy Corp. Long Term Disability Plan, 477 F.3d 833 271

Graden v. Conexant Systems, Inc., 496 F.3d 291 (3d Cir. 2007) 271

Greany v. Farm Bureau Life Ins. Co., 973 F.2d 812 (9th Cir. 1980) 132

Great West Life & Annuity Ins. Co. v. Knudson, 534 U.S. 204 (2002) 266; 284

Greenberg v. H & H Music Co., 506 U.S. 981 (1992) 142

Guidry v. Sheet Metal Workers Nat'l Pension Fund, 493 U.S. 365 (1990) 169; 174

Guilbert v. Gardner, 480 F.3d 140 (2d Cir. 2007) .58; 61

Gulf Pension Litigation, In re, 764 F. Supp. 1149 (S.D. Tex. 1991) 468

H

Hall v. National Gypsum Co., 105 F.3d 225 (5th Cir. 1997) 251

Hamann v. Independence Blue Cross, 543 Fed. Appx. 355 (5th Cir. Sept. 18, 2013) 268

Hamilton v. Starcom Mediavest Group, Inc., 522 F.3d 623 (6th Cir. 2008) 142; 147, 148

Hardt v. Reliance Std. Life Ins. Co., 130 S. Ct. 2149 (2010) 303

Harris Trust and Savings Bank v. Salomon Smith Barney Inc., 530 U.S. 238 (2000) . .221; 231; 233

[References are to pages]

Harrison v. Digital Health Plan, 183 F.3d 1235 (11th Cir. 1999) 300, 301

Hashimoto v. Bank of Hawaii, 999 F.2d 408 (9th Cir. 1993) 143

Hecker v. Deere, 569 F.3d 708 (7th Cir. 2009). . 240

Hecker v. Deere & Co., 556 F.3d 575 (7th Cir. 2009). 237, 238

Heimeshoff v. Hartford Life & Accident Ins. Co., 134 S. Ct. 604 (2013) 130; 250; 302

Held v. Mfrs. Hanover Leasing Corp., 912 F.2d 1197 (10th Cir. 1990). 300

Hellman v. Cataldo, 2013 U.S. Dist. LEXIS 117676. .256

Henderson v. Bodine Aluminum, Inc., 70 F.3d 958 (8th Cir. 1995) 251

Hi Lex Controls, Inc. v. BC & BS Michigan, 2013 U.S. Dist. LEXIS 73043 (E.D. Mi. May 23, 2013) 236

Hill v. Blue Cross and Blue Shield of Michigan, 409 F.3d 710 (6th Cir. 2005) 271

Hines v. Davidowitz, 312 U.S. 52 (1941). 309

Hogan v. Kraft Foods, 969 F.2d 142 (5th Cir. 1992) 301

Holmstrom v. Metro. Life Ins. Co., 615 F.3d 758 (7th Cir. 2010). 267

Holtzclaw v. DSC Communs. Corp., 255 F.3d 254 (5th Cir. 2001). 147

Hoult v. Hoult, 373 F.3d 47 (1st Cir. 2004). . . .169

Hughes Aircraft Co. v. Jacobson, 525 U.S. 432 (1999). 194; 224, 225; 477

Humphreys v. Bellaire Corp., 966 F.2d 1037 (6th Cir. 1992) 148

Hunter v. Caliber System, Inc., 220 F.3d 702 (6th Cir. 2000). 15; 265

I

In re (see name of party)

Ingersoll-Rand Co. v. McClendon, 498 U.S. 133 (1990). 141; 266; 314; 316

Intermodal Rail Employees Association v. Atchison, Topeka and Santa Fe Railway Co., 520 U.S. 510 (1997) 141; 146

International Union v. Murata Erie N. Am., 980 F.2d 889 (3d Cir. 1992) 296

Irving; United States v., 452 F.3d 110 (2d Cir. 2006) 171

IT Corp. v. General Am. Life Ins. Co., 107 F.3d 1415 (9th Cir. 1997) 197

Izzarelli v. Rexene Prods. Co., 24 F.3d 1506 (5th Cir. 1994) 275

J

J. Geils Band Employee Benefit Plan v. Smith Barney Shearson, Inc., 76 F.3d 1245 (1st Cir.). 298

John Blair Communications Profit Sharing Plan v. Telemundo Group, 26 F.3d 360 (2d Cir. 1994) 264

John Hancock Mutual Life Ins. Co. v. Harris Trust and Savings Bank, 510 U.S. 86 (1993). 190

Jones v. Allen, 2014 U.S. Dist. LEXIS 132672 (2014). 146

Jones v. Rather Packing Co., 430 U.S. 519 (1977). 308

K

Kane v. Aetna Life Ins., 893 F.2d 1283 (11th Cir. 1990) 132

Katsaros v. Cody, 744 F.2d 270 (2d Cir. 1984). . 206

Kayes v. Pacific Lumber Co., 51 F.3d 1449 (9th Cir. 1995) 196

Kennedy v. Plan Adm'r for DuPont Sav. & Inv. Plan, 555 U.S. 285 (2009). 169; 173; 211

Kenney v. Roland Parson Contracting Corp., 28 F.3d 1254 (D.C. Cir. 1994) 131

Kenseth v. Dean Health Plan, Inc., 722 F.3d 869 (7th Cir. 2013). 283

Kentucky Assoc. of Health Plans, Inc. v. Miller, 538 U.S. 329 (2003). 325, 326

Keys v. Eastman Kodak Co., 739 F. Supp. 135 (W.D.N.Y. 1990) 249

Keys v. Eastman Kodak Co, 923 F.2d 844 (2d Cir. 1990) 249

Keystone Consolidated Industries, Inc; Commissioner v., 508 U.S. 152 (1993). 221; 224

Kimbro v. Atlantic Richfield Co., 889 F.2d 869 (9th Cir. 1989). 147

King v. Burwell, 135 S. Ct. 2480 (2015). 95

King v. Marriott International, Inc., 337 F.3d 421 (4th Cir. 2003). 144

Kirse v. McCullough, 2005 U.S. Dist. LEXIS 17023 (W.D. Mo. May 12, 2005) 256

Koert v. GE Grp. Life Assurance Co., 231 Fed. Appx. 117 (3d Cir. Feb. 27, 2007) 296

Kowalski v. L&F Prods., 82 F.3d 1283 (3d Cir. 1996) 141

L

LaAsmar v. Phelps Dodge Corp. Life, Accidental Death & Dismemberment & Dependent Life Ins. Plan, 605 F.3d 789 (10th Cir. 2010) 267

Lampen v. Albert Trostel & Sons Employee Welfare Plan, 832 F. Supp. 1287 (E.D. Wis. 1993). . .197

Langbecker v. Electronic Data Systems Corp., 476 F.3d 299 (5th Cir. 2007) 240

Langley v. DaimlerChrysler Corp., 502 F.3d 475 (6th Cir. 2007). 60

Larocca v. Borden, 276 F.3d 22 (1st Cir. 2002) . 271

LaRue v. DeWolff, Boberg & Assocs., 552 U.S. 248 (2008) 243; 250; 252; 266; 271; 273; 276

Lee v. California Butchers' Pension Trust Fund, 154 F.3d 1075 (9th Cir. 1998). 251

Leigh v. Engle, 727 F.2d 113 (7th Cir. 1984) . . 193; 203

Lemishow v. Commissioner of Internal Revenue, 110 T.C. 110 (1998). 55

Liberty University, Inc. v. Lew, 733 F.3d 72 (4th Cir. 2013). 93

Lincoln Mut. Cas. Co. v. Lectron Prods., Inc., 970 F.2d 206 (6th Cir. 1992). 330

Livick v. Gillette Co., 524 F.3d 24 (1st Cir. 2008) 132

Lockheed Corp. v. Spink, 517 U.S. 882 (1996) . 113; 129; 194; 203; 218; 224, 225; 231

Loevsky v. Commissioner, 55 T.C. 1144 (1971) . 364

Longaberger Co. v. Kolt, 586 F.3d 459 (6th Cir. 2009) 234

Loomis v. Exelon Corp., 658 F.3d 667 (7th Cir. 2011) 237

LoPresti v. Terwilliger, 126 F.3d 34 (2d Cir. 1997) 196

Luna, In re, 406 F.3d 1192 (10th Cir. 2005) . . . 190

M

M&G Polymers USA, LLC v. Tackett, 135 S. Ct. 926 (2015). 114

Mackey v. Lanier Collection Agency & Service, Inc., 486 U.S. 825 (1988) 314; 316

Magin v. Monsanto Co., 420 F.3d 679 (7th Cir. 2005) 275

Malone v. White Motor Corp., 435 U.S. 497 (1978). 308

Marin General Hospital v. Modesto & Empire Traction Co., 581 F.3d 941 (9th Cir. 2009) . . 311

Martin v. Consultants & Adm'rs, Inc., 966 F.2d 1078 (7th Cir. 1992) 298

Martin v. Feilen, 965 F.2d 660 (8th Cir. 1992) . .203

Martin v. National Bank of Alaska, 828 F. Supp. 1427 (D. Alaska 1992) 226

Mass. Mutual Life Ins. Co. v. Russell, 473 U.S. 134 (1985) 243; 266, 267; 269; 273, 274; 276

Massachusetts v. Morash, 490 U.S. 107 (1989) . 323, 324

Masters, Mates & Pilots Pension Plan, In re, 11 Employee Benefits Cas. (BNA) 2629 (S.D.N.Y. 1990) 193

McBride v. PLM Int'l, Inc., 179 F.3d 737 (9th Cir. 1999) 146

McCravy v. Metro. Life Ins. Co., 690 F.3d 176 (4th Cir. 2012). 283

McDonald v. Artcraft Elec. Supply Co., 774 F. Supp. 29 (D.D.C. 1991) 256

McDonald v. Provident Indem. Life Ins. Co., 60 F.3d 234 (5th Cir. 1995) 275

McDonnell Douglas Corp. v. Green, 411 U.S. 792 (1973) 147

McGann v. H & H Music Co., 946 F.2d 401 (5th Cir. 1991). 87; 142, 143; 147

McMahon v. McDowell, 794 F.2d 100 (3d Cir. 1986) 203

McNevin v. Solvay Process Co., 32 A.D. 610 (N.Y. App. Div. 1898). 150

McNevin v. Solvay Process Co., 60 N.E. 1115 (N.Y. 1901) 150

McRae v. Seafarers' Welfare Plan, 920 F.2d 819 (11th Cir. 1991). 268

Meade v. Pension Appeals & Review Comm., 966 F.2d 190 (6th Cir. 1992) 301

Mello v. Sara Lee Corp., 431 F.3d 440 (5th Cir. 2005) 132

Mertens v. Hewitt Assocs., 508 U.S. 248 (1993).231, 232; 266; 277–279

Metro. Life Ins. Co. v. Glenn, 554 U.S. 105 (2008) 259

Metropolitan Life Ins. Co. v. Mass., 471 U.S. 724 (1985) 325; 328

Metropolitan Life Ins. Co. v. Taylor, 481 U.S. 58 (1987). 253, 254; 309, 310

Metzler v. Graham, 112 F.3d 207 (5th Cir. 1997). 204; 210, 211

Meyer v. Berkshire Life Ins. Co., 128 F. Supp. 2d 831 (D. Md. 2001). 296

Michaelis v. Deluxe Fin. Servs., 2006 U.S. Dist. LEXIS 265 (D. Kan. Jan. 5, 2006). 256

Moench v. Robertson, 62 F.3d 553 (3d Cir. 1995). 207; 265

Molina v. Mallah, 817 F. Supp. 419 (S.D.N.Y. 1993) 15

Moon v. Bwx Techs., Inc., 956 F. Supp. 2d 711 (W.D. Va. 2013) 284

Musmeci v. Schwegmann Giant Super Markets, 332 F.3d 339 (5th Cir. 2003) 58, 59; 196

Musto v. Am. Gen. Corp., 861 F.2d 897 (6th Cir. 1988) 131

N

Nachman Corp. v. Pension Ben. Guaranty Corp., 446 U.S. 359 (1980) 9; 243

Nachwalter v. Christie, 805 F.2d 956 (11th Cir. 1986) 132

Nat'l Fed'n of Indep. Bus. v. Sebelius, 132 S. Ct. 2566 (2012) 90; 93

National Sec. Sys., Inc. v. Iola, 700 F.3d 65 (3d Cir. 2012) 234

Nationwide Mutual Ins. Co. v. Darden, 503 U.S. 318 (1992) 248

Nazay v. Miller, 949 F.2d 1323 (3d Cir. 1991) . . 258

New Jersey State AFL-CIO v. New Jersey, 747 F.2d 891 (3d Cir. 1984) 246

New York State Conference of Blue Cross & Blue Shield Plans v. Travelers Insurance Co., 514 U.S. 645 (1995) 314, 315; 318–320

Nicolaou v. Horizon Media, Inc., 402 F.3d 325 (2d Cir. 2005) 143

Nor-Cal Plumbing, Inc., 185 F.3d 978 (9th Cir. 1999) 246

Northlake Reg'l Med. Ctr. v. Waffle House Sys. Emp. Benefit Plan, 160 F.3d 1301 (11th Cir. 1998) . 302

Novak; United States v., 476 F.3d 1041 (9th Cir. 2009) 171

P

Pacificare Inc. v. Martin, 34 F.3d 834 (9th Cir. 1994) 197

Patelco Credit Union v. Sahni, 262 F.3d 897 (9th Cir. 2001) 226

Patterson v. Shumate, 504 U.S. 753 (1992) . . 49; 174

Pegram v. Herdrich, 530 U.S. 211 (2000) . 188; 190, 191; 193

Pension Benefit Guar. Corp. v. LTV Corp., 496 U.S. 633 472

Perdue v. Burger King Corp., 7 F.3d 1251 (5th Cir. 1993) 15

Pilot Life Ins. Co. v. Dedeaux, 481 U.S. 41 (1987) 325, 326

Plumb v. Fluid Pump Serv., 124 F.3d 849 (7th Cir. 1997) 132

R

Ranke v. Sanofi-Synthelabo Inc., 436 F.3d 197 (3d Cir. 2006) 298

Rath v. Selection Research, Inc., 978 F.2d 1087 (8th Cir. 1992) 147

Reed v. United Transp. Union, 488 U.S. 319 (1989) 300

Register v. PNC Fin. Servs. Group, Inc., 477 F.3d 56 (3d Cir. 2007) 53

Reich v. King, 867 F. Supp. 341 (D. Md. 1994) . 205; 210

Reich v. Lancaster, 55 F.3d 1034 (5th Cir. 1995) . 197

Renfro v. Unisys Corp., 671 F.3d 314 (3d Cir. 2011) 237

Riley v. Murdock, 890 F. Supp. 444 (E.D.N.C. 1995) 206

Riordan v. Commonwealth Edison Co., 128 F.3d 549 (7th Cir. 1997) 249

Robbins v. DeBuono, 218 F.3d 197 (2d Cir. 2000) 169

Ruckelshaus v. Sierra Club, 463 U.S. 680 (1983) 303, 304

Rudowski v. Sheet Metal Workers Int'l Ass'n, Local Union No. 24, 113 F. Supp. 2d 1176 (S.D. Ohio 2000) 234

Rush v. Martin Petersen Col, 83 F.3d 894 (7th Cir. 1996) 296

Rush Prudential HMO, Inc. v. Moran, 536 U.S. 355 (2002) 325, 326

Ruttenberg v. United States Life Ins. Co., 413 F.3d 652 (7th Cir. 2005) 251

S

Schering-Plough Corp. ERISA Litigation, In re, 420 F.3d 231 (3d Cir. 2005) 275

Sereboff v. Mid Atl. Med. Servs., 547 U.S. 356 (2006) 266; 284; 287

Sexton v. Panel Processing, Inc., 754 F.3d 332 (6th Cir. 2014) 144

Sexton v. Panel Processing, Inc., 912 F. Supp. 2d 457 (E.D. Mi. 2012) 143

Shahid v. Ford Motor Company, 76 F.3d 1404 (6th Cir. 1996) 146

Shaw v. Delta Air Lines, Inc., 463 U.S. 85 (1983) 314–316

Shawley v. Bethlehem Steel Corp., 989 F.2d 652 (3d Cir. 1995) 145

Siskind v. Sperry Ret. Prog., Unisys, 47 F.3d 498 (2d Cir. 1993) 203

Sladek v. Bell Sys. Mgmt. Pension Plan, 880 F.2d 972 (7th Cir. 1989) 249

Slice v. Sons of Norway, 34 F.3d 630 (8th Cir. 1994) 132

Smith; United States v., 47 F.3d 681 (4th Cir. 1995) 169

Sommers Drug Store Co. Employee Profit Sharing Trust v. Corrigan Enters. Inc., 793 F.2d 1456 (5th Cir. 1986) 203

Spinelli v. Gaughan, 12 F.3d 853 (9th Cir. 1993).256

Sprague v. General Motors Corp., 133 F.3d 388 (6th Cir. 1998) 114

Stearns v. NCR Corp., 297 F.3d 706 (8th Cir. 2002) 114

Stewart v. KHD Deutz of Am. Corp., 75 F.3d 1522 (11th Cir.) 256

Stewart v. Thorpe Holding Co. Profit Sharing Plan, 207 F.3d 1143 (9th Cir. 2000) 196

Struble v. New Jersey Brewery Employees' Welfare Trust Fund, 732 F.2d 325 (3d Cir. 1984) . . . 264

Swinney v. General Motors Corp., 46 F.3d 512 (6th Cir. 1995) 146

T

Tatum v. RJR Pension Inv. Comm, 761 F.3d 346 (4th Cir. 2014) 206

Taylor v. United Techs. Corp., 354 Fed. Appx. 525 (2d Cir. Dec. 1, 2009) 237

Taylor v. United Techs. Corp., 2009 U.S. Dist. LEXIS 19059 (D. Conn. Mar. 3, 2009) 237

Terry v. Bayer Corp., 145 F.3d 28 (1st Cir. 1998) 258

Thomas v. Bostwick, 2013 U.S. Dist. LEXIS 134370 (N. D. Ca. Sept. 19, 2013) 174

Thomas, Head & Greisen Emps. Trust v. Buster, 24 F.3d 1114 (9th Cir. 1994) 198

Thomas Kiddie, M.D., Inc. v. Commissioner, 69 T.C. 1055 (1978) 348

Thompson v. Talquin Bldg. Prods. Co., 928 F.2d 649 (4th Cir. 1991) 330

Thurber v. Aetna Life Ins. Co., 712 F.3d 654 (2d Cir. 2013) 287

Tibble v. Edison Int'l, 729 F.3d 1110 (9th Cir. 2013) 237; 240; 264, 265

Tolle v. Carroll Touch, Inc., 977 F.2d 1129 (7th Cir. 1992) 141

Travelers, 514 U.S. 645 320

Trucking Employees of North Jersey Welfare Fund, Inc. v. Colville, 16 F.3d 52 (3d Cir. 1994). . .169

Trucking, Inc., 755 F.3d 468 (7th Cir. June 13, 2014) 169

Turner v. Fallon Community Health Plan, 127 F.3d 196 (1st Cir. 1997) 15; 251

Tussey v. ABB, Inc., 746 F.3d 327 (8th Cir.) . . 206; 237; 240; 265

Tuvia Convalescent Ctr., Inc. v. Nat'l Union of Hosp. & Health Care Emps., 717 F.2d 726 (2d Cir. 1983) 246

Tyco Int'l Inc., In re, 606 F. Supp. 2d 166 (D.N.H.) .240

U

U.S. Airways, Inc. v. McCutchen, 133 S. Ct. 1537 (2013) 130; 266; 284; 287–289

Unisys Sav. Plan Litig., In re, 74 F.3d 420 (3d Cir. 1996) 206

United Food & Commercial Workers v. Pacyga, 801 F.2d 1157 (9th Cir. 1986). 330

United State v. Roberson, III, 591 F.3d 1337 (11th Cir. 2009) 311

United States v. (see name of defendant)

UNUM Life Ins. Co. of Am. v. Ward, 526 U.S. 358 (1999) 314, 315; 320; 325, 326

V

Varity Corp. v. Howe, 516 U.S. 489 (1996). .9; 130; 191; 195; 203; 204; 266; 268; 270; 278; 281

Vincent v. Lucent Technologies, Inc., 733 F. Supp. 2d 729 (W.D.N.C. 2010). 261

W

Watts v. Organogenesis, Inc., 30 F. Supp. 2d 101 (D. Mass. 1998). 251

Weber v. Jacobs Mfg. Co., 751 F. Supp. 21 (D. Conn. 1990) 256

Wilczynski v. Lumbermens Mut. Cas. Co., 93 F.3d 397 (7th Cir. 1996) 251

Wilkins v. Baptist Healthcare Sys., Inc., 150 F.3d 609 (6th Cir. 1998) 271

Wilkins v. Hartford Life & Accident Ins. Co., 299 F.3d 945 (8th Cir. 2002) 302

Will v. General Dynamics Corp., 2009 U.S. Dist. LEXIS 105987 (S.D. Ill. Nov. 14, 2009) . . . 234

Williams v. Metropolitan Life Ins. Co., 609 F.3d 622 (4th Cir. 2010) 259

Winstead v. J.C. Penney Co., 933 F.2d 576 (7th Cir. 1991) 243

Wojchowski v. Daines, 498 F.3d 99 (2d Cir. 2007) 169

Wolin v. Smith Barney, Inc., 83 F.3d 847 (7th Cir. 1996) 298

[References are to pages]

Wooddell v. International Union of Electrical Workers, 502 U.S. 93 (1991). 256

Wright v. General Motors Corp., 262 F.3d 610 (6th Cir. 2001). 311

Wright v. Riveland, 219 F.3d 905 (9th Cir. 2000) 169

X

Xerox Corp. ERISA Litig., In re, 483 F. Supp.2d 206 (D. Conn. 2007). 234

Y

Yeseta v. Baima, 837 F.2d 380 (9th Cir. 1988). .196

INDEX

[References are to sections and appendices.]

A

ADEA (See AGE DISCRIMINATION IN EMPLOYMENT ACT (ADEA))

AFFORDABLE CARE ACT
Generally . . . 3.06; 3.06[A], [F]
"Cadillac" health plans (IRC § 4980I), excise tax on
  Generally . . . 3.06[D][6]
  "Applicable employer-sponsored coverage"
    . . . 3.06[D][6][a]
  "Coverage provider" . . . 3.06[D][6][c]
  "Excess benefit" . . . 3.06[D][6][b]
Employer mandate, IRC § 4980H
  Generally . . . 3.06[D], [D][1], [D][4], [D][4][f], [D][7]
  "Applicable large employers" . . . 3.06[D][4][a]
  Effective date . . . 3.06[D][4][e]
  "Minimum essential coverage"
    . . . 3.06[D][4][b]
  No offer penalty, IRC § 4980H(a)
    . . . 3.06[D][4][c]
  Unaffordable coverage penalty, IRC § 4980H(b)
    Generally . . . 3.06[D][4][d], [D][4][d][i]
    Amount of penalty . . . 3.06[D][4][d][iii]
    Minimum value . . . 3.06[D][4][d][ii]
Employment-based health care plans
  ERISA regulation prior to Affordable Care Act
    . . . 3.04
  Financing methods, implications of
    . . . 3.03[D][4]
ERISA
  Incorporation of Act's provisions by
    . . . 3.06[B]
  Regulation of employer-sponsored health plans prior to Act by . . . 3.04
Health Insurance Exchanges or Health Insurance Marketplaces
  Generally . . . 3.06[E]
  Essential health benefits package
    Generally . . . 3.06[E][2], [E][2][a]
    Actuarial value requirements
      . . . 3.06[E][2][c]
    Annual cost-sharing limits . . . 3.06[E][2][b]
  Types of Exchanges or Marketplaces
    Generally . . . 3.06[E][1]
    American Health Benefit (AHB) Exchange
      . . . 3.06[E][1][a]
    Small Business Health Options Program
      (SHOP) . . . 3.06[E][1][b]
Individual mandates, IRC § 5000A
  Generally . . . 3.06[D], [D][1], [D][2], [D][7]
  "Applicable individuals" . . . 3.06[D][2][a]
  Constitutionality of . . . 3.06[D][2][d]
  "Minimum essential coverage"
    . . . 3.06[D][2][b]
  Monetary penalty . . . 3.06[D][2][c]

AFFORDABLE CARE ACT—Cont.
Individual subsidies
  Generally . . . 3.06[D][3]
  Cost-sharing subsidy, PHSA § 1402
    Generally . . . 3.06[D][3][b]
    Amount of subsidy . . . 3.06[D][3][b][ii]
    Direct payment to insurer
      . . . 3.06[D][3][b][iii]
    "Eligible insureds" . . . 3.06[D][3][b][i]
  Premium tax credit, IRC § 36B
    Generally . . . 3.06[D][3][a]
    Amount of tax credit . . . 3.06[D][3][a][ii]
    "Applicable taxpayers" . . . 3.06[D][3][a][i]
    Direct payment to insurer
      . . . 3.06[D][3][a][iii]
Market reforms, substantive
  Generally . . . 3.06[C], [C][3]
  Expanding coverage, provisions
    Generally . . . 3.06[C][1]
    "Cherry picking," prohibitions on
      . . . 3.06[C][1][a]
    Young adults, coverage of . . . 3.06[C][1][b]
  Improving coverage, provisions
    Generally . . . 3.06[C][2]
    Lifetime and annual dollar limits on benefits, prohibition of . . . 3.06[C][2][a]
    Preexisting condition exclusions, prohibition of . . . 3.06[C][2][b]
    Preventive care . . . 3.06[C][2][c]
Problems with U.S. health care system prior to enactment of
  Generally . . . 3.05
  High costs . . . 3.05[B]
  Individual and small group markets, poorly functioning . . . 3.05[C]
  Uninsured individuals, large number of
    . . . 3.05[A]
Small employers (IRC § 45R), tax credit for
  . . . 3.06[D][5]

AGE DISCRIMINATION IN EMPLOYMENT ACT (ADEA)
Retiree health benefits and . . . 3.07[D]

ATTORNEY FEES
ERISA § 502(g)(1) . . . 7.10

C

CIVIL ENFORCEMENT PROVISIONS, ERISA
Generally . . . 7.01
Attorney fees, ERISA § 502(g)(1) . . . 7.10
ERISA § 502(a) causes of action
  Generally . . . 7.02; 7.02[D]
  ERISA § 502(a)(1)(B) . . . 7.02[A]
  ERISA § 502(a)(2) . . . 7.02[B]
  ERISA § 502(a)(3) . . . 7.02[C]
Exhaustion of ERISA § 503 claims review procedure
  Generally . . . 7.04

[References are to sections and appendices.]

**CIVIL ENFORCEMENT PROVISIONS,
ERISA**—Cont.

Exhaustion of ERISA § 503 claims review
procedure—Cont.

  Claims for benefits under ERISA § 502(a)(1)(B),
  exhaustion requirement for

    Generally . . . 7.04[A]

    Criticisms of requirement . . . 7.04[A][2]

    Exceptions to requirement . . . 7.04[A][3]

    Reasons for requirement . . . 7.04[A][1]

  Claims other than under ERISA § 502(a)(1)(B),
  exhaustion requirement for . . . 7.04[B]

Federal jurisdiction under ERISA § 502(e) and removal

  Generally . . . 7.05

  Complete preemption doctrine, removal under

    Generally . . . 7.05[B]

    Aetna Health Inc. v. Davila . . . 7.05[B][2]

    Early Supreme Court complete preemption
    cases . . . 7.05[B][1]

  Express ERISA claims, removal of . . . 7.05[A]

Judicial standard of review, generally . . . 7.07

Judicial standard of review applicable to claims for
benefits under ERISA § 502(a)(1)(B)

  Generally . . . 7.07[A], [A][5]

  Conflict, standard of review in cases of
  . . . 7.07[A][3]

  De Novo default standard . . . 7.07[A][1]

  Initial plan interpretation rejected, standard of
  review after . . . 7.07[A][4]

  Plan administrator granted discretion, deferential
  standard if . . . 7.07[A][2]

Judicial standard of review applicable to ERISA
claims other than claims under ERISA §
502(a)(1)(B) . . . 7.07[B]

Jury trial, right to . . . 7.06

Remedies (See REMEDIES, ERISA)

Standing, ERISA § 502(a)

  Generally . . . 7.03

  Beneficiary . . . 7.03[B]

  Fiduciary . . . 7.03[C]

  Participant . . . 7.03[A]

Statute of limitations (See STATUTE OF LIMITA-
TIONS)

E

EMPLOYEE BENEFIT PLANS (GENERALLY)

Amendments, plan

  Generally . . . 4.04

  Anti-cutback rule for pension plans, ERISA §
  240(g)

    Generally . . . 4.04[B]

    Accrued and prospective benefits compared
    . . . 4.04[B][2]

    Protected benefits . . . 4.04[B][3]

    Purpose of rule . . . 4.04[B][1]

  Procedure (ERISA § 402(b)(3)), plan amendment
  . . . 4.04[A]

Fiduciary liability under ERISA

  Generally . . . 6.07

**EMPLOYEE BENEFIT PLANS
(GENERALLY)**—Cont.

Fiduciary liability under ERISA—Cont.

  Co-fiduciary liability, ERISA § 405(a)
  . . . 6.07[B]

  401(k) plan fees and

    Generally . . . 6.08

    Disclosure regulations, fee . . . 6.08[B]

    Hecker v. Deere . . . 6.08[C][1]

    Litigation, excessive plan fee . . . 6.08[C],
    [C][1], [C][2]

    Retirement savings, plan fees and their impact
    on . . . 6.08[A]

    Tussey v. ABB, Inc. . . . 6.08[C][2]

  Nonfiduciary liability

    Generally . . . 6.07[C]

    Extension of *Harris Trust* to breach of fidu-
    ciary duty cases . . . 6.07[C][3]

    Harris Trust v. Salomon Smith Barney, Inc.
    . . . 6.07[C][2], [C][3]

    Mertens v. Hewitt . . . 6.07[C][1]

  Personal liability of fiduciary, ERISA § 409(a)
  . . . 6.07[A]

Fiduciary standards under ERISA

  Generally . . . 6.01; 6.04; 6.04[A]

  Determining fiduciary status

    Generally . . . 6.03

    Functional fiduciary, ERISA § 3(21)(A) (See
    subhead: Functional fiduciary, determining
    when person acting as)

    Named fiduciary, ERISA § 402(a)
    . . . 6.03[A], [C]

  Diversify (ERISA § 404(a)(1)(C)), duty to
  . . . 6.04[E]

  Exclusive purpose rule, ERISA § 404(a)(1)(A)
  . . . 6.04[C]

  Follow plan documents (ERISA § 404(a)(1)(D)),
  duty to

    Generally . . . 6.04[F], [F][1]

    Conflict with ERISA . . . 6.04[F][2]

  Liability, fiduciary (See subhead: Fiduciary liability under ERISA)

  Loyalty (ERISA § 404(a)(1)), duty of
  . . . 6.04[B]

  Prohibited transaction regime, ERISA §§ 406-408
  (See subhead: Prohibited transaction regime,
  ERISA §§ 406-408)

  Prudence (ERISA § 404(a)(1)(B)), duty of

    Generally . . . 6.04[D], [D][1]

    Employer stock, and investment in
    . . . 6.04[D][2]-D][2][b]

  Responsibility under ERISA, overview of fiduciary . . . 6.02

  Self-directed plans (ERISA § 404(c)), exemption
  from standards for (See subhead: Self-directed
  plans (ERISA § 404(c)), exemption from
  ERISA fiduciary standards for)

Functional fiduciary, determining when person acting as

  Generally . . . 6.03[B], [D]

  Employers

    Generally . . . 6.03[D][1]

    Fiduciary, as . . . 6.03[D][1][b], [D][1][c]

[References are to sections and appendices.]

EMPLOYEE BENEFIT PLANS (GENERALLY)—Cont.

Functional fiduciary, determining when person acting as—Cont.

  Employers—Cont.

    Settlor, as . . . 6.03[D][1][a], [D][1][c]

  Investment advice

    Generally . . . 6.03[D][4]

    Defined benefit plans, and . . . 6.03[D][4][a]

    Defined contribution plans, and . . . 6.03[D][4][b]

  Officers and directors, corporate . . . 6.03[D][2]

  Summary of . . . 6.03[C]

  Third party administrators . . . 6.03[D][3]

  Trustees

    Generally . . . 6.03[E]

    Directed trustees . . . 6.03[E][1]

    Investment managers . . . 6.03[E][2]

Operation of

  Generally . . . 4.01

  Amendments, plan (See subhead: Amendments, plan)

  ERISA § 510

    Generally . . . 4.05

    Burden of proof in claim, shifting . . . 4.05[D]-D][3]

    Defendant's burden of proof in claim . . . 4.05[D][2]

    Exercise clause or retaliation provision . . . 4.05[B], [B][1]

    Individuals protected by . . . 4.05[C]

    Interference clause . . . 4.05[B], [B][2]

    Multiemployer plan provision . . . 4.05[B], [B][4]

    Plaintiff's burden of proof in claim . . . 4.05[D][1], [D][3]

    Purpose of . . . 4.05[A]

    Whistleblower provision . . . 4.05[B], [B][3]

  Reporting and disclosure requirements, ERISA §§ 101-111

    Generally . . . 4.03

    Purposes of requirements . . . 4.03[A]

    Specific requirements . . . 4.03[B]

    Summary plan description . . . 4.03[C]

  Writing requirement, ERISA § 402(a)(1)

    Generally . . . 4.02

    Elements of written plan document, required . . . 4.02[B]

    Failure to satisfy, effect of . . . 4.02[D]

    Oral representations and estoppel claims . . . 4.02[E]

    Purpose of . . . 4.02[A]

    Satisfying . . . 4.02[C]

Pensions plans (See PENSION PLANS)

Prohibited transaction regime, ERISA §§ 406-408

  Generally . . . 6.06; 6.06[A]

  Administrative exemptions from

    Generally . . . 6.06[F][2]

    Class exemptions . . . 6.06[F][2][a]

    Individual exemptions . . . 6.06[F][2][b]

EMPLOYEE BENEFIT PLANS (GENERALLY)—Cont.

Prohibited transaction regime, ERISA §§ 406-408—Cont.

  Employer securities and real property, ERISA § 407(a) limitation on plan's acquisition and holding of . . . 6.06[E]

  Encumbered property, ERISA § 406(c) prohibition on transfers of . . . 6.06[D]

  Exemptions from

    Generally . . . 6.06[F]

    Administrative exemptions (See under this subhead: Administrative exemptions from)

    Statutory exemptions . . . 6.06[F][1]

  Remedies and sanctions . . . 6.06[G]

  Sanctions and remedies . . . 6.06[G]

  Transactions between plan and fiduciary, ERISA § 406(b) prohibited . . . 6.06[C]

  Transactions between plan and party in interest, ERISA § 406(a) prohibited

    Generally . . . 6.06[B], [B][2], [B][3]

    Commissioner v. Keystone Consolidated Industries . . . 6.06[B][4][a]

    Hughes Aircraft Co. v. Jacobson . . . 6.06[B][4][c]

    Lockheed Corp. v. Spink . . . 6.06[B][4][b]

    Party in interest, ERISA § 3(14) . . . 6.06[B][1]

    Supreme Court cases interpreting . . . 6.06[B][4]-B][4][c]

Self-directed plans (ERISA § 404(c)), exemption from ERISA fiduciary standards for

  Generally . . . 6.05

  Purpose of ERISA § 404(c) exception . . . 6.05[A]

  Regulations, ERISA § 404(c)

    Generally . . . 6.05[C]

    Control, opportunity to exercise . . . 6.05[C][1]

    Investment advice . . . 6.05[D], [D][2]

    Investment education . . . 6.05[D], [D][1]

    Investment options, broad range of . . . 6.05[C][2]

  Significance of ERISA § 404(c) exception . . . 6.05[B]

Welfare plans (See WELFARE PLANS)

EMPLOYEE BENEFITS (GENERALLY)

Defined . . . 1.01

Reasons employer offers . . . 1.02

Regulation of

  Generally . . . 1.03

  ERISA (See ERISA)

Tax rules governing

  Generally . . . 1.07

  Deferral, tax . . . 1.07[B]

  Exclusion, tax . . . 1.07[A]

  Roth treatment . . . 1.07[C]

[References are to sections and appendices.]

**EMPLOYEE RETIREMENT INCOME SECU-
RITY ACT OF 1974 (ERISA)** (See ERISA)

ERISA
Generally . . . 1.05
Administration risk, protection from . . . 1.05[D],
   [D][2]
Affordable Care Act
   Employer-sponsored health plans prior to,
     ERISA's regulation of . . . 3.04
   Incorporation of Act's provisions by ERISA
     . . . 3.06[B]
Attorney fees, ERISA § 502(g)(1) . . . 7.10
Civil enforcement provisions (See CIVIL EN-
   FORCEMENT PROVISIONS, ERISA)
Coverage . . . 1.05[C]
Default risk, protection from . . . 1.05[D], [D][1]
Employee benefit plans (See EMPLOYEE BEN-
   EFIT PLANS (GENERALLY), specific subheads,
   e.g., Fiduciary liability under ERISA)
"ERISA-qualified plans" . . . 2.05
Historical background
   Generally . . . 1.04
   Pre-ERISA regulation of employee benefit plans
     (See subhead: Pre-ERISA regulation of em-
     ployee benefit plans)
Internal Revenue Code and . . . 1.06
Numbering system . . . 1.05[B]; App. A
Preemption (See PREEMPTION, ERISA)
Pre-ERISA regulation of employee benefit plans
   Generally . . . 1.04[A]
   Failure to protect plan participants and beneficia-
     ries . . . 1.04[B]
   Income tax law, federal . . . 1.04[A][1]
   Labor law, federal . . . 1.04[A][2]
   State law . . . 1.04[A][4]
   Welfare and Pension Plans Disclosure Act
     . . . 1.04[A][3]
Purposes of . . . 1.04[C]
Remedies available under (See REMEDIES, ERISA)
Statute of limitations (See STATUTE OF LIMITA-
   TIONS)
Statutory framework
   Generally . . . 1.05[A]
   Title I . . . 1.05[A][1]
   Title II . . . 1.05[A][2]
   Title III . . . 1.05[A][3]
   Title IV . . . 1.05[A][4]
Termination of pension plans (See TERMINATION
   OF PENSION PLANS, subhead: ERISA, regula-
   tion of termination under Title IV)
29 U.S.C., table of corresponding section numbering
   in . . . App. A

F

401(K) PLANS
Generally . . . 2.06[A]
Nondiscrimination rules (See NONDISCRIMINA-
   TION RULES FOR QUALIFIED PENSION
   PLANS, subhead: 401(k) plans, rules for)

401(K) PLANS—Cont.
Plan fees and fiduciary liability under ERISA (See
   EMPLOYEE BENEFIT PLANS (GENERALLY),
   under,subhead: Fiduciary liability under ERISA)

H

HEALTH CARE
Affordable Care Act (See AFFORDABLE CARE
   ACT)
Retiree health insurance (See RETIREE HEALTH
   INSURANCE)
Welfare plans (See WELFARE PLANS, specific
   subheads, e.g., Employment-based health care
   plans)

I

INTERNAL REVENUE CODE
ERISA and . . . 1.06
Favorable tax treatment for employee benefits (See
   EMPLOYEE BENEFITS (GENERALLY), sub-
   head: Tax rules governing)
Termination of pension plans, regulation of (See
   TERMINATION OF PENSION PLANS, subhead:
   Internal Revenue Code, regulation of termination
   under)

N

**NONDISCRIMINATION RULES FOR QUALI-
FIED PENSION PLANS**
Generally . . . 9.01; 9.03
Affiliated service group rules, IRC § 414(m)
   Generally . . . 9.04[C], [C][2]
   Garland v. Commissioner . . . 9.04[C][1]
   IRC § 414(m)(2)(A) organization
     . . . 9.04[C][2][a]
   IRC § 414(m)(2)(B) organization
     . . . 9.04[C][2][b]
   IRC § 414(m)(5) management organization
     . . . 9.04[C][2][c]
Contributions or benefits (IRC § 401(a)(4)), nondis-
   crimination requirement in
   Generally . . . 9.03[A], [A][3], [A][4]; 9.08;
     9.08[A]
   Amounts rule
     Generally . . . 9.08[B]
     Defined contribution plans, summary of
       amounts rule as applied to . . . 9.08[B][4]
     Flexibility features . . . 9.08[B][3]
     Safe harbors for defined contribution plans
       . . . 9.08[B][1], [B][1][a], [B][1][b]
     Testing of defined contribution plans
       . . . 9.08[B][2], [B][2][a], [B][2][b], [B][5]
     Uniform allocation formula for defined contri-
       bution plans . . . 9.08[B][1], [B][1][a]
     Uniform points allocation formula for defined
       contribution plans . . . 9.08[B][1],
       [B][1][b]
   Other benefits, rights and features . . . 9.08[C]
   Special circumstances . . . 9.08[D]

[References are to sections and appendices.]

NONDISCRIMINATION RULES FOR QUALIFIED PENSION PLANS—Cont.

Employer
  Generally . . . 9.04[A]
  Affiliated service group rules, IRC § 414(m) (See subhead: Affiliated service group rules, IRC § 414(m))
  Anti-avoidance rule, IRC § 414(o) . . . 9.04[E]
  Common control, IRC §§ 414(b) and (c) employers under
    Generally . . . 9.04[B]
    Brother-sister group . . . 9.04[B][2]
    Combined group . . . 9.04[B][3]
    Controlled group definition, advantages and limits of IRC §§ 414(b) and (c) . . . 9.04[B][4]
    Parent-subsidiary group . . . 9.04[B][1]
  Identifying, generally . . . 9.03[B][1]
  Leased employees, IRC § 414(n) . . . 9.04[D]
  Separate lines of business under IRC § 414(r) as separate employers (See subhead: Separate lines of business under IRC § 414(r) as separate employers for purposes of)
401(k) plans, rules for
  Generally . . . 9.03[A][5]; 9.09; 9.09[E]
  Excess contributions, methods for correcting
    Generally . . . 9.09[C]
    Distribution of excess contributions . . . 9.09[C][1]-C[1][d]
    Qualified matching or nonelective contributions . . . 9.09[C][3]
    Recharacterization of excess contributions . . . 9.09[C][2]
  Safe harbors
    Generally . . . 9.09[D]
    IRC § 401(k)(12) safe harbors . . . 9.09[D][1], [D][1][a], [D][1][b]
    IRC § 401(k)(13) safe harbors . . . 9.09[D][2]-D[2][c]
  Special IRC § 401(a)(4) amounts rule for . . . 9.03[A][5]
  Special IRC § 401(k)(3)(A)(ii) nondiscrimination tests
    Generally . . . 9.09[B]
    Actual deferral percentage (ADP) . . . 9.09[B][1]-B[1][c]
    Actual deferral ratio (ADR) . . . 9.09[B][1][b]
    Alternative limitation, IRC § 401(k)(3)(A)(ii)(II) . . . 9.09[B][2], [B][2][b], [B][2][c]
    Highly compensated employees (HCEs), determining actual deferral percentage for . . . 9.09[B][1][a]
    125% test, IRC § 401(k)(3)(A)(ii)(I) . . . 9.09[B][2], [B][2][a], [B][2][c]
  Special nondiscrimination testing, generally . . . 9.09[A]
Highly compensated employees, IRC § 414(q)
  Generally . . . 9.05
  Compensation test . . . 9.05[B]
  Identifying, generally . . . 9.03[B][2]
  Objective test, implications of . . . 9.05[D]

NONDISCRIMINATION RULES FOR QUALIFIED PENSION PLANS—Cont.

Highly compensated employees, IRC § 414(q)—Cont.
  Ownership test . . . 9.05[A]
  Top-paid group election . . . 9.05[C]
Identifying plan, generally . . . 9.03[B][3]
Minimum coverage requirement, IRC § 410(b)
  Generally . . . 9.03[A], [A][2], [A][4]; 9.07
  Average benefit percentage test, IRC § 410(b)(1)(C)
    Generally . . . 9.07[D], [G], [G][2], [H]
    Classification test . . . 9.07[G][1]-G[1][b][iii]
    Nondiscriminatory classification test . . . 9.07[G][1][b]-G[1][b][iii]
    Reasonable classification test . . . 9.07[G][1][a]
  "Benefit" under the plan, meaning of . . . 9.07[B]
  Excludable employees
    Generally . . . 9.07[C]
    Collective bargained agreements, employees covered by . . . 9.07[C][3]
    Minimum age and service requirements, employees who do not satisfy . . . 9.07[C][1]
    Nonresident aliens . . . 9.07[C][2]
    Qualified separate lines of business, employees of . . . 9.07[C][4]
    Terminating employees, certain . . . 9.07[C][5]
  Percentage test, IRC § 410(b)(1)(A) . . . 9.07[D], [E], [H]
  Plans that automatically satisfy IRC § 410(b) . . . 9.07[A]
  Ratio percentage test, IRC § 410(b)(1)(B) . . . 9.07[D], [F], [H]
Minimum participation requirement, IRC § 401(a)(26)
  Generally . . . 9.03[A], [A][1], [A][4]; 9.06
  Purpose of . . . 9.06[A]
  Statutory requirement . . . 9.06[B]
Preliminary steps in applying, generally . . . 9.03[B]
Purpose of . . . 9.02
Separate lines of business under IRC § 414(r) as separate employers for purposes of
  Generally . . . 9.04[F]
  Purpose of rule . . . 9.04[F][1]
  Treasury regulations implementing IRC § 414(r)
    Generally . . . 9.04[F][2]
    Individual determinations . . . 9.04[F][2][c][iii]
    Line of business . . . 9.04[F][2][a]
    Qualified separate lines of business . . . 9.04[F][2][c]-F[2][c][iii], [F][2][d]
    Regulatory safe harbors . . . 9.04[F][2][c][ii]
    Separate lines of business . . . 9.04[F][2][b]
    Statutory safe harbor . . . 9.04[F][2][c][i]

[References are to sections and appendices.]

P

PENSION PLANS
Generally . . . 2.01; 2.02
Anti-alienation provision (ERISA § 206(d); IRC § 401(a)(13))
  Generally . . . 5.04
  "Assign" or "alienate" defined . . . 5.04[B]
  Bankruptcy estate and . . . 5.04[D]
  Exceptions to
    Generally . . . 5.04[C]
    Fiduciary breaches with respect to plan . . . 5.04[C][4]
    Loans to plan participants . . . 5.04[C][1]
    Qualified domestic relations orders (QDROs) . . . 5.04[C][3]
    10% exception for benefits in pay status . . . 5.04[C][2]
  Purpose of . . . 5.04[A]
Defined benefit plans
  Generally . . . 2.02[A]
  Benefit formulas
    Generally . . . 2.03; 2.03[A]
    Calculating compensation for purposes of (See under this subhead: Calculating compensation for purposes of benefit formulas)
    Fixed benefit formula . . . 2.03[A][1]
    Flat benefit formula . . . 2.03[A][2]
    Unit benefit formula . . . 2.03[A][3]
  Calculating compensation for purposes of benefit formulas
    Generally . . . 2.03[B]
    Career average pay . . . 2.03[B][1]
    Final average pay . . . 2.03[B][2]
  Defined contribution plans distinguished (See subhead: Distinctions between defined benefit and defined contribution plans)
  Older and younger workers compared and "time value of money"
    Generally . . . 2.02[C][7], [C][7][b]
    Assumptions of "time value of money" (See under, subhead: Older and younger workers compared and "time value of money")
  Pension benefit security rules
    Benefit accrual rules (ERISA § 204; IRC § 410) . . . 5.02[C][2]-C][2][c]
    Vesting requirements (ERISA § 203; IRC § 411) . . . 5.02[A][2], [A][2][a], [A][2][b]
Defined contribution plans
  Generally . . . 2.02[B]
  Defined benefit plans distinguished (See subhead: Distinctions between defined benefit and defined contribution plans)
  Older and younger workers compared and "time value of money"
    Generally . . . 2.02[C][7], [C][7][c]
    Assumptions of "time value of money" (See under, subhead: Older and younger workers compared and "time value of money")
  Pension benefit security rules
    Benefit accrual rules (ERISA § 204; IRC § 410) . . . 5.02[C][1]

PENSION PLANS—Cont.
Defined contribution plans—Cont.
  Pension benefit security rules—Cont.
    Vesting requirements (ERISA § 203; IRC § 411) . . . 5.02[A][3], [A][3][a], [A][3][b]
Distinctions between defined benefit and defined contribution plans
  Generally . . . 2.02[C]
  Distributions . . . 2.02[C][5]
  Funding . . . 2.02[C][2]
  Input or output as focus of plan . . . 2.02[C][1]
  Investment risk . . . 2.02[C][3]
  Older and younger workers compared and "time value of money" (See subhead: Older and younger workers compared and "time value of money")
  Pension Benefit Guaranty Corporation (PBGC) Guarantee . . . 2.02[C][4]
  Portability . . . 2.02[C][6]
Minimum funding standards (ERISA §§ 301-305; IRC §§ 412, 430-432)
  Generally . . . 5.05
  Funding basics
    Generally . . . 5.05[A]
    Defined benefit plans, funding . . . 5.05[A][2]
    Defined contribution plans, funding . . . 5.05[A][1]
  Pension Protection Act of 2006 (See subhead: Pension Protection Act of 2006, minimum funding standards and)
  Pre-ERISA funding of defined benefit plans . . . 5.05[B]
  Purpose of . . . 5.05[C]
Older and younger workers compared and "time value of money"
  Generally . . . 2.02[C][7]
  Assumptions of "time value of money"
    Generally . . . 2.02[C][7][a]
    Compound interest . . . 2.02[C][7][a][ii]
    Discounted present value . . . 2.02[C][7][a][iii]
    Positive interest rates . . . 2.02[C][7][a][i]
  Defined benefit plans . . . 2.02[C][7], [C][7][b]
  Defined contribution plans . . . 2.02[C][7], [C][7][c]
Pension benefit security rules
  Generally . . . 5.02
  Benefit accrual rules (ERISA § 204; IRC § 410)
    Generally . . . 5.02[C]
    Defined benefit plans . . . 5.02[C][2]-C][2][c]
    Defined contribution plans . . . 5.02[C][1]
  Minimum age and service requirements (ERISA § 202; IRC § 410) . . . 5.02[B]
  Vesting requirements (ERISA § 203; IRC § 411)
    Generally . . . 5.02[A]
    Defined benefit plans, for employer contributions to . . . 5.02[A][2], [A][2][a], [A][2][b]
    Defined contribution plans, for employer contributions to . . . 5.02[A][3], [A][3][a], [A][3][b]
    Employee contributions, for . . . 5.02[A][1]
    Forfeitures . . . 5.02[A][5]

[References are to sections and appendices.]

PENSION PLANS—Cont.

Pension benefit security rules—Cont.

Vesting requirements (ERISA § 203; IRC § 411)—Cont.

Normal retirement age, special rules for vesting upon . . . 5.02[A][6][a]

Plan termination, special rules for vesting upon . . . 5.02[A][6][b]

Schedules, summary of vesting . . . 5.02[A][4]

Special vesting rules . . . 5.02[A][6]-A][6][c]

Top heavy plans (IRC § 416), special rules for vesting of . . . 5.02[A][6][c]

Pension Protection Act of 2006, minimum funding standards and

Generally . . . 5.05[E]

At-risk plans . . . 5.05[E][3]

Benefit restrictions . . . 5.05[E][2]

Failure to satisfy minimum funding standards, effect of . . . 5.05[E][5]

Minimum required contribution . . . 5.05[E][1]

Prior to Act . . . 5.05[D]

Waivers, funding . . . 5.05[E][4]

Qualified joint and survivor annuity (QJSA) rules, ERISA § 205

Generally . . . 5.03; 5.03[C]

Annuities, generally . . . 5.03[A]

Exempt from, plans and benefits . . . 5.03[E]

Marriage requirement . . . 5.03[G]

Purpose of . . . 5.03[B]

Waiver with spousal consent . . . 5.03[F]

Qualified plans

Generally . . . 2.04

"ERISA-qualified plans" . . . 2.05

Nondiscrimination rules for favorable tax treatment (See NONDISCRIMINATION RULES FOR QUALIFIED PENSION PLANS)

Requirements, qualification

Generally . . . 2.04[A]

Enforcement of . . . 2.04[A][3]

Rules to protect plan participants, qualification . . . 2.04[A][1]

Rules to target tax subsidy, qualification . . . 2.04[A][2]

Roth treatment . . . 2.04[D]

Tax benefits of traditional

Generally . . . 2.04[B]

Deductibility of contributions to plans by employer . . . 2.04[B][1]

Distribution, contributions included in employee's income upon . . . 2.04[B][2]

Earnings on contributions exempt from tax . . . 2.04[B][3]

Economic effect of favorable tax treatment . . . 2.04[C]; App. B

Roll over of distributions . . . 2.04[B][4]

Types of qualified plans

Generally . . . 2.03[E]; 2.06

Cash balance plans . . . 2.06[C]

Employee Stock Ownership Plans (ESOPs) . . . 2.06[B]

"ERISA-qualified plans" . . . 2.05

PENSION PLANS—Cont.

Qualified plans—Cont.

Types of qualified plans—Cont.

401(k) plans . . . 2.06[A]

Individual Retirement Accounts (IRAs) . . . 2.06[D]

Pension plans . . . 2.03[E][3]

Profit-sharing plans . . . 2.03[E][1]

Stock bonus plans . . . 2.03[E][2]

Qualified preretirement spousal annuity (QPSA) rules, IRC § 417

Generally . . . 5.03; 5.03[D]

After normal retirement age, participant's death . . . 5.03[D][1]

Exempt from, plans and benefits . . . 5.03[E]

Marriage requirement . . . 5.03[G]

On or before normal retirement age, participant's death . . . 5.03[D][2]

Purpose of . . . 5.03[B]

Value of QPSA from defined contribution plan . . . 5.03[D][3]

Waiver with spousal consent . . . 5.03[F]

Regulation of

Generally . . . 5.01

Anti-alienation provision (ERISA § 206(d); IRC § 401(a)(13)) (See subhead: Anti-alienation provision (ERISA § 206(d); IRC § 401(a)(13)))

Minimum funding standards (ERISA §§ 301-305; IRC §§ 412, 430-432) (See subhead: Minimum funding standards (ERISA §§ 301-305; IRC §§ 412, 430-432))

Pension benefit security rules (See subhead: Pension benefit security rules)

Qualified joint and survivor annuity (QJSA) rules, ERISA § 205 (See subhead: Qualified joint and survivor annuity (QJSA) rules, ERISA § 205)

Qualified preretirement spousal annuity (QPSA) rules, IRC § 417 (See subhead: Qualified preretirement spousal annuity (QPSA) rules, IRC § 417)

Tax rules governing (See TAX RULES GOVERNING PENSION PLANS)

Termination of (See TERMINATION OF PENSION PLANS)

PREEMPTION, ERISA

Generally . . . 8.01; 8.02

Deemer clause, ERISA § 514(b)(2)(B)

Generally . . . 8.06

Prevalence of self-funded plans . . . 8.06[D]

Self-fund under Affordable Care Act and, incentive to . . . 8.06[B]

Stop-loss insurance in self-funded plans, role of . . . 8.06[C]

Supreme Court's interpretation of . . . 8.06[A]

ERISA § 514(a) and its requirements

Generally . . . 8.04

"Employee benefit plan" requirement . . . 8.04[C]

"Relates to" requirement

Generally . . . 8.04[B], [B][3]

[References are to sections and appendices.]

PREEMPTION, ERISA—Cont.
ERISA § 514(a) and its requirements—Cont.
  "Relates to" requirement—Cont.
    Shaw two-prong test . . . 8.04[B][1],
      [B][1][a], [B][1][b], [B][2]
  "State law" requirement . . . 8.04[A]
Express preemption under ERISA § 514
  . . . 8.02[A][1]; 8.03
Procedural posture of ERISA preemption claims,
  typical . . . 8.02[B]
Saving clause, ERISA § 514(b)(2)(A)
  Generally . . . 8.05
  "Regulates insurance"
    Current test defining . . . 8.05[B], [B][1],
      [B][2]
    Original test defining . . . 8.05[A]
Types of preemption, basic
  Generally . . . 8.02[A]
  Complete preemption for jurisdictional purposes
    . . . 7.05[B], [B][1], [B][2]; 8.02[A][4]
  Effect of preemption . . . 8.02[A][3]
  Express preemption . . . 8.02[A][1]; 8.03
  Implied preemption
    Generally . . . 8.02[A][2]
    Conflict preemption . . . 8.02[A][2][b]
    Field preemption . . . 8.02[A][2][a]

R

REMEDIES, ERISA
Generally . . . 7.08
Benefits under ERISA § 502(a)(1)(B), claims for
  Generally . . . 7.08[A], [A][1], [A][4]
  Other ERISA § 502(a) remedies, availability of
    . . . 7.08[A][3]
  Terms of the plan . . . 7.08[A][2]
Breach of fiduciary duty under ERISA § 502(a)(2),
  claims for
  Generally . . . 7.08[B], [B][3]
  LaRue v. DeWolff Boberg & Associates, Inc.
    . . . 7.08[B][2]
  Massachusetts Mutual Life Ins. Co. v. Russell
    . . . 7.08[B][1]
"Safety net," claims under ERISA § 502(a)(3)
  Generally . . . 7.08[C], [C][3]
  Challenges brought by plan participants (or for-
    mer plan participants)
    Generally . . . 7.08[C][1]
    CIGNA Corporation v. Amara
      . . . 7.08[C][1][c]
    Mertens v. Hewitt Associates
      . . . 7.08[C][1][a]
    Varity Corporation v. Howe
      . . . 7.08[C][1][b]
  Enforcement of plan reimbursement provisions,
    claims seeking
    Generally . . . 7.08[C][2]
    Great West v. Knudson . . . 7.08[C][2][a]
    Sereboff v. Mid Atlantic Medical Services, Inc.
      . . . 7.08[C][2][b]
    U.S. Airways, Inc. v. McCutchen
      . . . 7.08[C][2][c]

REMEDIES, ERISA—Cont.
Supreme Court's remedy decisions, making sense of
  . . . 7.08[D]

RETIREE HEALTH INSURANCE
Generally . . . 3.07
Accounting rules, retiree health benefits and
  . . . 3.07[C]
Age Discrimination in Employment Act, retiree
  health benefits and . . . 3.07[D]
Types of . . . 3.07[A]
Vesting of retiree health benefits . . . 3.07[B]

ROTH CONTRIBUTIONS
Generally . . . 1.07[C]; 2.04[D]; 10.04[B]

S

**SAFE AND UNSAFE HARBOR PERCENT-
AGES** ·
Treas. Reg. § 1.410(b)-4(c)(4)(iv) . . . App. C

STATUTE OF LIMITATIONS
Generally . . . 7.09
Breach of fiduciary claims (ERISA § 413), appli-
  cable to
  Generally . . . 7.09[A]
  General six year limitations period, ERISA §
    413(1) . . . 7.09[A][2]
  Six year fraud or concealment limitations period,
    ERISA § 413 . . . 7.09[A][3]
  Three year actual knowledge limitations period,
    ERISA § 413(2) . . . 7.09[A][1]
Multiemployer plan provisions of Title IV of ERISA
  (ERISA § 4301(f)), applicable to disputes under
  . . . 7.09[B]
Other ERISA claims, applicable to
  Generally . . . 7.09[C]
  "Reasonable" limitations periods set forth in plan
    . . . 7.09[C][2]
  State statutes of limitation, analogous
    . . . 7.09[C][1]

T

TAX RULES GOVERNING PENSION PLANS
Generally . . . 10.01
Distributions, plan
  Early distributions (IRC § 72(t)), 10% additional
    tax on . . . 10.04[D]
  IRC § 72, taxation of distributions under (See
    subhead: IRC § 72, taxation of distributions
    under)
  Loans, IRC § 72(p) (See subhead: Loans, IRC §
    72(p))
  Minimum required distributions, IRC § 401(a)(9)
    (See subhead: Minimum required distributions,
    IRC § 401(a)(9))
  Rollover distributions, IRC § 402(c) (See sub-
    head: Rollover distributions, IRC § 402(c))
  Roth accounts (IRC § 402A(d)), taxation of
    qualified distributions from designated
    . . . 10.04[B]

[References are to sections and appendices.]

TAX RULES GOVERNING PENSION PLANS—Cont.

Distributions, plan—Cont.
  Rules governing, basic . . . 10.04
Employer contributions, deductibility of
  Generally . . . 10.03
  Combined plans, IRC § 404(a)(7) deduction limitations on . . . 10.03[D]
  Defined benefit plans, IRC § 404(o) deduction limitations on . . . 10.03[C]
  Defined contribution plans, IRC § 404(a)(3) deduction limitations on
    Generally . . . 10.03[B]
    Compensation, IRC § 404(I) limit on . . . 10.03[B][3]
    Compensation for purposes of IRC § 404 . . . 10.03[B][1]
    Elective deferrals, compensation and . . . 10.03[B][2]
    Interaction with IRC § 415 limits . . . 10.03[B][4]
  Excise tax on excess contributions, IRC § 4972 . . . 10.03[E]
  Limitations, summary of deduction . . . 10.03[F]
  Timing of deduction . . . 10.03[A]
IRC § 72, taxation of distributions under
  Generally . . . 10.04[A]
  Amounts not received as annuity, IRC § 72(e) . . . 10.04[A][2]
  Annuity, amounts received as
    Generally . . . 10.04[A][1]
    Defined . . . 10.04[A][1][a]
    "Simplified method of taxation" under IRC § 72(d) . . . 10.04[A][1][b]
Loans, IRC § 72(p)
  Generally . . . 10.04[E]
  Advantages and disadvantages of . . . 10.04[E][1]
  Regulation of
    Generally . . . 10.04[E][2]
    Amortization requirement, IRC § 72(p)(2)(C) . . . 10.04[E][2][c], [E][2][c][iii]
    Maximum loan amount (IRC § 72(p)(2)(A)), general . . . 10.04[E][2][c], [E][2][c][i]
    Multiple loans (IRC § 72(p)(2)(A)), special maximum for . . . 10.04[E][2][c], [E][2][c][iv]
    Prohibited transaction rules, loans and . . . 10.04[E][2][b]
    Qualification requirements, loans and . . . 10.04[E][2][a]
    Repayment period, IRC § 72(p)(2)(B) . . . 10.04[E][2][c], [E][2][c][ii]
    Tax distribution rules (IRC § 72(p)), loans and . . . 10.04[E][2][c]-[E][2][c][iv]
Minimum required distributions, IRC § 401(a)(9)
  Generally . . . 10.04[F]
  Beginning date, required . . . 10.04[F][1]
  Defined benefit plans, from . . . 10.04[F][4]
  Defined contribution plans, from . . . 10.04[F][3]
  Distribution period . . . 10.04[F][2]

TAX RULES GOVERNING PENSION PLANS—Cont.

Minimum required distributions, IRC § 401(a)(9)—Cont.
  Post-death distributions
    Generally . . . 10.04[F][5]
    After distributions have begun, death . . . 10.04[F][5][a]
    Before distributions have begun, death . . . 10.04[F][5][b], [F][5][b][i], [F][5][b][ii]
    Five-year rule when death before distributions have begun . . . 10.04[F][5][b], [F][5][b][i]
    Life expectancy rule when death before distributions have begun . . . 10.04[F][5][b], [F][5][b][ii]
Qualification requirements for favorable income tax treatment
  Generally . . . 10.02
  Annual compensation limit, IRC § 401(a)(17) . . . 10.02[A]
  Catch up contributions, IRC § 414(v)
    Generally . . . 10.02[D]
    Application of . . . 10.02[D][2]
    Purpose of . . . 10.02[D][1]
  Contributions and benefits, IRC § 415 limitation on
    Generally . . . 10.02[B]
    Benefits, IRC § 415(b) limitation on . . . 10.02[B][3]
    Contributions, IRC § 415(c) limitation on . . . 10.02[B][2]
    De minimis benefit . . . 10.02[B][5]
    Phased in limit . . . 10.02[B][4]
    Purpose of . . . 10.02[B][1]
  Elective deferrals, IRC § 402(g) limitation on
    Generally . . . 10.02[C], [C][2]
    Excess deferrals . . . 10.02[C][4], [C][5]
    History and purpose of . . . 10.02[C][1]
    Qualification requirement, IRC § 401(a)(30) . . . 10.02[C][3]
Rollover distributions, IRC § 402(c)
  Generally . . . 10.04[C]
  Eligible rollover distributions
    Generally . . . 10.04[C][2]
    Hardship distributions . . . 10.04[C][2][c]
    Minimum required distributions . . . 10.04[C][2][b]
    Periodic payments . . . 10.04[C][2][a]
  Property, rollovers of . . . 10.04[C][5]
  Purpose of exception for . . . 10.04[C][1]
  Retirement plans, eligible . . . 10.04[C][3]
  Types of rollovers . . . 10.04[C][4]
Roth accounts (IRC § 402A(d)), taxation of qualified distributions from designated . . . 10.04[B]

TERMINATION OF PENSION PLANS
Generally . . . 11.01
ERISA, regulation of termination under Title IV
  Generally . . . 11.03
  Distribution of plan assets upon termination . . . 11.03[H]
  Guaranteed benefits . . . 11.03[E]

TERMINATION OF PENSION PLANS—Cont.
ERISA, regulation of termination under Title IV—
Cont.
  Pension Benefit Guaranty Corporation, generally
    . . . 11.03[B]
  Pension Benefit Guaranty Corporation insurance
    programs
    Generally . . . 11.03[C]
    Multiemployer program . . . 11.03[C][2]
    Single-employer program . . . 11.03[C][1]
  Pension Benefit Guaranty Corporation premiums,
    ERISA § 4006(a)(3)
    Generally . . . 11.03[D]
    Multiemployer per-participant flat-rate pre-
      mium, ERISA § 4006(a)(3)(A)(v)
      . . . 11.03[D][4]
    Single-employer per-participant flat-rate pre-
      mium, ERISA § 4006(a)(3)(A)(i)
      . . . 11.03[D][1]
    Single-employer termination premium, ERISA
      § 4006(a)(7) . . . 11.03[D][3]
    Single-employer variable-rate premium,
      ERISA § 4006(a)(3)(E) . . . 11.03[D][2]
  Pension Benefit Guaranty Corporation premium
    structure, critique of . . . 11.03[D][5]
  Pension Benefit Guaranty Corporation upon ter-
    mination, liability to
    Generally . . . 11.03[G]
    Termination premiums . . . 11.03[G][4]
    Unfunded benefit liabilities . . . 11.03[G][1]
    Unpaid annual premiums . . . 11.03[G][3]
    Unpaid minimum funding contributions
      . . . 11.03[G][2]
  Purposes of Title IV of ERISA (ERISA §
    4002(a)) . . . 11.03[A]
  Single-employer plan terminations (See subhead:
    Single-employer plan termination regulation
    under ERISA Title IV)
Internal Revenue Code, regulation of termination
  under
  Generally . . . 11.02
  Reversions (IRC § 4980), tax on
    Generally . . . 11.02[B]
    Benefit increase exception . . . 11.02[B][2]
    Qualified replacement plan . . . 11.02[B][1]
  Special vesting requirement, IRC § 411(d)(3)
    Generally . . . 11.02[A]
    Horizontal partial termination
      . . . 11.02[A][2]
    Vertical partial termination . . . 11.02[A][1]
Single-employer plan termination regulation under
  ERISA Title IV
  Generally . . . 11.03[F], [F][4]
  Involuntary termination, ERISA § 4042
    Generally . . . 11.03[F][3]
    Discretionary terminations . . . 11.03[F][3][b]
    Mandatory terminations . . . 11.03[F][3][a]
  Voluntary distress termination, ERISA § 4041(c)
    Generally . . . 11.03[F][2]
    Business continuation test . . . 11.03[F][2][c]
    Liquidation test . . . 11.03[F][2][a]
    Pension costs test . . . 11.03[F][2][d]
    Reorganization test . . . 11.03[F][2][b]

TERMINATION OF PENSION PLANS—Cont.
Single-employer plan termination regulation under
ERISA Title IV—Cont.
  Voluntary standard termination, ERISA § 4041(b)
    . . . 11.03[F][1]

W

**WELFARE AND PENSION PLANS DISCLO-
SURE ACT (WPPDA)**
Generally . . . 1.04[A][3]

WELFARE PLANS
Generally . . . 3.01; 3.02
Affordable Care Act (See AFFORDABLE CARE
  ACT)
Benefits identified . . . 3.02[A]
Employment-based health care plans
  Generally . . . 3.03; 3.03[A]
  Consumer-driven health plans . . . 3.03[C][4]
  Conventional health insurance . . . 3.03[C][1]
  ERISA regulation prior to Affordable Care Act
    . . . 3.04
  Favorable income tax treatment as reason for
    . . . 3.03[B], [B][2]
  Financing methods
    Generally . . . 3.03[D]
    Affordable Care Act, implications of financing
      methods under . . . 3.03[D][4]
    ERISA, implications of financing methods
      under . . . 3.03[D][3]
    Fully-insured plans . . . 3.03[D][1], [D][6]
    Self-funded or self-insured plans (See sub-
      head: Self-funded health care plans)
  Health Maintenance Organizations (HMOs)
    . . . 3.03[C][2]
  Point of Service (POS) plans . . . 3.03[C][3]
  Preferred Provider Organization (PPO) plans
    . . . 3.03[C][3]
  Self-funded plans (See subhead: Self-funded
    health care plans)
  Types of . . . 3.03[C]-C][4]
  Wage and price controls as reason for
    . . . 3.03[B], [B][1]
ERISA purposes, constituting plan for
  Generally . . . 3.02[B]
  Donovan v. Dillingham test . . . 3.02[B][1]
  Excluded plans . . . 3.02[B][2]
  Three-step inquiry . . . 3.02[B][3]
Flexible Spending Accounts (FSAs), federal taxation
  of
  Generally . . . 3.08[D][2]
  Health Savings Accounts (HSAs), special rules
    for . . . 3.08[D][2][e]
  Limits on contributions to . . . 3.08[D][2][d]
  Uniform coverage rule for health FSAs
    . . . 3.08[D][2][c]
  Use it or lose it rule
    Generally . . . 3.08[D][2][a]
    $500 carryover for health FSAs
      . . . 3.08[D][2][b][ii]

[References are to sections and appendices.]

WELFARE PLANS—Cont.

Flexible Spending Accounts (FSAs), federal taxation of—Cont.

Use it or lose it rule—Cont.

Modifications to rule for health FSAs . . . 3.08[D][2][b], [D][2][b][i], [D][2][b][ii]

2 1/2 month grace period for health FSAs . . . 3.08[D][2][b][i]

Retiree health insurance (See RETIREE HEALTH INSURANCE)

Self-funded health care plans

Generally . . . 3.03[D][2]

Stop-loss insurance for

Generally . . . 3.03[D][5]

Aggregate attachment point . . . 3.03[D][5][b]

Distinction between fully-insured plans and self-funded plans with stop-loss insurance . . . 3.03[D][6]

Specific attachment point . . . 3.03[D][5][a]

Taxation of benefits, federal

Generally . . . 3.08

Cafeteria plans, IRC § 125

Generally . . . 3.08[D]

Flexible Spending Accounts (FSAs) (See subhead: Flexible Spending Accounts (FSAs), federal taxation of)

WELFARE PLANS—Cont.

Taxation of benefits, federal—Cont.

Cafeteria plans, IRC § 125—Cont.

Full flex plans . . . 3.08[D][3]

Premium only plans . . . 3.08[D][1]

Consumer-driven health care plans, contributions to

Generally . . . 3.08[B]

Health Reimbursement Accounts (HRAs) . . . 3.08[B][2]

Health Savings Accounts (HSAs) . . . 3.08[B][1]

High Deductible Health Plans (HDHPs) . . . 3.08[B][3]

Employer-provided health insurance (IRC § 106), contributions to fund . . . 3.08[A]

Flexible Spending Accounts (FSAs) (See subhead: Flexible Spending Accounts (FSAs), federal taxation of)

Group-term life insurance, IRC § 79

Generally . . . 3.08[C], [C][1]

Exclusion for . . . 3.08[C][2]

WPPDA (See WELFARE AND PENSION PLANS DISCLOSURE ACT (WPPDA))